enigma books

Renzo De Felice

Professor of History, University of Rome

The Jews in Fascist Italy

A History

Preface by Michael A. Ledeen

enigma books
New York

Publisher's Cataloging In Publication Data

De Felice, Renzo, 1929-1996
    [Storia degli ebrei italiani sotto il fascismo]
The Jews in Fascist Italy : a history / Renzo De Felice ; with a preface
by Michael A. Leeden — 1st English ed.

    p. cm.

Includes bibliographical references and index.
ISBN: 1-929631-01-4

1. Jews—Italy. 2. Fascism—Italy. I. Ledeen, Michael Arthur, 1941-
II. Miller, Robert L. (Robert Lawrence), 1945- III. Title. IV. Title:
Storia degli ebrei italiani sotto il facismo

DS135.I8 F4513
945/.004924

051402-4295H5

Table of Contents

Part One

I.   The Italian Jews on the Eve of the Fascist Takeover

II. The Years of Adjustment: 1922-1932

III. In Hitler's Shadow: The Internal Contradictions
     of Fascism – 1933-1934

i

The photographs in the first section are from the original
1961 edition. Those in the second section
are from various private sources.

This translation is dedicated to the memory of:

Major Lawrence L. Miller, U.S. Army
North Africa 1942-1943; Italy 1943-1945; Allied Military
Government Rome 1944; Tuscany 1944-45; Trieste and
Venezia Giulia 1945-1947.

Acknowledgments

Enigma Books wishes to extend its most sincere thanks to the many
persons and institutions that made this edition possible:

The Italian Ministry of Foreign Affairs for its generous support;
Senator Paolo Riani, Director of the Italian Cultural Institute in
New York; Dr. Antonio Cosenza of the Italian Cultural Institute
in New York; Dr. Roberto Gilodi, Editor at Giulio Einaudi Editore;
Dr. Emilio Gentile of the University of La Sapienza in Rome; Dr.
Michael A. Ledeen of the American Enterprise Institute; Dr. Gisèle
Lévy, Librarian at the Unione Comunità Ebraiche Italiane in Rome;
Giorgio Fabre of *Panorama* magazine; Robert Stewart, Editorial
Director of Enigma Books; Jay Wynshaw; Stephen Dodson; Kim
Englehart; Catherine Dop; Asya Kunik; and Charles P. Miller. We
also wish to thank Dr. Stanislao Pugliese, Associate Professor of
History at Hofstra University, for co-editing the manuscript.

Glossary of Abbreviations and Terms

Abbreviations
of the most important archival sources used in this book

ACIR	Archivio Comunità Israelitica di Roma - *Archives of the Jewish Community of Rome*
ACS	Archivio Centrale dello Stato - *Central State Archives*
ASAE	Archivio Storico Affari Esteri - *Historical Archives of the Foreign Ministry*
ASMAI	Archivio Storico Ministero Africa Italiana - *Historical Archives of the Ministry for Italian Africa*
AUCII	Archivio Unione Comunità Israelitiche Italiane - *Archives of the Union of Italian Jewish Communities*

Abbreviations and important terms for the English edition

AOI	Africa Orientale Italiana - *Italian East Africa*
Catholic Action	Azione Cattolica - *Italian Catholic lay organization authorized by the Lateran pact, the concordat between the Italian Fascist government and the Holy See.*
CAUR	Comitato d'Azione per l'Universalità di Roma - *Action Committee for the Universality of Rome*
CENTRO	Centro di coordinazione antibolscevica universale - *Center for worldwide antibolshevik action*
CLNAI	Comitato di Liberazione Nazionale Alta Italia - *Committee of National Liberation of Northern Italy*
DELASEM	Delegazione per l'Assistenza Emigrati Ebrei - *Delegation for the Assistance of Jewish Immigrants*
D.L.	Decreto Legge - *Legal Decree*
Duce	"duce" – *In the original edition Renzo De Felice writes the title in lower case and quotation marks. In the English translation we have opted for the most commonly used spelling of the title without quotation marks.*
EGELI	Ente di Gestione e Liquidazione Immobiliare - *Office of Management and Liquidation of Real Estate*
EIAR	Ente Italiano Audizioni Radiofoniche - *Italian Organization for Radio Broadcasting, the national radio network until 1945*
FSI	Federazione Sionistica Italiana - *Italian Zionist Federation*
GIL	Gioventù Italiana del Littorio - *Italian Youth of the Lictor (Fascist Youth Organization)*

GL	Giustizia e Libertà - *Justice and Freedom anti-Fascist political movement founded by Carlo and Nello Rosselli*
GNR	Guardia Nazionale Repubblicana - *National Republican Guard, the police and security organization of the RSI*
GUF	Gruppi Universitari Fascisti - *Fascist University Groups*
INFC	Istituto Nazionale Fascista di Cultura - *Fascist National Institute of Culture*
HICEM	Hias-Ica - *Jewish Emigration Association*
Littoriali	*Fascist Youth Congress*
March on Rome	"marcia su Roma" - *In the original edition Renzo De Felice writes the term in lowercase and in quotation marks. In the English translation we have opted for the most commonly used form with an initial capital letter and without quotation marks.*
MVSN	Milizia Volontaria per la Sicurezza Nazionale – *Fascist Voluntary Militia for National Security*
ONB	Opera Nazionale Balilla - *Fascist Children's Organization*
OVRA	Organizzazione Volontaria Repressione Antifascismo - *Voluntary Organization for the Repression of anti-Fascism (Secret Police)*
PAI	Polizia dell'Africa Italiana - *Italian Colonial Police*
Palazzo Chigi	offices of the Ministry of Foreign Affairs
Palazzo Venezia	offices of Mussolini
PCI	Partito Comunista Italiano - *Italian Communist Party*
PNF	Partito Nazionale Fascista - *National Fascist Party*
PS	Pubblica Sicurezza - *Italian National Police*
Quadrumviro	Designation for the four original Fascist leaders: Mussolini, Balbo, De Bono, and De Vecchi
RDL	Regio Decreto Legge - *Royal Legal Decree*
RSI	Repubblica Sociale Italiana - *Italian Social Republic (neo-Fascist regime in Northern Italy 1943-1945)*
Salò	Repubblica di Salò - another designation for the RSI due to the location of many ministries in the town of Salò, on Lake Garda.

Preface

By Michael A. Ledeen

T he book you hold in your hands is an intellectual bombshell, the first salvo in a long and violent Italian cultural war that started in the early 1960s, when it was first published—and still lingers on. This intense debate was very similar to the one that erupted in France the following decade, with the publication of Alexander Solzhenitsyn's *Gulag Archipelago*. Just as Solzhenitsyn's works on Soviet totalitarianism transformed the political and cultural debates about Soviet Communism, so Renzo De Felice's work on Italian Fascism, of which *The Jews in Fascist Italy A History* was the first volume, eventually changed the way in which Italians viewed their past and, accordingly, their future.

In many important ways, De Felice was the preeminent intellectual figure of post-war Italy, for, almost single-handedly, he delivered a fatal blow to the Gramscian strategy of the Italian Communist Party to capture and manipulate the political culture. With courage, humor, and determination, De Felice destroyed the most cherished myth of the left: that Fascism was a purely reactionary phenomenon of the middle and upper middle classes, to defend their economic interests against the threat of a socialist revolution. According to this view, Fascism was imposed on the Italian people (as on the Germans) by a vicious clique of politicians, industrialists, and military figures, and was finally removed twenty years later by a vast popular insurrection (or, in Germany, by the Allied armies).

This mythology was doubly misleading. First of all, there were enormous differences between German National Socialism and Italian Fascism, not least of all the racist doctrines of the Third Reich and the vision of human nature that Nazi racism rested on. The Nazis believed that "race was destiny," that a person's race was biologically determined and forever immutable. Italian Fascists, on the other hand, believed that race was a spiritual matter, and that even unworthy persons (as, after the passage of the disgraceful Racial Laws in the autumn of 1938) could be transformed into a higher type. In other words, Italian racism was designed to change Italian national character, while Nazi racism was a method of imposing the innate superiority of the Aryan race on the rest of the world.

The second great myth in the conventional wisdom about Fascism was that it was imposed by terror wielded by a small minority. On the contrary, in both countries the regimes were enormously popular and represented genuine mass movements. Fascism and Nazism were not "foisted off" on the people, but were embraced by the overwhelming majority. Neither Italy nor Germany had any really effective resistance once the regimes were consolidated, and insofar as small groups attempted to overthrow the tyrants, they were as much the result of disastrous military campaigns as of moral opposition to evil.

Finally, both regimes were removed as a result of military defeat, and both Germany and Italy returned to democracy because the Allied armies imposed it.

De Felice proves that Fascism was widely popular for most of its history, and contained elements of a highly optimistic movement that was part and parcel of the French Revolutionary tradition. It was a highly misleading caricature to call Fascism "reactionary," not least because many of its most important leaders (including Mussolini himself) came from the ranks of Italian Socialism or radical syndicalism. The "revolutionary Fascists" were not industrialists or well-to-do businessmen defending their self-interest against left-wing radicals, but were, in large part, members of a rising lower middle class that constituted a new political force in post-war Italy. Indeed, Mussolini had little interest in giving free rein to Italian industry; the Fascist "corporate state" exercised considerable control over the business community. Like Soviet Communism, Italian Fascism viewed the state as paramount in all things, including spiritual convictions and religious practice.

De Felice also insisted—beginning with this book—that the differences between Nazism and Fascism were fundamental, and he strongly resisted efforts to lump the two into a single phenomenon.

For daring to write the truth, he was subjected to a campaign of cultural terrorism that would have destroyed any but the strongest men, and had the Left succeeded in silencing De Felice, it might well have confirmed its hegemony over Italian historical and political culture.

De Felice's lifelong study of Fascism—his monumental biography of Mussolini reached more than seven thousand pages of dense text, documents and footnotes—began with the study of the Italian Jews during the Fascist period. Published in 1961, this book marked a dramatic break in the studied silence of the Italian scholarly community on the Fascist period (indeed, the only "biography" of Mussolini in print at that time was an apology written by two Fascists, and there was no scholarly book at all on Italy's role in the Holocaust), as well as for De Felice himself. His battle with Communist orthodoxy began within his own spirit, and was first focused on the Italian Jews.

That an Italian scholar would devote so much of his time to Jewish history was most unusual. Although there has been a Jewish presence in Italy as far back as the earliest days of Rome (the oldest monotheistic house of worship in Europe is the synagogue of Ostia Antica, the old port of Rome), in modern times the Jews have constituted only a tiny part of the Italian population. During the Fascist period, there were but 40,000 Italian Jews, out of a population of more than 40 million. Moreover, unlike France, Germany, and Central Europe, the Jews were not a political or cultural "issue" in modern Italy. To be sure, there had been ghettos in the major cities, including Rome (the very word "ghetto" comes from Venice, after all), and there was considerable Catholic anti-Semitism, but Italy was remarkably free of the sort of mass anti-Semitism that had laid the groundwork for the Holocaust on the other side of the Alps. As *The Jews in Fascist Italy* recounts in considerable detail, not only did the Italian people not embrace anti-Semitism when the Racial Laws were passed in 1938, they considered it so alien to Italian tradition that the pro-Fascist consensus began to fall apart at that very moment. For most Italians, the Jews of the country were worthy citizens, as for most Italian Jews, Italy was home. Few other countries could boast the Italian openness to Jewish assimilation and the Jewish eagerness to assimilate.

Throughout his career, De Felice devoted a remarkable amount of time to the study of the Jews, from his early writings on Italy during the Napoleonic period, to a later book on the Jews of Libya. He was greatly concerned about the future of Israel, always went out of his way to accept invitations to lecture at Israeli universities, and provided space in his journal, *Storia Contemporanea,* to Israeli scholars such as Sergio Minerbi. All of this was unique in the Italian scholarly community. His interest in things Jewish had a significant impact on our friendship: he took pains to introduce me to Rabbi Augusto Segre, a shining light in post-war Italian Zionism, and a great scholar who lectured on Jewish questions at the Lateran University, and who later married Barbara and me in the old Sicilian Synagogue in Rome just a few years before his *aliyah.*

Renzo's interest in, and sympathy with, things Jewish was so striking that many, even including some of his closest friends, wondered if there were some family connection (so far as I know, there was none). There was no trace of religiosity in Renzo's private life, and he left instructions that there should be no religious funeral after his death. His attraction to Jews was a matter of moral conviction and cultural respect. I suspect that he saw his own struggle against the cultural totalitarians of the Italian intelligentsia as a continuation of the battle for freedom waged by the European Jews throughout the modern period.

The prize student of the Florentine Marxist historian Delio Cantimori, De Felice had been a member of the Communist Party until 1956. His *The Jews in Fascist Italy* was methodologically anti-Marxist, drawing its inspiration from the older ethical, cultural, and philosophical tradition of Benedetto Croce and De Felice's late father-in-law, Guido De Ruggiero. Instead of economic and social explanations, De Felice studied the political and spiritual drama of the major and minor actors in the tragedy, and found that the study of the Italian Jews was indispensable to understanding Fascism.

Jews played major roles both within the Fascist movement and in the anti-Fascist resistance, in each case far beyond their numbers. The grotesque finale of Italian Fascism should not blind us to the fact that, for many years Mussolini was a major supporter of the Zionist movement, particularly Jabotinsky's Revisionists (the modern Israeli Navy was born at the maritime school at Civitavecchia, thanks to the Fascist regime, after all). And, at the apogee of Mussolini's popularity, he shared his passions with a Jewish mistress, Margherita Sarfatti.

Unlike Hitler's National Socialism, Italian Fascism was not fundamentally anti-Semitic, and the Italian version of racism was very different from the Nazis'. The adoption of racism by the Fascist regime resulted from the internal logic of the alliance with Hitler, and from "lessons learned" in the colonial occupation of Ethiopia.

The strength of the consensus is perhaps best appreciated by the final ghastly chapters of the history of Italy's Jews under Fascism. With rare exceptions, the Italian Jews could not appreciate their true peril, and were easy prey for their enemies. Few believed they would be physically harmed, let alone exterminated, even when the Nazi armies occupied the country and the death convoys began to operate. Augusto Segre, who fought in the Resistance in those years, once told me, with tears in his eyes, how he went door to door in the Jewish quarter of Turin, his home town, warning them that the Nazis were coming, and urging them to leave the city and to seek refuge in the countryside. Hardly a soul heeded his advice, and many laughed at him and called him a crazy fool.

The claim that most Italians supported Fascism would have been bad enough, but De Felice was not content to insist on Fascism's broad popularity (in later years, he would provide a detailed picture of the "consensus" upon which Mussolini's success rested); he went on to show that two crucial sectors of the Italian political universe— the intellectuals and the young—had, with rare exceptions, even supported the racial laws and the repression of the Italian Jews. As always, his claims were accompanied by a huge body of evidence, above all documents from the archives of the Fascist regime (Renzo was the first scholar to base his writings on Fascism on the enormous documentation that became available, beginning in the mid-1950s), and interviews with those who played important roles in it.

Prior to the publication of *The Jews in Fascist Italy*, the Italian political and intellectual elites had wrapped themselves in the comfortable mythology that anti-Semitism wasn't "really" Italian at all; it was something imposed on Italy by Hitler, but the Italians never really believed it, and did everything they could to sabotage it once it had been established. De Felice stripped them of these comfortable lies, and exposed them to the criticism of their fellow citizens, and, worst of all, of their children. His exposé of the sins of the intelligentsia, many of whom went on to become stylish Leftists in the post-war period, provoked a storm of protest, as did his insistence that a handful of leading Fascists, including the court philosopher himself, Giovanni Gentile, had protested against anti-Semitism.

In short, *The Jews in Fascist Italy* shattered the oversimplified stereotype that had been fed to the war generation and their children. De Felice insisted both on documenting the sins of many who had claimed political virtue, and on carefully identifying those Fascists who found the internal fortitude to resist the embrace of Nazi anti-Semitism by a regime they had long supported.

The most dramatic moment in De Felice's career came in the early summer of 1975, with the publication of a small book with the unprepossessing title, *Interview on Fascism*, in which De Felice responded to a series of questions from me. He chose me because he wanted an interviewer who, while professionally qualified, was not involved in Italian political or cultural debates (I had written a book on Italian efforts to create a Fascist "international" before Hitler's rise to power in Germany, had published an article on the Italian Jews during Fascism which was in some ways critical of De Felice's own work on the subject, and was working on a book on D'Annunzio's occupation of Fiume at the end of the First World War). I had no idea that our short conversation would provoke an intellectual and political firestorm, and even Renzo's worst fears did not remotely approach the dimensions of the reaction. Our little book proved so explosive that the publisher held it in the warehouses for several weeks until the spring elections—in which the Communist Party was widely expected to become the most popular in the country—were over. Once released, it became an overnight best seller. For months, it was virtually impossible to read a newspaper, watch an evening of television, or listen to a few hours of radio, without running into a supercharged attack on De Felice, not only for the presumed "errors" of his historical analysis, but for "corrupting Italian youth." More than one critic suggested that he be forbidden to teach at Italian universities, and many accused him of "treason."

Why such a violent reaction to what was, after all, a debate over events more than half a century before? Because the intellectuals of the Left recognized immediately that if De Felice's interpretations prevailed, and Italians agreed that the "revolutionary" tradition had been mother to both Fascism and Communism, then, the neat moral/political dichotomy between Communism (good) and Fascism (bad) was blurred, with Fascism enhanced by its revolutionary past and Communism besmirched by its common ancestry with Mussolini's movement. But there was more to it than mere intellectual disagreement; if De Felice's theories were accepted, the Marxist hegemony over "correct" interpretations of modern history would be shaken, the spokesmen for the "official" culture would be discredited, and political legitimacy might be restored to groups and political parties of the Right.

As the great French historian François Furet has written, the European communists use the categories of "Fascism" and "anti-Fascism" both to distort the history of the recent past, and to categorize politicians and intellectuals as acceptable or morally bankrupt. De Felice's careful work exploded both of these enterprises. Therefore, De Felice and his ideas had to be destroyed.

The campaign against him was one of the great ironies of Italian intellectual life, because his wife, Livia De Ruggiero, had already lived through a similar ordeal with her father, the great Catholic philosopher, during the Fascist era. When Guido De Ruggiero published *A History of Western Liberalism*—a thinly veiled attack against Fascism—Mussolini himself denounced the book and its author in the pages of *Il popolo d'Italia*, signaling the beginning of an assault that sent De Ruggiero to jail. By the time he emerged, his health was broken, and he never recovered his full intellectual or physical powers. One evening, when I asked Livia how she was dealing with the attacks against Renzo, she said, "I wonder if I am going to lose the second man in my life the same way I lost the first."

It was a bitter fight, but the mass of evidence on De Felice's side swung the battle in his favor, and in the end he defined the

debate on the history of Fascism. De Felice was one of the very
few Italian historians to acquire an outstanding international reputation, and for the past fifteen years at the least, no serious scholar
of Fascism has been able to fundamentally challenge his analysis.
Interview on Fascism remains one of the all-time Italian bestsellers,
and has been translated and published from Japan to Argentina.

Much of De Felice's view of Fascism was born during his research on the Italian Jews, and he remained constant in his insistence that the role of the historian is to organize the facts, no matter how painful they may be, and then attempt to make sense out
of them. In doing so, he ran headlong into a political buzz saw that
felt profoundly threatened by such serene objectivity. They were
quite right, of course, to devote such energy to discredit him. It is
no accident, as the Marxists would say, that the success of De Felice's
view of Italian history has paralleled, and contributed to the collapse of Italian Communism, now a pathetic shadow of its formerly menacing self. The battle over Italian history proved to be
decisive in the war for the Italian future, and if there are now a
post-Fascist Right and a post-Communist Left, no small part of the
credit for these hopeful developments is due to the courageous
historian from Rieti who refused to be intimidated, and insisted on
telling the story of his country, regardless of the political and personal consequences.

This book should have been translated into English long ago,
and it is a singular honor to have been asked to present it to an
American audience for the first time. We are all indebted to Enigma
Books for having had the courage and the understanding to undertake this project, and I fervently hope this book will take its rightful
place among the fundamental works on the Holocaust.

Washington, D.C.
May 2001

Introduction
to the New Edition

A mong the nations of Europe, Italy has been known to be
relatively immune to racism. George L. Mosse, who, as an
American of German-Jewish origin, was well equipped to understand racism and, as perhaps the foremost authority on the subject—considered that Italy represented "a backwater area"[1] when it
came to race and prejudice. Two powerful obstacles to the spread
of this racism were Catholicism and the "humanistic" nationalism
of Mazzini and of most participants in the nineteenth-century
Risorgimento. This applies certainly to the nineteenth and most of
the twentieth century. The alliance between classical nationalism
and racism, which took place in other countries, was watered down
by Italy's recent history. In countries like Italy, where national unity
had been recently achieved, the nationalist-racist alliance appeared
with particularly aggressive and violent characteristics. Italy was also
able to avoid racist connotations from becoming attached to the
traditional kind of Catholic anti-Semitism that tended to become
highly politicized, due, in part, to the demise of the Church as an
independent state, and also, in part, to the inroads of liberalism,
secularism, and socialism which attracted the Jews.

The Italian Fascist Party began a growing debate on racism during the mid-1930s: in 1938 the Fascist regime launched its own
racist legislation, which should not be confused, as often happens,
with that of the Nazis. The heavy burden of responsibility that
Mussolini and Fascism must bear for this decision, among many
others, must not be reduced by any measure. Our aim is to reach a
better understanding of the nature of Fascist racist policy, the motivations surrounding its introduction, and the reasons for its ultimate failure.

A few years ago, Mosse wrote with characteristic objectivity
regarding Mussolini:

[He] was not a racist; like Adolf Hitler, he was a master politician, but he did not carry a heavy ideological load coupled with an apocalyptic vision. Hitler considered every major problem in eschatological terms, and his solution, of necessity, could only be absolute and "final." Mussolini saw the future as being undetermined and, because of his open-ended concept of the new Fascist man, certainly leading to a positive outcome. This approach allowed him to assume a cynically flexible position on the issue of race.[2]

Mussolini attempted to achieve certain objectives with the enactment of the racial laws of 1938. One was to re-energize Fascism. Another was intended as a "show of friendship" towards Germany, and Hitler in particular; Mussolini also wanted to emphasize for Italian as well as foreign observers the differences between Fascism and Nazism. This was the origin of what he called the "non-biological character," and the purportedly more "spiritual" attitude, he wanted to give to Fascist racism. Hence his insistence on the slogan, with respect to the Jews, "discriminate, but do not persecute."* Another motive that induced Mussolini to proclaim himself racist, after having ridiculed Hitler's racism a few years before, and to introduce racial legislation (which, it must be remembered, was not only aimed at the Jews but also encompassed the native population of the Fascist "Empire"), was the desire to regulate the interaction between Italian citizens in Africa and the Africans in order to avoid "conduct unbecoming" towards the natives that could lead to race mixing and harm Italy's prestige and authority in that part of the world. Mussolini was convinced, as many others were at the time, both in Italy and overseas, that declining birth rates and race mixing were typical symptoms of the "aging of the population" and of the moral and material decline of a nation.

By all accounts Mussolini's efforts to instill "racial consciousness" in the Italian people were clearly to be a dismal failure. Racism did not reappear in Italy after the war, except in some of its crudest expressions against foreigners (now commonly referred to

---

* "Discriminare, ma non perseguitare."

as being "different"). We shall, however, continue to refer to them as "foreigners." Significantly, not even the large number of women, mostly in central and southern Italy, who were raped by colored Allied soldiers during the Italian campaign (the "maroccaned" women) and the propaganda advantage that the RSI, the Fascist Italian Social Republic, was able to draw from these events, were enough to spark any racist reactions within the population. The opposite took place in the Rhineland after World War I, where a much smaller number of rape victims was enough to create racist tensions that included even large segments of the German left-wing parties. Racist-type incidents in Italy today, rather than being the expression of a true racist feeling (exhibited only by very small neo-Nazi groups), are best explained by the economic difficulties and moral crises of certain fringe youths and their craving to reach the spotlight through media attention. In addition, the visible increase in the number of immigrants from developing nations during the last two decades, who make up, especially in agriculture, an underpaid workforce often accused of causing unemployment among youths—even though these very youths who occasionally attack foreign workers would, in fact, never accept the kinds of jobs the immigrants are forced to take.

Anti-Semitism poses an altogether different historical problem. The classic Catholic tradition, because it remained latent and was therefore slowly weakening, managed to stay alive, or at least dormant, during the nineteenth and, in some instances, even in the twentieth century. This tradition encouraged the appearance of two imported varieties of anti-Semitism: the aesthetic-literary and the political. At the end of the nineteenth century, and again following the events of 1917, this tradition adopted the themes and ideas of foreign cultures (especially French, but also Austrian, Russian, and Romanian), displaying at first a potential rather than actual importance it never had before. Anti-Semitic ideas remained limited to small groups, but they help explain the underlying Fascist arguments used against "internal" Zionism (while for a long time Mussolini was pro-Zionist in his foreign policy, mostly to counter the British in the Middle East), which caused anxiety only in Jewish and anti-Fascist circles. The anti-Semitic legislation of 1938 received a hostile reception from most of the Italian people and even from most Fascists, for whom it represented a decisive step in Italy's alignment along German positions and towards war. It found less hostility in some smaller groups, which included not only Fascists but also Fascist fellow travelers and even Catholics, the very people who, in the past, subscribed to the aesthetic-literary and political forms of anti-Semitism.

Fascism, at its beginnings in 1919 and for many years thereafter, was neither racist nor anti-Semitic and many Italian Jews were Fascist Party members, with some occupying important political, financial, and cultural positions within the Party itself. When Mussolini decided upon his racist and anti-Semitic course, the approval of the new Party line, noisily endorsed by the majority of Fascists, can be directly attributed to conformist attitudes and to opportunism. The younger generation within the Party proved to be the exception: it accepted racist policy in the mistaken view that the failure of the "Fascist Revolution" was attributable to the absence of "racial consciousness" and to the "corruption of the soul" that propaganda identified as the hallmarks of Judaism.

All these issues make up the substance of this book. They are important because of the unique relationships, absent in any other country under a Fascist-type political regime, characterizing the tolerance and mutual acceptance which existed between the Jews and Italian Fascism up to 1938. Mussolini's colossal failure to instill a "racial awareness" among the Italian people can be explained by the high degree of assimilation of Italian Jewry during the first decades of the twentieth century and by the historical weakness of anti-Semitism in Italy even before it was rejected after facing the reality of the Holocaust. Today, the reality is a lack of anti-Semitism and that the situation is among the best, if not the best, in Europe.

Anti-Semitism is certainly an ancient illness, but it is also the result of many conscious and unconscious cultural layers and connections, more rooted in certain countries than in others, Italy being a noteworthy case. It is unrealistic to expect anti-Semitism to disappear in a few short years when one considers its long history. That sort of thinking often stems from a misplaced "reasonable optimism." To be pessimistic, however, is just as dangerous as being overly optimistic. To give anti-Semitism an exaggerated importance may result in bringing about its revival, in giving it a "facelift" at the very moment it is about to disappear and when only education in understanding the lessons of history and the responsible and accurate use of information can really counter it. For declarations of principle to be more than empty wishes, they require sound historical foundations, a true knowledge of the facts, and a clear vision, which is often absent, rather than emotional outbursts and simplistic theories that often obfuscate our understanding of the true facts.

Racism and anti-Semitism continue to occupy a very important place in the life of many nations. At the end of the Second World War, the widely held view was that anti-Semitism, being the result of a tragic infatuation and the cause of mass exterminations, was, at last, a closed chapter of history. Any new scholarship would only serve to further condemn its memory and justify, through its defeat, the inevitable triumph of rational thinking over the irrational.

Daily events demonstrate the exaggeration of this misplaced optimism, which was another one of those myths borne of the horrors of the war and the excitement surrounding its end, a myth meant to uplift man's spirit but unable to withstand rational examination. With respect to racism it is useful to reread the Montagu Commission's 1949 declaration written for UNESCO, which many geneticists correctly refused to endorse, according to which biological studies were able to prove the validity of "the ethical idea of universal brotherhood."[3]

When examining problems such as racism and anti-Semitism we must have the courage to say that "taking sides" for moral reasons is insufficient, just as mere emotional rejection is also useless. Only through rationality and the intimate knowledge of their inner workings can we effectively know and oppose them. Feelings of indignation and resentment are understandable but useless and potentially counterproductive, especially if they prevent a deeper comprehension of their meaning, their root causes and transformations. The same can be said of silence when faced with the horror generated by Fascist extermination, or by an overly optimistic vision that relegates anti-Semitism and racism to a past best forgotten and without any future. During the years immediately following the war this view contributed to creating a negative attitude towards any scholarship dealing with anti-Semitism, resulting in some issues being neglected or treated much too superficially.

Consider the case of assimilation, which plays a very important part in our understanding of the past and present transformations of anti-Semitism. The extreme example would be, in some cases, to consider the "Jewish Problem" as being nothing more than a part of the history of anti-Semitism rather than of the history of Judaism in general in its various national ramifications, therefore failing to understand the deep changes that took place within the Judaism of the Diaspora, as well as the changes affecting the attitude of large numbers of non-Jews towards the Jews.

Racism and anti-Semitism must be studied, we shall continue to insist, just like any other historical problem, with a clear view of their origins, their development, and their manifestations. One must avoid establishing simplistic parallels between extremely different situations such as European racism, civil rights problems in America, and apartheid in South Africa.

Two main pitfalls can affect the historian. One is to be overcome by indignation and therefore to confuse the issues and be afraid of analyzing the facts lest one appear insensitive to the plight of the victims of racism and anti-Semitism. The other is the fear of being accused of excessive "relativism" by creating degrees of responsibility for such monstrous crimes. The usual result is that many important aspects of racism and anti-Semitism will be ignored, including the ability to advance our understanding of their causes and mechanisms, even the most perverse ones that, by their very nature, cannot simply be chalked up to "hatred," "madness," or "evil" but require rational explanations. Another danger is to try to resolve everything through the simplistic formula that democracy, by its very presence, eliminates "evil," which, invariably, re-appears where democracy is absent. This implies that with strong democratic governments, past or present, anti-Semitism and racism were absent, except among some anti-democratic minorities. The historian who is unaware of these dangers and is not actively engaged in avoiding them is being derelict in his professional and ethical duties, as well as in his political responsibilities.

We have stated the need to go deeper below the surface of the facts and understand them from within, using all the tools at our disposal. Racism and anti-Semitism must therefore be considered as separate phenomena, even though the former has often absorbed and drawn elements from the latter. Similarly, they both differ from nationalism, even though in countries where the Jews were most numerous in the nineteenth and twentieth centuries, racism, anti-Semitism and nationalism appeared—with few exceptions, such as the Action Française—within a single movement, or at least closely related amongst themselves. George L. Mosse stated:

> The most effective alliance between racism and nationalism took place in central and Eastern Europe. In many countries such as Hungary, Romania, and Poland, the Jews were the most "visible" segment of the business middle class, and all the points . . . invoked by the proponents of a socialist nationalism could come into play. The presence of urban ghettos encouraged the belief in racial differences. In addition, in some nations, such as Germany during the industrial revolution, racist ideas held the national cohesion together at the very moment it appeared to be destroyed by the class struggle.[4]

Anti-Semitism, in its religious form, first pagan and then Christian, is much older than racism. Racism, in effect, appears only during the second half of the eighteenth century and becomes a coherent ideology at the beginning of the nineteenth century. About fifteen years ago Mosse wrote:

> It is possible to trace racism through various well-defined historical phases. The theories were elaborated during the eighteenth and the first half of the nineteenth century. From the second half of the nineteenth century up to the end of the First World War, racism grew more intense and acquired a clearer, more focused orientation. Between the two world wars it established contact with European mass movements and succeeded in putting into practice racist theories. Finally, after the Second World War, the racists continued to be vocal but were overwhelmed by the reaction against their own crimes.[5]

Mosse would probably be less optimistic if, summing up the historical overview, he were writing that last sentence today. His ability to understand the historical dimensions of racism, anti-Semitism and their points of contact remains far superior to that of most scholars. First of all, Mosse does not belittle or, worse, ridicule, as others have, those cultural and pseudo-cultural elements, typical of certain periods and their cultures, that contributed to create racism. These elements have various different components— esthetic, linguistic, anthropological, ethnological, eugenic, histori-cal, etc.—adapted to various local and political circumstances; they allow racism to penetrate all social circles and become one of the points of reference for many mass movements not only of the 20th century but also from 1850 onward.

An important contribution of the French Revolution during the nationalist phase of modern nation states was the late romantic theory of "ideal racial types." This theory heightened some "his-torical" contrasts between the great powers, most of all between Germany and France. It enhanced the "anti-modern," i.e., "anti-capitalist," variant of anti-Semitism that, consciously or not, had penetrated the lower middle and working classes. When racist ideas were combined with anti-Semitism, at those levels in particular, they resulted in the most repugnant and tragic outcome, especially when anti-Semitism became "secularized," i.e., "politicized," and migrated to upper-class acceptance of racism along with a few cultural *topoi* adopted from positivism.

Once exposed to racism, anti-Semitism held on to its original Christian characteristics and also acquired new political directions that modernized its older "social" aspects destined to grow in im-portance, based on the stereotype of the Jewish usurer. These di-rections were, in part, better adapted than the traditional stereo-types to all circumstances and political realities: democratic and non-democratic, left- and right-wing, Nazi and Communist, etc. The connection to racism also encouraged the ruling classes and the Catholic hierarchy to slowly distance themselves from anti-Semitism.

To better understand the increasingly political connotation ac-quired by anti-Semitism from the middle of the nineteenth century onward in many countries, and especially in France, it is vitally important to know that almost everywhere the emancipation of the Jews was not just the result of the principles of progress, freedom, and equality, but also of the idea, originating in the Enlightenment, revealing the Christian origins of the old prejudices. Once emancipated, it was thought, the Jews would finally shed their "disagreeable characteristics" and undergo an economic and cultural metamorphosis that would result in losing their "uniqueness." In addition to this belief, which was to flourish in the late nineteenth century in the pervasive climate of secular positivism, another set of ideas set forth by the Jews themselves explains, at least in part, the Zionist reaction: that the Jews would inevitably be integrated and then assimilated into society, and would eventually abandon their religion for a "higher" form of belief destined to unite in a single form of deism the deeper meaning of all the great monotheistic religions. It becomes clear how, in a context in which Christian tradition was still strong, racist tendencies increased and the Jews were spread politically among liberals, democrats, Freemasons, and socialists; the "failure of emancipation" made the Jews appear as a foreign body to many people and as the enemies of "civilization." The Jews were considered all the more "unnatural" because they claimed to be a nation even though they had no land of their own. This is a fundamental characteristic in an age when nation states were commonly considered to be based on three indivisible elements: culture, territory, and independence, and multiethnic states were expected to disintegrate.

For the lower middle class and the traditional ruling classes, the Jew, with his hard work, enterprising spirit, rationalistic and scientific culture, became the stereotypical enemy of traditional "well bred" values. The Jews were equated with the spread of modern ideas, and with denying the values of a society they wished to dominate. The "Dreyfus Affair," coming right after the uproar surrounding the bankruptcy of the Panama Canal Company, was very important in this context. The peasantry also became "politically" anti-Semitic as it felt threatened by modernization, and traditional laborers who were of "artisan" origins, saw the Jew as the symbolic "inventor" of financial capitalism, "high Jewish finance," and the factory. The best example is that of France, studied by Zeev Sternhell in a series of books that clearly demonstrate how French anti-Semitism, contrary to accepted views, was, up to World War I, the strongest in western Europe.[6] French anti-Semitism was rooted in both the right and the left; it was countered only by Catholicism, and therefore the anti-racism of the upper middle and upper classes for whom negative attitudes towards the Jews never went beyond the accusation of lacking in "elegance."

During the second half of the nineteenth century the connection between racism and anti-Semitism had already created a highly explosive mix (whose tragic and devastating effects were to appear in the next century). This mix, in short, accused the Jews of being the most absolutely "negative" race and the "enemy of civilization," a race with a single aim, as was put forth in the most notorious and "successful" pamphlet ever produced by anti-Semitism, *The Protocols of the Elders of Zion*: the subjugation of the world to its own political and economic power. During the nineteenth century, the most rabid racists established a sort of "hierarchy of Aryan racial purity" of the various peoples, giving the Aryans the "mission" of putting an end to this "Jewish project" and freeing the world from the "Jewish nightmare."

Nazism was to combine racism and anti-Semitism even more tightly, making them appear one and the same. To draw the conclusion that, at some point in their history, racism and anti-Semitism became one is a mistake and can result in seriously misunderstanding the situation today. This is true of Europe as well as of other continents, which we cannot possibly analyze in this book. Outside Europe, anti-Semitism and racism differ even more, each one having its own unique characteristics that must be carefully analyzed to avoid any misestimation.

Racism and anti-Semitism remain, as always, two fundamentally different phenomena. They each have divergent patterns of development while maintaining a single common denominator: both require an economic and moral crisis to gain access to mass movements.

After being stopped by the Second World War, political racism appears to have found some new forms of growing acceptance once again. The new form of racism requires precise economic conditions to become a political force and differs from the much older "anti-foreign" type, which rarely survives more than a few generations beyond the point of "contact" between different cultures. To quote Mosse: "Such a powerful movement, because of its strength and influence, leaves its mark for several generations."[7] The new racism feeds on the violence of interethnic national conflicts, as in the typical case of the former Yugoslavia, and even more on a series of events and mind-sets related to economic conditions resulting from the frustration and fear generated by economic tensions. The dismantling of the Berlin Wall and the disappearance of the Soviet system have created tensions echoed in the mass media, generating as always in times of moral and material strife, emotional waves that, in turn, create more prejudice and racist psychoses. The unemployed and the underemployed, as well as uprooted youths who have not found their own social status, are most likely to see the "foreigners" as a group of dangerous competitors denying them both work and the welfare benefits they expect from the government, and these "foreigners" as the root cause of the hardships they and the country must endure.

Appearances notwithstanding and despite many statements, the current situation has little in common with the "typical ideal" of the most completely formulated example of European racism: Germany after the First World War and under the Nazi regime.

Due to space limitations we will not examine the various differences to be found within European racism today. The French example, in particular before the 1990s, in a still positive economic context, was directed against immigrants from Africa and Asia, who are indispensable to the French economy. The same holds true for England, where forms of racism have appeared within a more difficult socio-economic context than in France.[8] The German situation is tied to the new reality after the crumbling of the Soviet system and reunification, with its racism aimed mostly at Turks and Yugoslavs who, in fact, have been working peacefully in Germany for many years, apart from the notable exceptions of recessions or economic crises as in 1966-1967 and 1979-1983, without igniting racist outbursts but now targeting the "asylanten"* even more.[9] One

---

* refugees.

important point must be made clear: there are few common denominators between current European racism and "historical" racism, and furthermore, there is a radical difference between the political and ethnic realities of the older variety and those appearing today. While it is correct to vigorously oppose violent racism we do not feel it justifiable to magnify the current racist psychosis beyond the precise set of circumstances that make it possible and "successful," and to therefore exaggerate its importance. To place the old and the new racism on the same level is to confuse chicken pox and the bubonic plague—which is not to say that even chicken pox should not be feared and cured.

Today's racism has virtually no ideology of its own, no negative or positive stereotypes except for that of the "foreigner," whose profile changes according to different circumstances; most of all, it lacks any notion of the kind of life and society it intends to bring about. Except for groups that are openly neo-Nazi, the fundamental characteristics and historical precedents of traditional racism, the "clash between spirit and culture," are extremely weak. The origins of today's racism are to be found in a fundamental fear of the future, or the inability even to imagine a future and therefore the fear of nothingness. Hence, and this is its main characteristic, an inability to find expression in a political mass movement, coupled with the impossibility of making connections beyond its own network. The new racism also lacks the *Gleichschaltung* (forcible standardization) that allowed Nazism, once in power, to indoctrinate large numbers of youths with its "racial ethics."

We shall now conclude by discussing anti-Semitism, which was thought to be disappearing and less of a reality than racism. Despite what has often been said up to the Second World War, anti-Semitism was very much a reality within democratic countries.[10] Take the example of the British and American attitudes during the Second World War, as revealed by Walter Laqueur, in delaying and minimizing the news regarding the death camps for fear of being accused of going to war "for the Jews."[11] Anti-Semitism, instead, appears to be receding and becoming less visible, a poor relation to racism, a sort of necessary link to a tradition rather than a truly essential and dynamic component.

The decline of anti-Semitism since the war is due to various factors, the most important of which are certainly the following.

First: the devastating effect that the Holocaust has had on anti-Semitism. The memory of the Holocaust, effectively nurtured by the Jews worldwide, has somewhat eclipsed in the popular memory and cultural sensitivity of significant layers of the population, the no less monstrous Nazi crimes towards the other "inferior races," focusing concentrated attention and revulsion on anti-Semitism for the most part.

Second: the slow and steady move by most of the Christian churches, and the Catholic Church in particular, towards a complete revision of their traditional positions, up to the recent and explicit condemnation of anti-Semitism in the New Catechism.

Third: the fact that most Jewish immigrants from the former Soviet Union, where anti-Semitism has reappeared with partly traditional and partly anti-Western and nationalistic characteristics, have gone to America and Israel. Consequently the racist psychosis, similar to that experienced earlier in France, that also appeared in Germany following the dismantling of the Wall and reunification, had only a minor anti-Semitic component. The fact that after the First World War in Germany anti-Semitism turned into a mass movement and the Jews were branded as criminals by a nationalism exacerbated by defeat and the threat of revolution from the left, was due to the relatively large number of Jews who, contrary to today, were living in Germany at the time. The poorest Jews, mostly from Eastern Europe, differing from ordinary citizens because of their language and appearance, joined either the progressive or "subversive" left-wing parties or the most nonconformist and least "proper" intellectual circles of Weimar society.

A new element has appeared in recent decades, intruding upon these "mitigating" facts, slowing the decline of anti-Semitism and introducing a completely new factor: the anti-Zionist and anti-Israel type of anti-Semitism of Arab origin. This new form of anti-Semitism arises from the old anti-Jewish feeling within the Islamic world and above all the struggle against Israel by the Arab countries and the Palestinian movement.[12] The result is strong hostility which has spread within the Third World towards the United States and anyone favorable to Israel's right to survival and security, even succeeding in securing a vote at the United Nations' General Assembly condemning Zionism as racism. It has also widely penetrated the left- and right-wing parties in Europe, mostly among those elements most hostile to the United States and its "globalist-capitalist ideology." The Soviet Union had long been anti-Zionist regardless of the fact that it supported the creation of the state of Israel for tactical reasons, and had also, through its support of Arab policies, encouraged the new anti-Semitism. The massive changes within the Soviet Union during the last few years have had vast repercussions on the situation in the Middle East and on European left-wing parties, creating an obstacle to this new anti-Semitism, limiting it to certain groups, less anti-Semitic than hostile to American-style capitalism, and frequently reacting directly or indirectly to the Vatican's attitude towards the Arab-Israeli conflict.

This is what we can say within the limitations of an introduction to the study of a single aspect of anti-Semitism. It is a fact that anti-Semitism in the West is declining and this, to be sure, is a very positive outcome. However, it continues to exist in those countries that formed the old Soviet Empire and inside the former Soviet Union itself and, with very different characteristics, within the Arab-Moslem world, where its success is tied to cultural economic and political factors, making any projections relating to its evolution or its timing impossible. Personally, I am convinced that we can be optimistic in this area, if only because, as anti-Semitism tends to decline in those centers where it used to be dominant, it also tends to disappear in other countries, even in those where it had deeper and older roots, which are now undergoing a crisis created by unstoppable global economic integration and the resulting inevitable modernization.

Bibliographical Note

he 50th anniversary of the introduction of the racial laws by the Fascist government in Italy, along with a general in terest in the history of the Jews, anti-Semitism and racism, inspired a number of events and gatherings in Europe directly or indirectly related to the Jews. This gave rise, between 1988 and 1992, to many scholarly meetings, scientific and nonscientific review articles and monographs, and various other works that had been in preparation for longer periods of time but happened to appear together.

As is often the case in such circumstances, these publications represent a wide variety of interest and scientific value, some by specialists in the field, others by first-time and independent scholars. Some restate well-known facts and events; many of the others add some new element—useful to deepening our knowledge of the facts but of little historical value—that only completes a well-known picture. Few of these publications ultimately stand out. The real value of most of these works resides in their basic dissatisfaction with the scholarship of Jewish history, especially in Italy, during the nineteenth and twentieth centuries, and they are, in fact, merely guidelines towards possible future directions of scholarship that only extensive research will confirm.

For this reason, be it correct or incorrect, we have accepted with pleasure the publisher's proposal to republish this work in the Tascabili Einaudi edition (it had been part of the Biblioteca di cultura storica), to give it a broader audience and perhaps stimulate in the readers of the earlier editions a renewed interest in the "revised and expanded" edition, where certain previously neglected issues had been barely touched or only on the basis of limited documentation. On the other hand, this new edition, while awaiting the results of the latest studies that have been announced in the last few years, is the reprint, without any new revisions, of the 1988 edition, because any new additions would have been limited to a few bibliographic changes and notes. Should we decide to produce a new edition, it will only be once the various scholarly announcements of these last few years have yielded significant results—if they actually do, because often, research stimulated by external events, and notably anniversaries, fails to produce any viable projects. We also expect to have a better sense— at the conclusion of our *Mussolini* biography, especially regarding the two-year period 1943-1945—of whether we will need to make any further changes to this work.

Having made this choice, we nonetheless wish to give the non-scholarly reader interested in an "active" reading of our book (a reading that will stimulate, deepen, and widen the topic) a few bibliographical indications of works which have appeared since 1988 and are of greater interest or expand upon certain aspects we have written about. Because they cover various periods, we have loosely divided these topics into four basic groups according to the date of publication.

General works:

E. Fintz Menascè, *Gli ebrei a Rodi,* Milan 1992; *Stato nazionale ed emancipazione ebraica,* a cura di F. Sofia e M. Toscano, Rome 1992.

Specialized studies:

S. Zuccotti, *L'olocausto in Italia,* Milan 1988 (original edition 1987); R. De Felice, *Il fascismo e l'Oriente. Arabi, ebrei e indiani nella politica di Mussolini,* Bologna 1988; K. Voigt, *Zuflucht auf Widerruf Exil in Italien 1933-1945* (I), Stuttgart 1989; C. Schwarzenberg, "Cinquant'anni fa: le leggi razziali e i provvedimenti antisemiti," in *Il diritto di famiglia e delle persone"* 1989, pp. 349 ff.; N. S. Onofri, *Ebrei e fascismo a Bologna,* Bologna 1989; A. Zambonelli, "Ebrei reggiani tra leggi razziali e olocausto (1938-1945)" in *Ricerche storiche,* December 1988 and September 1989, pp. 9 ff. and 7 ff.; M. Minardi, "La cancellazione: le leggi razziali e la persecuzione degli ebrei a Parma (1938-45)," in *Storia e documenti,* July-December 1989, pp. 65 ff.; A. Ara, "Gli ebrei a Trieste 1850-1918," in *Rivista storica italiana,* April 1990, pp. 53 ff.; T. Catalan, "L'emigrazione ebraica in Palestina attraverso il porto di Trieste

(1908-1938)," in *Quale storia*, August-December 1991, pp. 57 ff.; P. Saiani, "Propaganda antiebraica ed eccidi a Forlí (1938–1944)," in *Bollettino dell'Istituto storico provinciale della Resistenza di Forlí*, 1990, pp. 45 ff.; *Ferramonti: un lager nel Sud*, a cura di F. Volpe, Cosenza 1990; G. Caravita, *Ebrei in Romagna (1938–1945)*, Ravenna 1991; A. Stille, *Uno su mille. Cinque famiglie ebraiche durante il fascismo*, Milan 1991 (ed. orig. 1991); F. Del Regno, "Gli ebrei a Roma tra le due guerre mondiali: fonti e problemi di ricerca," in *Storia contemporanea*, February 1992, pp. 5 ff.; A. M. Canepa, "Pio X e gli ebrei: una rivoluzione," in *Nuova antologia*, July–September 1992, pp. 139 ff.; D. Bidussa-A. Luzzatto-G. Luzzatto Voghera, *Oltre il ghetto. Momenti e figure della cultura ebraica in Italia tra l'Unità e il fascismo*, Brescia 1992; S. Minerbi, *Un ebreo fra D'Annunzio e il sionismo: Raffaele Cantoni*, Rome 1992; P. Cannistraro-B. Sullivan, *Il Duce's Other Woman. The never-before-told story of Benito Mussolini's Jewish mistress and how she helped him come to power*, New York 1993.

Studies on the Italian attitude towards the Jews in occupied areas and during the Second World War

The Italian Refuge. Rescue of Jews during the Holocaust, edited by I. Herzer, Washington 1989; D. Carpi, "L'atteggiamento italiano nei confronti degli ebrei della Tunisia durante la seconda guerra mondiale (giugno 1940–maggio 1943)" in *Storia contemporanea* December 1989, pp. 1183 ff.; L. Picciotto Fargion, "Italian Citizens in Nazi-Occupied Europe. Documents from the files of the German Foreign Office 1941-43," in *Simon Wiesenthal Center Annual* (1990) pp. 93 ff.; J. Steinberg, *All or Nothing. The Axis and the Holocaust 1941-1943*, London-New York 1990; L. Picciotto Fargion, *Il libro della memoria. Gli ebrei deportati dall'Italia (1943–1945)* Milan 1991.

Publications of colloquia, special issues of magazines, publication of documents on the 50th anniversary of the racial laws:

"1938. Le leggi contro gli ebrei," in *La rassegna mensile di Israel*, January-August 1988; "Ebrei, anti-Semitismo e razzismo in Italia dall'Unità alla persecuzione fascista," in *Storia contemporanea*, December 1988; *Le interdizioni del Duce. A cinquant'anni dalle leggi razziali in Italia (1938–1988)*, a cura di A. Cavaglion e G. Romagnani,

Torino 1988; *L'abrogazione delle leggi razziali in Italia* (1943–1947), a cura di M. Toscano, Senato della Repubblica, Rome, 1988; "Juden. Ebrei e Antisemitismo in Tirolo e in Trentino," in *Materiali di lavoro*, 1988; *La legislazione anti-ebraica in Italia e in Europa*, Camera dei Deputati, Rome 1989; "L'offesa della razza. Anti-Semitismo e leggi razziali in Italia e nella Venezia Giulia," in *Quale storia*, April 1989; *Conseguenze culturali delle leggi razziali in Italia*, Accademia Nazionale dei Lincei, Rome 1990.

March 1993

Author's Introduction 1987

E ven books sometimes have their own history. The first edition of this book was published over twenty-five years ago, in 1961. When the first two editions were long out of print in 1972, we welcomed the many requests to publish a third revised and expanded edition.

As we wrote then, our aim was to fulfill two duties we felt were equally important. A moral duty, which was to explain once again and bring to light the facts surrounding Fascist anti-Semitism and the persecution of the Italian Jews for those who had not lived through or had forgotten these events. This was all the more true because at the time—and unfortunately the fact remains true today as well—too many people, in Italy and overseas, tended to underestimate, forget, and even refocus or deny the tragic fate of European Jewry and anti-Semitism between the two world wars. A few short years ago, anti-Semitism appeared defeated and reduced to a tiny group of fanatics, but it now seems to be regaining ground in its more political incarnation, probably the most dangerous one, because next to the religious, racial, and economic varieties it is the most insidious of all. Take, for example, the way this kind of anti-Semitism has successfully woven itself within the folds of the Arab-Israeli conflict, and how it can mingle irrational animal instincts with the "purest" of idealistic values. A scientific duty: to account for the details, new information, and, most of all, new documents that have come to us from many private individuals, as well as from Italian, foreign, and various other organizations we have been in contact with.

Rather than being "revised and expanded," this third edition was intended to be more "revised and updated." There were to be no major changes with respect to the point of view or the conclusion of the preceding editions. The scientific discussion after the first two editions, the political and, even less, the sensational aspects, did not interest us then and do not today, even though, after many years, new facts have come to light which will possibly serve as material for a study of the political and ideological climate in Italy after World War Two. Yet none of this has changed our view of the fundamental issues. The few studies and new documents published in the last ten years, relating, for the most part, to the attitude of the Holy See towards the policies of the Fascist government against the Jews and Nazi extermination have not prompted us to make any changes to our work even when they actually corroborated what we had already written.

This being said, the changes we *did* make were limited to factual revisions, a few necessary additions to explain certain events or to give a more complete picture, as well as bibliographical additions, which we found we owed our readers, both old and new. We have not altered the main text or our conclusions on particular events, even in those cases where changes appeared to be necessary at the outset. The intent was to give this work the particular—objective as well as subjective—flavor of the moment in which it had been thought and written. A moment in time not too distant from ours—as we have said—but already remote with respect to the historiography of Fascism.

Twenty-five years represents a long time for a book about contemporary history. We have found it impossible for this fourth edition to use the same criteria we used to revise and update the third. As far as we are concerned, there are too many major obstacles for such a reworking.

From 1972 to now, and during the last ten years, we have seen the publication of many books on the history of Judaism and its various aspects, assimilation, Zionism, the relationship of the Diaspora Jews with Israel, national realities, European anti-Semitism between the wars and its differences with those of the preceding and following historical periods, the Holocaust, the Anglo-American position regarding first Jewish refugees up to 1939–1941, and the issue of the Jews in countries occupied by Germany. Parallel to this purely historical literature, we find an even larger number of books and articles by journalists and writers, many of considerable interest and indicative of the great wave of emotional, cultural, ideological, and political feelings involving both Jews and non-Jews. These works have continued to restate many aspects of the Jewish problem, including the question of whether or not it can be resolved at all, and the historical events surrounding Judaism during the last two hundred years, as well as the Holocaust.

The Holocaust itself is discussed today not only and not so much with respect to its reality and the responsibilities of those who undertook it—the inconsistency of the arguments used by the revisionists is obvious—but mostly regarding the moral responsibility of the German people and their historical conscience in the face of the monstrosity of the Nazi genocide and, on the other hand, in the way the historian can confront these issues. This is the substance of a controversial struggle, the *Historikerstreit*, which has recently upset the German cultural and historical establishment, a struggle set out by Jurgen Habermas in such ideological and political terms that it fails to increase our knowledge of the Nazi period, and does not contribute to a more rational and historical approach, which is, in fact, what is now most wanting on the part of historians.

The disputes this journalistic and historical literature has inspired directly or indirectly—the many positions taken by scholars in their wake, even though they had never specialized in the history of Judaism; for example, François Furet—are now impossible to ignore, even when they do not directly involve the themes of this book, and even when their ideas have little or nothing to do with the work of the historian, whose only objective can be to reconstruct and effectively understand reality, and are therefore obviously unfounded. This literature, these disputes, these debates (and even a certain type of memoir), even though they refer to realities other than those of Italy, or address them from perspectives different from the historical political ones, use a kind of documentation that is in itself atypical or extraneous. A case in point is the study by H. Stuart Hughes, *Prigionieri della speranza. Alla ricerca dell'identità ebraica nella letteratura italiana contemporanea* (Bologna 1983), which not only studies the emancipated Italian Jewish identity, but also the particular characteristics of assimilation in Italy. All these works show a number of directions and ideas for future investigations and studies in order to verify their validity with respect to Italian realities, that cannot be ignored.

To give an idea of the progress made in studies on contemporary Judaism during the last twenty-five years, and especially the last ten years, it is impossible not to mention the fundamental work of

George L. Mosse on the connection in contemporary history between racism, anti-Semitism, and mass political movements, which has almost completely changed the characteristics of anti-Semitism in our time compared to the traditional types preceding the French Revolution. The line of research he opened, which was entitled *International Fascism: Racism in Europe,* as well as the apparently tangential *Masses and Man,* is the only one that succeeds in overcoming a whole series of dead-end issues to which a number of important scholars had previously been drawn; for example, the burning issue, that was also mentioned in the preface to the first edition of this book, by Delio Cantimori, concerning connections in the study of racism between the National Socialist theorists and such philosophers as Herder, Fichte, Hegel, and others and the need to truly understand the new face of anti-Semitism as it has evolved during the last two hundred years and the reasons for its spread, to the "right" as well as to the "left," and the different national characteristics it has adopted. It is significant to consider the results reached by Zeev Sternhell, following in the steps of Mosse, in the case of France.

If, from the general view on the subject, we shift to the more particular one of studies of the Italian situation, two issues stand out. The first is rather simple to state. Despite the many studies that have appeared, the anti-Semitic policy of Fascist Italy and the history of the Italian Jews between the wars continue to be—in and, above all, outside of Italy—unknown or misunderstood even by the most serious historians. That these characteristics have been so particular to Italy that they turn Italian anti-Semitism into something different from that of German anti-Semitism has not been properly understood, or has been quickly explained by the lack of seriousness inherent in the Fascist regime, by the skin-deep consensus that Fascism, contrary to the acceptance of Nazism in Germany, had found in Italy. This is also true, according to some, of the basically Catholic culture permeating the Italian people. At first the anti-Semitic policy of Fascist Italy was placed on the same level as that of Nazi Germany, even though it was limited by the differences of the Italian Fascist regime, by the opportunism of Mussolini, and by the fact that the full development of the policy was stunted by the collapse of the Fascist regime in 1943 rather than, as in Germany, in 1945. The amazement and the enthusiasm at the discovery, during the last few years, of the extent of the protection and help given to the Jews by the Italian population, and by the soldiers of the Italian army within the Italian-controlled zones of occupation, were explained by the "humanity" of the Italians. Such a sweepingly partial and simplistic explanation fails to clarify these facts and has been so extended by some that they have effectively minimized the responsibility of the Italian Fascist regime and of Mussolini himself, even with reference to the period of the Italian Social Republic (RSI); it ends up misstating all of Fascism's policies towards the Jews, to the point of making them incomprehensible. It is, therefore, necessary to restate certain facts and reconstruct an organic description of the entire policy of the Fascist regime towards the Jews, its particular characteristics, its evolution in time, its differences when compared to those of other "Fascist" countries, while at the same time understanding all of its internal and external motivations, whether permanent or contingent.

In light of what has just been stated, we must turn to the most recent studies on the subject.

No comprehensive works or studies of the larger aspects of the Italian reality of the subject have appeared during the last fifteen years. The only notable and partial exception is the broad research by Meir Michaelis, *Mussolini and the Jews*, published in English in 1978 and in Italian in 1982. This work unquestionably offers interesting new elements resulting from extensive research, especially in German archives, regarding the attitude of Nazi Germany towards the Fascist Jewish policy. With respect to the relations between Berlin and Rome on the subject, it does not change, but rather enriches the picture we painted about twenty-five years ago. In our opinion, the work by Michaelis has one serious limitation, which is to reduce the Jewish policy of the Fascist regime to a foreign policy "event," and in particular to relations with Germany. For Michaelis the *indirect influence* of Germany on Mussolini's intent to forge an ever-tighter relationship is the only cause for the introduction of the racial policy. This underestimates and, at times, ignores every other aspect of Italian racial policy, resulting in blurring and obfuscating the deeper differences that exist between the attitude towards the Jews during the liberal governments and the Fascist regime before the mid-1930s; the reality and the inner workings of

Fascism itself, and how these changed in time, as well as the repercussions that these changes had on the attitude towards the Jews,
and on the autonomous developmental process of a home-grown
anti-Semitism on the part of Fascism in general, and by Mussolini
in particular.

If—apart from the work by Michaelis—these last fifteen years
have not seen any works on broader aspects or particular moments
of the history of the Italian Jews under Fascism, there have been
many research studies, individual contributions, and memoirs, some
of them of great value, that have enriched our knowledge and proposed or indirectly suggested new problems and subjects to be investigated.

As for us, we must say that during these last few years we have
returned many times to issues and themes we consider important
and even fundamental to the problems addressed in this book. We
allude in particular to our study on the Jews in Libya, *Ebrei in un
paese arabo. Gli ebrei nella Libia contemporanea tra colonialismo, nazionalismo
arabo e sionismo 1835–1970*, first published by Il Mulino, Bologna, in
1978, and also our biography of Mussolini, in process of publication in this same Einaudi series, and more precisely the second book
of the third volume, *Mussolini il duce. 2: Lo Stato totalitario 1936–
1940*, published in 1981. In this work the problem of the "politics
of race" and the introduction of the anti-Semitic measures are described in broader and deeper terms than our knowledge of the
realities of Fascism and of the ideological and political evolution
of Mussolini allowed us to do twenty years before and again in
1972, when the third edition of this book was published.

To all these reasons stemming directly from the general history
of contemporary Jewry, and of the Italian Jews during the Fascist
regime in particular, we must add, in conclusion, another no less
relevant one, which, in truth, belongs to a different problem that is
essential to achieve effective historical understanding of Fascist anti-
Semitism and of the differences between the Fascist and Nazi policies, and, generally, between all the various "Fascisms" in power.
We refer to the so-called question relating to a "Fascist phenomenon" at the center of both a historiographic as well as a political
debate and its importance in the controversy surrounding the issue
of totalitarianism.

We shall not discuss here the arguments, theories, and interpretations of those scholars who still speak of a "Fascist phenomenon" that would include all the European "Fascist" regimes of the 1920s, 1930s, and 1940s (not to speak of those who would extend it beyond Europe and even beyond the Second World War), nor of those who are in favor of continuing to develop a typological analysis of the totalitarian political regime and, therefore, speak of a "totalitarian phenomenon." In this introduction we can easily limit the subject to Italy and Germany and to racism and anti-Semitism; for the older, third type of "Fascism," we invite the reader to consult, for deeper information than what is generally available, Haim Avni's *España, Franco y los judíos* (Madrid 1982).

A superficial examination of the writings of the proponents of the theory of a "Fascist phenomenon"—the original ones date from the years during and immediately following the Second World War—and the writers who more recently have revived and developed such arguments (attempting at times to integrate them with those derived from the theory of "totalitarianism"), and the historians who appeared on the neo-Marxist wave of the sixties and seventies, shows that these authors consider the differences in ideology, racist, and anti-Semitic policies as a secondary and marginal aspect of the "Fascisms," variations that would not substantially alter the main characteristics of the phenomenon. Even though racism and anti-Semitism, because of their uniquely central importance on ideology and concrete action, make up the core elements of Nazism, most of these authors do not analyze the decisive value that these aspects have in elaborating a "theory of Fascism" and therefore of a purported unity of the "Fascist phenomenon," they end up dealing with the problem by simply ignoring it. Others accept the fact that there is such a problem, "but attempt to find a 'common ground' to the Fascist movements beyond the obstacle" (Friedländer) or, as in the case of Michaelis, speak of the differences in quantity that would appear to have a bearing because Nazism was a Fascism taken to its most extreme consequences, and therefore racism and anti-Semitism should be added to the differences that allow us to consider all "Fascist" movements as related, first and foremost Nazism and Fascism. Only a few writers have attempted to integrate these into the larger picture of their phenomenological interpretation, but, it must be stated clearly, with unsatisfactory if not grotesque results. The typical case is that of W. Schieder, who has seen fit to speak of a Fascist racism comparable to the Nazi variety when writing about Africans, Slavs, and South Tyroleans.

The difficulties that should encourage scholars to abandon the idea of a "Fascist phenomenon" and to clearly point out the differences between Fascist and Nazi totalitarianism have been illustrated by, among others, Karl Dietrich Bracher (see, for example, "Il nazionalsocialismo in Germania: I problemi d'interpretazione," in *Fascismo e nazionalsocialismo*, a cura di K. D. Bracher e L. Valiani, Bologna 1986). Bracher has declared such a theory unconvincing and totally useless, showing the wide differences, both in their ideas as well as the concrete actions taken, between the Fascist and Nazi regimes, insisting in particular on the central position within Nazism of "racist positions that transcend nation states and are tied to the ideology of *Lebensraum*"—which is absent from Fascism. The most convincing and broad argument on why it is impossible to ignore racism and anti-Semitism as a fundamental question, in itself sufficient to cancel any theory coupling Nazism to other historical realities, has been made by Saul Friedländer in his presentation at the opening of the Colloque de l'École des Hautes Études en Sciences Sociales that took place in Paris in 1982 ("De l'antisémitisme à l'extermination. Esquisse historiographique et essai d'interprétation," in *L'Allemagne nazie et le génocide juif*, Paris 1985). In concluding, Friedländer summed up the problem in terms that leave no space for those who continue to speak of a "Fascist phenomenon," and he restates the absolutely central nature of anti-Semitism in the ideology and politics of Nazism, which puts an end to the possibility of avoiding a dividing line between Fascism and Nazism, with all the consequences, direct and indirect, that stem from this division and which all those who wish to scientifically study the Jewish policy of Fascism must take into account. Friedländer wrote:

> The historian who is not encumbered by ideological or conceptual blinkers recognizes that it is precisely Nazi anti-Semitism and the anti-Jewish policy of the Third Reich that give Nazism its particular character. The problems regarding Nazism take on a new dimension

that defies comparison. Both Fascism and totalitarianism disappear as sufficient concepts; the Freudian and Marxist interpretations reach their obvious limitations on this question . . . If we accept the fact that the Jewish problem was the center, the very essence of the system, a good part of the usual explanations lose their coherence and historiography is faced with an "anomaly" that defies its usual categories of interpretation.

We have taken some time in this overview of the literature dedicated directly or indirectly to Jewish problems and contemporary anti-Semitism, that have appeared since 1972, for two reasons: to give uninitiated readers a summary of these writings and to offer a few references to check and integrate what we have written in this book and demonstrate that, as we have already stated, we cannot simply offer a revision and amplification to what we wrote some twenty-five years ago. It is also impossible to summarize in the same way the studies on Italian Fascism. In 1961 these studies were just beginning. The only comprehensive work was the *Storia dell'Italia nel periodo fascista* by Luigi Salvatorelli and Giovanni Mira, a work that was certainly beneficial but, because of the unavailability, at the time, of necessary sources was, in effect, only an outline, an orderly description of known facts. The situation was no better at the level of more specialized studies. Therefore, everything had to be investigated and reconstructed practically from the beginning and in the absence of scientifically valid models. The only exception was the *Nascita e avvento del fascismo* by Angelo Tasca, the only study that offered new ideas and points leading to a real understanding of Fascism, but because it only examined its origins, it was received with suspicion by most of the "militant" culture of the period. The situation has changed considerably since then; the literature concerning Fascism has increased immeasurably, taking directions that we shall not discuss here, but maintaining a fundamentally political and ideological overview that one can attribute, in our opinion, to the absence of a comprehensive work appearing earlier. Due to obvious limitations, such as the lack of access to public and private archives which are accessible today, namely the *Storia* by Salvatorelli and Mira, and because of the cautionary advice imparted at various times during the 1960s by Delio Cantimori, even though it was formally accepted and paid lip service to, that in effect were disregarded and set aside but in point of fact changing its real meaning and forcing them to fit political-ideological grids that have nothing in common with true historical research. This is why we refrain from offering a second synopsis that would not help the reader by adding new elements for a clearer understanding of the material in this book.

We must now go back to the initial intent of these pages and explain how this new edition differs from those preceding it; how—once we had decided to forego the idea of a merely formal revision and an updating limited to the bibliography—we have solved the problems tied to the progress of research studies in these last few years on the subjects of Judaism and anti-Semitism in general and in Italy in particular.

It might seem that the best solution would have been to rewrite anew what we had written twenty-five years before. We have, however, always rejected such a solution, just as we have refused, on other occasions, to write an abridged version that would make this work more popular, more accessible, and easier to translate. This is essentially because, as we have already said, we are convinced that books have their own history, which cannot be modified. To engage in a complete rewrite would have meant to create an entirely different book, almost certainly no better than the older version. The conceptual underpinnings of the original volume would have always tended to reemerge, and, therefore, the new book would not have differed substantially from the original; it would have been heavier with detail, which while almost never essential would have no doubt cluttered the narrative and probably clouded the fundamental ideas it intended to illustrate. Some of these ideas, including the more significant ones we had already presented in 1961, could have appeared as the result of additions and discussions that came after the publication of the first three editions. But, overall, it would have meant writing a book that was the child of the older one and at the same time completely new, while—and we have no trouble saying this—the reasons we are intellectually and psychologically tied to this work are not so much due to its recognized scientific value, as the fact that when it was first published in 1961 it signaled a turning point in the historiography of Fascism, from one way of writing history to another. This was not so much because of the variety of the sources we used—which were made accessible through a number of circumstances, not the least of which was the moral value of the subject of the study—because we examined reality without, as Cantimori would have said, being overwhelmed by emotions, even the most noble and justifiable ones, nor conditioned by preconceived ideas and ideological scruples, which the historian—especially the historian involved in contemporary history—must at all costs avoid if he is to understand and explain the reality he is writing about.

Having rejected a rewrite, this fourth edition could not be limited, like the third, to a formal revision and a simple expansion of the bibliography, which would not have done justice to the progress made in the field since 1972. Therefore, there was a need for a deeper handling that would not alter the general plan or the size of the book itself. The revision would have to be limited in the text to those facts and problems essential to a real understanding of the historical impact of the Jewish and anti-Semitic Fascist policy and yet encompass the results of new studies and the most interesting single contributions in the notes.

To these changes we have added a revision that had been considered during the work on the third edition. We had decided not to include these revisions at the time because we felt that the text of how we had "lived" the subject ten years before could remain unchanged at the time. We now think it necessary to make these revisions.

As is often the case with youth, and we were younger then, we had not sufficiently kept our indignation in check nor avoided certain conclusions that can be attributed to hindsight: the knowledge of how events were to unfold, what certain events were to lead to, and the kind of allegiances some men would later adopt. Cantimori had immediately and constructively criticized this tendency of ours. Almost jokingly he reminded us of the old dictum of "a famous and very wise statesman and politician of times past": *Videbis, fili mi, quam parva sapientia regitur mundus* [You see, my son, how little wisdom rules the world], and observed that we should have better spent our energy—but then we did not have access to the documents that we have today—in attempting to explain in greater depth the personality of Mussolini and the strength of his own position regarding anti-Semitism and racism. He also warned us that even if loathing these policies is a duty, its too frequent repetition "for educational purposes" "can end up canceling its effectiveness." He concluded, going from general to detailed criticism, by saying "certain coldly analytical pages are far more effective to the reader who wants to know and learn about the subject than the more polemical sections of this book, even though these are so few, and books such as this one appear to me to have more impact than violent invective and biased reconstructions."

Twenty-five years later the words Cantimori wrote have lost neither their value nor, unfortunately, their relevance. Both have actually increased, because the "educational purpose" of a certain type of morality is now one of the most common means of attempting to deny the value of historical reconstructions and critical conclusions in order to replace them with tired political and ideological positions that obviously are meant to deviate from the main issue. This being said—and we address ourselves to our earliest readers, who may not understand or may actually misunderstand the disappearance of certain passages—the scruples that we had in 1972 in not making any changes or corrections have given way to the need to avoid creating the wrong impression in those new readers who do not have a thorough grounding in historical work, therefore unwittingly perpetuating a certain type of historical writing that is more the result of bias and unscientific attitudes.

This being said, we feel we have satisfactorily fulfilled our responsibilities towards our new and, above all, our old readers. In closing we can only once again renew our thanks to all those who during these twenty-five years, and then some, have transmitted documents, news, facts of all kinds to us, which helped enrich and deepen our work and the understanding of the reality this book seeks to render. Due to their number and to avoid any involuntary omissions, we apologize that we are unable to name all those who have understood the spirit of this work and have, in some way, helped; they are gratefully remembered. Once again, our deepest thanks to all.

December 1987

Part One

———◦•◦———

I.

The Italian Jews on the Eve of
the Fascist Takeover

1.

The Italian Jews

T he first task in examining the situation of the Jews in Italy during Fascist rule is to determine their actual numbers and and their importance in Italian life at the time.

Contrary to what would appear obvious, establishing the exact number of the Jews is not simple. The discussions among the Fascists themselves during the years 1938-1939 show how difficult the task actually turned out to be, even though they had conducted a special census, which was continuously updated and expanded, using all the sources and governmental instruments at their disposal, including the threat of severe punishment against whoever attempted to evade it or failed to answer truthfully every question to the government's satisfaction. The basis for the racial laws was the census of August 22, 1938, yet—as Giovanni Preziosi was to say in arguing with Telesio Interlandi—"this census could not be considered *the* census."[13]

Depending upon the definition used to describe "the Jew," the actual number of Jews undergoes many changes: the various censuses taken by individual Jewish communities include only those

Jews registered within the communities themselves, almost always without differentiating between Italian nationals and foreign Jews residing in Italy.[14] The official Italian government censuses—for our purposes those taken in 1911 and particularly in 1931—included only those Jews who practiced their religion. However, in 1911 some 874,532 persons said that they practiced no religion at all and 653,404 refused to answer, and in 1931—when the answer regarding religion was compulsory—17,283 persons declared that they practiced no religion at all.[15] Therefore those Jews who did not practice the Jewish religion or who, for whatever reason, did not identify themselves as Jewish were not counted. The racist census of 1938 in attempting to find out more was unable to do so completely—as even its organizers were to acknowledge—on the basis of extremely questionable criteria which cannot be taken at face value.[16]

This is the kind of problem we encounter in dealing with the Italian Jews; with the Jews living in the Italian African colonies, the foreign Jews living in Italy, and the Italian Jews living abroad, many more questions arise. This explains why, among the Fascists themselves in 1938-1939, we find very different numbers and how it is always difficult to understand which Jews they were referring to and how they arrived at those numbers: some spoke of 70,000, some of 100,000, 120,000, and even 180,000.

Given these facts, rather than attempting to guess or to enter into hypothetical calculations that are more or less subjective, we will offer the reader some basic figures and a few observations which can give a better idea, in particular of the numbers of Italian Jews, foreign Jews, and Jews living in the colonies.

The Italian Jews were, according to the official numbers of each census:

Census	Italian Jews
1911	32,825
1931	39,112
1938	47,252

The increase could lead us to believe that there had been a significant demographic leap, a myth that we must deal with at the outset. The increase in numbers from 1911 to 1931 is actually only superficial: it can largely be explained by the additional territories Italy annexed in 1918 (especially Trieste), which added about 7,000 Jews, and by the more scientific manner in which the second census itself was conducted. If we limit the comparison to the Italian borders of 1915—as Riccardo Bachi[17] correctly did—the "increase" between 1911 and 1931 is only of 2,098 persons, from which we must deduct those added back from the "gray" answers in 1911 and the foreigners, about 1,000, who had become Italian citizens in the meantime. The natural increase in the Jewish population, according to these numbers, is actually nil, if not negative, when compared to the national average.[18] Between 1931 and 1938 there was a slight demographic increase but not enough to justify the jump from 39,000 to 47,000 persons, just as it cannot be attributed to newly naturalized Italians, amounting to about 400. The sharp increase can be attributed in part to the inclusion of virtually all Italian Jews and, in part, to the racist criteria used in the 1938 census. Proof of this tendency, which confirms the regressive nature of Italian Jewish demographics, can be found in the following statistical table taken from the numbers put together by the office of Demography and Race—the total number at year-end 1938 is modified by comparison to the number provided by the August 22, 1938 census due to intervening adjustments.

Religion at birth	Religion at census						
	Jewish	Cath.	Other Christian	Other non-Christian	None	Without affiliation	Unknown
Jewish	37,203	1,498	53	6	98	31	53
Catholic	19	6,881	2	-	-	3	1
Other Christian	1	15	135	-	-	-	-
Other non-Christian	-	1	3	-	-	-	-
None	13	325	2	-	1,367	-	-
Without affiliation	2	16	-	-	-	58	-
Unknown	3	29	-	-	-	-	214

From these figures it becomes obvious that: *a.* almost one-tenth of those who claimed not to practice any religion during the 1931 census were of Jewish origin; *b.* the jump in numbers between 1931 and 1938 is explained by the religious nature of the criteria used in 1931 and the racial nature of the criteria used in 1938. The number of those who practiced the Jewish religion in 1931, 39,112, is actually higher than in 1938 when it was 37,241; the jump is attributable, besides 1,367 who said they practiced no religion at all, to the 7,019 Jews who since birth were considered Catholics (6,881), or other Christians (135) or of other non-Christian religion (3), as well as children of parents who had already converted before their birth or of parents of mixed religion but for the most part non-Jewish.

To have a complete picture of the Italian Jews we should add to these numbers those of citizens and residents of the Italian colonies and foreign countries. The available numbers are impossible to ascertain.[19] The number of residents in the colonies in 1938 also cannot be accounted for with any precision; the census of 1931—the differences within seven years can be considered negligible—gives a total of 511 persons: 385 in Libya (331 in Tripolitania and 54 in Cyrenaica), 108 in the Italian islands in the Aegean, 16 in Eritrea, and 2 in Somalia.

Even though covered by a different legal statute, the foreign Jewish nationals residing within the Kingdom of Italy were very important to reach a true evaluation of the number of Italian Jews.[20] Not only did their numbers increase steadily between 1911 and 1938 due to the arrival of immigrants from Eastern and Central Europe,[21] but almost half of the large number of those foreign Jews—a total of 10,173 according to the 1938 census—were permanent residents established in Italy for many years[22] and a part of the Italian Jewish communities, participating actively in their religious, cultural, and community life. For once, the racists and the Fascist authorities were not mistaken in considering foreign Jews as belonging to Italian Jewry. We shall use the same criteria in the two lists we have compiled indicating the Jews present in Italy in August 1938.

Finally, to close this brief statistical overview, there were 28,600 indigenous Jews in the old colonies: 24,024 in Libya (21,138 in

Tripolitania and 2,886 in Cyrenaica), 4,372 in the Italian islands in the Aegean, 193 in Eritrea, and 11 in Somalia.[23] To this group, which had, especially in Libya,[24] its own particular character, must be added, in 1936, the Falasha Jews of Ethiopia. Their exact numbers are uncertain, but the best approximation is about 40,000.

Having determined rather precisely the total number of Italian Jews, the next question is what *influence* did this minority—about one and one-quarter per thousand of the entire population of the Kingdom of Italy—have on Italian life?

According to the anti-Semitic racists, Jewish "influence" was gigantic, even crushing; they compared the Jews to an octopus extending its tentacles into every important segment of national life: culture, administration, politics, and, most importantly, the economy. According to Giovanni Preziosi they occupied a dominant position in Italy, since they control the nerve centers of national life." He was perhaps the only really coherent Italian anti-Semite of the twentieth century, a racist who did not repeat verbatim the words and slogans coined by others, but for over thirty years proceeded to "study" the Italian Jews, "even though they represent in our midst a very small minority—fewer than 50,000"— Preziosi wrote in 1920 and repeated again in 1944:[25]

> The Jews control the biggest banks in Italy; they occupy a high percentage of the boards of directors of our corporations; they are very numerous within the Senate and in the Chamber of Deputies; they occupy the highest and most important positions within the state administration. They are innumerable in the teaching profession, and some university departments have been effectively closed to anyone else. They own almost all the publishing companies in Italy. Many daily newspapers are under their control... And we should not forget that all business deals, even those having a patriotic theme, are directed by a Jew.[26]

The real picture is very different.

It is true that the Jews were active in proportionately higher numbers than most other Italian citizens in all intellectual activities: a whole series of historical and sociological studies has adequately explained the reasons for this Jewish presence; the historical mechanism that determined that the Jews in Italy were for the most part middle- and upper-middle-class. Using this historical and sociological point of departure and comparing the Jews to the rest of the Italian middle class, it immediately appears how unfounded the arguments of the racists and anti-Semites are, and how this supposed Jewish "supremacy" is proved meaningless. The best refutation of anti-Semitic propaganda can be found in the census of 1938 itself and in the official and secret decrees of Fascist racist policy.

If the middle-class identity of Italian Jews is a given fact, the only possible exception being the working class, living mostly in the ghetto of Rome, the economic activities of the Italian Jews ages ten and older, as assembled by the Office of Demography and Race using the census of 1938, does not reveal statistically, the presence of any Jewish "octopus." (See table below.)

	Owners	Professionals	Artisans	Managers	Employees	Temp. Employees	Workers	Total
Agriculture	218	-	-	7	22	-	5	252
Industry	662	-	264	267	1,527	41	1,027	3,788
Trans. & Comm.	85	-	4	28	311	28	168	624
Trade	4,785	-	-	71	2,304	118	139	7,417
Wholesale	758	-	-	33	876	31	38	1,736
Retail	2,474	-	-	27	1,015	51	33	3,600
Other	1,553	-	-	11	413	36	68	2,081
Credit & Insurance	32	-	-	93	861	16	5	1,007
Professional activity	1	1,508	-	-	86	5	1	1,601
Medical	1	417	-	-	11	-	-	429
Legal	-	554	-	-	55	-	-	609
Literary/scientific	-	47	-	-	-	-	-	47
Other	-	490	-	-	20	5	1	516
Public Administration	-	-	-	216	1,655	59	55	1,985
Private Administration	3	91	-	5	131	11	2	243
Religion	-	-	-	11	93	27	2	133
Domestic economy	-	-	-	1	11	54	1	67
Non-professionals	-	-	-	-	-	-	-	22,694
Owners & well-to-do	-	-	-	-	-	-	-	1,381
Pensioners	-	-	-	-	-	-	-	939
Students & pupils	-	-	-	-	-	-	-	6,704
Housewives	-	-	-	-	-	-	-	12,250
Other	-	-	-	-	-	-	-	1,420
Unknown	-	-	-	-	-	-	-	645

It is also obvious, when comparing the results of the 1931 census to earlier ones, that, generally, the Jews did not drastically improve their status within the previous thirty years, contrary to what the anti-Semites declared. The details reveal that the Jews were concentrated almost exclusively in central and northern Italian cities, and in fact in a very small number of urban centers, which makes the "octopus" assertion look improbable, as do any comparisons to a much more significant Jewish presence in other countries, as, for example, Poland.

The geographic subdivision can be found in the regional and provincial figures of the 1938 census; as do the difference between major centers and smaller centers—typical of a growing middle class—these few figures taken from the statistics of the Office of Demography and Race will be sufficient:

	Provincial centers	Other municipalities
Italian Jews	41,224	4,137
Foreign Jews	7,767	1,975
Total	48,991	6,112

In reality the Jewish "presence" was limited to just a few cities; in descending order: Trieste, Leghorn, Rome, Milan, Venice, Turin, Ancona, Florence, Genoa, Ferrara. The Jewish population could be described as really significant only in Trieste and possibly in Leghorn, Venice, Ancona, and Ferrara. It was certainly not from such limited bases that the Jews could expect to conquer Italy! The local figures in these cities—it remains unclear how the figures were arrived at, whether from the official census or other sources based on last names and lists of various kinds—which were published in the daily newspapers in 1938-1939, confirm the facts. A few numbers will be enough to prove our statement. In Trieste, the largest "Jewish city," out of 380 doctors and dentists there were 90 Jews; out of 142 pharmacists there were 7 Jews; out of 310 lawyers and magistrates there were 46 Jews; out of 135 architects there were 7 Jews; out of 390 engineers, builders, and entrepreneurs there were 33 Jews; out of 130 employees and professionals there were 15 Jews:[27]

these figures are anticlimactic when one thinks that this is the largest Jewish population in an urban center. The same pattern emerges in a city like Turin, considered "average" as to the numbers of Jews: according to *La stampa*,[28] which published a series of articles on the "massive" Jewish presence in the life of Turin and the surrounding province, in August 1938 the Jewish doctors numbered 203 out of 1,463, the engineers 79 out of 960, the accountants 34 out of 180, the industrial accountants 14 out of 332, the public accountants 38 out of 271, the notaries 9 out of 108, and the lawyers 124 out of 962. It must be noted that these numbers were compiled with "the criteria of not taking into account only typically Jewish last names," in mind a practice that, as was to become obvious from the massive number of denials that were to crowd the newspaper files during those months, actually created an artificial increase and contributed to the publication of completely false statistics.[29]

From any point of view these statistics demonstrate that the Jews in Italy did not hold the keys to economic and social power. Even in a profession such as stockbroker, which more than any other would appear to be typically Jewish, only 13% were Jews.[30] Similar proportions, as we shall see, are to be found among the Jews who were eliminated from public administration in 1938.

The inventories of Jewish estates that were published with massive publicity during the second half of 1938 by virtually all the newspapers lead us to different conclusions. First of all it is important to note that the numbers that were published had been obtained by the usual referencing of "Semitic"-sounding last names.[31] It is further significant that, when the Fascist authorities conducted a regular census on the subject, they did not publish the results with so much fanfare. Even if we consider the numbers that were published as valid, they end up proving the opposite of what the Fascists had intended: not only did they refer to a limited number of cities—those that had larger Jewish populations, as we have seen—but even in these cities Jews did not constitute the massive presence that had been announced. On the national level the proportions were even smaller. After so many virulent and indignant articles about Jewish economic superpower, it was almost comical to read such news items as the one about how the Jews in Milan had monopolized 14% of all imports.[32]

If the Jews indeed had a presence and played a role in Italy since the second half of the nineteenth century, it was not so much in the economic field as in the administration, becoming state functionaries, magistrates, military men, and then turning to politics and academia. As Arnaldo Momigliano rightly observed concerning this issue:

> My impression is that the passage from the ghetto to the middle classes took place more frequently in Jewish families through their entrance into the state administration and academia than because of commercial activities.[33]

As soon as we consider the detail of the history of the Jews and their integration into Italian society before and after their emancipation, Momigliano's statement becomes obvious. As he wrote again in 1933 while reviewing a book by Cecil Roth, *The Jews in Venice*, which caught the attention of Antonio Gramsci and, after some hesitations, garnered Gramsci's approval,[34] it is a development that characterized the parallel birth of national awareness in both Italians and Jews.

Numerically, therefore, the Jews amounted to a negligible quantity and their influence on national life—economic, social, administrative, and political—was less than overwhelming and geographically limited, so that even from the psychological and moral point of view the Jews could not be a problem in Italy. It can be said that from the second half of the 18th century the *Jewish question* no longer existed in Italy. For some time the Jews had successfully integrated themselves psychologically and legally into Italian society without any problems or opposition. This process had begun during the period overlapping the 18th and 19th centuries, first at the time of the "Jacobin" republics and later during the Napoleonic period,[35] to reach a rapid conclusion during the Italian *Risorgimento*,[36] which took place with the wide and enthusiastic participation of the Jews, who were welcomed and treated without any prejudice by the overwhelming majority of the Italian people. A united Italian state did not—we repeat—acknowledge a *Jewish question*. Isolated cases, such as the famous "Mortara case," which actually began within the State of the Church and immediately drew the attention of the new Italian authorities,[37] cannot be used as proof of a malaise that certainly did not exist. The Italian Jews, free and equal to all other Italian citizens in every way, were undisturbed and actually favored by the state whenever the practice of their religion and the respect for their traditions in an essentially Catholic country were in danger of being jeopardized. The Italian Jews were quickly integrated into the new Italian society,[38] becoming almost always fervent patriots.[39] The resistance and ostracism displayed by a few Catholic circles remained for the most part isolated instances, and generally met with the disapproval of the majority of the population.

The result of this integration was a rapid and massive assimilation of the Italian Jews, morally and materially, into Italian society, resulting in a deep attachment to Italy, the Italian state, and its future.[40] This attachment, in many cases, even caused a repudiation of their own Jewishness, as if being Jews meant that they were not able to be completely Italian.[41] When, at the close of the 19th century and at the beginning of the 20th, Zionism appeared within international Jewry, many Italian Jews expressed their opposition to its ideals.[42] The result of this assimilation was also to be found in material changes such as the rapid exodus from the ancient ghettos and a spreading throughout the country, along with mixed marriages, a certain detachment from the life of the Communities and from religious practice itself, accompanied occasionally by a number of conversions to Catholicism.

Because of its size, it is important to examine the material aspects surrounding assimilation. These had three focal points: mixed marriages, dissociations, and conversions.

The number of mixed marriages is the most difficult to ascertain even today: the Jew who married outside his religion had in effect repudiated his religion, and often the Communities were not informed of his marriage; nor can the figures relating to the permissions granted by the Holy See to marry "due to the difference in religious practice" be used, the majority of mixed marriages being performed exclusively in a civil ceremony and therefore not subject to this type of control.[43] Reliable numbers are not available for the first decades following Italian unification; for the years we are analyzing, a useful reference is the ad hoc count made by the Office of Demography and Race at the end of 1938. According to this count the status of mixed marriages would have been, as of October 24, 1938, as follows.

	Northern Italy	Central Italy	Southern Italy	Islands	Total
Marriages					
Total	5,363	1,885	156	53	7,457
With Jewish husband	3,285	1,077	84	32	4,478
With Jewish wife	2,078	808	72	21	2,979
Without children	1,803	574	52	17	2,446
Children					
Total	6,195	2,731	248	73	9,247
Jewish children	1,337	686	18	4	2,045
Non-Jewish children	4,689	1,951	226	69	6,935
Part Jewish & part non-Jewish children	169	94	4	-	267

These are extremely significant numbers not to be found in any other country. According to the 1938 census, of married couples involving Jews only 56.3% were both Jewish; the other 43.7% were mixed.[44] In a memo issued by the Office of Demography and Race we find the following notation: "The percentage of Jews of both sexes that marry persons of another religion and race is far superior in Italy to any other country in Europe";[45] in 1930-1937 this figure in Italy was 30%, while the same statistic in Germany was 11% in 1934, and in Hungary 14% in 1932. The real significance of these numbers could not have possibly escaped the Fascists themselves. In a secret memo dated September 1941 we read:

11

The Jewish situation in Italy did not present the extreme danger it did in other countries, due to the limited number of Jews residing in the Kingdom, and because of the high rate of mixed marriages between Jews and Aryans. This reality created a special situation whereby the Jews who had infiltrated Aryan society with emotional and material ties had effectively reduced the feelings of antagonism towards themselves, even more so due to the fact that many Jews, given their positions of prominence reached within the state administration, the armed forces and industry, had been able to create a favorable, rather than hostile, attitude among their peers. The true feeling of suspicion towards the Jews, if exception is made of the very small group of anti-Semitic researchers, was present in Italy only within the lower classes against the most humble Jews, those who worked at the trades that were typical of the ghetto.[46]

The Fascists themselves were forced to admit that anti-Semitism did not exist in Italy, but that there was a definite tendency towards assimilation on the part of Italian Jews—at least within its largest group in the middle class—which encountered no resistance among non-Jews. It is important to note that within mixed marriages, the non-Jewish spouse was usually the bride, who could have been discouraged by a religious attachment to Catholicism if not by an anti-Semitic motivation.

It is even more difficult to reach a number for "dissociations", and we are not helped in this task by any findings during the period of racial persecutions. The figures published by Dante Lattes[47] are of little value in this regard; they involve only those official dissociations—on the basis of Article 5 of the Rules of the Jewish Communities, which deals with the cases of those who declare they no longer wish to be considered Jewish—and add to these the true renunciations of the faith, those who in fact actually change their religion. Despite the fact that many elements are missing, mostly regarding de facto dissociations, these numbers can be of interest, especially if we consider that, for the category of renunciations, we can rely on figures from the office of Demography and Race. According to Lattes, the dissociations and renunciations from 1932 to 1937 would have been 988: 86 in 1932, 149 in 1933, 196 in 1934, 455 in 1935, 37 in 1936, and 65 in 1937.[48] As for the renunciations—often followed by conversions—we have numbers from the office of Demography and Race as of the end of 1938 but referring to the month of August. The dissociations are classified below according to the years since they took place.

Years	Italian Jews	Foreign Jews
Less than 1	371	150
1	130	35
2	97	22
3	90	14
4	69	16
5	59	15
6-9	237	40
More than 10	818	142
Unknown	213	45
Total	2,084	479

These numbers almost certainly include the official dissociations that we mentioned above. From these tables we can infer that the religious consequences of these tendencies toward assimilation were not so much a conversion to Catholicism or to other organized religions as a distancing oneself from the older religion, a consequence that is within the logic of assimilation in general. It is necessary to examine this tendency in greater detail.

During the *Risorgimento*, at the time of emancipation and equality, Italian Judaism lived through an extremely lively and vital period of debate: those in favor of assimilation and the defenders of Jewish identity, innovators and traditionalists, freethinkers and the strictly orthodox clashed in heated debates over the values and mission of Judaism within the new historical and social circumstances. As Attilio Milano wrote regarding this period of great interest and change, once Italian unity was achieved,

> there followed some twenty-five years of fog, which descended over all the thoughts and actions of the Italian Jews and influenced everything that concerned them; this fog concerned their identity as Jews

13

and was the result of the excessive attention they had drawn by being suddenly and completely emancipated.[49]

It is a harsh and extreme judgment, betraying the bias of its author; coming from a Jewish source it remains significant. In reality, from 1870 until Fascism and even beyond, for some up to the racial persecutions, the vast majority of Italian Jews enthusiastically took the road to assimilation, immersing themselves into the vast Italian majority. Having left the ghettos and their traditional activities, having gone to live among the "others," having successfully entered the workforce in jobs that had been previously closed to them within the administration, teaching, the armed forces, etc., and being welcomed everywhere without problems and even with friendliness, most of these Jews became psychologically and intellectually *Italianized*. As another Zionist writer was to observe: "if integration here and there did not always seem to have worked, it was a work in progress, an ideal to strive for."[50] To those who would taunt them because of their origins, the Jews would answer that Italy was a composite of various races and that the Jews were a part of Italy just like the Piedmontese, the Tuscans, the Neapolitans, or the Sicilians. After immersion in the Italian culture of the time, many left the Jewish faith in part or completely. Spiritual ties to world Jewry were loosening while the psychological and even material differences became greater, especially with the largest and most fervent group, located in Eastern Europe. For many, the only ties with world Jewry were merely a question of humanity, which did not go beyond some form of financial support, which was given sometimes grudgingly.[51]

At the end of the last century the Italian Jews had lost all contact with the Jews in the rest of Europe and the world; they had become isolated and separated from the great Diaspora, from the large areas in central and eastern Europe that were the cultural and traditional heartland of Jewish life, where the basis for the great renewal and spiritual rebirth known as Zionism was beginning. Italian Jewry, or to be more precise the Italian Jews, considered themselves closed within the borders of the country they were living in, ecstatic at their own successes in politics, science, industry, the arts, journalism, and were well on their way towards the most complete assimilation, paving the way for the next generation to be completely absorbed and having their identity canceled. The voices of the rabbis were weak and almost never went beyond the walls of the Beth ha-Knesset, almost always and everywhere, deserted, often controlled by the Boards of Directors of the Communities, which were invariably made up of Jews who were assimilated or favorable to assimilation.[52]

A typical example of this psychological and intellectual attitude can be found between 1874 and 1922 (the dates are significant) in the magazine *Il Vessillo israelitico*,[53] a monthly published in the town of Casale Monferrato. It is important to note that this attitude was not limited to wealthy and well-educated Jews:

> In contact with liberal institutions, the social reality that had accompanied Jewish life during the period it lived within the enclosure of the ghetto quickly disappeared; religious feeling, which had remained for centuries the great element of cohesion and strength for the Jewish communities, weakened when it did not altogether disappear; this evolution was to become, in time, the norm after having been limited at the beginning to the upper social classes.[54]

The problem and the precise forms the integration and assimilation were to take remain to be investigated despite the great importance that it had and still has for a true understanding of the internal history of the Jews as well as their relationship with the social, cultural and moral reality of Italy. Mario Toscano appears to have best summarized the current status of these investigations:

> On the basis of the most recent research, Italian Jewry up to the beginning of the new century is marked by an accelerated process of integration into national life, without traumatic forms of rejection of its own identity, but rather rich in nuances centering around the weakening of Jewish religious identity at the very moment when religion became the identifying factor of Jewish diversity. Within the religious emptiness that characterized the newer generations of Jews, the examples of secularization and modernization of liberal society favored the dissemination of new values as substitutes and contributed to integrating the Jews even more. These values would give the

masses an egalitarian type of ethic and a messianic anxiety of redemption, within the cult of the new liberal monarchy that was their
homeland and gave the seal of approval to the Jewish Italians as
belonging to the Italian nation. Jewish consciousness weakened, faced
with these extremely strong solicitations coming from the entire society around them, and religious belief appeared to be an archaic
residue; traditional culture was unable to renew and modernize itself,
and the acceptance of the modern meant forgetting one's origins,
with many variations, from neglect to outright rejection.

With reference to the Italian Jewish community in general, many
attitudes of a number of middle-class Italian Jews can be traced to
their compromise between patriotism and weakened religious practice, and the origins of the decline of Jewish consciousness can be
found in the intellectual world analyzed by Stuart Hughes.[55]

We have spent some time on this aspect of recent Italian Jewish
history because we feel it essential to the understanding of three
other key features of the history of the Italian Jews regarding Fascism: the almost total absence of anti-Semitic motivations within
Italy; the spreading of Italian Jews among Italian political parties
of all tendencies and therefore taking a position for or against Fascism as Italian citizens rather than Italian Jews; the appearance and
slow growth of Zionism among Italian Jews, its significance and its
position towards Fascism and vice versa.

There is little reason to discuss the almost complete absence of
anti-Semitic motivations. Classical anti-Semitism is driven by religious or economic motivations, and both were almost completely
absent from Italy. The main reason was the small number of Jews,
which made them an infinitesimal minority even in the cities of
greater concentration. If we compare Italy to Austria, a country
where anti-Semitism was not that violent and, in many ways, only a
reflection of the influence of neighboring countries, we find that
in 1935 there were 195,481 Jews, of whom 176,034 lived in Vienna,
out of less than 6,000,000 inhabitants. Anti-Semitic motivations
were further absent from Italy for religious reasons due to the lack
of fervor of the Jews themselves, since a majority did not practice
their religion, and because of a certain innate tolerance on the part
of the Italians. The economic motivation was also almost com-

pletely absent because of the weakness of the Jewish presence in the national and local economy. The only exceptions were a few small groups with almost no influence over public opinion and some Catholic circles that were using anti-Semitic attitudes as part of their wider criticism of secularism; the left-wing parties failed in any case to find an anti-Jewish public opinion within Italy. If there was anti-Semitism in Italy, it was limited to smaller groups that were socially outside the mainstream and did not go beyond a few traditional stereotypes that had their origins in the darkness of centuries: the "cheap" Jew, the "dirty" Jew, the "crooked" Jew, the Jew socially disconnected from the rest of the people, etc. The negative characteristics associated with the ghetto Jews no longer applied to the new social and civil context, which associated the Jews with other, more positive images, such as business acumen and organizational capabilities, intelligence, honesty, etc. We shall address anti-Semitism in more detail below; our purpose here is only to note its conspicuous absence.

The scattering of the Jews among the numerous Italian political parties of all shades is a natural consequence of assimilation. In the absence of anti-Semitism, it was logical that the Jews should avoid flocking into a single political party, movement, or pressure group dedicated to the defense of their civil rights.[56] It was also obvious that the Jews would scatter politically into all parties, depending upon their social and ideological interests, with the exception of those that were structurally incompatible with Judaism, namely the parties, movements and circles that were openly inspired by the Catholic Church. All parties from left to right had some kind of Jewish membership. There was possibly a preference for the left; however, even before making such an assertion pending a study of the issue, the reasons are easy to explain: the entrance of the Jews into mainstream Italian life during the *Risorgimento* and the period immediately following the unification of Italy took place through the followers of Garibaldi, the democrats, and the Masonic radicals; in the right-wing parties one found groups and individuals that were more reactionary, that harbored prejudices and aversions against the Jews as such, and as newcomers; the centuries-old injustices and the spirit of human solidarity that can be

17

found among the Jews, as well as a certain petit-bourgeois attitude rooted in scientism and positivism, brought the Jews to socially and politically advanced political parties, or at least those that, like the nationalist party at its inception, gave that impression. Undeniably, however, many Jews joined and sympathized with moderate or right-wing parties that defended their economic, cultural, and moral interests. Fascism was to attract many Jews into its ranks from the beginning. In conclusion, the Jews were essentially behaving politically not as a community but as individual citizens, just like other Italians, even though their political choices were influenced by a few specific factors—just as for all other Italians, be it within localities and regions, or religious, social, and cultural communities.

The reality of Italian Judaism, dominated by assimilation, was to be further influenced by Zionism between the end of the 19th and the beginning of the 20th century. Under the double pressure of two factors, on the one hand the savage explosions of anti-Semitism that occurred in Eastern Europe and to a lesser degree in France, and on the other hand the strong personality of Theodore Herzl, Zionism had, by the end of the 19th century, become a force outside Italy. Its penetration in Italy was slow, as we have pointed out, and incomplete, and even today it can be said that half of the Italian Jews are not active Zionists.

Zionism, as it developed quickly from Herzl's initial ideas,[57] sent to the Jews of the world two important messages: to provide a national home in Eretz Israel in order to build their own political and social autonomy, and to proclaim their Jewishness, meaning their religion, culture, tradition, and national will.[58] These ideals were to find very quickly, in Italy, small groups of supporters and followers in Florence, Leghorn, Pisa, Milan, Genoa, Padova, Trieste.[59] The first ones were in Leghorn, Ancona, Ferrara, and Modena, but they were quickly overshadowed by those of Florence and Trieste. In Florence, centered around the famous Rabbi S. Z. Margulies, one of the most vivid personalities of Italian Jewry, and a "young and energetic prophet of Zionism,"[60] Alfonso Pacifici, its members reached the point of actually speaking Hebrew among themselves. In Trieste, the group centered around the *Corriere Israelitico* and another young leader, Dante Lattes, who became its driving force.

This group was less numerous than its counterpart in Florence but was the initiator of the Zionist movement in Italy. Thanks to the enthusiastic efforts of these circles, Zionism became the new face of Italian Judaism, and its struggles also reached Italian public opinion at large. Newspapers and magazines were published,[61] cultural initiatives flourished that discussed the various aspects of the Jewish problem head-on and with uncharacteristically dramatic force;[62] as Pacifici wrote in 1912:

> We must disturb the people's conscience, inject anxiety into even the most indifferent souls, to create that vibrant feeling of expectation that is the mark of renewed vitality within people who were at risk of dying from inertia.

The *Corriere Israelitico* and (after its merger with *Settimana Israelitica* in 1915 at the start of the First World War) the new *Israel* published in Florence beginning in 1916, were, for the most part, the instruments of the Italian Zionists in their struggle against assimilation and to reclaim "a universal Jewish life, the aspirations of Israel, the greatness of the Jewish past, the nobility of its thoughts."[63] Dante Lattes was to be the leader and the main mover of this effort, "the spearhead" of Zionism. As Milano has written, Jewish journalism had been until that time on the defensive: "Its defensive posture protected more or less efficiently the traditional and spiritual Jewish heritage but could not stop the continuous desertions of individuals from the ranks; with Lattes, journalism became resolutely aggressive: it confronted the Italian Jews directly with the problems of their time, and did not hesitate to unveil their own weaknesses in the face of these problems."[64]

Zionism, in spite of these efforts and the enthusiasm of its leaders, had difficulty in reaching out to the Jews in Italy and did so very slowly. It took on, over time, outside a few circles, a markedly "philanthropic" character. The majority of Italian Zionists, including those who belonged to the Italian Zionist Federation, all understood it as an "oriental" issue, a way of saving other Jews who were being oppressed or persecuted. For them Zionism came down to a form of financial contribution to encourage emigration from Eastern Europe and moral solidarity with Jewish victims of oppression.

Very few took Zionism to mean a moral and material movement that would include the happy as well as the unhappy Jews, the free Jews and those who were oppressed. For the majority, Zionism, on the ideological and cultural level, did not go beyond a certain curiosity for history, tradition, and folklore and a greater attachment to these elements. The standard tone of Italian Zionism was set by *L'idea sionistica*, the official publication of the Zionist Federation, published in Modena in the first decade of the 20th century.[65] It made two major points:

First, "the emigration of the Jewish proletariat from Eastern Europe, to colonize many lands in Palestine and Asia Minor that were uncultivated or neglected, under a Charter granted by the government in Constantinople, and the guarantee of the European powers to assemble the Jews in various homelands." Second, "the moral and intellectual elevation of the Jews in the countries they lived in." As for the Jews in Italy: "Zionism does not intend to give us a homeland because we already have a beautiful and noble one, nor has it any political or religious aims, and therefore it cannot be regarded as a racial or religious challenge."

This care to keep Zionism on a strictly philanthropic and apolitical level was demonstrated by the end of the publication *L'idea sionistica*, which decided to shut itself down at the outset of the war between Italy and Turkey because its editors feared being accused of harboring sympathies for the Turkish Empire, with which the international Zionist movement was negotiating at the time to seek wider entry into Palestine.[66] The coming of the First World War was to find the Italian Zionist movement still very weak. Its situation did not improve very much after the war in spite of the famous "Balfour Declaration," which was accepted by the Italian government, which recognized Zionist claims to Palestine as legitimate.[67]

Zionism was to be reinforced by a new energy and new important ideas, promoted by Angelo Da Fano, first in Gorizia and then in Modena, and then by the *Avodà* group in Rome, enriching the already existing ones. It remained an important movement but still in the minority, more intellectual than practical, as the numbers of the *aliya*, the Jewish emigration to Palestine from Italy, clearly demonstrate. Between 1926 and 1938 the total number of Italian immigrants into Palestine amounted to 151,[68] mostly from Florence and Trieste, the two largest, most vital and consistent centers of Zionism in Italy.[69]

The Zionist movement was able to find a small number of true followers, and its value was more cultural and ideological than practical.[70] Zionism, despite its efforts, was unable to reverse the trend toward assimilation. To attract larger numbers of followers, it had to wait for the end of the Second World War and its murders, its horrors, and its disappointments. However, Zionism did have initial success, paradoxically, under Fascist rule. Among the younger and more active Zionists, the repressive and tyrannical Fascist regime inspired a reaction towards greater political consciousness. Long before racial persecution in Italy, the freedom requested for Jews in other countries was now demanded for those in Italy itself; those ideals of freedom and social equality that could not be found in Italy were by contrast wished for the society and the state being built in spite of the opposition of nature, men, and governments in Palestine. Zionism went from being a Jewish movement to becoming a factor for the Italian Jews as well. It is no accident that one of the first Italian immigrants to Palestine was Alberto Spagnoletto, an anti-Fascist persecuted by Fascism, along with Enzo Sereni and his wife.[71]

2.
Racism, Anti-Semitism, and
Anti-Zionism in Italy

Italy has never really experienced racism or racist sentiment among the general public, even within its most provincial and middle-class culture. The very roots of racism are conspicuously absent. This explains how in 1936-1937, and even more in 1938-1943, when Fascism introduced its racist policies aimed at instilling a "racial consciousness" among the Italian people, even though the campaign was supported by enormous propaganda efforts and powerful slogans, it failed to sway the Italian public. Only a small number of unsavory characters (who were often paid) wound up being in favor of the racial policies.

This result was to be expected. Racism[72] as a mass psychological phenomenon, as well as a "cultural" fact, is the direct consequence of national antagonisms, or, better, of nationalism itself, of which it is a component. Thus, racism finds its origins and its focal points in those "elastic" border areas that are ethnically vague, zones of mixed nationalities, or where strong minorities are present and where there are violent confrontations between various national groups. Modern nationalism began in Germany and more precisely in East Prussia, a region of deep national divisions between Germans, Poles, and Lithuanians. Its founders and theoreticians, from the time of Herder and Kant to that of Hitler and Rosenberg, through the Romantics and the Social Darwinists, had in fact theorized the German push towards the east and possibly towards the west, for example the struggle against the "negrified" France.[73] All this was absent from Italy, a country basically homogeneous from the ethnic point of view, with borders, at least up to 1918, that were well defined and consistent with the ethnic boundaries. Therefore, a homegrown racism was essentially nonexistent, and any imported racism found no followers. This indifference to racism was reinforced by two other factors of a moral and cultural nature that appeared in the 19th and 20th centuries. Italian culture, and even more, the psychological makeup of Italian culture, was and remains either essentially Catholic or predominantly secular, both being, at least in their Italian manifestations, fundamentally opposed to racism.[74] Catholic ethics, as has been repeated at various times by major Catholic writers, e.g., Taparelli, d'Azeglio, Ozanam, and Toniolo, and by the hierarchy of the Catholic Church, for example, the encyclicals *Immortale Dei* and *Il fermo proposito*, are both clearly anti-racist and consider Europe and the world as one single human group. Secularism is also, in its philosophical and political foundations, clearly opposed to racism. As Gioacchino Sera noted: "the secular ideal of equality among men affirmed and upheld by the French Revolution . . . is the strongest obstacle for many scholars, even those of a more naturalistic bent, to the existence of psychological differences between the races."[75] It follows that there were no racist motivations among the Italian people and the study of race as such would be limited to the field of science, especially the anthropological school of Paolo Mantegazza and Giuseppe Sergi, without ever acquiring any ethical, psychological, or political significance.

The exceptions to this rule are few, of minimal significance and almost invariably imported from abroad. However, this did not prevent Fascist propaganda after 1938, and in particular the infamous magazine *La difesa della razza*, from trumpeting their significance as important and original theories.[76] The only Italian racist theoretician of any consequence in the 19th century was probably Petruccelli della Gattina, for whom the history of the Italian idea was "a history of the Italian race understood in its various manifestations"; he contrasted the "Semitic origins" of the Church with the origins of the Empire, which were clearly of "Frankish origin."[77] Besides this author, racism within Italian culture was entirely influenced by foreign doctrines[78] at the end of the 19th and the beginning of the 20th centuries. Racism had something of a development around the First World War, mostly within nationalistic and futuristic circles. The word "race" appeared frequently in the confused and contradictory pronouncements of these groups. In reality theirs was not a truly racist position but rather an adaptation of the ideas of Barrès and Maurras, where racism lost its positivist and biological justifications and was reduced to a sort of super-nationalism. For them "race" really meant "origins"; it no longer had a biological value but was rather the equivalent of *civilization*, national *tradition* and also simply, *nation*. Two well-known examples will illustrate this tendency. For Alfredo Rocco nationalism would "re-establish the primacy of the Italian race against the excesses of individualism" and was nothing but "the defense of the nation as a permanent and unalterable entity along the centuries, set against the extreme political and economic dissolution produced by individualism." "Nationalism believes that those races where the survival of the species is systematically sacrificed to the interests of individuals are ultimately destined to perish. And it does not want the Italian race to perish." *Race* for him actually means *nation*, "a social aggregate made up of men of the same race," which is actually a moral and historical continuum. The biological concept of race is alien to his thinking and actually, while attempting to distinguish in 1914 the Italian concept of nationalism from French nationalism, Rocco insisted upon the "internal character" of the latter, because it meant to "reinvigorate the race," while Italian nationalism maintained an "external character" and sought imperialistic "wealth" and the "expansion of the race."[79]

With Filippo Tommaso Marinetti and the Futurists the concept of race becomes more complex. It is everything and nothing at the same time; it is the springboard of nationalism and of Italian imperialism generating its power source in a spiritual manner that transcends any "biology of race." Two excerpts from speeches given by Marinetti in November 1919 will suffice:

> I am a futurist, which means a spirit inebriated with the power of Italian blood. This blood contains the virtues that can dictate new laws of common good and strength, new paths of light and heroism to the world . . . One of my passions has always been the great future of the Italian race, capable of extending its spiritual domination over the world.[80]
>
> Futurism carries within it a moral foundation more cosmopolitan than nationalist, despite its nationalist appeal, its calls to the Italian race, its willful amorality, and remains difficult to categorize within strict and coherent racist parameters of the classical type.[81]

We can conclude that, despite a few passing infatuations in rather small but vocal circles for racist interpretations of human activity and behavior, especially during the years overlapping the two centuries,[82] Italian culture, and particularly political doctrine,[83] remained immune to racist aberrations coming from abroad—so immune that when the racist campaign was launched in 1938, its more realistic proponents and even some Fascist leaders felt the need to underline the deep differences between the "spiritual" value of Fascist racism and the "materialistic" Nazi type.

Until the 1930s, the Jewish problem in Italy had almost never been addressed in racial terms. If there were any such references to the Jews as a biological and anthropological race at the end of the 19th century, based on foreign influence, they were quickly dismissed by scientists, politicians, and journalists. Cesare Lombroso, for example, vehemently rejected theories that he called "the most disgusting human secretions," "a cold breath of savage hatred," quickly demonstrating their absence of scientific value and unmasking the true aims, which had nothing to do with science but were purely political, drawn from particular situations having nothing in common with Italy: in Russia, Germany, and particularly in Austria.[84] If in the second half of the 19th century and the first decades of the 20th, the "Jewish race" is discussed in Italy it is not in any racist biological sense,[85] but somewhat mistakenly as a reference to the traditions and culture of the Jews as a group present within many nations.

There was no real anti-Semitic movement in Italy during the last century that can be compared to those of other countries; at the most there were small manifestations of an innocuous and traditional type, which were disappearing under the pressure of assimilation.[86] Some high-level anti-Semitic incidents that were quickly silenced and forgotten, for instance the campaign waged by Pasqualigno against I. P. Maurogonato to become part of the Minghetti government in 1873,[87] clearly show how these outbursts were alien to the Italian mentality and sensibility.

During the second half of the 19th century we can say that Italy knew only Catholic anti-Semitism originating from old "theological" beliefs within the Church, with the Jews cast as "God killers" and enemies of Catholicism—the anti-Semitism of the country parish priests and some of their bigoted followers. Then, during the last two decades of the century, anti-Semitism was reinvigorated by other influences and pressures that were more secular and politically inspired, giving it a new life in certain quarters. There is little reason to linger on the traditional, "theological" aspects of Catholic anti-Semitism, since they are well known and of little interest here. It is more important to analyze in greater detail the renewed vigor that was displayed at the end of the century, not only because it remained alive much longer, but also because many of its ideas were to become part of the anti-Semitic ideology of the Nationalists and Fascists, who clearly used them in the propaganda of the years 1938-1943.

In discussing the reign of Pope Leo XIII, Arturo Carlo Jemolo makes a passing reference to the position of the Holy See regarding the "Dreyfus case," noting the contradiction between the "openly anti-Dreyfus attitudes of many religious associations and of most of the Catholic press" in France (however, this applies to Italy as well) and the fact that Dreyfus was considered innocent inside the Vatican. The Vatican only went as far as a direct reprimand of anti-Dreyfus Catholic associations for having tolerated such an attitude and "more than anything, too many words and too many actions that were clearly anti-Christian."[88] In fact, a careful study of the reign of Leo XIII reveals that it represents the key moment in the Jewish policy of the Catholic Church and, going deeper into the analysis, that there was no contradiction in that position.

During the years preceding the Dreyfus case, the Jewish problem within Italian Catholic circles in particular, and more precisely the relationship between Jews and Christians, had always been considered of secondary importance. With the liberal ascendancy and the emancipation of the Jews, traditional popular religious anti-Semitism had virtually disappeared everywhere. The hierarchy of the Church, with few exceptions, while it did not declare itself openly in favor of emancipation and equality with the Christians and without modifying its traditional position towards the Jews, had actually tried to bury the problem in an attempt to forget it, limiting itself to merely making declarations of principle, always tempered by the explicit condemnation of violence against the Jews. Only a few die-hard clerics who were upholding the most traditional attitudes of Catholicism and the position taken by Balmes were openly against the principle of religious tolerance and emancipation.[89]

An important change took place halfway through the reign of Leo XIII: around 1884 the Catholic press resumed steady attacks on the Jews. There were many reasons for this change, some of them particularly Italian, while others were the echo of the problems and attitudes common to France.[90] Two stand out, however, and appear essential for different reasons. Faced with the intransigent attitude of the clergy and the anti-Italian policies of the Vatican, since the closing years of the pontificate of Pius IX, the entire country had been influenced by anticlerical sentiments. The secular ruling class reacted,

> strongly encouraging anticlericalism and joining, above and beyond the divisions of political parties and factions, in a single organization, Freemasonry, which attempted to mobilize the masses around an ideology that was at the same time patriotic and anticlerical, tilted towards positivism and neoclassical aesthetics.[91]

Around 1880 this tendency became so important that it influenced one way or another a great number of people across all social classes.[92] During those years, parallel to the development of anti-clericalism and Freemasonry, more extreme factions were gaining social acceptance as they elaborated their platforms and from various quarters took the first steps towards the creation of a truly radical democratic party. The efforts of Antonio Labriola, for example, were ultimately to result in the foundation of the Socialist Party; it will not seem unusual that the Church, deeply threatened by these events, would attempt to defend itself. The new attitude of certain Catholic groups towards the Jews must be examined in this context.

The pontificate of Leo XIII was, for the most part, dedicated to regaining what the Church had lost in earlier decades. As Pietro Scoppola correctly noted, Leo XIII attempted to reposition the Church within the new historical reality "by bravely using the tools offered by the modern world," to give it "the full exercise of that leadership and guidance it had held uninterruptedly during past centuries."[93] The main event of this new policy was undoubtedly the *Rerum novarum*. In practical terms not all Catholics understood the message of this encyclical with the same honesty and good intentions that the Pope had expressed: for many the "social policy" of the Church amounted to nothing more than a device to split the working class, pushing it into an anti-socialist attitude as a "tactical" tool to oppose "the reds." On the other hand, many Catholics, primarily the Jesuits of *La civiltà cattolica*, interpreted the encyclical *De secta massonum (Humanum genus)* only as a device directed against Freemasonry, isolating it in order to destroy it or at least to seriously weaken its political power. As with *Rerum novarum,* these Catholics completely overlooked the deeper and more social meaning of *Humanum genus:* the freeing of the masses from the pseudo-social demagogy of the radical and Freemason middle class in order to set them on the path to real emancipation. Entrenched on this line of resistance and simple all-out defense, these Catholics accepted and spread all the most absurd stories and anti-Masonic "revelations," even the completely discredited writings of Leo Taxil and Carl Hachs, towards whom Leo XIII had shown little enthusiasm, and if he was not openly condemning them, in the overheated atmosphere of the times, it was only to avoid being accused of having become a tool of the Freemasons himself.[94]

After 1887, when it appeared possible that Freemasonry could expand its influence in Italy once it had overcome its own internal struggles, the Catholics went to great lengths to put a stop to this threat by trying to influence popular sentiment, which in Italy remained fundamentally religious and Christian. The Pope had never, in *Humanum genus* or any other pronouncement, made any anti-Semitic references nor accused the Jews of being the soul of Freemasonry. Catholic journalists, however, did not hesitate to use even such an argument, and, by emphasizing the participation of a number of Jews in Freemasonry, in anticlerical organizations, and in radical and socialist parties, wound up identifying all these movements and forces with the Jewish element to the point of considering them by-products of Judaism.[95]

The second, less important but still significant, motive behind the wave of Catholic anti-Semitism can be found within the economic structure of the Church itself, which had changed under Leo XIII from a feudal economy to the capitalist model.[96] The process of bringing about so vast a change as entering the mainstream of capitalism at such a late date was bound to create a certain level of antagonism and competition between the Church and existing financial institutions and companies, which included many Jewish managers.

The attitude of the Church in the Dreyfus Affair and its Jewish policy in this context no longer appears contradictory and has its own internal logic. Modern Catholic anti-Semitism is best analyzed by Antonio Gramsci when writing about Catholic social thought:

> It is most certainly a political and historical element, but of a very particular nature: it is a reserve issue, not in the front line and therefore to be easily "forgotten" and "silenced" practically at any time, yet without forgetting it completely, because the occasion may arise for it to be trotted out again.[97]

Seen and historically understood as a "back-burner" religious issue, Catholic anti-Semitism during the last hundred years takes on a very specific meaning. The *phases* of its recurrence, its sudden explosions and disappearances, which would otherwise be incomprehensible, become clear with the final dramatic crisis of the Fascist period. All civilized men and true Catholics in particular, many of them secular and religious, ran tremendous risks and even sacrificed their lives to save Jews from persecution during those sad years. They were denied—as François Mauriac, a man whose Catholic credentials cannot be doubted, was to write—"the comfort of hearing Simon Peter, the successor of the man from Galilee, condemn with clear and unequivocal words rather than diplomatic allusion, the crucifixion of these innumerable *brothers of the Lord*,"[98] and we can add that these civilized and true Catholics were to witness choices by other Catholics that, in spite of the many subtle *distinguos*, ended up only in enhancing anti-Semitism and Fascist persecution.

But let us return to the Catholic anti-Semitism of the period of Francesco Crispi at the end of the 19th century. We have already identified its general characteristics. It is important first to take a closer look at its historical roots before we delve into some of its more significant manifestations. Besides the traditional and well-known Catholic position regarding the Jews and Judaism, two elements must be considered rather closely.

The tendency to turn Judaism into a sort of all-encompassing matrix for a whole series of movements, forces, organizations, etc., was nothing new at the time, even though it was to reach its full development as a theory. At the end of the 18th century Catholic writers had systematically written about a conspiracy bent on the destruction of Christianity and its replacement by deism and anarchy. The originators of this conspiracy were said to have been the philosophers, Freemasons, and Jansenists, and its major achievement was the French Revolution. At the time there were writers who added a fourth culprit to the three responsible for the conspiracy: the Jews. For example, the anonymous author of *Memorabili avvenimenti successi sotto i tristi auspici della Repubblica Francese*, published in Venice in 1799, did not hesitate to cite as one of the causes of the French Revolution "the underground maneuverings of the Jews." Such a thesis would, from then on, never be discarded by clerical circles, and even became part of a popular anti-Semitic poem of the time. It was revived by the reactionaries and the clerical party in 1848 in an attempt to convince the people that even the most moderate liberal demands were in fact inspired by the Jews. This position would reappear in the strongest terms thanks to the Jesuits at the end of the 19th century. The Jesuits simply mixed the three traditional conspiracies, to which others, such as liberalism and socialism, had been added, as tools of Judaism, making it the main culprit of all the catastrophes that had beset Europe during the preceding century.[99] For the Jesuit Father Raffaele Ballerini, the French Revolution itself, which had taken two years and much heated controversy before emancipating the Jews, was actually the product of a Jewish conspiracy.[100]

To this older "theoretical" ideology were added a whole series of more recent, and mostly foreign, elements, originating in Austria, and also, to a lesser degree, in France. Italian Catholic anti-Semitism acquired new issues during the years 1880 to 1900 from the anti-Semitic slogans and ideas of the Austrian Christian Social Party, which was closely connected to Italian clerical organizations, especially in the region around Venice. In most cases this was inspired by August Rohling, a professor of Catholic theology at the University of Prague, and by the political pamphlets of the *Deutsches Volksblatt* and people like Georg von Schönerer and Karl Lueger and finally Edouard Drumont.[101]

The Jesuit magazine *La civiltà cattolica* became the main mover in this campaign. It began with an extremely long refutation of Corrado Guidetti's *Pro Judaeis* that lasted two years and contained most of the argumentation on the issue later developed in greater detail. The magazine returned periodically to this topic with long background studies that were to provide material for the Catholic and especially the Italian clerical press. *La civiltà cattolica* dedicated much space to the Jews in many notes, chronicles, and reviews. Standing out were three articles published in 1890 under the title *Della questione giudaica in Europa*, which contained the new Catholic position on the matter. These articles were reprinted in booklet form and widely distributed.

The basis of these ideas was the centuries-old traditional view of the decay of the Jewish religion, which was said to have prompted the Jewish people to commit the "ultimate crime," the murder of God, or "deicide," therefore deserving divine punishment, which assured its survival[102] until it accepted conversion to the true faith. Such a conversion was to be, according to the Jesuits, extremely slow, and made more difficult because of the materialism and degeneration of Judaism created by Talmudism. "The Jew persists in remaining a Jew because he is awaiting the fulfillment of a dream, the messianic dream that will lift him to world domination."[103]

Such an aspiration through the spirit of the Talmud, which teaches "besides an awful kind of ethics, actual hatred for all humanity,"[104] explained why the Jews "are the sworn enemies of the prosperity of the nations in which they live"[105] and of Christianity.

> From the very first centuries of the Church, the Jews proclaimed they were entitled to dominate all pagans and Christians . . . they therefore created that sect that after many names is now known as the Freemasons . . . The mission of the sect is to rebuild the reign of Israel over the ruins of Christianity and of any other religion that worships the true God.[106]

This was to be a universal reign, "built on the earthly pleasures of the flesh and on estrangement from the religion of God," that the Jews were determined to bring about and nothing would stop them, not even the most horrific crimes.[107] Yet the Catholic Church, after having "always treated the Jews with exceptional tolerance and compassion" and doing "whatever it could and can do for the freedom of the Synagogue,"[108] was always opposed to extending equal rights to the Jews "to which they have no right," and always insisted that they be separated from the societies in which they lived and that their lives be regulated by special laws to prevent them from harming the Christians.[109] But through fraud and duplicity, hiding behind the idea of freedom, the Jews had finally succeeded in obtaining their own emancipation.

This unfortunate occurrence, according to the clerical writers of the time, is the origin of almost every ill that since then had descended upon humanity or was likely to do so soon, in the words of the Jesuits. Father Raffaele Ballerini wrote in this regard:

> What were the consequences of Jewish emancipation in every country where it came to pass? Two obvious and ominous ones: a pitiless war on the Christian religions and notably the Catholic religion; and then an unlimited and unbridled spread of usury, monopoly, thievery of all kinds to the detriment of the peoples that enjoyed and still enjoy personal freedom.[110]

Father Francesco Saverio Rondina, another Jesuit, illustrated the situation after the Jews, once emancipated, went "from being our equals to being our masters":

> The Jewish nation does not work, but rather benefits from the substance and the work of others; it does not produce but lives and prospers on the fruits of the work and industry of the nations that accept its presence. It is the octopus with its multiple oversize tentacles grabbing and drawing everything unto itself; it has the banks as its stomach . . . and its suckers are everywhere: in contracts and monopolies, in credit institutions and banks, in the postal and telegraph system, in shipping and railroad companies, in municipal and state finances. It represents the kingdom of capital, the aristocracy of gold that has replaced that of inventiveness and blood.[111]

There was also a subtle attempt, as we can see, to add to the central religious anti-Semitic theme, economic motivations that were intended to increase popular and anti-capitalist discontent against the Jews. In typical fashion Rondina accuses the Jews of being responsible for the many bankruptcies in which numerous small investors had lost their meager savings.[112] During the closing decade of the 19th century Italy was, according to *La civiltà cattolica*, a country rocked by chaos, violence, immorality, all of this orchestrated by a huge Jewish machine of unlimited power.

It can be said that Italy, from 1859 to now, has become the kingdom of the Jews, who have been clever at hoodwinking the idiot masses, passing themselves off as the most ardent patriots in the country . . .[113] The over 50,000 Jews who are infesting the country are for the most part concentrated in the Veneto, around Mantua, in the old states of the Este, and around Ferrara. In this region, which can truly be referred to as Jewish Italy, they hold the high ground in every way. Not one lira is spent without their approval. Business, industry, foreign exchange, rural property as well as city property are all under their control. One only needs to point out that four-fifths of the territory of the province of Padua is owned by Jews, and they control the remaining fifth through the mortgages they handle. Ancona, Leghorn, Florence are all living under the harness of the Jewish usurers. They dream of the day when the most luxurious villas, the most lucrative farms and the best-known palaces of the nobility will fall under their control due to the collateral for loans that they represent for the ill-advised and imbecile owners who are incapable of shaking them loose...Let us not talk about Rome, which was occupied not so much by the bayonets of the Italian army as by the great Jewish net that has caught all sorts of big and small fish, who then are gobbled up in a succession of pitiful cries, problems, and miseries. Usury reigns supreme in this capital of Jewry rather than of Italy; and along with usury, fraud, robbery and criminal societies. . . Milan, Turin, Venice, Modena, Bologna, Florence live by a public opinion manufactured in the ghettos and the synagogues. The so-called independent newspapers are all more or less Jewish-inspired, controlled by the government. Let's not even talk about Rome, where it's impossible to pick up a liberal sheet that is not in the hands of Israel.[114]

The less important clerical press—for example *La Chiesa* and *Il Cittadino*, both published in Genoa—that followed the path of *La civiltà cattolica*, reached in their attacks extremes of sectarian hatred, idiocy, naiveté, and false statements that were truly incredible. *La Voce della Verità*, published in Rome, even went so far as to accuse

Jewish anticlericalism of the murder of King Umberto I.[115] The solution that this press proposed officially was—no less!—the abolition of equal rights and the reintroduction of the old rules.[116] The model to be followed was Russian Czarist legislation[117] and the openly violent anti-Semitic policy of the Austrian Social Christian Party.[118] The progress of anti-Semitism was chronicled with unambiguous satisfaction,[119] even though Christian moderation was always invoked and violence and anti-Semitism were rejected. In the last of the three famous articles, the writer of *La civiltà cattolica* even went so far as to accept proposals coming from the most extreme clerical quarters to confiscate Jewish property as "national property."[120] Others found the solution to the Jewish problem in the restoration of the secular power of the States of the Church.[121]

A few books published or translated during this period by clerical publishers contained even more vicious attacks and more drastic remedies. It will be enough to cite the translation of the book by Ferrant Martinez, *L'ebreo, ecco il nemico! Appello ai cattolici* [The Jew is the Enemy! An Appeal to Catholics], translated by Abbot D. G. Foatta, published in Prato (1891), and the work of G. Pananzi, *L'ebreo attraverso i secoli e nelle questioni della moderna società* [The Jew Through the Centuries and in the Problems of Modern Society], (Treviso 1898).

Obviously, not all Catholics subscribed to such positions. It can safely be said that such attitudes remained limited to clerical fundamentalist circles and the Jesuits, with a few noteworthy exceptions. The mass of liberal Catholics, and even some organizations such as the Christian Democrats of Romolo Murri, rejected this positioning of the Jewish question. In fact, the Jewish question was almost never brought up by the liberals, in contrast to what clerical groups were doing in an organized and repetitive way. From the liberal press and the allusions it made from time to time, it appears that they addressed the issue in a completely different way.[122]

Two articles by Count F. di Kuefstein should be considered separately; they were published by *Rassegna italiana* in February and March 1883.[123] Rather than originating from the anti-Semitic explosion within the clerical movement of the time—motivated more by the political struggle and also, in a way, by the adaptation of the Church and its most vital elements to the new capitalist economy—these articles must be placed in the context of the difficulties experienced by many Catholics, both psychologically and morally, in adjusting to the capitalist process then in full swing. The "Christian" concept of economics Kuefstein proposed is a return to the full moral, religious and economic doctrine of St. Thomas Aquinas,[124] which in reality is the theoretical defense of the semifeudal backward state of the Austrian and, to a somewhat lesser degree, Italian peasantry. The Jew, in this view, is made responsible for competition and capitalist concentration.[125] Over the centuries Jews had never accepted the laws of the corporative and feudal economy of Christianity, and, at the risk of seeming contradictory, they were responsible for the appearance of vast anti-capitalist mass movements.[126] Both articles, written according to the typical frames of reference of Austrian Social Christian thought (in particular the anti-liberal struggle of the *Vogelsang*), made strong claims to scientific impartiality. In these writings the occasional specifically positive Jewish trait, as Werner Sombart would say, would be praised. They can be considered, despite the conspicuous presence of divine *condemnation* always in the forefront, as a sort of *deus ex machina*,[127] as examples of racist and economic anti-Semitism more than of traditional religious anti-Semitism.

At the start of the 20th century the more responsible quarters of the Catholic press reduced the volume and frequency of their attacks on Judaism. This was not the result of a change of policy; the violence of the struggle had certainly not abated.[128] The developments of the national and general situation determined its lower intensity.

In Europe the secular, economic anti-Semitism that attracted vast popular support was in full swing and took a decidedly racist direction, forcing the Church to review the theoretical basis of its own Jewish policy. The reduced strength of the middle-class radical and republican parties and the alliance between moderates and Catholics, the Gentiloni pact, etc., and their strong position in high finance, noticeably reduced the attacks against liberal Masonic Judaism.

New issues were brought progressively to the forefront, along with the traditional ones that they would, in time, overtake. Socialism was seen as a product of Judaism, and, to a lesser degree but nevertheless present in the provincial press, capitalism was seen as a typically Jewish product[129]—the very issues, together with race, which were to be used by Fascist anti-Semitic policy.

A few facts and some typical incidents will confirm our point that nothing new came out of the Church's slow withdrawal from its attitude and that of its most authorized spokesmen, if not in a tactical reduction of the anti-Semitic position, at least its shift to other issues pending a new explosion. First of all, there were the public congratulations sent by Pope Benedict XV and his secretary of state, Cardinal Gasparri, on March 23, 1918 and June 20, 1919, respectively, to Monsignor Jouin, curé of St. Augustin in Paris and founder in 1912 of the *Revue Internationale des Sociétés Secrètes*, whose mission it was to fight the Jewish threat. The monsignor even edited and published a translation of the notorious *Protocols of the Elders of Zion* and was the author of *La judéo-maçonnerie et la révolution sociale* and *La judéo-maçonnerie et la domination du monde*. Following the October Revolution, the connection between Judaism and Bolshevism was constantly and systematically made.[130] Finally, in 1928,[131] there came the condemnation and shutting down of the Society of the Friends of Israel, which counted among its members cardinals, bishops, and laymen and had as its program the conversion of the Jews to Catholicism.[132]

With the coming of the 20th century, Catholic clerical anti-Semitism was soon joined by the nationalists, the revolutionary labor unions, and the Fascists. This new anti-Semitism was to remain less significant than the clerical variety but beholden to it for a whole series of reasons, attacking the Jews as anti-Christian, the Freemason Jews, the Jews as leeches of the national wealth, the anti-national Jews, the Bolshevik Jews, etc., and yet lacking the systematic nature and importance of the religious argumentation. The absence, in Italy, of any truly pressing Jewish problem implied the total absence of any anti-Semitic mass excitement. The extreme weakness and cultural and ideological confusion of Italian nationalism and the movements it inspired, pushed the anti-Semitism of the nationalists into the background rather than making it a main feature of their political action and ideology. Many times they even denied that anti-Semitism played any role in their political positions.[133] It entered into the Italian nationalist canon through the slogans of French nationalism and the need to compete with the clerical right wing than out of deep conviction; with very few exceptions, anti-Semitism was reduced to something ill-defined, remaining superficial, a feeling rather than a real conviction. A 1904 article by Alfredo Oriani is typical in this respect; after admitting that "in Italy there is no anti-Semitism," the writer refers to the Jews: "our people have never really hated them, and today they could not be singled out within the anonymous crowd if a secret unidentifiable instinct, less recognizable than a memory, did not point to them."[134] For the majority of Italian nationalists who fed on futurism, D'Annunzio, irrationality, the worship of beauty, of violence, of drunkenness, and other confused feelings, even anti-Semitism remained at that same level of confusion. The Jews were not "beautiful"; they lacked the spirit of adventure and courage; they were pacifists, "bourgeois," miserly; they failed to recognize higher values than those of money; they lacked higher passions and, most of all, love of country; they were, in the end, the opposite of that "new man" the nationalists purported to represent.[135] Alfredo Oriani continued in the same article: "the Jew is not a farmer and his small industry is not creative, his trade is a mystery, his coin is a weapon, his help means death . . . because money is the most terrible of weapons and the Jew knows how to use it." The originality of the Jew died in Palestine: "after Jesus, the Jews have never really created anything: in philosophy, science, art, politics, they can know and use everything, but they can't create."[136] For Enrico Corradini the Jews were the antithesis of the new Roman consciousness of Italy; they did have revolutionary messianic fervor, but it was a subversive type of revolution, the denial of everything grand and beautiful; they were natural revolutionaries, their revolution was popular and plebeian, aimed at destroying all individual and aristocratic values:

> The first praise for the popular king is in the Bible. The first socialism is in the Bible. The first violence by the weak against the

aggressor, the first time the humble despise the proud is to be found in the Bible. And they were never to be as furious anywhere else. Only in the Bible can the prophet be found, the frenetic titan of the crowd, the demagogue of socialism, the most unjust of the just, the violence of the meek, the proudest of the humble, drunk with madness, with all the injustice, with all the violence, with all the pride, with all the hatred, with all the fury of destructiveness of the most plebeian democratism gone mad.[137]

The demonstration of this fact for the nationalists, including those who were not anti-Semitic, and even for some Jews, the presence of so many Jews in Freemasonry and the old parties, liberals, radicals, and socialists, against whom they had the strongest quarrel and, after 1917, within the victory of monstrous Bolshevism, was proof enough.[138] To this we should add that the nationalists supported a settlement between Church and State that was opposed by the Freemasons and the secular parties where the Jews were most active; anticlericalism, said Rocco, had been downgraded into an anti-religious fight, mostly because the Freemasons and the secular parties had become "instruments of religious hatred of many non-Catholics, especially Semites, who represent their core."[139]

Up to World War I, according to the historical anthology and the essays on Italian anti-Jewish writing published by Roberto Mazzetti at the peak of the racist campaign,[140] anti-Semitism remained a relatively limited manifestation within nationalist circles, to an elite of sorts, using traditionalist or vaguely spiritualistic rhetoric, politically ineffective and loosely defined.[141] The essay by Pietro Ellero in 1915, "La vita dei popoli," illustrates this idea and was to be praised twenty years later by the Fascists.[142] We can speak of a more aggressive and pointed nationalist anti-Semitism only immediately following the First World War. There is no trace of it before then, even in Giovanni Preziosi's articles in his magazine *La vita italiana*. As we shall see, before 1919-1920, the nationalist attack against the Jews was not anti-Semitic and remained almost exclusively limited to attacking Zionism.

Before the end of the First World War, even Preziosi did not make anti-Semitism the main focus of nationalism, nor did it have any political characteristics.[143] The first writings by Preziosi in 1907–1908 show no anti-Semitic references; in 1911–1912 the future theorist of anti-Semitism had no qualms about publishing articles in the magazine _L'Italia all'estero_, edited by Rodolfo Foà, who was Jewish. Founded in 1913, the magazine _La vita italiana_ welcomed articles by Jews and well-known Freemasons for many years. Even in 1916, during the publication of the second edition of his most important work, _La Germania alla conquista dell'Italia_, Preziosi's attacks were aimed at pan-German ideology and hegemonic policies of Germany over the world and over Italy in particular. He accused the Banca Commerciale and Giuseppe Toeplitz of being secret instruments to conquer and dominate Italy politically and economically— these are still the "German" Banca Commerciale and the "German" Toeplitz; for them to become the "Jewish" bank and the "Jew" Toeplitz, we will have to wait three or four more years. In _La vita italiana_ anti-Semitic attacks were extremely rare and of a traditional type during that time; in any case the author was Maffeo Pantaleoni, not Preziosi himself, even though, given his prior training as a priest, Preziosi would have been familiar with those themes.

In a well-known letter written in August 1920, which Preziosi was to reprint many times, Maffeo Pantaleoni thanked the director of the magazine for having opened his eyes regarding the "world conspiracy" by the Jews through the article on the _Jewish international_ published that same month in _La vita italiana_.[144] In reality Pantaleoni was the author of the first attacks on the Jews in Preziosi's magazine; for example, in the issue of December 1916, the commentary entitled _Le due mozioni alla Camera, quella degli "arrivisti" e quella dei "barbaro giudaici"_ [Two bills in Parliament, the one sponsored by the "activists," and that of the "Judaic barbarians"]; if they still lack the _worldwide_ aspect of the "conspiracy," their _Italian_ nature is made very clear. Besides the publication in _La vita italiana_, the articles were republished as a book by Pantaleoni in September 1919, one year before Preziosi's basic anti-Semitic statement.[145] It should be noted that Pantaleoni was the one who introduced Preziosi to the _Protocols of the Elders of Zion_, and Pantaleoni, again, we believe, who "launched" Preziosi's career in Italian cultural life during the First World War.

In 1918-1919 *La vita italiana* was still not specifically anti-Jewish. It did not take a clear position against Zionism, limiting its comments to the dangers it could create "when the Jews shall have their state in Palestine" and the question of a "dual nationality" for those Jews who did not emigrate to the banks of the Jordan.[146] It gave Zionism much space in the magazine[147] and opened the discussion regarding various problems of interest to Italy while stating that in Italy "Judaism is able to live a peaceful parallel life" to the national one, and could actually make positive contributions to Italian policy in Eastern Europe and the Mediterranean.[148]

It was only in 1920 that Preziosi suddenly changed his position, giving anti-Semitism more and more space in his magazine until it became, in 1922, the main theme of his political action. The timing of the positioning of the main nationalist, and later Fascist, theoretician of political anti-Semitism is the best proof of the absence of any anti-Semitic tradition in pre-Fascist Italian politics, as well as the explanation of the meaning of anti-Semitism for Preziosi and certain nationalist and Fascist circles. Political anti-Semitism was characterized by the belief in the existence of an international conspiracy of which the Jews were the main movers (for example, the Wilsonian pacifism of the League of Nations, the collaboration between a few great powers that were democratic, plutocratic, and Masonic, international socialism "without a country" and Bolshevism), bent on dominating the world and imposing its will, especially on the poorer and more dynamic nations such as Italy, which was "the real victor in the war." In practical terms nationalism was to see, during the years immediately following 1918, its hopes that the world war meant a period of internal economic prosperity and territorial, political, and economic expansion beyond the old borders, as well as international prestige for Italy, dashed. The denial of these dreams and the harsh reality of the post-war period could not just be explained away with the slogan of the "lost victory"; to gain political value and justification it was necessary to introduce something grandiose, irrational, mind-boggling, monstrously subtle and strong that would serve to explain the failure, justifying it to the Italian public and eliciting its indignant reaction, using some untapped and hidden lever that was already planted in their minds.

The explanation of the "Jewish conspiracy" satisfied all these motivations and easily lent itself to becoming an ideology that could be set up as a *political system*, especially in a country where politics were *ideologically* weak and, in general, full of antihistorical clichés and as many messianic expectations.[149] In his August 1920 article and its sequel one month later, Preziosi's blueprint is clear: his entire production over the next twenty-five years will only be a series of variations on the theme, additions and updates of the same picture.

Who were those responsible, at the international level, for having "cut the wings" of the Italian victory by ignoring its sacred demands? Lloyd George, Clemenceau, and Wilson. The explanation provided by Preziosi is swift and categorical: after a lengthy description of the big picture and how high finance, journalism, and international politics were all controlled by the Jews and having published the list of the major Jewish "leaders" in these fields, he goes for the jugular:

> Politics today is led by the Jews through their influence over the statesmen; Lloyd George is himself of Jewish origin; Wilson is in the hands of the Jews; Clemenceau was tied to a Jewish crowd; during the Paris peace conference Wilson was the guest of a Jew; Lloyd George was the guest of a Jew; the only person admitted to the top-secret meetings of the four, during the conference, was the Jew, Mantoux.

All the details of the picture must be complete: "Jacob H. Schiff created the *American Neutral Conference Committee*, which eventually became the League of Nations, and financed the press campaign against "the old diplomacy," "imperialism," etc."[150] That was addressing only the bourgeois and plutocratic front; but Judaism uses many disguises and any instrument that will propel it to power:

> Let us not even consider Marx and Lassalle, whose real names were Mordecai and Feist Lasall; but is not Trotsky (whose real name is Braunstein), the soul of today's Russian revolution, and Kerensky, who was its prime promoter and whose real name was Zederblum, not also Jews? Were not Radek and Joffe, those two importers of

revolution into Germany, also Jews? Is Litvinoff not also a Jew whose real name is Finklestein? And are the names of the major revolutionaries who are keeping the world in chaos today not Jewish—Enver Pasha, whose real name is Annar Pasha, and Bela Kun?[151]

The *inquest* goes on for Germany, the USA, England, France, and wherever proof is insufficient he resorts to invention or uses "news" from the most discredited German papers. Not to mention Italy: "Even Italy is a victim of the Jewish international. Let us recall how, during the conquest of Libya, high finance and Jewish journalism were against us . . . "[152] Everything throughout the world, according to Preziosi, is controlled "by the spirits of that very ancient international made up of Jews scattered all over the world after the destruction of Jerusalem during the reign of Emperor Titus."[153]

In the articles written in 1920–1921 Preziosi seems to show some hostility towards anti-Semitism. It is first of all for him, "a Jewish game," and secondly his attacks on the Jews are based on precise "facts" and are not to be confused with anti-Semitism. It does not exist in Italy; "in no country are the Jews more at home than in Italy": it is up to the Italian Jews not to foment it. "We will not deny the Jews political freedom, provided they do not become the instruments of Italian decay in favor of foreign and anti-national political and economic interests . . . we are far from demanding that the Jew be hunted down."[154] This was written in 1920; the attacks by Preziosi and *La vita italiana* in general became harsher during the following months and the last hesitations were cast aside: "Freemasonry and democracy are the main tools of international Jewry; Bolshevism's high command in Moscow and its propagandists overseas are also, with rare exceptions, all Jews."[155] The Jews who are members of Freemasonry, the democratic parties, the Socialist and the Communist parties, are all enemies of Italy. Beginning in 1922 any existing restraints disappeared among the writers of *La vita italiana,* which became the foremost anti-Semitic magazine in Italy and gave material to other nationalist magazines such as the *Rivista di Milano, L'idea nazionale* and most notably *Don Chisciotte.*[156] The "hunting down of the Jew" had not yet adopted the methods of Eastern Europe and Germany, methods that Preziosi repudiated at first as "a colossal lie," then accepted and justified later as a natural "reaction." There were incidents of violence by Fascist squads and individuals, which had anti-Semitic overtones. Preziosi limits his action to denouncing the power of the Jews within public administration[157] and implicitly calls for the elimination of the Jews from these posts altogether. By 1922 Preziosi had completed his makeover and anti-Semitism had become a definite political slogan for *La vita italiana*.

We must now briefly examine this itinerary from 1920 to 1922. We have seen how Preziosi and his magazine changed during this time; the "ideological sources" and "documents" he refers to require further investigation. His anti-Semitism was neither personal nor the result of Italian experiences, which were nowhere to be found or, with reference to the clerical variety, were of a different nature and were really aimed at the anti-Christian element within Judaism.

We find that in 1920 Preziosi used the infamous *Protocols of the Elders of Zion*, one of the most notorious forgeries of all time,[158] translated from Russian to German in 1919 for the first time. This was the main *ideological* and documentary source used by Preziosi who, having accepted it at face value, translated it and used it as his exclusive strong point. To the *Protocols* must be added the entire arsenal of pamphlet writing of those years from Germany, France, and Great Britain, which was constantly referenced in Preziosi's writings, as well as at a higher level, if we may use that term, the writings of Georges Sorel; for instance *Quelques prétentions juives* [A Few Jewish Pretensions] published in 1912, which Preziosi used copiously to prove the Jewish origins of socialism. The use of anti-Semitic argumentation from French, German and the nascent Nazi party publications, grows markedly in 1921 and 1922 in the pages of *La vita italiana*. In the July 1921 issue, in an article entitled *Plutocrazia e bolscevismo giudaico sgretolano il fascismo* [Plutocracy and Jewish Bolshevism Crush Fascism], Maffeo Pantaleoni even attacked Mussolini, accusing him of being if not exactly in agreement with, at least of being gullible in the face of the intrigues of, Italian Judaism.[159] At the same time that it launched its attack on the "Jewish"

Banca Commerciale, on the "Jew" Toeplitz, on the "Jews" Treves, Modigliani, Della Torre, Luzzatti, Schanzer, Alessio and their "agents," Nitti-"Cagoia"* and Orlando being at the top of the list: according to *La vita italiana* they were not part of Italian internal and foreign policy but, rather, belonged "to the other country." Public opinion was encouraged to display its aversion to all of them, and for the Jews in general they began demanding "proportionate" representation, at least for the most delicate positions.[160] By 1922, as we have said, the conversion of Preziosi to full-fledged anti-Semitism was complete, as evidenced in *La vita italiana*, from July and especially August onward.[161]

In this issue we find not only the famous article by Preziosi on "Gli ebrei nelle amministrazioni dello Stato italiano" [The Jews in the Italian state administration] and an article entitled "Come l'Alta Banca Internazionale Ebraica continua a rivoluzionare il mondo" [How high international Jewish finance continues to revolutionize the world], but more importantly another article that is the key to Preziosi's entire position in the coming years. It is entitled "Gli ebrei, la passione e la resurrezione della Germania (Il pensiero di un tedesco)" [The Jews, the Passion and Resurrection of Germany (The Thoughts of a German)], signed by "un bavarese" [a Bavarian].[162] Thanks to the statements of Preziosi and his friends, repeated in Germany and never denied, we now know that the author was Adolf Hitler himself.[163] The article was accompanied by a short editor's note, which subsequently was to disappear from reprints during the years of the racist campaign, that said: "In publishing this important article we refrain from any comment on certain positions and ideas of the author. Each one of our readers is able to reach his own conclusions." A significant note showing that at the time Preziosi felt unable to adopt the Nazi ideology *in toto*, considering it counterproductive even for Italian public opinion, be it nationalist or Fascist. This note does not change the substance of what he believes; if we take into consideration

---

*NDT: "Cagoia" was a scatological and disparaging nickname coined by Gabriele D'Annunzio against Prime Minister Francesco Saverio Nitti during the Fiume crisis of 1919.

Preziosi's career, undoubtedly the presence of an article by Adolf Hitler in *La vita italiana* can only mean that Italian political anti-Semitism had linked itself to the most brutal positions of world-wide anti-Semitism. We feel we have given a clear enough view of the most extreme stance of nationalist anti-Semitism on the eve of the Fascist takeover.

Even though important, it is clear that Giovanni Preziosi's position and *La vita italiana* cannot be compared to that of the Nationalists nor even of the Fascists. Even during its obscure beginnings between 1920 and 1926, the position of *La vita italiana* was never adopted by the majority of the Nationalists and Fascists and remained an isolated case without a following in the country, but dangerously tolerated by Mussolini even after the March on Rome and a harbinger of things to come. Yet although public opinion was unaffected by the infection that Preziosi represented, some drops of his poison did find their way here and there. Italy was not to become anti-Semitic because of Preziosi and his miserable little group, but the Italian public, as it rejected anti-Semitism, became unconsciously accustomed to hearing its slogans and some of its ideas. While many felt these were "exaggerations," which certainly could never apply to the "good" Italian Jews, there might however be some truth to them somewhere. The July 5, 1923 issue of the magazine *Israel* was to publish this sad comment in an article entitled "La stampa antisemita in Italia" [The anti-Semitic press in Italy]: "These are only secondary publications, but it is a fact that anti-Semitism, which once appeared to be remote to this civilized and peaceful people, gentle and intelligent, has managed to find its dark path into Italy."

The most brutal, gross, and violent anti-Semitism encountered strong opposition in almost every section of the population. Without detailing the various statements, we will mention as an example, what the famous journalist Mario Missiroli wrote in two well-known columns, "Opinioni," in the daily *Il resto del carlino*; his response symbolizes, in a way, the average thinking of the time. For Missiroli "anti-Semitism is to human dignity a crime worse than war itself," and against these persons we must react "with courage and fairness."[164] The notorious *Protocols* were indignantly rejected by the vast majority of the press as childish and gross fabrications,[165] and the same can be said for the equation of Judaism and Bolshevism.[166]

But some drops of poison did penetrate unconsciously into almost every quarter, even those that were more mature and seriously involved both politically and ideologically and that should have been immune. For example, Missiroli himself, even as he condemned anti-Semitism, thought that Judaism was "the pessimistic and abstract negation of history, intimately persuaded that freedom and redemption from sin are denied to mankind, striving for control over nature and truth," and that it fostered "asceticism, theocracy, despair, and rebellion" and was "the origin of internationalism," as well as at the origins of the First World War.[167] The socialists used some anti-Semitic arguments concerning the Jews' "wealth" and antisocial attitude as well as "exploitation" by the Jews.[168] But among all the "reasons" used by the anti-Semites the one to capture the imagination concerned "Jewish banking," its international connections and its negative influence on Italian life—an "argument" that cannot be traced exclusively to the *Protocols* and the Preziosi group because, in less strident terms, it had been disseminated in Italy since the beginning of the century and accepted in many quarters. Accusations against Jewish banking and finance thus were turned into truisms for many, to the point that even the publication *L'Unità*, edited by Gaetano Salvemini, used some of those themes.[169] These accusations appeared to be confirmed in one of the most obvious aspects of the Italian national economy. The lack of capital in Italy at the beginning of the 20th century gave banks an overwhelming importance compared to industrial enterprise and had, especially after 1907, made industry heavily dependent upon the major banking institutions. This trend had intensified during and after the First World War, bringing even heavier banking intervention in industry and a very obvious overlapping clash of stock markets and financial interests versus the industrialists. So at war's end the "banking quadrumvirate," Banca Commerciale Italiana, Credito Italiano, Banco di Roma, and Banca Italiana di Sconto, controlled most of the industrial production within Italy. In this heightened context,[170] a few large industrial groups already owned major daily newspapers—Ansaldo owned *Il messaggero* in Rome and *Secolo*

XIX in Genoa, while ILVA owned *Il Mattino* in Naples. These same groups then began their bid to acquire banks, just as Ansaldo did in buying the Banca Italiana di Sconto. Some banking institutions were suffering from their own aggressive investment policies of earlier years, and in this situation it is not surprising that large Italian banks should become the targets of criticism by broad segments of public opinion and that they should be accused of being at odds with national interests, among other things, and pursuing the interests of International Banking controlled by *International Jewry*, "which had men such as Toeplitz and other bankers as its 'trusted agents' among us . . . "

At the time of the March on Rome there was, therefore, no popular support for anti-Semitism[171] despite the efforts of certain groups and publications, but it can be said that a few clichés and assorted legends had found their way into popular culture during previous years regarding the Jews and Judaism that, while failing to spark any anti-Semitic excitement or state of mind, did create in some parts of society a measure of antagonism towards the Jews rather than the friendly and impartial attitudes characterizing the preceding forty to fifty years, and some anti-Semitic slogans and calumnies were no longer rejected *in toto* with the same indignation as before.

If racism and anti-Semitism failed to succeed in Italy, in spite of everything, anti-Zionism did have increasing success within certain circles at the beginning of the century and right after the First World War.

At the turn of the century, when Zionism developed and expanded, it was well received except among certain clerics. As long as Zionism remained a utopian ideal almost everyone approved of it, thinking that from a historical and cultural standpoint it was a "brilliant" device to rid Eastern Europe of its bloody pogroms and anti-Semitism. King Victor Emmanuel III himself, along with several Italian statesmen, did not hide his "approval" and his "sympathy" for Zionism, both remaining platonic, naturally.[172] A few clouds began to appear during the war between Italy and Turkey, separating Zionism from a section of Italian public opinion. The Nationalists saw in the Zionists the potential or real allies of the Turks, in an "obvious" syllogism: the Zionists were negotiating Jewish immigration into Palestine with the Ottoman Empire; they are therefore friends with the Turks and enemies of Italy. This reasoning triggered a number of statements, sometimes quite harsh, against Zionism and the Jews in general. The self-imposed censorship of the publication *L'idea sionistica* and many pro-Italian statements made by Jews were ineffectual.[173] For most Nationalists and many others, whose attacks appeared in *La nazione* published in Florence and *Il mattino* in Naples, *Israel*, in the words of Francesco Coppola in *L'idea nazionale*,[174] was against Italy. Paolo Orano was among the fiercest in this campaign, besides Coppola,[175] and the protests and resignations of many Jews from the Nationalist Association did not succeed in putting a stop to it. With the outbreak of the First World War, Turkey was again an enemy of Italy; then came the famous Balfour Declaration, which Italy accepted, and Zionism for a brief period recaptured some sympathies, as did certain pro-Zionist initiatives: the liberation of oppressed Jews and the Jewish national question became something of a point in the agenda of the allies in the fight for the liberation of peoples against the Central Powers and their oriental allies.[176]

Among the most significant positions taken in those years in favor of Zionism was that of Enrico De Marinis in an article published in the daily newspaper *Roma* of March 23, 1917: "Gli ebrei e la guerra" [The Jews and the War], as well as those of Francesco Saverio Nitti and Guglielmo Marconi in an interview in the *American Jewish Chronicle* of June 22, 1917. Nitti, after reiterating that Italy did not have a Jewish problem and that "perhaps no nation can compare to Italy in its great admiration for the Jewish race," promised unequivocally that "if the Jewish people tell the Powers that the reestablishment of Palestine is necessary to its prosperity or an essential factor for the future well-being of the Jewish race, Italy will be ready to defend its cause."

At the end of the war, however, anti-Zionism reappeared. As Francesco Ruffini was to write, the misunderstandings and prejudices against Zionism quickly became generalized, radical and pervasive.[177] Very few escaped these attitudes.[178] A journalist like Missiroli condemned anti-Semitism and at the same time was also opposed to Zionism, as we have shown. The nationalists considered Zionism a "betrayal" and a "rejection" of the Italian homeland by the Jews, or at best their claim to having two homelands was, for Missiroli, and many other sincere democrats and radicals, an old-fashioned and irrelevant view of one's country and its true meaning. Missiroli wrote: "Zionism is a dream, and not even a good dream at that. According to the Zionists the homeland no longer exists: it is an old ideology that the French Revolution destroyed. The homeland is not a gift of nature but our own continuous masterwork."[179]

From this type of idea, inspired by Ernest Renan, Missiroli, like many others,[180] criticized the Zionists for not being able to fulfill their human destiny within their *own* country. Everything else became secondary to these two divergent but, in effect, practically parallel concepts of patriotism and homeland: even the possibility, many times repeated by Italian Zionists and pro-Zionists,[181] that a Jewish Palestine that was friendly towards Italy could become a significant outlet for the Italian economy and an important ally to foster Italian political and economic penetration of the Middle East. With the deepening internal and international crisis, to the so-called patriotic anti-Zionism was added the additional ingredient, within nationalist, revolutionary trade unionist and Fascist movements, of anti-British and anti-Zionist opinions. Zionism, it was believed, was a sort of Wilsonian invention to mask imperialistic British interests in the eastern Mediterranean. In practical terms, anti-Zionism, as it appeared within extreme nationalist circles, joined and cross-fertilized anti-Semitism itself.

Many socialists were not immune to this growing trend. For instance, a typical article by Claudio Treves in *Il resto del carlino* of May 23, 1920, where the socialist leader went back on every one of his previous pro-Zionist positions:

> Alas! Life often denies the fictions that support our hopes! Zionism was a daring and beautiful idea in defiance of destiny, a promise of reawakening after centuries of death! It was the indomitable heretical spirit that seeks in every homeland a larger homeland that transcends everything and spreads the pollen of every revolution.

All this will be laid to rest by diplomacy and its creation of a national territory under British protection . . . They [the Zionists] saw only England and the ghost of the League of Nations behind it . . . This is not the way to build the new Jerusalem. This is not the way to announce the promised reunion to those who are scattered throughout the world.

We must also briefly examine two important expressions of anti-Zionism, Catholic and nationalist, during the post-World War I period. Both were to exist even after the March on Rome, and both strongly contributed to some of the future positions of Fascism in power towards Zionism in general and its Italian expression in particular.

Catholic anti-Zionism was directly connected to the positions adopted by the Holy See and certain Italian Catholic circles during the second half of the 19th century regarding the problems of the Holy Places. With the disintegration of the Ottoman Empire and the beginning of Western influence and penetration in Palestine, the Catholic Church aggressively promoted the defense of the Holy Places and of the "rights" of Christianity over them, as well as the need to exclude from the Holy Places themselves any non-Catholic presence. This idea gained such a strong following among Italian Catholics that in 1887 they created a national association in Florence to help Italian Catholic missionaries, the *Associazione nazionale per i missionari italiani*, whose mission it was to give spiritual and material support to Italian missions and maintain religious faith and patriotism among Italian nationals overseas. At the outset the association favored, as proposed in an article by Fedele Lampertico in the November 1, 1891 issue of *Rassegna nazionale* and reprinted as a booklet several times,[182] the abolition of "religious hegemonies" within the Holy Places and their replacement by a "police force of all European countries" and the "defense of Catholic interests," to be reached not through a single state but through tutelage and representation, "universal and therefore Catholic." As Italy's international importance increased and Catholics gradually entered the administration of the Italian state, this initial position changed into a demand that Italy be awarded the tutelage of the Holy Places, since it was a Catholic world power with centuries-old interests in Palestine. The Association then began in 1902 to establish various Italian schools and institutions in the Holy Land, administered by Catholic religious orders,[183] that had the double mission of protecting Catholic interests and affirming the Italian "presence."[184] The Association and the Catholics in general took positions very close to those of the nationalists. In a booklet entitled *L'Italia e la Palestina* published by the association in 1917 one can read, for example:

> The great events of the last few years, the Libyan action, the occupation of Rhodes and the islands of the Dodecanese, the various initiatives undertaken in Asia Minor, the prestige afforded to Italy by the Alliance, the expedition in Albania, the dispatching of troops to Salonica, finally the Italian contingent together with the sister nation's troops, alongside the British army at the foot of Judea, have all pushed Italy along the paths toward the Orient. We hope that she will not need to pause during this march, and that she will remain in the land of Jesus with full rights, in accordance with its history and its centuries-old traditions.[185]

While this Italian Catholic effort toward the Holy Places was underway, Zionism was gaining ground and approval. The Jews, who up to then had not been involved in the Palestinian equation, began to enter the fray, morally, economically, and politically, with increasing importance, changing its scale and its goals. After the Balfour Declaration and the international agreements of 1920-1921, the Jewish "presence" in Palestine became a new factor that altered and influenced the picture considerably. This explains the opposition of the Holy See,[186] as well as of many Catholics, to Zionism. Very quickly this opposition took extremely violent and overt forms. At the forefront of the anti-Zionist campaign were notably the newspapers *L'osservatore romano*, *Corriere d'Italia*, and *Rassegna nazionale*. Concentrating on the period immediately preceding and following the March on Rome, we must note the attacks against Zionism in *L'osservatore romano* during Chaim Weizmann's visit; the anti-Jewish pronouncements of the patriarch of Jerusalem Monsignor Barlassina in April and May 1922, and the ensuing disputes in the press;[187] the campaign in the *Corriere d'Italia* against "Jewish encroachments" in

Palestine; and the general positions taken by *Rassegna italiana* on the Holy Places between 1922 and 1925. We will only mention the violently anti-Zionist campaign in *L'avvenire d'Italia*, published in Bologna, and the harsh attacks during the Turin congress of the Popular Party by Rufo Ruffo in April 1923, focused on the "grabbing" of Palestinian lands by many Jews and the presence among the Jews of a number of pro-Bolshevik elements.[188] For all these writers and speakers, Zionism was not favorable to the concept of equality for all "races and religions" in Palestine, but rather attempted to secure for the Jews an overwhelming position of privilege and therefore a "purely Jewish Palestine."[189] The region was undergoing a real "Jewish invasion," conducted with a "visible hatred of humanity and Christianity," and in these conditions "Christians cannot condone a policy tending to impose an intransigent Jewish majority on the Holy Places."[190] The Jewish question would not be solved with Zionism and the Jewish National Home. "The real solution," wrote Romolo Tritoni, a frequent contributor to *Rassegna italiana*, "is to be found in the assimilation taking place in the West and in accelerating Jewish emancipation where it is still lagging and protecting its emigration, without necessarily establishing a political state."[191] The national home would hurt both Jews and Europeans, exciting the Moslem world against them, and was bound to damage the "question of the Holy Places, which is, for Italy, more important than Zionism."[192] This problem could be resolved "fairly" under the British mandate;[193] there were some, like A. Corsaro, who advocated the more radical solution of giving the Holy Places to Italy: "Palestine should be Italian politically, or at least under an Italian protectorate."[194]

On October 11, 1924, following these statements, the Catholic Union for the Holy Places and pilgrimages to Palestine issued a note to the Italian government and the League of Nations requesting that they "reject and stop the Zionist movement in its nationalistic tendencies," giving "the unalterable right of Christianity, exposed to vexing and lurid clashes with Judaism." It is interesting to note that in this message sent by the Catholic Union for the Holy Places as confirmation of the requests for "tutelage of the Holy Places" against the "Zionist peril" were other "arguments"; for example, the scattering of the Jews for two millennia was the indication of "a supernatural form of justice that is imposed upon the God-killing race."[195]

In conclusion we can say that immediately after the First World War and following the March on Rome, the majority of the organized Catholic movement, its press, its organizations, the Popular Party[196] itself, were less than favorable to Zionism, and displayed not only a complete lack of understanding toward it and no willingness to listen—like the rest of the Italian press and public opinion as well—but together with this aversion, it slowly adopted the Nationalist[197] and even anti-Semitic argumentation.

Nationalist anti-Zionism, during the postwar years, kept on repeating the usual slogans about the Jews not being patriotic; their support of Zionism, the Nationalists maintained, was the best proof that the Jews placed the interests of their race ahead of those of their homeland. The Nationalists used their usual method of identifying everything with one single issue and considered, in stark contradiction to the obvious facts, that all Jews were Zionists. As their newspapers and magazines repeated incessantly (see, for instance, the articles on Zionism and Palestine of July 1925 by Francesco Scardoni in *La tribuna*, as well as the positions taken by Francesco Coppola and his group in *Politica*), for the Nationalists you could not be a good Zionist and a good Italian at the same time; the Zionists therefore could not have two homelands and should give up their Italian citizenship. In addition to this ultimate demand there were other lesser ones. They argued that Zionism opened the Jewish question rather than resolved it, and that while a Jewish religion exists a Jewish nation does not, and Jews from various countries would all be "foreigners to each other," that Zionism is only "a pure invention of the intellect by some Polish or Hungarian Jew," and a hoax made up of national rhetoric of the democratic war and Wilsonian peace.[198] Besides these positions, the Nationalist arguments against Zionism were pro-Arab and anti-British. For those who were pro-Arab, Zionism was going to provoke disorder and agitation in the Near East, and to support it meant to undermine Italy's position in the region and within the Arab world in general. For the anti-British camp, Zionism was a political and financial trick of the British to grab and hold on to Palestine through the excuse of the mandate. The Nationalists at this point were actually taking many of the Catholic positions, for example the defense of the Holy Places, and of Catholic interests against the intrigues of the Jews, American Protestantism and Anglicanism, as well as atheistic Bolshevism.[199] The cross-fertilization is obvious; as we have seen, the Catholics tended to appropriate certain Nationalist arguments, and both Catholics and Nationalists were to merge their positions into what would become a few years later the subject of a book by Alessandro Besozzi, *Italia e Palestina*, in which all points of view from Coppola and the magazine *Politica* especially and those of the Catholic Union for the Holy Places become one and the same. Zionism was condemned in the end from every point of view. It was not only claimed to be anti-historical, but also a product of British imperialism, which "gathered Jews from all parts of the world and sent them to Palestine to set up another bastion for its hegemony in the Orient"; "all anti-Catholic machinations and the testing ground of all the socialist and communist madness," it is at odds with the interests of Italy; "the Zionist movement . . . will never be favorable to our requirements as the Catholic power in Palestine . . . and it represents a constant and dangerous threat to Italy." Under these conditions "we must save our spiritual values in Palestine, our traditions, our culture, our pride, our language, our interests, and our potential as Catholics and Italians," we must free Palestine "from the hegemony that is Zionist, Moslem, Orthodox, Anglican, American, British, French, and Spanish." The only way to achieve this is "to open up to Islam, making the Moslems economic partners in our colonies, keeping their interests in mind in the evolution of politics in the Orient," and only Italy can accomplish this "since she has contributed to the liberation of Palestine. Furthermore, Italy is the most civilized, enlightened, free state within Europe, giving an excellent example of its tolerance, at home and in the colonies, of every form of religion, freedom of thought, offering every guarantee of good government for Palestine."[200] Besozzi's position was not as extreme and did have tangible value; as we shall see later, the idea of a transfer of the mandate from Britain to Italy will remain as a permanent demand at least up to 1936-1937 in certain Catholic-Nationalist circles on the fringes of Italian foreign policy, where it was to have some influence at various points and even considered, in the changed Palestinian reality, an agreement with right-wing Zionist groups to bring it about.[201]

After the First World War, anti-Zionism was much more of a reality than racism or anti-Semitism in Italy; with a few unimportant exceptions, Zionism was misunderstood, misinterpreted, considered with suspicion if not aversion. The anti-Zionist struggle now appears to have played an important part in preparing Italian public opinion for those anti-Semitic slogans and prejudices, that, as we have noted previously, while they did not create anti-Jewish opinions or tensions as such, certainly weakened public opinion and prevented a rejection of the first symptoms of Fascist anti-Semitism and racism, convincing Mussolini that the Italian people in a way would not really oppose his racist measures. Significantly, an article written by Giulio Provenzal on December 8, 1918, just after a pro-Zionist meeting in Rome, shows an indirect but important influence of anti-Zionism over various parts of Italian public opinion and the reactions it elicited from some Jews who expected anti-Zionism to evolve into anti-Semitism. Provenzal, after stating that he was "convinced of the right of the Jews to claim Palestine and that the world is favorable to their return to the place from which they had been violently expelled," wrote that he did not participate in the Rome meeting because he was convinced that such events "create a misunderstanding within the masses."[202] To avoid such misunderstandings it must be clear that such demonstrations were intended to show solidarity with those Jews "who are living in conditions where they are deprived of freedom and orderly existence," namely those living in Eastern Europe. These events do not involve Italian Jews, whose homeland was Italy and had demonstrated it since the beginning of the *Risorgimento* and the First World War. Solidarity with stateless Jews should not "create the false impression that Italian Jews, religious or not, freethinkers or believers, are not first of all Italians and expect good will from their non-Jewish compatriots."

3.

The Fascist Attitude:
Its Initial Contacts with the Jews

The Fascist attitude toward the Jews at the time of its origins during the years from 1919 to the March on Rome is not readily apparent. Fascism, at its "origins" or during its periods of "maturity" and its "decline," was unquestionably a unified movement as it appeared to the outside world (the Fascists eagerly embraced the myth of the monolith), as well as having tragic consequences for Italy and the Italian people. But clearly Fascism was also something very complex and composite in its internal reality and dialectics. Viewed from the outside there was "Fascism," but on the inside there were "the fascisms" or, better, "the fascists," with their personalities, their origins and above all their personal positions, interests, alliances, strengths, policies, ties, and preferences in the face of political, economic, and spiritual realities in Italy and abroad. The strength of these Fascisms and their interplay was always very strong. No one observing Fascism from the outside at the time imagined the power of these Fascisms, nor do many, even serious historians of Fascism today, who still tend to judge Fascism by its consequences for Italy and the world and underestimate its intimate reality, which is actually the Italian reality of those years in many respects. Mussolini himself was the unopposed Duce in appearance only; he was constantly at loggerheads with these power groups and their struggles. In the beginning, for example, the "pacification pact" and the congress at the Augusteo; during the period when Fascism was in power and during the final period (whether it was July 25, 1943 or the fall of the RSI)—sometimes holding them at bay, but many times held at bay and conditioned by them himself. No aspect of politics or even of Fascist reality was spared the interplay of these forces. We are convinced that this observation applies to every phase of Fascist rule, especially to its policies toward the Jews. Undoubtedly Jewish policy was ultimately incoherent and in need of definition. The study of this policy demonstrates that it is impossible to show the relation of cause and effect by blaming this absence of coherence and definition on the coarseness of Fascism itself, its ideology, its cultural confusion, the histrionics of Mussolini and his ever-present opportunism, or finally, the dictates of the Nazis. The various phases of Fascist Jewish policy acquire a logic of their own once they are placed in the context of the internal struggle within Fascism and the various Fascisms: each of these phases coincides exactly with one of the moments of the internal struggle, be it an episode of the struggle between the national factions within Fascism; between local leaders; the various administrative branches of the state; a particular issue of Fascist foreign policy; the personal ambitions of young or "excluded" leaders; or foreign intrigues to influence Fascist policy.

This is true in general and even more so for the period of the origins, when Fascism was everything and nothing, a sum total of personal and private interests, local realities, states of mind, illusions and compromises. In 1938, when the racist campaign was underway, self-styled historians and careerist journalists, national and local party leaders, all went hunting in the press archives of the previous decade to find articles, speeches, comments—often vague and unrelated to the current situation—in order to *prove* that racist policy and anti-Semitism were already within Fascism at its beginnings, or to show that they were present during the struggle "before the March on Rome." But Fascism at the beginning did not have a position of its own regarding the Jewish question, only a series of individual positions. An examination of the dozens of newspapers and news sheets that were more or less Fascist during that time, for instance *L'Assalto, Audacia, Il Maglio, Balilla, Intrepido,* would only be a long and futile exercise. It can easily be summed up that for this press, anti-Semitism and the Jewish question were never very important; the comments and asides that one finds are, as usual, of the Nationalist type, and not so fiery at that. For a long time Preziosi found no real following among the Fascists.[203] Besides the traditional anti-Semitic topics, they do not go beyond the usual Nationalist accusations that the Jews are the ones inspiring Freemasonry, socialism, Bolshevism, and the attacks on high finance and Jewish banks. The attacks on Zionism are more pointed, especially on certain internal or international occasions, such as the 1920 Zionist congress in Trieste. But never, even in the newspapers in cities with the largest Jewish population, does anti-Semitism use violent or even excited language; nor can one find any real racism in those publications. Beyond the Fascist-influenced press, if we look at the memoirs of Fascists and anti-Fascists of the period it does not appear that anti-Semitism had any importance, not even where the Fascist squads perpetrated their most violent acts.[204] This is also the case of the writings of the most vocal Fascist anti-Semites after 1938, for example Farinacci's *Storia del Fascismo*;[205] also in books by Jewish authors who would have been more sensitive to the problem, for instance, the book *1920: Paginette della vigilia* by Attilio Reglio. There was actually some mention of the patriotism of Italian Jews, their heroic conduct and their sacrifice during the First World War and even during the Fascist revolution itself.

This is not surprising. Italy was not a fertile ground for mass anti-Semitism, as we have previously noted. The heterogeneous nature of Fascism at its beginnings, certainly more than Nationalism, which was not without its radical, libertarian, and socialist elements, failed to spread some of the arguments and motivations that no doubt existed within. It must also be noted that many Jews were present in the ranks of the Fascist party from its earliest days and their presence was a sort of guarantee of the loyalty and patriotism of their fellow Italian Jews and an obstacle to the appearance of real anti-Semitism. Many Italian Jews also contributed financially to the Fascist party.

Let us examine, as best we can, the position Mussolini adopted personally as well as the press he controlled directly, *Il popolo d'Italia* and *Gerarchia*, the latter a magazine edited by Margherita Sarfatti, who was Jewish. The opinion that the Italian public and the Jewish readership could have had, in the chaotic state both Fascism and the country were in during those years, regarding Fascism's position towards the Jews and the *Jewish problem* in particular, was mostly the result of Mussolini's attitude and what was appearing in his own publications.

A few definite facts come to light after examining these publications:

a. Mussolini did not personally harbor, even after rising to power, any real prejudice against the Jews; he did not view them with either sympathy or antagonism; he recognized that the Jews were successful and clever, especially in the financial and economic fields;[206] he held them in high esteem as a people;[207] he was not immune to anti-Semitic remarks and prejudices, but these were not that important and did not go beyond what was common to the men of his generation and cultural mold.

b. This traditional anti-Semitism had no practical consequences for him: it did not prevent him, for example, from personally publishing articles in publications directed by Jews, such as in 1908 in *Pagine libere*, owned by Angelo Oliviero Olivetti, and to have Jews as his very close friends and coworkers, such as Cesare and Margherita Sarfatti and the lawyer Ermanno Jarach during the years we are discussing.

c. This traditional type of anti-Semitism did not have a *racist* bent, as the propagandists of the racial policy were to claim after 1938.[208]

d. Anti-Semitism had no political significance until 1936-1937; the Mussolini of the "origins" and of the years up to the racial campaign would never adopt the extreme views of Preziosi, who never had any real influence; nor would Mussolini be on friendly terms with him and toward whom he felt no sympathy, as well as toward other foreign and Italian propagandists of extreme anti-Semitism.

e. Mussolini felt a kind of reverent fear of *Jewish power* in the world.
    The rare opinions Mussolini expressed regarding the Jews during this period must be examined in light of the above. These opinions have, as far as we are concerned, been given too much importance by some scholars of Fascist persecution, possibly because of the way the Fascists themselves had used them extensively in 1938-1945.[209] We do not give them as much weight, due to their contradictory and irregular nature; if they have any significance, especially the famous statement of June 1919 in *Il popolo d'Italia*, it shows how unclear Mussolini was about the subject and how dependent he was journalistically on Nationalist and anti-Bolshevik propaganda of the time.[210] The very small number of

articles, and the fact that they were not even carried in *Gerarchia*, Mussolini's theoretical magazine, indicates how insignificant the topic was to the ideology Mussolini was building. The most important positions, due more to their length than anything else, were in *Il popolo d'Italia* of June 4, 1919, October 19, 1920, and June 25, 1922.

In the article entitled "I complici" [The Accomplices], of June 4, 1919, Mussolini uses the recent events in Russia to attack world Jewry, which he calls the "soul" of both Bolshevism and capitalism:

> If Petrograd does not fall, if Denikin gives up, this is what the big Jewish bankers of London and New York want, tied through their race to the Jews who in Moscow and Budapest are taking their revenge on the Aryan race that has condemned them to being scattered for so many centuries. In Russia eighty percent of the *Soviet* leaders are Jews; in Budapest, out of 22 people's commissars, 17 are Jews. Could Bolshevism be the revenge of Judaism over Christianity? The question is worth pondering. It is possible that Bolshevism may drown in the blood of a catastrophic *pogrom. World finance is in the hands of the Jews.* Those who control the money of nations actually control their politics. Behind the puppets in Paris are the Rothschilds, the Warburgs, the Schiffs, the Guggenheims who carry the same blood as the dominators of Petrograd and Budapest. The race will never betray its own . . . Bolshevism is supported by international plutocracy. This is the truth, in substance. International plutocracy, controlled and dominated by the Jews, has a supreme interest in seeing Russian life accelerate its process of molecular disintegration. A Russia that is paralyzed, disorganized, hungry will be tomorrow the place where the *bourgeoisie,* yes the *bourgeoisie,* my dear proletarians, will celebrate its spectacular horn of plenty.[211]

The oversimplification of this view is obvious, but what is most obvious is the reference to the oldest slogans of French anti-Semitism. Only a year and half later, Mussolini himself will reject and turn these ideas upside down in the article of October 19, 1920, "Ebrei, Bolscevismo e Sionismo italiano" [Jews, Bolshevism, and Italian Zionism]. Two events awakened his interest: the anti-Semitic measures in Hungary and a statement by the Italian Zionist Federation. On the first he writes:

> We must not be surprised by these draconian measures. Just remember that Bela Kun, the head of Hungarian Bolshevism, was a Jew, that Szamuely, the unholy leader of the red terror, was another Jew, and that four-fifths of the People's Commissars were Jews. The sun has set on Bolshevism, and in Hungary we will not hear about Bolshevism for quite a while. The Jews are paying heavily and will pay even more dearly for the crimes committed by a few of their brethren.

Nothing new up to this point, but Mussolini goes on:

> Bolshevism is not, as is thought, a Jewish phenomenon. But it is true that Bolshevism will mean the complete ruin of the Jews in Eastern Europe. This great and possibly imminent danger is acutely felt by the Jews all over Europe. It is easy to foresee that the collapse of Bolshevism in Russia will be followed by a *pogrom* of unheard-of proportions . . . [212]

His opinion on the weakness of the October Revolution and Bolshevism has not changed with respect to the preceding article of one year earlier. But the idea of the Jewish nature of Bolshevism itself has changed. What was the reason for this change? We think it was linked to a variety of reasons: better information regarding the facts, new suggestions from many influential Jews surrounding Mussolini, who were helping Fascism and *Il popolo d'Italia*, even financially, and most of all, the new phase Mussolini wanted Fascism to enter: no longer an elite revolutionary movement, but a national party "on the basis of a collective responsibility" and "made" to govern.[213] This change implied a widening of the appeal of Fascism and the identification of the nation with the state. The numerous Jews inside the Fascist Party and many who were important in national, and especially in economic, life, persuaded Mussolini, who was influenced by the groups closest to him and tended to exaggerate the importance of Jewish strength in Italy, into believing that they were tied to an organized world opinion and therefore could no longer be considered on the fringes of the nation but should be fully integrated into it. This is the reason for the new position taken by Mussolini. The second part of the article in *Il popolo d'Italia* confirms our interpretation. Mussolini states on the one hand that "Italy does not know anti-Semitism and we are convinced it shall never know it," but on the other hand he attacks Zionism and denies the existence of any "specific problems" of Italian Jews,[214] contrary to what was stated by the FSI [Federazione Sionistica Italiana]. However, this attack is also accompanied by a real "opening" towards Italian Jewry:

> " . . . in Italy we make absolutely no difference between Jews and non-Jews, in every field, religion, politics, the army, the economy . . . Italian Jews have the new Zion right here, in our beautiful land, which many of them have defended heroically with their blood."

This "opening" was immediately followed by a warning to the Zionists in particular and to Italian Jews in general. Mussolini knew that many Jews had little sympathy for Fascism and actually were members of the various anti-Fascist parties: "Let us hope Italian Jews will continue to be intelligent enough not to provoke anti-Semitism in the only country where it has never existed before." Less than a year and a half later, when the prospects of coming to power were more and more realistic, his language becomes even more explicit. In commenting on the murder of Walter Rathenau by German right-wing extremists, Mussolini reduces anti-Semitism to a variety of pan-Germanism and resolutely condemns it as such.

> Rathenau conducted his policies out of necessity. However, German right-wing groups were unable to forgive Rathenau two things: First, his conduct of foreign policy, where he did everything possible to fulfill the clauses of the Versailles Treaty. Second, his Semitic origins. For the German right-wing extremists, who see themselves as being of the purest Aryan race, it was intolerable to have a Jew directing and representing Germany to the world. There is in Germany, on the subjects of Aryanism and Semitism, an extremely violent climate. It makes no difference that the Jews of Germany behaved very honorably during the war; it makes no difference that

many of them feel so completely assimilated as to establish, under the presidency of Dr. Neumann, the League of German National Jews, who have cut every tie to their religion and their race (to a request for assistance to the Jewish colonies in Palestine, the presidium of the League of German National Jews replied as follows: "We are too German and too poor to give even a single pfennig for the reconstruction of Palestine"); it makes little difference that more or less, with the exception of the "Mizrahi" in Berlin, the German Jews are German. All this doesn't save them from the hatred of the pan-Germanists, who can only hate the *Judenrepublik* in Berlin.[215]

These are the three most important statements by Mussolini on the *Jewish problem*. There is nothing original in any of them: on the one hand he inherits the most outdated nationalist and anti-Semitic "theories," mostly from Italian and European sources (essence of Judaism, high finance, Bolshevism), and on the other hand, the pronouncements of Orano and, in a way, of Sorel on Zionism.[216] A careful reading of *Il popolo d'Italia* and Mussolini's speeches of this period reveals some other mentions,[217] but none will add to a careful examination of the article of October 1920. It contains, along with the article of June 1919, the entire official position of the Duce-to-be concerning the Jews, the Jewish question and Zionism before the March on Rome. There is nothing new to be found in any other mention or anti-Jewish comments in *Il popolo d'Italia* made by anyone other than Mussolini.[218]

After having examined—at least in its most important themes and its significant statements—what the Fascist attitude at its "beginnings" was toward the Jews, we must now look at the position of the Jews toward Fascism during the same period. This type of examination has a double objective: on the one hand, because it completes the description; on the other—we restate this because it is important—it shows how the Jews behaved just like all other Italians, even toward Fascism.[219]

Mussolini had had several Jews within his immediate entourage since 1919; yet Jewish approval of and membership in the Fascist party went further than that. Some Jews played a key part, at least as much as we can ascertain such delicate matters, in financing the first Fascist groups. In the initial and, up to now very unclear, financial requirements of *Il popolo d'Italia*, a key role was played by Commendatore Elio Jona,[220] and according to many rumors, as we shall see later, and the direct accusations leveled by the anti-Fascist Jews of Tunis during the Italian racial measures, one of the most important financial backers of Fascism was none other than the very much insulted Giuseppe Toeplitz. It was the case even in the provinces, especially those areas where the "reds" were strongest: Leghorn, Pisa, Ancona, and in the Romagna region. Around Ferrara, many Jews clearly actively backed Fascism and the squads led by Italo Balbo, and some large Jewish landowners played an important part in this effort.[221]

Some numbers, impersonal as they may be, are quite significant; among the participants present at the foundation of the Fasci di Combattimento in Milan on March 23, 1919, the famous "sansepolcristi,"* there were at least five Jews, one of whom, Cesare Goldmann, actually provided the space for the meeting; three Jews appear as official martyrs of the "Fascist Revolution": Duilio Sinigaglia, Gino Bolaffi, and Bruno Mondolfo. It is true that many Jews joined the Fascist party at the very beginning, before it had shown its true face, and left the party shortly thereafter. For instance the "sansepolcrista" Eucardio Momigliano, who was to quickly become a strong anti-Fascist and a leader of the Unione Democratica,[222] but this does little to change the general picture. Suffice it to say that 230 Jews took part in the March on Rome, or at least received the certificate confirming their participation, and at that time about 750 Jews were members of the PNF [the Fascist Party] or of the Nationalist Party that was folded into the PNF in March 1923. These numbers were compiled by Demography and Race in 1938 in order to proceed with the discriminations. The full picture, with the entire membership, can be examined in the following chart.

---

* The meeting took place in Piazza San Sepolcro, hence the name "sansepolcristi" of those Fascists who were present.

	Italian Jews 21 years old, having become Italian citizens after birth and residing in Italy since 1/1/1919	Italian Jews 21 years old and over
Party members before October 28, 1922		
With party card year XVI and with March on Rome certificate	1	193
Without party card year XVI and with March on Rome certificate	1	23
Without party card year XVI and with out March on Rome certificate	2	121
With party card year XVI and without March on Rome certificate	3	402
Total	7	739
Party members from Oct. 29, 1922 to Oct. 28, 1928		
With party card year XVI and with March on Rome certificate	-	3
Without party card year XVI and with March on Rome certificate	1	1
Without party card year XVI and without March on Rome certificate	6	288
With party card year XVI and without March on Rome certificate	16	1,478
Total	23	1,770
Party members from Oct. 29, 1928 to Oct. 28, 1933		
With party card year XVI and with March on Rome certificate	-	4
Without party card year XVI and with March on Rome certificate	-	-
Without party card year XVI and without March on Rome certificate	12	516
With party card year XVI and without March on Rome certificate	89	4,299
Total	101	4,819
Party members from Oct. 29, 1933 and after		
With party card year XVI and with March on Rome certificate	-	-
Without party card year XVI and with March on Rome certificate	-	-
Without party card year XVI and without March on Rome certificate	12	351
With party card year XVI and without March on Rome certificate	99	2,154
Total	111	2,505

Party members since an unknown date		
With party card year XVI and with March on Rome certificate	-	1
Without party card year XVI and with March on Rome certificate	-	-
Without party card year XVI and without March on Rome certificate	1	85
With party card year XVI and without March on Rome certificate	2	206
Total	3	292
Total party members	245	10,125
With March on Rome certificate	3	225
Total non-party members	593	22,161
With March on Rome certificate	-	2

Even if we consider the "racial" motivations behind these statistics, they indicate even more the strong following Fascism had among the Jews,[223] perhaps stronger than was previously thought, but easily explained by the "upper class" nature of the Fascist party at the beginning and, on the other hand, the middle-class character of Italian Jewry. This middle-class Jewish identity also explains how, if so many were attracted to Fascism, so many others were attracted to parties and movements that were strongly anti-Fascist, shunning, for the most part, any middle positions that were either agnostic or characteristic of a "wait and see" attitude. Unfortunately those types of statistics are not available, and we can only infer from various elements, such as the number of Jews within the committees and parliamentary groups[224] of the largest anti-Fascist parties and of those participating in public anti-Fascist demonstrations. A typical example is the "Croce manifesto" of May 1925, which comes somewhat later in time: among its supporters there were at least 33 Jews.[225] From these elements it is clear that many Jews, especially the intellectuals, were among the most determined adversaries of Fascism from the beginning. The most militant Zionists were also mostly anti-Fascist; they understood that Fascism in power would become their implacable enemy, and even after the March on Rome many did not hesitate to state their opinion on this matter. For example, during the local elections of 1923 in Piedmont, Emmanuele Segre publicly refused to be the Fascist candidate when the Fascists of

Nichelino[226] offered him the spot, stating that he was a "fervent Italian" but also "a Zionist, as a real Jew should be" and sensed an incompatibility between Fascism and Zionism: "I see the beauty of the Fascist ideals . . . but I think . . . I detect a Fascist tendency to oppose Zionism."[227]

The massive presence of Jews among the anti-Fascists explains why the first Mussolini government elicited, even among the least politically involved Jews, more disgust than fear that the anti-Semitic comments circulating among the Fascists and their Nationalist allies could lead to open anti-Semitism. The most recent Fascist policy and propaganda, as well as the quick but pointed comment made by Mussolini during his first speech in parliament on June 21, 1921 did not justify such fears.[228] Actually, some of the appointments he made after his rise to power confirmed this impression: the Undersecretary of the Interior was Aldo Finzi, who was Jewish and a former aviator in the *Serenissima* squadron led by D'Annunzio, a Fascist squad member, member of parliament, and of the Fascist Grand Council; and another Jew, prefect Dante Almansi, was named codirector of the police with Emilio De Bono and was confirmed in this post despite having earlier tendered his resignation.

The Zionists were the most alarmed. The editorial of their magazine *Israel* in the issue following the March on Rome, is typical in this regard. The article of November 2, 1922, entitled "Nel nuovo ministero italiano" [In the New Italian Government], stated:

> Italian Zionists are particularly pleased to see the Hon. Colonna di Cesarò become part of the government, as he was president of *Pro-Israel* and recently renewed his good will toward Zionism by consenting to introduce President Weizmann at the Collegio Romano . . . Other members of the new government come from those political parties that had been very much opposed to the policies followed by earlier governments on matters concerning the Near East and especially the problem of the Mandates on Syria and Palestine . . . Since some very particular points appear to complicate their attitude toward the Jewish-Zionist problem, we will not make the mistake of thinking that these parties and their leadership intend to cover with their name many small attempts that have apparently been taking

place for some years to import into Italy, with the usual lies and traditional prejudice found elsewhere, the bad seed of anti-Semitism . . .

The editorial writer of *Israel,* following this cautious but strong introduction, went on to remind his readers that Italy had never known anti-Semitism and concluded with a clear invitation that was also a wish:

> We want to renew the most sincere and natural wish of Zionist policy: that this glorious rebirth of the ancient scattered people . . . shall find the cordial support of all nations and of all parties within each nation . . . We also hope that the new government will want to keep unchanged the traditional and much-welcomed support of Italy for Zionism.

And so, in fear, suspicion, and mutual distrust, were to begin the relations between a large portion of Italian Jewry and Fascism finally in power.

II.

The Years of Adjustment:
1922-1932

4.
A Difficult Beginning

The years immediately following the March on Rome were not very favorable for the relationship between the Jews and Fascism.[229] Up to 1926-1927 Fascist-Jewish relations were influenced by the deep political crisis affecting the country, and in particular the double attempt by Fascism to eliminate its political adversaries as well as destroy democratic institutions while it tried to gain a more focused sociopolitical identity and present itself as the sole center of political power. During the Mussolini government's first months in power, the tiny but very active anti-Semitic group, especially the publication *Don Chisciotte*, edited by Filippo Tempera,[230] began an insidious campaign to persuade Mussolini and the Fascists to fire Bonaldo Stringher and Giuseppe Toeplitz from their positions at the head of the Bank of Italy and the Banca Commerciale Italiana, respectively. The purpose of this campaign was not to set Fascism on the path of an active anti-Semitic policy; its promoters actually sought to reduce the influence of the Banca Commerciale Italiana in favor of other financial groups. However, until it became clear that Mussolini would not support this attempt, the campaign did in fact muddy the waters between Fascism and the Jews and encouraged a few Fascist groups to take a very cautious, if not ambiguous or even antagonistic, attitude toward the Jews. This gave rise to mutual feelings of distrust if not of outright aversion, and from time to time some incidents, while not serious in and of themselves, contributed to the atmosphere of continued tension. On both sides there were some harsh attitudes and misunderstandings that, in this context, were not conducive to relaxing tensions and bringing the parties to some kind of understanding. The Jews were often too quick to interpret as evidence of anti-Semitism actions that were dictated by the regime's antidemocratic logic or the desire to uphold the authority of the state on every occasion that affected not only the Jews, but all other minorities as well. On the Fascist side there was a marked tendency to interpret as evidence of anti-Fascism many of the moral and cultural aspects of Judaism, viewed as being external to the national character and tending toward internationalism. During these first years there were relatively few direct relations between the leadership of the government and the Fascist Party on the one hand and Jewish community leaders on the other. For a long time relations were limited to personal contacts between Jewish community leaders (Angelo Sacerdoti in Rome, Federico Jarach in Milan, Felice Ravenna in Ferrara, etc.) and a few Fascist leaders, as well as some Fascists who were Jewish. The only official contact of national importance was the conversation between Mussolini and the Rabbi of Rome, Angelo Sacerdoti, which took place at the end of November 1923. At the close of the meeting an official communiqué was published and Sacerdoti gave an interview. The communiqué stated:

> During the conversation, Dr. Sacerdoti pointed out to the Hon. Mussolini that foreign anti-Semitic political parties wish to reinforce their own anti-Semitism because of the so-called anti-Semitic attitude of Italian Fascism, which they would like to use as a model; His Excellency declared emphatically that neither the Italian government nor Italian Fascism ever intended and do not plan an anti-Semitic policy, and he deplores that foreign anti-Semitic political parties attempt to use for their own ends the attraction exercised by Fascism throughout the world.

This idea was to be repeated during the interview given by Sacerdoti,[231] which confirmed that the same kind of assurances had been given in private "as soon as the Fascist Party was in power" by a "member of the government" in order to relieve any "worry that existed at the time in certain circles within the Jewish community."[232] Besides this conversation between Mussolini and Sacerdoti, there were only "technical" meetings between the leaders of the Consortium of Jewish Communities and the relevant officers of the ministries, especially the Ministry of Public Instruction and the Ministry of Religious Affairs, which were without any political or public significance. The Mussolini-Sacerdoti meeting produced no concrete results: both Jewish and Fascist opinion did not attribute any significance to it and remained entrenched in their respective positions. Only those who closely followed such matters noticed that Mussolini's words were followed by decisions confirming their substance: exemption from school taxes for foreign students, who were mostly Jewish and matriculated at Italian universities, confirmation of military leave for Jewish holidays, etc. Through the declarations of top Fascist Party leaders,[233] the party refrained from attacking the Jews, even though it tolerated the attacks by the major dailies and other newspapers supporting Fascism, and took punitive measures against those Fascists and newspapers which deviated from Mussolini's "line." A case in point, in 1926, was that of the Milan weekly *Il Fascio*, whose editor, Mario Giampaoli, was the Fascist federation leader in the city and a prominent figure within the party. On August 14, the weekly published a vitriolic article entitled "Noi e gli ebrei" [The Jews and Us] under the byline of C. M. Boesmi. The Fascist writer's opinion was that "the Jewish movement" could still represent a danger:

> The existence of this people lost within Europe represents, and will continue to represent, one of the major stumbling blocks and among the worst dangers for European security . . . They accumulate capital for their own benefit, they manipulate our money, and therefore our future . . . they squeeze our existence in their hands and can reduce us to hunger when they wish and slander us with impunity.

The *Fascio* article also wanted to oppose Jewish capitalism with an "active and fruitful capitalism" without Jews: "We must begin by driving away the Jews from the Latin race . . . For nations to be at peace a national home must be created for the Jewish nation . . . Each one in his own home." It was, obviously, a very harsh attack; and Mussolini's own reaction must have been just as hard: on September 4 *Il Fascio* dissociated itself completely from Boesmi's article. The editor, Giampaoli, wrote a "correction."

Among those things that are unacceptable for an Italian is the idea of creating a Jewish Question in Italy . . . The young Boesmi should know that there is a huge number of unworthy non-Jews devoid of the noble sentiments, generosity and patriotic feelings of a Jew who may be influenced by hatred that cannot always be admitted.

The episode was certainly the most noteworthy of its kind during those years due to the personality of the editor of *Il Fascio* and the complete repudiation of the article. It indicated the existence of numerous anti-Semitic elements within Fascism, and Mussolini's decision to proceed unhesitatingly against them was a prelude to a new phase in the relationship between Fascism and the Jews.

This being said, it must be pointed out that after the March on Rome, many Fascists, above all those who came from the Nationalist movement, still looked upon the Jews as an opposition group, closely tied to Freemasonry, to the anti-Fascist parties, to foreign interests, and for some—an opinion held only by Preziosi and his small group at *La vita italiana*,[234] and a few others—to the Jewish international, to high international finance and those groups and organizations that were more openly anti-Fascist and anti-Italian. These accusations, although less frequent than before October 28, 1922, were to be repeated for several years by the Fascist and even more by the pro-Fascist press, hypocritically exploiting the fact that many Jews were among the top leaders of the anti-Fascist parties. The main newspapers in this campaign were Farinacci's *Cremona nuova*, the Nationalist *La tribuna*, *Il Piemonte* in Turin and *L'Impero* in Rome. It was easy to find in their articles clear allusions to "Judaism, which takes the internationalist path too easily" and "social-communist Judaism," or "Masonic Judaism." At certain times, as with the approval of measures against Freemasonry in 1925,[235] such attacks became rather violent; other more serious newspapers also published more or less open and violent attacks, as the March 20-21, 1927 article by Ermanno Amicucci in *La nazione*, published in Florence, against "Jewish banking" as well as other respected cultural magazines.[236] Even more frequent were the smaller "colorful" attacks and *bons mots* coming from the oldest traditional clichés of anti-Semitism: for instance in October 1926, both the satirical weekly

Travaso delle Idee and *La sera,* published in Trieste, sarcastically referred to Francesco Saverio Nitti as an "honorary Jew who deserves to be promoted to rabbi."

The Consortium, the Communities, the various Jewish organizations, the magazine *Israel,* and prominent Jewish individuals kept on repeating, to no avail, that such generalizations were impossible to justify and that all Jews were not the enemies of Fascism. The Fascists kept on repeating that Claudio Treves was a Jew, that Giuseppe Emmanuele Modigliani was a Jew, that Arnaldo Momigliano was a Jew, that many Jews were involved in the main anti-Fascist initiatives and were among the anti-Fascists who had left Italy, and that the Italian anti-Fascists overseas were finding support among Masonic and Jewish organizations (on April 3, 1927 *La tribuna* violently attacked international Judaism in an article "Andiamo adagio" [Let's go slowly]). For the publication *Il lavoro d'Italia,* at the beginning of 1928, the Jews were "the last bastion of anti-Fascism." Beyond these declarations, the aversion to "anti-national" Zionism extended to almost all Fascists. The anti-Jewish debate was not limited to these issues: another complaint was the Jewish, Zionist or non-Zionist, tendency to distance the Jews from the life of the nation and its institutional bodies, demanding privileges—according to certain journalists—that appeared to be more "proof" to the Fascists of the "foreign character" of the Jews, who were inclined to feel more akin to their coreligionists the world over.

Even the presence of many Jews among the Fascists was insufficient to mitigate this kind of thinking. The murder of Giacomo Matteotti, and the period immediately following it, saw many Jews leave the Fascist Party, and an even more significant drop in new Fascist Party (PNF) memberships: between 1919 and the March on Rome new Fascist and Nationalist party memberships totaled 746, while between October 29, 1922 and October 28, 1928 there were only 1,793 in all.

In this context more serious incidents added to the press campaigns and individual attacks. Many Jews were beaten by Fascist squads. The most serious incident took place in Tripoli, where the authority of the state was not as well established, the sense of responsibility of the Jews less pronounced, and the actions of the Fascists more violent and out of control, with the additional ingredients of a difficult general climate influenced by local disputes. After a few preliminary signs at the end of May, the first incidents took place on August 19, 1923. For insignificant reasons—it appears that a soldier had overturned, by accident or deliberately, the worktable of a Jewish peddler—Jews, Fascists, and passersby engaged in a fight in the Jewish quarter, and the carabinieri intervened. The next evening the Fascists staged a "punitive action" that was promptly followed by other smaller incidents in which even some Arabs became involved, with more violence and looting that were presented by the Fascists almost as a Jewish revolt. In the end one Italian soldier was killed, many were wounded, and there were numerous arrests among the Jews. These incidents were widely known within the colony and in Italy and had broad repercussions within the Jewish community in Tripoli.[237] Rabbi Elia Artom tried unsuccessfully in a letter to the *Corriere di Tripoli* to defuse the situation and place the incidents in perspective, showing how absurd it was to place the blame on the entire Jewish population.

> . . . It is clear that judging from the facts themselves and the positions of the ultra Fascist press . . . certain Fascist elements display an attitude whereby they completely despise the entire Jewish population of Tripoli and deny any feeling of dignity and legal due process.[238]

The episode did have serious legal consequences and, even worse, left much local rancor in its wake that, in the long run, was to have a negative influence, as we shall see, upon the relations between the local authorities and the Jewish community and within the community itself. In February 1924, Minister Federzoni, accompanied by Count Volpi and Italo Balbo, toured the Jewish quarter of Tripoli, and on April 11, 1926 Mussolini himself visited the same Jewish quarter; on both occasions the officials were greeted with all the customary honors and "warm" feelings from the people, but the events of the years to come were to show that these demonstrations were not spontaneous and that the community in Tripoli did not forget the violence it had endured.[239]

So much for the Fascist side. On the Jewish side the years 1926-1927 were to be marked by three different, if not contradictory, attitudes.

On the one hand, the Jews tried to keep the Consortium and the Communities outside politics, stressing at every occasion that they could not be responsible for the attitudes of individual citizens and should not be identified with them.[240] The Jewish organizations were careful to praise any measures taken by the government and the Fascist Party in favor of the Jews that brought about a relaxation of tensions, and to show themselves to be, while avoiding excessive conformity, "good Italians."[241] At the same time, however, any evidence of anti-Semitic attitudes was quickly and resolutely pointed out and disapproved of.

On the other hand, the magazine *Israel* and the more active Zionists attempted to clarify the true meaning of Zionism and its acceptance by Italian Jews and to show how the creation of good relations between Italy and Jewish groups in the eastern Mediterranean and in Palestine would be all to the advantage of the Italian economy and its government.

The third part of this period saw the Zionists and others, some even spontaneously, begin a cultural and moral action to reclaim and renew typically Italian Jewish values and traditions to rekindle a Jewish self-consciousness which had been dampened by assimilation.

The first of these attitudes speaks for itself, since its purpose was purely defensive and was the direct consequence of an active Fascist minority among the Jews. The other two require some explanations.

The Zionist attitude had its roots in the period preceding the Fascist ascent to power and would play an important role in the future relations between Fascism and the Jews. It must be examined in greater detail. For its role in "clarifying" the true nature and the various goals of Zionism as well as the complete openness on the part of the Zionists to be identified as such and be Italians at the same time, we shall quote, besides the two small volumes by Dante Lattes entitled *Zionism*, a short history and program for Italian Jews, an article in *Israel* of July 23, 1925 entitled "Sionisti e Italiani" [Zionists and Italians]:

75

They [the Zionists] are citizens (in the legal sense) of the various states in which they reside or to which they are connected through the nationality of which they are subjects, and nationals of the Jewish nation, of Israel, that even though scattered, has maintained . . . the bonds of its unity, apart from trying to create its own political center.

As for the "propaganda" aspects of the advantages that a pro-Zionist Italy would reap from such a policy, we must refer to the cited speech by Dante Lattes at the first congress of Italian-Oriental and Colonial Questions in Trieste in September 1922. Italian Zionists had, at that time, clearly begun their effort to reach an understanding between Italy and Zionism, as Italy's foremost Zionist wrote at that time.

Should England and France follow with great interest this new social, agricultural, national and spiritual, economic, and cultural experiment, Mediterranean Italy, the natural bridge between Europe and Asia, among the lands of the tragic Jewish Diaspora and the land of Jewish reconstruction, the Italy that works and hopes for a better and more equitable future for proletarian and oppressed people, the Italy that wishes to realize the dream of its martyrs, its poets, thinkers and dreamers, the Italy that needs to expand its trade and must do so among the Mediterranean nations, in those countries whose coasts are closest, cannot remain indifferent or absent from these new sources of life and these new markets. It is not just the desire of us Italian Jews, but of all Jews in the world who admire and love this free and generous land and are grateful for the wholehearted support it has given to their requests; it is the desire of all Jews that Italy participate in the renaissance in the Orient.

He then went into greater detail:

I am authorized by the World Zionist Organization . . . to ask that Italy find new ways and means to collaborate with the Jews to ensure the rebirth of Palestine in all those forms that can be useful to both sides. Palestine does not wish to be, and should not be, the monopoly of just one power; the Jews wish and have an interest that nations should benefit and draw advantage from the new page of history about to open in Palestine, that all nations should compete in their contribution to the reawakening and reconstruction of the Jewish national home.[242]

This first official "opening" would serve as the model for Italian Zionist action during the following years, as is shown by, among others, the various positions taken by the publication *Israel* and the Italian Committee for Assistance to Jewish Immigrants in Trieste.[243] The Italo-Palestinian Chamber of Commerce was created in this spirit to develop commercial relations between Italy and Palestine, to channel through Italian ports, and Trieste in particular, the transit of Jewish emigrants, to create cultural relations between Italian universities and the Hebrew University of Jerusalem (whose inauguration was attended by the Italian Consul and that received a friendly message from Giovanni Gentile) as well as, generally, to disseminate within the public at large, various articles in the best cultural and public affairs publications, the successes of the Jews in Palestine and the economic and commercial opportunities they opened to Italian capital.[244]

As for the third aspect of Jewish life and activity during these years, the effort to create a greater consciousness and involvement within the community in Italy, much has been written recently, but its real meaning—or at least one of its essential meanings—has gone unnoticed by the majority of Jewish writers who have approached the subject.

Undoubtedly the reclaiming of certain values and traditions, of certain commonly accepted rights, such as the study of the Hebrew language and culture, a religious and moral education attuned to Mosaic law and Jewish tradition, the observance of the Sabbath and other holidays, the continued right to divorce for Jews from the "new provinces" (Trentino, Venezia Giulia, and Dalmazia),[245] and others, had begun before the March on Rome and was a consequence of the Zionist rebirth and its struggle against assimilation.[246] It is also true that this claim developed mostly after 1922, reached its peak during the years we are analyzing and, significantly, involved groups having little or nothing to do with Zionism. This is precisely the point that we feel has not been sufficiently studied when limiting the discussion to Zionist action. Without limiting the merits of Zionism, in our opinion the Jewish "awakening" and the "reclaiming" of Jewish values, this closing of Italian Jews within themselves, is largely due to the aggressive success of Fascism and the passive reaction of most Italian Jews to its success. Significantly, Fascist Jews without exception immediately opposed such a psychological and ethical stance as a rejection of "being Italian" by identifying the nation with the state and the state with the party, and therefore a rejection of Fascism itself.

For many Jews who were not active Zionists, to find refuge in Judaism, in its religious, moral and social values, meant to reject the "values" that were advanced by Fascism. For the most committed Zionists, to demand separate grammar schools and secondary schools where future generations would be molded, and to have separate textbooks and religious teaching meant not only to struggle against assimilation but also implicitly accepting Jewish culture as being inferior to the Italian.[247] For the majority of Jews this meant to reaffirm one's own moral and intellectual freedom, to reject the very real dangers of the "Gentile educational reforms," giving the clergy undue influence over both religious belief and teaching itself; to be able to continue studying freely one's own history. The history of the Jews after the Diaspora is the mirror image of the lands and the nations where they were living, and not just free from anti-Semitism, but according to a truth that went beyond anti-Semitism and influenced the entire historical context. It is no accident that the Jews were supported in these demands only by liberal politicians, such as Francesco Ruffini, Alessandro Casati, and Vittorio Polacco and by those Fascists who were still aware of certain values, like Gentile. The best proof was offered at the Jewish Youth Convention at Leghorn on November 2-4, 1924.[248]

The heads of Italian Zionism[249] and the most important Jewish leaders took part in the convention but also Jews who were neither Zionists nor active in any official way in Jewish affairs. The meeting between the two groups, or better, the clash between them, gave the convention its meaning and shows the emergence of the anti-Fascist and liberal tendency within those Italian Jews who participated and were not Zionists. The speeches given by Alfonso Pacifici, Guido Bedarida, Giuseppe Colombo, Alberto Olivetti, and Enzo Sereni, as well as the talks by the Zionists and the program laid out by Alfonso Pacifici, were all meant to be "working groups" for Zionist organizations in various fields; for a majority of participants most preliminary problems were already solved or agreed to: to defend Italian Judaism, preventing it from "degenerating" through assimilation and to work at creating a Jewish Palestine. "For us," said Enzo Sereni, "the only salvation for Jewish life is in Eretz Israel: anything other than that is false and mistaken . . . without Palestine there is no free Jewish life possible." Beside these two objectives any other seemed meaningless; even the situation in Italy took second place, it merely became the place where one worked: the great problems of freedom and morality in civil and political affairs would be resolved *there*, not here. "Here," said Sereni, "you have no political labels to fear and do not have to deny any part of our program." The non-Zionists were vocal against this position, in particular Nello Rosselli. His speech gave rise to an intense debate stretching far beyond the three days of the Leghorn convention.[250] Even though somewhat long it must be considered very carefully as the most complete theory of passive anti-Fascism coming from those Jews who, while not Zionists, could identify in a return to their own Jewish identity a way to defend themselves and react against dictatorship. Rosselli began by saying, "I didn't come to Leghorn to discuss the problems of cultural or administrative organization of Jewish groups in Italy," and then went on to say:

> Before addressing such questions . . . we must know what we are getting into, who we are . . . I am a Jew who doesn't go to the temple on the Sabbath, who doesn't speak Hebrew, who is completely unobservant. And yet I am attached to my Jewish identity and I want to defend it against any kind of deviation that may be a broadening or a reduction of itself. I am not a Zionist. I am therefore not an *integral* Jew.

Rosselli's address became more passionate and explicit:

> For the Zionists, for the integral Jews there is only one issue: the Jewish issue. Everything in their private lives begins, returns, is resolved, and flows into their Jewish identity. Jewishness permeates their entire life; there are no problems of morality, society, nation, religion that are not seen in relation to Judaism.
>
> For many others, and for me (because I am speaking here only of myself), the Jewish issue is of interest only in its religious aspects: as a Jew I feel a need for religion. However, all the other problems of life appear to me one by one, with an intensity, an anxiety, I would like to add, as great as the problem of religion and completely separated from the issue of being Jewish. I personally do not feel the Jewish problem as being the fundamental, the only, problem affecting my life. Some people may dislike or despise this confession of mine; it remains, however, a fact. One cannot dictate to certain deep-seated feelings; we are what we are; we must accept what we are.
>
> There is a considerable difference between myself and the integral Jews. We are not following the same path, let us say so openly, our goals are not the same; I could also say that our very personalities are fundamentally different . . .
>
> Let me repeat that I consider Judaism a religious concept of life. For me the national question that many of us see as closely tied to Judaism has no connection to religion. I have explored my own soul; I can't say that this idea of the motherland to be reconquered, of the land where the Jewish people will reunite, has moved me at all, not even once. I would add more: inside me there is the foundation of my entire being, the consciousness of a citizen who is part of his own country, who loves his homeland, criticizes it, rejects it, adores it, who really feels its presence, who has no intention of discussing whether this is or is not legitimately his country.
>
> But, you will ask me, how then do you feel Jewish? What is this Jewish identity you cling to so strongly? You don't feel that being Jewish is something that penetrates your entire life and gives it its passion from the first breath to the last—and is the right feeling? You are religious, and at the same time you say you don't follow the religious rites. So why then do you say you are Jewish?

I do say I'm Jewish, I cherish my Jewish identity because (and here I am quickly explaining what would require much more time) my belief in only one God is indestructible, and no other religion has expressed this belief so clearly—because I have the vivid consciousness of my personal responsibility and therefore of the fact that I cannot be judged by anyone other than my own conscience and God, because I reject any form of idolatry, because I see the tasks of this life with Jewish seriousness, and with Jewish serenity the mysteries of the afterlife—because I love all men as Israel tells us to love them, and I therefore have the social view that comes from our best traditions, because I have that religious sense of family that appears from the outside as a foundation of Jewish society . . .

With such an introduction it is easy to see how Rosselli, like Croce, could identify Judaism with the religion of freedom and reach only one conclusion: today "our religious practice" comes between us and our country; while we wish "to give religion the reality of our life, this reality for many of us is not far from here, it can only be here"; the ambiguity torments and eats away at us.

Those things that remain unsaid weigh heavily on our conscience. And those things that are said without conviction, without faith, that are said almost outside ourselves . . . The integral Jews find their peace or look for their peace in Zion. We, and I also, must find our peace, the happiness of our own lives. This can only come from the foundations of our individuality: in Judaism and Italian identity.

For Rosselli the former feeds the latter, Judaism plays the role of guarantor reinforcing Italian patriotic faith. Firm in this belief, he actually warned his co-religionists not to give up the struggle in Italy or disarm, and not to transfer completely their energies and ideals to Eretz Israel. Even though he did not say so explicitly in Leghorn, the final words of his speech are an echo of his brother Carlo's slogan a decade later: "Today in Spain, tomorrow in Italy." Words that seem to echo those of the Passover Haggadah: "This year we are here, next year we shall be in the land of Israel; this year we are slaves, next year we shall be free in the land of Israel."

Let me keep my hope in the day when we shall be able to believe and strengthen our faith by comparing it to others and understand it even more, and at the same time to live our own life completely and broaden our own identity. Let me hope for that day. Then the Jew, that Jew who decided to live his life in his native land, in his country of yesterday if not the day before yesterday, certainly in his country of today and tomorrow, will live his entire religion, will follow it with fervor, and will be consciously proud of it, will not attempt to lose his faith or hide it but to spread it, to talk proudly about it with everyone. Because, my friends, the truth cannot be suppressed, and he who feels he possesses the truth cannot resist the overwhelming desire to share it with everyone.

Few people had the clear thinking and self-consciousness of Nello Rosselli even during the darkest years of the Fascist regime. His position remained the most thoughtful and advanced among those who did not become active anti-Fascists; nevertheless, it reveals a state of mind that was far from isolated. Confirmation of this at a different level, can be found in the diaries of Emilio Artom, an obscure high-school teacher.[251] That Rosselli's position was the right one can be found in the gradual approval, especially after 1938, by most Zionists, of their slowly coming to accept how the cause for the struggle for freedom of the Jews could not be separated from the cause of freedom in general. Enzo Sereni was among the first to understand this in spite of his own Zionist intransigence. In Leghorn, better than anyone else he had understood the substance of Rosselli's position, and, while critical, had not rejected it, and even attempted to mediate it. Of course, by then he was also a convinced anti-Fascist, and his complete dedication to Zionism was in part the consequence of his disappointment at the utter defeat of the liberal-democratic movement and the bankruptcy of those ethical and cultural values which had been its foundation and which he had defended as much as possible within the pages of *Scritti Politici*, along with many other Jewish writers.

5.

Toward an Agreement

I n 1926-1927 relations between the Jews and Fascism improved dramatically. In Italy, with the defeat of the parliamentary opposition (the "Aventine" deputies), the creation of the Special Tribunal, the beginning of the Fascist takeover of the state bureaucracy and the muzzling of Fascist extremism,[252] Mussolini was creating the foundations of his regime and "normalizing" the political situation. In this new climate, the active opposition having been decapitated and the passive opposition reduced to silence or at least to "mumbling," the "Jewish opposition" began losing its momentum and its significance, for the little importance it effectively had during the first few years after the March on Rome as well as for the greater importance many Fascists attributed to it in good or in bad faith. Within the general reorganization of the country, normal relations were felt to be necessary by both sides. In addition to these reasons, attributable to internal politics, there were others influenced by foreign affairs. Even under the form of a mandate, the "Jewish national home" in Palestine was a reality that Fascism, for economic reasons as well as political prestige, could absolutely not ignore. The Mediterranean policy and the push for the "mare nostrum" were already a reality. Nor could Italy be ignored by Zionism and the Jewish Agency; within the precarious Palestinian situation, Italy could become an important balancing factor against British influence. It must be added that within the League of Nations, Italy, through the Marquis Alberto Theodoli,[253] held the presidency of the Commission on Mandates and, in 1927, the transfer of the Palestinian mandate to Italy was discussed with some insistence (the first to mention the idea was Lord Rothermere in the *Daily Mail*).

The first sign of an improvement came in April 1926, when Dino Grandi, then Undersecretary for Foreign Affairs, in an interview with the Jewish Telegraph Agency, confirmed what Mussolini had told Sacerdoti three years before: there was no Jewish question in Italy; the enthusiastic collaboration of the Jews in Italy's struggle for unity and during the First World War demonstrated that they shared the same ideals as all Italians; foreign Fascist movements are anti-Semitic but it is impossible to "equate even in their ideas" their positions with those of Italian Fascism "due to the existence of different conditions within each country."[254]

This first step was quickly to be followed by other initiatives. Mussolini had a meeting with Weizmann the same year.[255] The meeting had been prepared by Dante Lattes since the two political leaders had first met on January 3, 1923,[256] and, in spite of a few stinging attacks by both participants,[257] it was a cordial and positive discussion.[258] Weizmann explained the Palestinian situation in its various aspects and underlined the importance of Italian ports, especially Trieste, for Jewish emigration. Mussolini, while letting it be understood that he thought the Zionists were being used as pawns in the power struggle by Great Britain, offered his help in colonizing Palestine, saying, "You are aware that we could build your state *de toutes pièces*," and as a start requested that contracts for work in the port of Haifa be awarded to Italian companies. In general, Weizmann, as he was to write in his memoirs, felt that Mussolini "was not against the Zionist idea, nor against our activity in Palestine; he was suspicious of the British, who according to him used the Jews in the eastern Mediterranean to block Italian preeminence in the *mare nostrum*."

Another step in the same direction took place less than one year later at a meeting between Mussolini and David Prato, as Prato was leaving to become the grand rabbi of Alexandria in Egypt. During a cordial exchange, Mussolini expressed his satisfaction at the nomination and the prestige it meant for Italy, and reiterated the absence of Fascist anti-Semitism, underlining the importance of the "extremely loyal" Italian Jews in the Near East.[259] During the next few months three more events were to confirm that relations between Fascism and the Jews, and indeed between Fascism and the Zionists, were on a new path. At the beginning of June 1927 Mussolini received Dr. Victor Jacobson, a delegate of the Zionist executive committee.[260] At the same time he authorized the creation of an Italy-Palestine Committee similar to those already existing in other countries. On October 19, he received the President of the Zionist executive committee, Nahum Sokolov. This last meeting closed the official round of cooperation: up to then Mussolini had been the one taking the initiative, but now the moves were being made by some of the most prominent Jewish personalities in the world and the Duce had the satisfaction of being praised in the highest terms of his career. In an interview published in *Il giornale d'Italia*, Sokolov not only voiced an extremely favorable opinion of Mussolini, but also admitted that Fascism was "immune" to any anti-Semitic prejudice. Asked why Jews were generally against Fascism, he answered emphatically: "Freemasonry? Anti-Fascism? Italophobia? What do these have to do with Zionism? We should not be confused. There are Jews in every area, but there is only one area that is truly Jewish—Zionism." He added that there had been uncertainties and wrong information regarding Fascism, but "today we begin to understand the essence of Fascism; today it is being studied carefully; and we begin to doubt many of the old dogmas of the past." And as if that were not enough he added: "The real Jews did not take positions against you."[261]

In this new climate, while the Italy-Palestine Committee added new important members[262] and began its activities under the protection of the Palazzo Chigi[263] (the Italian Ministry of Foreign Affairs) and the Consortium of the Communities began negotiating with the government to reach new legislation that would settle the relationship between the state and the Jews, and while the ministries began granting the first concessions (such as making sure that public examinations did not coincide with Jewish holidays), on the Jewish side there were many declarations of solidarity with Italy and the regime and favorable to Mussolini himself. We will only recall the more significant ones that appeared overseas. In *The Reflex* in Chicago and *Réveil Juif* in Sfax, Guido Bedarida informed international Jewish readers of Mussolini's declarations to Sacerdoti and Sokolov.[264]

The internal repercussions on Italian Jews of this new climate appeared quickly; a stronger sense of security was felt by most, uncertainties and suspicion melted away, new memberships in the PNF rose with the same intensity as those of the nation as a whole: from October 29, 1928 to October 28, 1933 there were 4,920 new members. Opposition to Fascism, active or passive, was reduced to small proportions, almost the same as those of the rest of the Italian middle class. Even the Jewish intelligentsia, which had at first appeared to be less flexible than that of Gentile Italy, felt the changes as well. When at the end of 1931 Fascism imposed the loyalty oath on university professors, only three Jewish professors refused: Giorgio Errera, Giorgio Levi della Vida, and Vito Volterra.

Based on what we have written one should not think that in the new situation, between 1926 and 1928, attacks on the Jews and Zionism disappeared and that the relations between Jews and Fascism were without difficulties. Attacks and harassment were to continue for a long time, even though to a lesser degree and less frequently. In its January 26, 1928 issue the publication *Israel* complained in the editorial "Stampa non buona" [Bad Press] of the attacks by several newspapers, some Fascist-inspired—a few days earlier there had been an article inspired by Farinacci "Azioni in rialzo" [Higher Values] published in the newspaper *Il regime fascista*, where the Jews were accused of setting their own interests ahead of the rest of the nation and—as we have already shown—a harsh attack in *Il lavoro d'Italia*. For many Fascists, Zionism in particular would remain particularly unacceptable. In 1928 the good relations just established with Zionism had a brief but dramatic moment of crisis and were about to turn negative once again.

By meeting with Weizmann, Jacobson and Sokolov, Mussolini had not intended to sanction an Italian Zionist movement (against which he harbored, along with the great majority of Fascists, all the old prejudices and hostilities) but, as Guariglia put it, to "look inside" international Zionism and use it as an anti-British tool to extend Italian influence in the Near East.[265] This explains how, just one year after 1927, when every issue seemed to have been resolved, Italian Zionists at the Zionist congress in Milan reaffirmed their "nationalistic" positions, giving rise to strong protests and harsh attacks, and a particularly harsh article in *Il popolo di Roma* on November 29, 1928 entitled "Religione o nazione?" [Religion or Nation?] written, it appears, by Mussolini himself.[266]

The article pointed out that, whereas before the Milan congress all Italians thought that "the Jews of Italy were Italians who believed in Moses and expected the Messiah," the descriptions of the congress published by *Israel*[267] showed that in reality "the spectrum offers some variations we should ponder that could lead to a change of opinion." One could see appeals to reaffirm Jewish consciousness and awaken the ghosts of assimilation and absorption and expressions such as "one Jewish people," "Jewish race," "Jewish ideals," used "without the slightest allusion to religion." In the face of such language,

> Christian Italians will perhaps be a bit surprised and disturbed to find that there exists in Italy another people, which declares itself completely foreign to our religious faith but also to our nation, our people, our history, our ideals. A guest people, who live among us like oil over water, together but never mixing, to use the expression of the deceased rabbi of Florence, Marguiles. This is serious enough . . . We then ask the Italian Jews: are you a religion or are you a nation? This question is not intended to begin an anti-Semitic movement, but rather to lift a dark shadow covering a problem that exists and can no longer be ignored. We shall draw the necessary conclusions from this answer.

As can be imagined, the article caused an uproar. Many Jews and cultural personalities such as Carlo Foà, Mario Attilio Levi, Giorgio Mortara, and Giorgio Del Vecchio quickly wrote to the newspaper, declaring their own dedication to Italian patriotism and loyalty to Fascism as well as their anti-Zionist stance. Dante Lattes also wrote to the paper, sending a declaration drafted quickly by the executive committee of the FSI that denied the existence of any dissent and affirmed that "no political intent" linked Italian Zionists "to the Jews of other countries or to those in Palestine" and that they felt "linked without limitations to the destiny of Italy, of which they wish to be faithful citizens, equal to all others in pursuit of their duty."[268] After many of these letters were published, on December 15, the anonymous writer who started the entire dispute, meaning Mussolini himself, reappeared with a letter-article entitled "Replica ai sionisti" [Answer to the Zionists], which can be summed up as follows: the reply by the FSI was not satisfactory because there was no doubt that Italian Zionism was part of universal Zionism and its goal was a Zionist state in Palestine; for the moment this could not be considered serious, but in the future, once the Zionists had reached their objective, things would inevitably change.

> As long as Palestinian Zionism remains in what I will call its national preparation phase, we can accept in good faith that this does not disturb the relationships between the Jews and their fellow citizens in other countries; but once Zionism goes on to create a national state, such relationships will be radically reexamined by governments because you cannot belong to two homelands at the same time, or be a citizen of two states.

This statement concluded the debate in *Il popolo di Roma*. It went on for some time in other newspapers, and many took advantage to broaden the issue from anti-Zionism to anti-Semitism pure and simple and to openly criticize the new Jewish policies of Mussolini. Such was the case, for instance, of Ardengo Soffici in a Note in the issue of December 31, 1928 of *Il Selvaggio*. Soffici sounded a warning, basing his argument on, among other documents, the infamous and discredited *Protocols of the Elders of Zion*:

> Regarding the Zionist congress that recently took place in Milan and where the participants talked less about religion than about the Jewish people, the Jewish nation, Fascist newspapers questioned with some amazement what this means and whether the Jews living in various countries, and therefore also in Italy, should be considered citizens with a different religion or foreigners, meaning citizens of the Jewish nation.
>
> The amazement of these Fascist journalists actually amazes us even more. How can this be? There are still people among us who are not aware that the Jews are first and foremost Jewish, that the Jewish nation has always existed and always shall exist, but that it is first and foremost an imperialist nation, since for centuries it has worked at creating a universal empire? Fascists who are unaware of this are also ignorant of the fact that Freemasonry, Protestantism, Democracy, Anarchy, and Revolution of all kinds, from the political

to the philosophic, literary, and artistic are only pawns cleverly used by the Jewish nation to reach its goal?

This goal has been reached in part, as the Milan congress and other such meetings show, and where it is no longer fearful of uncovering most of its cards. International banking and high finance are in Jewish, or by extension in the Freemasons', hands, and the same can be said of the press of almost all of Europe and America, not to speak of more than one government, where Bolsheviks, Freemasons, Liberals, Socialists, Radicals, Republicans and Democrats, etc., make things happen and cooperate to serve the King of Israel. With such leverage it's easy to imagine what good things can be done: and we are seeing it.

The uproar created by this series of attacks was so great that there were moments when the publication *Israel*, as the official voice of Italian Zionism, was close to being shut down: it was only because of an urgent visit to Rome by its editor and a moderating move by Bottai toward Mussolini (who had probably sought the controversy only to "ring the bell"[269] and nudge the Zionists to tone down their initiatives in harmony with the internal, and most of all, international aims of the regime) that the danger was averted at the last minute. Some non-Zionist Jews even took the initiative to suggest that *Israel* should, of its own accord, cease publication, a proposal that was to be frequently repeated in later years. At the same time, the Italian Zionist Federation (FSI) was also in grave danger. This was not the only serious risk for *Israel* during that period; one year later the same circumstances and the same last-minute salvage operation were to repeat themselves. The reason for the new threat to shut down the magazine (in practice *Israel* stopped publication for a few issues and was replaced by a "bridge solution" of two series of the *Rassegna mensile di Israel*) was the article by Alfonso Pacifici, "In regime di 'concordato'" [Under the Concordat Mode], that appeared in the issue of February 28, 1929.

The negotiations to reach a settlement between the State and the Church had raised some fears in many Jews. The concern was that the settlement could worsen the legal position of the Jews, or at least bring about a greater intervention by the State into the religious and administrative affairs of non-Catholic minorities. Some pessimists, or simply anti-clerical people, feared negative national economic consequences, especially for the stock exchange.[270] There was even a rumor that the Catholics had demanded that the Jews be banished from Italy and the synagogues shut down.[271] In this climate Pacifici asked himself in his article if the settlement "will cause changes in the relations between the Italian State and its Jewish citizens and the centuries-old institutions that assured the diverse expressions of Jewish community life." The text of the settlement, he continued, encourages the State to "ignore" the exercise of non-Catholic tolerated religions, but in practice this was not possible. Following the Austrian example, it was possible to think "that a consequence of the new religious regime in Italy with respect to Jewish life will be greater involvement and less agnosticism by the State than in the past." This led to a pessimistic assessment of the settlement and the implicit feeling that it would usher in the victory of the Church. This angered Mussolini because someone was criticizing his work and doubted the success of the settlement itself.

The two crises of 1928 and 1929, of which the former was the most serious but the latter was actually more dangerous and unknown to most people except for its use by the anti-Fascist émigré circles in France,[272] did not alter the course of events. Mussolini and those responsible understood that it would be dangerous to persecute the Zionists and preferred to play a deeper "game" within Zionism and use the existing political divisions within them to enlist their help for the anti-British policy. On the other hand, developments in the religious settlement convinced even the most fearful and suspicious Jews of how exaggerated their own fears were in practice. The presentation made in Parliament by Minister Alfredo Rocco on April 30 regarding authorized religious[273] practice was followed by Mussolini's speech in parliament on May 13, in which the Duce declared:

> We respect the sacred character of Rome. But it is ridiculous to think, as it has been said, that it will be necessary to close the synagogues. The Jews have been in Rome since the times of the kings;

perhaps they provided the clothes after the rape of the Sabines. They were fifty thousand at the time of Augustus and they asked to weep over the dead body of Julius Caesar. They shall not be disturbed.

Thus he quelled even the last fears. The new law regulating the Jewish Communities that was approved in 1931 completed the effort and opened a new phase in the relations between Jews and Fascists. In a few short months every last misunderstanding and opposition disappeared. The possibility that a "Jewish problem" should appear in Italy seemed to both sides as remote as it was unthinkable. The only anti-Semites left among the Fascists were Preziosi and very few isolated elements on the fringes or outside state and party bureaucracy; even in the publication *Il regime fascista*, of the same Roberto Farinacci who, in 1938, would be among the more extreme proponents of racism and anti-Semitism, attacks on the Jews diminished and became less acute,[274] and (in July 1930) it published a very harsh attack on Nazi racism and anti-Semitism. On February 25, 1931 during a visit to the temple in Leghorn, Costanzo Ciano even publicly stated that there were too few Jews in Italy. It will not be surprising that even in the Zionist publication *Israel*, which still drew some occasional criticism (for instance, the anonymous editorial, personally written by Mussolini, "Matrimoni misti e malinconie inattuali" [Mixed Marriages and Past Delusions] in *Il popolo d'Italia* on May 29, 1932), there appeared more and more pro-Fascist articles and opinions. The best such example is the editorial in the October 27, 1932 issue on the tenth anniversary of the March on Rome, appropriately entitled "Decennale" [Ten Years]:

> ... after ten years of the Fascist regime, the spiritual life of the Jews in Italy is more intense, much more intense than before ... in an historical period such as that of Fascism it becomes easier for the forgetful to reestablish the threads of their conscience and for the attentive to reinforce their conscience through study and good deeds.

If *Israel* and the Italian Jews were praising Fascism in such terms, Mussolini for his part was not disappointing them. During the summer of 1932 the Milan publisher Mondadori published the well-known *Colloqui con Mussolini* by Emil Ludwig, thus presenting Italian and international Jewry and public opinion in general with an unequivocally clear position taken by the Duce that left no room for ambiguity. It would take the incredible dose of effrontery Mussolini was capable of to simply forget his own words only seven years later! In the *Colloqui*, Mussolini was as explicit as he ever would be. He condemned racism unequivocally, calling it a "stupid mistake." He was just as vocal regarding anti-Semitism: "Anti-Semitism doesn't exist in Italy . . . Italian Jews always behaved as good citizens, and as soldiers they fought bravely." Replying to Ludwig's observation about the rumor that he would block their participation in the Academy of Italy, Mussolini almost made a promise: "Absurd. It is only that up to now we had not found the person. Now, Della Seta, one of our greatest scientists, is a candidate . . . " He concluded with remarks on the international scene and, alluding to Germany in particular, he referred to anti-Semitism as "the sacrificial lamb,"[275] words that appeared to close the subject permanently.[276]

6.

The New Establishment of the
Jewish Communities

When Fascism came to power the Jewish Communities (known under various names, such as community, university, fraternal union, association) did not have an organizational or a homogenous legal status.[277] Their main function was to provide religious worship and instruction, as well as charity; these goals were pursued under statutes and bylaws that preceded the unification of Italy and were very different from one another. The Sardinian laws of 1857 were in force in Liguria and Piedmont as well as in Emilia and the Marche, where the same law had been introduced in 1859-1860. In Tuscany they were still organized according to the laws of the Grand Duchy of 1814-1818; in the Veneto and the other Venetian regions of Venezia Tridentina and Giulia, the Austro-Hungarian legislation was still in effect. Elsewhere, in Rome, for instance, the Communities had been elevated to the status of nonprofit organizations after Italian unification or, as in Milan, in the form of associations without legal status. On the national level, the Communities, since 1911, had been establishing tighter coordination: a Consortium had been created in 1914 that had become organized legally in 1920. The Consortium, which the Communities were not obligated to join, had the following functions: "to provide for all such things that may be of interest to the Communities with respect to their goals, Jewish culture and the preservation of the artistic and cultural heritage, the general interest of the Jewish identity"; "to elicit from the authorities proper measures for the Communities that, due to changing local conditions, are either in danger or in the process of disappearing"; "to help in the establishment of new Communities as the need arises."

The more the organization and legal status of the Communities was heterogeneous, the more the possibility of representation and access were difficult within the Consortium. Beyond this, both the majority of the Communities and the Consortium, not having regular cash flow and having to rely on the donations of their members, were constantly beset by economic problems that ended up making any activity impossible.[278] Also, their respective power and areas of responsibility with respect to the lay administration and the Rabbinate were unclear, which gave rise to clashes and friction.[279]

In this situation, clearly many who were active within the Communities and the Consortium, and who were trying to adapt to the new needs and moral as well as material requirements that were the consequence of the Jewish awakening underway, welcomed a new establishment that would include the organizational and legal status of the Communities and the Consortium and their relationship to the State. Those opposed were a small number of ultra-Orthodox Jews and militant anti-Fascists, who for different reasons feared the interference of the state in Jewish affairs and preferred to continue with the old system in order to avoid it.

The "reorganization" of the state that Fascism undertook in 1926-1927 appeared to the leadership of the Italian Jews as an opportunity to try to obtain the desired reforms and, considering the new political climate, to tighten the relationship between the Italian Jewish community and the Jews living in the Italian colonies and in the eastern Mediterranean in general—Salonica, Alexandria, etc.—who were traditionally close to the Italian Jews and included many Jews of Italian nationality or origin.

The first idea to move in this direction came from or was suggested to the Rabbi of Rome, Angelo Sacerdoti, when he attended the inauguration of the Hebrew University in Jerusalem. Back in Italy, Sacerdoti discussed the idea with other community leaders and it was decided to submit the project to the government.

There are few details regarding the initial approaches and preliminary talks that took place. We must assume that on the Jewish side much importance was attached to the second part of Sacerdoti's plan, in that he presented the first part of the plan as a prerequisite to the second half: to achieve Italian predominance in the eastern Mediterranean adequate financial backing was necessary and the Italian Communities required legislation that could allow them to increase their own resources through a compulsory tax to be levied on all Jews. What is certain is that, beginning in 1927, Sacerdoti sent Mussolini a memorandum on these issues[280] and that he had a few meetings with the Duce alone and with the president of the Consortium, Angelo Sereni. The result of these meetings was positive: in 1927 the Consortium named a commission, including Mario Falco, Giulio Foà, and Angelo Sullam, to prepare a project that would be submitted to the government "as the wish of Italian Jewry for unified legislation."[281] The project was presented to Minister Rocco in November 1928.

The government, at the same time, was preparing and passing new measures for the recognized religious faiths and for the revision of the Civil Code. Even before the measures on recognized religious faiths were approved, Minister Rocco, on March 22, 1929, accepting the wishes of the Consortium, named a commission to "prepare legislation for the reform and integration of the regulations of Jewish universities in the various regions of the Kingdom." The commission was made up of Senator Adolfo Berio as President, Giuseppe Raimondi representing the Ministry of the Interior, Nicola Consiglio representing the Ministry of Justice, and three Jewish representatives, Angelo Sacerdoti, Angelo Sereni, and Mario Falco. In October of that year the commission had completed its work and presented the proposed legislation to the Minister with a long memorandum.[282] On the basis of this draft, which the government modified in minor ways,[283] the Legal Decree of October 30, 1930, number 1731, was prepared and passed by the Council of Ministers on October 16;[284] this, along with the laws of September 24, 1931, number 1279 and of November 19, 1931, number 1561, together made up the new law of the Communities.[285]

While the Fascist government accepted practically without changes almost all of the Jewish proposals, the reform of the Civil Code was a different matter. The Consortium not only was unable to have article 402 (which legally punished offenses perpetrated against the Catholic faith) extended to include the Jewish faith,[286] but also failed to secure approval for its point of view in matrimonial law.[287]

The main points of the new law[288] were the following:

a. Goals: The Communities[289] were given responsibility to provide for local religious needs (religion and instruction) and, if required, for charities among their members; they were required to be part of the Union of Italian Jewish Communities, whose function it was to represent the Communities and the Jews to the government and the public for all matters of Jewish interest in general; to participate in the social and religious activity of Judaism and maintain contacts with Jewish communities abroad, "especially with those that traditionally are close to the Italian Jews and to Italy"; and to be responsible for the conservation of Jewish traditions and the historical Jewish heritage.

b. Members: While, as it was clear, the Communities were automatically part of the Union of the Communities, "all Jews that reside within the Community are legally members." To leave the Community a member was obligated to formally declare the intention of abandoning Judaism.

c. Financing: The financial means to fulfill these goals were to be found, besides the treasuries of the Communities and of the

Union, in a contribution imposed upon every member of the Communities, to be established from year to year on the basis of the income of each member and the budget of the Communities themselves. The collection of the contribution would follow the model of the collection of municipal taxes.

d. Lay leadership: The administration of the Communities was elected directly by all its members. The council of the Union was elected by the delegates to the congress of the Communities.

e. Spiritual direction: The rabbis (recruited by direct appointment or through an examination) were the spiritual directors of the Communities. The head rabbi of each community had a consultative vote in the council and the leadership committee of the community. Five head rabbis, elected by their colleagues and by the deputy-rabbis, would take part in the congress of the Union (having a consultative vote), and among them, the congress would elect three leaders to the Rabbinical Council (which would have to be called for all cultural and spiritual matters).

f. Government control: The Communities and the Union were under the tutelage and scrutiny of the state. The Minister of the Interior had to approve the nominations of the rabbis.

The new law was welcomed favorably by the overwhelming majority of Italian Jews. Only some rabbis would have preferred to play a larger role in the direction of their Communities. All the major groups welcomed it with great satisfaction.[290] On October 17, the day after the law was approved by the Council of Ministers, the president of the Consortium cabled Mussolini the "enthusiastic gratitude" of the Italian Jews;[291] the Communities all sent similar messages. The January 20, 1931 issue of *Israel*, which had followed the preparation of the new law very closely, was completely dedicated to the new legislation.[292] The editorial, "La nuova legge delle Comunità" [The New Law of the Communities] spoke of the new law in positive terms as "a good law" and added:

> The new law reflects truly the clear and cordial relations, sealed by centuries of living together and by the most recent decades of complete cooperation in common goals, that, much to Italy's credit,

characterize the relations between the great Italian community and the small but historical Jewish community that is part of it, rich in glorious cultural traditions, social institutions, charitable works and study.

There was only minor criticism of the law. Within the same issue of *Israel* President Angelo Sereni and Rabbi Sacerdoti were even more full of praise: "the new law, which I have no hesitation in calling better than any law recently enacted in other countries," wrote Sacerdoti, "will lead to a rebirth of Jewish institutions in Italy." The Revisionist Zionists were also favorable in their publication, *L'idea sionistica*. As Amadeo Revere wrote:

> The new legal establishment of the Communities elevates, quite obviously, all of Judaism to a new position of dignity and responsibility, giving it the place it deserves and the necessary authority to the Rabbinate. This dignity and authority of the Rabbinical body had been missing or had been questioned by some in the past. The light-hearted and irresponsible period of the lay-Masonic mentality among the leadership of the various Communities was not the best means to improve the tone of Rabbinical authority.[293]

There were also many favorable comments coming from Jewish Communities overseas: Grand Rabbi David Prato cabled his appreciation and gratitude from Alexandria to the Italian Minister to Egypt.[294] There was some resistance and bad feelings—more sentimental and local in nature—from cities and towns such as Asti, Pitigliano, Reggio Emilia, and Senigallia, where small communities had been dissolved and attached to larger ones close by because of the new legislation. More serious, but without any real consequences, was the resistance of the Orthodox Jews of Fiume, who were much more reluctant than any others to accept the new law.[295] The switch from the old ways to the new took place more or less "without shocks," as the new commissioner of the Union to the government was to state at the Union congress of 1933. There were some critics, mostly young Zionists, unhappy with the new law.

On the Fascist side the new law was almost completely ignored, while a few foreign newspapers, especially those in the Italian language in America,[296] gave it wider coverage, treating it as a simple news item; only the *Corriere padano*, published in Ferrara, printed an enthusiastic article.[297] Even *La vita italiana* did not dare voice any kind of protest; the article of April 1932, by Gianfrancesco Sommi Picenardi, entitled "Israele contro Roma?" [Israel Against Rome?], in other ways violently anti-Jewish, approved the new law and distinguished between international Jews and Italian Jews:

> It is true that Italian Jews are showing their gratitude, and their gratitude and attachment to the Regime separates them further from the influence and the temptations of that vague and dangerous intellectual internationalism that has in Paraf one of its greatest supporters. It aims at mobilizing the Jews who are citizens of various nations to serve a cause foreign to—when it is not actually turned against—the interests and aspirations of national populations that assimilate them, and that wishes to oppose the New Jerusalem to the Rome of Fascism and the Vatican.

The Catholic press also refrained from making any comments about the new law. The anti-Fascist émigrés in Paris and elsewhere outside of Italy were the most vocal in their criticism. The day after the council of ministers approved the law, the *Manchester Guardian* wrote that Fascism, "following its passion to label every one of its citizens," had sought by the new law to catalogue even the Jews, creating a racial definition that had never before existed in Italy.[298] Filippo Turati had written in his July 9, 1929 letter to Rabbi Sacerdoti:

> Oh! Those poor Jewish Communities that are about to be "concentrated" following the "totalitarian" fashion, and abandon their centuries-old autonomy! When all of this will be over, you, as head of the Jewish Community of Rome, will be the head of all the Communities. Just as the Pope is Pope because he is the Bishop of Rome, so you will also be, as Grand Rabbi, the Pope of the Italian Jews with the government's approval. This will probably be an advantage for you, but I doubt it will be as advantageous for Judaism, if this word means a free spirit of liberation and independence with respect to every power with the exception of that of Jehovah.[299]

The comments of the anti-Fascist movements followed the same lines.

As soon as the new law was approved and even before it was enacted, the first positive effects could be felt in the improved relations it created. In various cities during the new school year 1930-1931, despite some technical difficulties, Jewish religious education began in the municipal schools; in Milan, for example, it was introduced in five grammar schools and one high school.[300] Following a discussion between Angelo Sacerdoti and Mussolini on April 7, 1931, a modified version of the state textbook for elementary school children was approved so that they would not have to study texts "where there are many passages referring to Catholic religious rites and teachings."[301] Other small examples show the improvement in the relationship: it was decided, contrary to previous city planning, that the dome of the Rome synagogue would not be demolished. The government remained obdurate about the problem of the Sabbath. During the second half of July *Israel* began a campaign to honor the Sabbath.[302] At first it seemed it would have positive results; in Tripoli local authorities excused some Jews from being present at government schools, but at the end of 1932 an order from Governor General Pietro Badoglio reinstated the obligation to attend school on Saturdays.[303] Aside from the Saturday problem,[304] the approval of the new law on the Communities ensured that all problems between the State and the Jews, by the end of 1932, were heading toward a friendly resolution.

7.

Palestine and Italian Public Opinion

Serious incidents between Arabs and Jews took place in 1929 in Palestine.[305] The reaction of the Italian press to these incidents is particularly interesting, giving a rather precise picture of the attitude of mainstream Italian public opinion toward the "Jewish home" in Palestine, the Arabs, and British policy. This attitude was and remained part of the broader Jewish question itself and can be equated with the public's attitude toward anti-Semitism.

The large-circulation newspapers, the Fascist press and the Catholic press offer the best picture of public reaction. The Italian Zionist and Zionist-Revisionist reactions deserve some mention as well, even though we shall examine them later.

The events in Palestine were followed with great interest by the press, and major newspapers sent their own correspondents to follow the news on the spot; the *Corriere della sera*, for instance, sent Orio Vergani. The large circulation press did not take negative attitudes toward the Jews. As an example, in *Il resto del carlino*, G. M. Sangiorgi underlined the "European character" of Zionist colonization. The British were criticized the most, and accused of not having fulfilled the mandate given to them by the League of Nations; Virginio Gayda in *Il giornale d'Italia* wrote of England as "betrayer of the Jews." This general feeling is best illustrated by the following excerpt from an article entitled, symptomatically, "I 'pogroms' in Palestina" [The Pogroms in Palestine] published by *Il resto del carlino*:

> The tragic events in Palestine offer only one, rather thin, consolation: that this time the authors of the savage pogroms are not civilized whites but fanatics and Arabs. This, however, does not change the facts, and rather increases the responsibility of those who were supposed to prevent or at least suppress these acts without hesitation. The massacre of hundreds of Jews is not just a sudden explosion of fury: it had to be the result of something prepared over time with the connivance of those very Arab policemen who, even though they are in the pay of the British, looked on and did not react as the anti-Semitic violence took place . . .
>
> The Jewish emigration to Palestine, if we set aside the idealism of returning to the ancient lands of their ancestors, is also a gigantic experiment of Western—meaning white—colonization of a land that had been left impoverished by lazy Turkish rule and the inept agricultural capability of the Arab-Bedouin tribes, and it should, without any religious prejudice, teach us something about the anti-Semitic revolt. The Arabs took advantage of the obvious weakness of the British—the stomach of the Empire, being too full, is suffering from indigestion—to attempt to destroy the magnificent work done by

the Jews: first the massacre of a people outnumbered by one hundred to one, then devastation and looting. And here British responsibility is very serious, because the government in London had guaranteed the security of life and property for the Jewish "home" . . .

Arab anti-Semitism is an anti-European revolt; it is not further proof, as some would have us believe, that Zionist colonization is artificial and sterile. It is, on the contrary, proof that the Jewish works have grown and extended themselves. This would be a superficial and low form of criticism, which not even anti-Semitism can excuse: one cannot compare Zionist and Arab civilization.

Even Paolo Orano appreciated the value of the work done by the Zionists and the Jews in general in Palestine and centered his criticism on England and the League of Nations.[307]

The few critical declarations were from the Italian nationalists. On October 23, 1929 *La tribuna* unhesitatingly proclaimed: "The pipe dream of a true Jewish state, a dream that England kept alive for some time for reasons of imperial opportunity, can be considered erased forever."

The same kind of position can be found in the openly Fascist press. Even though—for obvious reasons tied to colonial policy—maintaining a more conciliatory attitude toward the Arabs, the Fascist newspapers did not display any antagonism toward the Jews. *Il regime fascista* of July 28, 1929 even made some pro-Zionist declarations. About the movement it wrote:

Zionism, in Italy at least, is not well received. Prejudices that by now should only be the revolting memory of a distant past surface from the savage subconscious and prevent one from considering with sympathy a movement that has as its goal the reclaiming of a homeland for an Israel that is scattered all over the world and that in some gray areas of civilization is still subject to civil and religious limitations and the object of ferocious persecution.

And writing about a possible Jewish state in Palestine added:

Anyone with a minimum of good breeding cannot but agree that this historical-political possibility can in no way threaten human rights. We actually welcome the realization of an ideal that has accompanied Israel like the sun of hope in its centuries-old pilgrimage throughout the world.

The fiercest attacks were obviously directed at the British.[308] In general Fascism took a much less pro-Jewish position than these writings would lead one to believe. Even without Lord Rothermere's new proposals, in January and September 1929, in the *Sunday Pictorial* and the *Daily Mail*, and again the following September, that the Mandate on Palestine should be transferred to Italy, it is a fact that Mussolini thought he could take advantage of the dramatic situation in Palestine to gain a foothold in the region with the excuse of the ineffectiveness of the British and the need to defend the interests of Catholicism. It was no coincidence that Virginio Gayda in the September 1929 issue of *Gerarchia*, Mussolini's own magazine, wrote: "Palestine is also the sacred land of all Christianity. Its natural status should be that of internationalization, with the participation of Italy and France along with England in its governance."[309] The newspaper *Il Tevere* was even more to the point and spoke of Italy as a possible "mandatory power."[310]

The Catholic newspapers were the only part of public opinion and the press that was decidedly opposed to the Jews. The larger dailies such as *L'Italia* in Milan, *L'avvenire d'Italia* in Bologna, the *Unità cattolica* in Florence, and the *Corriere d'Italia* in Rome, the magazines, the local small papers, and the parish bulletins as well as the bulletins of the religious orders, were unanimous. The same could be said of many lecturers—Father Giovanni Semeria, Ernesto Vercesi, Gaspare Ambrosini, P. Molaioni, etc.—and the many Catholic unions and associations for the Holy Places.[311] There was no real difference in their positions: they all condemned "Zionist imperialism," to which they attributed all blame. The most moderate voice was that of *L'osservatore romano*, which maintained a dignified and "Christian" attitude while clearly stating that "Zionist policy has lifted the wind and whipped up a storm."[312] For the other Catholic publications the Jewish-Arab fight was "without a solution," and "a radical solution can only be found by stopping the Zionist organization."[313] And in this "the Christians are in agreement with the

Moslems." Adopting the ideas of the Archbishop of Caesarea, Ernesto Vercesi noted that the "only difference between Christians and Moslems" was "that while the Moslems want to suppress the foreign mandate and the Balfour Declaration . . . the Christians want the Mandate to continue for some more years but are in agreement with the Moslems on the rest."[314]

So just like the Fascists, for the Catholics, England's responsibilities were enormous regarding the problems in Palestine.

> As for the question of the Holy Land, the Mandatory Power, even though it had the duty to establish order and maintain the most elementary rights, remained totally absent. The mandate regime is supposed to prepare nations for political maturity . . . England, on the contrary, introduced two new elements of disorder: Zionism and Anglicanism.[315]

It was therefore necessary to revise the mandate:

> . . . another power without commitments or ties to Zionism should take up the task of the mandate over Palestine; this could be Italy, or Spain, or both together—or better, because it corresponds to the aspirations of every Catholic, a tripartite agreement, between Italy and Spain under the direction of the Holy See.[316]

These were obviously the old Catholic ideas that had resurfaced and tried to become part of Fascist expansionism in the Mediterranean.[317]

Local newspapers were much more violent, and their anti-Zionism quickly turned into blatant anti-Semitism. This should come as no surprise given what was stated previously. On the one hand it is almost impossible to avoid anti-Semitism in a debate on anti-Zionism, especially when, as in the case of the Catholic critics, such a debate takes on religious overtones; on the other hand, during those years even the most intelligent and important Catholic cultural figures—stimulated possibly by a few French political writers, and by the Nationalists—had written several books in Italy that more or less openly espoused dangerously anti-Semitic ideas. The best example of this trend is the novel *Gog* (1931) by Giovanni Papini, who in December 1925 in an interview published in the

Warsaw [Jewish] daily *Nasz Przeglad* was full of praise for the Jews and Jewish colonization in Palestine. *Gog* contained the character of Benrubi, Gog's secretary, and was replete with the worst kind of anti-Semitism, as the praise he drew from Preziosi demonstrates,[318] as well as Vichy radio on April 27, 1943, which used *Gog* in an anti-Semitic broadcast.[319]

Local Catholic newspapers provide the best examples: *Fede e Ragione* in Fiesole, *Luce* in Varese, *La stella di san Domenico* in Turin, *L'Araldo* in Bari, and *L'Ordine* in Lecce. Two essays, chosen at random, will give an idea of the level and the arguments they used:

> Zionism seeks to enact in Palestine the ideas of the French Revolution; this is how we explain the fact that almost all the 164,000 Jews sent there by Herzl's Zionism are Bolsheviks . . . [320]
>
> The two-thousand-year dream of the Jews—the majority of whom have become atheists and Bolsheviks—is to exterminate the Catholics and Catholicism, with the universal social revolution and the Jews' return, for the most part to Palestine to turn it into a Jewish nation against God's will, so that this may allow them to better destroy over there, any remaining vestige of the divinity of Christ and of Christianity.[321]

The most extreme of all these publications was *Liguria del popolo*; even *La vita italiana* appeared serious and moderate by comparison. Every issue was full of anti-Semitic hatred taken from every source (first and foremost from the *Protocols*). The most fantastic stories appeared in its columns; a typical example was a series of articles published at the end of 1928 and the beginning of 1929, "L'immane pericolo ebraico-massonico-bolscevico-protestante" [The Monstrous Danger from Jews-Freemasons-Bolsheviks-Protestants]. Anti-Zionism became quite simply another form of vulgar anti-Semitism.[322] *Liguria del popolo* made no pretense of hiding its ideas: in December 1931 it published an article full of lyrical praise for the growing anti-Semitic violence in Europe, writing, "obviously in many nations of Europe people are facing up to the social dangers of international Jewish Masonic Bolshevism . . . "

The majority of the Italian press overseas was financed by the Fascist government, and their attitude clearly shows how the government tried to present its policies to Italians who were living far from their homeland and were exposed to contrary opinions or at least were capable of judging freely for themselves.[323] It appears that most of the Italian press adopted a wait-and-see attitude and, while generally favorable to Zionism, it took a moderate position: England was the nation truly responsible for the disorder in Palestine. As for the aspirations to an Italian mandate, these were never presented as coming from Italy but rather as suggestions by Lord Rothermere. Some newspapers—*Il Progresso Italo-Americano* in New York, for example—besides pointing to British responsibility, pointed to the religious intolerance on both sides. Even in newspapers that were the most critical of Zionism—which was generally thought to be too close to British policies[324]—it was never suggested that the Jewish settlement policy should be stopped: as the daily *Italia* in Montreal wrote, the objectives were to make sure that the economic independence of Palestine would not be compromised from the start and avoid the establishment of monopolies.[325]

As for Italian Judaism, its attitude was resolutely pro-Zionist. Some caution was demonstrated by the most openly Fascist Jews, who blamed Great Britain exclusively for what had happened in Palestine.[326] The Fascist Jews found themselves sharing the same opinions as the Revisionist Zionists, who had organized themselves in Italy in 1925-1926.[327] In 1929 they did not yet have their own press, but their attitude was clear and confirmed by the first issues of *L'idea sionistica*, which began publication in May 1930. The very first issue published an anti-British stand by Jabotinsky and detailed criticism of the report by the Commission of Inquiry established by the British government to shed light on the events of August 1929; the new magazine completely espoused the ideas of the Russian Zionist leader. The Italian Zionist Federation and the magazine *Israel*, while they did not hesitate to criticize specific aspects of British policy, maintained a line common to most Zionists, and tried to find support among non-Zionists and non-Jews. The FSI published the Zionist position regarding the Holy Places in mid-September 1929. After repeating the declarations by Sokolov on the Zionist movement's respect for the Holy Places both Christian and Moslem, "Palestine is holy for the great religions of humanity" and for "the inviolable rights of conscience and religious freedom," the FSI stated:

> ... the Jews ask for no other privilege than to rebuild, with their own efforts and sacrifices, a land that was once the site of a prosperous and enriching civilization; they do not ask for favorable treatment as to political or religious rights; they consider that it is obvious that all inhabitants of Palestine, Jews and non-Jews, should be perfectly equal in every respect.

III.

In Hitler's Shadow:
The Internal Contradictions
of Fascism – 1933-1934

8.

Hitler Takes Power:
The Initial Consequences

I n 1932-1933 relations between Fascism and the Jews in Italy appeared to have been permanently and most positively resolved. Internally, all pending issues had been smoothly agreed to or were about to be solved in a peaceful and comprehensive manner. Both sides did not fail to voice their pleasure and exchanged frequent expressions of satisfaction and friendship. Of course there remained, both among the Fascists and the Jews, people who were opposed to the new state of affairs, but these were isolated individuals, excluded from the political decision-making process. On the Fascist side, the opponents were essentially Preziosi, his little group at *La vita italiana* and a few others who lacked both Preziosi's sense of the macabre and his dedication, while they were even farther on the fringes of the PNF than he was. The mouthpieces for their more or less coherent pronouncements were the magazines—*Antieuropa* directed by Asvero Gravelli and *La nobiltà della stirpe* directed by Stefano Maria Cutelli—both with extremely low circulation. On the Jewish side the small group remaining in opposition, or at least passively defensive and not openly antagonistic, were the anti-Fascists, mostly outside the mainstream of Italian Jewish life but members of the various underground anti-Fascist parties. The connection between Fascism and Italy, which was gaining ground among the Italian people more and more, also influenced the Jews, especially after the new establishment of the Communities, and Mussolini's stance against anti-Semitism—while dark clouds were gathering over the Jewish people all over Europe —appeared to herald for Italian Jews a new and particularly happy period.[328] Even those who were not anti-Fascists but did not share this general optimism were not opposed to the new relaxation for these reasons, but rather precisely because they understood the precariousness of the international situation and the possibility of a deterioration of relations between the Jews and Fascism. They sought—for the good of Italian and international Jewry—to avoid at all costs any such deterioration, confirming their faith in Fascism by their attitude. As Dante Lattes was to write, they were "to fulfill the double duty toward Italy and Israel," if not as fellow travelers of Fascism, then as its collaborators in a kind of "diplomatic peace task" which was dedicated to avoiding any worsening of the international situation that could have negative consequences for the Jews, and more generally for peace.[329] For different intersecting reasons many would adopt this position: the Zionists of the FSI and *Israel*, the Zionist Revisionists of the newly formed Regrouping of Italian Zionist Revisionists, and the magazine *L'idea sionistica*.[330] At the international level various signs led a majority of Italian Jews to feel that things were improving: the dwindling anti-Zionist campaign against Jewish colonization in Palestine and the many meetings of Zionist leaders with Mussolini,[331] as well as, for those in the know, the new relationship that the Palazzo Chigi was beginning to have with the two most important Zionist organizations, as we shall see further ahead.

Not even the very first inklings of a Fascist "racial" policy were enough to spark any fears or doubts. These signs were not at all threatening; they contained nothing racist as such (to find the first signs of this trend we must wait for the "conquest of the Empire"). This was confirmed by the explicit condemnations of true racism and of German racism in particular, which were clearly linked to a Fascist policy of eugenics and good health for the general population tending to improve the medical status of the Italian "race" (the fight against tuberculosis and similar infections), or of an anthropological and demographic nature (Italians who were to be "more beautiful looking" and "three centimeters taller"). The search for a "moral" improvement of the Italian people also had no anti-Semitic overtones; its anti-bourgeois bias was actually aimed indiscriminately at all Italians.[332]

At this time no accusations can be found against Fascism for being anti-Semitic,[333] even within the anti-Fascist press overseas. In spite of the fact that there were many Italian Jews among the émigrés who were very well informed about the situation of the Jews in Italy and quick to detect any anti-Jewish nuance, the only warnings were to avoid being too optimistic, seeing everything in rosy colors, and the complacency of many Italian Jews in being content with the situation and retreating into "Jewish matters" only. A typical example was the interview given by Carlo Sforza to the American Hebrew agency published in the "Italia" newsletter of the Anti-Fascist Concentration in Paris.[334] Count Sforza in the interview said anti-Semitism "gagne du terrain parmi les Nazis et les Fascistes en Italie" [is gaining ground among the Nazis and Italian Fascists], but underscored the idea of a need to unite in the anti-Fascist struggle:

> The Jews should not fight only for Jewish causes. They should not play into the hands of their enemies because they consider their problems separate from the other problems of freedom. By combining their legitimate interests with the common cause of freedom, they will achieve two results at once: they will participate in the liberal awakening in the world, and at the same time they will reduce anti-Semitism.[335]

The advance of Nazism in Germany had a few supporters in Italy who applauded the possible establishment of a Fascist-type regime in that country. With very rare exceptions, even among those Italian supporters of Nazism, most were openly opposed to its trademark anti-Semitism, and in this they joined the overwhelming majority of Italian public opinion and the press of all shades.

The only voice immediately applauding Hitler and Nazism and not withholding approval of the positions and anti-Semitic violence of the Nazis belonged, of course, to Giovanni Preziosi. Already in September 1930 *La vita italiana* had published an enthusiastic article entitled "Hitler" by its editor which fully endorsed Nazi racism and anti-Semitism, followed by other equally favorable articles. Apart from Preziosi and *La vita italiana,* for a few years even the most extreme fringes of the Fascist press would not approve of Nazi racism and anti-Semitism; nor, for a few years, would Fascism itself be favorable to Hitler's cause. In fact, Fascism looked with some sympathy at a kindred movement whose success would confirm the rejection of liberalism, democracy, and socialism and open new possibilities for Mussolini's "revisionist" policies, it also remained basically suspicious for various reasons: because of its claims on Austria, because of the fear that it might, in spite of Hitler's declarations to the contrary, aim at "reuniting" Alto Adige to the Reich, and generally because of the extremism and aggressive character of its policies and ideology.[336] Some statements favorable to Nazism did appear here and there in *Il Tevere, Il bargello, Il regime fascista,* and *La nobiltà della stirpe,* but these articles were not written by the Fascist leadership, and even less by the government. Nor were these writings very explicit and systematic; above all, they were not openly racist, the prevailing tendency being to clearly condemn Nazi racism[337] and criticize anti-Semitism for being too extreme, even though it was not altogether unjustified, given the German context, which was so different from that of Italy. *Il Tevere,* for example, published various editorials[338] and articles that were favorable to Nazi anti-Semitism; but when it sent its correspondent, Corrado Pavolini, to Germany in 1930 he was careful not to adopt Nazi anti-Semitism, and spoke of an "intense hatred," "almost revolting if one thinks that even the Jew is, after all, a human being," and comparing it to the situation in Italy, "where anti-Semitism does not exist."[339] The same can be said for *Il regime fascista,* where—between 1930 and 1932—approval for this aspect of Nazi ideology was even less explicit and where Jews were frequently mentioned in favorable terms.[340] With very few exceptions, we can conclude that the position taken by Mussolini in his *Colloqui* would remain for a long time (as the publication of the *Dottrina del Fascismo* and its various reprints would demonstrate until 1937)[341] the official position of Fascism. Italian Jews were solidly supportive of this position, as is clearly shown in an article by A. Revere, "Hitler e gli ebrei" [Hitler and the Jews], in *L'idea sionistica* of June-July 1932, which was entirely based on Mussolini's declarations to Ludwig.

Hitler's nomination as Chancellor on January 30, 1933 did not alter Mussolini's attitude, but its consequences were quickly felt in Italy. The shadow of Nazism began to darken over the heads of the Italian Jews.

Mussolini did not change his position with respect to Italian Jews and Judaism in general. The Duce avoided, for the moment, any temptation to imitate Nazism—still considered junior to Fascism—and on more than one occasion criticized Hitlerian racism and its practical effects, even attempting to stop the enactment of German measures and to play the role of official "mediator" between Hitler and international Jewry.

A letter from Angelo Sacerdoti to Alfonso Pacifici of March 7, 1932 is an interesting document because it focuses on Mussolini's position and the related feelings of the Italian Jews at this time, especially the hopes they placed in the Duce himself:

> Saturday evening I met with His Excellency Mussolini, and I transmit to you, confidentially, the results of the conversation, which you are authorized to relate to the President of the German Zionist Federation, whose letter was read to me by Lattes. He told me that he had already made approaches to Hitler to tone down the anti-Semitic hate campaign, and that, through the Italian representative, Hitler had promised that once in power he would officially declare that he only saw German citizens and would therefore give up anti-Semitism. But Mussolini added during our talk that once the "devil was on a rampage" it would be hard to control the situation and that in any event the moments preceding the takeover would be quite dangerous. He asked me for more information and if I thought the situation was that serious, and he appeared very much impressed and truly worried by the gravity of what I related to him. He asked me if Neumann, the president of the German-Jewish Federation, had attempted to contact Hitler. In parting, he promised to follow the matter and said he would ask his Berlin representative but was unable to tell me right then what he could do in our favor. I was impressed by the human emotion he displayed and that he really wanted something to be done.
>
> Please relate all this to the president of the German Zionist Federation. I have already informed Dr. Munk, who wrote to me last December. May God help us! I did what I could.[342]

111

All of Fascism, however, was not to follow Mussolini down this path.

Hitler's clash with the Jews awakened in some the old, and not altogether silenced, anti-Semitic tendencies. Others, knowing that in almost every other Fascist party in other countries (especially the French, Belgian, Danish, and British) and within extreme right-wing movements (in Austria, Hungary, Romania, etc.) Fascism used anti-Semitic elements to ease its political penetration where anti-Semitic ideas were strong and active, feared that the Nazis with their extreme anti-Semitism could quickly replace Fascism and the feelings of kinship it had within those parties and movements. Still others, seeing so many Jewish refugees from Germany and Eastern Europe coming and settling in Italy, worried that such a massive influx of Jews would reinvigorate the anti-Fascist opposition and create a dangerous form of economic and professional competition for the Italian population itself at a time when Italy had not yet recovered from the debilitating effects of the American depression. Others still, sensing the quick rise of Nazism, decided to join it and reestablish positions within the PNF that they had lost during the years following the Aventine crisis or, simply, to further their own careers. Others, finally, who were almost certainly in the pay of the Nazis to support their policies, overcame the coolness of Mussolini and of many Fascists toward the Nazis, and sought to establish a close relationship between the two regimes. In light of these two opposite tendencies and of the various nuances of the pro-Nazi tendency in particular, we must examine the changes in position taken by Fascism toward the Jews and, specifically during the years 1933-1934, the reappearance of anti-Semitism within the Italian and Fascist press. An important factor must be considered in this context: Mussolini and many Fascists rejected or specifically condemned Nazi racism, but they also wished to avoid casting a shadow on the good relations between Fascism and Nazism and between Italy and Germany (it must not be forgotten that Mussolini had been in regular contact with Hitler for many years through Major Renzetti).[343] This explains the lack of enthusiasm and the hesitation characterizing the moves Mussolini made toward Hitler, which were not devoid of a certain typical elementary Machiavellian calculation. On the one hand, the Duce, wanting to be the mentor of his German "pupil," as well as an impartial mediator, suggested that Berlin moderate its attitude toward the Jews; while on the other hand he advised Berlin to save face and not give in completely.[344] This gave rise to a fear—even among the more aware and responsible elements of the Fascist party—of taking a position and getting involved in such a large and important issue.[345] There was also the desire to avoid angering the new German friends too much; the effort was made to *understand* their motivations and justify them due to "the specific situation in Germany" (as if anti-Semitism and racism could not be examined in and of themselves but only "historically"), and the idea—even among those who were not affected by more or less explicit anti-Semitic prejudices—of the "unquestionable" guilt of the German Jews, or, at least, their "innate sense of victimization," as well as, finally, hypocritically hiding behind the explanation that Nazism was "still young" and that under the guidance of Fascism it would find the right path and measure for its Jewish policy.[346] This uncertainty and contradiction can easily be found throughout the official Fascist press which was not openly pro-Nazi—*Il popolo d'Italia* first and foremost—at least during all of 1933. In 1934, due to the crisis in the German-Italian friendship and the arrest of a group of anti-Fascist Jews in Turin, the positions became progressively clearer.[347] There were many renewed attacks in 1934 aimed at "anti-Italian" Zionism and at anti-Fascist Jews; however, even in official PNF newspapers the opposition to Nazi racism became more focused and decisive as well as in the writings of Mussolini himself, who raised his voice and published several articles in *Il popolo d'Italia*.[348] Following these positions taken by the Duce, the disgust Italians felt toward the Nazi aberrations on the race issue burst forth, even in Fascist newspapers, especially during the second half of 1934, and from every quarter the differences between the two ideologies and regimes on this issue were highlighted. Among the most vocal in the Fascist press on anti-Semitism were Balbo's *Corriere padano*, *Antieuropa* (October 1933-March 1934) and *L'Italiano* (November 1934), all of which dedicated two issues to the debate against Nazi racism.

In spite of Fascist control of the press, the large-circulation newspapers that were not tied to the party took an even clearer stance. Beginning in 1933 they were all opposed to what was happening in Germany and unambiguously condemned Nazi anti-Semitic policy and racism in general; the Italian translation of *Mein Kampf*, for example, was used to harshly criticize the Nazis. Apart from comments regarding events in Germany, a few examples will illustrate this series of critical writings. For *La stampa della sera* in Turin of March 7, 1933, the accusations against Jewish intrigue were items belonging to a "sideshow," and the morning edition of the same paper[349] referred to Alfred Rosenberg's theories as "funny stuff" that was laughable at best. The daily *L'Ora* in Palermo did not hesitate to write "we don't believe in racism at all," and added "it is really incredible and quite unacceptable that under the guise of Nazi domination, Nordic superiority, and Aryan expansionism" Hitler would attempt to disguise "a new and sudden rise of Wilhelmine imperialism."[350] *Il popolo di Lombardia* of Milan was even more explicit: "Racism is outside history; it denies it, or to put it better, it ignores, neglects, and is indifferent to it. It reduces history to a branch of propaganda." Attacking *Mein Kampf* directly, it added:

> This way of seeing things is far removed from our own. Racism upsets every one of our ideals. An Italian will talk about origins, family, but rarely does he ordinarily use the word "race" in referring to his own people. Because Italians are made of history, their own history teaches them that a complex and long-standing civilization is not born of a race, but, if anything, is the product of the coming together of races and peoples.[351]

The Catholic press was more varied in its reactions. The vast majority of Italian Catholics were against Nazi aberrations; however, the same uniform attitude and judgment is not found in the most respected Catholic newspapers. Besides the infamous *Liguria del popolo*, which used all kinds of calumnies and anti-Semitic absurdities[352] and was an extreme and isolated case within Catholic circles, one finds differing positions in the press, as well as some uncertainty and contradictions. A few Catholic newspapers took a position clearly against Hitler's racism and anti-Semitism; others had a more ambiguous attitude. Besides those publications that found it necessary, in the years between 1933 and 1935, to revive the oldest accusations of "ritual murder" against the Jews,[353] some Catholics found themselves in a difficult position: even though they wished to ignore anti-Semitic tendencies still lingering, the issue preventing a decisive condemnation of Nazism was the preeminent role the Nazis took in the struggle against Communism, to the point that the Church sympathized with it, and in July 1933 a concordat had been signed between Berlin and the Holy See. The break between the Vatican and Germany took place slowly over the years, due more to circumstances and the unfolding of Hitler's policies, than to initiatives coming from Rome. The Vatican's initial reaction was to have the Congregation of the Holy Office condemn, on February 9, 1934, the works of Alfred Rosenberg and Ernst Bergmann, singling out the anti-Christian character of Nazi racism—"it breaks and rejects the dogmas of the Catholic Church, and even the foundations of the Christian religion; it supports the need to create a new religion." The Catholic press was therefore somewhat uncertain whether to stress Nazi racism more than anti-Semitism, which lumped together both Judaism and Christianity and was fundamentally opposed to the Church.[354] This uncertainty was not limited to the wide-circulation press that fortunately induced only a few Catholics to think that an action on two fronts was possible, against both the persecutors and the persecuted—that is, against Nazi racism and the Jews. A Catholic publisher, La Morcelliana of Brescia, symptomatically published in 1934, with an introduction by Giuseppe Ricciotti, a translation of the sermons of the archbishop of Munich, Cardinal Faulhaber, while at the same time another Catholic publisher, Vita e Pensiero in Milan, published a translation of a book by Hilaire Belloc that was certainly not favorable to the Jews.[355]

The Jesuits of *La civiltà cattolica*, more than any others, were unable to repress a certain anti-Jewish rancor. This impression is confirmed by two articles by Father Enrico Rosa entitled "La questione giudaica e l'antisemitismo nazional socialista"[356] [The Jewish Question and National Socialist anti-Semitism]. After condemning Nazi "exaggerations" the author clearly states:

It [Hitler's Germany] has veered from the most open Masonic pro-Semitism to the wildest and most extreme anti-Semitism that actually ends up being counterproductive when it comes to the rightful and justified restrictions placed on Jewish arrogance and ascendancy at all social levels that the old liberalism had fostered and that was related to sectarian Protestantism aimed at harming the Catholic religion . . . [inasmuch as] . . . it is not the result of religious thought or Christian conscience and morality, but rather of the spirit of incredulity and even of immorality and the subversion of religion and society that characterized its already-mentioned predecessors. . .

We do not deny that they could also appear excusable, and even perhaps worthy of praise, if their political opposition could keep within the limits of a tolerable resistance the intrigues of the political parties and Jewish organizations . . . The most inexcusable mistake made by the anti-Semitic writers of the *Manual* is their constant tendency to extend the accusations against Judaism to those who should not be accused: the Popes, the Catholics and Catholicism itself.[357]

Fundamental anti-Semitism could also be found in other Catholic publications. *La Rassegna romana*, edited by Egilberto Martire, for example, in a note entitled "Pro Iudaeis," signed "t. t.," in its May-June 1933 issue, "vigorously" deplored the anti-Jewish campaign by Hitler's government, but also deplored the protest demonstrations against the Nazis being held in America, England, Belgium, France, Spain, and Mexico, that had been attended "often in the front row by eminent Catholics and venerable members of religious orders." The writer "t.t." wrote acidly regarding this issue—mentioning as an aside that "Bolshevism is ninety percent Jewish":

Why so many vocal protests when one touches the Jew? What feelings, what interest, what power motivates such reactions? Can we only conclude that it is unbridled love for Free Thought or ardent admiration for David's Psalms or the Ten Commandments? Must we believe that it is only the human instinct of compassion for a scattered people of downtrodden outcasts and miserable slaves?

We don't think so. The eighteen million Jews in the world today (a religious and ethnic minority, as they say in Geneva) produce the leadership of most civilized countries; produce the most daring, feared and powerful leaders of industry, of finance, of business—meaning of money.

Therefore with all due respect for these protests, for their final objectives, for the authority of the men that are participating in them—many of whom are the purest apostles of loyalty and humanity—we must conclude, with honest and calm sadness, that in the end all is repaid.

After which we can go back to praying fraternally *pro Judaeis*. Praying doesn't cost anything; but it is worth more than a meeting at the Trocadero. For certain.[358]

Less than a year later, *La rassegna romana* devoted a hard and clear article by Pericle Perali to the problem of race and its ramifications in Italy, but it should be noted that it followed[359] the condemnation of racism by the Sacred Office in July, but in reiterating this condemnation, did not even remotely address the subject of anti-Semitism.

This was the general attitude of the Italian press toward the first news of Nazi racism as it reached Italy.[360] The reactions of the Italian Jews can be summarized, besides the comments made by *Israel* in addition to those of the Italian newspapers, through an approach toward Mussolini by the Rabbi of Rome, Angelo Sacerdoti, on April 20, 1933 and the interview Sacerdoti gave to *Echo de Paris* about six months later. First, Sacerdoti wished to inform Mussolini of "the feelings of bitterness and worry among the Italian Jews because of the serious situation facing their co-religionists in Germany."[361] With the second initiative Sacerdoti tried to react vigorously when faced with the first symptoms of the appearance of the Nazi poison in Italy.[362] He did so by recalling that there was no homegrown anti-Semitism in Italy and mentioning Mussolini's own remarks on the subject:

> The first [reason for there being no anti-Semitism in Italy] is that patriotic Italian Jews joined Fascism in large numbers at its founding. The second is that Fascism is Mussolini; his ideas are Fascist ideology. Mussolini never even had the smallest anti-Semitic after-thought; he cannot even conceive of it.

On the other hand he referred to the patriotism and Italian identity of the Jews of Italy ("I am Italian, I feel Italian and my country is Italy, where my ancestors established themselves many centuries ago") and at the same time rejected any inference that an accusation of Zionism could make them somehow less Italian than other Italians. To the interviewer's question, if as a Zionist he had two homelands, Sacerdoti answered unhesitatingly: "You cannot draw such a conclusion, otherwise I would have to ask you whether, as a Catholic, you have two homelands: France and Rome."

9.

The Italian Government
and the German Anti-Semitic Measures

Less than two months after Hitler took over the Chancellery, on March 29, 1933, the Nazi Party published its famous proclamation against the Jews.[363] Reactions of universal horror and indignation were immediately expressed all over the world. The Italian ambassador to Berlin, Vittorio Cerruti, quickly sent a cable the same day to Mussolini, who—as Cerruti was to write later—"had bitterly condemned the Führer's anti-Semitism in my presence."[364] Describing the situation that the German Jews would be faced with, Cerruti expressed the opinion that "a friendly but strong word from Your Excellency to Hitler" could be the only hope to revoke those measures. Mussolini's answer came immediately: the Duce asked Cerruti to transmit a personal message to Hitler, in which, after stating that his initiative was due only to his feelings of sympathy and the desire to help the always difficult and delicate beginnings of the new regime and warning that anti-Semitism could unite the "enemies of Germany, including Christians," against him, he wrote:

> I feel that the party's proclamation against the Jews, while it will not reinforce National Socialism within the country, will increase the moral pressure and economic retaliation by world Jewry. Without the

new element of the proclamation the campaign would have weakened and disappeared after a short time. The Fascist regime has endured several similar campaigns and has overcome them either through the tactic of indifference or a counteroffensive to establish the truth in a clear manner. I believe that the government should ask the party not to apply its proclamation and wait for the government, using all methods at its disposal, radio, press and diplomacy, to reestablish the truth. The German Jews themselves should be asked to tell the truth, but after the declaration it will be difficult for them to do so. Every regime not only has the right, but the duty, to remove from positions of responsibility those elements that are not completely trustworthy, but to do this it is not necessary, and can actually be damaging, to frame the problem as a race issue—Semitism and Aryanism—when it is actually a simple defensive measure of revolutionary development.

On March 31, Cerruti went to the Chancellery with this message.[365] The meeting was inconclusive: Hitler did not hide his personal irritation at the Italian initiative and confirmed his intention to go down the path drawn by the proclamation of two days earlier in so many words. Right after the meeting, Cerruti cabled its result back to Mussolini:[366]

> Hitler received me at noon, thus delaying a Cabinet meeting for fifteen minutes.
>
> Von Neurath and Papen, with whom I spoke before entering Hitler's office, both begged me to convince him. Papen had already told me the evening before that Hindenburg himself, during a one-hour meeting with Hitler in his presence, had been unable to persuade Hitler, even when he mentioned the 12,000 German Jews who had died during the war. Hitler, it appears, had been induced to adopt the measures in question during conversations he had in Bavaria with the notoriously rabid anti-Semite Julius Streicher, who had been named President of the Central Committee to counter the campaign of vilification promoted by the Jews.
>
> Given that my mission was confidential and friendly and that my visit was to remain without publicity, I expressed myself in the same terms as Your Excellency's cable—Hitler listened to me up to the

point in which the attitude of the government toward the party came up and interrupted me to say:

1. No revolution had been more orderly than this one in Germany and there had only been two dozen persons killed in the entire country, of whom only 2 or 3 were Jews;

2. No violence had taken place against the Jews as such;

3. It was his duty to eradicate the Bolshevik plague from central Europe by acting without quarter;

4. It was not his fault if German Marxists were predominantly Jews and if the thinkers and propagandists of Marxism were Jews all over the world;

5. He asked me if it were not possible to say that exemplary order could be maintained in Germany (I answered in the affirmative) according to absolute justice;

6. In spite of this, Germany had been subjected to a campaign of vilification, especially in America and England, but, so far, not in France; he cared little about the smaller countries, because they could be pressured in various ways;

7. He had decided to go ahead with the anti-Jewish boycott in Germany to force the foreign Jews to stop their vilification campaign;

8. He knows the psychology of the Jewish international whose methods were liés and cowardice;

9. The forceful measures he had taken would have an immediate effect. He was certain of it and assured me that the boycott would not go beyond three to four days, because by that time the vilification campaign would have stopped in America as the one in England had already ended.

I went back to reading the message from Your Excellency until its conclusion, after which Hitler told me that Italy was fortunate as a country because it had few Jews. This was the reason why Italians in general and Your Excellency as well, in spite of your clear views, and for whom he confirms his endless admiration, cannot understand the danger that Judaism, intimately tied to Bolshevism, represents. In a short time America, according to information he has just received, will have to face the same problem to free itself from the menace of Marxism and will require even more energetic measures.

I spoke about two other issues: commercial relations, which would suffer due to foreign countries buying and selling in Germany without singling out Jews and Christians, and the strength of the national government, which was so great that to revoke the measures would be seen as act not of weakness but of magnanimity.

Hitler answered: "As my friends you would interpret it this way, but not so my enemies." As for economic considerations, he said that the boycott would be so short as to have no real consequences. In taking leave of me Hitler asked me to tell Your Excellency that he appreciated the steps taken, but feels it necessary to continue on the road he had marked out, which is the result of long studies of the situation and corresponds to the need to fulfill the task he has imposed upon himself to rid central Europe of Bolshevism.

Von Neurath was waiting for me in an adjoining room and I quickly informed him of the meeting. He begged me to immediately call Rome to suggest to Your Excellency that Italy also make some kind of official declaration similar to that of England condemning the anti-German campaign.[367]

The failure led Mussolini to ignore von Neurath's suggestions; instead, to placate Hitler's anger and avoid unfortunate consequences in the relations between the two countries, he asked Cerruti to immediately inform von Neurath that he was ready, should the Germans want him to, to issue instructions to Italian diplomats overseas to deny "erroneous rumors of persecution against the Jews in Germany and other violence."[368] In spite of this and in spite of the refusal of the "pupil" to listen to him, Mussolini did not lose interest in the issue; it was too serious and full of potential complications to disappear, and as if that were not enough, the Duce's desk was piled high with requests from Jews all over the world seeking his help on their behalf. We have mentioned the initiative by Angelo Sacerdoti; five days earlier a telegram from London had reached the Palazzo Venezia sent by the World Alliance to Fight Against Anti-Semitism, requesting a declaration that Fascism was dissociating itself from Nazism.[369] As early as April 5, one of the most influential leaders of Italian Jewry, Commander Federico Jarach, a large industrial entrepreneur from Milan, had requested the Palazzo Chigi to intervene in favor of the German Jews, or at least allow them to take refuge in Italy. The Ministry of Foreign Affairs had authorized their entrance the very next day, "as long as [the refugees] do not engage in politics directed against Italy or Germany";[370] this favorable decision paved the way for the ones that followed under the pressure of public opinion and from Italian and international Jewish organizations, which were taken by various appropriate offices to facilitate the transit, the stay and, despite some resistance,[371] the exercise of their profession in Italy. While Jarach was pressuring the Palazzo Chigi, the Union of the Communities approved and transmitted to Mussolini a resolution expressing "the strong wish that they [German Jews] should quickly return to normal living conditions, that unjust restrictions be lifted and they be given the same rights as all citizens" and it was also requested "that all civilized nations agree to a solemn pact that will, by preventing the return of brutal explosions of hatred, protect the Jews from persecutions and inhumane restrictions."[372] The world press, almost at the same time, published a declaration by Chaim Weizmann saying that Mussolini was not averse to a plan to send part of the German Jews to Palestine.[373]

In this context, Italy's prestige as well as Mussolini's own would not allow him to ignore the problem. Fearing that a second failure with Hitler might damage his own prestige, Mussolini from now on would proceed very cautiously and never directly. Rather than quickly taking a new initiative toward Berlin, he preferred to contact the international Jewish organizations and the Nazis to appear in the role he liked best, that of mediator.

While Cerruti kept him constantly informed about events in Germany and German public opinion,[374] and while by facilitating the transit and the establishment of refugees in Italy[375] he attempted to lessen the enormity of the problem,[376] Mussolini asked Angelo Sacerdoti to officially contact the "Jewish world" so that, in case of a moderating attitude by Germany toward the Jews, it "would agree to take a position of benevolent neutrality toward the new Germany." This difficult initiative went through various phases, about which we are now well informed thanks to the documents of the Ministry of Foreign Affairs.

Sacerdoti, faced with such a difficult task (due to the bitterness of the unfolding conflict between Nazism and the Jews and because of the difficulty in setting up negotiations "in the name of a Jewish world that is not organized and therefore has no representative organizations"), preferred to turn the matter over to Weizmann by organizing a meeting between him and Mussolini on April 26. The meeting produced no results: Weizmann was involved in preparing a vast plan for German Jewish emigration to Palestine,[377] and furthermore it was difficult for him to take such a risky position with so few possibilities of success. Sacerdoti did not give up. He traveled to Geneva and Paris, where two Jewish conferences were taking place—on the problem of the Jews in Upper Silesia and on the committees on emigration—and contacted the representatives of the Board of Deputies of British Jews, the Consistoire des Israélites de France, the International Jewish Alliance, the Zionist Organization, and the Agudat Israel. The results were not very different, as Sacerdoti was to write in a report to Mussolini dated July 10:

> Some are worried about the difficulty in reaching concrete results, some want to be able to contact their respective governments before giving a positive answer . . . in any case at the end of the conversation they all agreed to use their personal influence to obtain from the Jews of the world through local organizations and the Jewish press a change in attitude toward Germany as soon as the circumstances of the Jews in that country were to return to normal.[378]

It became immediately clear to Mussolini and the Palazzo Chigi that, based on these positions, without an initial gesture of relaxation coming from Berlin, it would be impossible to mediate any negotiation. In preparation for the second international Jewish congress set to convene in Geneva at the beginning of September, Sacerdoti asked Alessandro Chiavolini for new instructions. The opinion at the Palazzo Chigi, according to a note to Mussolini of August 21, was that "at the moment there seems to be no possibility that the anti-Semitic measures enacted by Germany will be revoked . . . however, the initiative by Commendatore Sacerdoti could serve to reduce the confrontation between the

Jewish world and Germany." Before making a decision, Mussolini wanted to wait for the end of the Zionist congress in Prague; then he told Sacerdoti that he could mention "the probable friendly intervention by the Italian government" toward the German government, especially so that the Jews might "take with them at least part of their possessions when they left Germany to go to Palestine."[379] Despite these very limited negotiating points, Angelo Sacerdoti and Dante Lattes attempted, from September 5-8 in Geneva, without making commitments or creating too many expectations for an initiative coming from Mussolini,[380] to have a moderating effect and avoid taking harsh positions that would preclude the possibility of the Duce's interceding with Hitler.[381] It was not much; it meant that Italian Jews would be authorized by Mussolini to accept the positions that had been reserved for them in the Executive Committee of the World Jewish Congress and the Committee of the Jewish delegations[382] and above all, be able to help their co-religionists, who were arriving in Italy in increasing numbers;[383] it also meant that Jews in general kept open the possibility of Mussolini's intervention with Hitler. For Mussolini it meant he could claim to be the friend and protector of the Jews. The Duce did move, in fact, along these lines for the entire year 1934 and beyond: even on May 3, 1937, when the policy of understanding with Germany was a fact and he was already thinking about the next measures against the Italian Jews, he told von Neurath that he had suggested that Schuschnigg accept the "collaboration" of the Austrian Nazis but noted "there had to be a difference in the systems of Austria and Germany, because it would be impossible to impose an anti-Catholic and extreme anti-Semitic policy in Austria."[384]

There would be four significant stages in this policy in 1934: Mussolini's meetings with Weizmann in February, with Hitler in June, and with Goldmann in November, and the authorization extended to Sacerdoti and Orvieto to attend the third World Jewish Congress in August. The meeting with Weizmann took place at the Palazzo Venezia on February 17 and was to be the most important one between the two leaders. In general[385] it clearly shows how, at that time, Mussolini was far from being favorable to close relations with Hitler and was leaning toward the policies of the "four power pact" and defending Dollfuss in Austria.[386] From the point of view of Jewish policy that we are focused on, the meeting's result was to consolidate what had been discussed the year before. We shall discuss the Palestinian aspects of the meeting later on; for the moment it will suffice to remember that Mussolini made no mention of pressuring Hitler in favor of the Jews again—nor did Weizmann make any such request—but did promise to welcome them into Italy. Weizmann, who had been briefed by the Marquis Theodoli in preparation of the meeting[387] regarding the current problems of the Italian chemical industry, which was dependent upon Germany, promised in exchange "to help Italy free itself from the Germans in several aspects of the chemical industry" by placing at Italy's disposal a few secret patents of military and agricultural interest—this took place during a separate meeting at the Excelsior Hotel between Weizmann, Theodoli, and Paravano—and by setting up plants in Palestine that would also provide materials for Italy.[388] The immediate result of the meeting was that Mussolini ordered the Central Director of PS (Pubblica Sicurezza—the Italian National Police) to allow about three thousand German Jews, especially scientists, medical doctors, technicians, and professionals, to establish residence in Italy[389] and gave orders to help them during their stay in Italy in their professional activities (the matriculation, attendance and possibilities for the younger generation to study in Italian schools and universities was particularly liberal).

The second moment, chronologically, was the Mussolini-Hitler meeting—the first between the two—in Stra and Venice on June 14 and 15. We do not have detailed information regarding this meeting. But we may infer, based on two items, that during the course of these talks Mussolini again mentioned to Hitler that, in his opinion, the Nazi anti-Semitic campaign was a political mistake. It is no coincidence that Mussolini would tell his entourage later that, more than a meeting, it was a clash, and "rather than speaking about current problems, Hitler recited to me from memory his *Mein Kampf*, that brick that I was never able to read";[390] less than a month later, on July 14, *Il popolo d'Italia* underlined the deep differences between "culture" and *kultur* with respect to racism. These are vague traces but they are strangely confirmed in a news item published in Jerusalem's *Doar Hayóm* of June 20 stating that in Venice Mussolini had suggested Hitler moderate his attitude toward the Jews to protect Germany's economic position.[391] It is no wonder, given this background, that soon after, on August 20-23, the third World Jewish Congress opened in Geneva, Mussolini authorized Angelo Sacerdoti and Angiolo Orvieto to give speeches about "Judaism" and "the civilization of Rome" as elements which had formed modern civilization, with the clear intent of welcoming cooperation[392] between Italy and the Jews, and to vote in favor of resolutions condemning Nazi racism and in favor of the extension of the anti-German boycott, among others.[393] Between the two events in Venice and Geneva there had been the failed putsch in Vienna, the assassination of Dollfuss, and Italy's troop concentration along the Brenner Pass. And it was no coincidence that a few days later, on September 6, during a visit to the Fiera del Levante where he visited the Palestinian pavilion, Mussolini acrimoniously rejected Nazi racism: "Thirty centuries of history allow us to gaze with sovereign disdain at some of the doctrines coming from behind the Alps, propagated by the progeny of people who did not know how to write the documents of their own life at a time when Rome had Caesar, Virgil, and Augustus." Finally, during the next meeting on November 13 with Nahum Goldmann, Mussolini made statements and precise commitments as he never had done before, so much so that this meeting with the president of the Committee of Jewish Delegations is the final and most significant act of this phase in the relations between the Duce and international Jewry, taking into consideration the manipulative aspects of every one of his political actions and the particular moment in German-Italian relations. It demonstrates what his "true" feelings were toward the Jews in general before falling completely into the mindset of the inevitable alliance with Hitler and the need for Italy to remove all possible elements, not only of friction, but also of any differences with Germany.

Goldmann had requested the meeting[394] through Baron Pompeo Aloisi, who presided over the Commission of Three of the League of Nations to resolve the problem of the Saar and make sure the plebiscite took place successfully. Goldmann had had many contacts with Aloisi regarding the 7,000 Jews in that region, who, should the vote be favorable to Germany, were at risk, if not of becoming Nazi subjects, at least of losing all or part of their possessions. Aloisi had tried unsuccessfully to find a solution to the problem. Goldmann thought of going directly to Mussolini, who on another occasion had already shown his good will. As he was to write later on:

> The Italian government, and Mussolini in particular, were then far removed from any anti-Semitic prejudice. One example among many will illustrate this fact: about six months before my conversation with Mussolini, I had been informed that Austrian Chancellor Dollfuss, who was completely under Italian influence, wanted to make changes to the Austrian constitution. He wanted, in particular, to change the constitutional clauses that guaranteed equality of rights to the Jews. I contacted the Duce through Baron Aloisi, the Italian representative to the League of Nations, asking him to intercede with Dollfuss to avoid any change in the equal rights of Austrian Jews. The Duce told me that he had sent Dollfuss a letter through Baron Suvich, then Undersecretary for Foreign Affairs, who had traveled to Vienna on an official visit, asking Dollfuss not to infringe upon the rights of the Jews. This news was confirmed later by my Jewish friends in Vienna.

Angelo Sacerdoti was present at the friendly meeting between Mussolini and Goldmann. Regarding the Saar, Mussolini, after a few barbs against the League—"a conversation club, a senate of talkative old men, who speak endlessly, and speak and speak"— and after a very harsh attack on Hitler—"an imbecile and a scoundrel, a fanatical scoundrel, an unstoppable talker"—came to the point: "I will force Germany to let the Jews leave the Saar with their money." The conversation then turned to the condition of the Jews in Austria and Poland. Mussolini made a firm commitment in both cases: he promised to ask Schuschnigg to ensure that a Jewish problem would not arise in Austria, and as for Poland, he promised a similar move if the Poles were to turn to him regarding the problem of minorities. The conversation then turned to the Palestinian situation again, with clearly pro-Zionist declarations by the Duce: "You must create a Jewish state. I am a Zionist myself. I already said so to Dr. Weizmann. You need a real state, not the ridiculous National Home that the British offered you. I will help you create the Jewish state."

And some actions, at least, did follow the words. Because of Italian intervention an article was added to the agreement signed in Rome on December 3 between France and Germany for the Saar, giving the Jews the right to leave freely, and with all their possessions, the territory of the Saar within one year of the plebiscite. This actually took place after the vote of January 13, 1935 that returned the region to Germany.[395]

10.
Anti-Semitism Threatens Italy

While Mussolini was involved in this international activity, which—while timid and unsophisticated—can only be considered for its intentions rather than its results, as favorable to German Jews and those European Jews who were directly threatened by anti-Semitic attacks, he was interpreting, for once, the feelings of the overwhelming majority of the Italian people, anti-Semitism was slowly reappearing in some circles and in a few Fascist publications.

Even during the first half of 1934 when it reached its apex, the campaign was limited to the usual proponents and publications which advocated anti-Semitism. After the initial uproar, even though it quickly abated, the controversy managed to poison the feelings of the Italian people. But while the public overwhelmingly rejected the attempt to transplant the bad seed of anti-Semitism into Italy, it wound up inadvertently absorbing some of this campaign of lies.

The example of what was happening in Germany because of the Nazis was certainly the root cause of it all. This originated both in the anti-Jewish policy as well as the much more totalitarian character, when compared to Italy, adopted by the Nazi regime, leading many Fascist extremists to think it a good idea to import, in whole or in part, the German model to finally give rise to the much-awaited "second wave." If, however, it could not simply be transplanted—something many were unwilling to accept—at least it could use anti-Semitism to pressure Mussolini to restart the "forward march of the revolution." Some certainly wanted to ride the issue to further their own careers; for others, the fear of so many refugees flocking into Italy[396] could perhaps become a threat, possibly bringing along with their own aversion to Nazism a similar attitude toward Fascism; all these elements played a role, as we have already shown. Undoubtedly, beyond these suggestions and worries, there was also the determined and direct intervention of the Nazis. Once in power, Hitler dispatched a growing number of Nazi agents into Italy to "work the landscape" politically, and spread propaganda for Germany, engage in espionage, and identify, among the Fascists, those who were active supporters of Nazism. In Alto Adige this activity was very deep and continuous; Hitler never gave up his claims over that region. Elsewhere, on the other hand, as shown dramatically by the documents of the Foreign Ministry, the Nazis had, from 1933 on, a whole series of agents, the first links in the chain that in a few years would choke the entire country. We already know from the report by Angelo Sacerdoti, quoted previously, that there existed in Italy an organization known as the Pan-Aryan League. One of the assignments of its agents was anti-Semitic propaganda and should come as no surprise; there are many indications that this was the case. We have mentioned the violent incidents against the Jews in Meran; another episode must be mentioned. The postcard reproduced in Document 7 was distributed, along with others, in La Spezia in January 1934 by a German who was gathering funds for "Fascists imprisoned overseas."[397] In these conditions we can easily infer that the Nazis had a hand in the anti-Semitic campaign by certain groups and publications in Italy in 1933 and most of all 1934. This inference seems all the more legitimate when we consider that the maximum effort by the anti-Semites took place when, after an initial moment of euphoria, relations between Berlin and Rome began to deteriorate, as well as from certain veiled accusations which—even though they were to be partially denied—came from inside the Fascist party regarding one of its most vocal publications. We refer to the debate in February-March 1934 between *Il Tevere*, edited by Telesio Interlandi, and the *Corriere padano*—whose editor was at the time Nello Quilici—which was controlled by Italo Balbo. A bitter polemic ensued in which the *Corriere padano* branded *Il Tevere* as the official arm of the National Socialists in Italy,

> having taken up the heavy task of serving Hitler, attacking the Jews and those thought to be Jews, whether they were guests in Italy or Italians, at the very moment when Hitler and his press were heaping on the Duce and Italy the bouquet of insults we are well aware of . . . a Jewish question doesn't exist in Italy. *Il Tevere* wants to force it to appear.[398]

The first signs of the anti-Semitic campaign appeared as soon as the Nazis took power in Germany.[399] The initial attacks, tentative at first but becoming progressively harsher, began in *Il Tevere*. *Ottobre*, also published in Rome, and *Il regime fascista*, controlled by Farinacci, followed these closely. The latter newspaper, after having written for some time about how the Jews were, directly or indirectly, the leaders of very important economic groups and having reiterated the usual ideas regarding international and Jewish banking, actually favored on May 26, 1933 the introduction of a quota for Jews in Italy. After an introduction regarding Jewish psychology, Jewish internationalism and the similarities between Judaism and Bolshevism, the writer continued:

> It is natural that, given such a mindset, there should appear among us—Catholic Fascists—the need that the smallest number possible of Jews should be present at the nerve centers of national life, and, if anything, given the proportionate number, we should pick those we know well for their past attachment and loyalty to our Regime.

But *Il Tevere* was to blow harder in that direction: the more the overwhelming majority of Fascists and Italians were indifferent to

130

its campaign, the more it became strident and intense, on its way to becoming the Italian equivalent of *Der Stürmer*. As it retraced events of five to six years before, everything became fair game for an anti-Semitic attack, even the visit to Italy of "Jewish" film director Max Ophüls to make a movie or the re-christening by Lloyd Triestino of a ship on the Trieste-Palestine route with the name *Tel Aviv*.[400] The attacks in *Il Tevere* did not spare those who refused to follow its bizarre political line,[401] nor did it spare Mussolini's foreign policy. While it is not certain, though it can be inferred, that *Il Tevere*, *Ottobre*, and *La scure*, etc., did not know that at the third World Jewish Conference—which they had violently attacked[402]—there were two Italian representatives authorized by the Palazzo Chigi and that the Duce was very aware of this participation. It remains quite certain that, as they wrote favorably[403] of the "alarm" caused by the authorization given to young German Jews to attend the universities, they also certainly knew they were attacking Mussolini's policies by doing so, which were— on this issue, as we have seen—even more liberal than those of France.

During the first months of 1934, *Il Tevere*'s campaign became particularly violent. On January 18, *Israel* had published a synopsis of the speech given by Augusto Levi on the occasion of the re-opening of the Zionist Group in Rome. *Il Tevere*'s comment on January 30 about the article in *Israel* isolated certain declarations, in particular a condemnation of assimilation, in an extremely violent editorial entitled *Ebrei* [Jews], which stated:

> At this point we should demand to see the speaker's identity card. If he is Italian, and we have no doubt that he is, he is deeply mistaken—if not guilty of a bad deed—by encouraging his co-religionists to not "assimilate themselves completely." This means that he hopes and desires that the Jews remain foreigners in the country in which they live and prosper and where they have obtained citizenship. When the Jews were considered foreigners in the nations in which they lived, it was the time—alas—of the ghetto. Is it possible that the Jew who refuses to "assimilate," who refuses to become a one hundred percent citizen, can be nostalgic for the ghetto days? These are absurd questions to ask, especially in Italy.

Faced with the indifference and even the revulsion of most Italians for racist pronouncements and for anti-Semitism itself, *Il Tevere* fell back deftly on anti-Zionism, which could more easily gain acceptance among Italians, who could see something foreign in it that could easily be used to prepare the introduction of full-blown anti-Semitism later on.

Having found the right chord for the issue of the "Italian" identity of the Zionists, *Il Tevere* did not let up its efforts. On February 5 it published a "letter to the editor" by an attorney named Giorgio Sacerdoti who, after stating that he considered himself "an Italian Jew and not a Jewish Italian," expressed "my complete satisfaction and my agreement with the content of the short article" and attacked Zionism by defining it "a crime against Italianism," and closed with an "appeal" to Italian Jews: "Shake yourselves once and for all and don't allow the mindless actions of a few individuals darken with suspicion the true patriotism and real Fascist creed of the majority." The letter was immediately reproduced by many newspapers, which described it as "noble" and used it as an excuse for attacks on Zionism. *Il Tevere* kept on beating the drum and within days published other "approvals" coming from "Italian" Jews.[404] Faced with a growing controversy, the Union of the Communities issued a press release on February 14, signed by its President, Felice Ravenna:

> The Union of Italian Jewish Communities, faced with a discussion underway in a Rome newspaper regarding the patriotism of Zionist Jews, solemnly declares that all Italian Jews, whether or not they are Zionists, are sentimentally, traditionally and through their convictions equally moved by the purest of Italian sentiments, of which they have given and shall continue to give shining proof and demonstrating beyond any doubt that, whatever their attitude is with respect to Judaism, being Italian is for them just as pure and fervent.
>
> The Union is making such a declaration public not because it fears a return to a time of coercion and violence that has long disappeared and been forgotten, to Italy's credit, but as a warning and a protest against continuing controversies that have no basis in fact

and to reaffirm the prefect harmony existing between the Zionist idea and the greatest attachment to Italy.

On the 15th *Il Tevere* immediately criticized the release, which had been repeated in most of the press, with a comment entitled "Sionismo e patriottismo ovvero: carta canta" [Zionism and patriotism or: paper sings], where after calling references to a period of coercion and violence useless, inappropriate and unwelcome, and repeating its own accusations of Zionism as being anti-patriotic, stated clearly:

> *Il Tevere* will welcome, provoke, and cultivate controversies such as this one as long as they help, as they do, clarify and defend the national feelings of the Italian people, against sly undertakings by all forms of internationalism, without exception.

The controversy was not about to quiet down with this exchange of "statements." On the one hand, as we shall see, the dispute was usually published in more general terms by other newspapers; on February 16, *Il giornale d'Italia* published a letter by Giuseppe Ascoli, Sergio Fiorentini, Raimondo Musatti, and Alberto Rossi requesting that the Union produce a "convincing demonstration" of what had been stated in its press release and therefore "to publicly declare, in a precise and categorical way, how it is possible to say that a pure and true feeling of belonging to Italy can co-exist when there are also aspirations toward another nationalism." The Zionists, under this new attack—up to that point they had been accustomed to following and commenting on the controversy in *Israel*[405]—reacted with a letter of their own (signed by Riccardo Bachi, Silvio Colbi, Paolo Fano, Maurizio Mendes, and Attilio Milano) published in the February 21 issue of *Il giornale d'Italia*,[406] followed by a second letter to the same newspaper signed by Bianca Ravà Pergola. At the same time a new anti-Zionist letter was published in *La stampa* in Turin, written by a student from Alessandria, Adriano De Benedetti; on February 24, *Il Tevere* published a second, more violent letter from Giorgio Sacerdoti. The controversy—which was now being followed by the entire press—bounced to every part of Italy as *Il Tevere* kept it going with daily editorials and articles and did not spare anyone from attack, even accusing *Il giornale d'Italia* and *Corriere padano* of Zionism because they had both welcomed and published letters from Zionists or simply for reporting the news honestly. And so the controversy spread even further.[407]

By the beginning of March the dispute had reached its zenith and soon began to die down and spread to wider and more important issues such as those voiced in the letter by the five Zionists to *Il giornale d'Italia* and the *Corriere padano*. As it petered out, the debate threatened to move on to items that were not to the liking of *Il Tevere* and the various proponents of anti-Zionism. Even among those who were openly anti-Zionists and certainly not suspected of tenderness toward the Jews, some began saying that it was unnecessary to keep this issue alive at all. A typical example was the editorial of October 7 in *Ottobre*. The editorial "buried" Zionism as an issue, saying that it was a trick not worthy of discussion and denying that to be anti-Zionist meant to be anti-Semitic; some "Roman colleagues" were chastised for having started an "inappropriate" controversy regarding Zionism and its compatibility, more or less, with Fascism:

> We say inappropriately, because of the same reasons all the participants felt, once they entered the inhospitable terrain where the controversy was mired and quickly removed themselves or reconfirmed their position. Why start at all? To give a reason to Mrs. Agar or Madam Rebecca to bother the public with letters full of ghetto chatter? Is the price of paper so cheap for some Fascist or Fascist-sympathizing publications?

Which was a clear and somewhat awkward way of pulling back. An unforeseeable occurrence saved *Il Tevere* this time by pushing the Zionist controversy into the background but in some way appearing to confirm the conclusions of its instigators, and allowing them to extend it to all the Jews and turn the controversy itself into a real fracas. The new dispute involved not only ideas and interpretations, but also facts, and involved the entire press. We refer to the arrest on March 11, 1934 of Sion Segre, an anti-Fascist from Piedmont and a member of the Giustizia e Libertà movement, while he tried to smuggle anti-Fascist material into

Italy along with another Jew, Mario Levi, who was able to escape into Switzerland. The news was made public only on March 30, after an investigation allowed the police to arrest fourteen other anti-Fascists. As soon as this became news, *Il Tevere, Il regime fascista,* and the press jumped on the item, emphasizing how most of the fourteen persons arrested were Jews: Sion Segre, Attilio Segre, Giuliana Segre, Marco Segre, Leo Levi, Riccardo Levi, Carlo Levi, Giuseppe Levi, Gino Levi, Carlo Vercelli, and Leone Ginzburg.[408] On this and on an utterance attributed to Mario Levi as he fled across the border, "Cowardly Italian dogs!", *Il Tevere* began the second phase of its anti-Semitic campaign. This is how Interlandi's newspaper editorialized on March 31 under the telling title "Lascianà abbà Biruscialaim Quest'anno al Tribunale Speciale" [Next Year in Jerusalem. This year in front of the Special Court of Justice]:

> This small platoon of anti-Fascist and anti-Italian Jews ('Cowardly Italian dogs!') comes appropriately after a controversy that could have appeared insignificant . . .
>
> What was the objective of the debate we have kept going these last few months that was so lazily received by the public and the press? It sought to establish, with Jewish documents in hand, that the Jew does not assimilate because he sees in assimilation a reduction of his identity and a betrayal of his own race; that the Jew demands a dual nationality—let us even say a dual homeland—to remain a 'productive element,' that is, to go about his business and maintain beyond the borders a center of attraction and dissemination above any nation; that not even war (and therefore Fascism) assimilated the Jews into the nation for which they fought: the Jewish press speaks of Jews who fought each other in the name of foreign countries.
>
> All this is now covered by the dramatic stamp of the OVRA; and so that no one would miss the significance of these names, we shall, even though we might be called naïve, remind the reader that the best anti-Fascism past and present can be found within the Jewish race: from Treves to Modigliani, from Rosselli to Morgari, the organizers of anti-Fascist subversion were and are "the chosen people."

Much of the press—including *Il popolo d'Italia* reprinted the comments by *Il Tevere*—and many other similar comments appeared in various newspapers (in particular, *Ottobre* of April 1, *Il popolo di Romagna* of April 3, and *La rivoluzione fascista* of April 5). No newspaper obviously dared say that the entire matter had been set up as a provocation—when the special court sentenced the accused, there would be only two persons condemned: Ginzburg was given a four-year sentence and Sion Segre three years with two years' probation. The outrage expressed by some Jews at the idea that the entire Jewish community of Italy stood accused because of the actions of a small group,[409] the declarations of loyalty to Fascism by individual Jews and entire Communities, and the disassociation from responsibility by the Jewish press and the Union of the Communities—all these drew spiteful, insulting and accusatory responses as well as more or less obscure insinuations from *Il Tevere* and *Il regime fascista*. Farinacci's newspaper answered the declarations of loyalty in an editorial series published on April 8, 10, and 28, most significantly the one on April 10 entitled "Decidersi" [Decide], stating that the Zionists had to be cast aside: "We must, therefore, make a decision. We have reached a point at which everyone must take a position. Also because those who declare themselves Zionists have no further right, in this country, to hold onto any honors, positions, favors, etc., etc." Even more threatening—and even more subtle than others, as it rejected the spectre of the Nazis' excesses, which could have prevented someone from following its line—in an article entitled "Risposta ai signori dell'Israel" [Answer to the gentlemen of Israel] the same *Il regime fascista* answered, on April 18, as proof of loyal friendship toward the Italian Jews, with an invitation to them to "decide," to break the "ambiguity," to reject and turn their backs on Zionism forever:

> If they wish to avoid the appearance in Italy of every form of deplorable anti-Semitism (we don't go as far as saying the horror of the pogroms of Holy Mother Russia and the revolting Hitlerian mayhem, because to react against that type of infection all you need to be is Italians and Fascists), Italian Jews only need to follow the advice we gave them: decide!

The anti-Zionist campaign at this point once again lost momentum; even though it did not stop altogether, it was now limited to a small number of discredited publications. It would have taken steps by the government enacting at least some of the restrictions demanded by the anti-Zionists for the campaign to continue with some kind of credibility. The fact that this did not take place and that Mussolini took positions which were clearly anti-German where race issues were concerned—it is also possible that some moderating pressure had been exerted on the likes of Farinacci and Interlandi—quickly reduced the anti-Zionist crusaders to silence and back to the old more or less generic attacks on Jewish internationalism, high level finance, and Jewish racism as the origin of all racism, etc.

The controversy should not be seen as a defeat for the Fascist groups that had initiated it and kept it alive for over four months. Besides the usual drop of poison that was planted in the minds of the Italian people,[410] as the campaign began to subside, a very dangerous fire had been set among Italian Jews, and this fire threatened to spread and destroy from within their most solid organizational and administrative structures. Gaetano Salvemini, who was far removed in America and followed events in Italy closely, quickly understood the seriousness of what had been happening during those months and condemned it in worried terms to American and international public opinion.[411] In 1933, and even more in 1934, anti-Semitism—which undoubtedly included anti-Zionism—was no longer a marginal and individual occurrence within the Fascist party; although it still had few supporters, it had become one of the motivating issues of some groups. For the moment, Italian foreign policy and the struggle between forces within the party kept these groups at a disadvantage; however, external conditions and power plays could change all this in the not too distant future. Fascism, in any event, had to deal with them, because of a reality that could no longer be ignored: Hitler's rise to power in Germany and the commitment demonstrated by Nazism to replace Fascism as the leader of Fascist-type political parties by using anti-Semitic and racist ideology. Mussolini found it absolutely necessary, but at the same time difficult, to oppose this initiative, in part because of the strong influence wielded by Nazism among the Fascist movements and also because they were already anti-Semitic themselves. The PNF's refusal to accept racism and anti-Semitism as its policy would play into the Nazi grasp for political hegemony. This was the reason for the "need" to make some concessions, such as accepting the principle that "in many places" "some Jewish groups" should be attacked because they had "installed themselves as in a conquered land by openly or secretly using a negative influence over the moral and material interests of the Homeland which had given them its hospitality, creating some kind of state within the state, using every right and avoiding every duty," and consequently, even though the Jewish problem could not "become a universal hate campaign against the Jews," "each country, according to the principle of national sovereignty, is the only entity able to decide what attitude to take toward its citizens, the groups, races, and religions residing within it."[412] These merely verbal concessions of the moment quickly appeared inadequate to produce the desired results and inevitably influenced Italian Fascism by creating the impression that no inalienable principles were in the balance but only subjective problems, *sub iudicio*, which could be handled piecemeal.

11.

The Italian Jews React

The anti-Zionist campaign from January to April 1934 had very serious consequences among Italian Jews. It was at the origin of the deep split that years later would divide the them and create a crisis for many Communities and for the Union itself. The split would not be completely mended by the fall of 1938, when the racist policy was unleashed, but only during the tormented crucible of the dramatic war years and Nazi occupation, when all Italian Jews would find themselves united in the common struggle for survival.

We have recorded some Jewish reactions to the campaign against Zionism during those months. These were only the first and most publicized reactions. The press and public were not informed of many others, including the most serious ones, which took place "at a distance" after the controversy had subsided. As in the campaign by *Il Tevere* and other anti-Zionist newspapers, it is possible to identify two moments in time, before and after the arrests in Turin, two phases that were followed by the more serious third phase, going beyond the chronological boundaries of this chapter. Too many factors came together at the same time to spark a crisis. Personal and general issues, noble and less than noble, played a role, and it is not surprising that under such blows, made even more dangerous by the example and the threat coming from Germany, Italian Judaism, rather than rallying around in one solid block, became weaker and more divided. This is a further demonstration of the high degree of Italianization—meaning to identify with the national mentality and life in Italy—it had reached. Without a doubt, we can identify among the main reasons the success of Fascism among the Jews, a Fascism that had not yet become disenchanted and convenient but was nationalistically active and in some cases aggressive, drawing strength in those years from the comparison with Nazism. Those Jews who strongly supported Fascism felt Zionism was incompatible with their own Fascist allegiance, while to others, who were less convinced and more cynical, it appeared as a useful target to attack, and a way to further their own careers by drawing attention to themselves. For the vast majority it was only a source of big and small "gripes"—contributions to the refugee fund and to Eretz Israel, observance of the Sabbath, sending children to Hebrew school, etc.; in short, being Jewish. It was also seen as a considerable risk: why pit oneself against the "master," why be seen in a bad light, why become a suspect and "invite" retaliation? These motivations came on top of many others, such as the antagonism between the Zionists themselves—the General Zionists and the Revisionists—as well as the desire of some young people to take a leadership position inside Italian Jewry and its organizations. All these factors clashed internally and, above all, between the internal and international situation of the Zionists and the leaders of the Union, who had to strike a balance among all these pressures and counter-pressures and the ever-growing interference on the part of the government.

When *Il Tevere* began its campaign at the end of January and the letter by Giorgio Sacerdoti was published, the president of the Union, Felice Ravenna, and Angelo Sacerdoti both thought it was one of the usual attacks that would deflate within a few days and draw minimal interest. They both agreed to leave it unanswered so as not to give it any undue importance. But once the campaign got underway with the letters of support by Rubens Samaia and Mario Rossi, the Union received a letter from three Zionists in Milan demanding a quick and decisive response. They further threatened an autonomous action if this did not happen in defense of the good name of Italian Zionism,[413] even raising the possibility of a duel because one of the co-signers, Leone Carpi, an attorney, wanted to challenge Giorgio Sacerdoti. An appropriate answer was now urgent. This was the background when the press release was published on February 14. On the 12th it was submitted for approval to the head of the Prime Minister's press office, just to be sure. Its publication gave rise—during the meeting of the committee of the Union on February 21—to some protests from those who said "we should not participate in controversies that could lead the Union beyond a simple declaration," and that the Union should "try to find that discipline that will increase its own prestige." The Union, faced with a growing controversy and many statements by numerous Jews, both Zionists and anti-Zionists, had to attempt to quash it as soon as possible, as a preventive and conciliatory measure toward the heads of the Communities and of the Zionist movements, and, above all, to instill in everyone a greater sense of discipline. During the ensuing weeks, as the controversy showed no sign of abating, the Union decided to take a position in three Italian Jewish publications: *Israel*, published by the Zionists, *L'idea sionistica*, published by the Revisionists, and *Davar*, published in Milan—which did not represent any specific Jewish group and was above all a cultural and advertising magazine, but that nevertheless had been targeted by *Il Tevere*—to avoid having them feed the controversy, directly or indirectly. At the same time the Union, finding it difficult to control the Jewish press, began planning its own official publication, discussing it first with Dante Lattes and then with Umberto Cassuto. The former refused to become its editor because he was a militant Zionist and was "opposed to linking my work with a vague program that could possibly clash with my own ideas and journalistic activity of thirty years to further the cause of Italian Jewry." The negotiations with the latter were also unfruitful for many reasons, in particular the Union's difficulty in securing adequate financing for the new publication. During these first weeks there were disagreements and differences of opinion between members of the committee and the council of the Union: some would have preferred a more determined attitude, and in particular that Zionist activity be reduced to a form of assistance. It was not yet a serious split, but already the first cracks began to appear.[414]

The real crisis exploded violently after the arrest of the Turin anti-Fascist group. As soon as the news became public, individuals began to "dissociate themselves," to voice "indignation" and accuse the Union. Commander Jarach in Milan, president of the local Community, paid a visit to the Prefect to transmit the "feelings" of the Milanese Jews and to "defend the Jewish reputation," issuing a press release rejecting the actions of the anti-Fascists in Turin and asking to be received by the Duce to express the devotion of Italian Jews. Other communities took similar steps; some Jews quickly issued declarations to the press and local Fascist groups along the same lines. From Verona a proposal was sent to the Union—in the centuries-old ghetto tradition to blunt the effects of anti-Jewish measures—to offer alms, intended to ensure peace and loyalty, to local charitable institutions. In Turin more than anywhere else, reactions were very dramatic: not only was there an initiative to the Prefect similar to the one in Milan with offers of assistance, but even going so far as to request the expulsion of anti-Fascists from the Communities and the dispatch to the Duce of a declaration of "absolute and enthusiastic devotion and dedication" handsigned by all "Italian Jews worthy of Italian nationality"—thus excluding the Zionists. From Turin other harsh accusations were leveled at the Union: "as usual this Union has revealed itself to be derelict of duty toward sensitivity and reality." Beyond these individual reactions, Turin was to experience, by reflection, the first symptoms of a crisis that soon would engulf the entire country and involve the Union itself in Rome. The Community council of Turin was forced to resign, the Community itself was placed under the administrative control of a commission, and as an "indispensable" temporary measure, the publication *Israel* was to be suspended and replaced by a new national and Fascist publication. Distrustful of the Union, a group of Fascist Jews led by Ettore Ovazza, a participant in the March on Rome, a Fascist squad member and new Community commissioner, began to prepare for the publication of a new newspaper, whose masthead was a program in and of itself—*L'unità italiana* [Italian Unity] soon changed into *La nostra bandiera* [Our Flag].[415] And as if this were not enough to complicate matters, even the Zionists, under the accusations hurled at them from all sides, counterattacked. *Israel,* partly because of the greater sense of responsibility of its editor and to avoid government measures, remained moderate, limiting itself to rejecting the accusations in the press, condemning those arrested— "joining everyone in deploring this very sad episode we await the sentence of the judges: Italian justice doesn't discriminate against anyone, Jews or not"—and hoping that "as sad as it is, this episode should remain just that, an episode" and not be arbitrarily generalized.[416] The President of the FSI used much stronger terms in writing to the President of the Union. In a long letter, after reiterating that the Zionists had maintained discipline regarding the debates of the Union and, on the other hand, criticizing the "condescending lack of generosity" which, according to him, the anti-Zionist campaign had shown among those "who must lead the Jewish community in Italy," he rejected any notion of press control and any regimentation of cultural institutions by the Union itself, and concluded threateningly:

> The Zionists will not threaten to secede as long as their belonging to the Community does not involve sacrificing their faith and dignity: they have never ostracized anyone, nor have they asked for help or favors. However, one must be careful that the fear of a schism on one side does not create another break on the other.[417]

The Union was therefore under fire from the anti-Semites, the Fascist Jews who generally were also anti-Zionists, the Zionists, and the government. In the meantime Angelo Sacerdoti, in the Union's name, had contacted the government at the beginning of April and met with Undersecretary of the Interior Guido Buffarini-Guidi. Following this meeting the council of the Union decided to combine the cultural and assistance associations to the Communities, to study efficient ways to control the Jewish press, and to take the measures the government would require in the future toward Zionist groups. These decisions were approved by the presidents of all the Communities at an emergency meeting in Milan and submitted to the Council of the Union in Rome on April 24. They were approved by nine votes in favor, one opposed, and one abstention.[418]

When the council began to enact with extreme caution, while keeping all traumatic changes to the bare minimum, these serious but no doubt necessary decisions, the first issue of *La nostra bandiera* was published in Turin at the beginning of May. The importance of this initiative by Ovazza and his group was obvious: it was an anti-Zionist position originating from within the Italian Jewish community and a declaration of no confidence in the Union itself, or at least in its current leadership. The publication of *La nostra bandiera*—which was immediately praised by Farinacci—announced on both levels the existence of a serious crisis within Italian Jewry.

What Ettore Ovazza and his group wanted was clear from the very first issue of their newspaper.[419] First of all they were ultra-assimilationists: "In general a Jewish press has no reason to exist in Italy. A cultural press could be somewhat understandable."

Further, they were decidedly Fascist:

> We are soldiers, we are Fascists: we feel equal to all other citizens especially in our duties toward the common homeland . . . Benito Mussolini with his great and immense accomplishments as a statesman has given Italians of the Jewish faith a law that is today among the most equitable of all those regulating our communities among all the countries in Europe. We will facilitate for all our co-religionists

143

the understanding of the current Fascist legislation on the issue. We have a clear and well-defined legal situation today: to abuse it or be unworthy of it is a crime that deserves the hard justice of the Regime.

Above all, they were anti-Zionists:

There is an international commitment, which includes Italy, to give a "national home" to our co-religionists who are forced, because of the inequality of the countries they live in, to find a safe haven . . . But this original Zionism deviated little by little into a project to create a Jewish nation in Palestine . . . The fact that with the money of the entire world, and in particular with money from England and America, they were able to create some communities for refugees, while it constitutes a great demonstration of solidarity, for political significance and the concept of nationality, it means absolutely nothing. The reconstruction of a Jewish nation in Palestine is an historical anachronism and an artificial undertaking that must be opposed. In 1492 the Jews expelled from Spain spread into all the regions of Europe and North Africa . . . They have been since then the faithful citizens of the countries where they found refuge and a homeland. For us Italians, the problem has a special meaning, because nowhere as in Italy has any European nation given the Jews a homeland with such equality for all its children. It is unacceptable that in our country there could be people who can think with nostalgia about a land that is not Italy. Zionism is a magnificent tool to develop a colonial land with the money of the Jews from all over the world. We shall help, and continue to help, these populations that are thus reborn to a new life, but while we reaffirm the impossibility of creating and revitalizing an independent Jewish nation, we do recognize the need to urgently reexamine the whole situation at the international level. The best ally of racist policy today is nationalistic Zionism. We are firmly convinced that anti-Semitic policy would never have reached such extremes had it not had among its issues that of the so-called national home. The very Jewish ideal, from the strictly religious point of view, preaches the return to Zion as a spiritual return . . . We decidedly reject the nationalist Zionists, who are respected and live with the same civil and political rights as other citizens in Europe, and who actually are turned toward Palestine . . . Anti-Semitism, where it does exist, is not a strong enough reason to require the creation of a Jewish nation . . . The Fascist government has always taken part in every international action aimed at strengthening this Jewish colony in Palestine. Italy contributes with its economic and cultural activity to the exchanges with the Orient and Palestine. But as Italians and as Jews we cannot go further than that. We repeat it once again: Palestine for us is a land under British mandate where a program of Jewish colonization has succeeded marvelously well.[420]

We have included these extended quotations because they are necessary to understand the motivations of *La nostra bandiera*. The Ovazza group was, in fact, within the orbit of the Fascist authorities—the prefecture and the Fascist federation of Turin and undoubtedly the Ministry of Foreign Affairs, even though it may not have had the backing of certain sectors of Fascism and the government[421]—and it is not impossible that the authorities were already thinking about a new organization of Italian Jews.[422] It should be said that the Turin-based group of *La nostra bandiera* was made up of people acting in good faith. In spite of the tragic end in store for many of them and for Ovazza himself, most had, during the years 1938-1939—contrary to other Jews who occupied positions of leadership within Italian Jewry—a dignified and at times proud attitude (for instance General Liuzzi), and none of them can be accused of being either corrupt or adventurous. In some there was perhaps a certain degree of fear and exaggerated respect for the authorities. Most of them, as Fascist true believers, were deeply assimilated (but not detached) Jews, and yet they remained unresponsive to many deep moral and cultural issues within Zionism. They were convinced, on the one hand, of Fascism's good faith toward the Jews, both Italians and non-Italians, and, on the other hand, of the precariousness of the political situation of Palestine, determined as it was by British interests. They thought, in good faith, that Fascist Italy represented the best possible solution for the Jews and that Zionism, consciously or not, was playing a game that was ultimately beneficial to England and to the internal and external enemies of

Fascism. This would explain their position, based on assumptions that can neither be condemned nor discounted, but only evaluated and understood historically.

The publication of *La nostra bandiera* added to the troubled waters of Italian Jewry. The Union was faced with new and more serious difficulties. A first meeting between Jarach and Ovazza resulted in the decision to request a new meeting with Buffarini-Guidi.[423] The meeting took place on May 15, and President Ravenna himself went to the Viminale Palace. This is how he reported back to his colleagues in the council that same day:

> I was received today at 6:30 p.m. by His Excellency Buffarini-Guidi, who was very cordial, and, I might emphasize, gave to the entire discussion a very affectionate atmosphere. At first, I strongly protested against the veiled accusation of not understanding national feeling. I stated that we cannot tolerate such an unconscionable accusation, since all members of the council have given throughout their lives proof of their attachment to Italy. He answered exactly: "We know you and your colleagues, stay calm: I think I have understood that the younger group who feel they are the vanguard patrol would like to use the issue to trip you up, but don't be worried. It is best that you see the Duce in about fifteen days, and he will issue the orders you want. I will warn His Excellency Mormino myself." I informed His Excellency about the organization of the Cultural Circles and he expressed satisfaction, even though I said that these had never deviated from the correct path of spirituality and Jewish culture.
>
> I mentioned the meeting with the head rabbi, Dr. Sacerdoti, and recalled that we had proposed to create a newspaper of the Union; he said that he personally approved and would inform me through His Excellency Mormino as soon as possible.
>
> As for the Zionist groups that, according to him, involve issues at the highest level, he said the head of the government would give me his reply during the coming meeting.[424]

Nothing concrete in practical terms, only general assurances which did not reveal what the true position of the government was: in the absence of an official act of approval and a few decisions that gave a clue—such as the nomination of Ovazza as government commissioner for the Community of Turin to prepare new elections—nothing to show that there were any misgivings toward the Union. This created an impasse and a crisis: while the initiative of the Turin group was approved in Leghorn, Mantua, Ancona, Padua, and Verona, and the election of the Community council in Turin was successful—General Guido Liuzzi was elected president—and *La nostra bandiera* demanded a "clear explanation" that would expand upon the press release of February 14.[425] The project to create a new publication of the Union was finally shelved. Among the members of the council uncertainty began to surface through a series of final or announced resignations.[426] The consequences of this deteriorating situation were felt very quickly, even more because on February 22, *Il Tevere* took a position ("Ciarle sionistiche") [Zionist chatter] against "the agitation of Italian Zionists," accusing them in substance of betraying Italy and invoking the example of Nazi intransigence. By mid-June the Union was forced to issue to the presidents of the Communities a short declaration on Zionism that accepted most of the positions of the Turin group.[427] A few weeks later new negotiations began between General Liuzzi, Ovazza and the Rabbi of Turin, Dario Disegni, to find a solution to the dispute.[428] At the same time the attitude of the government confirmed its approval. President Ravenna again returned to see Buffarini-Guidi:

> . . . Asked . . . if the Union could get an token of approval for its work, he answered that he had seen nothing to the contrary and that there was no reason to modify the cordial and benevolent attitude of the preceding meeting. He added that there was no reason to give undue importance to certain articles, some of them not very friendly, in certain newspapers. He said, with a very appropriate turn of phrase, that our life is measured in centuries, and if there is from time to time a demonstration against us we should not worry about it too much.[429]

This simply meant that Mussolini, having used the crisis of January-April, had decided—after giving the Zionists a "beating" that was more over principles than truly repressive—to "fascistize" even the associations of Italian Jewry.

A basis for agreement was reached by year-end thanks to the mediation of Angelo Sacerdoti between Rome and Turin: Ovazza, Liuzzi, and Dario Nunes Franco were to become part of the council of the Union and Liuzzi of the committee (others would resign to create the vacancies), the Turin group was to cease publication or transform *La nostra bandiera* into a cultural magazine, and the Union was to start its own biweekly magazine.[430] On January 9, 1935 the council of the Union welcomed its three new members. This did not resolve the crisis, it only closed its first phase; other less dramatic but even more serious events were soon to follow.

IV.

Fascist Foreign Policy
and Zionism

12.

Mussolini and Zionism

The anti-Zionist and anti-Jewish dispute in 1933 and mostly during 1934 in Italy originated outside Mussolini's entourage. The Duce actually made no attempt to stop it or repudiate it and the measures agreed to by the Union with Buffarini-Guidi were intended to counter Italian Zionism. Mussolini, however, at the same time, was helping the German Jews, and held friendly and repeated meetings with major Zionist leaders, like Chaim Weizmann and Nahum Goldmann, expressing much sympathy in speaking with them, making promises that were kept only in part—such as those concerning the Saar and Austria. This attitude could appear contradictory, misleading, or even underhanded. The facts do not bear out such a conclusion. Besides the boastful wisecracks—"You know that we could build your State from scratch"—and the histrionics of certain demagogic declarations—"I, myself, am a Zionist" to Weizmann and Goldmann—that are typical of his personality, Mussolini's policy toward international Zionism, like his policy toward German Jews, had its line and its logic which appears to contradict only on the surface his attitude toward Italian Zionism.

For Mussolini, Italian Zionism and international Zionism were two separate problems, the former belonging to internal policy and the latter to foreign policy. We have mentioned one of the official policy statements issued by the PNF: "Italy's attitude toward Zionism is different as to whether it is the Zionism in Palestine or the participation of Italian citizens in the Zionist movement..."; ev-

149

erything confirms this position. Typically, when on May 15, 1934 Buffarini-Guidi received Felice Ravenna, the problem of Zionist groups was set aside and left to the personal decision of the Duce because it was a "problem of high-level policy."

Mussolini harbored all the prejudices and suspicions common to the Nationalists and Fascists, and to many others as well, toward Italian Zionism. The belief that the Zionists had two "homelands" that were not at the same level, and that the one preferred would be Palestine, was deeply disturbing to his own monolithic and exclusive concept of homeland, turning the Zionists automatically into disagreeable suspects. In addition, another belief was that since the prevailing homeland would be Palestine, the Zionists would easily be influenced by British polices and "gold." Mussolini had a deeply rooted aversion for any international organization—an aversion that also affected international Fascist organizations, which he always suspected and tolerated only because of unavoidable political necessity—and a fear, not totally unjustified, that since most foreign Zionist organizations were democratic and anti-Fascist, the Italian Zionists would become the tools of anti-Fascism, or at least the importers and promoters of dangerous ideas in Italy.

Mussolini's attitude toward international Zionism was, if not sincerely sympathetic—as previously shown, some of its characteristics were not very conducive to gaining his acceptance—at least of some benevolent approval. Beyond the idea that the Jewish question and the anti-Semitism that was either latent or active in much of Europe could be the causes of serious international problems and that, therefore, "settling" the Jews in Palestine could solve these problems, he saw in Zionism—especially in its most right-wing and anti-British elements—a useful vehicle to further Italian interests in the eastern Mediterranean and above all to create problems for Britain in the area. The idea of a revision of the Mandate in Palestine and its transfer to Italy was almost certainly never adopted by Mussolini, who was fully aware of how difficult it would be to enact and, should it have been possible, of the kind of problems Italy would have to face. These would have certainly been more explosive than those the British were confronted with, involving only two adversaries, the Arabs and the Jews, while Italy would also have to deal with the Catholic Church. However, the idea, set forth mostly by Catholic nationalists, did flatter his ego and, especially if it were to be promoted by non-Italians, would increase his prestige and the effectiveness of his policies. The Zionist card, just as at a later date the Arab card—the Grand Mufti of Jerusalem in particular—was for Mussolini a pawn that could also be used in his Mediterranean game, as demonstrated by the agreement with Great Britain in 1937. That relations between Italy and Zionism during the 1930s did have such characteristics appears confirmed in the *Ricordi* [Memoirs] by Raffaele Guariglia, who for many years was in charge of Section V, Oriental affairs, at the Palazzo Chigi.[431]

The Zionists obviously did not reject the "relationship" with Fascist Italy. Before Mussolini "fell under Hitler's influence," Italy was one of Europe's most liberal countries toward the Jews, and it was not advisable to take an adversarial position that might anger her, always in the hope that Mussolini could persuade his German colleague to greater moderation. Later, as it became apparent that Italy was sliding toward an alliance with Berlin, there were even better reasons to maintain good relations, if only to delay the alignment with Germany on racial policy and avoid any interruption in relations between Palestine and Italy, which were now vitally important economically, and because of the transit of refugees through the port of Trieste. Above all, good relations with Italy meant avoiding seeing Italy play the Arab card and Palestine remaining the sole domain of British policy: a balance between the British and Italian influence in Palestine, or at least an Italian presence, was very important to the Zionists. Finally, for the right-wing groups, like the Zionist Revisionists, who were close to Fascism in many ways, friendship with Italy was fundamentally important: their shared, decidedly anti-British attitude, guaranteed they would find in Italy and on Italian soil necessary help and the opportunity to organize.

All these reasons were valid when applied to international Zionism, and were even more so for the Italian Zionists. We have already shown, in quoting Dante Lattes, that for them it was always a three-sided battle: for Israel, for the safety of their co-religionists in Nazi-controlled Europe, and for peace—should it crumble under the blows of Nazism, it would inevitably first overwhelm Italian Jewry. Writing about the mission he and Angiolo Orvieto undertook in 1935 in England to attempt to avoid the application of sanctions, Dante Lattes stated very clearly:

> It was obvious to us that this measure would be damaging to the Italian nation and would exasperate the people until it affected the Jews of Italy because of that lingering prejudice in public opinion and within the leadership of the regime that part of the blame could be attributed to international finance, which was Jewish and provoked rivalries, envy, and conflicts, and because of the fear that Italy, ostracized by democratic governments, would wind up in the arms of Hitler's Germany, the mortal enemy of the Jews.[432]

This statement by Lattes clearly confirms, with even more historical accuracy, what Weizmann wrote in his memoirs regarding his own investigations in London and Paris in 1934 after his meeting with Mussolini to bring about a rapprochement between those governments and the one in Rome.[433]

13.

The First Phase:
Prelude to War in Ethiopia

During the years immediately following the March on Rome there were no major changes from the pre-Fascist period in Italian policy toward Palestine and Zionism. If there was a stiffer attitude, it was because of the question of the Jewish National Home and growing suspicion of Great Britain.[434] A general pro-Arab stance ensued; however, we must not forget that a major reason for this policy change was the personal involvement of the Marquis Theodoli,[435] president of the Commission of the League of Nations on Mandates, who had always been openly opposed to Zionist demands and represented the Catholic position regarding the Holy Places while being at the same time receptive to Arab demands—so much so that Weizmann could write that "he could always be counted on to veto any constructive proposal in our fa-vor."[436]

The first signs of change in this policy appeared in 1926-1928, once Salvatore Contarini, who had pursued the pre-Fascist policy, was fired from the Palazzo Chigi. As Mussolini's personal involve-ment was felt even in foreign policy, the first changes appeared. But given its marginal character, the policy toward Palestine, within the scope of Mussolini's general foreign policy, would remain for a long time under the supervision of Raffaele Guariglia and Mariano De Angelis, the Italian consul general in Jerusalem, who was very knowl-edgeable concerning the Palestinian problem and had initiated Ital-ian contacts with Zionism. In 1926 Mussolini began showing inter-est in the eastern Mediterranean; that year, Arnaldo Mussolini [the Duce's older brother], said clearly in an interview with the North American Alliance that Italy had ambitions regarding the eastern basin, particularly Albania, Syria, Smyrna, and Adalia, "which should belong to us."[437] For some time Palestine was not directly included in this new policy, even though the discussions Mussolini had with Weizmann, Jacobson, and Sokolov and the authorization to create an Italy-Palestine Committee in 1926-1928 confirm renewed inter-est in the region and in Zionism. During this period, and for a few more years, the new policy, as Guariglia wrote, was a "deeper inves-tigation" into Palestinian events and the developments of Zionism, a deeper economic and cultural penetration of Palestine to influ-ence the Jews who were living there.[438]

As long as relations with Great Britain were good and Mussolini's arrows were aimed at France, this attitude was the norm. As Brit-ish-Italian relations worsened and the 1929 crisis demonstrated that it was impossible to mend the clash between Arabs and Jews, the British position became more difficult and the idea arose that on the Fascist and Zionist side there was a need to create stronger relations.[439] The decisive step in this direction was taken by the Zi-onists, possibly in 1932-1934, with some gestures toward Mussolini. At the beginning of 1931 Mussolini had authorized the Palazzo Chigi to have Lattes and Sacerdoti inform Weizmann that the Ital-ian government would welcome Zionist Congress meetings in the town of Abbazia. The Congress met in Basel instead because the

Zionist left wing had rejected the offer, despite the fact that Weizmann had personally promoted the idea.[440] The Duce's attitude, as well as that of most of his deputies during the German crisis, dispelling many uncertainties and creating some hope[441] while overlooking certain prejudices, was to be the determining factor. The Zionist press quickly underlined Italy's pro-Jewish stance, contrasting it with that of the Nazis. As *Haaretz* in Tel Aviv was to write on April 19, 1933:

> We have learned from Rome that Mussolini has warned Mr. Göring and Mr. von Papen, who are in Italy to negotiate political issues with Mussolini, against persecuting the Jews in Germany. It has been stated that Minister Balbo has protested against the persecution of the Jews in Germany and that Italian Jews have organized protests against Germany.

Mussolini, who avoided involvement in the effort to stop the press campaigns by *Il Tevere* and *Il regime fascista*, was worried about their repercussions on the Jews in Palestine. The Jerusalem daily, *Doar Hayóm*, published an attack directed at *Il regime fascista* on July 5, 1933, demanding a quota for the Jews in Italy.[442] Rome immediately sent instructions to the Consulate in Jerusalem to deny the allegation in Farinacci's newspaper and reassure De Angelis at the same time:

> This Ministry will continue to favor the avoidance by the Italian press of any declarations that could create tendencies within the Jews of Palestine that would be contrary to their pro-Italian attitude.[443]

Mussolini's three meetings of 1933-1934 with Weizmann and Goldmann would prove that Zionism could not expect much from Italy beyond certain prejudices and attitudes inherent to his regime.[444] Mussolini would never take a strong position in favor of the Jews if they did not, in turn, take a decidedly anti-British position, which was obviously impossible. However, these meetings did demonstrate that the Zionists would only be the losers in shunning his friendship and influence. Mussolini could influence the exodus of Jewish refugees from Europe and portray himself as a mediator between Arabs and Jews to find a solution to the Palestinian problem. These were cards worth playing, if only to avoid seeing Arab influence gaining in Rome.

In his conversation of February 17, 1934, Weizmann moved on both levels, encouraged by the fact that that very morning, and it could not be a mere coincidence, taking its cue from a recent article in the *Mercure de France*, *Il popolo d'Italia* in an editorial entitled "Una soluzione" [A solution] had, without too much of a commitment, considered the possibility of "creating in Palestine not just a 'home,' an ambiguous term devoid of political significance, but a real state." In using both lines of discussion, Weizmann demonstrated that he understood Mussolini perfectly well, since he was constantly seeking spectacular personal successes.

Victor Jacobson's summary of the conversation shows that in speaking about a Jewish state Mussolini said, "I have already spoken to the Arabs.[445] I think we can reach an agreement. The problem will be the question of Jerusalem. The Arabs say that the Jews should have their capital in Tel Aviv." Weizmann replied deftly:

> One thing is very clear: if Jerusalem doesn't become a Jewish capital, it must not become an Arab capital because of the Christian world. Jerusalem is the meeting point of three religions. But the sanctity of Jerusalem for the Moslems is a relatively recent invention, while for the Jews, Jerusalem is the city of David and for the Christians it is the center of the Holy Land.

Therefore, in the tense situation of the time, which certainly would not have permitted the Jews be given Jerusalem, Weizmann actually was "offering" it to Mussolini in order to deny it to the Arabs and to impress the Duce with the idea that he could be, in the eyes of world opinion, not just a mediator but the leader who restored to Christianity the care of the Holy Places—in case his initiative should actually succeed in resolving the Palestinian crisis and persuading the Arabs to recognize Jewish requests. In exchange Weizmann not only assured Mussolini of the friendship of the Jews but also, knowing how badly Mussolini wanted improved relations with the British and the French after the collapse of the Four Power Pact, promised to make inquiries in this direction: "I think we can be of help in England by preparing for collaboration."

The news that Mussolini had received Weizmann created a stir in Palestine among Jews and Arabs. The Arabs were very impressed, so much so that rumors were spread that the article published the same day in *Il popolo d'Italia* had been written by the Duce himself, and the Palazzo Chigi had to instruct De Angelis to reassure the Arabs: Mussolini had not written the article and in any case "it offers not an effective but only a symbolic solution" and summed up a proposal already made by others to resolve the Jewish problem.[446] In spite of these assurances, the Arab Palestinian press would speak of the pro-Zionism of Mussolini and Italy for a long time to come.[447] The Zionist reaction was more cautious; for them friendship with Italy was thought to have many advantages but it was not realistic to expect Mussolini to take a decisive position. He would move only with concessions that the Jews could not make, unless they abandoned the British and League of Nations policy, which was contradictory, unsatisfactory and open to criticism but also relatively safe, and switch to Mussolini's policy, which was without any guarantees and extremely dangerous. Herman Swith said as much in *Haaretz* of December 29, 1934 in an article entitled: "Il Duce, la Palestina ed il Congresso Ebraico Mondiale" [The Duce, Palestine, and the World Jewish Congress]:

> It is stupid to say that Mussolini loves or hates the Jewish people. He simply loves Italy. However, the Duce, unlike other statesmen, is interested in the Jewish question without much sentimentality, nor does he show prejudices, hatreds, or disdain. For Mussolini the Jews are a pawn on the world chessboard, not terribly important, but not altogether useless. This is Mussolini's attitude toward us, no more and no less.[448]

This responsible and cautious attitude was not common to all Zionists and Jews. Some, blinded by the myth of Mussolini's power and wisdom, which was widespread even overseas, looked up to the Duce and Italy as the only nation able to resolve the Palestinian question and free the Jews from their problems. Among many cases we shall only mention two that are in the documents of the Italian Foreign Ministry. Wilhelm Gross, a lawyer, wrote to Mussolini from Stryj in Poland in April 1934, and in a picturesque Italian full of poetic expressions requested his support for Jewish demands in Palestine, reminding the Duce that the Jewish people would never forget such a commitment and would build in its heart "an arch more precious and lasting than the Arch of Titus."[449] Another request came in November of the same year from a Moses Lehman in New York, who asked that Mussolini establish the Jews within the Italian colonies.[450]

These requests came only from individuals, and their confidence in Mussolini only indicated a certain state of mind. The relations, beginning in 1932, between the Italian government and the anti-British, right-wing Zionist Revisionists, as we have seen, were much more significant.

We have already mentioned the letter written in 1922 by Jabotinsky to Mussolini and the first organizations of Zionist Revisionists in Italy around 1927, as well as the publication of their magazine *L'idea sionistica* in 1930. On the international level, initial contacts of the Zionist Revisionists and the Italian Foreign Ministry came a few years after the founding of the Italian Revisionist movement in 1932 and began to take shape in 1934. Thanks to a long memorandum from Raffaele Guariglia to Undersecretary of Foreign Affairs Fulvio Suvich on November 4, 1935, we have detailed information as to how things developed in 1932 in a series of reports which are part of the documents of the Historical Archives of the Foreign Ministry. In spite of its length, we include the Guariglia report, an extremely important document that sheds light better than any description concerning not only the course of events, but the thinking of the two interested parties.

In April 1932 Mr. Jabotinsky, head of the Zionist Revisionist Group, proposed in a letter to Prof. Sciaky of the Liceo Galileo in Florence a project to create a Central School of Instructors for the military preparation of Jewish youth and mentioned that France would agree to allow the Center establish itself on its territory. The project was also submitted to this Royal Ministry.

We did not follow up on the project at the time due to the problems that such a Center located in Italy could create for us in the Arab world and the few guarantees that the Revisionist movement appeared to offer. However, this movement, due to energetic promotion by Mr. Jabotinsky, has been growing and becoming more important; during the Vienna Congress last September, which took place after the secession by the Revisionist group from the World Zionist Organization, the Revisionist group adopted the name "New Zionist Organization" and gave its program a decidedly nationalist bent, its goal being the creation of a completely Jewish state that would be free and independent.

It should be noted that during the Congress of the World Zionist Organization (the Jewish Agency), which took place at Lucern at the end of August and the beginning of last September, the opposing factions within the parties at the congress demonstrated a lack of cohesion within the organization, which is split into two major groups: one does not wish to consider the Jewish people as a nation but rather a religious community, while the other, which includes the least extreme members of the revisionists who have not left the Jewish Agency, tends to advocate the creation of a Jewish state. The same General Zionists, led by Dr. Weizmann, who only conceives of Palestinian Zionism within the British Mandate, were persuaded to accept the most important points of revisionism and now agree to the inevitability of a future Jewish state but also insist that the Mandatory Power allow Jewish emigration into Transjordan.

The movement led by Jabotinsky is fundamentally opposed to the British Mandate and is based, in imitation of Fascism, on youth, whose organization is known as Betar. This is the second year that this organization has sent its students to the Maritime School at Civitavecchia: Italy's agreement to Mr. Jabotinsky's wish to establish a Central School for Instructors for the military preparation of youth in Italy would be a second step after admitting Jewish students at the Civitavecchia School and would help in the liberation of Palestine from the British Mandate. Should Your Excellency feel that it would be in the interest of Italy to allow the creation of such a center, the approval of the Royal Government could be extended, with the caution required by our foreign and colonial policy and above all the need to avoid taking any anti-Arab attitudes.

A few days ago I had a private conversation with Mr. Jabotinsky, who was traveling through Rome. He confirmed the favorable attitude toward Italy and Fascism on the part of Zionist Revisionism, since its position toward general "Zionism," which is now under the control of the democracies, is the same as the position and function Fascism has toward liberal and socialist democracies.

He also told me that our fears of alienating the Arabs are exaggerated. Arabism in the Mediterranean—he thinks—is the past reliving its own legend, lacking the main element necessary to any movement of ideas, which is a cohesive force. Zionism has such a force and represents the future.

Mr. Jabotinsky is a very intelligent and forceful man with a strong personality, devoid of that Jewish mysticism that has been so negative for the Jews up to now.

I feel we should help and favor Revisionist Zionism, because we should encourage those in the Mediterranean who request Italy's support and because official Zionism of the democratic-liberal, socialistic, plutocratic type is a British trademark and completely controlled by the British government.

As for the repercussions on the Arabs, I agree with Mr. Jabotinsky that our fears were and are exaggerated.[451]

It clearly emerges from Guariglia's report that Italian interest in Zionism had only an anti-British motivation, and the Fascist government, convinced that it could not use the entire Zionist movement (because of the commitments of Weizmann and the leadership group to the British system and because of the fundamentally democratic character of Zionism itself), chose to support the Revisionists, who were decidedly opposed to the system and ready to fight using every possible means, including force of arms.

The opinion that Revisionism was ideologically very close to Fascism was widely held by the Revisionists themselves[452] and this Italian policy line was supported by the Ministry of Foreign Affairs.[453]

Initial contacts between the Palazzo Chigi and the Revisionists began in 1932[454] but actually grew in 1934 with the opening of the Jewish section of the Maritime School at Civitavecchia and developed further in 1935-1936 when the Revisionists broke with the Jewish Agency and created their own organization.[455]

Against this background collaboration between the Italian government and the Zionist Revisionists developed over time.

The school at Civitavecchia began operating in December 1934, coinciding with the arrival of the four young Revisionists, who had been authorized to attend courses in the schools run by the PNF.[456] The authorization request, which at first had been submitted to Grand Admiral Paolo Thaon di Revel, president of the Consortium of Professional Maritime Schools, had been quickly approved by the Foreign Ministry and other competent ministries. The first course, taught by Commander Nicola Fusco, the director of the regular school in Civitavecchia, ended the following April:[457] out of twenty-nine cadets, twenty-four passed the theoretical examinations. In the meantime, with funds coming from a supporter of the Revisionist movement, a large four-mast training yacht had been purchased, the *Quattro Venti*, hopefully renamed *Sara I*, which displaced 635.46 tons and had an engine of 501.28 hp. The *Sara*, flying the Italian flag, went on its first cruise in the western Mediterranean in the fall, visiting Seville and Algiers. While it was in Algiers on October 23, 1935, the ship was suddenly recalled by an order from the Italian government. There were two reasons for this: it appears that in Seville the young cadets did not hide their aversion for the Nazis and Germany, inciting protests and creating anxiety; furthermore, in Algiers, the appearance of twenty Jews in uniform had frightened the Italian consulate, which informed Rome on October 22 that the whole thing was "damaging to our relations with the Moslem world."[458] Following these incidents and worries, the Foreign Ministry was uncertain whether to renew the school's authorization, but in the end decided to. The second course was attended by fifty cadets (twenty-four Poles, eight Czechoslovaks, five Germans, four Lithuanians, three Romanians, three Austrians, one Hungarian, and one citizen of Danzig); the cruise was limited, by governmental decision, to Italian ports and to Nice and Marseilles.[459] In order to increase the budget and finance the school because of irregular payments by the Revisionist center, a large fishing boat was added—the *Sara* also carried cargo during its cruises. The young graduates of the school were usually employed on board Palestinian, Polish, Romanian, Lithuanian, and Norwegian ships; a few were clandestinely smuggled into Palestine. During the third year, 1936-1937, the Revisionists attempted to go to foreign ports during the summer cruise despite the fact that it was forbidden because of a fake sale of the *Sara* so that it would no longer appear to belong to the Civitavecchia school and could sail under a French flag. The incident was disturbing to the Foreign Ministry, to the point that in July 1937 it seriously considered canceling the school's authorization. The result was that in September 1937 the *Sara*, after calling at Malta, arrived on the Palestinian coast, to the excitement of the Jewish community.[460] The year 1937-1938 was to be the final one of the school: the loss of the *Sara* was to be added to the difficulties caused by the obvious change of attitude by the Fascist government toward the Jews, and therefore the cooling of relations with the Revisionists.[461] During the preceding year's cruise, as the ship returned to Italy with a substitute captain—the real captain had to leave the ship for a number of reasons, including disputes with the Revisionist political supervisor, who wanted to give the cruise a truly political and propaganda flavor[462]—it ran aground on January 26, 1938, south of the mouth of the Golo, near Bastia.[463] The survival of the school was becoming extremely precarious under these conditions, and while Jabotinsky, who was very encouraged by the results obtained so far, was preparing to enlarge the school and launch an ambitious subscription loan all over the world for "the sea of Israel,"[464] the decision was made to shut the school down after quickly ending the courses and giving exams to the cadets. This ended the most tangible form of collaboration between Revisionism and Fascism, which lasted over three and a half years and, but for the change of direction decided by Mussolini, would certainly have been extended to the air force and the army.[465] Its significance is obvious: besides naval preparation for a few hundred Jewish youths from all over Europe, many of whom became the nucleus of the Israeli navy, it was necessary for Fascism to train a group of youths who were to become propagandists for Italy and Fascism all over the world, and especially in Palestine.[466] For the Revisionists it was very important to appear as the active branch of Zionism, giving it a navy and the ability to travel around the Mediterranean every summer with a group of young

Jews, militarily trained and organized, as a symbol of the future state.

The Maritime School at Civitavecchia was the first and most important step in the relations between Italy and the Revisionists, but it was not the only one. While the courses in Civitavecchia were taking place and the *Sara* sailed the waters of the Mediterranean every year, the relationship between Jabotinsky's agents and the Italian government in Rome and in Palestine, through the Italian consulates, was very close, so much so that it was the cause of protests and denunciations from the British and the Arabs.[467] If such relations did not go beyond a certain point it was due to the Italian fear of going too far down a road that could bring favorable results but also cause growing difficulties with the Arabs, with whom Mussolini was increasingly seeking closer relations,[468] thus forcing London to reach a "general agreement" with him in the Mediterranean, as well as a visibly growing anti-Jewish attitude in Italian foreign policy.[469] Various requests from the Revisionists for economic and military collaboration were ignored,[470] as well as a request by Jabotinsky for a meeting with Mussolini in July 1936.[471] Revisionist attempts at collaboration ended as soon as it became clear that Mussolini had decided to adopt anti-Semitism and align himself completely with the Nazi ally. At the beginning of 1937, as we shall see, when the Tripoli incidents took place, an alarmed Jabotinsky immediately contacted the Palazzo Chigi to obtain "real information" on what was happening,[472] indicating very clearly that he was not about to swallow, without reacting, an Italian anti-Semitic campaign just because he needed the friendship and the help of the Fascists. The Revisionist leader was to reiterate this position a few months before his death in 1940, even before Italy's entry into the war, harshly condemning Mussolini's anti-Semitism and its true motivations.[473]

14.

The Second Phase:
the War in Ethiopia and Zionism

T he world crisis created by the Italian Ethiopian conflict had deep repercussions on the relations between Italy and Zionism. The Fascist government, on the one hand, attempted with renewed vigor to foment problems for England in Palestine and gain the sympathy of Zionists in general, and on the other hand tried to use Zionism to avoid sanctions and in particular their application even by Palestine. It is clear that this did not change the Italian government's opinion of Zionism itself.[474] The authorization given in April 1935 to the Ministries of Foreign Affairs and the Interior for the Jewish Agency congress to take place at Abbazia[475] must be understood within this specific context. The same can be said about the mission given at the end of 1935 to the CAUR (Comitati d'Azione per l'Universalità di Roma) [Action Committees for the Universality of Rome], in agreement with the Palazzo Chigi. Corrado Tedeschi was to travel to Palestine and renew contact with the Zionists, both General and Revisionist, and persuade both of them, especially the former, to take a friendlier attitude toward Italy.[476] The crux of the mission was to convince the Zionists that Italy rejected any type of anti-Zionism, and explain that, if some Italian newspapers took such a line, it was without the knowledge of the Italian government and would not be repeated, because Italy was friendly toward the Jews and was engaged in a policy of sympathy toward them; in addition, the Italian government accepted "as correct," the *fait accompli* of the "National Home" for the Jews in Palestine and was respectful of the importance and weight of world Zionism. "In return . . . the Jews must logically understand that any change in a Mediterranean country must take into account the importance of Italian policy; in sum, not only England but also Italy is present and vigilant in every Mediterranean question."[477] The declarations by Mussolini on August 8, 1935 to the Grand Rabbi of Alexandria of Egypt, David Prato, were in the same vein: a warning to the Zionists to stop flirting with England and decide to create a true Jewish state in Palestine. Mussolini agreed to the proposal that Prato had been requesting for many years, i.e., that within the Palazzo Chigi there would be a Bureau of Jewish Affairs headed by a Jew, to develop and coordinate cultural, economic, and religious initiatives which would make the Jewish communities in the Near East centers for Italian penetration in those countries and create a sort of Federation of Sephardic Jews (or "Leghornese") that would be the vehicle for such penetration.

Prato's idea was not new, and had been considered by the Ministry of Foreign Affairs in order to counterbalance British penetration and presence in the Near East beginning in 1918-1920, first under Sonnino and then under Nitti and Sforza; it had been encouraged since 1916 by the Italian Zionists and had Weizmann's approval. When Mussolini came to power not only had it been proposed once again indirectly—as a possible cooperation of the Jews in the development of Italian trade in the Levant—by Lattes and Moshé Beilinson; it had also been revisited by the Zionist executive itself with a view of organizing a Sephardic Congress in Rome at the end of 1923. Canceled in part due to the opposition of the Colonial Office and the lack of interest of the Palazzo Chigi at the time, it had been discussed between 1926 and 1929 by David Prato, who had even talked to Mussolini about it. Once again the discussion was unsuccessful because, it seems, of the hostility shown by Grandi,[478] with the exception of the creation of a Rabbinical College on the island of Rhodes for the instruction of rabbis for the Levant. This position did not change even after Dino Grandi left the Foreign Ministry. During the summer of 1933 Mussolini had approved the creation of a Bureau of Jewish Affairs, to be headed by Prato himself, but two unexpected events had prevented its implementation: the rejection of Prato's resignation by the Community in Alexandria and the furor caused by the press campaign against the anti-Fascist Turin Jews who had been arrested. To revive this project just before the war in Ethiopia became so clearly self-serving that, even with Mussolini's approval, it was shelved once more. Due to the circumstances, it was best that Prato remain as head of the Community at Alexandria of Egypt, and no search was made to find a replacement. Prato had proposed the name of Carlo Alberto Viterbo but his past political associations made him unacceptable, and probably no other candidate would have been acceptable in any case. The idea of a convention of "Leghornese" Jews was also cast aside even though it had been approved in principle by Mussolini.[479] The extremely intense diplomatic activity undertaken by the Italian government at the end of 1935 and the beginning of 1936 towards the Zionists and the leaders of Italian Jewry at various Jewish conferences during those months and toward world Zionist leaders should also be placed within this context.

According to the documents we have seen, the Italian consul general in Jerusalem, De Angelis, was the first to believe the sanctions against Italy[480] by Palestine[481] could be reversed, possibly because of suggestions coming from some Palestinian Jews who interpreted the application of sanctions by the Palestinian government as reducing Palestine from a mandate to a British colony.[482] In a cable to the Italian Foreign Ministry dated October 18, 1935 De Angelis noted:

> Should the Royal Government feel it necessary to avoid this mandated country from becoming involved in the sanctions, I would like to point out that some initiatives could be taken with Dr. Weizmann, who is the only Zionist leader able to speak with some authority to the British government. He is in London at this time.[483]

The proposal from De Angelis came just as another initiative had been decided in Rome: to encourage Italian Jews to ask their British co-religionists to pressure the British government to avoid sanctions of any kind. This shows that Mussolini believed the Jews indeed had great political influence and were a real international power.

The London mission, which was to be duplicated in Paris and Geneva, was entrusted to Angiolo Orvieto and Dante Lattes. An encrypted cable from Suvich to Grandi announced their arrival on October 30.[484] In London the two met with Balfour's niece, with Montefiore, with Weizmann, and with an influential journalist of the *Times*; they were unable to speak with Herbert Samuel, who was campaigning for re-election. They told everyone that sanctions would in effect throw Mussolini into Hitler's arms and that the first to suffer would be the Italian Jews. Further details of these London meetings are not available. There is more information regarding the meeting with Weizmann a few days earlier with two anonymous "trusted representatives" of Dino Grandi, whose cable to Rome on October 31 is worth quoting in its entirety:

> I sent some people I trust to see Dr. Weizmann before he left London and had them explain to him the problems mentioned in Your Excellency's cable n. 412 regarding the application of sanctions by the Palestinian government. I also pointed out that—beyond the damage it would do to Palestine to brutally interrupt its trade with Italy, which under the present circumstances should be favored and increased—the extension of the sanctions to Palestine seriously threatens its status as an independent country under mandate. Palestine would certainly be treated as a British colony. Palestine should be excluded from the sanctions not just from the point of view of its economic interests but also because of the moral and political interests of Zionism.
>
> Dr. Weizmann, as reported to me by my representatives, indicated he was convinced by these reasons. They gathered the impression that Dr. Weizmann would take action in favor of our point of view.
>
> During my last conversation with Vansittart I also discussed this point at length, explaining the legal issues preventing an extension of sanctions to Palestine and repeating what I had said regarding Egypt: that we could only consider as a hostile act on the part of Britain the adoption of sanctions by a country that has neither the duty nor the right to associate itself with sanctions. A British extension of sanctions would not just go against the Pact of the League of Nations but also against the relaxation of tensions and the improvement of Italian-British relations that the British government declares so emphatically it is seeking.[485]

Contrary to the impression reported by Grandi's two trusted emissaries, the meeting with Weizmann did not produce any practical results, as is now known, and the initiatives by Orvieto and Lattes met with the same fate. We have no record of the answers they were given during their meetings, but we can possibly gain some insight from the various declarations made a few days later by Professor Selig Brodetsky of the political department of the executive center of the Jewish Agency. Lattes quickly transmitted these declarations to Guariglia in Rome.[486] Speaking at the sixteenth congress of Zionist Women of England, Brodetsky said:

> The Jews have no quarrel with Italy. The manner in which Italy treats the Jews, be they its own citizens or immigrants, has been and is admirable. I would like to see a few other countries use the Italian model in their treatment of the Jews who live in their midst. *For the rest, we do not wish to become involved in international discussions.*

This statement, which, at least in part, coincided with the declarations made a few days before by Montefiore to the Deputies of British Jews, was published in the *Jewish Chronicle*; we think it reflects the substance of the answers given to Orvieto and Lattes.

The failure of the Orvieto-Lattes mission and the impression of success maintained until the end in Rome because of the pressure brought upon Weizmann, especially after reassuring information had been received from Grandi, left a bitter taste at the Palazzo Chigi, perhaps even with Mussolini himself, who could not understand how such a "distinguished" initiative could be ignored. Orvieto and Lattes were thanked by a letter from Suvich, but from then on certain people began repeating the line about the "Jewish-Masonic conspiracy" against Italy. Some declarations against Italy by individual Jews, and the presence of various Jews in League of Nations offices, were seen as proof of the existence of such a conspiracy. Baron Aloisi's diary is quite clear about this, even if a bit messy, and demonstrates how these accusations originated from the end of November 1935 to April 1936 and were even being spread at the highest levels of Italian diplomacy.[487] Aloisi writes about the attacks in *Gringoire* in Paris that he inspired against "certain Jewish and Freemason characters at the League of Nations who are working against us,"[488] and even of a fifty-minute meeting on March 31, 1936 between Mussolini and a certain Babault (Georges Batault?) who had published a few anti-Semitic articles in November in the *Revue Hebdomadaire*,[489] where Jews and Freemasons were accused of wanting a war.[490] These accusations were immediately repeated in Italy by the usual group of anti-Semites; Preziosi went so far as to write in *La vita italiana* of March 15, 1936 that Eden was "the right-hand man of international Jewry" after having stated two months earlier that Italy was at war with the Jewish groups led by Cassel-Breitmeyer and Wernher-Beit, who had been the first to warn England, according to him, against the danger the Ethiopian action held for British interests in the Blue Nile.[491]

However, these anti-Semitic darts were limited for the moment, without consequences for Italian Jews or Fascist policy toward Zionism. The Italian government and the Palazzo Chigi itself continued to encourage contacts between the representatives of Italian Jews and foreigners to demonstrate that Italy had no anti-Semitic prejudice and to attempt to gain the sympathy, or at least the neutrality, of the Jewish organizations and communities scattered around the world, and in particular within the Mediterranean basin.[492] At the end of February 1936, Orvieto and Lattes attended the Paris conference of the executive committee of Jewish delegations,[493] and between August 8 and 15 of the same year, along with Felice Ravenna and Guido Zevi, they were at the first World Jewish Congress in Geneva.[494] The instructions of the ministry in both cases were the same as they had been for three years—to seek moderation:

> While being able, as Jews, to agree to the recommendations and votes that would be proposed . . . to deplore discrimination, established or just being used against the Jews in some of those countries—Germany, Austria, Poland, Romania—they should avoid putting themselves forward and in any case should work diligently, possibly toward having a moderating effect.[495]

In spite of the activity displayed by the Italian delegates, these contacts would not produce any tangible results, with the exception of a few general statements favorable to Italy and its "sympathy" and "understanding" for Jewish problems which had become customary in contrasting the liberal policy of Mussolini to that of Hitler and his imitators, which was becoming more extreme in persecution. The political atmosphere of the time was not conducive to improving relations between Fascism and Zionism, especially once the first signs of a new phase in relations between Italy and Germany appeared. The Jews, at least those who were more forward-looking, were troubled and sickened by what they saw and therefore not in the best frame of mind to begin changing their relationship to Fascism.

15.

The Third Phase: Breaking Relations

B y mid-1936 and during the first months of 1937 relations between Fascist Italy and Zionism entered what was to be their final phase.

On June 9, 1936 Mussolini named his son-in-law, Galeazzo Ciano, as the new Foreign Minister. The "change of command" at the Palazzo Chigi would immediately have deep repercussions on Zionist policy. The change was motivated by three reasons.

Fulvio Suvich had been a moderating influence at the Palazzo Chigi, and as the good citizen of Trieste that he was, had always cautioned Mussolini against Germany. In a note to Mussolini dated February 7, 1936 he emphasized, regarding the Austrian problem, that the Italian-German closeness of relations of those months should remain limited to "a psychological coming together," and clearly added "it is best that other countries be told that this closeness has no wider meaning."[496] Whatever policy was ultimately pursued, one point was firm for Suvich: Austrian independence had to be defended at all costs. "To sacrifice Austria"—he wrote to Mussolini—"would be a colossal mistake." Beyond any moral considerations, "the day Austria is annexed to Germany, and Germany is at the Brenner Pass and the Julian Alps, will be the day our path will be clearly marked, because we will be tied by solidarity with the anti-German group against the German threat." As we can see, Suvich did not even consider an agreement with Berlin as a possibility. "It would be a dangerous illusion to think that Germany, once it arrives at the Brenner and at Tarvisio, will stop at these positions and not attempt to go beyond them . . . It would require for us to ignore German history and the mindset of the German people to think that Germany would not make every effort to cross the one hundred kilometers that would then separate it from the Adriatic." On the other hand, "no agreement will suffice or be respected in the face of German expansion." Ciano, taking over from Suvich with the added, if only formal, powers of a full minister, in part because of his easy-going nature and inexperience, in part because he overestimated Italy's potential, changed this policy line. As Guariglia writes, he criticized the policy followed during the Italian-Ethiopian war "for not having been conducted in closer contact with Germany" and "for having used the German bugaboo to modify the Franco-British attitude as well as that of the League of Nations toward us."[497] As soon as he arrived at the Palazzo Chigi, Ciano began—"with fervor" writes Guariglia—a policy of concrete approaches toward Germany. If at a later date Ciano changed his mind, having realized that he had walked into the jaws of the lion, that is a different problem, does not mitigate his enormous responsibility for having taken Italy down the road toward an alliance with Hitler. This path was taken at full throttle: October 1936, Ciano's trip to Berlin; May 1937, von Neurath visits Rome; June 1937, Marshal von Blomberg visits Italy; August 20, 1937, Mussolini speaks in Palermo about the Rome-Berlin "Axis"; September 1937, Mussolini travels to Germany; October 1937, Hess visits Rome; November 6, 1937, Italy joins the Anti-Comintern Pact; December 11, 1937, Italy leaves the League of Nations; March 1, 1938, Ciano publishes an article in '*Wille und Macht*'; March 12, 1938, Anschluss; May 1938, Hitler visits Italy . . . While traveling the legs of this journey at unconscionable top speed, and as the alliance between Italy and Germany became daily more obvious in every field, Mussolini, began preparing, now under the influence of its most extreme proponents and of the alignment of every political area to the policies of the two friendly nations soon to become allies, the abomination of anti-Semitic policies. Clearly, in this climate, Fascist foreign policy interest in Zionism also decreased daily.

Ciano, while pursuing his policy of closer relations with Germany—we must remember that in Milan on November 1, 1936 Mussolini declared that "the vertical line Berlin-Rome is not a diaphragm, but rather an axis around which all the European states who seek collaboration and peace can collaborate"—attempted to bring about a gentlemen's agreement with England, concerning the problems in the Mediterranean, that would recognize each country's interests.

Through these negotiations with England, Italy was putting an end—at least officially—to the policy of penetration in Egypt and in Palestine[498] and to anti-British propaganda among the local populations.[499] The protocols signed in Rome on April 16, 1938 ratified, at the close of this negotiation, the mutual undertaking to respect the Mediterranean status quo. Palestine was not mentioned in the agreement, but that very day an exchange of verbal notes took place between the two governments in which Italy agreed that the new policy applied to that country as well:

> The question of Palestine has been discussed between the Italian Foreign Minister and His Majesty's Ambassador in Rome during their recent conversations. As a result the Italian Foreign Minister has verbally assured His Majesty's Ambassador that the Italian Government will abstain from creating difficulties or embarrassment for His Majesty's Government in the administration of Palestine. His Majesty's Ambassador has verbally assured the Italian Foreign Minister that His Majesty's Government intends to preserve and protect legitimate Italian interests in that territory.[500]

This was one more reason for relations with the Zionists to become less attractive and more of a risk to the Palazzo Chigi, and it appeared that they should no longer be pursued or developed.

While the Palazzo Chigi articulated this dual policy toward Berlin and London, it began concentrating its interest on the Arabs, who were given many signs of friendship, and, secretly, some help as well. On March 18, 1937 in Tripoli Mussolini brandished the "sword of Islam" as if to symbolize his "patronage" of all Arabs. Under these circumstances, relations with the Zionists became not just difficult but dangerous and of little value.

171

The suspicion the Zionists felt toward Italy and Fascism increased in this new climate, and on the Italian side, the few moves that were still being made were ignored. A timid proposal, in the form of an opinion poll for the creation of a Zionist center in the region of Lake Tana (in Ethiopia) in 1936 never got beyond the exploratory phase.[501] The same happened a year later to a proposal to create a banking institution in Palestine with Italian capital.[502] The requests coming from the Revisionists were also ignored, as we have already noted.

The most typical incident of this new period was the meeting between Ciano and Nahum Goldmann. During the preceding years Mussolini had agreed to hold meetings with major Zionist leaders without any difficulty. Now, however, it became more and more difficult. In November 1936 Goldmann requested a meeting with Mussolini, then, having understood that it would not be granted, asked instead for a meeting with Ciano, saying that he wanted Weizmann to have the opportunity to meet with the Duce. Ciano turned down the request. In March 1937 the request was put forth once again. After many hesitations by the Palazzo Chigi regarding the date of the meeting—Goldmann had requested March 25 or 26, Ciano had answered that during that month it would not be possible, Goldmann then proposed April 5, 6, or 7, with the same response—it was finally set for May 4. The result was practically nil: Ciano spoke only in generalities, limiting himself to polite assurances and denying that the anti-Semitic campaign by some Italian newspapers during those weeks had any meaning or was a prelude to a change of Fascist policy toward the Jews. A note by Guariglia of the same day summed up the meeting "for the record":[503]

Ciano received Goldmann at 10. After the meeting he told me:

1. that he was very satisfied by what the Foreign Minister had told him, that we have no intention of changing our policy toward Zionism; that Italy is not thinking of adopting racist policies; that some press articles and books are the opinions of isolated individuals;

2. that the Zionist Executive is against the partition of Palestine; its objective is to gain time with the current mandate system and to

promote Zionist immigration into Palestine in proportion to the capacity of the country to absorb it. They would accept partition only to avoid a worse outcome and if all of southern Palestine would be within the Jewish zone.[504]

The Zionist card had lost its value in the eyes of the Fascists: alliance with Germany, a pro-Arab policy, and a Mediterranean agreement with England had modified the view the Palazzo Chigi had of Palestine. The efforts of those Jews who, feeling the storm rising above their heads, tried to ward it off by attempting to convince important Fascist leaders that Italy could at last replace Great Britain within the mandate over Palestine, came to nothing.[505]

Fascism quickly stated officially that within this new political line there would no longer be any place for Zionism. On February 16, 1938, upon publication of the famous *Informazione Diplomatica* n. 14, which signaled, in its hypocrisy, the anti-Semitic campaign inside Italy and which shall be examined later, one paragraph mentioned the Palestinian question:

> Official circles in Rome feel that the universal Jewish problem can be solved only in one way: to create somewhere in the world, not in Palestine, a Jewish State, a State that truly reflects the meaning of the word and is therefore capable of representing and protecting through normal diplomatic and consular channels, all the scattered Jewish masses from various countries.

Ciano, in his diary for February 15, says he made it clear that the Jewish State proposed by Mussolini would not be in Palestine, "in order to protect our relations with the Arabs."[506]

Immediate Zionist reactions were, in spite of some formal caution, quite violent. The Jewish Agency issued an official press release on March 1, where, after "taking note, with satisfaction, of the opinion of the Fascist government that the universal Jewish problem can be resolved in one way only, the creation of a Jewish State," protested against the Fascist "veto" that this state should not be located in Palestine:

> How can we forget that Italy solemnly approved both the Balfour Declaration and the mandate in Palestine? . . . How can one explain

this new thesis of the Fascist government, which has maintained until now a benevolent and encouraging attitude toward the Zionist work in Palestine, whose goals have been extremely clear at all times: to find a solution to the anguishing Jewish problem in Europe by returning the Jews to the land of their ancestors with the opportunity of rebuilding a free and independent national life? On the other hand, is it really necessary to reaffirm that the Jews have never thought of creating a Jewish State anywhere else but in Palestine?[507]

Later, on the Zionist side, there were attempts to mend the breach and negotiate with Rome in some way, to avoid the *Informazione Diplomatica* from being used by the Arabs against the Jews in Palestine. Various initiatives in this direction had failed. In April Goldmann tried to secure another interview with Ciano but it was not granted.[508] In Jerusalem various Zionist representatives tried to contact Rome through the Consulate General[509] but were politely and coldly rebuffed by Mazzolini. A mission to Rome by Professor Chaim Wardi, lecturer in Italian at the Hebrew University of Jerusalem, did not go beyond the office of the Vice Director for Oriental Affairs at the Palazzo Chigi, who, responding to the request for an Italian "gesture" that would indicate the Zionists were not being abandoned by Italy to the sole mandatory power, answered that such a gesture did not appear necessary for now and invited him to come back in a few months[510]—this at the beginning of July 1938, one week before the publication of the famous manifesto of the racist "scientists"!

The relations between Fascism and Zionism had come to an end.

V.

The Crisis Deepens:
1935-1937

16.
The War in Ethiopia

The years 1935 to 1937 were crucial for the Fascist attitude toward the Jews as well as every other aspect of Fascist policy. At no other time did Mussolini appear to be so popular in Italy and Fascism so secure. The success of the war in Africa—which at first gave rise to uncertainty and aversion in many circles—galvanized the feelings of the Italians. The popular demonstrations of those years were undoubtedly sincere; the "day of the wedding ring"* was truly an act of faith and popular consensus, just as were the eight billion lire underwritten for the national bond in September 1935; the sanctions were greatly resented as being unfair by the overwhelming majority of the Italian people, and the victory and the foundation of the Empire were welcomed with an enthusiasm that equaled only the hope that they were based on. The historian can only agree with the words of a man who was among the very few who really felt the mood of Italy at the time, the head of the OVRA, Guido Leto:

> It can be safely and dispassionately said that during the years 1935-1936 the overwhelming majority of the Italian people supported

---

* In Italian the word for wedding ring, *la fede*, also means "faith"; to give one's most cherished possession made of gold was a highly symbolic, almost mystical, gesture. [NDT]

175

Mussolini, if not Fascism, and that Mussolini had even greater support from Italians residing overseas.

Politicians who had been cool to Fascism or shown opposition to the regime were changing their position, expressing approval or reserving judgment, while approval from people of all social strata poured in from everywhere.

The successful African campaign had created a spiritual consensus that exploded spontaneously during the demonstration in Piazza Venezia and other Italian cities on May 9, 1936, when Mussolini proclaimed the founding of the empire. Even the cautious judgment maintained by the King and almost all the members of the Royal House during the campaign disappeared, and many hoped that Mussolini would revise his policies to return to the Italian people, even gradually and in moderation, those fundamental freedoms which had been taken away.[511]

There were only a few small groups left opposed to Fascism, often unconnected to one another and rarely in touch with the anti-Fascist movement overseas. The latter was also divided and in crisis.[512] The Communist Party itself was on the defensive, so much so that it fell back on a sort of new tactic to "re-enter" politics, seeking an alliance with "Fascists who were in the opposition," in the name of the original Fascist principles.[513] The opposition was reduced, as Mussolini himself said, to a "meager group of intellectuals estranged from national life" who could do no harm and whose anti-Fascist action did not go very far beyond—with rare exceptions that fell immediately under the ax of the OVRA—keeping alive, in various workplaces, the principles of freedom and democracy and slowly influencing, from the teaching posts they often held, the souls and minds of some youths through daily contact with culture—the real culture, not the one issued by the Ministry of National Education—and its values.

Only the Spanish Civil War broke this solidarity with Mussolini. It gave new strength to anti-Fascism at home and overseas, reawakening some working-class elements—especially the longshoremen on the Genoa waterfront—and alerting others. The mass of the Italian people, somewhat disillusioned, not having seen its expectations fulfilled, and moreover, being called upon for renewed sacrifices, remained faithful to Mussolini.

For the discontent to spread and take shape, one has to wait for the alliance with Germany and the inherent danger of a war on very short notice.[514] Only then would a large number of Italians irrevocably distance themselves from Mussolini and Fascism—but it is best to stress that Mussolini and Fascism were not always seen as one and the same; many Italians during the war were pro-Mussolini while being, obviously not actively or effectively, anti-Fascists.

It is impossible to ignore this broad picture if we wish to understand the attitude of the Jews during those years. As Italians living among Italians, they behaved once again like all Italians and, in their vast majority, took the same positions. The greater contacts they had with foreign countries compared to other Italians did not influence them to the contrary. Beyond the fact that, even overseas, there was great sympathy for Italy and for Mussolini and that the Jews generally moved within expatriate Italian circles where such sympathies were very strong, two other important factors contributed to their continued faith in, and sympathy for, Fascist Italy: what was known and being said of Mussolini's help for their German co-religionists, and the very favorable conditions under which they were living in Italy, because of the government and popular feeling, even when compared to other European countries, including the democracies. The repeated statements by Mussolini that there was no Jewish question in Italy nor could one appear, together with the sense of how far removed anti-Semitism was from the minds of the Italian people and how indignantly they expressed their reactions to foreign excesses, created a sense of security in everyone's mind. The anti-Semitic tirades of some Fascist newspapers were not enough to end this sense of security: these were only present on the fringe, and while serious, they were not worrisome, and would never be approved by the Duce and the Italian people. Most would not change this attitude even when Fascism and Nazism came closer together; for most Jews, Germany was one thing and Italy another, and in Italy "certain things" would never happen. Anyone who warned of such possibilities was either an alarmist or an enemy of Italy, or at best someone who had been influenced by those who had witnessed the German horrors and was used to seeing dark shadows everywhere.

It is within this climate that the events of the years 1935 to 1937 should be considered; on the one hand, they were to be, for the majority of Italian Jews, years of peaceful work, of hope, faith, and commitment to the collective feelings of their homeland; on the other hand, they were also, for a small group of those same Jews who understood the edge of the abyss on which they, and Italy itself, were standing, years of relentless anxiety, which became heavier as the phases of Fascist policy tightened the links of the chain that was inevitably drawing Italy closer to Germany. Only in 1937 did this linkage become obvious to everyone, while at the same time the attacks against the Jews increased progressively and became more focused. If up to then these attacks had been the prerogative of small, well-identified circles, they now were material for growing numbers of people and found their way into newspapers and magazines that had not carried them until then, so much so—as shown in the preceding chapter—as to bring about the worried protests not only of the Italian Jews but also of the international Zionist organizations. And, worst of all, anti-Semitism was converting many high officials of the regime, led by Mussolini himself. Given the documents we have studied, and we do not think any new elements can be brought up reversing the terms of the problem, in this conversion, the pressure coming from Germany and the Nazis was decisive but not direct. The Nazis repeated their warnings about the "Jewish menace" during meetings with the Fascists and upheld their anti-Semitic policies; however, not until 1943 did they officially pressure Rome to persecute the Jews. The alignment of Italian policy with that of Germany was regarded as necessary and desired by Mussolini and the majority of the Fascists as a requirement for a "totalitarian" building of the Axis. Typically, those most opposed to the alliance with the Germans, Balbo for example, were also opposed to the anti-Semitic measures. To attempt, as do many today, even among the Jews, to attribute to the Nazis *direct* responsibility for the Italian racist campaign is not only not supported by any tangible proof but amounts to an attempt, as Italians, to evade a measure of responsibility. Just as in Germany, there have been, and still are, Germans who deny the existence of the death camps and seek to minimize the Nazi horrors, there are also those in Italy who are revolted by the very idea that some Italians, even though they were Fascists, could have committed such a monstrous crime and could think, at least up to September 8, 1943, even on a level that did not involve the spilling of blood, of introducing into Italy a policy so foreign to the mentality, the tradition, and the disposition of the Italian people. They want to shake off collective responsibility and blame it on the Nazis and seek in Hitler's "order" a kind of alibi that, had any such order been given, would excuse nothing.

We do not mean to imply that there was no Nazi pressure brought to bear on Italy to align itself with Germany's racial policies, but that these pressures were indirect. There was constant harping on the "Jewish menace," insisting that the *facts* demonstrate to Mussolini the impossibility that between allies there could be such a glaring difference in attitude, which could have resulted in the absurdity that while Germany was expelling and exterminating its Jews they could find refuge in Italy and, worse, that at the same table could be seated working together a bureaucrat or industrialist or Nazi general who had persecuted the Jews and an Italian Jewish bureaucrat, industrialist, or general. More pressure was brought on Mussolini by those Fascists who were notoriously anti-Semitic, such as Preziosi, Nazi agents, or men who had embraced the Italian-German alliance because of conviction or self-interest, turning it into their political "trump card." It should also be remembered that the anti-Semitic poison dripping for so long into Italy by the likes of Preziosi and Interlandi, as well as various Nazi agents, began to take hold precisely during these years. While the old pre-Fascist functionaries within the bureaucracy, the diplomatic corps, and the army were disappearing by attrition or through decisions of the leadership, with them the nucleus of the original Fascist leaders also left the scene and while they could easily be blamed for many things, being too favorable to the Germans was never one of them. A new generation was coming to the forefront of Italian life, morally corrupted and culturally deprived by fifteen years of Fascist regime, having experienced nothing but Fascism, and who had not

179

gone through the energizing effects, good or bad, of the First World War—whose only wartime experiences were the easy and barbarous ones of Ethiopia and Spain. Having developed within this atmosphere, they thought as propagandists and careerists at heart, and if on occasion they felt that things were not happening as they should in Italy, rather than investigating the root causes, they attributed it to "sabotage," to the Italian inability to go all the way, or to the lack of socialization of the regime and were inclined to react by turning a sympathetic eye to the monolithic character and the "perfection" of Nazi Germany. This symptom should not be ignored; to take just one example, it appears very clearly when one reads the reports from Italian diplomats overseas. As generations rotated, these reports tend to become less and less interesting and lose, with rare exceptions, any personal input, bouncing back to Rome what Rome was saying or wanted to hear said. These diplomats did not hide their anti-Semitic prejudices and when writing about their visit to the leaders of the local Jewish community, limited themselves to commenting on "the lack of cleanliness of the people and their dwellings . . . which explains why for many centuries these people have been seeking in vain a fixed place in the world"; contrary to their older colleagues who castigated what was happening in Germany under their very eyes, they reported more and more dryly on the Nazi anti-Semitic campaign and its horrors and actually ended by praising it:

> This is the only great and revolutionary example in contemporary history of *filtering* a people, isolating the extraneous molecules . . . with this colossal effort National Socialism is confident that it can bring the Reich to a sublimation of its characteristics, to a reawakening of its deepest roots.[515]

All this being said, the official relations between Fascism and the Jews in 1935-1937 were good, and in some cases, excellent.

The Jews, as we have stated, participated in the general enthusiasm for the African conflict. Besides those mobilized, many went as volunteers, just as, but in much smaller numbers, for the Spanish Civil War—a Jew, Alberto Liuzzi, who died in Spain was decorated with the gold medal for military valor.[516] For the religious support of all these fighting men in Africa, the War Ministry and the Union of the Communities reached an agreement to create a "military rabbinate" that named three chaplains.[517] The participation in the "day of the wedding ring" and the offering of gold was also extremely broad. The Jews took part in this not just as individuals, but also as a community; some of them offered "all those gold and silver objects that were not prevented by a specific ritual from being given as gifts."[518] Offerings from Jews came in from overseas as far away as the Belgian Congo and Rhodesia.[519] The victory and proclamation of the empire were welcomed by the Jewish press with real enthusiasm, as the triumph of lawful right and truth over arbitrariness and lies[520] and were celebrated even in the temples.

The conquest of Ethiopia was seen by many Jews not simply as a national event but also as affecting Jewish life. In the region near Gondar and Lake Tana lived the Falasha, a people of the Cushitic race who practiced the Jewish religion. From the beginning of this century Italian Jews had shown interest in these African co-religionists and had established some relations with them. There had even existed in Florence, for some time, a Pro-Falasha Committee. The conquest of Ethiopia increased this interest, making the relationship stronger and closer and actively working at lifting the moral, civil and religious life of the Falasha. This was not just illustrated and widely discussed by the Jewish organizations and the press[521] but also quickly set in motion. At the beginning of June 1936 the Union contacted the Minister of Colonies, Alessandro Lessona, and it was decided that the Union would be in charge of assisting and organizing the Ethiopian Jews and would immediately dispatch its representatives to meet with the Falasha and organize two Communities, at Addis Ababa and Dire Dawa.[522] This difficult mission was entrusted to the attorney Carlo Alberto Viterbo, a member of the Union council, and Dr. Umberto Scazzocchio, former secretary of the Rome Community and a resident of Asmara. Viterbo left at the end of July for Italian East Africa. Arriving in Asmara he was received on August 22 by Viceroy Marshal Rodolfo Graziani, who expressed his sympathy and understanding for the Jewish people and assured him "that all religions would be respected within the borders of the empire and the Falasha people, well known for dedication to hard work, would certainly benefit from the benevolent attention of the Government." With a decree of September 19, the Community of Addis Ababa was created and Viterbo was named its commissioner by the government. At the end of November, after laying the foundations of the new Community, Viterbo traveled to the region where the Falasha lived. In the meantime, in August, they had declared their loyalty to General Pirzio-Biroli.[523] The project of creating a second Community at Dire Dawa was temporarily set aside. Accompanied by the director of the Falasha school of the capital, Emmanuele Taamrat, Viterbo crossed impracticable areas on a mule, at times outside the area under Italian military control, visited the largest Falasha villages—Dembia, Sechelt, Belesa, Uoghera—and met with the leaders and populations of the villages and military authorities.[524] The first tangible contacts between Italian and Ethiopian Jewry were thus established. In the years up to the outbreak of the war these would continue with some regularity, and various Falasha came to Italy to study.[525]

Fascism responded to this activity by the Jews with sympathy on the surface while secretly preparing racist and discriminatory measures. In August 1935 Mussolini once again had a meeting with Rabbi David Prato to discuss the problems of Italian-Egyptian Jewry.[526] In 1936 Mondadori published the first two volumes of the *Cronache del Regime* by Roberto Forges Davanzati; the radio programs broadcast by EIAR, without softening in any way the violent attack of December 1934, "Natale cristiano e solstizio razzista" [Christian Christmas, and Racist Solstice], were aimed at Nazi racism, "an historical and spiritual absurdity because it seeks to erase two thousand years of history and faith."[527] In February 1937, on Rhodes, the "quadrumvir" Cesare Maria De Vecchi held a friendly meeting with leaders of the local Jewish community.[528] Mussolini himself traveled to Libya one month later to receive the famous "sword of Islam" and visited the Jewish quarter of Tripoli, displaying a lot of sympathy for the people—so much so that a French journalist, Maurice Montabré, reporting on the trip for *L'Intransigeant* on March 19, 1937, could write, half joking, "Will it be said now that Mr. Mussolini is the 'protector of Zion' just as he is the 'protector of Islam'? And will Germany take umbrage of the former as much as England was worried about the latter?" And in June of the same year, to deny the accusation of anti-Semitism prompted by the publication of the book by Paolo Orano, *Gli ebrei in Italia* [The Jews in Italy], and the journalistic dispute that followed, the Duce even declared to *Il Progresso Italo-Americano*, whose editor Generoso Pope had traveled to Rome especially for the interview:

> I can authorize you to declare and inform the American Jews as soon as you return to New York that their worries for their brothers living in Italy are unwarranted and are only the result of mean-minded information. You are authorized to point out that the Jews of Italy have received, are receiving, and shall continue to receive the same treatment as that awarded to any other Italian citizen, that no form of racial or religious discrimination is on my mind, and that I remain faithful to the policy of equality in eyes of the law and freedom of religion.[529]

The daily routine of official relations between the Jews and the government caused no reason to doubt these declarations. We have seen how the military Rabbinate had been created in 1935 and how, in 1936, the relations with the Falasha had been approved and facilitated. Many other episodes should be added to these, for instance the authorization to reprint school texts for the Community schools,[530] but it would be useless: up to 1938 the Italian government and Mussolini had kept secret their decision to introduce anti-Semitic legislation into Italy and actually denied such intentions, several times, behaving toward the Union and the Communities as though nothing was happening.

17.

The Tripoli Incidents

B efore discussing the publication of Paolo Orano's book and other anti-Semitic declarations in the press during this period, it is necessary to describe the incidents that took place in Tripoli between the end of 1936 and the beginning of 1937. These incidents, which caused much comment overseas, have been considered by many as one of the first signs of Fascist anti-Semitism.

But, in our opinion, they cannot be categorized as such and there are many reasons that prove this point. First of all, the Tripoli incidents, as they occurred, were not thought of as signs of anti-Semitism even by the vast majority of Italian Jews. Second, they were not considered as such—a very telling fact—by the most anti-Semitic Fascist newspapers and magazines, which completely ignored them, just like the overwhelming majority of the Italian press. Third, the government official involved was Italo Balbo, who at the time was governor of Libya—a man who could certainly not be accused of anti-Semitism, and who was thought of overseas as "pro-Semitic" and suspected, by some, of being a Jew himself, and was among the most important leaders of Fascism. In a few months Balbo would be the first one, as was typical of this proud and honest man—rightly described by his biographer Antonio Aniante as "the Trotsky of Fascism"[532]— to take a position clearly and without hiding it from anyone, against all discrimination and persecution. Shortly after the Tripoli incidents, during the visit to Libya by King Victor Emmanuel, Balbo would discuss the announced anti-Semitic measures directly with the King—"I'm here in Africa and I hear certain things about the Jews. We certainly won't be imitating the Germans!…"[533]—and he would repeat the same views to Ciano a few months later.[534] During the meeting of the Grand Council of October 6, 1938, he would be the one to resolutely oppose the measures decided by Mussolini. Considering all these factors, it is absurd to think that Balbo would light a fuse in Tripoli with such obvious results. But even without these initial reasons, a dispassionate and objective examination of this sad episode will immediately reveal that the Tripoli incidents were caused exclusively by local disputes, which had nothing to do with anti-Semitism, and even while deploring the violent methods used by Balbo—it should also be remembered that the incidents took place in a colony and not in Italy, and that the Jews were indigenous to Libya and not Italian citizens—it seems that the objective responsibilities were not solely attributable to government actions in this instance.

There had been some serious incidents in 1932 between Fascists and Jews in Tripoli. The situation improved quickly, during the intervening years, without completely erasing all reasons for friction.[535] The Libyan Jews were numerically strong and very much attached to their traditions, even to ancient practices that had long before been shed or modernized by Italian Jews, and were more apt, if not to clash, at least to stand out in a society undergoing rapid change such as Libya during those years. Old privileges that the Jews of Tripoli had enjoyed since Turkish domination were thought to be absolute rights which they were not willing to give up. The "pacification" conducted with a rather heavy hand by Badoglio and Graziani inside Libya had caused much suspicion and bitterness which were colored by local nuances because, while they appeared in a society where there were hardly ever any incidents, the Jews were living—in social and material conditions that were far superior—within a society where Arabs represented the overwhelming majority. To this we should add that the Jewish minority, particularly in the Tripoli Community, lacked a leadership of undisputed prestige and was torn by internal dissension. A number of emigrants to Palestine left during the years 1932-1933, demonstrating a complex state of affairs that worried central and local Italian authorities.[536] For several years, the local government attempted to face up to the situation by acceding to many demands made by the Libyan Jewish Community, mostly through the social promotion of newer generations. A determined effort was made to broaden elementary and secondary instruction: in the ten years from 1922-1923 to 1932-1933 the Jewish school population in Tripolitania increased from 1,340 to 3,209.[537] The pupils of these schools were allowed, at first, to not attend school on Saturdays. A ruling issued by the governor in the middle of the 1932-1933 school year made Saturday school attendance mandatory and its avoidance punishable by dismissal. The decision caused a lot of animosity; some families accepted it, while many others refused to send their children to school on Saturdays, and the result was a certain number of dismissals.[538] The president of the Union immediately went to Tripoli, and the incident was temporarily smoothed over by transferring all decisions on the issue to the school superintendent. A real solution was necessary, and not only regarding the school issue. The Union also wished to create two new Communities at Misurata and Derna but the government rejected the request, worried as it was about the difficult situation facing those of Tripoli and Benghazi.[539] Under these conditions the Union decided to send an experienced rabbi in an attempt to bring the situation under control for those Communities and create the foundation of a Grand Rabbinate of Libya. The choice was the Rabbi of Padua, Gustavo Castelbolognesi, who had been in Tripoli in 1933 for the school crisis, and he was duly appointed.

The Castelbolognesi mission[540] was immediately viewed with sympathy by the central government, which even paid part of his travel expenses of one thousand lire from the Ministry of Colonies, and it coincided with the beginning of Balbo's tenure as governor. Castelbolognesi met the new governor as soon as he arrived on February 19. The very friendly meeting produced no results; Balbo wanted to gain time and, for the moment, was reluctant to solve the Saturday problem.[541] Time and patience were required to find a solution to all pending questions, and Castelbolognesi had neither, since he was to return to his home base in Padua. This created further complications: while Padua's Community wanted him back, Tripoli's Community did not want to see him leave, and the government, impatient with the Union's inability to solve the problem and find an acceptable candidate for Tripoli's rabbinical opening, did not hide its discontent, refusing even to pay for Castelbolognesi's return home. At the end of March he quietly went on "leave" and once he had settled matters in Padua, returned to Tripoli in November. The situation had deteriorated because of the extension of the obligation of school attendance on Saturdays to Benghazi; even the request for a Grand Rabbinate, rather than calming the people down, had embittered them further, leading many Jews to believe that this could bring about excessive centralization and bureaucratization of religious life. Some even wanted to create a Libyan Union of the Communities in Tripoli and a High Rabbinical Court.[542]

Balbo was mostly interested in increasing economic and social activities that were already in place—silver and ivory works, a trade school, etc.—and the creation of new structures, such as day care centers, in order to reduce the large number of Jews who had "no known occupation." He found himself quickly engulfed in a series

186

of problems far removed from his temperament and psychological make-up, since he was used to the assimilated and civilized Jews of Italy and of Ferrara in particular. These problems appeared to be absurdities for the most part, attributable to closedminded attitudes and resistance to his own innovative efforts, which also ran the risk of creating difficulties with the Arabs, who were always scrutinizing him and were ready to interpret any concession made to the Jews as signs of favoritism, which was not part of his plan and would have amounted to a political mistake. Any concession made to the Jews would have made another one to the Arabs necessary and vice versa. He was to tell the king during the aforementioned conversation: "The Arabs yell and then they need the Jews as much as they need bread and air. You see, here in Libya, they quarrel, they hate each other, they curse each other—but they wind up being allies on every occasion."[543] Nevertheless, the local government—at Sacerdoti's request from Rome, where he had approached Mussolini[544]—tried to fulfill the suggestions made by Castelbolognesi. As a long report to the Union concerning his activity in Tripoli from November 1934 to May 1935 shows, the local authorities tried to balance the budget of the Community, find a location for the day care center, authorize the school administration to lend space in the schools for Hebrew language instruction, and, in general, solve many small practical problems; no objections were made to the creation of the Grand Rabbinate as well.[545] However, Balbo and the local authorities were firm regarding the Saturday problem. For them it was a question of principle, of order and uniformity. When Castelbolognesi repeated his request, Balbo was final: "I can tell you right away on this issue that the answer is definitely no." The refusal was accompanied by a promise to create a section for Jewish students. "The special section for Jews in secondary schools without the regular Saturday time schedule will be created. I promise you that." In the meantime the school superintendent was ready to accept the stopgap solution of weekly excuses from the parents.[546] However, the Saturday issue was important not just to the schools. Toward the end of December the problem came to a head for the freight forwarders who refused to work on Saturdays and either lost customers or had to pay additional storage fees in the general warehouse.[547] Here as well, a short-term solution was found, through an agreement among all freight forwarders and a government regulation increasing the free storage of merchandise from three to five days. These were all temporary solutions. In March, Balbo told Castelbolognesi in no uncertain terms that he would need to push for assimilation and persuade the Jews to open their stores on Saturdays; Castelbolognesi answered dryly that, as a rabbi, it was his duty to defend and encourage the true Jewish religious traditions.[548]

While the issues were caught in a quagmire of opposite demands and fundamentally conflicting positions, a seemingly unimportant incident was suddenly to bring everything to a head. An ordinary love affair between two young Jews, the man being thirty-five and the girl only fifteen, ended in a shotgun wedding in front of witnesses, but, because of the high social position of both families, between April and May 1935 it turned into a serious incident. The rabbinical court was asked to rule on the validity of the marriage ceremony; however, the problem immediately involved both the Community and the Italian authorities. Balbo, due to the fact that the girl was under age and at the insistence of her father, informed Castelbolognesi that the marriage would have to be annulled; the Community, already divided by deep dissension, immediately went into crisis. The crisis was officially unrelated to the question of whether or not the marriage was to be annulled, but it must have weighed heavily due to the political significance attached to the intervention by the governor and the importance of the families concerned. The wealthier and more modern Jews, already assimilated or in the process of assimilation, would have preferred a more flexible attitude that would convince the local and central governments of their pro-Italian allegiance and make their moral and legal status akin to that of their co-religionists in Italy. Along these lines, in previous years, when Badoglio was governor, requests had been made so that Jews from Tripoli could serve in the army; the answer was that this should take place step by step and "take into account the degree of evolution of the psyche of the Jews of Tripoli."[549] In this new case Castelbolognesi only made sure that the decision of the rabbinical court would be in accordance with rabbinical laws. This lack of "good will" irritated Balbo, who informed the rabbi in so many words: "the commission [of the Community], not you, is following the government's recommendations."[550] Castelbolognesi answered by submitting his resignation to the Union. President Ravenna, who was now very worried by the turn of events, asked him to reconsider, pointing out that the situation was serious enough without the added irritant of a "political" resignation and that he should consider withdrawing it.[551] Perhaps he had been "excessively harsh" with the leadership of the Community and should actually try to find a solution by meeting with Balbo alone, to convince him that his position was based on "the deepest Italian feelings" and that it was not such a good idea to clash with the traditionalism and orthodoxy of the Jews, running the risk of turning the Jews of Tripoli into "a rebel group when they had always been absolutely loyal."

Unfortunately things were getting out of hand: at the beginning of June, on the same day the rabbinical court issued its decision validating the wedding, an order coming directly from Balbo banned Castelbolognesi from Libya. Felice Ravenna and Dante Lattes immediately traveled to Tripoli to try and patch up this serious dispute. Balbo, with whom they met on June 28, 1935, remained unmoved.[552] First, he harshly attacked the work of Castelbolognesi, who was seeking to portray him as an anti-Semite—he, who was the greatest friend of the Jews, from Rothschild down to the mayor of Ferrara and many others. From the rabbi he would have expected "action that would elevate the civil and social status of the Jews of Tripoli and draw them closer to Italian civilization, persuading them to shed some of their old habits that, when compared to the western Jews and to the intense pace of the modern world, appeared somewhat out of date"; instead he had found in him an obstacle to this task. As for the specific episode of the wedding that had caused the decision to ban Castelbolognesi, Balbo found it "detrimental to the moral education of the Jewish population" and feared that, should it be repeated, it would lead to a relaxation of family morality and the eventual dissolution of the family. It was of no avail to try to explain that the rabbinical court had issued its judgment within the boundaries of rabbinical jurisprudence. After discussions lasting for two hours the following statement was issued:

> His Excellency the Governor of Libya has met for a long and cordial discussion with attorney Felice Ravenna, President of the Union of the Jewish Communities of Italy, and examined with him the conditions of the Jews in Libya. The Governor expressed much gratitude to attorney Ravenna for the hard-working, well-disciplined and moral Jewish population, which is actively participating in Mussolini's new Italy beyond the seas.[553]

The statement was obviously intended for the outside world; all the deeper issues were still open and unresolved. This state of affairs did, in fact, bring about the serious incidents of 1936-1937.

It was decided by the General Commissioner of Tripoli to enact a decree dated November 14, 1936 stipulating that, as of December 1 all stores selling goods to the public located outside the old city of Tripoli, as well as those located in Corso Vittorio Emmanuele between Piazza Castello and Piazza dell'Orologio, would have to be open every day except Sundays. The decree caused unhappiness and negative reactions in Jewish circles, and as the time for its enactment neared there were some small disturbances that were immediately and harshly suppressed: on December 2, two Jews—Sion Barda and Nahis Saul—who had participated were each publicly flogged with ten strokes of the *kurbash*, and a third person, who could not withstand flogging, according to a medical examination, was sentenced to three months in prison.[554] The uproar in international Jewish circles was enormous: newspapers and well-known individuals protested, among them David Prato and the Ashkenazy Grand Rabbi of Jerusalem.[555] In spite of these protests, the decree was upheld and enforced with extreme harshness: those who did not open their stores on Saturdays had their license revoked and the most unruly among them were flogged.[556] But the floggings were few, not two hundred and fourteen as reported by Reuters and *Tunis Soir*, as the Rabbi of Tripoli Hai Gabizon admitted in a letter to *L'Avvenire di Tripoli* dated December 23, 1936. Balbo also, contrary to what he had thought of doing at first and to what certain foreign newspapers had written, took no action against the

Rabbi of Tripoli, even though he had advocated ignoring the decree. These were, in sum, the Tripoli incidents of 1936-1937[557] and their beginnings in 1932. There is no doubt that the measures taken against the protesters were excessive and not at all civilized—even though flogging the natives was quite a normal practice for most colonial powers—but we still cannot consider the Tripoli incidents as examples of anti-Semitism; just a few months later some Arabs were flogged in Misurata as well. We believe that these incidents were only an unhappy episode of colonial policy, where the unyielding loyalty of a minority of Jews to the dictates of their religion and customs clashed with the energy of a man who was used to commanding and dealing with highly civilized and assimilated Jews. In the final analysis, most cautious foreign commentators regarding the Tripoli episodes of 1935 and 1936-1937 came to that conclusion.[558]

18.

The Growing Press
Campaign Against the Jews

The year 1935 was rather quiet when it came to anti-Semitic propaganda. Following the ups, and now mostly the downs, of Italian-German relations, even the newspapers that in earlier years had been attacking the Jews, now toned down considerably. At the beginning of the year these same newspapers took positions against Nazi racism.[559] Rather than real anti-Semitic attacks, all of 1935 would be marked by a series of minor jabs. Besides the usual champions of anti-Semitism—*La vita italiana, Liguria del popolo,* etc.— the only serious attack was published at the end of the year by *L'azione coloniale,*[560] but more than an example of internal anti-Semitism, it was a reflection of the anti-Jewish policy being followed by some Italian representatives at the League of Nations at the time. This general opinion is confirmed by the many reports and news items regarding the trial held during the spring in Bern about the authenticity, or lack of it, of the *Protocols,* which ended with a few Nazis being found guilty of having distributed the infamous pamphlet in Switzerland.

Things got progressively worse in 1936: the improvement of German-Italian relations and the Spanish Civil War had immediate repercussions. Satirical newspapers began the trend, in particular *Marc Aurelio,* with many others quickly following suit. The issue used most frequently was the Jewish origin of Bolshevism or, at least, the massive presence of Jews within it. In October this thesis was revived by no less than *La civiltà cattolica* in a long article entitled "La questione giudaica" [The Jewish Question] which must be considered unmistakably as preparatory to the encyclical of the coming March, *Mit brennender Sorge,* against Hitler's racism. In this article, the Jesuits tried to differentiate between Catholic and Nazi anti-Semitism.[561] The writer simply updated the articles of 1890 by underlining the relationship between Judaism and Bolshevism. This was an unambiguous and not a contradictory relationship according to the author; the Jews were in fact "masters of money," and, at the same time, the soul of socialism and communism because of their wish to dominate the world.

> The fastest way to reach that goal is through brutal and dictatorial Communism. The idea is to replace the still limited and relatively weak capitalism of Europe and America with a world pan-capitalism having absolute power . . . At the root of the rage of the Jew to get rich and speculate with money, which is the key to enjoying all the wealth in this life, there is an almost materialistic, or rather, temporal concept of life . . . Also within the Jewish anxiety and the all too frequent participation of Jews in the social revolutions of the moment, there is their materialistic and temporal messianic concept . . . For the rationalist and revolutionary Jew who doesn't believe in the Scriptures, the latent messianism of his soul is transformed in the aspiration for the ideal reign of justice that the Communists dream of, to be pursued at the cost of death and ruin, as Rathenau admitted and as was practiced by the bloody Bela Kun and Szamuelly in Hungary, by the Bolshevik Jews in Russia, and by others among the foreign agents who are now so horribly active in Spain.

The solutions the author proposed included isolation, stating that it was important to "make them harmless, with methods attuned to modern times, but excluding any type of persecution."

The tendency to consider the Spanish conflict as a struggle in defense of Catholic civilization against Communism was embraced by *La civiltà cattolica* and also by many Fascist and Catholic circles. A prime example is the short volume published in 1936 in Empoli by the member of parliament, Alfredo Romanini, *Ebrei-Cristianesimo-Fascismo* [Jews, Christianity, Fascism], widely acclaimed by many well-respected members of the Catholic clergy[562] and, in spite of its lack of interest and value even compared to the most antiquated anti-Semitic literature, can be considered the first truly contemporary Italian anti-Semitic pamphlet.

In spite of their importance, the examples of *La civiltà cattolica* and Romanini were not the most telling signs of the changing climate. The most important and significant statement once again appeared in Roberto Farinacci's newspaper, *Il regime fascista.*[563] On September 12, 1936 an unsigned editorial appeared entitled "Una tremenda requisitoria" [A terrible indictment]. Using a speech given by Goebbels a few days before at the Nazi congress in Nuremberg, where Hitler's minister had violently attacked Communism and pointed out that in Spain and France all the leaders of "subversion" were Jewish, the anonymous writer, after reminding the reader that Fascism had been in the forefront of the anti-Bolshevik struggle, addressed the issue of the Italian Jews:

> We must confess that the Jews, who are an infinitesimal minority in Italy, even if they intrigued in a thousand ways to grab posts in finance, the economy and the schools, did not resist our revolutionary march in any way. We must confess that they always paid their taxes, obeyed the laws, and did their duty during the war as well.
>
> However, they do have a passive attitude that can give rise to suspicion. Why have they never said a single word that could convince all Italians that they fulfill their duties as citizens out of love, not out of fear or because it's useful?
>
> Why are they not open about their intention to share their responsibilities with the Jews of the world whose only objective is the

193

triumph of the Jewish international? Why have they not revolted against their co-religionists who are responsible for mass murders, the destruction of churches, and the spreading of hatred, and are the bold and mean-minded exterminators of Christians?

There is the feeling that soon all of Europe will be in the midst of a religious war. Don't they realize it?

We are already convinced that from many quarters people will cry out: we are Fascist Jews. It's not enough. They must furnish the mathematical proof of being Fascists first and Jews afterward.

It was a very harsh attack, more so than the one of 1934; this time it was not officially leveled, as before, against the Zionists but against all Jews. The impression and the comments it generated were enormous. And Farinacci did not stop there. Just as in 1934, some Jews wrote to *Il regime fascista* and other newspapers to refute these accusations. Seizing upon one of these statements, on September 19, *Il regime fascista* answered in an editorial with the threatening title "Perché provocarci?" [Why provoke us?]. Farinacci, in his unsigned editorial, laid down his cards:

We are not anti-Semitic out of predisposition. This is so true that it was far from our intention to engage in any real anti-Semitism; in our little articles we were seeking only one very definite result: to avoid pushing away from us, at this time of intense international Jewish turmoil, all our compatriots of the Mosaic religion.

That Farinacci had little sympathy for the Jews was a well-known fact, but he had never, in his previous statements, gone so far alongside Preziosi—whose magazine had already been portraying itself as the "monthly publication of *Il regime fascista*"—as to engage in open anti-Semitism. The Jews, faced with such blatant words, reacted in two ways, as in 1934: some quickly proclaimed their absolute loyalty and dedication to Fascism, while others tried to fight the accusations. Farinacci honored the most noteworthy among the first group, Commander Jarach, President of the Community of Milan, by publishing his rebuttal in its entirety on September 20. The others received their answer in a new editorial in the same issue of *Il regime fascista*, "Non divaghiamo!" [Let us not stray from the point!], in which he stated pointedly: "There exists in Geneva a world Jewish Parliament, where even Italy is well represented." To prove the existence of the Jewish international, he "revealed" that a Spanish Communist had been arrested in Poland with a large amount of money collected from Polish Jews.

Faced with such massive attacks,[564] quite unlike those of 1934, and their spread to other Fascist newspapers, the highest official authorities representing Italian Jewry had to take a position to try to stop the campaign and rebut accusations that could impress a public unaware of what went on behind the scenes, and to avoid having their silence appear as lacking in arguments to answer Farinacci, or worse, as proof of stubbornness. On September 24, *Il regime fascista* published a long letter from the President of the Union, Felice Ravenna, that was firm and noble but, for obvious reasons, too cautious.[565] In the letter Ravenna, after reminding the readers that Mussolini never used the issues of race or religion and that Italian Jews had always done their duty, recalled that the "Italian contribution" to the Jewish International had only been to help their co-religionists who were being persecuted in other countries, that the Italian delegates to the World Jewish Congress in Geneva had been expressly authorized to participate by the Fascist government, and that during the proceedings "the name of Italy had been widely cheered." These were not, however arguments that could stop a man like Farinacci; he followed up Ravenna's letter with two thick columns of commentary in which he not only reiterated and sharpened his previous accusations but, for the first time, hinted at possible anti-Jewish measures in Italy as well:

> It's true, yes, that the Duce has not felt the need, so far, to introduce differences of race or religion in Italy, but a few Italian Jews want to be different from Italians of other religions by participating in campaigns for Zionism and in the proceedings of the World Jewish Congress.

That "so far" was, in fact, the announcement of the impending racial campaign.

A more forceful position appeared almost at the same time in a very long article, "In risposta alle pubblicazioni di *Il regime fascista*"

[Reply to the articles in *Il regime fascista*]. In *La nostra bandiera*, "Il patriottismo ed il fascismo degli ebrei italiani" [The patriotic and Fascist feelings of Italian Jews]—the issue is dated February 16, but was actually published several days later—disputes Farinacci's editorials up to those of the 19th and 20th. Even though it took its lead from him and criticized the Union, as we shall see below, and even though it was written in strictly Fascist terms, the answer of *La nostra bandiera* did not mince any words. It was not just defensive, nor limited to recalling Mussolini's recent statements against anti-Semitism in general and the fact that it did not exist in Italy, and proclaiming the Fascist loyalty of many Italian Jews; it also decidedly took the counteroffensive: accusations against the Italian Jews were labeled as "maneuvers by international anti-Semitism in its own crazy attempt to drag Fascism in its wake,"[566] maneuvers that also included some Italian participants. The attacks appearing in the Italian press were nothing but "the echo of the vehement anti-Semitic and anti-Jewish crusade proclaimed in Nuremberg." *La nostra bandiera* added, in a somewhat contorted but nevertheless clear passage, that even before the recent Nuremberg congress that had seen the beginning of the campaign in *Il regime fascista*, the anti-Semitic crusade had been proclaimed in Italy "due to other probable influences which cannot, however, be documented." And at this point, it went on to note how "strangely" identical the arguments used by *Il regime fascista* were to those being circulated by the agency *Oriente*, "which seems to aspire to become the mouthpiece of the artificial Italian anti-Semitism just making its first appearance."[567]

At its apex, the anti-Semitic campaign was suddenly halted. There were some more short comments in a few newspapers and even some violent remarks, but for a few months, until the following April, when Paolo Orano's book was published, it died down. To keep it going until Mussolini was ready to make a decision was practically impossible even for someone like Farinacci, and this time there would be no major incident that could revive it as in 1934. It is also possible, perhaps, that the attacks in *Il regime fascista* had a specific purpose going well beyond the more general wish to keep the issue in the forefront; it cannot be excluded that they were intended to keep the pressure on Mussolini in anticipation of Ciano's trip to Germany in October.[568] Beyond this target, with secret agreements not going past a few specific problems—collaboration in Spain and the policy toward England—the initial purpose of the attacks had disappeared.

While the press campaign died down, its poison was beginning to spread. A few incidents began before Farinacci's attacks; we mention them only now for the sake of clarity, and because they were used politically only around mid-November 1936. An anti-Semitic demonstration, the first in Italy in many years, had taken place in Ferrara in June. On the walls of some houses appeared graffiti such as "Viva il Duce—Morte agli Ebrei" [Long live the Duce—Death to the Jews]. According to the investigation conducted by the carabinieri at the request of the Ministry of the Interior, it surfaced that there was some malcontent in the city of Ferrara against the Jews. According to the report dated July 8, 1936 and seen by Mussolini on the 10th, written by the commanding general of the carabinieri, Riccardo Moizo,[569] the immediate causes of the graffiti were the many failing grades given to students during final exams: the students were protesting against the school principals, who happened to be Jewish. This unhappiness among the students was actually part of a certain popular anger against the influence of Jews in city affairs, and, according to some, was the beginning of an anti-Jewish campaign. The Jewish population in Ferrara, according to the report, numbered about eight hundred persons, all of them generally "active, diligent and thrifty," who "had never been singled out as having any political affiliation, nor does it appear that they can be tied to any abuses or prejudices; they are loyal to the Regime and national institutions." But because of these very qualities, many have reached "good social and economic status and positions of leadership": the mayor, the head of the provincial administration, the secretary of the provincial economic council, the judge at the local court, two high school principals, the principal of the day care centers, two directors of the Bank of Italy, the president of the school of agriculture, and the president of the Fascist provincial association for commerce, as well as various members of local commissions, were all Jewish. This, according to the same report, was the root cause of the discontent. The episode did not reach the Italian press but did find its way to Mussolini and the Fascist Grand Council during its meeting of November 18. There is unfortunately no record of the reactions of the Grand Council members nor of the positions they took—there is no trace of it in the "Foglio d'ordini" [Marching Orders] of the PNF—just as we do not know whether Mussolini introduced the issue to the Grand Council himself or at someone else's request. Such information would give us a much better understanding of the episode. There are various possible interpretations of this incident, as a spontaneous demonstration of anti-Semitism, as a way of applying pressure organized by anti-Semitic Fascists, or as a struggle between Fascist groups, in particular an attack against Balbo by anti-Balbo forces, since he was notoriously pro-Jewish and had personal ties to many of the most important Jews in Ferrara. The most likely explanation is that the graffiti at Ferrara were part of a pressure operation.

There is no doubt that during the closing months of 1936 and the beginning of 1937 Nazi agents and Fascist groups supportive of the policy of alliance with Germany made significant efforts to foster anti-Semitism and create an anti-Jewish obsession within public opinion to be used on Mussolini, whose uncertainty and hesitation on the subject were well known, and manipulate him into breaking relations with the rest of the world and make the decisive commitment of complete alignment with Hitler. We have seen the hints in *La nostra bandiera*; to these we may add the letter addressed by Eucardio Momigliano to Sommi Picenardi, about the general accusation of *La nostra bandiera* that also mentions a specific case. The letter not only alludes to the "underlying anti-Semitic campaign" conducted by Preziosi, a few satirical journalists and "one or other Roman daily suffering from chronic financial problems," but also mentions a specific incident that took place in Milan during that time: "In the last few days a Milan art magazine was offered the sum of 70 thousand lire to begin an anti-Semitic campaign within the art world." During the Nazi Party congress at Nuremberg the Germans had sent invitations to various Fascist leaders, selecting them from among those who appeared most favorable to anti-Semitism. According to the Cairo newspaper *Al*

Abram, of February 21, 1937, during this time Tullio Cianetti, taking part in a Nazi rally for the labor front alongside the infamous Julius Streicher, had made specific declarations—not carried by the Italian press—in favor of a German-Italian agreement against the Jewish peril.[570] It is clear that from the beginning of 1936 the German press showed increasing interest in the development of anti-Semitism in Italy, noting with "strong sympathy" how in Italy there was a new awareness as to the seriousness of the *Jewish peril*.[571]

The anti-Semitic campaign started vigorously once again in April 1937. We can say that from this moment on, until the fall of Fascism on July 25, 1943 and beyond, until April 1945 when the final vestiges of Fascism were swept away, it would never stop. The kick-off was the publication of Paolo Orano's famous pamphlet, *Gli ebrei in Italia* [The Jews in Italy]. Rumor had it that Mussolini had ordered the book written,[573] which is possible, even though he did not fully approve of it; here we need only to examine briefly the arguments used by Orano as the reasons for his attack and what its consequences were to be.

Written with a certain amount of care (contrary to the anti-Semitic literature that was to follow), with an intelligent observation here and there, an apparent scientific bent and, above all, the pretense of being impartial and even of not having any anti-Semitic prejudice, *Gli ebrei in Italia* added nothing new to what Orano had written in his own *Cristo e Quirino* [Christ and Quirinus], and, more recently, by the likes of Farinacci and Interlandi, whose conclusions were adopted by the author. Beyond the usual anti-Semitic clichés—the Jews want to dominate through gold, their educational diplomas and subversive doctrines, the Jews as racists, the Jews as importers into Italy of the worst intellectual fads from abroad, etc.— Orano went in two main directions with his discussion: on the one hand against the Zionists—singling out *Israel* and Dante Lattes— and on the other hand against the Fascist Jews—for example, Ettore Ovazza. His arguments against Zionism were not new and essentially repeated those used by the Nationalists first and later by the Fascists: the state of Israel would only be a tool of England; in helping Zionism Italy would be helping British expansionism and taking a position contrary to its interests against the Arabs without considering Christian rights or the Holy Places—"the Cross and the Fasces are tied by the closest spirit and together are facing a Jewish England and a Judaism that is Britishized"; to be a Zionist means going against the interests of Italy. The attack on the Fascist Jews was more original, and in a certain sense had more weight than that against Zionism. The latter was not very popular among Italians, and a campaign against it could easily be orchestrated without offending many people. It was much more difficult, on the other hand, to justify a campaign that was aimed against all Jews indiscriminately, even against those who were not Zionists but were "excellent Italians," laden with decorations for the most part, and wearing Fascist regalia. Their main fault was to speak up as Jews.

> Individual identification and separation lead us to suspect a hidden need to advertise oneself and at the same time to prove the mistake of what the Nation takes for granted, that the Jews do not share in the same patriotic feelings as other Italians, an assumption that no one ever made . . . Why . . . set forth these civic titles to be used in defense of the Jewish religion? . . . If indeed with regard to the Homeland, the Nation, Italy, they are Italians just like anyone else, why keep apart to show off their merits?

Paolo Orano concludes that this attitude on their part leads us to suspect that they are predisposed to not feeling morally obligated to uphold the cause of national interests, so this is for them a significant sacrifice in order to make themselves more worthy of praise and recognition than others. Having disposed of the Zionists and the Fascist Jews in this manner—at one point Orano states that when Ovazza writes one sees the reappearance of the same idea of the "chosen people" that originated with Lattes—the author of *Gli ebrei in Italia* concludes categorically. Not only must the Jews take a position "against the international Israel, against Zionism, against the secret apostles, the messianisms designed to excite," they must also abandon any kind of individuality that is not strictly religious:

> No more and never again Jewish sports organizations, no separation and no isolation of children, youths and adolescents of both

sexes. For the communities the day of giving back has come. We all agree that they smell stale, are rarefied, and in a word, unhappy. There is no reason why one should ask and see whether an Italian is a believer or not, whether he practices religion or not, Catholic or Jewish. The Synagogue should be sufficient for prayers that are different, and for dissonant choruses.

"It is the problem that must be done away with. Fascist Italy doesn't want it. It would be unnecessary to say more"—these were the parting words in Orano's book. It is no surprise that such a totalitarian demand, asking that the Jews no longer be themselves, would raise such an enormous outburst in all circles and would be interpreted as a forerunner of the next extremely serious developments in the Jewish policy of Fascism.[574]

Some Jews tried to respond to the attack calmly; but their voices were quickly overtaken by the din of ever-growing accusations.[575] *Gli ebrei in Italia*—which was reprinted in an expanded edition in December—was immediately the subject of many reviews. In most of them—sometimes taking the form of investigative essays on Italian Judaism, as in the Turin daily, *La stampa*—Orano's conclusions became even more explicit, and the reviewers demanded that they be drafted into laws. Some cases, scattered here and there, are worth singling out. *Il giornale d'Italia*[576]—which wrote about the ethical and social anti-Semitism of Orano and, somewhat cautiously, to complete the picture, mentioned *Il mito del sangue* [The Blood Myth] by Evola, which had also just been published, and its racist interpretation—summed up the substance of Orano's pamphlet:

> Zionism in our country is an absurdity; the connection to the Judaism of the liberal, democratic or socialist countries is criminal; the activities of the Communities and of the newspaper *Israel* seek to keep up the pride of race and the Jewish tradition when one knows that religion is but an external formality; the hospitality given in the Veneto region to German Jewish refugees is deplorable.

Il corriere della sera, among the most moderate dailies, made a list of all the "mistakes of the Jews," and sensing the way the wind was blowing concluded: "The greatest of all mistakes is to worry about the integrity, the purity of the race; the Jews, by putting the stress on this word, are thus making it a problem that demands a solution."[577] *La stampa* was also particularly violent; in the conclusion of a report over three long articles[578] it not only supported and proposed to disband, or at least radically transform, the Communities but—by adopting the words of an extremely violent article in the April 4 issue of *Quadrivio*—demanded a very strong effort to fight, before anything else was done in the intellectual sector, the Jewish "mongrelization" that was polluting Italian life.[579]

> If the Fascist State is totalitarian, it cannot accept a privileged group of citizens, covered by special laws, can, using the pretense of charity and cultural connections with foreign countries, engaging in truly independent foreign policy actions that are not inspired by Italian interests but by those of world Judaism . . . If the Fascist state is totalitarian, it cannot tolerate Italian culture being, as it is, polluted by Judaism . . .

And there were those who kept repeating subtly that the road to follow was that of the Germans, even though not in forms that were "revolting to our character."[580]

Up to this point the attacks had been made by a notoriously anti-Semitic or semi-official or "large circulation" press; it was an extremely serious matter, but one could hope—and many Jews and non-Jews held such a hope—that it was only a device to keep the matter "warm," to "steer" public opinion and that things would not go too far beyond this point. The "Macchiavellianism" or the "wisdom"—depending on the point of view—displayed by Mussolini remained the underlying belief; nothing irreparable could happen until the Duce had spoken, and, as we have seen, in prior cases he had never issued his opinion, or if he had it was to reassure the Jews and world public opinion, not in support of the attacks. But when even *Il popolo d'Italia*, upon reviewing Orano's book, wrote that one was faced with a "new problem" that had appeared during the last decade, when the spiritual position of Italian Jews, who had until then always lived in perfect harmony with the rest of the population, appeared to be changing,[581] a cold feeling overcame all those who understood what this position could mean coming from Mussolini's personal newspaper. The questions posed by *Il popolo d'Italia*, "Do they consider themselves Jews in Italy or Jews of Italy? Do they feel like guests in our country or part of the population?," also led one to think that Mussolini had already solved the problem and had, in the end, opted for a negative answer.

Reactions came quickly. A wide segment of the press interpreted the review in *Il popolo d'Italia* as the signal; if there had been any hesitations, they now disappeared, and those who had been cautious at first now became more violent, each one wanting to be seen as the first and the best at gaining points in this new "battle" of Fascism. Few, as we shall see, among newsmen, writers and persons of culture were able to avoid this psychosis; most of them would go all the way. The Jewish side had two types of reactions: a few, either because they still could not believe that the bad seed of state-sponsored anti-Semitism could grow even in Italy, or because they were disgusted and resigned, locked themselves in dignified silence and those who could do so began to consider emigrating; others, either because they felt they could still convince Mussolini of the good faith, the Italian sentiments and the Fascist loyalty of the Italian Jews, or that in doing so, they could acquire some distinction that would set them apart from the fate of their co-religionists, were quick to publicly display their Fascism and their Italian allegiance and openly condemned Zionism and Jewish internationalism. Similar behavior had appeared on other occasions. This time, however, the declarations were published all over the main newspapers, especially in *Il popolo d'Italia*. That newspaper published several dozens of them, some individual, others submitted collectively,[582] and many others—some of them containing vibrant and indignant protests—remained unpublished in the paper's archives when Mussolini suddenly ordered a stop to the campaign.[583] Many, the great majority, even though they pledged loyalty to Italy and the Duce and decidedly condemned Zionism and the Jewish international, remained dignified and quite proud, a sure sign of good faith. Others were less dignified if not abject: some people asked for the disbanding of all Zionist organizations and even the suppression of the entire Jewish press.[584]

These declarations, whether they were sincere or expressions of opportunism, were so numerous that in a few weeks' time they threatened to become counterproductive for Fascism. In an editorial in the June 8 issue of *Il regime fascista* entitled "Tutti in linea!" [Everyone line up!], Farinacci tried to turn things around by using humor, observing:

> There is a lingering suspicion that in the near future the only Jews to remain unaffected by the demolition work by the co-religionists scattered around the world will be ourselves who have never been circumcised; but in this world everything is possible.

On the same day Mussolini ordered Pini, the editor of *Il popolo d'Italia*, to quickly put an end to the campaign.[585]

Before examining Mussolini's position it will suffice to say that during the second half of 1937 the anti-Semitic campaign was somewhat toned down.[586] Those still engaged were *Il Tevere* and *Quadrivio*, continuing their attacks against everything that had anything to do with the Jews,[587] and also, obviously, *La vita italiana*.[588] Following the dispute regarding the book by Orano there would be other books published, such as the one by Gino Sottochiesa, *Sotto la maschera d'Israele*[589] [Under the mask of Israel].

However, the fire coming from Fascist propaganda was adjusted to the target: rather than the social-ethical direction contained in Orano's book, it went in the more racist direction. The books by Giulio Cogni on racism and the values of the Italian race[590] were published during this period, as well as a book and many articles by Julius Evola on the blood myth.[591] The fire coming from *Quadrivio* magazine was particularly strong, since it had gone down the road of anti-Semitism as well as of racism since the beginning of the year, publishing articles about the topic in a special section spread over many issues. It is interesting to note that within these racist disputes the major angle tended to show an Italian type of racism, which was spiritual in the manner of Evola rather than the "German type" used by Cogni. There were several harsh rejections[592] of the latter during these months, such as that of Ezio Garibaldi in *Camicia rossa* ("All'insegna del puro sangue ariano") [In the name of pure Aryan blood], for whom this was all "nonsense."[593]

Between April and June anti-Semitism had become—for all practical purposes—a broken arrow: on the mass level it had failed to make any headway among the Italian people. Accustomed for decades and centuries to living with the Jews without clashes or difficulties, Italians could not comprehend why they should suddenly hate them and persecute them. Besides those who understood the political significance of the matter and rejected it as a tragic Fascist set-up, the Italian people asked themselves why on earth they should persecute the Jews: everyone knew someone who was Jewish and knew that, contrary to what was being said, they were good Italians and often good Fascists, as was obvious from their innumerable declarations of attachment to Italy that had been and continued to be published in the Fascist press. Perhaps there were some anti-Fascists among them, just as probably all the Zionists were anti-Fascist. The Fascist "man in the street" or the man corrupted by so many years of Fascism reasoned: let those be punished and their organizations banned, let's shut down their newspapers, but why, because of a few bad elements, should we harm so many innocent and excellent Italians? Typically even at the time of the most violent attacks in the press, these were aimed against the Zionists, contradicting Orano's theory that lumped together Zionist and Fascist Jews. Beyond the most intense moments of the dispute, even in the press, a few brave voices began to reappear, somewhat timidly, and the silence of many others was also extremely eloquent. Adriano Tilgher had the courage to attack the *Protocols*, which had just been reissued by Preziosi, calling them the fruit of the imagination of a fanatical and reactionary anti-Semite.[594] Most of the press, even the Fascist press, decided not to mention them, and instead reviewed the book *Noi ebrei* [Us Jews] published by Abramo Levi, which countered Orano somewhat, and even published Jewish reactions "as witnesses"—just as many bookstores refused to put the *Protocols* in their windows—so much so that Farinacci in his *Il regime fascista* wrote about a "conspiracy of silence" and of "clandestine circumcisions."[595] When in September *Il giornale d'Italia*, a strong promoter of the German-Italian alliance, reported on Hitler's closing speech at the Nuremberg Nazi party congress, it cut all the anti-Semitic allusions and attacks,[596] demonstrating that the alliance between Italy and Germany would have been more easily accepted by the Italian public if it was kept in the dark regarding Nazi anti-Semitic violence and made less aware of the danger that it could be transplanted into Italy. Pro-Fascist and Fascist newspapers overseas were careful not to mention the campaign underway in Italy in order to avoid jeopardizing the prestige that Fascism still enjoyed, especially among immigrant groups. Even *Il merlo*, published in Paris, though pro-Fascist and supported financially by Rome,[597] criticized the anti-Semitic campaign sparked by Orano's book.[598]

Once the goal had been set—the passage of anti-Jewish legislation—other ways of reaching it had to be found. Simple anti-Semitism was too personal, too explicit, foreign by nature, in spite of the years of preparation to popular Italian psychology, and had failed during the very first attempt to impose it. It was then decided to take the racist route, which had been shunned at first because it could create problems with the Church—with whom a common denominator could be found in some type of anti-Semitism—and even with the Germans, who boasted of being the true Aryans and made no attempt to hide the fact that they considered Mediterranean peoples inferior. Against these risks— which, as we shall see, were tentatively avoided by emphasizing a more spiritual than biological racism and by inventing the "race of Rome"—racism had the advantage of being much more impersonal and totalitarian because it implicated the Jews indirectly, and placed them in a much wider context with a pseudoscientific explanation that was therefore, by its very remoteness from Italian popular culture, to fall upon a less naturally hostile environment.

The slowing of the anti-Semitic campaign during the second half of 1937 must be understood in this context, as well as its reemergence within a racist sub species.

19.

Repercussions on Italian Jewry

On January 24, 1935 the newspaper *Israel* commented on the inclusion within the council and the board of the Union of the Communities of representatives of the group *La nostra bandiera*:

> With the new members it appears that the Council of the Union has made an effort at conciliation; to us it appears—besides any personal assessment of individuals, which we purposefully will not make—that this group is being accorded too much importance given its lack of following among those who dedicate their spiritual energies to Judaism and actively participate in Jewish life.

A rather harsh comment, revealing the fear of the Zionists that the active presence within the Council or the administration of Fascist Jews of *La nostra bandiera* could mean giving a decidedly anti-Zionist orientation to the Union itself, placing it increasingly in a crossfire. It appears less justifiable to say that, as *Israel* writes, the Fascist group was being overestimated. Besides the fact that this group was, by its very makeup and the names of some of its members, politically more important than its active numbers, in fact the movement begun in Turin was not so negligible and, moreover, was increasing in size. The 1,200 subscribers of *La nostra bandiera* at its peak, in mid-1937, provide a good indication.

Under these conditions to exclude *La nostra bandiera* from the Union would have been a considerable mistake: it would have provided Fascist anti-Semites with "proof" that the Union was a nest of Zionists and anti-Fascists; created suspicion within the government and run the risk of a secession that would have split the Union and drawn away many Jews and even entire Communities who were acting in good faith. The road toward an agreement was the wiser, even though the more difficult, one to take; it avoided, for the moment, this triple danger and allowed the Union some time to test the good faith and the true intentions of *La nostra bandiera*.

It became immediately apparent that this was not an easy path to follow; to have attempted it forcefully and in good faith is to the credit of the Union's leadership during those years. By taking this approach, not only was it able to deflect further suspicion and attacks from the Fascist side and slow down the machinations of the Ovazza-Liuzzi group, but—most importantly—by opening up the leadership of the Italian Jewish movement to them, it was able to avoid the suspicion and opposition of the most assimilated Jews, who were even farther removed from community life, regarding the true orientation of the organizations that headed the community. Because of this cautious attitude, when in mid-1935 the Ovazza-Liuzzi group left the Council and the Union's board to start its own secessionist organization sometime later, the consequences of their departure would be minimal, and those breaking away had very few supporters among their co-religionists, so that the Fascist government found it useless to back them and continued to recognize the Union.

What the members of *La nostra bandiera* wanted became clear at the Council meeting of January 9, 1935. General Liuzzi immediately explained their program. The path followed by the Union up to then had been "excessively quiet," while Italian Jewry needed more clarity than harmony. "The international Jewish worldly type cannot endure, because every place imposes its own specific political and religious characteristics." The Union had to reinforce the spiritual Jewish conscience—honesty in front of man and God. As for the community establishment, it was not, according to Liuzzi, Fascist, "because authority rises from below rather than above," and was outside the corporate State. It was therefore in need of radical reform. This reform should be "moral" at first and would have to "join the religious spirit with that of Fascist Italy"; the authority of the rabbis—who must all be Italian citizens—had to be "elevated" and "regulated" so as to favor the ambitions of the "best ones." The longer term program *La nostra bandiera* proposed to the Union was summed up by Liuzzi as follows:

> 1. The Union of the Communities will have political-administrative functions and a leader picked by the Government.
>
> 2. A certain number of Communities—different from the current ones, since a revision is necessary—have essentially religious

functions; their leaders are rabbis named by a Grand Rabbi. A secretary, named by the Union based on a list proposed by the head rabbis, should work alongside the rabbis.

3. Administrative centralization and the dismantling of all existing superstructures—cultural circles, various associations. Review and updating of all Charities, many having lost their reason for being.

4. Jewish religious life will no longer be separated from social life.

5. As for Zionism, a return to the program of the first Italian Zionists—the agenda of Carlo Conegliani of 1901—which today's Zionists have completely abandoned.

To be clear on this last point of the program Ettore Ovazza spoke about Zionism, reiterating that for Fascist Zionists it could only be purely ethical and philanthropic:

> We have come here to set Jewry on the road toward clarity and Italian ideals; we represent the conscience of Jewish youth that has lived through the War and the Fascist Revolution: we are not here to be Internationalist Jews. We only recognize Zionism from the philanthropic point of view.

At the very first meeting of the new council, the biggest problem was discussed; the Zionists were defended by Carlo Alberto Viterbo:

> Our Zionism is an appendage of our Jewish identity . . . we try to be honest, clear, to avoid ambiguity, but we cannot fight those who share our own tradition of faith handed down by our teachers . . . it is a mistake and otherworldly to deny the Italian identity of the Zionists, an Italian identity they have been wrapped in for thousands of years, an Italian identity that they cannot tear away from themselves because their attachment to the Homeland is not loyalty but love . . . Many Zionists fought in the Great War, and many are Black Shirts. But we Zionists also love Israel. Zionism as we understand it is not just philanthropic but also made for ourselves, because from the rebirth of Israel there is a new livening of the language, the culture, of our most noble traditions.[599]

Even before concentrating on practical issues, there were major differences and centered on the very idea each opposing group had of Judaism and of being Jewish. Such a fundamental difference in conception made any kind of dialogue difficult. Even discussing practical questions where there was agreement, such as helping the German Jews, became extremely problematic: Ovazza and his followers wanted the collection of funds to be made only by the Communities, while Viterbo wanted them extended to the Keren Kajemeth and the Keren Hayessod, which were rejected by the others because these were international organizations. Under these conditions, from the first meetings of the new leadership group any possibility of cooperation—despite the attempt at mediation by Sacerdoti and Jarach—appeared minimal. Liuzzi and Ovazza were insisting that a radical reform of the 1930 law, that Liuzzi simply characterized as "anti-Fascist by definition," be proposed to the government. While not opposing the idea in principle, the other members expected it to be carefully examined and any irreparable steps avoided, obviously fearing that in the new general political context, a reform of the law could lead to a complete dismantling of the organizational structure of Italian Jewry, reducing it—as Fascism had done previously with various confederations, trade associations, and similar groups—to a mere showcase, without any autonomy or capability of its own, as a tool of the local and international policies of Fascism. This cautious and responsible attitude taken by the majority of the Union was just one more indication for *La nostra bandiera* that went to prove the majority's hostility to any real political and moral renewal of Italian Jewish life and of its wish to bury Liuzzi's program, which had been approved, in principle, by the Council and the Board.

This state of affairs went on for four months[600] until it came to a head during the Council's meeting of May 2, 1935 with the resignations of Liuzzi, Ovazza, Nunes Franco, and Max Ravà.[601] The crisis, however, continued to drag on for a long time. The majority of the Union wanted to avoid a complete break and began new discussions to reach an agreement,[602] while the group *La nostra bandiera* was undecided and divided as to how to proceed.

General Liuzzi, who had busied himself by informing the Ministry of the Interior via the prefecture of Turin, presented his own plan to the government; anticipating an answer—which failed to come[603]—he obviously did not want to take a strong position in any direction. Even Ovazza and the others, as the attitude of *La nostra bandiera* during those months shows—the publication had been transformed, as previously agreed with the majority of the Union, into a Jewish cultural monthly—were unsure of the kind of position they should take, since they received no tangible and clear sign of governmental approval. The entire year 1935 went by in this climate of uncertainty and of more or less official negotiations.

In the new political situation that appeared in January 1936, the Ovazza-Liuzzi group, following the advice of the prefect of Turin, who encouraged General Liuzzi to "revive the struggle against the Union, whose leadership, he knew, was not liked in Rome," decided to go on the offensive, encouraged by the moderate success that its position had had in Turin and other Communities, in particular Rome, Florence, Leghorn, Venice, and Milan. The first act of this offensive was the publication in the January 15, 1936 issue of *La nostra bandiera*—which became once again an aggressive biweekly with that issue—of a *Precisazione di programma* [Clarification of our program], meant to explain the group's position toward the Fascist government and especially towards Zionism. *La nostra bandiera* reiterated its total loyalty to Fascism and its policies and the need for the Union to also take this position more vigorously. The group appeared more flexible toward Zionism than could have been anticipated. International Zionism was condemned, but the colonization of Palestine and its desire to become a nation was not rejected but actually accepted—perhaps to avoid a break with the overwhelming majority of Italian Jews who were deeply attached to the ideals and successes of the Jews in Palestine, or perhaps because within the group itself the majority was sincerely reluctant to shun those ties and those achievements, or, finally, because it hoped to obtain governmental backing by supporting in toto the Palazzo Chigi and its policy toward Zionism.[605] Palestine was defined as the "land of refuge of persecuted Jews without a homeland"—just as Italy was called "a dam and a Mediterranean beacon against the spread of Northern anti-Semitism"—and spiritual center for the Jews, just as the Holy See and Mecca were for Catholics and Moslems, "without weakening in any way their sense of belonging to their own homeland." Palestine should not continue to be an "extension" and an "appendage" of England and should be given the means to live independently. To achieve this goal, the program of *La nostra bandiera* called for increased economic and cultural relations between Italy and Palestine.

Immediately after this program was published, the Liuzzi-Ovazza group insisted that the resignations of its members within the branches of the Union, which had been suspended until then, become effective.[606] It then began, within the columns of *La nostra bandiera*, a relentless campaign for the reform of the 1930 law and consequently of the structure of the Communities and of the Union; in particular, it demanded the revision of the articles regarding the electoral system and "the lack of hierarchical organization within single organizations as well as within larger ones." After this preparation,[607] at the end of May, General Liuzzi published a pamphlet entitled *Per il compimento del dovere ebraico nell'Italia Fascista* [How to Fulfill Jewish Duties in Fascist Italy] intended as a summary of all the proposals of *La nostra bandiera*.[608]

Following an introduction stressing "the real and worrisome decline of Italian Jewish potential," which was attributed to the conservatism and pacifism of the Communities and the absence of a "superior and effective Italian Jewish authority," both lay and religious, so that, according to him, Italian Judaism was apathetic and far removed from the national spirit and the Fascist ethic, Liuzzi went on to examine the various "problems" which had to be urgently discussed and resolved to ensure "doing one's Jewish duty in Fascist Italy." He was very emphatic about the need to adopt these proposals right away:

> The current situation is too serious for there to be any hesitations: either live or die! And to live, it is vital and urgent for our Communities to find within the Union a higher authority having the responsibility for their revitalization, and for them, to have as lead-

ers, new men with the knowledge and the ability to act, having, that is, a Jewish soul not only true to the Italian past but deeply and unmistakably Fascist for the future.

Misunderstandings and mistakes, old Masonic roots and international ties must be, once and for all, swept away by us all as errors and betrayals that are now either no longer valid or defunct. Here again the objective is to fight and win, in the interest of the homeland, as well as our own.

Even a cursory reading of the various "problems" that made up General Liuzzi's booklet clearly reveals that, in practice, the program offered to the Communities and to Italian Jewry in general was a sham.[609] Rather than a program, it was a vague collection of ideas that showed, if not a lack of knowledge, at the very least a lack of clarity as to what Italian Jewish life was all about, both morally and materially. The only clear point was that *La nostra bandiera*, frightened by the signs of a possible change of the situation in Italy, thought it could ward off the danger by leading Italian Jewry into taking an extreme Fascist position, being more Fascist than official Fascism itself. Liuzzi was convinced that to do this, "fundamental reform" was required of all Jewish organizations, and he demanded that his group be given a free hand for everything and anything, from selecting the "new men" who were to enact the reform, to the forms and limits it would take—the old leaders were characterized as "men overtaken and defeated," and it was clear that *La nostra bandiera* would not even consider the possibility of accepting their cooperation. Faced with such a program it is no surprise that, not just the Union and the Zionists immediately spoke up against it, but also many rabbis and the vast majority of the Communities and of the Italian Jews, even those far removed and many others who had been sympathetic to the movement *La nostra bandiera*. It was one thing to feel Italian and Fascist, in many cases, and another to sacrifice organizational autonomy—which in the long run meant giving up on the possibility of a Jewish life and one's own Jewishness—to *preempt* a danger that most did not yet believe in; those who did believe in it knew that it would not be kept at bay with half measures and a dispute that only encouraged the anti-Semites and those who backed an alignment with Germany, even on anti-Semitic policy.

The Union immediately reacted to Liuzzi's booklet and, at a Board meeting of June 11[610] and a Council meeting on June 28 and 29, issued a notice dated July 9, 1936 instructing all the Communities to reject the accusations made and pointing out the inconsistencies contained in the proposals made by the Fascist group *La nostra bandiera*. The notice was moderate in tone but firm in its content,[611] stating that the Union had always "tried to fulfill the tasks that it had been assigned" and "in various ways" had attempted to reawaken Jewish life in Italy, "unifying and stimulating its energies" and not neglecting any of its duties. As to the specific accusations leveled at it, if the Union had shown interest in the problems of Jews in other countries it had always done so with the approval "of the supreme authorities of the State" and on the basis of the elementary right to provide for the safety of its co-religionists who were being persecuted; the accusation of avoiding common social life was false; actually there were no Jewish professional or athletic organizations, the only initiative of this kind had taken place in Rome within the "after work" organization of the Capital and had been disbanded some time before; even more untrue were the accusations of "old Masonic roots" and of claims of "international ties":

> In truth, we could smile at such suspicions with a clear conscience if we didn't also know that the enemies of Israel are always lurking to seize upon even the faintest accusation coming from one of our own, and if our mission as representatives of the Jews of Italy did not compel us to vigorously reject any possible doubt regarding our clear conscience, our exemplary loyalty as Italians.

Finally Liuzzi's proposals were rejected, demonstrating that besides the "secular" they would have affected the "spiritual" and tended to create an Italian synagogue that would be "foreign to the body and the history of Israel."[612]

In spite of the intensive campaign by *La nostra bandiera*[613] and very detailed penetration work among the various Communities, Liuzzi's program did not attract many supporters. The only result of this effort was to sow further uncertainty, disorientation, rancor, fear, and weariness among Italian Jews who were faced, just when the anti-Semitic campaign was becoming even more massive, with an almost complete lack of general direction and proper representation with the state administration. Even though the Union was strongly supported by the great majority, it was to find itself in an increasingly difficult position: it could not and did not wish to adopt drastic measures against the Ovazza-Liuzzi group to avoid an even deeper split and giving the government an excuse to step in with unforeseeable consequences. On the other hand, the situation kept deteriorating into a deadly impasse that was affecting all Jewish associations, and which had to be broken. The death of Angelo Sacerdoti—followed in February 1937 by the passing of Felice Ravenna—deprived Italian Jewry of the one man who could possibly have succeeded at a three-party mediation between the Union, *La nostra bandiera*, and the government. Attempts by both groups to secure Mussolini's personal intervention in their favor also yielded no results: both the request for a meeting by President Ravenna in September and by General Liuzzi in October went unanswered.[614]

Under these circumstances, *La nostra bandiera*, seeing that it was impossible to obtain a declaration by the Communities against the Union or at least to persuade the government to take action against the Union leadership, decided on January 24, 1937 to create, in Rome, a "Committee of Italians of the Jewish Faith." The consequences of this split could have been disastrous and encouraged a series of private initiatives that could end up being very dangerous. The group *La nostra bandiera* was made up of persons acting in good faith, as we have seen, who through their ultra-Fascist actions, deluded themselves into thinking that they would deflect the suspicion of some Fascists away from the Jews. Resolutely anti-Zionist and opposed to any form of Jewish "internationalism," despite the fact that many of its members were removed from the activities and the very culture of Judaism and had only vague and superficial knowledge of what these were, the group was led by honest and determined persons who were not about to forget their own Jewish character. It was no accident that *La nostra bandiera* openly and resolutely fought Nazi anti-Semitism and racism and their Italian mouthpieces, and

215

in spite of its own belief in Fascism, at least until the crisis of the summer of 1937, never completely turned its back on the idea of a "true" Jewish State in Palestine and even took a position against the harsh measures taken by Balbo in Libya to find an authoritarian solution to the Saturday problem.[615] Within Italian Jewry, as in all the associations of this world, there were some elements that were less honest and less committed. Once the unity of the Italian Jews had been broken, others could easily attempt to splinter it further, and for much less honest motives than those of the majority of the members of the Committee of Italians of the Jewish faith. Under the fire of anti-Semitism, some people might attempt to seek personal advantage following the example coming from Rome, giving rise to new initiatives and movements which could damage all of Italian Jewry or at least increase the pessimism and confusion that already existed. During the following months a few individual initiatives would prove that this was not just an idle fear; fortunately they received little publicity and had even less of a following, the most notable being the creation of an Italian anti-Zionist movement.[616]

The immediate consequences of the foundation of the new Committee were disastrous: the majority of the Communities remained loyal to the Union, some did join the new organization or at least did not hide their sympathy for it—Alessandria, Florence, Leghorn, Mantua, Rome, Turin, Venice; others avoided taking a position—Abbazia, Bologna, Rhodes, Tripoli; some Jews and Jewish groups overseas voiced their decision to join the Committee.[617] Among the founders of the Committee were some important persons within Italian Jewry. Under these circumstances the council of the Union decided to resign on April 6, 1937.[618] Commander Jarach—who in the meantime had succeeded as President to the deceased Felice Ravenna—sent his resignation to the General Director for Religious Cults at the Ministry of the Interior. At this point there was an unexpected twist: Buffarini-Guidi invited Jarach and the Union council to not insist on resigning and to remain in place.[619] A paradoxical situation ensued, which has become clear to us today—Mussolini, who had already decided on the anti-Jewish campaign, preferred to deal with the "disloyal" men of the Union rather than the ultra-Fascists of *La nostra bandiera*; it would be more difficult for him, at least morally, to take action against the Italian Jews if the latter had been in charge, but this created even more confusion at the time.

The Union then tried to take action by asking all the Communities to gather around it, condemning some of them for having joined "a committee of private persons."[620] Such firmness was more for the sake of appearances than a real position during a particularly difficult moment, at the time of the anti-Semitic campaign stemming from the book by Paolo Orano and while the secessionist Committee[621] was actively campaigning for members[621] and demanding that, according to the bylaws, there be a second congress of the Union[622] as quickly as possible. The government, in turn, while confirming its confidence in the Union and, having failed to uphold the secessionist Committee,[623] refused to oblige the Union and dissolve the Committee itself or at least take measures against dissident Communities.

Italian Jewry, chaotically divided internally and exposed externally to the massive campaign of vilification and calumny that we have described, appeared to be on the brink of disaster. The Union had no real authority, and in attempting to reduce any false moves or misunderstandings that would provoke attacks, was by now almost completely inactive.[624] The Committee was also in crisis: at the end of August, Ettore Ovazza had resigned as director of *La nostra bandiera*, which was now embracing opportunism and turning away from every value and principle of Judaism,[625] and the entire movement followed the newspaper's lead. With Ovazza, the Committee lost one of the most sincere and honest persons of the group, which was fundamentally attached to its Jewish identity and which, in good faith, and in accordance to its Fascist position, was convinced that it could ward away from the Italian Jews the gathering storm. The Communities were torn by dissent and their activities were reduced to a minimum. Here and there, finally, some conversions and abjurations were already showing that the more fearful ones could not withstand the test and to save themselves would deny their own faith.[626] The very tone with which Italian rabbis addressed their brothers for the Jewish New Year[627] led one to believe that Italian Judaism was by now in the midst of an irreparable crisis. But, as we shall see in the next chapters, the more the material crisis became serious and dramatic in the months and years ahead, the more we witness a healing of the moral blows, a strengthening of conscience and tightening of the will. The very deep split of the 1930s was healing as the persecutions accelerated. And even though there were desertions and betrayals, the persecution served more than any other issue to revive the consciousness of the majority of Italian Jews, which had been following the path toward complete assimilation. In the common resistance to oppression, in mutual help, in the proud defense of one's very being against calumnies and excesses, in maintaining against Fascism one's own Jewish identity and at the same time one's Italian identity, in seeing themselves understood, helped, and sustained by the overwhelming majority of the Italian people, many of those assimilated Jews actually recaptured their own Jewish identity and, at the same time, their full balance as Jews and as Italians.

Part Two

VI.

The Preparation
of the Anti-Semitic Measures
January to November 1938

20.

Mussolini's Position

The position taken by Mussolini toward the Jewish question and the Jews in general during the period of the origins of Fascism and how this affected Fascist internal and foreign policy during the years following the March on Rome has been examined earlier. The Duce, at the same time, clearly made a difference between Italian and foreign Jews and, in particular, between Italian and international Zionism. While not entirely devoid of some elementary forms of anti-Semitism—which were quite common to most men of his generation and background[628]—Mussolini, for many years, cannot be considered an anti-Semite. The idea of state-sponsored anti-Semitism was far removed from his mind until 1937. Italian Jews under Fascism enjoyed the same kind of "freedom" as other Italians; persecuted foreign Jews found in Mussolini, if not quite a protector, at least a politician who helped them and opened Italy's doors as few other heads of state had done. For a long time

Mussolini was unsympathetic toward Zionism because of its relationship with Great Britain, but he also displayed no special antagonism towards it. He saw Zionism as one of many pawns to be used on the international and, in particular, the Mediterranean chess board. He harbored a kind of suspicion toward the Jews, which was the typical attitude of all nationalists: the diffidence of the provincial mind toward anything cosmopolitan and international; anything that, one way or the other, created a link that was not specifically national. High finance and the "Jewish international" represented a reality he did not wish to confront and that, he felt, did not have very strong roots in Italy. He considered Italian Jews as being Italian: they had fought well during the First World War, often coming from occupied provinces, and many had been and were good Fascists. From his long involvement in the Socialist world he knew full well that the fact that they were Jews had no bearing on the anti-Fascism of a Treves or a Modigliani. He does not appear to have dwelled upon the relationship between Jews and Freemasons at all for many years. For a good fifteen years the Jews in Italy were not discriminated against and were able to reach the ranks and positions they sought and aspired to. Some commentators have taken the fact that no Jew was appointed to the Italian Academy as proof of prejudice against the Jews.[629] But we do not consider this relevant since many other talented Italians were also not appointed as Academicians. In fact, few Jews could have been considered as candidates and, among these few, most had either refused to swear allegiance to Fascism or were not agreeable to the Fascists.[630]

Mussolini's attitude toward racism and Nazi anti-Semitism was even clearer. He had spoken out against both many times and had allowed attacks and criticism to appear unchallenged. We can find a sort of "race myth" in his speeches and thinking right after the March on Rome, but it has nothing in common with Nazi racism. The goals and limits of Mussolini's racism never went beyond a health-related policy linked to demography and eugenics. Besides wanting to replace the bourgeois mentality of the "tiny Italy" with the imperial consciousness of Rome—in other words, not going beyond the physical and moral regeneration and improvement of the Italians themselves—nothing in Mussolini's pronouncements and actions on the subject of race will appear until the end of 1937, including the Fascist Grand Council decisions of March 3, 1937, to even hint at a true biological racism and a Nazi-type policy.[631]

The evolution in Mussolini's position did not begin until the second half of 1936. There were many separate underlying causes, as well as Mussolini's future position, that must be examined in order to understand the course of anti-Semitic policy during the years 1938-1945. Only then can we understand the underlying reasons of the attitude of Fascist authorities toward the Jews in 1938-1940, and again in 1940-1943, and even in 1943-1945, during the RSI period, including single episodes and clarify the entire anti-Semitic policy of Fascism.

The initial reason—but not necessarily the most important one—for Mussolini's change can be found in a few anti-Fascist and anti-Italian positions taken by individual Jews and Jewish organizations during the wars in Ethiopia and Spain.[632] Mussolini, who had lost all sense of proportion during those years of Italy's moral isolation, tended to generalize from those statements and to believe that the Jewish international, allied to the enemies of Fascism, was on the war path against him. The failure of the initiatives taken in Geneva, Paris, and London by a few Italian Jews must have confirmed his view. He saw further confirmation—and this is the second reason—in the fact that some Jewish industrialists and businessmen who had been supporting him and his policies unconditionally, began to criticize and grumble about the absurd and unsustainable new path on which he intended to take the Italian economy. In speaking with Yvon De Begnac in October 1941 he said characteristically: "I felt the Jewish hostility towards Fascism when we began applying our emergency policy to the economy."[633]

To this first group of reasons explaining Mussolini's attitude toward the Jews we must add events that influenced him indirectly: once Ethiopia had been conquered, the policy regarding "race" entered a new phase beyond those related to health, demography, and eugenics. Due to the presence of many Italian soldiers and colonists in those lands, Mussolini wanted to avoid race mixing on a large scale, not just through legislation, but also by instilling ideals of racial "consciousness" and "dignity" in the Italian people. The need to take action became even more pressing once news began filtering back more and more insistently from the AOI regarding the "awful behavior by civilians and military personnel toward indigenous women," the "irresistible sexual hunger shown by our citizens,"[634] and the serious repercussions this had on Italian relations with the natives and on law and order. At one point, the problems became so serious that Mussolini ordered the colonists' and the military's mail in East Africa be opened to discover those who were guilty of such "crimes" against race. It finally reached the point where three Italian women, who had had sexual relations with the natives, were ordered flogged and condemned to five years in a concentration camp.[635] A series of documents further indicates that Mussolini attributed revolts in various regions of the Empire to this type of behavior, because of the lack of "racial dignity" of the Italians toward the natives. Ciano's diary has two significant annotations,[636] one on January 8, 1938:

> The Duce is worried about the Empire: the Goggiam is in revolt. According to the Duce, Pirzio Biroli is responsible as well as the lack of racial preparation of the Italians. The behavior of many of our people has made the natives lose respect for the white race.

The other is dated July 30, 1938:

> ...the Duce feels the race issue to be fundamental after the conquest of the Empire. The insurrection of the Amhara is due to the lack of racial preparation of the Italians.

The following instructions, written by Mussolini on November 18, 1937 to the Duke of Aosta, who had just been named Viceroy to replace Graziani,[637] are even more telling, as is the section on Ethiopia in the speech Mussolini gave to the national council of the PNF on October 25, 1938.[638]

> The lack of racial consciousness has had serious consequences in Amhara. It is one of the reasons for the rebellion of the Amhara. The Amhara had no plan to revolt against Italian domination and no reason to do so. The proof is that during the Ethiopian campaign 5,000 Amhara, fully armed, welcomed comrade Starace with enthusi-

asm and obedience when he got off the plane. But when they saw the Italians going around more ragged than they were, living in the *tucul,* kidnapping their women, etc. …they said: "This race does not bring civilization." And, since the Amhara are the most aristocratic race in Ethiopia, they rebelled.

Perhaps the Catholics don't know these things, but we know them. This is why the racial laws of the Empire will be more rigorously applied and those who misbehave will be banned, punished, imprisoned. To hold on to the Empire, the natives must have the very clear and overwhelming feeling of our superiority.

On a formal level racial policy toward the populations of the Empire had nothing in common with the problem of the Jews. But its impact upon it, though indirect, should not be underestimated. The racial question for Mussolini became political, as a result of new relations between Italy and Germany, but also had a "spiritual" dimension: that is, to give Italians a new racial consciousness that would turn them into a race of conquerors capable of handling the tasks that an "Imperial Italy" must now take upon itself in the world. In both areas the struggle against the bourgeois "spirit" and "mentality" was, in his view, an essential element implicating the Jews directly, as the embodiment of such a spirit and mentality, and indirectly because, through anti-Semitic policy, it defied and attacked the prejudices and inadequacies of the Italian bourgeoisie.

To these secondary reasons there are three major ones in order of their growing importance: the influence of Mussolini's entourage, the myth of the "new civilization," and the new phase of relations with Germany.[639]

Even though the last factor undoubtedly played a major role, the influence of the entourage should not be underestimated.[640] Many Fascists, especially those of the new generation, were receptive to more or less strong forms of anti-Semitism. We have discussed the new generation of diplomats; there were similar examples of functionaries in other ministries, notably the Interior Ministry. Some significant examples show how Mussolini was surrounded by individuals who were for the most part anti-Semitic, were prejudiced, or at least displayed little sympathy for the Jews.

The attitude of King Victor Emmanuel III is noteworthy. He can certainly not be labeled as an anti-Semite, but did display some kind of prejudice, and was not particularly sympathetic toward the Jews. He later would not oppose the first anti-Semitic measures. The way the King sidestepped a question in 1938 that had been put to him by Italo Balbo regarding the first rumors of possible anti-Jewish measures in Italy is revealing. When Balbo, who was also a "quadrumvir," asked Victor Emmanuel III whether Italy was going to imitate the Germans in this area, the King answered:

> Listen Balbo, I never bite off more than I can chew in advance, but on this issue I warned Mussolini and told him a few times: "President, the Jews are a nest of hornets, let's not stick our hands in there." He said I was right and even went further: he let them flock into Italy. I can't tell you how many complaints came in from our professionals and merchants in seeing these German and Austrian Jews arrive…even a bit arrogant and invasive, they tell me. And Mussolini remained silent and tolerant. Now, I know he wants them out because during the war in Africa, and I can't blame him for this, America, England, and France were against us with an acrimony I can't describe. You know him as well as I do, even better than I; Mussolini holds a grudge about this hostile attitude…and then he's a bit jealous, I think, that German anti-Semitism has been so popular among the Arab nations of the eastern Mediterranean.

That was the extent of his answer to Balbo's comments.[641]

There is nothing anti-Semitic in this conversation, but neither is there any rejection of anti-Semitism on moral grounds, nor even some minimal sympathy for the Jews. The King would not change his attitude even after approving the racial laws. When the Pope protested to him about those laws, it appears he answered that he "didn't like priests" and that he was for the Jews only out of a human sense of pity.[642] In truth it all appears to be very limited.

Many others close to Mussolini had little sympathy for the Jews. Emilio De Bono, who would oppose the measures at the Grand Council meeting, appears to have done so not out of any particular human or moral impulse, but only because he felt they were politically mistaken, stating ironically that he was himself an anti-Semite:[643]

It seems that they do everything possible to make enemies. The thing about the Jews is exploding like a bomb! But if you had discovered the destructive Jewish influence a long time ago why didn't you speak up before? Why did you wait for the German example? This is how the public will think. How then will they excuse so many inconsistencies? I am stupid to take it to heart. It's Mussolini's fault, but those around him, rather than moderate his impulses, are egging him on. It appears we have to discuss it at the Grand Council. I will also speak, I, who have always been an anti-Semite. What is always missing is good measure and equilibrium. The negative man is Starace.

And if we go from the "old" men, like De Bono, to the "young" ones, like Galeazzo Ciano, the picture does not change. He states his views in his diary: "I don't like the Jews, but I don't see the need to take such action in Italy."[644] The diary itself is full of little anti-Semitic annotations: the Soviet chargé d'affaires in Rome is a "little Jew,"[645] the attitude of Hore Belisha can be explained as the "vanitas Judaica," etc.[646] It should be noted that at the Grand Council the "anti-Semite" De Bono was opposed to the measures against the Jews, while the "moderate" Ciano was careful not to oppose them, even though in private, according to his diary, he thought they were not expedient and even clearly said so. [647]

…Nor do I think it convenient for us to unleash an anti-Semitic campaign in Italy. The problem doesn't exist in our country. There are few of them and with few exceptions they are good. And in any case one must never persecute the Jews as such. It just cements the solidarity of all the Jews in the world. They can be hit under any other pretenses. But, I repeat, the problem doesn't exist for us. And perhaps, in small doses, the Jews are necessary to society like yeast is necessary to making dough for bread.

Almost no one within the entourage would take a strong position to dissuade Mussolini. Balbo was the exception and, ironically, during the entire tragic Jewish issue the one person Mussolini would later refer to with respect. Speaking with De Begnac in 1941, he said "Balbo defended them with extreme civic courage."[648] Most of the others accepted the Duce's directives slavishly, jumping blindly to fulfill them, in the hope of furthering their own careers.

As for Starace, we have seen De Bono's harsh opinion placing him, along with Bottai, among the most extreme members of the Grand Council. Thanks to Starace the PNF was ready in time for the new measures and it was under his supervision, along with the Ministry of Popular Culture, that the manifesto of the racist scientists would be published. The same can be said of Bottai, the "moderate" and "rebellious" Bottai: at the Grand Council meeting he even impressed Ciano for the violence of his anti-Semitic attacks and for "his intransigence."[649] Among the government ministers, he was to immediately embrace the crusade with the greatest zeal, even producing a theory to support it in a series of memos to his employees.

Compared to them one is almost tempted to feel some respect for a Farinacci or a Preziosi; at least they were consistent, according to their viewpoint. They believed that an anti-Semitic policy was necessary in Italy, and if they sought to influence Mussolini long before he was leaning in that direction, it was out of conviction, not cowardice or flattery.

Preziosi, as we have seen, was an old-time anti-Semite; he was *the* anti-Semitic theorist and had written about the subject for years in his own magazine, and later in *Il regime fascista*. He had relations with right-wing Nazis after the First World War and had been their political promoter since 1933. Even though he was aware that Mussolini did not like him, he persevered for years in this parallel action, converting to it, first Farinacci ("Preziosi," Mussolini would say, "has been leading Farinacci around"),[650] then attempting to draw in all those he could persuade.[651] Farinacci had never liked the Jews, but he cannot really be called an anti-Semite: in 1924 there was a rabbi among the main editors of *Cremona nuova*;[652] in 1932 he interceded with Minister Solmi to recommend that a Jew be named as chairman of a university department;[653] once the racial campaign had started he kept a Jewish secretary employed[654] and even agreed to "Aryanize" some Jews.[655] For him anti-Semitism was necessary to give the alliance with Germany a totalitarian character; it was essentially a political question and he did everything he could to eliminate the last major obstacle between the two regimes. He never concealed from Mussolini, whom he knew did not like him and for whom for many years he would be the "bête noire" within Fascism,[656] his view that the racial campaign was merely a political question and, as far as we know, never joined in the disquisitions and ideological explanations of racism, as many others would. A letter he wrote to Mussolini from Cremona on August 5, 1938, reveals the political character of his anti-Semitism and is the best epitaph for the manifesto of racist "scientists" of the preceding July. He wrote:

> My thoughts are, quite frankly, that the racial problem, seen from the anthropological point of view, appears unconvincing. The problem remains, in essence, a political one. I am convinced once again that when scientists try taking a hand at politics, they wind up tainting every problem. On the philosophical and scientific levels one can forever debate; but in politics, when reasons of state exist, one acts and wins.[657]

Without a doubt, the influence of such an entourage was considerable. Those close to Mussolini were either completely in favor of a total German-Italian understanding (on September 29, 1937 Ciano will write in his diary "No one can accuse me of being hostile to the pro-German policy"), or were fearful and did not have the courage to contradict him; neither the former nor the latter did anything to prevent anti-Semitic persecution. The few who were against it were overwhelmed by the sheer numbers of their opponents and by their reputation of being extremely anti-German.

The myth of the "new civilization" played a greater role along with the totalitarian bent Mussolini imposed on the regime after the war in Africa. It is impossible to describe in detail both issues within the confines of this work. For an analytical reconstruction the reader may wish to consult what we have written in our biography of Mussolini.[658] In this context it will be sufficient to say that during the second half of 1938 the Duce always tended to explain the "crisis of civilization" which, according to him, was overtaking Europe and to project a "new civilization" which, still according to him, Fascism had to bring about through the "spiritual races" history had shaped and which existed within the various western peoples. These spiritual races, acting as bodies and antibodies, struggled amongst themselves. Victory depended upon historical circumstance, and therefore it became the moral and political duty of the spiritual elite, namely the aristocracies, to educate and transmit their Greco-Roman and Judeo-Christian values to the masses. The first, believing in heroism, in struggle, in creativity within pain, in the need for demographic development; the second in justice, in peace, and in the cynical and superficial modernity that kept man too far from nature, making him more and more individualistic, egotistical and anti-social, pushing man to strive and prosper without faith, and not be truly engaged in anything; while the future belonged to people who believed, people who were non-materialistic, who had the collective sense of life which always overcomes individual egoism and constitutes true idealism, not abstract and sentimental, but dynamic and virile. He was convinced that the historical mission of Fascism was to fight the bourgeois spirit and mentality, which was responsible for the decay of the spiritual race of Judeo-Christianity, and also to fight against the Jewish spirit and therefore the Jewish race because its culture was at the root of the bourgeois mentality. This was a purely ideological conviction, giving Mussolini a political advantage that cannot be underestimated, it allowed him to single out and oppose his own spiritual racism to the biological variety represented by Nazism. The result, aside from not appearing as an imitator of Hitler, would allow him to reject the more humiliating racial implications for Italians and position himself as the advocate of a completely different racism with objectives and motivations which were spiritual, rather than materialistic.

Though by now he felt compelled to choose racism and anti-Semitism, Mussolini did not want it to be simply a slavish copy of the Nazi racist concept with its resulting legislation. There were many reasons to reject such a solution: prestige, internal politics, world image, etc. All of them were valid, but even taken together they cannot overshadow another overriding reason encompassing them all: that of underscoring, in spite of everything, the differences between Fascism and Nazism, to maintain the ideological autonomy of the former from the latter, and to fit in with his own spiritualist vision of the "new civilization."

In his search for coherence, right after the publication of the "manifesto of the scientists," Mussolini approved[659] of an editorial published in *Critica fascista* in which,[660] contrary to other comments written at the time, the discussion on racism was placed on the level of moral unity and national education that was being followed by Fascism. The editorial approved of the fact that the manifesto did not wander into philosophical or religious areas and that an effort was being made to read it differently than most people, who, were prone, through lack of moral or political sensitivity, to a spirit of conformity and pro-German zeal, stating that:

> the declared lack of philosophical or religious intent, while it clearly and openly marks the directions, limits and the realistic balance of the Italian racist concept, in harmony with the essential ideas of Caesar's and Christian Rome, should not follow an interpretation or, worse, a merely materialistic application of the declaration. The foundations of Italian racism are and must be essentially spiritual, even though it begins, appropriately, with purely biological data.

And three years later, during the summer of 1941, Mussolini would find that the position closest to his own, as well as to his political goals, was expressed by Julius Evola in his *Sintesi di dottrina della razza* [Summary of Racial Doctrine], published a few months before and which he read between August 25 and 29 in Germany.

Evola was a strange kind of Fascist intellectual, virtually unknown to most at the time. He began writing in the *Corriere d'Italia* and *Lo Stato democratico* of the Social Democracy of Colonna di Cesarò, then in *Critica fascista*, where his articles provoked excited reactions by *L'osservatore romano* and the Catholic and moderate Fascist press for having supported the idea of a revolutionary Fascism. In this vein he raised the problem of the incompatibility between Fascism and Christianity in his book *Imperialismo pagano* [Pagan Imperialism], published in 1928, where he stated that if Fascism truly possessed an "imperial will" it must return to the pagan tradition, while the Church should be deprived of its power and subordinated to the state. Thanks to an introduction by Giovanni Preziosi,

Evola finally reached *Il regime fascista*, directed, by Farinacci where, beginning in 1934, he wrote a cultural column entitled "Diorama filosofico."[661] At that time he came in contact with Nazi elements, even though, it should be pointed out, his racism was never identified with the Nazi variety and he was criticized by the Nazis on many occasions.[662] The most significant work by Evola up to that point had been *Rivolta contro il mondo moderno* [Revolt Against the Modern World], published in 1934. He owed his fame to *Il mito del sangue* [The Blood Myth], which was published in 1937, where he explained racial theories beginning with the Romantic period up to the Nazis. Only four years later did he explain his personal doctrine in *Sintesi di dottrina della razza*, contrasting the biological and anthropological concept of racism with that of an internal race, a race of the spirit, promoting the Ario-Roman race, which was to be a "central guiding race"; and even writing about a race "new and ancient in time, that can be called *race of the Fascist man or the race of Mussolini's man.*"

Mussolini, who, since 1935, was already acquainted with some of Evola's ideas and had expressed his approval to the magazines and dailies that had published them, decided to meet the author upon reading the *Sintesi*. According to Evola:

> . . . having read the book he summoned me and praised it beyond its true worth, telling me that it was precisely the kind of doctrine he needed. It allowed him to consider problems similar to those confronting Germany, and therefore to "align himself," while maintaining an independent attitude by using the spiritual orientation, that primacy of the spirit, that was missing in much of German racism. More precisely, the theory of the Ario-Roman race and its corresponding myth could integrate the Roman ideal that Fascism had put forth in general, as well as create a basis for Mussolini's plans to change and uplift the average Italian through the state, and derive from him a new kind of man.[663]

At this juncture we must account for the final reason for Mussolini's change in attitude with respect to racism and anti-Semitism and his decision to turn them into elements of Fascist ideology and foreign policy, after having derided the Nazis for many years, harshly at times, in his public pronouncements. These must be examined, bearing in mind two important factors: all the other reasons we have described until now were fundamentally secondary —even though their importance should not be underestimated — and that the decision made by Mussolini to introduce state-sponsored anti-Semitism into Italy stemmed from the belief that, in order to give credibility to the Axis, it was necessary to eliminate the most glaring difference in the policies of the two regimes. While others, including Farinacci, certainly contributed to convincing Mussolini of this, their role must not be exaggerated: there is no doubt that the decision was essentially a willful choice Mussolini made and external pressures had only an added, but secondary, importance. It is also true, as we have seen previously, that the Germans played no part in influencing the decision by specific requests. In 1936-1937, when Mussolini started down the path that would lead him to the racial policies and state-sponsored anti-Semitism, he would not have tolerated a direct intervention of this kind coming from Hitler, nor would Hitler have made any such attempt. A massive and personal intervention would not occur until the second half of 1942 and the beginning of 1943, when Italy's situation was so precarious that it was inconceivable for Mussolini to refuse to bow to German demands. No document or eyewitness account has surfaced from that period to the present suggesting, before that date, that any such direct intervention took place,[664] nor can any individual steps taken by the Germans to pressure low-ranking Fascist functionaries or party members without any influence — or who claimed at best, an influence that they did not, in fact, have on political decisions taken in Rome — be considered important. There is actually a precise notation by Ciano that the contrary was true, on December 3, 1937, when the racial campaign had already been decided, he wrote:[665]

> The Jews are accusing me in insulting anonymous letters of having promised to Hitler that they would be persecuted. Untrue. Never have the Germans spoken to us about this issue.

According to Attilio Tamaro, undoubtedly a well-informed source, the racial legislation was a sort of "token" Mussolini gave to Germany.[666] This somewhat romantic interpretation may serve as a psychologically justifiable explanation; but it does not even appear necessary as a way of explaining a decision that without a doubt was in the logic of events. Racism and anti-Semitism occupied too conspicuous a place in Nazi ideology to be ignored and were too much a part of the reality of German policy for an eager ally not to adopt. The politics of denial, of trying to avoid the problem with minor diplomatic gestures, could suffice during the initial phase of coming together, but could not sustain a true alliance nor lend credibility to the possible German-Italian alliance in the eyes of the world. To give instructions to all ministries to avoid appointing "citizens of the Jewish faith on possible missions and assignments to Germany" could be sufficient as a token during the preliminary phases of German-Italian negotiations on November 23, 1936, when this order was issued by the Palazzo Chigi;[667] but with the progressive strengthening of the Rome-Berlin relationship it would have been silly to think it could be enough. In addition, as Mussolini would say, "if one speaks to the Führer using that kind of racist jargon it is invariably effective"[668] and therefore an Italian alignment on anti-Semitism would automatically overcome certain German suspicions toward Italy. When Ribbentrop came to Rome on November 5-7, 1937 to sign the anti-Comintern pact—an important diplomatic milestone on the way to the Pact of Steel—Mussolini and Ciano, during the meeting on November 6 informed him, among other matters, of the progress of the anti-Semitic campaign in Italy:

> We are conducting a rather determined and intensified anti-Semitic campaign under the direction of a man who is quite popular in Italy, the Honorable Farinacci; who already has two publications in Rome, *Il Tevere* and *Quadrivio*, with many followers, especially within the academic world.[669]

Our interpretation is not contradicted by available documents regarding the relations between the Italian and German police forces on the subject of the Jews, at least from the end of 1936 onward. The cases we have found[670] do not indicate a common action between them regarding the Jews but only a normal exchange of "courtesies" and information between two friendly police forces. It is significant that in one of the cases we have examined, "Jewish groups" are mentioned as well as contacts by the subject in question with Trotsky, indicating an anti-Communist action rather than an anti-Jewish one, as had been coordinated by Himmler and Bocchini during his first trip to Germany in March-April 1936.[671] On that occasion the two police chiefs had agreed to a coordinated collaboration in the struggle against Freemasons and Communists. Italian documents regarding the meeting[672] indicate that the Germans tried to connect the anti-Communist and anti-Freemason action to the anti-Jewish one. "In their opinion the Jewish problem, besides being closely connected to world Communism, whose leaders, in effect, are all Jews, and with Freemasonry, is paramount to the others in many respects." Bocchini did not follow the Nazis down this path and let the matter drop almost completely:

> The Italian Delegation pointed out that the Jewish question in Italy has different characteristics as to the size of the mass, which is irrelevant in proportion to the population of the Kingdom and because the infiltration within the institutions of the State and the Regime is very small.

Under these conditions, Italian cooperation could only be generic; the Italian police would provide its German counterpart with a "general information bulletin" and would keep in mind "all the issues that could be of particular interest to the Reich." Therefore it would provide the German police with information of interest regarding German-Jewish refugees, as demonstrated in two cases in December 1936 and June 1937. Confirmation of Fascist reluctance, at this time, to engage in anti-Jewish action is substantiated by the fact that if the Jews were discussed during the Himmler-Bocchini conversations, no detail of these conversations was carried into the text of the agreements, where, at the most, paragraph 5 can be understood as referring to the Jews, since the two police forces would receive "from one another suggestions regarding the implementation of police measures against Communists, Freemasons, and *emigrants* and would act accordingly insofar as the legislation of the respective countries makes it possible, and where there would be no state-related objections."

The preparation and enactment of the Italian racial measures was followed and "encouraged" by the Nazi press.[673] Significantly, even in personal and confidential German documents, the preparation and enactment were always described as a spontaneous adaptation on Italy's part. Among many documents proving this point, two stand out in particular: a letter to Farinacci from Ludwig Pauler, one of the most important individuals in Nazi journalism, and a speech by the head of the race office of the Nazi party on the occasion of the visit to Germany by the director and deputy director of the Office of Racial Studies of the Ministry of Popular Culture. Pauler wrote to Farinacci on August 19, 1938 immediately following the manifesto of the "scientists":

> The Fascist extension into the clear foundation of race, which has been very well prepared, has been extraordinarily satisfying to Germany. I saw it coming and have expected it, because the natural sciences must also become part of the political scene. Proof that Nordic blood is preponderant in the Italian people was demonstrated by the achievements of Fascism in every field. This century and one thousand years beyond, will be decided by the racist-populist revolution that is embodied in our two peoples.[674]

Doctor Walter Gross, head of the Nazi party race office, was even more explicit the following December:[675]

> The only uneasy issue between the Nazi and Fascist programs had been, until recently, the absence of racial policy. Now this point has been eliminated and the Nazi party is very pleased, not just about Italian racial policy, but also because it has developed along its own original lines, which its leaders feel are more attuned to the different conditions in the country and its people.

Following Mussolini's change on the issues of racism and anti-Semitism, we can sum up the unfolding of the main events and their timing: the progression is extremely clear, especially when compared to German-Italian relations, and, generally, to the most significant events of those years:

1935	November 2	The League of Nations approves sanctions
	December 14	*Gringoire* attacks the Jews in the League of Nations
1936	March 30	Mussolini receives Georges Batault
	April 1	Mussolini orders a more markedly pro-German orientation[676]
	September	Campaign in *Il regime fascista*
	October	Ciano's trip to Germany
	November 23	Ciano gives instructions to avoid sending Jewish officials to Germany
	December 23	Mussolini begins dismissing Jewish journalists from *Il popolo d'Italia*[677]
1937	March 3	Mussolini tells Pini: "Farinacci is falling in line"[678]
	March 23	The first racist articles are submitted to the editors of *Il popolo d'Italia;* Mussolini tells Pini: "As you know, I am a racist."
	April	Opening of the campaign on Paolo Orano's book
	May 4 to 5	von Neurath visits Rome
	May 25	*Il popolo d'Italia* takes a position on Orano's book
	September 5-12	A delegation of fifty Fascists led by Farinacci attends the Nazi congress at Nuremberg
	September 25-29	Mussolini visits Germany
	November 5-7	Ribbentrop visits Rome: Anti-Comintern pact, Mussolini and Ciano inform Ribbentrop about developments of the racist campaign
	December 29	Preziosi seeks Ciano's help to coordinate the anti-Semitic campaign[679]
1938	January	The anti-Semitic campaign begins in the Italian press
	February 16	Publication of *Informazione diplomatica* n. 14
	March 13	The Grand Council approves the Anschluss
	April	Ciano refuses to see Goldmann
	May 3 to 9	Hitler visits Italy
	June	Visit to Italy of a delegation of the Nazi race office led by Dr. Gross;[680] first restrictions to Jews participating in international meetings
	July 14	The "Manifesto on Race" is published

July 21	Instructions forbidding any Jews to participate in international conventions and meetings
July 26	Press release on race by the PNF
September 7	Decree against foreign Jews
September 29-30	Munich: Hitler and Mussolini discuss race issues[681]
October 6	The Grand Council approves the persecution

State anti-Semitism began, it must be noted and not underestimated, mostly, but not exclusively, because of Mussolini's wish to eliminate the most glaring source of friction and discord with his ally.[682] It was also to acquire, as it did in his view, its own character and not simply turn out to be the Italian version of Nazi legislation.[683] There can be no doubt on this subject, and those who have stated the contrary did not even bother to examine, even superficially, what the purpose of the legislation "for the defense of the Italian race"[684] represented in fact; how it was put in practice by the authorities concerned and what, in general, Fascist policy was on that issue. Having said this, we are not implying that Mussolini and Fascism deserve any praise or that their responsibility is in any way reduced: the action stands out, obviously, in all its inexcusable seriousness and wickedness; we only wish to reconstruct all the facets of this chapter in the history of Fascism and of Italy's most recent history.

It is clear that Mussolini was opposed to Nazi racist aberrations. He made many statements on this issue during the years preceding the alliance with Germany. His position did not change during the negotiations for the alliance itself, nor after it became a reality, nor even during the harshest moments of the war. Once the alliance was consummated he avoided any public signals that could endanger the alliance or be used by enemy propaganda. In private he never made a secret of his dissenting opinion for such aberrations and for those who supported them in Italy.[685] The fact that he remained silent was not intended to be an unlimited and final acceptance; in his unconscionable, easy-going manner, he always deluded himself into thinking that "after" the war was over, when, in victory, Italy would no longer be required to form a united front with Germany against the enemy, the issue would be reexamined.

In June 1942 he still harbored the illusion that "Rosenberg's theories" would not succeed after the war and should be revamped.[686] Nor did his temporary silence mean unconditional acceptance of everything the Germans were doing against the Jews: in the Italian military zones of occupation in France and the Balkans, Italian commanders saved thousands of Jews from the Germans with Mussolini's full approval and support, and he rejected pressure to the contrary coming from the Nazis. Even during the RSI period, attempts were made to avoid delivering to the Germans Jews who had been arrested and placed in concentrated areas.

Italian racial legislation had its own characteristics and should not be placed on the same level as Germany's or its satellites, Vichy France included.[687]

Mussolini's racist remarks in his speeches, or as noted by Ciano in his diary and by others, have been interpreted generally in too drastic a manner in attempting to find echoes of Rosenberg, Streicher, and Hitler. Bruno Spampanato and, most of all, Yvon De Begnac, have recounted some of Mussolini's conversations where he purportedly conveyed his concept of race. He is reported to have told Spampanato:[688]

> I have been a racist since 1922, but with my own kind of racism. Health, the preservation of the race, its improvement, the struggle against tuberculosis, sports for the masses, children at summer camps—was the kind of racism I had in mind. But there is also a moral racism that I preached, the pride of belonging to this millennial ethnic group born between the snow of the Alps and the fires of Mount Etna. Our racism overseas? Showing pride in Italian prestige, the ingenuity of our civilization. There is nothing objectionable in all this. When I occupied Albania I turned it into a state associated with Italy with equal rights even though Albanian life is far behind our three thousand years of Mediterranean civilization. I turned the Libyan colony into four provinces of the Italian state. I treated the subjects of the Ethiopian Empire as no colored men had been treated before...The manifesto on race could have been avoided. It was an abstruse exercise by a few journalists and professors, a ponderous German essay translated into bad Italian. There is much distance be-

tween what I have said, written, and put my name to on the subject. I suggest you look into the very old issues of *Il popolo d'Italia*. I have always considered the Italian people as the magnificent product of the fusion of various ethnic groups based on a geographic, economic, and, especially, a spiritual unity. It is the spirit that has driven our civilization to expand in the the world. Men of different blood were the carriers of a single splendid civilization. This is why I am far removed from Rosenberg's myths That is also a position that must be corrected.

And some four years before to Yvon De Begnac:

My personal point of view on the question of racism was clearly stated recently by Missiroli. "Extreme moderation," no more and no less. I am repulsed by all fanaticism, but we had to take a position facing a structured opposition. I am not complaining about it. Our conception is, in any case, completely alien to any political or religious motivation. Races exist and, beneath the races, the stock; and, beyond the stock, the people.

This is an unalterable fact. There are no superior and inferior races. We must not give in, especially in this area, to materialistic tendencies. Races are, sometimes, like nations: we become allies with some and fight against others. Naturally, in such cases, it is not a real war that is fought, weapons in hand, it is the worse kind of war: so dangerous that to avoid its consequences, resorting to a real war may appear useful.

Is there such a thing as the Italic race?

I don't think so in spite of the "evidence" of the scientists. All the races filtered through the snaking Italian alembic, acquiring our conception of life. No one lasted very long encamped on our squares. A bit of Jewish blood doesn't harm anyone. Imredy is intelligent perhaps because of this.

Missiroli touches upon the right point when he speaks of the spiritual values of Judaism in contrast to those upheld by Roman civilization and by Christian civilization. Yes, in Israel there is truly the drama of the doubling of life. One side tends toward the sublime, the other frighteningly toward reality, especially after the crucifixion of the Messiah.[689]

Within both of these long tirades by Mussolini, there is, especially in the first one, a strong desire to justify his actions; but by and large they seem to represent his true position on the problem of race. In support of this opinion, besides a whole series of other minor reports and a careful reading of the various official positions taken by the Duce, two significant documents must be considered.

Among the material stored at the Central State Archives in Rome there are a number of books coming from Mussolini's library, the "Mussolini Collection." Two of these books are of great interest from the point of view of this investigation: the *Vita di Gobineau* (Milan 1933) by Lorenzo Gigli and the *Sintesi di dottrina della razza* (Milan 1941) by Evola. Mussolini read both books The one by Gigli between December 15 to 23, 1933, and the Evola, as we have seen, "between August 25-29 XIX (1941) in Germany." The dates are recorded with certainty by two annotations in Mussolini's handwriting on the cover pages. The cover page of the *Vita di Gobineau* also shows the annotation of two pages: 64 (opinions on D'Azeglio) and 97 (the homeland that is in substance denied by Gobineau). Both volumes bear many underlined parts and markings in Mussolini's handwriting. These clearly indicate, even after almost eight years, not only the continuity of Mussolini's thinking, but also substantially confirm what can be found in the official positions taken by the Duce and the reports coming from those close to him during those years.

For our purposes the markings and underlined passages in the book by Gigli are relatively few. Besides those on page 97 it is worthwhile noting those of page 82 underlining the statement that "The only agent of history is race" and two other markings which already indicate Mussolini's point of view: a thick mark on page 85 shows how he had been impressed by Gobineau's conception of honor and of the civilizing idea it implied; on page 110 the statement that Germany is by now "deprived" of Aryan elements is also underlined.

The marks and underlined passages within the book by Evola are more frequent and significant. Among the more significant ones :

p. 82 it is necessary to keep spiritual tension alive, the superior fire, the internal shaping soul, which elevated matter up to that very shape, creating a race of the spirit in its image as an equivalent race of the body and the soul.

p. 96 [vigorously underlined]: dynamic theory, rather than static, of race and heredity.

p. 100 elevation of relatively inferior races through various heredity cycles.

p. 125 [underlined in red]: An idea, since it acts with sufficient intensity and continuity in a given historical climate and a collective society, winds up creating a "race of the soul" and, with its continuing action, gives rise in the generations that immediately follow, to a new standard physical type, that can be considered, from a certain point of view, as a new race.

On page 95 are underlined the well-known statements by Salaman regarding the "Jewish type" and the "German type."

Without getting into the "scientific" merits of Evola's theory and, in particular, regarding the passages underlined by Mussolini, nor into the Duce's cultural knowledge, these passages seem to confirm that Mussolini conceived of race and racism in a completely different manner from the Nazis, a "creational" and "spiritualistic" manner that had nothing to do with anthropology and biology.

It is within these various parameters that the anti-Semitic racial policy of Fascism should be placed. There is no doubt that the famous slogan, "discriminate, but do not persecute,"* reflected Mussolini's true intentions. Italian anti-Semitic legislation was, compared to that of other countries, much less personally oppressive and there is no doubt that Mussolini, once he had decided upon the racial campaign, aimed more than anything at pushing the Jews out of Italy, not to persecute and exterminate them. In February 1940, with the war already started, he thought of expelling all the Jews from Italy, at a rate of ten each day (obviously to avoid shocking

---

* In Fascist terminology, the terms "discriminate" and "discrimination" were used to describe those Jews who, for a variety of reasons, benefited from some type of exemption. [Translator]

public opinion with a mass exodus and, perhaps, secretly trying to "checkmate" the Germans). The project was shelved due to Italy's entry into the war, but no obstacles were placed on Jewish emigration. Not only did emigration continue officially for a long time, but Italian authorities were informed of many of its "clandestine" aspects; the DELASEM handling it was in constant contact with Bocchini first, and then with Senise; it was authorized to receive financial help from foreign countries, especially the USA, and was even given special terms by the Ministry of Currency and Exchange for currency transactions at a higher rate than the official rate of the U. S. dollar. Not only was emigration greatly favored but more than one eye was closed even toward those Jews coming more or less clandestinely into Italy to flee the Nazis. For a long time the internment and concentration camps for Jews were used only for foreign Jews and those considered "politically dangerous" and, except for the rather primitive hygienic facilities because of their locations, life was not too harsh in most of them. Many Jews do not have horrible memories of the camp at Fossoli.

It can be said that Mussolini started the racial campaign, besides seeking to eliminate any major differences with Germany, more against the "Italians" than against the Jews. Towards the latter he thought, in his moral crudeness and his simplistic view of spiritual values, that once one part had been allowed to emigrate, eliminating those that were "politically unreliable," the others, those who were "patriots," would require a generation in the new Fascist climate for them to become "Italians." Speaking in October 1941 to Yvon De Begnac he even turned his idea into a theory:[690]

> The Jew who is a patriot loses the argumentative characteristics of the race. When it comes down to helping the Homeland in crisis, General Pugliese, of the Naval Engineers, without asking to be reinstated to his rank, brought the ships sunk at Taranto by the British flyers back to the surface. I have Aryanized these men of heart. I took the same decision regarding a heroic recipient of a gold medal in Spain, Lieutenant Jesi, and also for the son-in-law of a General who is fighting with determination in North Africa. No one asked me for such decisions. I am encouraging people to leave more and

more. The Ministry of Currency and Exchange has been instructed to facilitate financial transactions for those emigrating. Many have settled their claims with the relevant courts. The procedure is that each one is free to use the law to the limits of what is allowed. Former Prefect Almansi, who is in constant contact with me, will become Aryan, and I am committed to it, as soon as he has resolved the difficult problem I have asked him to study. It will be settled in one generation. Mixed marriages are slowly eliminating Jewish traits. A small percentage will not hurt in the veins of the Italians in the future.

His real "obsession" was the "Italians," those Italians who refuse to feel Italian, who did not *feel* that they belonged to their own "race," who were always ready to "sell out." Out of a "race of slaves" he wanted to create a "race of lords."[691] One day, speaking with Ciano about the anti-Semitic campaign he let slip an utterance that betrays his entire insane and criminal racist infatuation:

All this will increase the hatred of foreigners toward Italy. That's fine: I will do everything I can to turn my back on France and England, from whom we can only expect more rot.[692]

And another day he observes again:

The revolution must now affect the habits of Italians. They must learn to be less "friendly," to become hard, implacable, odious. In other words: masters.[693]

We have shown how, in rethinking his racial policy, Mussolini even criticized the manifesto of the "scientists." Again De Begnac tells us that already in 1941 he was critical of certain "excesses" in the press campaign against the Jews.[694] Yet there is no doubt that the racial campaign gained momentum from 1938 to 1943, although it is useless to speak of the last two years because the RSI was, for all practical purposes, a province of Germany rather than a sovereign state. The most intelligent explanation of this fact was probably given by Giuseppe Bastianini in his memoirs, where he noted that the anti-Semitic measures would certainly have fallen by the wayside "if [Mussolini] had not had the impression that, from some quarters, they were trying to pressure the feelings of the Italian people, who were undoubtedly stunned by these measures, to begin a political maneuver intended to thwart him."[695] The almost unanimous rebellion of the conscience of the Italian people against the racial measures, even when Mussolini's own sister and his own children were to protect their Jewish friends "mercilessly," threatening to even give them a bed in their own room if they were not allowed to emigrate or settle their affairs legally.[696] The help and solidarity offered in every shape and form by all social classes must have appeared to Mussolini as a real betrayal, the refusal to become a "master race" an attempt to bend and thwart him. His obstinacy begins here, increasing daily, growing stronger because of the defeats he suffered and the inextricable and suffocating ties of an alliance that had brought his Axis allies inside his own domain. And they behaved like the real "master race."

In conclusion, there were many causes for the persecution and many individuals responsible, from those who made it possible to those who, out of cowardice, let it happen even though they disapproved of it. The paramount responsibility, however, undoubtedly belongs to Mussolini, because of the unconscionable megalomania of his wanting to transform the Italians and, with the Germans, to transform the world in the name of principles and ideals that, while not identical to those of the Germans and often, in fact, opposed to them, were still the denial of every principle and of every ideal.

21.

Preparing Public Opinion

I n 1938 the Italian press was in the vortex of an obscene racist and anti-Semitic crescendo. Once the persecution had been decided the most important goal was to make it appear "necessary" in the eyes of the Italians and this task was assigned to the press. In the vanguard, as usual, were *Il Tevere* and *Quadrivio* and, at a somewhat more qualified level, *Il regime fascista*. *Il Tevere* was up to the task of initiating every campaign and introducing anti-Semitism into every area and every field. To its editor, Telesio Interlandi, one of the shadiest characters of Fascist anti-Semitism,[697] any excuse was good enough to attack the Jews. The path opened by these three publications was quickly followed by local and youth newspapers experiencing financial difficulties that were exposed to pressure by the Ministry of Popular Culture and local Fascist federations. Their editors hoped to gain points and further their careers or at least erase some past black marks.[698] Among those were *Vent'anni* in Turin, *L'eco di Bergamo*, *La Vedetta d'Italia* in Fiume, *San Marco* in Zara, *Il Polesine fascista* in Rovigo, *La scure* in Piacenza, *Eccoci* in Cremona, *Il solco fascista* in Reggio Emilia, *Il popolo di Romagna* in Forlì, *La libertà* in Sassari, *Fronte unico* in Rome. A few weeks later the major dailies followed suit, beginning with *Il resto del carlino* and *La stampa*. By March-April the entire Italian press was "in line." There were even some impromptu initiatives and we shall only mention the two most important ones, both in Rome: *Il giornalissimo*, a weekly edited by Oberdan Cotone, and the infamous *La difesa della razza*, edited by Interlandi, that began as a fortnightly on August 5. The din quickly became so loud that even De Bono noted in his diary:[699] "the press . . . is more disgustingly slavish than usual."

It would be impossible within the scope of this book to account for all the writings against the Jews and "in defense" of the race that appeared in the Italian press during those months; a large volume dedicated exclusively to this one subject would not be enough. We shall only illustrate a few main "themes" and follow the more significant campaigns that best illustrate how the public was being prepared for the various anti-Semitic measures. Two important moments shall set the boundaries of our investigation, the publication in mid-July of the manifesto of the "scientists" and the meeting of the Grand Council on October 6, 1938.

The first change involving the press in general came in 1938 when all news items that could be identified as "pro-Jewish," so to speak, and regarding the patriotism of Italian Jews, vanished completely from the papers. For instance, news that a Fascist Jew who was dying wished to be dressed in Fascist uniform and draped in the tricolor flag, which in another period would have occupied much space in the entire press, was published by very few papers at the bottom of the page without any typographical highlighting.[700] On the contrary, much space was devoted to all petty crimes committed by Jews and, even more, to the anti-Semitic measures enacted in other countries. The year 1938 began with the decrees enforced in Romania by the Goga government. Much space was dedicated to the pro-British position of Zionism and how it behaved as a stooge of Albion, as well as any other news item that could be used to reinforce anti-Semitism. At random we discover a political item in *Il popolo* in Turin on January 17: "ten thousand Jewish volunteers in the ranks of the Spanish Reds," and a scientific item in *La sera* in Milan on January 10: "the children of mixed marriages with Jews are predisposed to catch tuberculosis… ." Much was made of the power and the invasion of Italy by the Jews.[701] *Il Tevere* was in the forefront of every aspect of the dispute, and specialized in the "defense of the culture of the Italian race," paving the way for the coming elimination of the Jews from official culture. The "Jewish musical octopus," internationalism in the arts, the struggle against jazz and Jewish-Negro music, were its main themes, soon repeated by many smaller local and Fascist papers. Obscure little writers and two-bit critics took advantage of this opportunity to vent their animosity and envy. One of the favorite targets of the attacks, during the first days of January, was the "Jew Pincherle," meaning the novelist Alberto Moravia. The attacks were not just intended against the Jews; anyone defending them or not considered a worthy Fascist became quite simply a pro-Semite, a pro-Zionist. This would be the case of Benedetto Croce. In *La Critica* of January 20, 1938 he published a letter from the humanist Antonio Galateo defending the Jews. Immediately a fellow named V. Ratti decided to attack him in *L'artiglio*, published in Lucca (February 5).

However, the dispute in *Il Tevere* was not just an "intellectual" one; it aimed at satisfying everyone: the petit bourgeois who always dreamed of a vacation in Positano and the lower-class Romans who saw prices increase on all food items that became scarce. The first group was represented by a "letter" from "some citizens of Positano," according to whom it seemed that this small town was full of Jewish refugees from Germany who were having a grand time;[702] for the second group there was another "letter" complaining that at Campo dei Fiori (in Rome), Italians "always lose" and the Jews "always make a profit"; "they are wholesale suppliers of that market, resellers at the outside stands and clever buyers."[703]

During the first weeks of 1938 the most anti-Semitic newspapers began two campaigns which must be mentioned because of their importance. The first started in *Il regime fascista*, directed against those newspapers, *Il piccolo* in Trieste first and foremost, that were not eager enough in their support of anti-Semitism and were actually critical of its supporters; and the second, initiated by *Il Tevere* and continued by *Il resto del carlino*, against the authorization and the easing of the rules allowing Jewish refugees to attend Italian schools and universities and, more broadly, against their being granted any "shelter" in Italy.

We mentioned in the preceding chapter that the republication the year before of the *Protocols* by Preziosi had elicited very little support, few critical reviews, and much silence. The situation during the first few days of 1938 had not changed much, in the January issue of *La vita italiana* Preziosi echoed what Farinacci's paper had already written:

> ...all book stores have either refused, or have not requested it or keep the book hidden; it is a much sought after book that sells well. And the newspapers? Except for *Il regime fascista* and *Il Tevere*, you can count on the fingers of one hand which papers wrote about the book and then only a few short lines. They did not even add it to the "books received" list.[704]

If anyone even took the trouble to mention the *Protocols*, it was only to criticize the book. Besides the article by Adriano Tilgher in *Il lavoro* in Genoa, at the end of December, there was a statement by the Hon. Niccolò Castellino, "Noi fascisti e la Germania" [We Fascists and Germany] in the *Nuova antologia* and another in *Il giornale d'Italia*. These statements had similar-sounding themes: "in Italy a Jewish problem does not exist and cannot exist"; "Italian Jews represent within their own race one of most homogenous and high quality branches." In addition to these voices there appeared a long article on January 1 by Rino Alessi in *Il piccolo* in Trieste entitled "Un problema" [A Problem]. Another article was published on January 6 and 7 in *Il piccolo* in Rome. Both were reprinted and favorably received, especially the former, by various papers (*Il popolo di Lombardia* and *Roma fascista*). Preziosi, Farinacci, and company decided to move agressively to muzzle these voices and discourage any others. While *Il piccolo* in Rome had shown little inclination to accept the *Protocols* as being true, Rino Alessi's paper had gone further. In analyzing the Jewish problem broadly, taking into account its European developments, especially in Romania, and its repercussions in Italy, Alessi stated that he rejected the interpretation of race as a biological factor and affirmed in so many words that "the Fascistization of the world…cannot be interpreted or dragged down by the noisy contingencies of anti-Semitism." The editor of *Il piccolo* clearly wrote that the only measure worthy of Italian civilization and its history would be to forbid the influx of Jewish refugees into Italy. Preziosi and Farinacci counterattacked violently. The former answered in his magazine, with an interview published in *Il giornalissimo*, a letter and a short piece in *Il regime fascista*, where he accused Alessi of being dependent upon the Jews and reaffirming the authenticity of the *Protocols*. But it was Farinacci who led the campaign.

It was clear from the first article, "Controffensiva" [Counteroffensive], on January 12 that *Il regime fascista* aimed not just at shutting up its opponents by forcing them to concur that a serious Jewish problem existed in Italy. In attacking Alessi and *Il piccolo* in Trieste, *Il regime fascista* began a violent struggle against the Jews of Trieste, the only Jewish community in Italy that was somewhat strong socially and within local politics. This incident is too important not to be summarized, at least in its broader strokes.

Since 1934, Starace had been observing the situation in Trieste and wanted to eliminate the Jews from "positions of authority and leadership" within the city. These plans had been temporarily set aside, when, during the second half of 1937 following the wave of the anti-Semitic campaign a few months before, they were revived in Rome and among some Fascists in Trieste. A report dated September 24, 1937 addressed to the national secretariat of the PNF indicates how these groups were initially targeting *Il piccolo*.[707] The report stated that the Fascist revolution had worked only half way in Trieste: of its two main enemies, the *Red-Slavs* and the *Jewish-Democratic-Freemasons*, only the former had been wiped out. This partial success had been achieved "not with the direct help, but with the quiet acquiescence" of the second group of "enemies" that, as the report continued, had claimed credit for "succeeding, not only in keeping its formerly held positions, but expanding and deepening their scope in all the aspects of city life." "From that moment on the only ones to be able to live in Trieste are those belonging to the vast and shady de facto criminal organization." It was therefore necessary to wipe out (and the report requested Rome's intervention in the matter) this "hybrid area of Masonic Judaism dressed in black shirts," beginning with its symbol and most "insidious weapon," *Il piccolo*, owned by the Jew Teodoro Mayer.[708] This situation had a whole series of precedents and connections: those promoting anti-Semitism in Trieste were obviously persons who, since they were outside the social and municipal leadership of the city, wanted to eliminate the Jews to grab their positions. The manipulations of Farinacci and Preziosi also played an important part and, most of all, the struggle between the two most important local factions within the Fascists, Francesco Giunta and Giuseppe Cobolli-Gigli, to seize control of the city. The anti-Jewish campaign was really a campaign of Fascists against other Fascists, with the Jews merely as an excuse. This immediately leads us to understand why Farinacci went on the war path with such violence against *Il piccolo*, initiating a dispute that appears to be out of proportion and, in some ways, counterproductive since, rather than keeping Alessi's protestations at the local level, they were elevated to the national level and to persons who would otherwise probably have never heard of these events.[709] The local situation in Trieste explains why Rino Alessi, at first, did not respond to Farinacci's attack, as he tried to avoid widening the dispute that risked spreading from generalities to the particular situation and threaten the Jews of Trieste as well as the very survival of *Il piccolo*. This, however, was Farinacci's very purpose and silence would not stop him. After waiting for an answer for a few days, on the 21st *Il regime fascista* attacked once again with a very violent article, "Seconda replica" [Second Answer], that focused on the situation in Trieste and furnished "documentary

248

proof" that it was controlled by the Jews. After listing all the public and private jobs and posts that were in Jewish hands (the same technique would soon be used by Nello Quilici for Ferrara and by others in smaller cities), the article concluded:

> Keeping the proportions in mind, among the 250,000 Catholics and the 4,000 Jews, we can conclude that the latter have nine-tenths (900 out of 1,000!) of the jobs encompassing the intellectual, economic, financial, and union leadership of Trieste.
>
> But Trieste is not an anomaly. We know the conditions in other Italian cities. And at the right time we shall publish the first and last names and the posts they occupy.
>
> We shall then ask with greater strength and authority to *Il piccolo* in Rome, *Il piccolo* and *Il popolo* in Trieste, to *Il lavoro* in Genoa if they still cling to the same point of view.

It was not yet a demand for "proportional representation" and quotas, but that was the essence of the dispute and Farinacci would make those demands as soon as the *Informazione Diplomatica* n. 14 was published.[710] This time it would be impossible to keep silent. On the 25th Alessi answered with a long article, eloquently entitled "Situazioni che non pesano" [Situations that Don't Matter], that was firm and dignified and deserves to be reprinted in its entirety. Having examined the situation in general, the editor of *Il piccolo* wrote:

> If the rule that citizens should be judged by their thoughts and actions giving life a purpose still applies today, *Il regime fascista* must admit that there is only one situation that is important to us; the honorable preoccupation of being worthy of a history that has its own dates and its inalterable markings. On May 24, 1915 our house was burned down and completely destroyed; the newspaper's publisher was condemned to death and his possessions were confiscated. Six years ago, when we celebrated the first half century of our activity, the Duce honored us with these words: "I want to be present at the celebration of the first fifty years of *Il piccolo*." "May *Il piccolo* continue on its mission of guarding our borders into the next fifty years. This is my wish." Just three weeks ago, certainly not because

of our request or solicitation, we received the gold medal of merit for culture and national education from the Fascist government. We add that we would not be writing this, even though they are dear to us as persons working with a clear conscience, if we did not feel pushed into self-defense.

No statistics, for whatever reason they were compiled, can place any doubt on this simple truth: that for over a half century *Il piccolo* has served the interests of the Nation with men who have the right to feel Italian as much as those who, with their thoughts and actions, consider Italy and only Italy as their only irrevocable Homeland.

If today, by adopting a concept of race that differs from that of the first fifteen years of Fascist life, one wishes to ignore the ethnographic makeup of our peninsula and the Roman tradition that recognizes the right to citizenship to anyone who, out of coherence and loyalty of thought and action proves that he deserves it, is now to be replaced by the racial testing of anthropological laboratories, it will be best not to waste too much time before erasing from the history of Trieste, as a city separated from Italy, the entire quarter century when Felice Venezian was directing with true Italian sentiments the policies of the Adriatic; to melt down the bullet that, on the Carso, took the noble life of Giacomo Venezian, one of the purest founders of Italian nationalism; to tear away two gold medals out of the six that honor with their glorious dead, the group of volunteers from Trieste, etc.

Il regime fascista must agree, because the history of this "faithful city of Rome" demands that kind of respect, that if there are Jews in Trieste who fit the description, we shall not be the ones to ask for mitigation of the law and of opinion. There are also those Italians of Jewish origin who do not deserve the humiliation of being subjected to generalized statistics after having been given, when Fascism was already leading Italy to its destiny, the honor and responsibility of public positions and to join with their names, those who died for Italy at war, on the walls of the noblest chapel of Italian patriotism: the cell of Guglielmo Oberdan.

Farinacci could be stopped neither by silence nor even less by strong and clear words. Two editorials in *Il regime fascista* of January

28 and 29 reiterated the "language of numbers" and rejected the reasons given by Alessi with two dry statements, that these were things of the past and it was best not to discuss them again and that Rino Alessi was chasing butterflies "under the arch of Titus through which the Jews were not allowed to pass." At the same time various other Fascist newspapers joined in the attack against *Il piccolo*. A new reply by Alessi, "In carreggiata" [On the Way], on the 29th was of no consequence. In the coming months the dispute between *Il piccolo* and *Il regime fascista* would see a few more weakening skirmishes:[711] *l'Informazione Diplomatica* n.14 and the manifesto of the "scientists" proved to Alessi and the Mayers the uselessness of a struggle doomed in advance and that could only hurt the Jews in Trieste. In July *Il piccolo* was sold by the Mayer family to a new publishing company[712] and Rino Alessi was fortunate to keep his job as editor. With the creation of a new company, the only large "Jewish" newspaper in Italy disappeared along with the only relatively free voice[713] in Trieste.

At the same time *Il Tevere* and *Il resto del carlino* were running their campaign against foreign Jews in Italy. The pace was set, as usual, by Interlandi's newspaper on January 14 with an article "Quelli che vengono" [Those Who are Coming] in which it was claimed that the student refugees coming to Italy constituted a grave danger because they remained in Italy after getting their degree, thus hurting the Italians and taking away jobs and careers:

> The foreign Jew with an Italian degree is preferred by our companies for, shall we say, innocent reasons; he knows more languages and adapts more easily and is more humble than an Italian... he has, in one word, the famous *characteristics* of the Jew. Mindful that much of the business world is filled with Jews and the foreign Jew finds the kind of solidarity that he needs. Once settled in Italy and having found a job, they wind up being naturalized, increasing the ranks of the local Jewry and becoming carriers of new Jewish poison (especially in the field of literature).

The campaign was taken one step further by "Camicia Nera," the pen name of an editorial writer at *Il resto del carlino*. The first editorial that took its cue from what was happening in Bologna was published on January 28; others followed on the 29th, 30th, and on February 1 and 4. The ideas put forth by "Camicia Nera" were, in substance:

1. Italian universities should be closed to new foreign Jewish students.

2. Foreign Jewish graduates or those about to graduate should find it difficult to exercise their profession in Italy. To ensure this we should deny them Italian citizenship, regardless of the number of years spent in our country.

The campaign was a prelude to what would be publicly announced in July, forbidding admissions of foreign Jews to all schools during the 1938-1939 school year. *Il Tevere* immediately voiced its support, since it had launched the campaign in the first place as well as other publications, especially youth newspapers.[714]

The *Informazione diplomatica* n. 14 of February 16 did not receive much coverage by the press in such an atmosphere. The real upheaval began with the publication, on July 14, of the manifesto of the "scientists" and the PNF press release on July 25 commenting on the manifesto itself. Not surprisingly, even Ciano noted the event in his diary: "emotion."[715] Virtually taken by surprise on the first day, the newspapers, for the most part, published the manifesto without any comment, or at the most reprinted the commentary from *Il popolo d'Italia*, which was less than half a column long and encouraged the Italian people to be aware and proud of their race. The skirmishing began during the next few days and all the newspapers dedicated their editorials first to the manifesto, then to the press release. In this mass of articles, which, it should be noted, were often anonymous, we shall single out only the one in *Il regime fascista* of July 17, "Razzismo" [Racism] by Maurizio Claremoris, which was sycophantic and sought to deny the "universalist" interpretations of Fascism by "souls buried in aspic, that, through multiple nuances, have successfully reconciled their innate social democratic instincts and the old Sturzian[*] faith with Fascism,"[716] and

———————

[*] *Sturzian*: the followers of Don Luigi Sturzo, one of the founders of the Partito Popolare, the forerunner of the Christian Democratic Party. [NDT]

those of Virginio Gayda, one of the most prominent political commentators of the time, in *Il giornale d'Italia* on July 24 and 27, seeking to identify racial policy with national policy. During the second half of July and all of August and September there was a gradual crescendo over the controversy: the manifesto and the PNF press release were immediately taken literally and there was not a daily paper that did not attack the Jews in general vociferously demanding that measures be taken against them.

Generally, there were various kinds of attacks: besides the usual platitudes about "Judaic characteristics," and the anti-Fascism of the Jews, many newspapers published, for example, the list of the Jews who some time before had signed the "Croce manifesto" on Zionism and the Jewish international. Foreign commentary favorable to Italy's new policy was given much space, as well as the measures taken by other countries against the Jews and their immigration.[717] Ordinary crimes committed by Jews in Italy and abroad were also given a lot of attention. When the Grand Council met on October 6, 1938, Fascist propaganda capitalized on the "foreign exchange scandal" of Sacerdoti-Godio. Because of his popularity, a former president of the *Roma* soccer club, Fascist propaganda underscored, as much as it could, the "Jewish origins" of Renato Sacerdoti.[718]

The attacks, in general, had two major objectives: on the one hand, against "Jewish superpower" in Italy, and on the other against "pietism," meaning those who did not "understand" the policy on race, which included the overwhelming majority of the Italian people. We shall analyze this last feature of anti-Semitic propaganda during the coming months.

There was not a newspaper, nationally or locally, that did not undertake its own investigation of the Jews, foreign and Italian, criticizing how many they were, what they owned, the positions they held, the business activities they engaged in. The action that was clearly positioned as a "defense" by the regime against this "invasion" and this "superpower," was conducted at all levels. Foreign Jews were the first targets. The campaign in *Il Tevere* and *Il resto del carlino* against the students was now broadened indiscriminately to all foreign Jews, up to the decisions of the Council of Ministers of September 2. It was obvious that this was just the first step. *Il Tevere* made the point that same day in its editorial comments, the very title being a statement in and of itself, "Primo: gli ebrei stranieri" [First: the Foreign Jews]: "It begins with the foreign Jews. Those remaining are the so-called Italian Jews. The fate of these other foreigners is also cast."

Along with the foreign Jews, the Jews in schools, both teachers and students, were also under fire. Here as well, the decisions of the Council of Ministers on September 3 were given several weeks of preparation by a violent campaign using the slogans of "The Jews out of the universities!" and "The Jews poison Italian youth!" In many cases lists of Jewish professors were published; some youth newspapers and GUF publications stood out during this campaign. Once decisions of the government were made public, and went even further than what many people expected (since they not only hurt the Jewish teachers but also the students themselves), this barbaric anti-cultural and uncivilized act found its own supporters. *Il Tevere* triumphantly published a new editorial, "Secondo: gli ebrei d'Italia" [Second: the Jews of Italy], calling the race laws "providential." *Critica fascista* was of the same opinion, meaning the "cultured" Bottai, in the September 15 issue, "Primo: la scuola" [First: the Schools]) and along with him, Rino Alessi, who had quickly fallen in line in *Il piccolo* on September 3 with "Resurrexit" and, along with them, many other "men of culture."

Besides the foreign Jews and the Jews in the educational system, all Jews were targeted in a sort of "Jew hunt" that spared nothing and no one. It was a methodical action leaving not a single little corner untouched. According to *Il telegrafo* of August 11, the article regarding the Jews in the *Enciclopedia Italiana* had been written "by Jews, by Zionists or some other anti-racist scholars" and should be completely rewritten. Some newspapers attacked those publishers who continued to publish books by Jewish authors,[719] while others were denouncing Jews who held public or political positions.[720] *Il regime fascista* even published the letter from a disgusted reader in Bologna complaining that in his city there was still a "via dei Giudei" [Jewish Street].[721] By September all these attacks, which until then had been left to the "creativity" and "spontaneity" of the various news editors, were to be carefully orchestrated. *Il popolo d'Italia* took on the task by itself.[722]

It began with a series of specific attacks against Jewish lawyers, Jewish doctors, Jews in the press, Jews in agriculture, Jews in the trades, Jews in commerce, Jews in the theater and cinema, Jewish accountants, Jews in industry, Jews in finance and the stock exchange, Jews in the navy, etc. Even sports publications attacked Jewish trainers and Jewish athletes. As the days passed, and the meeting of the Grand Council set to deal with the race issue came closer, the attacks became more personal, vilifying well-known Fascists, like Gino Arias and anyone with a "Jewish name." Some very prominent individuals, such as the doctor and Fascist deputy in parliament Eugenio Morelli and Marshal of Italy Enrico Caviglia, were denounced as "Jews" despite many denials, and these attacks continued drawing protests from newspapers which could not be termed pro-Semitic.[723] In a competition of zealously slavish behavior, possibly the most revolting that ever took place in Italy, some writers who were even more anti-Semitic than the policy of the regime itself were not satisfied with the measures already taken and loudly demanded their "totalitarian" and intransigent application, more intransigent than the manner in which the government was prepared to enact them. For example, using a news item of a few Jews who had been stopped at the border as they attempted to take their possessions with them, *Roma fascista* wrote, for example, on October 5, "Facciamoli passare nudi" [Let's Make Them Leave Naked]:

> All the Jews, the pro-Jews and the people who are suspected when leaving Italy must only take a few pennies, their clothes and their ugly snouts. But should the clothes be used to hide even one penny, then let's strip them naked and naked we'll kick them across the border by booting their backsides.

After such a preparation, the decisions of the Grand Council were welcomed by the entire press with unqualified "enthusiasm." Reading the editorials of those days it appeared that Italy had, through its racial policy, resolved all of its most delicate and vital problems. There was, however, little time for satisfaction: from October 6 to November 10, when it was made public and the moment the decisions of the Grand Council became law, the press was once again invited to stoke the fires of the issue and attack the obvious disgust and increasingly visible public aversion to the racial policy. This second aspect, the struggle against "pietism," shall be discussed further ahead. The majority of Italian newspapers actually went in two main directions: on one hand, praising the regime's "moderation," while, they claimed, the Jews responded by hurling invectives against Italy and Fascism the world over and by warmongering.[724] On the other hand, they repeated the slogan of the negative influence of Judaism on national life. During the second half of October, the news of the arrest in Trieste and Florence of two anti-Fascist groups that included the Jews Eugenio Colorni and Dino Philipson, was played up in this climate: Farinacci gave his editorial in *Il regime fascista* of October 18 the title of "Agli imbecilli" [For the Idiots], to prove what had been preached for months, namely, that the Jews, with the exception of a handful who were good Italians and good Fascists, for whom the Grand Council had done "what was logical it should do" (discrimination), were all dangerous enemies of the homeland. Not everyone approved of such "moderation." The ultraracists of *Il Tevere, Quadrivio,* and *Il giornalissimo,* and many journalists who dreamed of making the transition from their provincial papers where they starved, to the big national dailies, were hard at work to show their zeal in every possible way, loudly demanding harsher measures that were obviously inspired by those enacted in Germany. On October 24 *Il Tevere* published a letter from a group of shopkeepers in Rome, asking that there be a sign on non-Jewish stores informing their customers that it was an "Aryan" store; ten days before, the *Corriere emiliano*, representing other local papers (*La provincia di Como, Corriere adriatico, La scure,* etc.) had demanded the death penalty, Al muro! [Against the Wall!] for the "traitors of the national treasure," meaning against those Jews who, when forced to emigrate, attempted to smuggle their possessions out of Italy. They also complained about the "big papers," which did not sufficiently condemn these incidents and used them for their journalistic purposes. *Il lavoro fascista* also demanded, on November 2, that "the Aryan worker who wishes to leave his job as the employee of a Jewish company should be able to do so without fear, for this gesture of patriotic pride, for this gesture of legitimate courage"…of losing his retirement fund; and again in *Il giornalissimo:* "Discriminazione e incriminazione" [Discrimination and Incrimination] did not hide its disappointment that there were Jews who benefited from being *discriminated* and, in its issue of October 28, did not hesitate to threaten them. The assembly of journalists of Tuscany was up to the standard, and we shall close this list of moral miseries when, on October 23, it voted a position paper demanding the exclusion of "all those belonging to the Jewish race, without consideration of any type of discrimination" from the lists of its profession.[725] For all of them, the only policy on race was the one invoked by *Quadrivio* on October 16: "total and permanent separation." Assimilation was a dangerous illusion:

> The baptisms, the marriages celebrated according to the Catholic ritual, the break with Jewish tradition, this is all sensational but doesn't have anything to do with race, it doesn't change the blood, it doesn't cancel the Jew. The Jews will reappear in due time beneath the thin crust that hides them from the eyes of the naïve.

The naïve were not just the "pietists" but Mussolini himself, and whoever harbored the fantasy that there were "good" and "bad" Jews.

The magazine *La difesa della razza* took a unique position. It was, edited by Interlandi, who in September had published a short book eloquently entitled *Contra Judaeos*; *La difesa della razza* wanted to be mostly a magazine of popular scientific racism. Various scholars of anthropology, zoology, demography, medicine, biology, sociology, statistics, etc., were to contribute, as well as historians and literary critics; with few exceptions its tone was anything but scientific and anti-Semitic controversy was its real thrust. The documentary parts, especially, used material most often originating from Germany. In general, *La difesa della razza,* despite the clamor with which it was "launched" and the praise it initially garnered, failed to fulfill that "educational" function the Fascists expected. Notwith-

standing wide distribution, it only reached a very limited readership. To analyze this influence it is interesting to study its incoming
mail, called the "questionnaire." Even though the magazine would
be published regularly up to the eve of July 25, 1943, its real importance as an instrument of racist and mass anti-Semitic propaganda
was limited to its first issues. Because of the difficulty in finding the
entire spectrum of publications of the time, *La difesa della razza*
became, after the fall of Fascism, the symbol of the anti-Semitic
campaign; in reality its importance was not only very limited, but
the content offered only a pale reflection of what the press campaign against the Jews amounted to. The true picture of the campaign is reflected only in the daily newspapers. In a certain sense *La
difesa della razza* is already placed on a slightly "higher," less violent,
level and, even though this may seem a bit exaggerated, the tone of
its articles does not have the immediacy of the personal attacks on
the Italian Jews of the dailies.

If the press played an essential role in the psychological preparation of the anti-Semitic measures, other forms of propaganda
were also important, the radio first and foremost. Racist propagandists could reach every home through the airwaves of EIAR, even
people who did not read the newspapers,[726] and hold the attention
of those who refused to read what was published in the press.

Although it is impossible to account for all the lectures, conversations, speeches, and similar activities taking place in Italy during
those months, sponsored by the various Fascist federations and their
local groups, we can identify the most active organizations in this
area.

The most important being the Academy of Italy. On September 3, 1938 a commission of academicians was created, including
Rodolfo Benini, Francesco Coppola, Roberto Paribeni, Raffaele
Pettazzoni, and Giuseppe Tucci, who were given the task of studying "what had been through the centuries, the symptoms and the
influence of Judaism in Italian life, from ancient Rome until today."[727] The results of this "study" were to be made public on November 20. The occasion was the tenth anniversary of the founding of the Academy, to be commemorated at the Capitol. King
Victor Emmanuel III was present at the ceremony and academi-

cian Roberto Paribeni read a report on "L'ebraismo nella storia e nella vita di Roma antica" [Judaism in the history and the life of ancient Rome], the first essay, produced by the commission appointed two months before.[728]

In October, a vast plan for the documentation, study, and dissemination of the problems of race was set up by the Istituto nazionale di cultura fascista (INFC).[729] Two types of initiatives were established: a course in nine lessons on various aspects of racial policy[730] and the publication of six racist booklets.[731] This took place in Rome, while elsewhere a vast propaganda and educational operation, with the participation of the Gruppi Universitari Fascisti (GUF) and school authorities, was immediately launched.

Initiatives were promoted by the Comitato d'azione per l'universalità di Roma (CAUR) and their magazine *L'idea di Roma*[732] and the Centro di coordinazione antibolscevica universale that published a newsletter *Antibolscevico*.[733]

The GUF had the widest propaganda activity. In September, Starace issued his orders: at every GUF office there would be a section for Demography and Race.[734] On short notice these head offices and their subsections, scattered all over Italy, became focal points for an extremely virulent anti-Semitic campaign. In reading the press of the time it becomes immediately clear that the GUF took on a promotional role in the anti-Jewish struggle, especially in smaller communities, setting up lectures, lessons, publishing special magazine issues and even, in some cases, periodical bulletins. The most active were to be the GUF of Campobasso, Taranto, Macerata, Trieste, and Perugia, which on October 17, 1938 published a special issue of the bulletin *L'Assalto* on the problems of race. The most active of them all, however, was the GUF at Catanzaro. This bore the name of S. Mussolini, and not only organized many lectures but also published a monthly, then fortnightly, newsletter entitled *Razzismo*.[735] It should also be noted that at the Littoriali of 1939 there was a contest for a racist essay entered by many GUF members.

22.

Fascist Party and Government Initiatives
up to September 1938

In the rapid overview of the manner in which the 1938 racial measures were presented to the Italian people by the press and Fascist propaganda in general, we have only mentioned various official declarations accompanying the first measures themselves (the two *Informazioni diplomatiche*, the manifesto of the "scientists," etc.). These official announcements were mainly intended as propaganda tools to prepare public opinion; the manifesto of the "scientists" had the same purpose, so much so that in 1939-1940 the Fascists were seriously thinking of publishing a real "Declaration on Race." For several months these were the only official standards by which to gauge, in Italy and overseas, the shifting positions of the PNF and the government, both being obvious instruments of Fascist propaganda. Actually, due to the nature of the offices issuing these declarations, they automatically acquired a unique political value, transforming them into *instruments of government*. We have chosen to place the issue of government declarations in this section rather than earlier, which may create some difficulty for tracing the way propaganda presented the anti-Semitic measures for readers who did not live through those sad years. For the same reasons, we delayed in mentioning the disputes with the Catholic press and the attacks on "pietism." The purely political and official disputes between the Fascists and the Catholic Church, while part of the action of the PNF and the government, appear to mirror popular resistance to Fascism's anti-Semitic campaign.

We have seen how, in describing Mussolini's initial position in foreign policy and in the relations between the Duce and his closest staff—those at *Il popolo d'Italia*, for example—the very first anti-Semitic actions began as far back as the second half of 1936. The first "official" act was the publication of the *Informazione diplomatica* n.14. Mussolini had announced even before to his staff that he was about to take a position on the question of the Jews and race,[737] but had actually never done so. The *Informazione diplomatica* n. 14 was published on February 16, 1938 and had been written entirely by Mussolini; Ciano's contribution, as we have said previously, was limited to the paragraph on Palestine.[738] It stated:

> Recent journalistic disputes may have created the impression in certain foreign circles that the Fascist government was about to begin an anti-Semitic policy.
>
> In official Roman circles we can say that this impression is completely mistaken and the disputes are considered the result of world anti-Fascist opinion normally controlled by Jewish elements.
>
> Official Roman circles feel that the universal Jewish problem can be resolved in only one way: by creating in some part of the world, but not in Palestine, a Jewish State, a State in the real sense of the word that can therefore represent and protect, through normal diplomatic and consular channels, the Jewish masses scattered about in various countries.
>
> The fact that there are Jews in Italy doesn't necessarily imply the existence of a specifically Italian Jewish problem. On the other hand, while there are millions of Jews, the Jews in Italy are between 50 to 60 thousand out of a population that is almost 44 million.
>
> The Fascist government never thought, nor is it now contemplating, taking political, economic, or moral measures against the Jews as such, except, obviously, for those elements hostile to the Regime.
>
> The Fascist government is absolutely opposed to any form of pressure, direct or indirect, to extract religious abjurations and artificial assimilation. The law that regulates and controls the life of the Jewish communities has worked well and shall remain unchanged.
>
> The Fascist government plans to watch over the activities of the Jews who have recently entered our country and make sure that the role of the Jews in the collective national life is not disproportionate to the personal merits nor the numerical importance of their community.

Ciano relates that Mussolini himself termed it "a masterpiece of anti-Semitic propaganda."[739] Written in a deceptively conciliatory tone, the initial statement denying any governmental intention of instituting measures against the Jews was followed by many qualifications that actually were tantamount to announcements. For whoever understood a little of the Fascist technique of presenting the most delicate problems, it obviously presaged the coming measures. The last paragraph in particular is extremely clear: it says, in effect, that Mussolini was preparing measures against foreign Jews who were refugees in Italy and wished to introduce proportional representation for Italian Jews.

Obviously this was Mussolini's intention, confirmed by all the documents of the period in the archives. The legitimate question is why Fascism kept its true intentions secret for so many months and even denied several times of having any anti-Jewish regulations in mind. We think the answer can be found in a number of reasons. First, Italian public opinion was not yet prepared for the introduction of the measures and it was thought best to delay their enactment until after the ad hoc propaganda campaign, when Italians presumably would be sufficiently "convinced" that such measures were necessary.[740] Second, well aware of the unpopular reactions the measures would elicit overseas and from the Holy See, it was decided to delay taking an official position as much as possible, hoping that some unforeseen event would somehow justify them in the eyes of international public opinion. It was symptomatic that, even when the initial measures were taken against foreign Jews, their continued arrival into Italy was ignored, as if Mussolini hoped in this way to buy a more benevolent, or at least less hostile, attitude from Jewish organizations and publications abroad. By the end of December, when the first measures against Italian Jews had been introduced and there could be no further doubts as to his policies, the Duce answered questions from the Ministries of the Interior and Foreign Affairs as to how they should treat foreign Jews wishing to visit Italy as tourists, for health reasons, or to attend conventions and scientific meetings, by saying that he was in favor of allowing them into Italy and that his decision was motivated by the need to ensure the success of the 1942 Exhibition.[741] The third and final reason was that many were of the opinion that it was better that Mussolini conceal his intentions until the very last moment, in order to avoid damaging consequences to the national economy. Many feared that once the government's intentions became clear, numerous Jews would liquidate and then export their capital surreptitiously and therefore harm the Italian economy.[742] There is undeniable evidence confirming this fear. When *Il regime fascista*, on April 19, attacked the Trieste Committee for Assistance to Jewish Emigrants and the transit of these emigrants through the port, Ciano quickly stopped Farinacci by sending him a confidential note dated June 4:

> I inform you that the Italian Committee for Assistance to Jewish Emigrants is useful to us, not just to maintain but also to increase the flow of Jewish emigrants on our ships on the Palestine line, a good, lucrative traffic for the Steamship Company and that we must continue to fight to keep it from going to foreign competitors. You understand, therefore, that in the future, it's best to "pretend to not know" that such a Committee exists.[743]

After the publication of *Informazione diplomatica* n. 14, no further official positions were taken for about five months. The preparation of the measures was in full swing; a few telling symptoms began surfacing during the second half of June. At that time, requests arrived at the appropriate offices regarding the lists of Italian delegates to some conventions and international scientific meetings. There was no official rule against Jews participating in these meetings; that decision would only be made on July 21. Nevertheless all Jewish names were deleted from the lists. From the documents of the Presidency of the Council of Ministers[744] we know that Mussolini personally took care of the matter and crossed out the names of the Jews in his own hand and, when unsure, requested that they be investigated. Among the names crossed out were Roberto Almagià, who was scheduled to go to Amsterdam for the international geographic conference and to Zurich for the historical science convention; Camillo Crema, an engineer, who was to attend the international society for the study the chemistry of the earth meeting in Helsinki; and Doctor Italo Olivetti on his way to Berlin for a conference on technical instruction. The head of the public health organization of Albania had invited Professor Maurizio Ascoli to hold a series of lectures on the therapy of malaria in Tirana, under which invitation Mussolini had written: "Choose a Christian among the 44 million of same."

Finally, on July 14, came the publication of the manifesto of the "scientists."[745] It was generally racist in tone; of the ten points only one, the ninth, spoke of the Jews:

9. THE JEWS DO NOT BELONG TO THE ITALIAN RACE

Nothing remains of the Semites who reached the sacred soil of our Homeland throughout the centuries. The Arab occupation of Sicily has left nothing besides the memory of some names; the process of assimilation was always very rapid in Italy. The Jews are the only people who never assimilated in Italy because they are made up of non-European racial elements that differ in absolute terms from the elements that are at the origins of the Italians.

It was immediately clear to everyone, long before it would be underscored by the press, that the purpose of the manifesto was to create an ideological and scientific platform for state-sponsored anti-Semitism.

It is pointless to discuss the "scientific" value of this manifesto; its absence of foundation, in this sense, has been proved many times over, and even the most extreme promoters of the anti-Semitic campaign did not give it much importance in this area. It is more interesting to try to reconstruct its secret history, since no mention of it can be found in the documents we have examined. The manifesto was published anonymously, as is well known, by *Il giornale d'Italia* and then by the entire press. Only on July 25, 1938, eleven days later, did a PNF press release reveal the names of its authors and supporters and announced that it had been written "with the sponsorship of the Ministry of Popular Culture."[746] Actually, things went somewhat differently and this may explain the delay in making public the names of its authors, half of whom were only young university assistants (Lino Businco, Lidio Cipriani, Leone Franzi, Guido Landra, Marcello Ricci), and among the others (Arturo Donaggio, Nicola Pende, Franco Savorgnan, Sabato Visco, Edoardo Zavattari), only Pende was well known. The manifesto was not, it appears, the one written by the group of ten whose names were published on July 25. The original text was broadly edited, certainly by Mussolini,[747] and probably by functionaries of the Popular Culture and the secretariat of the PNF. This is clear not just from Ciano's diary, but also from the request made by Pende immediately following the 25th, to issue a "new declaration of the race commission" that Pende[748] had sent to Mussolini, as well as the commotion in Fascist circles[749] because of some statements made by Pende himself, which, though very cautious, were considered extremely dangerous and of instigating "pernicious consequences to Italian and foreign public opinion." There were protests to Dino Alfieri, the Minister of Popular Culture, against the rewritten manifesto, and, it appears, even to Mussolini himself by at least two "signers," Pende and Visco.[750] Their protests, however, were not taken into consideration and there was even a direct threat against Pende to put a gag on any future scientific communications of his, even on matters other than race, by the entire press.[751] Their agreement was obtained through the real threat of ostracism and the tacit acknowledgment on their part that they had originated the manifesto, which otherwise would have had only the signatures of a few younger men and persons of middle scientific importance, losing the semblance of authority conferred upon it by the names of Pende and Visco. However, even though this does not reduce the moral responsibility of all the signers of the manifesto, it does explain how some real scientists ended up, in fact, approving a text that, from every point of view, scientific, political and moral, remains one of the worst and shabbiest episodes of the Fascist period.

After the publication of the manifesto on July 14 and the press release of the 25th, the persecution machine began to function openly. Before the publication of the PNF press release, a change was announced at the Interior Ministry: the Central Demographic Office became the General Directorate for Demography and Race. This was how the famous "Demorazza" was created that would decide the fate of tens of thousands of foreign and Italian Jews for the next five years. Prefect Antonio Le Pera, along with Buffarini-Guidi, actually directed Italian anti-Jewish policy during that period. Among the first decisions taken by the new General Directorate, the most important was the de facto census of all Jews present in Italy[752] and a memorandum signed by Buffarini-Guidi and circulated to the ministries and major state organizations for them to proceed with a census of all their employees belonging to the Jewish "race."

On August 5 a new issue of *Informazione diplomatica*, n. 18,[753] officially announced what had barely been hinted at in n.14. After a few general paragraphs on Italian racism and Fascism's position on the issue, the *Informazione* stated:

> To discriminate does not mean to persecute. The Fascist government has no special plan to persecute the Jews as such. What this means is something different. There are 44,000 Jews in the metropolitan territory of Italy; the proportion would be one Jew for every thousand inhabitants. It is clear that from now on the participation of the Jews in the total life of the state must be, and shall be, adjusted in the same proportion.

The first measure, announced along with this declaration, forbade foreign Jews from matriculating at the schools of the Kingdom for the year 1938-1939.

Once it was in place, the persecution machine began churning like a vortex, so much so that, in a few weeks many decisions and measures were reviewed and modified several times due to the speed and shallowness with which they were introduced. What the zeal of individual ministers and functionaries could accomplish during this preparatory phase of the measures and during their enactment was apparent in the way various ministries and state agencies answered the memorandum from Demography and Race during the first days of August.[754] Most ministries limited themselves to acknowledging receipt of the memorandum and proceeded with the census. Foreign Affairs answered on August 17 that it had completed the census, and had recalled to headquarters those functionaries and employees who were unmistakably Jewish, placing them on furlough; ordered investigations of the doubtful cases; fired all local Jews employed in foreign countries as occasional workers, and finally, had made necessary investigations regarding the wives of functionaries posted abroad, "to avoid the kind of family hybridism that would create the impression abroad that the rules adopted by the regime are not of a binding nature." The Ministry of War answered on August 23 that it had proceeded with the census and excluded Jews from admission to military schools and academies and those already admitted would be expelled at the first opportunity. It is symptomatic that the Ministry of War specified that in all cases it would use reasons such as family, health, disciplinary, academic grades, etc., which clearly indicates a tendency to avoid admitting that it was eliminating the Jews from the army because of their origins. The answer from the Ministry of the Navy was about the same, and went even further, stating that officers had been ordered to declare their religion and this would appear in their "personnel files."

The ministry that wanted to stand out through its zeal was National Education. On July 20, as soon as the manifesto of the "scientists" was published, the ministry hurriedly informed Demography and Race that it would conduct its own census of all its employees of Jewish origin. As soon as approval was finally given, after being delayed at first, Giuseppe Bottai immediately let loose in every direction. On August 6 he sent a series of memoranda, tailored to the type of school to which they were addressed, to the deans, superintendents, and persons in similar positions, recommending that they distribute *La difesa della razza*, which must be "the focus of great interest on the part of the professors and their disciples." To the deans, Bottai wrote:

> Every university library must carry it and the professors must read it, consult it, comment upon it, to acquire the spirit that inspires it, to become its supporters and to spread its message.

And to the superintendents:

> In elementary school, with the tools adapted to the mentality of childhood, an atmosphere conducive to an initial, embryonic racist consciousness, will be created; while in secondary school the higher mental development of adolescents, already exposed to the humanistic tradition through the study of classical languages, of history and literature, will help explain the main points of racist doctrine, its goals and its limits. The dissemination of the doctrine shall continue in high school where studious youths, with the help of the humanistic and scientific knowledge already acquired, shall

deepen it and prepare to become, in turn, its disseminators and supporters.

Bottai invited the president of the Central Board of Historical Studies to give a racist orientation to the curriculum and ensure that historians would also follow that line.

The activities of the Ministry of National Education did not stop with these "learned" memoranda: on August 9 the superintendents were advised to exclude Jews from any temporary post or school assignment; on the 24th it announced that a list of textbooks, written by Jewish authors, which were to be replaced would soon be sent to them.[755]

Fortunately not everyone was as zealous as Bottai, and not everyone was ready, just to look good in the eyes of the master, to forget and trample the most elementary notions of due process and humanity. Evidence that such men still existed even within the highest circles of the regime is furnished by a confidential memorandum sent by Vincenzo Azzolini, the governor of the Bank of Italy, to the heads of all its offices on September 19, with a copy to the Interior Ministry being forwarded the next day. It states:

> I have been informed that in the next few days there will be requests by the Tax Police and other political authorities, addressed to some branches of our bank and other banking institutions, in order to obtain information regarding the existence of cash deposits or stocks and valuables in the names of Jews.
>
> The requested information also concerns contents in metal safety deposit boxes and seeks information on the movement of funds with the intention of taking appropriate measures to avoid the exodus of capital and valuables overseas.
>
> This being said, I inform you, with the full approval of the interested ministries, that the Banks must adhere to the firm rule that they can in no way neglect to strictly follow the most rigorous observance of banking secrecy.[756]

Actually it was during the very first days of the racial campaign, when no legal decree had yet been enacted, that the first orders to exclude all Jews from public positions were issued. On August 17

Buffarini-Guidi telegraphed all the prefects, telling them that belonging to the "Italian race" was the "essential and unalterable prerequisite to holding public positions" and therefore they had to ensure, with the gradualism they were to judge necessary, the substitution of those who were of a different race.[757] Pavolini issued the same orders a few days later to the secretaries of National Unions and the presidents of the Provincial Unions.[758] Finally, during the last days of August the removal from the presidency of the Assicurazioni Generali and the Riunione Adriatica di Sicurtà of Edgardo Morpurgo and Arnoldo Frigessi di Rattalma, both of them Jewish, took place along with the installation of their replacements, two "Aryans." According to Pietro Grifone, this fulfilled the wishes of some financial groups to seize control of two important companies and remove two of the most vocal adversaries of the new pro-German political and economic policy.[759]

The decrees approved by the Council of Ministers on September 2-3 closed this initial phase of the racial campaign. As we have previously noted, they concerned foreign Jews and the school system and dealt a very serious blow to Italian Jewry in general. Foreign Jews were forbidden to establish residence within the Kingdom, in Libya, and the Aegean; those who were already residing there had to leave within six months. The measure, already serious by itself, was worsened by article 3, that revoking Italian citizenship to foreign Jews who had been granted it after January 1, 1919.[760] As for the educational system, the Jews were excluded from teaching any classes at any level, and pupils of the "Jewish race" were forbidden from attending public schools; for those in elementary schools, special sections were set up within the localities where their number was not less than ten; for those in secondary schools, the Communities would be able to set up private schools; in both of these types of schools, teachers who had been dismissed from service would be given priority. An exception was made for students, including foreigners, already matriculated at the universities, who were allowed, in a transition period, to complete the studies they had already begun.[761]

23.

The Project to Settle
the Jews in Italian East Africa

T he decree against foreign Jews only mentioned Italy, Libya, and the islands of the Aegean; it did not mention the AOI, Italian East Africa. It is a significant omission and when read alongside some notations in Ciano's diary it sheds light on Mussolini's thinking at that time. The international press and some governments had interpreted *Informazione diplomatica* n. 14 to mean that Mussolini was thinking of creating the Jewish State, mentioned in the *Informazione*, in Italian East Africa, more precisely in the area of Lake Tana where the Falasha lived. The Palazzo Chigi had not answered requests for more information. There is no doubt that in 1938 Mussolini was thinking of settling some Jews somewhere in Italian East Africa. As of August 30, 1938 Galeazzo Ciano noted:

> The Duce tells me of his project to turn the Migiurtina into a concession for Jews from everywhere. He says that the land has considerable natural resources the Jews could exploit.[762]

Less than a week later on September 4:

> Regarding the colony for the Jews to be concentrated in, the Duce is no longer speaking of Migiurtina but of the Upper Juba that offers better living and working conditions.[763]

These notes from the Ciano diary have been confirmed by the publication of a few pages from the diary of Colonel Giuseppe Adami, head of the central cartographic office of the Empire,[764] who during the second half of 1938 was given the task by Duke Amedeo of Aosta, the Viceroy of Italian East Africa, whom Mussolini had asked to undertake the study of the possibility of settling a first group of 1,400 Jewish heads of families in Africa, to be followed by others. According to Adami, who was writing in the third person:

After informing him that he would be given a very interesting and important task, the Duke of Aosta with his usual clarity, gave the following instructions: he was to find an area capable of housing, at first, a colony of 1,400 Jewish heads of families, with the potential to settle double that number and expand further from there. It had to be an excellent area from the point of view of health conditions: no malaria, no tse-tse flies, no mandef, etc.; it should have good weather, lots of water, land lending itself to agricultural and industrial development, off the main traffic lines, with peaceful local populations, prevalently pagan, where there would be the smallest number of Coptic churches and mosques to avoid any religious disputes. The Duke of Aosta, having explained these ideas quite thoroughly, added that the request for such land came from Mussolini, in agreement with the British government, to welcome Jewish families who were being increasingly expelled by the Nazis from Germany, Austria, and Czechoslovakia. The numbers of Jews forced to leave were such that worried the British government because it felt it would be dangerous to allow a mass arrival into Palestine where even living conditions would become difficult. By directing the migration into Italian East Africa, a location offering marvelous land compared to Palestine, they could perhaps avoid friction with the Arab world and help the daily life of the Palestinian colony. The Duke dismissed the head of the cartographic office with a friendly smile, adding that he expected him to discover a small "Garden of Eden."

Based on these instructions Adami went in search of the right territory and thought he had found it in the Borana region, near Aresox in southern Ethiopia, about one hundred kilometers from Kenya. It was an area of about eight thousand square kilometers, at one thousand two hundred meters above sea level, with weather conditions Europeans could adapt to. An area that, as Adami was to write in his report to the Duke of Aosta on December 5, 1938, would allow the raising of much livestock, good agricultural production, cotton, castor oil, tobacco, and with local forests of middle and high trees so "it can be concluded that, in the chosen area, a large settlement dedicated to agriculture and cattle raising could prosper." Colonel Adami's report was immediately sent to Mussolini, who apparently liked it and sent a copy to the British government. But we have no follow-up information, nor did Mussolini pursue his idea.

These reports explain the silence regarding Italian East Africa in the decrees approved by the Council of Ministers of September 2 and their clear mention in the Grand Council declaration of October 6. Nor should this be surprising; in spite of Mussolini's anti-Jewish stance during those months and the decision to proceed against the Jews with the greatest harshness, his cynical attitude in mentioning that he wanted to group the Jews in Migiurtina is typical: "among the other [natural reserves, this region has] shark fishing, which would be very convenient because, at first, many Jews would end up being eaten." Mussolini never considered exterminating the Jews and actually favored a territorial solution that would allow them to be placed outside Europe and end the Jewish question without too many traumatic excesses and without, as far as he was concerned, provoking the anger of the Germans or the Anglo-Americans. The Nazis were considering something similar during those same months but thought of creating a grand reserve in Madagascar.[765] They had set up an emigration center in Vienna that was to continue for two more years. Ribbentrop would mention this Nazi project to Ciano in June 1940.[766] It would be interesting to know whether both projects appeared autonomously or if one influenced the other.

One thing is certain: the idea of settling a number of Jews in Italian East Africa, at first mostly Austrians, Germans, and Poles, then some Italians, was connected to similar ideas circulating at the time even in democratic countries. There had been discussions about sending the Jews to South Africa, Rhodesia, Kenya, and Madagascar, and even to create a Jewish state in East Africa under the joint protectorate of England, Italy, and France. On the other hand, there were projects to colonize the Empire and attempts to find overseas, especially in the United States, some of the required capital to make it happen. Italian diplomats and agents had mentioned it to representatives of the Jewish Agency beginning in mid-1936, initially presenting it as a first provisional step toward the creation of a Jewish state (but not in Ethiopia), because of the "historical" presence of the Falasha in Italian East Africa. Two other factors were even more significant: the favorable reaction within certain Jewish groups to the idea of a transfer of Jews to Italian East Africa, especially the "Gildmeester Auswaderer-Hilfsaktion," which negotiated the problem with Italian authorities until the end of 1939—even obtaining the authorization for a fact-finding commission to be sent on location. By this time, Rome had decided to end any emigration project to the Empire, despite the interest expressed by Roosevelt, and to a lesser degree even by Chamberlain, about the possibility of settling Jewish refugees from Europe in Ethiopia in agreement with Mussolini.

Roosevelt wrote Mussolini a personal letter on this issue on December 7, 1938, which was delivered to the Duce during the next few days together with a supporting memorandum by Ambassador William Phillips. Assuming that a solution was not found quickly "based upon the spirit of justice and humanity" to the problem of those who were no longer allowed to live in their native lands, international relations would further deteriorate and "the cause of peace [would be] further compromised." The President of the United States requested the Duce declare himself favorable to settling the Jews on the Ethiopian plateau and to ask "that the other states controlling other parts of the plateau" do the same, giving assurances that he would publicly support such a plan. One month later when Chamberlain came to Rome with Halifax to discuss the state of British-Italian relations, he very cautiously explored Mussolini's intentions.

In both cases Mussolini's response was that—besides the fact that "the general attitude of Jewish circles toward Italy was not such to induce the Italian government to welcome into its territory a large mass of Jewish immigrants"—the problem had now taken on a European scope and could no longer be resolved by Italian efforts alone. As he wrote to Roosevelt on January 11, 1939:

> The Jewish question exists, in different forms, in almost every state in Europe and must therefore be considered as a general European question for it to be constructively resolved.

In my opinion the only countries that can welcome and organize a large Jewish emigration are those having on their territories vast unpopulated spaces and huge resources which can be adequately used and exploited...

But what I have always considered and still consider as the most practical solution is the creation, somewhere in the world, of a truly Jewish state. The experiment of the Jewish Home in Palestine has failed due to historical conditions that were totally unfavorable to the creation of a Palestinian Jewish state, but the idea of creating such a state elsewhere should not be abandoned. Even if this were to be a state with a small territory, the Jews would have with it, as all other peoples, their own center and their national base. The Jews who become citizens of this state would therefore have a nationality and a definite status and even though they may be established in other countries, would find in this state the normal assistance and tutelage all foreigners enjoy. Only in this manner would the Jewish problem stop being in Europe the insoluble problem of the only minority deprived of a nationality.

As Sergio Minerbi has noted in his study, which is the best concerning the entire matter of the problems tied to the project of settling the Jews in Ethiopia and its various phases,[767] whether he was answering Roosevelt or speaking with Chamberlain, Mussolini always brought up the need for a "vast plan," a "concrete plan," for Jewish emigration, as if he did not wish to close the door on other ways of pursuing the discussion, perhaps hoping to be the *deus ex machina* for a solution to the problem. It is our opinion that, by this time, the Duce no longer believed in such a solution, even though the idea of a new and even greater success than that of Munich fascinated him. And not so much because—as it appears Ciano feared—he did not wish to appear as the "protector of the Jews" in Hitler's eyes, but because the British and American attitude had convinced him a real solution was no longer possible. After the *Kristallnacht* (November 9-10, 1938) the number of Jews wishing to emigrate had increased enormously. It was impossible to still envision their settling in Italian East Africa, for financial, economic, and political reasons,[768] because in spite of the worsening situation, the western powers showed no intention of taking any responsibility. They attempted to pass the "hot potato" along to Mussolini but Jewish emigration was not facilitated nor were restrictions to entry visas abolished; they hypocritically referred to "refugees" more than to "Jews"; no responsibility was accepted and they took pains to avoid appearing, in the eyes of their own public opinion, as too pro-Semitic in order not to be accused of fomenting a war to help the Jews. Even in the letter he wrote to Mussolini, Roosevelt never used the term "Jews," and he referred only generically to those who could no longer live in their countries of origin. Chamberlain, in discussions with Mussolini and Ciano on January 13, 1939, had not hid, according to Ciano, the implication that new Jewish immigration to England could "give rise to anti-Semitism already appearing in many parts of the country."[769] There is no reason to doubt what Ciano writes, recent studies, beginning with those by Walter Laqueur regarding the attitude of London and Washington toward the news filtering through during the Second World War on the progress of the Final Solution,[770] have shown how much, with the war now going on, the British and American governments strove to avoid appearing too pro-Jewish, or worse, of being influenced by the Jews. Since no one wished to accept mass immigration into one's country as a solution, immigration to Palestine would have ignited violent reaction on the part of the Arab world, creating a crisis in one of the most critically important areas politically, economically, and strategically for England, and therefore for the international system centered around her. It is very significant from this point of view that the project of settling the Jews in Ethiopia was still being considered by Washington and London until after mid-1943. Not only, therefore, after it had been scrapped on the Italian side, but even after Italy had lost the Empire. A safe haven, a place where the Jews could settle, had to be found, but without attracting the hostility of the Arabs while there was a danger of war with Germany and also later, during the war. Nor was it out of the question that the project would be considered after the war. In 1941 an important official of the United States' Department of State, speaking with a high level Zionist leader, said that for the Jews "after the war there would be a sort of Vatican in Palestine and a real territory in Abyssinia."[771]

Given these facts, we feel it is impossible to say that Mussolini wished to keep an open door for a possible initiative of his own. He certainly did not lack the political instinct to understand that it was impossible to find a solution to the Jewish problem, nor the realism to see that to step forward in an attempt to solve it would only have damaged his prestige and his relations with Hitler, uniting most of the Jews against him, while alienating much of the sympathy of the Arabs. In January 1939, when he answered Roosevelt's letter and met with Chamberlain and Halifax, the Duce had, in our opinion, abandoned any such idea. If he did not say so clearly, it was only for tactical reasons, to encourage London to enter into a "general agreement" with Italy regarding the Mediterranean.

24.

Fascist Party and Government Initiatives up to November 1938

With the measures enacted on September 2 and 3, 1938 the racial campaign was in full swing and it was clear that other measures would soon follow *altering* the legal and civil *status* of the Italian Jews. The Fascists made no secret of this. It was announced right after the session of the Council of Ministers that the Grand Council of Fascism would soon be convened to establish the "cornerstones" of the new policy on race. The meeting was set for October 1, and then postponed to October 6.

During this time the office of Demography and Race and the various ministries completed the necessary documents and information to prepare the next measures. The census of the Italian and foreign Jews present within the Kingdom was carried out and the statistical and nominal work of placing the data assembled into categories was underway. The identification of Jewish functionaries, or those presumed to be,[772] lay the groundwork for a future census of Jewish property, possessions, and institutions.

At the same time it was decided to prevent "the flight of hard currency" by the Jews, to stop the exportation of capital, and to end any Jewish "presence" in all sectors of national life. For example, bookstores were regulated to prevent the display of books by "non-Aryan" authors, publishers were to stop publishing such books, the EIAR was to avoid broadcasting music by Jewish composers, etc.

At the top levels of government, and Mussolini in particular, efforts were centered on removing the last two obstacles on the path of full state-sponsored anti-Semitism. These were the King and the Holy See.

The operation was swift and effortless when it came to Victor Emmanuel III. Mussolini dispatched Buffarini-Guidi to San Rossore, the estate where the King was staying at the time. The meeting was very brief and ended just as Mussolini had expected; Victor Emmanuel put up token resistance, but then, once Buffarini-Guidi had illustrated how the Duce intended to position anti-Semitic policy, he immediately agreed, limiting himself to an empty wish that those who had been patriotic be duly recognized. Buffarini-Guidi reported to Mussolini on the meeting in a memorandum dated September 12 that proves without a doubt the King's acquiescence to decisions made by the Duce:[773]

> Duce,
>
> I am pleased to inform you of the conversation I had at San Rossore with H.M. the King on the occasion of the swearing-in ceremony of a few Bishops.
>
> The King, once informed of the anti-Jewish policy enacted by the Regime, was in the kind of mood you had predicted. While he expressed full approval regarding the measures taken against the Jews of foreign nationality, he voiced reservations regarding the decisions against the Italian Jews.
>
> He asked me to show you two letters; one from Colonel Ugo Modena, Chief of Staff of the Fossalta division, asking to be treated with leniency in general, and one from Lieutenant Valfredo Segre, of the Legionnaire Air Force, that was enclosed with the return of his medal of valor.

I immediately told the King what you had instructed me to say: for the Jews of Italian nationality there would be precise discriminations, whereby various categories, those decorated for valor, the volunteers, and those wounded in the four wars, wounded for the Fascist cause, etc., would all be recognized for their contributions.

The King was then fully reassured and said: "I am really pleased that the President* will proceed with these exceptions, recognizing the merits of those Jews who have distinguished themselves for love of country" and, he added, "I was certain that the great sensitivity, the deep intuition and broad generosity of the President would have influenced such a policy."

The King then spoke to me about the Jewish Doctor, Stykold, who, he said, was one of the greatest clinical professors in Italy today, and he hoped that he could remain in our country and exercise his profession.

The obstacle of the Holy See, or, better, of Pius XI, was to be much more difficult to overcome.

Many scholars have analyzed this extremely important episode of the relations between the Church and the Italian State during Fascism, which has also drawn the attention of various specialists in Fascist anti-Semitic persecution. The 1959 study by Jesuit Angelo Martini published in *La civiltà cattolica* is the most important of these studies. Based on documents in Vatican archives, this work was undertaken by an expert researcher and offers a virtually complete, often meticulously detailed, history of the Vatican's attitude toward Fascist racial policy from mid-1938 to the death of Pope Pius XI. We shall refer to them extensively here, adding some new documents. The studies by Martini, while important, have two major flaws in the manner in which they approach the issue. First, they do not take into account an aspect that we consider essential: the different and often contrasting positions within the higher echelons of the Vatican, and the catholics in general regarding the Jewish question. Second, they analyze facts relating only to Vatican policy

----

* King Victor Emmanuel III always referred to Mussolini by his official title of President of the Council of Ministers.

during those months without explaining the underlying spirit of this policy.

With *Mit brennender Sorge*[775] of March 1937, the Catholic Church had condemned Nazi racism as atheistic and materialistic; Italian racism, as we have seen, appeared to be different and in many ways could have "blended" with the position taken by the Church itself. This was, without a doubt, the feeling within some Catholic circles. It is no accident that regarding the manifesto of the "scientists" *La civiltà cattolica* of August 6 wrote:

> Those familiar with the tenets of German racism will immediately notice the wide difference between those proposals and the ones by the group of Italian Fascist scholars. It would confirm that Italian Fascism doesn't wish to be identified with Nazism or German racism, which is intrinsically and explicitly materialistic and anti-Christian.[776]

Even more pointedly, the day after the publication of the manifesto, Jesuit Angelo Brucculeri published an article in *L'avvenire* in Rome on July 17, "Razzismo italiano" [Italian Racism], that amounted to an enthusiastic approval of the manifesto itself.[777]

Even without reducing the issue to these very visible positions, clearly the colonial aspect of Italian racist policy was generally approved by Vatican and Catholic circles, just as the former and part of the latter also approved the "anti-Semitic" aspects of "discriminate, but do not persecute." What was more worrisome (the Jesuits of *La civiltà cattolica*, as we mentioned earlier, were ready to gloss over this issue and not go beyond the literal interpretation of Italian racism) was that, with the manifesto of the "scientists," Italian racism would acquire a "theoretical position" and "an ideology with intangible axioms." Furthermore, Fascist policy did not consider the Jews as a religious group but rather as a race, thereby including those Jews who had converted to Catholicism. Had the Fascist measures not encroached upon the rights of the Church and its own prestige under the Concordat by denying it the right of tutelage of all those who placed themselves under its protection, there is little doubt that they would not have incurred its opposition. Vatican circles, with the exception of these two specific aspects, "understood" the reasons given by the Fascists. Even today, Father Martini accepts the thesis of "understandable resentment" of Italian government leaders "who had withstood, during the years of the Ethiopian affair, the political and economic difficulties created by the nations of the League, if not directly, at least not mitigated for Italy's benefit by Jews or Jewish organizations with international power and influence."[778] Therefore, even the most responsible Vatican circles did not hide their feeling that the racial measures had "some good aspects" and should not be viewed unfavorably.

The excellent studies by Father Martini, while showing how the Holy See tried, in every possible way, to convince the Italian government to modify its racial legislation, failed, however, to demonstrate clearly the following:

First, that the tough and aggressive position taken by the Pope did not reflect that of the entire Sacred College, and of all the most qualified Vatican circles, to such an extent that Farinacci, probably through Preziosi, had an informer of sorts in one of the Cardinals, possibly Vicenzo Cardinal La Puma.[779]

Second, this position was more aggressive at the beginning, when the Vatican did not yet know Mussolini's true intentions and feared that the consequences of racial policy would be the introduction of divorce in Italy, the annulment of marriages between Jews and Catholics, and the sterilization of the Jews.[780] Some high Vatican officials, who vigorously opposed Fascism, had played an important part against it, possibly because of the problem of the Catholic Action.

Once Mussolini's true intentions became clear, Vatican opposition was reduced to a single point: marriages of Jews who had converted [to Catholicism]. There is absolutely no doubt as to this final point. The Italian embassy to the Holy See sent two reports dated October 7 and 10, 1938, and in particular the latter, to Foreign Minister Ciano, which he then forwarded to Mussolini. These reports clearly indicate the true attitude of the Vatican.[781]

The October 10, 1938 teletype to the Palazzo Chigi, which was transmitted to Mussolini on the 13th, stated:

As I already have had the honor to inform you, the Grand Council resolutions on the defense of the race have not been viewed negatively in general within the Vatican, with reference to the reservations from the short comment in the *Osservatore Romano* of the 7th of this month, as to the consequences the new resolutions would have on matrimony as it is regulated by the Church.

These impressions were confirmed by Monsignor Montini, Substitute for Ordinary Affairs at the Secretariat of State, that the major, if not the only, worries of the Holy See, concern cases of marriage with converted Jews.

Faced with Mussolini's refusal to consider its other requests, mostly regarding article 7, the Church was satisfied, at least in part, by the Italian government's cancellation of article 2 of what was to be the Legal Decree of November 17, 1938 n. 1728 (which practically defined as "concubinage" the marriage of a Jew to an Aryan, even though he or she may have converted.) The Holy See not only always kept the dispute on strictly legal grounds, with the Concordat in mind, but, once the Concordat had been broken by the Fascists, it only lodged a formal diplomatic protest. In order to save the Lateran Treaty—it is significant that the Holy See never canceled the 1933 Concordat with Hitler, even though he violated it regularly—and everything it meant in Italy, first and foremost the Catholic Action, Pius XI accepted an extremely serious violation of the Concordat and approved, if not legally, at least implicitly in the conscience of many Catholics, the principle of the persecution of the Jews. Still, many priests continued to celebrate "mixed" marriages[782] in spite of the Fascist law prohibiting them, and Pius XI immediately took action to secretly help and rescue the Jews.[783] The fact that in later years this aid and help were to be greatly expanded, at a certain point even at risk to the lives of many priests, does not appear to alter the situation from the moral point of view—as expressions of human and Christian solidarity for those oppressed. The Holy See, overall, had a timid response to the Fascist racial decrees; it was intent not on defending the Jews, but on defending the very specific prerogatives of the Catholic Church in Italy; this was its attitude. Yet within the Catholic leadership in Italy some were determined defenders of the Jews, while others were staunch supporters of Fascist anti-Semitism.

This being said, we shall limit ourselves to describing the significant events and positions in the dispute that pitted the Fascist government against the Holy See during the second half of 1938; for more detail we recommend the works of Father Angelo Martini.

The first official position against Fascist racism was taken by the Pontiff himself. On July 28, 1938, three days after publication of the PNF press release, Pius XI, upon receiving the students of the College of Propaganda Fide, stated how racism was alien to the Italian tradition and disapproved that Italy should imitate Germany. Mussolini, stung in his pride, responded two days later during a visit to an assembly of the GIL (Gioventù Italiana del Littorio), that "even on the question of race we shall forge ahead." At the same time Ciano informed the Apostolic Nunzio, Monsignor Francesco Borgongini-Duca, that, should the Holy See persist in its criticism a clash would become inevitable. During this first exchange of views it became clear that the Vatican was mostly worried about the marriages of converted Jews. There were to be other meetings during the following weeks, between Ciano, Buffarini-Guidi, Starace and Monsignor Borgongini-Duca, Father Pietro Tacchi-Venturi, and Father Lamberto Vignoli. The meeting of the Grand Council of October 6 took place in this atmosphere, with much posturing and the most violent sparring taking place at a distance.[784] Once the programs had been presented, the negotiation phase began.[785] On November 2, Buffarini-Guidi transmitted to Father Tacchi-Venturi the draft of the Legal Decree, written to enact the resolutions of the Grand Council regarding matrimony. During the course of these negotiations, characterized by some very dramatic moments, the Holy See succeeded in obtaining the cancellation of article 2 of the draft, regarding concubinage,[786] but failed to have article 7, which in effect became article 6 of the Legal Decree of November 17, 1938 n. 1728, recognize the marriages of Jews who had converted to Catholicism as valid.[787] Pius XI declared, to no avail, that this was in violation of the Concordat. He wrote a personal letter to Mussolini and one to the King on November 4;

both were to be unsuccessful. Mussolini did not even answer and actually let it be known that "his impression was that the Vatican was pulling the chain too hard" and he was ready, should the Pope keep this up, to fight the Church to the bitter end. The King answered that he had forwarded the letter he had received to the Duce, on November 7.[788] Once the Council of Ministers approved the law on the 10th, the Holy See delivered an official note to the Italian embassy on November 13, protesting the violation of article 34 of the Concordat. The note was followed by an article published the next day in *L'osservatore romano* entitled "A proposito di un nuovo decreto legge" [Regarding a New Legal Decree] that repeated the main points contained in the note. During the coming weeks, until the Pope's death,* there were other inconclusive negotiations that were always limited to legal issues tied to the Concordat. In five months of negotiations the Holy See never addressed the matter of anti-Semitism as such. Even in the midst of the strongest arguments, these were only against racism, never anti-Semitism. Pius XI made the only clear reference to anti-Semitism at the start of the controversy in speaking to a group of Belgian pilgrims. On that occasion he said, "No, it is not possible for Christians to take part in anti-Semitism" and "anti-Semitism is inadmissible; spiritually we are Semites."

These clear and unequivocal statements were considerably weakened and reduced to a simple declaration of principle by a third statement: "We recognize everyone's right to defend himself, to take measures to protect himself against any threat to his legitimate interests."

This position was not very different from that of the Jesuits of *La civiltà cattolica*,[789] so much so that we feel most of the Catholic hierarchies did not wish to be perceived as lending tacit support to Fascist racial policy, fearing that, as in the German example, it could evolve into an anti-Christian policy also because the immediate purpose of the Church was to defend the rights it had been granted by the Concordat, as well as its own prestige. At the same time, the

---

* Pius XI died on February 10, 1939.

Church was not opposed to a "moderate" anti-Semitic action based upon reductions of civil rights.

Finding no real opposition with the King or the Holy See—the only two institutions with enough power to create obstacles had they taken a firm and determined attitude—Mussolini went into the meeting of the Grand Council of Fascism assured of his position. He knew that even within the supreme body of Fascism there were some unhappy opponents who did not hide their displeasure, especially Balbo, who was to try until the end to be aggressive within the debate, attempting to obtain a reduction in the anti-Semitic measures, and condition his approval of racist anti-Semitic principles on the granting of Italian nationality to the Libyan population.[790] Mussolini knew full well that the Grand Council would have approved his policies.[791] At the beginning of September he had personally written—the original hadwritten text exists—the statement that would be submitted for approval and that he continuously corrected and expanded over the course of one month, weighing each word and making many significant changes to the text. From the various versions that we have of the statement, it appears that he revised it up to a few hours before the meeting on October 6. The copy sent through Sebastiani to Starace, who also made a few formal corrections the morning of the 6th, not only differs from the final text approved by the Grand Council and handed to the press, but is also very different from another text we have seen that must have been written even later, during the breaks in the meeting itself. The complete text of some of these versions is in Document 22.[792] The most important variations, even apparently insignificant changes, have a definite meaning in reconstructing the Duce's personal position; they are typically in Mussolini's handwritten copy. At the end of the paragraph entitled "Jews and Judaism" the phrase "all anti-Fascist forces are led by a Jew," was changed into the more general "by Jewish elements." To understand how Mussolini was trying to avoid expressions that gave the impression of persecution, one can turn to the example in the first paragraph of subparagraph *d* where the word *measures* replaced the word *sanctions* at the last minute. Some changes, no doubt, indicate that besides Mussolini other persons took part in preparing the text of the declaration, and that these persons attempted to inject statements reflecting their own political views or, in some cases, give it a more or less oppressive tone. As an example, we can almost certainly attribute to Ciano, just as he had made changes to the *Informazione diplomatica* n. 14, the addition to the handwritten version by Mussolini (who did not mention it), the clearly negative reference to Palestine in the paragraph *Jewish immigrants in Ethiopia*, and perhaps even the fact that any mention of agreements with the "leaders of world Jewry" was deleted. More importantly, in the handwritten text and the version given to the press, it was forbidden for nondiscriminated Jews to own or manage companies employing more than one hundred persons, while in the final working text it was specified "one hundred persons or more of the Aryan race." Clearly, it is our understanding that at the last minute someone tried to prevent the loss of their plant by Jewish industrialists, by making it possible, as a solution, to hire their own co-religionists as employees. The reader will recognize other such variations by comparing the different texts we have published. Here we wish to stress the most significant changes made within the published text when compared to the preceding versions, and most of all, the handwritten ones made by Mussolini.

An important deletion—"the ten proposals elaborated by the Fascist Academics"—was made in the first part of the opening statement adopted by the Grand Council, after a copy of the declaration was given to Starace. This may be interpreted in various ways: to avoid taking a position that had been criticized from many quarters, especially overseas, as scientifically inconsistent; to prevent a head-on clash with many Catholics; to remove a clear reference to one of the "signatories" of the July 14 manifesto, who having changed his mind, could be tempted to retract his own signature.

Another important change, also made after Starace had received the text, was to increase the age from sixty to sixty-five as the limit for foreign Jews to be expelled. Two paragraphs stating that foreign Jews in "poor health" and with "three or more underage children to support" would not be forced to leave, were crossed out. The situation of foreign Jews now became worse compared to the original version, the next paragraph—the *b* of the published text—introduced by exempting from expulsion those who had "entered into a mixed Italian marriage before October 1, XVI," [1938] what amounted to a much less stringent approach compared to Mussolini's original text. The comparison shows the important addition of a time limit—October 1, 1938—for the measure stating that the children of a mixed marriage who did not practice the Jewish religion would not be considered as belonging to the Jewish race. The paragraph regarding "discrimination" was completely changed. Any statistical references to possible "discriminated persons" were deleted, but the categories of those eligible were broadened. The text sent to Starace is identical to Mussolini's handwritten copy except for paragraph 7, which, as far as Mussolini was concerned, only referred to the families of the "squadristi" of the years 1919 to 1922, while the new version added the families of the squadristi of 1924 and the Fiume Legionnaires. The final typed text we have seen does have one significant change: the families of the veterans of the four wars who had been awarded the cross for valor were also "discriminated". Since we know that during the meeting of the Grand Council, De Bono, Federzoni, and most of all Balbo, struggled to get all veterans discriminated without exception, this last minute inclusion leads us to believe that this text had been agreed upon during the meeting of the Grand Council itself, perhaps during one of the breaks. Within the same paragraph, and again at the last minute, one of the final sentences written by Mussolini began: "An album (in Starace's copy the word used is *listing*) of Jews belonging to the categories mentioned above will be compiled and the reasons they were not subjected to discrimination will be made public. A change of name or other forms will also be possible." Again regarding this same paragraph it must be noted that the final text shows an yet another change to point number 7: the squadristi of 1924 are limited to those of the second semester only. The paragraph entitled "The Other Jews" also underwent many changes: in Mussolini's handwritten text those "not discriminated" could not employ domestic servants of the "Italian race," but the rule disappeared later on; Mussolini's text did not exempt the "not discriminated" from military service. This is the secret evolution of the most relevant aspects of the compilation of the declaration made by the Grand Council.

The Grand Council meeting did have another characteristic that was just as "secret" in the pressures brought upon Mussolini from various quarters at the last moment: the final attempts by the Jews themselves to avoid the measures and by those who were opposed to the laws. The file of the October 6 meeting is important and its contents speak for themselves.[793]

It contains a clipping from the *Kölnische Zeitung* of September 9 with the article "The Exodus of the Jews from Italy," describing the various tendencies and decisions the Grand Council was expected to take. Lines within the clipping are underscored, possibly by Mussolini himself:

> Some predict harder measures, others do not think that the Fascist government will go beyond the measures it has taken until now and that, above all, exceptions will be made for older veterans and comrades who have proved themselves.

There is also a note regarding the surgeon Mario Donati, a well-known doctor and Fascist who had converted some time before and had married a Catholic. Two documents regarding the Jews— the resolution passed on October 4 by the Council of the Union of Jewish Communities[794] and sent to the Duce to reiterate the Italian character and the loyalty of Italian Jews and a short booklet, *Commemorazione dei Defunti. I valorosi che caddero per la Patria* [Commemoration of the War Dead. The Men of Valor Who Died for the Homeland]—just published for the same purpose by "a group of Jewish veterans from Rome," with short biographies of Jews who had died for Italy, between 1866 and 1921, and Fascism. There is also an excerpt of pages 133-34 of the article "La difesa della razza" [Defense of the Race] by Nello Quilici, published by *Nuova antologia* on September 16. This excerpt, using the city of Ferrara without naming it, as an example of the "Jewish invasion" of Italy and the progressive increase of Jewish influence during the sixteen years of Fascist rule, stated at the same time: "What is extraordinary is the fact that the Jews have used the anti-Jewish campaigns to consolidate their very rapid conquests, taking advantage of the traditional simple humanitarian chivalry of the 'good Italians.'"

It was obvious that documents 2, 3, 4, and 5 were intended to prevent Mussolini from enacting measures that were too harsh, while the first one was Mussolini's own answer to these rumors: foreigners are looking at us and will judge us according to our firmness.[795]

The Grand Council meeting took place in Rome at the Palazzo Venezia during the night of October 6-7 (between 10 p.m. and 2:45 a.m.). In attendance were: Mussolini, who presided, Giacomo Acerbo, Dino Alfieri, Francesco Angelini, Italo Balbo, Giuseppe Bottai, Guido Buffarini-Guidi, Tullio Cianetti, Costanzo Ciano and Galeazzo Ciano, Emilio De Bono, Alberto De Stefani, Paolo Thaon di Revel, Roberto Farinacci, Luigi Federzoni, Dino Grandi, Feruccio Lantini, Giovanni Marinelli, Mario Muzzarini, Edmondo Rossoni, Luigi Russo, Arrigo Solmi, Antonino Tringali, and Giuseppe Volpi. Starace, in his capacity as Secretary of the PNF, was also keeping a record of the proceedings. The only absentee was De Vecchi who, it seems, was opposed to the measures at first,[796] but who declared at the meeting of October 18: "had I been present at the meeting of the Grand Council of Fascism of October 6 XVI, I did not attend due to service requirements, I would have fully agreed with the decisions taken regarding the problem of race."[797] The PNF bulletin number 214 of October 26, 1938 states that, besides Mussolini who spoke repeatedly, other speakers were Balbo, Farinacci, Starace, Bottai, Federzoni, De Bono, Buffarini-Guidi, Angelini, Solmi, Volpi, Cianetti, and Alfieri. According to Ciano[798] we know that Balbo, De Bono, and Federzoni[799] were against the measures, while the others were all in favor. The most detailed account is in Bottai's diary:

> Mussolini "attacked" aggressively. It is a kind of internal debate that moves ahead among harsh words against possible opponents, present and absent. "I have been thinking about the problem since 1908," he says. "This, if necessary, can be documented. You should also read my speech in Bologna of April 21, 1921 about 'this Aryan and Mediterranean blood line of ours.' He then grabs some loose

pages from a magazine: "Listen to what happened in a city of the Val Padana." They are pages from the article written by Nello Quilici in *Nuova antologia* that prove the Jewish penetration of the political, administrative, and cultural texture of Ferrara. The "blow" is aimed directly at Balbo, who tries to strike a pose. He alludes to the problem in Trieste. He quickly talks about the Empire. "The problem must be resolved at once and clearly. If we don't fix it we lose the Empire." He reminds us of the cases in Goggiam; he talks of the cases of white men living with black women. He gets back to the Jews. "What remains of anti-Fascism is of Jewish imprint. The hostility to Hitler during his trip to Italy was due to the Jews. It was a Jew in Florence, Giacomo Lumbroso, who wrote and distributed the leaflets calling on Italians to 'demonstrate' against Hitler under the patriotic pretense of the Anschluss." He speaks about the Manifesto. "I practically dictated it myself." He rapidly describes the situation of the 470,000 Jews in Germany: they have their own cultural association, newspapers, magazines, theaters. There is no deep persecution. The Jews have been separated and isolated." He derides those who warn about the reactions against us by Jewish high finance. "It's overblown. If it were not we'd still go after the problem." He deplores the attitude of the Church. "I tell you that this Pope is dangerous to the future of the Catholic Church."

Once the declaration had been read (a document that he says can be called the "Race Charter," more important than the "Labor Charter") he gives the floor to Farinacci who, having noted the absence of De Vecchi, which he interprets as a wish to abstain, then loses himself in clichés. Balbo and De Bono after him try to mitigate the decisions by widening the categories that were favorable to the veterans. Long debate. Mussolini wavers, wanting to let some things go.

I make my report on the schools. I support the need to be firm once the measures have been adopted. "By readmitting the Jews into teaching we would lower, I conclude, the moral level of the schools. They would hate us for having excluded them and would despise us for letting them return." My view is accepted.

Federzoni is one of the "soft" ones. Starace is among the "hard" ones.[800]

De Bono also noted:

> The race problem was not properly discussed—Sectarianism. I spoke in favor of the veterans, supported by Balbo and Federzoni; against: Starace, Buffarini, and Farinacci; my views won in the end. But there are many, many cases to look into. Enough, we shall see.[801]

Balbo was the one who openly attacked the measures the most and not only supported the discrimination of all Jews who had been decorated with the cross of merit but also fought for Jewish children being allowed to attend school.[802]

Mussolini, supported by Starace, Buffarini-Guidi, Farinacci, and Bottai was definitely against any softening[803] "Discriminations don't count. The problem must be confronted. Now anti-Semitism has been inoculated into the blood of the Italian people. It will continue to circulate and develop by itself. Then, even if tonight I am conciliatory I shall be extremely harsh when preparing legislation." In the final analysis, those opposed to the measures succeeded in making sure that the veterans decorated with the cross of merit would be included among those discriminated. A careful reading of the final typed copy of the text and the declaration published the following day leads us to believe that perhaps Balbo was able to by-pass part 4 of the paragraph entitled "The Other Jews," which allowed for non-discriminated Jews the creation, not just of elementary, but also of secondary schools. The approved declaration was as follows — the bulletin of the PNF, contrary to other instances, does not specify whether it was unanimous or by general acclamation:

> The Grand Council of Fascism, following the conquest of the Empire, declares that racial problems, as well as the need for racial consciousness, have become an urgent issue. It recalls that Fascism has had for the past sixteen years, and continues to have, a positive impact in its efforts toward the qualitative and quantitative improvement of the Italian race, an improvement that could be dangerously compromised with incalculable political consequences through race mixing and bastardization.
>
> The Jewish problem is simply the metropolitan facet of a more general problem.

The Grand Council of Fascism establishes that:

a. matrimony between Italian men and women with elements belonging to the Camite, Semite, and other non-Aryan races is forbidden;

b. employees of State and Public Entities—civilian and military personnel—may not engage in matrimony with foreign women of any race;

c. matrimony of Italian men and women with foreigners, even though they may belong to the Aryan race, must be submitted for the prior approval of the Interior Ministry;

d. measures against those who would diminish the prestige of the race within the territories of the Empire will be reinforced.

Jews and Judaism

The Grand Council of Fascism reiterates that world Jewry—especially following the abolition of Freemasonry—has led anti-Fascism in every field and that foreign Jews and dissident Italian Jews have been, in certain important moments, such as in 1924-25 and during the war in Ethiopia—unanimously hostile to Fascism.

The immigration of foreign elements—which has greatly increased since 1933—has worsened the attitude of Italian Jews toward the Regime, which is not sincerely accepted since it is antithetical to the psychology, the policy and the internationalism of Israel.

All anti-Fascist forces are led by Jewish elements; world Jewry in Spain sides with the Bolsheviks of Barcelona.

Prohibiting entry and the expulsion of foreign Jews

The Grand Council of Fascism is of the opinion that the law barring entry of foreign Jews into the Kingdom could no longer be delayed and that the expulsion of the undesirables—according to the terminology used and made popular by the great democracies—is indispensable.

The Grand Council of Fascism has decided that, beyond controversial cases which will be examined by the appropriate commission at the Interior Ministry, the expulsion will not be applied against foreign Jews who:

a. are over 65 years of age; or

b. have entered into a mixed Italian marriage prior to October 1, XVI. [1938]

Jews with Italian Citizenship

The Grand Council of Fascism has established the following, whether a person belongs to the Jewish race or not:

a. anyone born of two Jewish parents is of the Jewish race;

b. anyone born of a Jewish father and a mother of foreign nationality is considered of the Jewish race;

c. anyone born of a mixed marriage who practices the Jewish religion is considered of the Jewish race;

d. someone born from a mixed marriage, who is of a religion other than Judaism is not considered of the Jewish race as of October 1, XVI.

Discrimination Among Jews Who are Italian Citizens

No discrimination shall be applied, except in all cases for teaching in schools of every grade and level, to Jews who are Italian citizens—who have not been penalized for other reasons—and who belong to:

1. families of War Dead in the four wars Italy has engaged in during this century: Libyan, the Great War, Ethiopian, Spanish;

2. families of volunteers in the wars in Libya, the Great War, Ethiopia, Spain;

3. families of combatants in the wars in Libya, the Great War, Ethiopia, Spain;

4. families of the Dead for the Fascist Cause;

5. families of those wounded, disabled, maimed for the Fascist Cause;

6. families of Fascists members of the Party during the years 1919, '20, '21, '22, the second semester of 1924 and the families of Fiume Legionnaires;

7. families with exceptional merits that will be ascertained by a special commission.

The Other Jews

Italian citizens of the Jewish race who do not belong to the categories mentioned above, while a new law is being drafted regarding the acquisition of Italian citizenship, will not be able to:

a. be members of the *Partito Nazionale Fascista*;

b. own or manage companies of any kind employing more than one hundred persons;

c. own more than fifty hectares of land;
d. serve in the armed forces in peacetime or in war.
    The exercise of the professions will be subjected to further measures.

The Grand Council of Fascism has further decided:

1. that the Jews dismissed from public jobs will receive their normal right to a pension;
2. that any form of pressure on the Jews to obtain abjurations is strictly forbidden and will be severely punished;
3. that no changes be made to the free exercise of religious ceremonies and the activities of Jewish communities according to existing laws;
4. that along with elementary schools, secondary level instruction be allowed for Jews.

Emigration of Jews to Ethiopia

The Grand Council of Fascism does not exclude the possibility of accepting, in order to stem Jewish immigration into Palestine, a controlled immigration of European Jews into some areas of Ethiopia.

This and other conditions extended to the Jews may be canceled or made more stringent, depending upon the attitude that Judaism takes toward Fascist Italy.

Chairs of Racism

The Grand Council of Fascism is pleased to note that the Minister of National Education has created chairs for the study of race in the most important universities of the Kingdom.

To the Black Shirts

The Grand Council of Fascism, while it notes that the problems of race have generated exceptional interest on the part of the Italian people, announces to the Fascists that Party directives on the subject are to be considered fundamental and binding for all, and that the laws that will be prepared very soon by each individual Minister will be guided by the directives of the Grand Council.

The publication of the Grand Council's program was quickly followed by the various laws and decisions that were to transform it into an integral part of the laws and regulations of the state. The D. L. of November 17, 1938, number 1728, was the cornerstone and it was published in the *Gazzetta Ufficiale* on November 19, becoming law on January 5, 1939. This decree actually turned into laws the most important points of the Grand Council meeting.[804]

Just like the declaration of the Grand Council, the decree was to have many different versions. Besides those regarding articles 2 and 7 concerning relations with the Holy See, that we have already mentioned, there were four important changes to the original document. Article 4 (later to be number 3) initially took into account only the cases of civilian and military employees of the state and the employees of the provinces, communes, and entities with state participation; employees of PNF organizations or others under party control and those of the trade associations and satellite entities, were added at the last moment. The same took place with article 14 (later to be number 13) which initially did not state that the PNF and its organizations or those it controlled could not employ persons belonging to the "Jewish race." Also article 16 (later to be number 15) became more stringent in its final version because secondary family members, those twice removed, were not considered as family members of the person having rights to being discriminated and to the non-application of articles 10, 11, 13*h* of the final text.

The situation of wealthier Jews was improved markedly because the original language of article 12 was dropped:

> At shareholders' meetings of corporations, those belonging to the Jewish race may not participate with a number of shares the value of which is more than one third of the total value of the shares of capital represented by those participating in the meeting. The shares owned by persons belonging to the Jewish race, beyond the limit indicated above, do not give voting rights, nor shall be tabulated when determining majorities required by law or the by-laws to validate the results of the meeting.

The purpose of this article is obvious; through it, as pointed out in the *Report on the Draft of the Legal Decree Having Provisions for the Protection of the Italian Race*, "its purpose is to eliminate the possibility that capital belonging to the Jews, who have been excluded by other legislation from the management of large companies, could become predominant in the decision-making process of corporate entities."[805] Its cancellation was certainly due to the desire to avoid the flight of Jewish capital overseas.

The D. L. of November 15, 1938 number 1779 was also very important, concerning the persecution's effect on the schools.[806] The rules for forced retirement and the dismissal of Jews eliminated from public administration positions were regulated by various legal decrees, the first of which (concerning military personnel) was approved by the Council of Ministers on December 22.[807] The PNF, however, was not to be outdone by the state: another Decree, dated November 21, excluded from the party itself "Italian citizens who, according to the laws, are considered as belonging to the Jewish race."[808] The decree did not mention those "discriminated," who were already being identified as such,[809] and according to Ciano's diary[810] we know that Starace wanted to expel all Jews without exception from the party.[811]

Besides these legislative measures, others were enacted in the administrative area. Among the most important we shall mention a confidential memo from chief of police, Arturo Bocchini, to all the prefects, dated October 24, ordering that foreign Jews seeking to enter Italy as tourists, for pleasure, health, or business reasons could not stay beyond three months. Instructions were issued to favor the maximum number of exits of foreign Jews, or those who had become so due to the new measures, who were residing in Italy and to avoid their possible return.[812] A note from the Ministry of National Education of October 18 stated that it was forbidden to accept donations or grants coming from Jews[813] for scholarships, prizes, etc. Another note from the Ministry of Justice of November 19 prohibited notaries from compiling any sale of real property or companies where a Jew was the contracting party[814] until further notice. In a very short time the ministries and public offices were swamped with a tidal wave of circular notices and communications regarding the Jews, often contradicting one another, sometimes seeking only to oppress and wound the Jews in their beliefs and cherished customs;[815] sometimes simply written without giving any thought as to their consequences to the state administration and the national economy. It was not difficult to find this kind of shoddiness within the various legal decrees being quickly approved to enforce the decisions of the Grand Council. To mention one case in particular, article 10 of the decree of November 17 limited Jewish property to no more than five thousand lire of agricultural assessment and no more than twenty thousand lire for urban buildings. But it did not foresee that such a sudden reduction in value could dangerously expose financial credit institutions who were due higher amounts from Jews. This caused an alarmed report from the governor of the Bank of Italy on December 3 to the Presidency of the Council of Ministers.[816] In this mess, much was left to the personal initiative of various functionaries, to their zeal, their servility, their fear, and their conscience.[817]

At the same time every state office and institution (State Audit Court, Council of State, National Research Council, State Bar, National Institute of Statistics, Commission for emigration and colonization, etc.) proceeded to eliminate from their organization charts all Jewish functionaries, employees, and part-time personnel.

25.

Italian Public Opinion

D espite the massive and sycophantic preparation by the press and direct action by the PNF, the anti-Semitic measures were not popular with the majority of the Italian people. The drops of anti-Semitic poison administered over the years notwithstanding, it was during the launching of the racial campaign that Fascist propaganda failed the test for the first time and that, for the first time as well, large numbers of Italians who had been Fascists until then, or, at least, were followers of Mussolini but certainly not anti-Fascist, began to see Fascism and Mussolini himself in a different light.

If many in the leadership joined in the campaign against the Jews out of cowardice or opportunism, their numbers became smaller in the lower echelons of the social strata and among those having political or administrative responsibilities. All the calumnies and monstrosities against the Jews being served daily by the press could not convince the great majority of the Italian people that the Jews in general and Italian Jews in particular were truly as dangerous as they were said to be, and that Italians should "defend" themselves from the Jews in such a cruel and savage manner. Many began to open their eyes to Fascism on this occasion and revise their opinions. Those who had shunned politics up to that moment and had, so to speak, "delegated" it to Fascism, began, during the second half of 1938, to think for themselves once again. A typical case has been narrated by one of the best Italian historians. From a modest background, neither he, much less his mother, had bothered much about politics until then. She had never, as a good old-fashioned mother, strayed very far from the kitchen and its chores. When she learned about the 1938 laws this simple woman told her son unhappily: "Now I understand that in our country anyone with a conscience can only end up in the 'confino'";* and so it was that this young man who, until then, had been only interested in his studies, became an anti-Fascist.

Those who had been affected by the hammering of propaganda did not react immediately against the measures. They were revolted at the sight of the bargaining that would soon ensue regarding the "discriminations" and "Aryanizations," and, in general, all kinds of "arrangements" that many Jews were forced into to escape the harshness of the laws and the arbitrary manner with which they were carried out. The corruption, the immorality of Fascism, quickly became obvious to everyone, causing disgust, solidarity with the Jews, and loss of confidence in the state. Just as in 1936, Guido Leto, the head of the OVRA, seems to best translate the new climate in Italy at the time in this paragraph from his memoirs:

---

* To be sent to the *confino* meant to be "confined" to certain remote areas in internal exile.

The Italian people had never related to the Jewish problem nor even had any definite idea of a racial problem.

Beyond a few cities where some Jews, gathered in specific neighborhoods, as in Rome, could be the target of jokes, more for fun than out of meanness, it was very difficult for an Italian to see the difference between an Aryan and a Jew, or even have a minimum of curiosity in knowing the race and religion of persons he was friendly with or with whom he had business relations.

The racial problem was truly non-existent for all Italians.

The enactment of the racial laws brought about a number of cases worth remembering. First of all, the experience of the gradual, if not readily apparent, erosion of state authority caused the citizens to fear the severity of Fascist laws less and less.

The idea began spreading, and it was not altogether wrong, that all one needed were some strong political connections to dare defy the law...

A whole army of specialists appeared and grew larger. They gravitated around the Jew as the target of the new laws: discriminations, Aryanizations, and help of all kinds had been promised. Money was being paid in thousands of cases and not always for nothing; there was fraud, it's true, but in general the organization, even though it had no statutes, functioned and counted for its immunity on the discretion of the beneficiaries.[818]

Within the more responsible and politicized circles, in some ways already influenced by anti-Fascism, state-sponsored anti-Semitism was the straw that broke the camel's back. While many young members of the GUF seeking to advance their careers and be noticed played the racial card with extreme irresponsibility and cynicism, many other GUF members decided to switch sides and quickly became anti-Fascists.[819] If many men of culture were unable to resist the call of Preziosi, Interlandi, and the Ministry of Popular Culture, many others, including Fascists, were to rise in disgust—as in the case of Marinetti—or at least tried to help the Jews by protecting their jobs through some trick, or helping them find some kind of work in private companies or other institutions.

The press of that period tells a vivid story. A careful reading shows, among the hundreds of news items, the ill-defined expressions of popular "indignation" against the Jews and their expulsion from cultural societies, sports clubs, regional associations, the Naval League, etc. Among the scores of letters—but how many of them were real?—from readers who demanded new and even more drastic measures deploring evasion and connivance,[820] we can discover other information and letters showing how the majority of public opinion reacted adversely to the racial policies. The "mail" received by *La vita italiana* and *Il Tevere* and other rabidly anti-Semitic publications is particularly eloquent in this regard. From a letter sent to *Il Tevere* on October 12, we find that in the Central National Library in Rome *La difesa della razza* has been "sabotaged" and cannot be found for reading. The *Facts and Comments* column written by Preziosi in *La vita italiana* proves once again that many months after the racial laws had been passed, the *Protocols* were being "sabotaged" by many booksellers who did not display them in their windows or even claimed they did not keep them in stock. Sometimes the news items concern Fascist circles: in a letter to *Il telegrafo* of September 8 we are told that at the literature convention of the *Littoriali* [Fascist Youth Congress] a young Fascist who had begun a violent attack against Jewish authors, demanding that Italian literature be saved from their "corrupting virus," was interrupted by the president of the commission, "a philosophy professor," who strictly forbade him from making any further reference to Judaism.

These are minor instances, it is true, but they give the flavor of the extremely virulent campaign going on within the press and the PNF against the "pietists," meaning those who disapproved of state-sponsored anti-Semitism, and commiserated with or helped the Jews. On other occasions Fascist tactics had been to officially ignore discontent and fight it by not even mentioning any dissent, while attempting to prove that the entire nation was monolithically in favor of Fascist policy. Now, faced with such a broad-based reaction, to ignore and keep silent were both impossible. The aversion to anti-Semitic policy was not strong just in certain circles which had never been completely favorable to Fascism, but also among those who had always accepted Fascist policy, and even among the Fascists themselves. There were many "pietists" within the ranks of the PNF. In June 1939, Starace was forced to forbid party members from submitting any kind of recommendation in favor of the Jews and threatened to withdraw their party card.[821] Within the first few months of the racial campaign, the PNF, on many occasions, had to take action against those "pietist" Fascists. The newspapers inform us that in December the party card had been revoked against three Fascists—two in Milan and one in Ancona—because of "incurable bourgeois attitudes" and "unbecoming pietistic acts in favor of a Jew."[822] The biggest outcry was the case of *Artecrazia*, a futurist publication in Rome edited by Mino Somenzi, but actually controlled by Filippo Tommaso Marinetti, one of the most prominent Fascist personalities within Italian culture. It was known that Marinetti was not an anti-Semite. He had clearly stated his opinion in 1936 during a meeting of the board of the PEN Club.[823] In the first few weeks of the racial campaign some of his remarks during a radio conversation regarding modern art demonstrated how much he was opposed to those who sought to deny any value to a whole series of contemporary works, just by calling them "Jewish." His position had caused quite a stir, but because of a notice placed in various newspapers a scandal had been averted.[824] However, a scandal suddenly did break out and could no longer be avoided in December 1938 with the publication of issue number 117 of *Artecrazia*. The entire magazine was dedicated to the "Italian quality of modern art" and to racism. And it was certainly not to praise the latter. The magazine began with an editorial by Somenzi entitled "Razzismo" [Racism]. Without mincing words, and in a few sentences, it branded with fire both anti-Semitism and its supporters and deserves to be quoted in its entirety:

> It burst out suddenly, like a bolt from the blue. It has taken the shape of a cataclysm as so much is said, written, and talked about it, in every shape or form.
>
> In the end it means more or less that 60,000 Jews have to pack up or switch nationality. An inanity, a small mark on the round and virile face of some 50,000,000 Italians. And yet much noise is being

made; they are bringing back stories that are 4,000 and more years old, as though they were true or had just happened the day before yesterday and are still newsworthy and must be urgently re-discussed so that humanity can sleep tranquilly. In reality everyone is sleeping very well and no one wants to try and understand. If we listen to the majority we must adopt the existing laws, if not create new ones. No one knows what is so new, only that at the end of the day, a small number of Jews, good or bad as they may be, should no longer have anything more to do with us. Of all the answers only one counts: "because they are Jews." Very simple, nothing really complicated. And yet there are so many complications!

To say, for instance, we are this or we are that, means resurrecting so many centuries of culture, with that coda of falsehoods that history serves up as truth. Then there would have to be discussions for many more centuries to come. Is it possible that for such a small matter they would want to end up looking like madmen? And madmen and fake madmen do exist, who roll up their sleeves like charlatans from morning to night on Italy's squares as though they intended to ward off the end of the world. The people look at them with gratified smiles and say, "if they are crazy, they are doing it on purpose, and if they are doing it on purpose, besides the Jews...I smell a rat."

Yes gentlemen...I smell a rat. But which rat? Well, we shall see.

As if this were not enough, two articles followed the editorial, one with the eloquent title "Arte e...razzia" [Art and...Plunder] and the other on "Italianità dell'arte moderna" [The Italian Character of Modern Art]. This second article was signed "Artecrazia," and, given the context, it was thought to be by Somenzi; however, there was no doubt that Marinetti himself had played a large role in writing it. The incident quickly became common knowledge and created much embarrassment and a sensation. The small number of copies of the issue that had not been seized, as it was immediately ordered, continued to circulate clandestinely for a long time. If the editorial by Somenzi had been very clear, the article signed "Artecrazia" was even more violent. For the sake of brevity we shall not discuss the claim that with anti-Semitism the real targets were actually modern art and therefore Marinetti himself,[825] but it is impossible not to quote the closing lines of the article, one of the most violent attacks ever written by Fascists about the corruption and hypocrisy of Fascism:

> Today what serves your purpose is the war against the Jews, but between a Jew, war veteran, squad member, Fascist legionnaire and a pseudo-Fascist Communist, swindler, ruffian, ready to serve any master and any party for a price, as long as they are in power, I am decidedly in favor of the first.
>
> When they speak of the *Jewish anti-Fascist International* I am puzzled. I ask myself whether this international includes the 60,000 Jews who reside in Italy, who according to the Duce himself have never been and are not a danger, or does it include you, who serve the regime so poorly and all its best men?
>
> And I ask myself, even more puzzled, if it's not you, rather than the Jews, who through these recurring campaigns have taken on the task of sweeping away these last, very few authentic Fascists of the day before, who are somehow still walking around freely and preventing, ignored and hungry, the triumphant march of innumerable profiteers and eleventh-hour heroes?

The *Artecrazia*-Marinetti "case" was to have an echo in the *Camicia rossa*-Garibaldi case. Ezio Garibaldi also was not an anti-Semite, yet the unequivocal tone of his "Discorso di attualità" [Discussion on Current Events] in the June-October issue of *Camicia rossa* also caused much outcry. Garibaldi strongly attacked the manifesto of the "scientists" and the "cognonerie" (from the name Cogni) of the various Italian racists, but most of all he attacked the cheap anti-Semitism of the Interlandi types, demonstrating that it was merely a translation into Italian of the stupid arguments of the *Stürmer* school that were being published in Germany. Garibaldi's position was less solid than that of Marinetti; after a few arguments,[826] the "case," was put to rest also because of the low circulation of *Camicia rossa*. The matter was resolved by a dry press release from Starace—published at the beginning of May 1939 in Bulletin n. 1318 of the PNF—where it was stated that Garibaldi had not been a party member since 1930.

The incidents involving Marinetti and Garibaldi were extreme cases; the press was, in its overwhelming majority, vehemently anti-Semitic; there were to be very rare cases of newspapers that were critical of some isolated aspects of anti-Semitic and racist propaganda in general. Some newspapers were able to resist the latest trend and, while not criticizing the measures, also avoided praising them as they were about to be enacted, and avoided the anti-Semitic uproar. We can accurately say that the only daily that did not print the manifesto of the "scientists" was *L'Ambrosiano* in Milan. In general, the opposition of the Italian people appears only indirectly within the press through the attacks against the "pietists," and against those who defended the Jews.

Beginning in August these attacks became more frequent and indicate how much the PNF and the Ministry of Popular Culture were worried about the openly critical attitude of the Italian people toward the racial policies. From hints here and there that fell between the lines, "the screams and lamentations emanating from this terrestrial foreign and domestic mentality" and about the existence of "a swarming behind the scenes of Jewish and pro-Jewish circles," to the still undefined accusation regarding unspecified attempts "to thwart the Fascist measures for the defense of the race and prevent them from fully succeeding" during the initial period,[827] to the open warning about this "dangerous" mentality. The "pietists," the "honorary Jews," the "tender hearted," the "little tenderly souls" were being targeted in the editorials of many newspapers. The "pietists," in general "the usual eggheads devoid of true Fascist faith or without the regular party pin on their lapel," were being warned, accused of being in bad faith, and most often called naïve.[828] Then, once the "benevolent" warnings were clearly lost, they were followed by more threatening ones:

> Sentimentalism doesn't exist in politics and among the first rules of modern man there is also the one that says he should not be an idiot.
>
> The individual who sobs about the "painful history" of the Jews and seeks absurd humanitarian arguments with the thinking of a Protestant spinster and demands innumerable exceptions for "individual

and pitiful cases" is an anti-Fascist, all the more an enemy because his lack of backbone will not allow him to change his mind even if he wished to do so. As an anti-Fascist, he must be cast from our entire life.[829]

And then, on to the open and direct threats:

"But where are the poor Jews going to wind up?"

Here is a silly question and an embarrassing one for us Fascists to hear repeatedly for a month or so, from women, men, from too many people…

To hell, comrades, they should go to hell, your "poor Jews," to pay for the evil they have perpetrated on the world for twenty centuries.

And you, comrades, should join them in excellent company…

You, comrades, you sentimentalists of the coin and of maliciousness.

To hell with the Jews, comrades, is where we would like to see you; and a spoonful of castor oil, we mean the kind that is aged in the barrel, of course, should help you slide there faster.[830]

By November not a single newspaper refrained from attacking the "pietists." "Pietism" was synonymous with the bourgeois spirit and anti-Fascism, and the "moral mongrel mentality" of some Italians was held up to ridicule and Fascist assault. To add weight to this campaign many dailies[831] on November 26 published some thoughts by Starace. "Pietism" was declared to be the antithesis of the Fascist sprit, a typical expression and a trademark of bourgeois attitudes. For a few weeks it almost seemed that the struggle against the Jews was to become secondary to that against those who were "pro-Jewish," the "moral mongrels," against the bourgeoisie itself.[832] Then, the campaign, without disappearing completely, suddenly quieted. Someone at the Ministry of Popular Culture must have realized that to go further down this road meant admitting that the "pietists" were not limited to a few "intellectualists," a handful of "tender little souls," a few individuals tied to the Jews by economic interests, a few superficial individuals who had not understood the deeper meaning of the racial policy, but that they were, in fact, the majority of the Italian people.

Trieste 1925-1927: Jewish refugees in transit.

above
Vladimir Jabotinski (wearing glasses) with teachers and cadets at Civitavecchia. *(Provided by Commander Nicola Fasco.)*

below
Civitavecchia school cadets march through town.

Giovanni Preziosi

Roberto Farinacci lecturing on the topic
"The Church and the Jews".

First page of the "Declaration on Race" of September 1938 in Mussolini's handwriting.
(Central State Archives. Rome.)

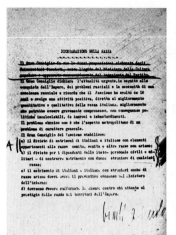

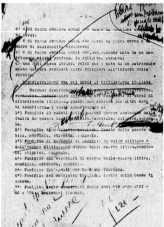

C. C. P. ROMA

DICEMBRE

3

1938-XVI
ERA FASCISTA

ANNO VII
Numero

117

LIRE
UNA

periodico di tutte le arti moderne diretto ___ Roma Via degli Scipioni 175-A Tel. 35-178

Italianità dell'arte moderna

RAZZISMO

E' scoppiato all'improvviso come un fulmine a ciel sereno. Ha assunto le proporzioni di un cataclisma tanto se ne dice, se ne scrive e se ne parla a proposito e a sproposito.

A conti fatti si tratta, poco più o poco meno, di 60.000 ebrei che devono far fagotto o cambiare nazionalità. Una inezia, un baffo impercettibile sulla faccia tonda e virile di ben 50 milioni di italiani.

Eppure, dicevo, se ne fa un gran strepito. Si tirano in ballo certe storie di 4000 anni fa e forse più, come se fossero cose vere o fatti avvenuti l'altro giorno e ancora oggi di scottante attualità, urgenti da risolvere perché l'umanità possa prendere sonno.

In realtà tutti dormono i sonni più beati e nessuno vuole sforzarsi a capire.
Stando a sentire i più, bisogna aggiornare i testi competenti se non curarne addirittura di nuovi.

Cosa vi sia di nuovo neppure si sa. Si sa solamente, alla fine dei conti, che pochi ebrei, buoni o cattivi che siano, non devono avere più nulla da spartire con noi. Dei " perché " ne basta uno: perché sono ebrei. Semplicissimo; quindi nulla di complicato. Eppure.... quante complicazioni !

Voler dire per esempio: perché noi qui, perché noi là, comporterebbe la riesumazione di tanti secoli di culture con quel corollario di belle che la storia propina per verità. Poi vi sarebbe ancora da dire e da discutere per molti secoli futuri.

Possibile che per una cosetta da nulla vogliamo passare per pazzi ?
E pazzi o finti pazzi ve ne sono che si sbracciano come ciarlatani dannati dal mattino alla sera, sulle piazze d'Italia come se si trattasse di scongiurare la fine del mondo.

Il pubblico li sta a vedere: sorride di compassione e si domanda: Se non sono pazzi lo fanno apposta e se lo fanno apposta, ebrei a parte,.... gatta ci cova.

- Sissignori.... gatta ci cova.
- Ma quale gatta ?
- Beh ! Staremo a vedere ....

MINO SOMENZI

UMBERTO BOCCIONI - futurista - (1913) - muscoli in velocità

December 1938 issue of *Artecrazia* banned because of Marinetti's attack on the racial policy.

above and left
Exodus from Italy: the ship
Esperia leaves Genoa for Haifa
in September 1938.

PROVVEDIMENTI PER LA DIFESA DELLA RAZZA ITALIANA

DENUNCIA

dei diritti pertinenti ai cittadini italiani di razza ebraica sugli immobili di cui ai commi d ed e
dell'art. 10 del R. decreto-legge 17-11-1938-XVII, n. 1728, alla data dell'11 febbraio 1939-XVII

(TERRENI E FABBRICATI)

above and right
Personal questionnaires for the
Jewish census of 1938.

MINISTERO DELLE FINANZE

SCHEDA PERSONALE

(Cognome e Nome dell'impiegato od agente)

(Paternità) (Maternità)

(Data e Luogo di nascita)

(Cognome e Nome del coniuge)

(Qualifica e grado gerarchico)

(Ufficio in cui l'impiegato presta servizio)

a) Se il padre sia di razza ebraica (*)

b) Se la madre sia di razza ebraica (*)

c) Se sia iscritto alla comunità israelitica (*)

d) Se professi la religione ebraica (*)

e) Se professi altra religione e quale (*)

f) Se la conversione ad altra religione sia stata effettuata da lui o dai
propri ascendenti, e quali, ed in quale data

g) Se il coniuge sia di razza ebraica (*)

DICHIARO CHE QUANTO SOPRA RISPONDE A VERITÀ

addì

FIRMA DEL TITOLARE DELLA SCHEDA

above left
Anti-Semitism: a store in Ancona featured in the *Corriere adriatico* of December 17, 1938.

above right
Anti-Semitism: a hotel at Cortina d'Ampezzo featured in *Il popolo d'Italia* of January 15, 1939.

— Ho un cugino che abita vicino a Piazza San Sepolcro Credete che possa essere una benemerenza?

left
Anti-Semitic cartoon mocking the search for discriminations in Ancona's *Corriere adriatico* of November 16, 1939.

left and below
The free internees' "payroll" at Lonigo,
near Vicenza in February 1943.
(Central State Archives. Rome.)

The school at Ferramonti.

Life at the
Ferramonti Camp in 1942

Images provided by Noemi Fajrajzen.

Inauguration of the Synagogue built by internees.

Camp life (but playing cards was...forbidden).

Passover 1942.

Inside some flimsy barracks.

Leaders of rescue organizations and of the Union of Jewish Communities during the Fascist regime.

above
Father Benoît-Marie,
a Capuchin monk who sheltered
thousands of Jewish refugees in
Rome in 1943-44, had previously been
active on the French Riviera with
Angelo Donati.

left
Dante Almansi

below
Angelo Sacerdoti

above
Lelio Vittorio Valobra

left
Angelo Donati

Jews drafted for forced labor service digging on
the banks of the Tiber. Rome, June 1942.

To find direct documentation of the opposition of the Italian people to state-sponsored anti-Semitism we must turn to other sources, namely, to the reports compiled by the police and, even more, to the reports coming from the administrators of the Fascist federations and Fascist party informers. The content of these reports varies, obviously, according to their author's intelligence, his degree of independence or servility to the political leadership. Each one, however, clearly indicates that the Italian people did not swallow the racist pill. Some random examples will be sufficient. Turin was a "middle" city as far as the Jews were concerned and perhaps the city most "critical" of Fascism compared to the rest of Italy. A report sent to the national secretariat of the PNF dated September 4, 1938 describes the general mood there:

> In general these radical measures are met with approval, many people hope to benefit from them, and the feeling of compassion for the Jews within public opinion will only be temporary.[833]

Another report, dated December 21, indicates things were not moving in the direction that had been forecast at first:

> Uncertainty and discontent regarding the Jewish problem lingers on with almost everyone. No one identifies with the racial campaign as it has been conducted, and people are wondering, but not out of pietism, where it is going and what results are expected from the measures taken and those to come in the future. I have been informed of sermons given in some churches in town, sermons dealing exclusively with the racial problem, which is not viewed favorably by the Catholic Church. In Catholic circles the entire anti-Jewish policy is being criticized and such criticism, well known to the public, is creating a solidarity with the Jews that surfaces everywhere.[834]

To this very unfavorable picture, Piero Gazzotti, the Fascist federal secretary of Turin, will send a different view to Starace on December 30 by writing "no one is talking about the Jewish problem anymore"; but he then had to agree that:

> the only true item in all this news relates to Catholic circles, where the racist policy is being either openly or surreptitiously criticized and solidarity with the Jews is not hidden.[835]

The picture does not change when switching from Turin to Milan, a city that was beyond a doubt much more favorable to Fascism. We have a very valuable eyewitness account in a long report to the Duce dated November 29 by Fascist federal secretary Rino Parenti, an important member of the party leadership.[836] The report seeks to counter criticism coming from Mussolini to Parenti, through the prefect of Milan, regarding Parenti's work over the last few months, relating mostly to the position of Cardinal Ildefonso Schuster, who had taken a well-known stand against racism in one of his homilies, published in the November 15 issue of *L'Italia*. In this report there are also various hints regarding the situation in Milan and Lombardy in general. Despite its defensive tone and the attempt to minimize the consequences of the cardinal's stand, Parenti stresses that the cardinal had demonstrated on other occasions "his unequivocal support" of Fascist policy. Besides the rhetorical statement that "I can assure you that on this issue as well, I, my Fascist colleagues, and the people of Milan, shall continue along the straight and narrow path," in spite of all this, it is obvious that even in Milan "the lamentations of the protectors of the Jews" were as common an occurrence as "the usual sentimental Aryans who make it their business to defend every useless cause."

The picture remains identical moving from Turin and Milan to Trieste, where, according to rigorous Fascist logic, opposition and aversion to the Jews should have been stronger than in any other city in Italy because in Trieste the Jews occupied important political, administrative, and, most of all, economic positions.[837] Yet, significantly, on November 20, Starace, following confidential information he had received, sent the following note to the Fascist federation secretary of Trieste, adding a P.S. in his own handwriting, "Grazioli, Careful!":

> Given that the Duce's Trieste speech had led us to believe that a less restrictive solution to the race problem could be possible, the anti-Jewish measures have had important consequences in the city due to the large number of Jews (6,329) and to the fact that much of business was based directly and indirectly upon capital and persons belonging to that race. To the economic factor we can also add a

sentimental one, since most inhabitants of Trieste have not forgotten the vast amount of work done by the Jews to defend Trieste's Italian character, even though, in some cases, it was because of vested interests. Those financing irredentism were Jews and the majority of volunteers from Trieste in the Italian army during the war between Italy and Austria were also Jewish. Some names, such as that of Commendatore Morpurgo and former Mayor Salem, did enjoy everyone's respect. The measures have nevertheless been received with little enthusiasm. As things stand, it is the general wish, even among Catholics, that, given the patriotic past of many Jews from Trieste, the discriminations should be awarded somewhat generously and those discriminated should enjoy a sufficiently happy life.[838]

These examples accurately illustrate the true feelings of Italian public opinion and it is therefore unnecessary to refer to other cities. The most important issue of public opinion at the time was the attitude of the Catholics.[839]

Documents previously cited show how the Catholics took a position clearly opposed to the anti-Semitic measures. There is ample proof of this and it remains a constant until 1945. To the direct reports we have quoted, others can be added from the Catholic press in June-July 1938, as well as over the course of the following months. Even using the necessary caution to avoid being shut down by Fascist authorities, the most important Catholic dailies, especially *L'Italia* in Milan and *L'avvenire d'Italia* in Bologna, were repeatedly critical during the initial hints of the racist campaign. Commenting on Paolo Orano's book, for example, Clemente Ghezzi's article, "Ebraismo e Cattolicesimo sul terreno storico-dottrinale" [Judaism and Catholicism on the historical-doctrinal level], in the June 1, 1938 issue of *L'Italia,* wrote clearly of the "painful and legitimate disorientation" that it had caused among Catholics, and mentioned, by comparison, Ettore Ovazza as an "honest and friendly Jewish person." Ghezzi's critiques did not end here. Alluding to the Fascist measures which were being prepared, he concluded his article with the following words:

We believe that the best, the most decisive, the most significant battle that we, practicing and convinced Catholics, can wage against Judaism must be a general mobilization of spiritual forces capable of moving the Infinite Heart of the Crucified Master for the salvation of what was once His People.

Mario Bendiscioli was just as vocal in his article, "Il problema ebraico" [The Jewish Problem], in the same newspaper two days later:

> The Church cannot allow the complete religious condemnation of the Jewish world, meaning the Old Testament, because it constitutes one complete organism, even though inferior, with the New, carrying the entire Christian Revelation.
>
> The fact that the Jewish people have resisted every assimilation, persecution, and dispersion shows the continuation of those eminent and singular qualities of cohesion that made it the guardian of divine Revelation before Christ. It is no doubt the reflection of this religious mystery that makes so many Catholics hesitate accepting a simply political Jewish problem, looking at Judaism as a national and not a religious issue.
>
> Where Judaism has been fought as a racial issue it has also been attacked in its universally sacred religious substance. The example of German anti-Semitism teaches us many things in this regard.

The attitude of the Catholic press became more cautious after the first government measures. The tension between Italy and the Holy See following the publication on July 30 in *L'osservatore romano* of the Pope's speech (which was forbidden to be reprinted by Italian newspapers, parish bulletins, and newsletters of the various archdioceses),[840] to the students of the Propaganda Fide College induced the Vatican to avoid any positions that could further poison the situation and encourage the government to take repressive action against the Catholic Action and the Catholic press itself. Veiled criticism of racism continued to appear frequently enough, and, significantly, Catholic newspapers were careful to avoid joining the anti-Semitic chorus, limiting themselves to factual accounts on the developments of Fascist policies. In November when the news of the Nazi *Kristallnacht* violence against the Jews, following the assassination of von Rath, reached Italy, the more serious Catholic newspapers did not hide their disapproval and disgust.[841] A few days later they repeated the complaints of the Holy See because of the Fascist government's violation of the Concordat regarding matrimony.[842]

So much for the press. The vast majority of Italian Catholics, and even the clergy, went much further in their opposition than what appears in the press and far beyond the position of the Holy See. It surfaces in reports from Fascist federations, and, indirectly, in the attitude of the press and Fascist propaganda in general.

Notwithstanding Mussolini's personal anti-clerical mood during those days and his threats to strum the "Ghibelline chord"* of the Italian people if it became necessary, or his spiteful and unbending attitude toward the Holy See, the Fascists wanted to avoid a clash with the Catholics. Besides serious international complications, such a conflict would not have been limited to the active Catholic membership of the Catholic Action, but would have probably spread to vast sections of the country, widening from "racist" aspects to other issues of Fascist policy and above all the policy toward Germany. The fact that this was the real line taken by the government is clearly demonstrated by a telephone conversation between Alfieri and Goebbels on November 23 (from the archives of the Ministry of Popular Culture). The day before, *Der Angriff,* one of the most vitriolic Nazi newspapers, had published a severe attack on Cardinal Schuster, regarding his criticism of Italian racial policy a few days before. *Der Angriff* accused the Cardinal of being the spokesman for a clerical clique that for over one year had sought the destruction of the Rome-Berlin Axis, and asked, "how long will this political sabotage, that is all for the pleasure of the democracies, continue to enjoy a free hand?" Alfieri strongly protested against this article during the phone call,[843] proving to Goebbels (who in the end agreed to stop the campaign), how misplaced it was. Alfieri used three arguments: Catholic newspapers had very low circulation within Italy; an intervention at this time would complicate matters because extreme pressure is being put on those very newspapers; and finally, it would be giving them too much importance

* During the middle ages the Ghibellines were the supporters of the Emperor against the Pope, whose political followers were known as the Guelphs.

to think they could seriously endanger the strength of the Axis. The fear on the part of the Fascists to be drawn into an open conflict with the Catholics is clearly implied under the diplomatic and outwardly assured tone of the phone call.

The Fascists preferred to try to influence Catholic public opinion as Preziosi and Farinacci were to do, by using its own ammunition and putting forward traditions and anti-Semitic pronouncements that, as we have seen, were certainly not difficult to find among the Catholics themselves. The action had begun at a supposedly high level during the first months of 1938[844] with the publication in April of the book *I rapporti fra la Chiesa Cattolica e gli Ebrei* [The Relations Between the Catholic Church and the Jews], written by a well-known personality within the world of journalism using the pseudonym "Nomentanus." This book was quickly followed by others in the same vein. Among these were *Ebrei-Chiesa-Fascismo* [Jews-the Church-Fascism] (Tivoli 1938) by Mario Lolli and *Io cattolico e Israele* [A Catholic and Israel] (Rome 1938) by "Catholicus." The content of all these works was the same: the Church had always persecuted the Jews; Fascism was therefore not doing anything new and remained within the Catholic tradition. The discussion quickly reached the pages of the newspapers that were suddenly filled with detailed articles on how the Church and the Popes had treated the Jews in past centuries, replete with "learned" quotations from the canon and the Church Fathers. It was beginning to look as though the Fascists were in fact the real Catholics. On August 28 *Il regime fascista* went so far as to publish the editorial "Lezione di cattolicesimo ai cattolici"[845] [Lesson in Catholicism for the Catholics]. Preziosi's *La vita italiana* even republished, in its September issue, all the articles that had appeared in *La civiltà cattolica* in 1890 that had also been reprinted in Farinacci's newspaper. The latter also decided to personally explain to the Catholics why they should approve of anti-Semitism just because they were Catholics. Not satisfied with the articles and editorials he was publishing almost daily in *Il regime fascista*, Farinacci even gave a lecture in Milan on November 7 at the Triennale Theater on the topic, "La Chiesa e gli Ebrei"[846] [The Church and the Jews]. During this lecture—certainly the most complete and clever attempt to "theorize," from the Fascist point of view, the convergence of Fascist and Catholic anti-Semitism—Farinacci showed how "anti-Judaism" had been, until a few years before, a constant theme of Catholic thought and policy, and affirmed that "if, as Catholics we became anti-Semites, we owe it to the teachings of the Church during the past twenty centuries," and he concluded by asking threateningly why the Church had changed its tune during the last few months:

> What has happened for the official Church today to feel no longer anti-Semitic but pro-Semitic? We can't believe that it was just the Jews boasting to Simonini what Simonini revealed to the Jesuit Father Barruel: "in Italy alone we have more than eight hundred priests...and we don't think it impossible to even have a Pope in our party." Why do the Communists, the Freemasons, the Democrats, the declared enemies of the Church, offer their services and praise it so highly today? To use it against Fascism. But Fascism is a friend of the Church because it is Catholic and Roman...These questions of ours create, for us Catholics, a deep spiritual tragedy. We cannot, in a few weeks, renounce the anti-Semitic consciousness that the Church itself gave us over thousands of years. But we shall overcome this tragedy of ours, convinced of our political mission. We reiterate that the Christian spirit is the highest form of energy upholding mankind and the European peoples, and leads them into combat in the service of God. We would not like the Church to shed its mission as a fundamental educator by taking on political questions that are exclusively the province of Fascism. Yes, because Fascism obeys history and maintains and enriches for future generations the legacy of Rome.

The purpose of Farinacci's speech was clear, on the one hand he was showing the Catholics that anti-Semitism was their religious duty, and on the other he did not spare them any threats in case they remained unconvinced. And this time it worked. The majority of Catholics were certainly not moved to embrace the cause of anti-Semitism by Farinacci's arguments; the Catholic hierarchies and the press chose to avoid any risks and, while not accepting it, any public dispute over anti-Semitism ended almost instantly.

The anti-Semites, however, were not about to stop even though the opponents of anti-Semitism had. As we have seen, anti-Semites existed among the Catholics and within the Clergy itself.

There is no need to mention the anti-Semites of *La Liguria del popolo*; based on what we have seen, their position was predictable. The same is true of *Italia e Fede*, whose editor Giulio De Rossi Dell'Arno was not satisfied with having written that Fascism "had felt the Christian need to at least save the Italian people from the threat of chaos" and had therefore "locked the Fascist homeland within the racist fortress," "raising all the drawbridges in front of all the horrors of cosmopolitanism" so as to regenerate "completely, in its physical and spiritual values, the Roman species" and thus return it "to the civic duties of Imperial and Catholic Rome."[847] He even denied that racism was the same as paganism and did not limit himself to these ideas within his own newspaper, but repeated them in a pamphlet published in 1940, appropriately entitled *L'ebraismo contro l'Europa* [Judaism Against Europe]. We shall not discuss Catholics, such as Gino Sottochiesa, who was rightly named by Richard Webster as a Fascist agent provocateur among the Catholics,[848] or Monsignor Giuseppe Beccaria, the King's head chaplain, who said he was pleased to be among the readers of *La difesa della razza* and sent it his best wishes.[849] We cannot, however, ignore the positions taken by authoritative publications, such as *La civiltà cattolica* and *Vita e pensiero*, and by a few important members of the clerical hierarchy.[850]

Il regime fascista, on August 30, 1938, in referring to the Jesuits, "Un tremendo atto d'accusa" [A terrible indictment], wrote that there was "much to be learned from the Fathers of the Society of Jesus" and that "Fascism is much inferior in its goals and its development compared to the rigor of *La civiltà cattolica*." Unfortunately Farinacci's paper is, for once, quite close to the truth. Referring to 1938 alone, it is a fact that *La civiltà cattolica*'s reviewer criticized the work of Simon Laemmel against Nazi anti-Semitism:

> The author exaggerates. He forgets the continuous persecutions by the Jews against the Christians, in particular against the Catholic Church, and the alliance with the Freemasons, the Socialists, and other

anti-Christian parties; he exaggerates in concluding that "it would not only be illogical and anti-historical, but a real moral betrayal if today Christianity failed to protect the Jews." Nor can we forget that the Jews have drawn upon themselves in every period of history, and draw upon themselves still, the people's understandable aversion with their too frequent abuse of power and hatred of Christ himself, his religion, and the Catholic Church.[851]

It called Hungarian anti-Semitism "a movement to defend national traditions and the true freedom and independence of the Magyar people."[852] *La civiltà cattolica* was brought to task because Preziosi and Farinacci had republished its 1890 articles; its answer appears forced and too weak to dispel the painful dismay caused by this reminder.[853] The true position of *La civiltà cattolica* appears identical to its earlier demand for a "segregation or distinction that fits our times," a position that was, in the final analysis, not much different from Mussolini's "discriminate, but do not persecute."[854]

As for *Vita e pensiero*, a magazine published by the Catholic University of Milan, it also basically justified the anti-Semitic policy of Fascism. Here there are no statements similar to those in *La civiltà cattolica*, but the spirit inspiring its staff is the same. Typically, no sooner had Pope Pius XI died, than the magazine quickly pointed out that

> the deceased Pontiff was not for democracy, nor was he pro-Jewish, or anti-totalitarian; he just preached, in the highest sense of the word, Christian doctrine, that is what it is and doesn't accept any kind of label.[855]

Which demonstrates that Pius XI's position was too rigid for them. Clearly, on anti-Semitism, the *Vita e pensiero* group took the same positions as Fascism through the public statements of its best-known spokesman, Father Agostino Gemelli, especially during a lecture he gave concerning William of Salicet on January 9, 1939 at the University of Bologna. William is seen as the medieval champion of the "synthesis between the individual and society, Church

and State, religion and politics, science and faith, Church and school."
This synthesis was destroyed during the intervening centuries because "Judeo-Masonic conspiracies" had, according to Gemelli,
given rise to the clash that characterized Church and State during
the nineteenth century. It was just an excuse to applaud Fascism
and "the Duce of Italy, that a high and august voice has called
peerless" and to launch an attack on the Jews.[856]

One quotation will suffice:

> It is a tragic and no doubt painful situation for those who cannot
> belong to this magnificent homeland because of their blood and their
> religion; a tragic situation where we see once again, as many times
> before in past centuries, enacted the terrible sentence that this deicidal
> people has called upon itself and that consequently is wandering
> around the world, unable to find the peace of a homeland, while the
> consequences of that horrible murder follow it everywhere and for
> all time.

It will come as no surprise, following such a sampling of Father
Gemelli's prose, to discover that Farinacci, in *Il regime fascista* of
January 10, quickly concluded with satisfaction, "Non siamo soli"
[We are not alone], and praised the Bologna speech by Gemelli, nor
two months later when he actually asked Mussolini to name this
"man who is really one of us" to the Academy of Italy.[857]

To conclude this sad page of Italian Catholicism under Fascism, we can only recall the homily by Monsignor Giovanni Cazzani,
Bishop of Cremona, on the occasion of the Epiphany in 1939. As
in the lecture by Father Gemelli of a few days before, it also contained a clear attack on the Jews. But the Bishop went somewhat
further, noting how the Church did not deny the right of the state
to persecute the Jews and would be careful not to defend them:

> The Church has never failed to recognize the right of the State
> to limit or forbid the economic, social, and moral influence of the
> Jews when they become damaging to the tranquility and well-being
> of the Nation.
> The Church has said and done nothing to defend the Jews, Jewry,
> and Judaism.

The Church, without any political agenda, has condemned a doctrine that denies the fundamental dogmas of our faith.[858]

This is the way Italian public opinion reacted through its most important representatives to state-sponsored anti-Semitism during the first months of its implementation.

26.

Italian Jewry and
the First Anti-Semitic Measures

I talian Jews in their overwhelming majority were caught completely off guard by the enactment of the first racial measures. For the mass of the Jews, just as for most Italians (except for a few anti-Fascist Jews, who clearly understood the direction Fascism was taking with its continuous linking up to Germany), not even the reopening of the anti-Semitic press campaign at the beginning of 1938 and the publication of the *Informazione diplomatica* n. 14 were enough "pieces of information" to acknowledge that Fascism had decided to follow the German example. Even for those in the highest circles, closest to the government, among the administrators of the Union and the largest Communities, there was, for a long time, no clue about the incipient danger.

Persecution was so far removed from the mentality, the history, and the traditions of Italy, so unjustified from any point of view, that most Italian Jews could not even conceive of it intellectually. The new and acrimonious press campaign unleashed at the beginning of January was long seen as one of the many campaigns destined to fade away sooner or later, as had always happened over the years. The *Informazione diplomatica* n. 14 itself was generally understood as confirmation that Mussolini had no intention of engaging in anti-Semitism and was interpreted mostly as a foreign policy initiative. The publication *Israel*, which certainly withheld no criticism, was very stern in its comments regarding Palestine, but remained positive in its interpretation of other issues, stating that it "disappoints the malicious-minded persons who expected the Fascist government to consider the adoption of more or less anti-Semitic internal measures."[859] All Jews felt considerable aversion toward the Germans and therefore toward the Italian-German alliance. Almost no one made the connection between this alliance and an imminent turn toward anti-Semitism in Mussolini's policies. What Emilio Artom was still writing in his diary on January 10, 1938 is fairly typical.[860] He did his utmost to find a solution to the problem of anti-Semitism, seeking the answer in its origins and development, but never imagining a direct Nazi influence: "Those who want to believe that it is being imposed by Germany do not convince me." He was rather thinking of a "secret international plot." In September the first laws took many by surprise. From the report of September 4, 1938 to Starace we learn that "Jewish circles were not prepared and, consequently, reality is disorienting and infuriating them; this has automatically created numerous anti-Fascists."[861]

The congress of the Union that took place in Rome on March 21-22, 1938, appeared to have returned some peace and quiet within Italian Jewry and to have improved relations with the government.[862] The secession of the Committee of Italians of the Jewish Religion had been solved with the formation of a new board with new directors, many of whom had represented the now dissolved Committee. The new leadership of the Union, in particular its president, Commander Federico Jarach—confirmed by the congress after the withdrawal of the candidacy of General Emmanuele Pugliese, and the Vice President, attorney Aldo R. Ascoli—appeared to have the full confidence and sympathy of the government, as demonstrated in the report of a long meeting Ascoli had on May 18 with Commendatore Mario Montecchi, the General Director for Religious Affairs at the Interior Ministry.[863] As Ascoli was to say on that occasion, it was a commonly held view that "a national Judaism, operating within the law, and respectful of all the decisions made by the Fascist government, will be able to live tranquilly within the national community" by adhering exactly to the regime's policies.

In this atmosphere the manifesto of the "scientists" in July and the first government measures appeared to most Jews and to the Union itself as so many bolts from the blue.[864] Many within the leadership even refused until the end to believe in the inevitable and thought that, on the contrary, by taking a submissive attitude that was at the same time unmistakably Fascist, it would be possible to avoid the measures or at least secure some mitigation. There was, no doubt, a good deal of opportunism in such an attitude; however, we do not believe that it should be condemned out of hand. For many Italians, the anti-Semitic campaign that began in 1938 was the first real political shock since the assassination of Matteotti in 1924. It was the first incident that opened their eyes to Fascism, and marking the beginning of their divorce from it. We do not see why most Jews should have had more foresight than other Italians as to how things would turn out in the end. Their confidence in Mussolini had been well placed from a strictly Jewish point of view: had Mussolini not helped the refugees from Germany, helping the Jews as few other European governments had, and at least officially always denying the existence of a Jewish Question in Italy? Nor should we forget that, as for all recently emancipated minorities, a break with Fascism meant, for those unaware of the values that were the antithesis of Fascism, breaking with Italy. While such a break was difficult for the majority of Italians, it was psychologically even more so for the Jews, who owed their emancipation and their complete equality to Italy. They were Italians to the core, by birth, culturally, educationally, and in some way doubly Italian because Italy for them, besides being what it was for all other Italians, also meant emancipation and civic equality attained only a few decades before. Not only were most Jews taken by surprise by Fascism's anti-Semitic policy and felt wounded by it morally more than materially, but since they were deeply Italian, it was impossible for them to simply turn their backs on the homeland now rejecting and persecuting them. The realization that Fascism did not represent Italy, and had not made a mistake or misunderstood them, was slow and painful. Fascism had consciously and cynically prepared and undertaken their persecution and it was now useless, naïve, and shameful to attempt to convince it of their "good faith" through demonstrations of loyalty, which it obviously did not deserve and in which the Jews no longer believed. For the less assimilated Jews, for the committed Zionists, the persecution was, from this point of view, not as serious as it was for most of their other co-religionists;

the persecution denied them less, and in some ways gave them back a lot more. To give up on Italy by emigrating or to give up being completely Italian in Italy was much easier for them than for those who were completely assimilated. The booklet by Immanuel Romano, *La questione ebraica* [The Jewish Question], which we mentioned at the beginning of this book, typifies such a position and illustrates well the different psychological situations involving the assimilated and the non-assimilated Jews.

For the Jews of a certain social and cultural level, who were aware of moral rather than political values, and had lived with this understanding through sixteen years of Fascism, it was just as easy to go into exile as to remain at home and accept the new situation, adapting to it morally, materially, and politically. This was not so easy for the others, those who had until then lived through Fascism "as Italians" and had to accept by themselves the reasons for their great misfortune. In reading the next chapters, perhaps some readers will be shocked or will smile and commiserate in finding out that some Jews would have preferred that the Union "collaborate" with the Fascist government; that some others, on various occasions, asked to be allowed to get into uniform to fight in the Second World War in the ranks of the Fascist army; and others still, during the most crucial moments of the war, agreed, even though they were the victims of persecution, to help the Italian armed forces. Indignation and commiseration, in our opinion, are completely out of place. In almost every case such episodes are the best proof of the tragedy of Italian Jewry and the moral monstrosity of persecution, a monstrosity that no "tolerance," no "humanity," no "well-meaning help" by the Fascists (compared to what was being done by the Nazis or other governments that were even more extreme in their persecution than the Fascist government), will ever be able to mitigate. It shows how, for the majority of Italian Jews, the persecution was not just a material fact, but also and mostly perhaps a moral issue. The financial damage, the broken careers, can be compensated; the wounds, in time, may heal; the bereavement for dead relatives can be soothed, compared to the dreadful proportions of the tragedy affecting all of humanity; what cannot be compensated, soothed, and repaired is the moral tragedy of those who felt Italian, wanted to be and were Italian, and in a few weeks were denied all of this without any reason.

As we have said, the manifesto of the "scientists" surprised everyone. President Jarach immediately met with Buffarini-Guidi and Alfieri, but from both he obtained only general assurances and an invitation to stay calm "because any alarm must be considered unjustified."[865] Thus began the series of pilgrimages during those months to those responsible for Fascist policy and their more or less hypocritical answers. The council of the Union could only proclaim its "painful amazement" and reaffirm the loyalty of the Jews to the Italian homeland.[866] There were certainly protests against the manifesto; many Jews wrote to *Il popolo d'Italia*, *Il regime fascista* and to other newspapers which generally did not print their letters.[867] Many did not believe the worse was still to come.[868] Even *Israel* felt that the manifesto merely announced a tendency to discourage mixed marriages.[869] However, the *Informazione diplomatica* n.18 was to dispel these illusions. The editorial in *Israel* is clear on this matter, even though it shows how, even within the most responsible Jewish circles, the full extent of what Mussolini was preparing had not been fully understood. The editorial in *Israel* indicates a "hopeful resignation":

> Discrimination can have painful consequences; to endure them with strength will be a new measure of dignity, of faith to one's own being, and of real love for Italy, that Jewish citizens will continue to serve with unlimited devotion in every field, in every condition, in every circumstance, wherever and whenever they may be located.[870]

While considering the extreme sensitivity of the time and the position of *Israel*, these are not, we think, the comments of someone who expects to be completely excluded; especially if we consider that the writer, shortly after, criticized the attitude of the press, as if its opinions were different from those of the government: "The hopeful expectation of the government's proposals toward the Jewish population in Italy is somewhat disturbed by the attitude of the newspapers, which is often exaggerated and partial."

From this moment on, and for another fifteen months, Italian Judaism entered a critical phase. The Union was by all accounts in a difficult situation, practically "out of the race," and run by men who, with few exceptions, felt that the best defense was the acceptance of government will. It did not succeed in having its own "policy," limiting itself, at first, to proving the Italian loyalty of the Jews and having Rabbi Aldo Lattes[871] approach Italo Balbo, who was known to be against the measures; and, second, to tackle only the most urgent practical problems, such as the organization of the schools, assembling data and material for the discriminations, and providing assistance to Jews who had been expelled. Even in these specific areas—we shall examine the most important aspects of this action in the following chapter—if much was accomplished it was due to the initiative and dedication of individuals and not through direct action by the Union. From a long letter dated December 29 from Vice President Ascoli to President Jarach in Milan, it appears that at the Rome headquarters nothing was known about the Assistance Committee for the Jews in Italy that was being handled by a member of the administration. By acting in this manner it is clear that the Union was losing much of its influence as the engine of Italian Jewry and created, de facto, a dangerous void at its center. In practical terms it followed and accepted the measures, without being able to even influence their elaboration—it would have been wishful thinking to believe such a thing possible—but it was unable to hold together the various Communities and Italian Jewry in general. From July to December the Union's activities, which were directed mostly by Vice President Ascoli, because Commander Jarach was often in Milan on private business, were limited almost exclusively by accelerating events to publishing periodic motions and press releases stating loyalty to Italy and the Regime,[873] to a few timid protests relating to acts of anti-Semitic violence that took place or had been threatened here and there, to the attitude of the press,[874] and to holding meetings with the leadership of the Regime who were directly involved in preparing the racial measures.[875]

However serious the crisis gripping the Union was, that of the individual Communities and of Italian Judaism was just as devastating. They were crushed by tremendous turmoil under the blows of anti-Semitism and racial policy. Disoriented and stunned by so many massive attacks, not all Jews were able to resist with firmness and dignity. From the columns of *Israel* on September 8, Dante Lattes, in his article, "Nell'ora della prova" [In Times of Trial], sent to all Jews a noble and heartfelt appeal to firmness and responsibility:

> The Jews of Italy are confronted with a challenge that requires the help of their entire millennial faith. They must rethink their long history and the way their forebears, at various times, were able to overcome a great many trials so that even this grave and difficult situation can be overcome with dignity. The discrimination that has been decreed against them must be accepted without discouragement, however painful it may be. Everyone bears a heavy responsibility. To suffer with steadfastness is not enough: we must suffer together, dividing the weight so that it doesn't become too heavy, unbearable, and tragic. God will help us if we know how to help others, if the strongest can sustain the weakest, if "your poorer brother can live with you," sharing your bread and sharing your heart.[876]

Not everyone accepted or even understood these words. In that tragic hour, some went so far as to condemn the one who addressed such a "noble" appeal. In Florence the editorial offices of *Israel* were ransacked by a group of Fascist Jews; in Milan *Davar* wanted to stop publishing and cursed its brothers at *Israel,* accusing them of being responsible for the persecution. In its September issue, which actually appeared after the meeting of the Grand Council, *Davar* published two editorials. The first, "Il Gran Consiglio e la Razza" [The Grand Council and Race] maintained that the persecution must be accepted in the Fascist spirit, which, according to *Davar,* cleared "the way of misunderstandings and ambiguities," and it approved, through the discrimination of those who had served, "the assimilation of the Jewish element into the Fascist element":

> For the highest ideal, the Nation, we have accepted; for this very ideal may every personal rancor cease that has nothing to do with the administration of justice: the wisdom of the Chief has won once again. And so we shall be able to: "follow the straight and narrow path" so that we may "believe, obey, and fight."

After this unambiguous attempt to save themselves by throwing their co-religionists to the wolves, *Davar* went on in a second editorial entitled "Lettera aperta al settimanale Israel" [Open letter to the weekly *Israel* to attack the Zionists and by extension those who were not about to shed their Jewish identity. The defense of Jewish tradition was characterized as a "betrayal," an attempt to separate the Jews from the Italian nation. "First and foremost among our errors," it wrote, had been to show no interest in their activities. But now the time to settle accounts had come; the Zionists, the "Orthodox," should accept their responsibilities, separating themselves from the others, but they should entertain no illusions of finding solidarity and understanding among the *real* Italians:

> It must be made very clear, starting now, that among Italian Jews there can be no cover up, just as there cannot be, among us, any theoretical or practical internationalism that can link one Jew to another inside and outside the borders of the Homeland. The enemies of Italy, Jewish or not, are our enemies; its friends are our friends, even though some religious differences can give a false impression to the contrary.

These sad words would weigh heavily on the conscience of those who had identified with them at the moment and among those who had accepted them, and would best be forgotten if they did not demonstrate so well the kind of moral confusion engulfing so many Italian Jews. Many of the public renunciations that took place during those tragic months can be traced to these statements: 460 abjurations during the first nine months of 1938; 1,771 during the last three months; 2,231 renunciations in 1938; plus an additional 1,649 during 1939.[877] Disavowals, renunciations, dissociations—sometimes, but not always, accompanied by a conversion to Catholicism, which, in general, took place within the upper classes of Italian Jewry and involved even some of the top leadership. Disavowals, renunciations, dissociations, that in some cases was the finale in the long process of separating oneself from Judaism and embracing assimilation, but that in many cases were dictated by the hope of escaping persecution, save their possessions and their positions.[878] There were also among them Jews who were sincerely Fascists and who thought that they were proving their attachment to Italy and Fascism and their complete independence from international Jewry by making such a decision.[879] It must also be pointed out that among the well-known individuals of the regime who were of the "Jewish Race," most of them reacted with great dignity, often choosing to emigrate, generally to Latin America; for example, Gino Arias, Giorgio Del Vecchio, Giorgio Mortara, Gino Olivetti, and Margherita Sarfatti.

The loss of almost four thousand persons who emigrated in proportion to all of Italian Jewry was a very serious drain; and yet despite this, beyond the initial moments of disorientation and chaos, Italian Jewry found the moral strength that allowed it to overcome the harsh trials of the years to come. To the many fearful, those who felt it their duty to place Italy ahead of Israel, there were also many who endured persecution in dignified silence while remaining faithful to their religion, but also those who had dissociated themselves *de facto*, if not *de jure*, and who found, during the persecution, if not religious faith, the pride and consciousness of their Jewish identity. If Ettore Ovazza renounced, it was to demonstrate that his position was far removed from "any internationalism hostile to Italy and Fascism" and in particular from Zionist policy,[880] while someone like Guido Liuzzi felt, in the same circumstances, more closely attached to Italian Jewry, whereas up to that point his involvement had been superficial, and he had not spared it any criticism. His participation in the fate of his co-religionists was public and not a secret within his heart. In offering all his help and collaboration to the Union of Jewish Communities, he made his position, regarding the true character of the measures passed by the Fascist government, known to the King[881] and to the most responsible leaders of the regime.[882]

Between these two—obviously extreme cases—moved the mass of Italian Jews; in dismay at first, but with clearer ideas as time wore on. Those who could, quickly opted to emigrate overseas, especially if they had children of college age.[883] Those who could not or did not wish to emigrate, tried to find a new way of life that would allow them to live in Italy, taking advantage of the new laws and, most of all, counting on the solidarity of their "Aryan" compatriots. Many others, still disbelieving events, preferred to wait and see how things turned out. In one way or another, all attempted to find a solution to their problems.

To document the magnitude of this problem statistically, it will suffice to state that in a few weeks the following people had to solve the problems of their livelihood: 200 teachers at every level and grade, 400 government functionaries and employees, 500 private employees, 150 permanent members of the armed forces, and about 2,500 professionals, forced to interrupt or reduce to a minimum their normal activities. The students affected by the Fascist measures were about 5,600—200 university students, 1,000 secondary school students, and 4,400 elementary school pupils. Foreign Jews are not included in these numbers, many of whom obviously had been residing for decades in Italy, with relatives and jobs.

It is not within the framework of this book to examine how individuals found solutions to their problems. It is important to note how Italian Jewry, after the first months of persecution, showed ever greater cohesion and inner solidarity, quickly finding the necessary equilibrium to overcome the difficulties suddenly encountered and save its moral well being and, as we shall see later, find within itself not just the energy to survive as individuals but the right men to guide it through this trial and ensure its survival as an organized entity. The kind of moral reactions that surfaced during those first unsettling moments for Italian Jews were demonstrated by the dramatic suicide on November 29, 1938 of publisher Angelo Fortunato Formiggini, who flung himself from the top of the Ghirlandina tower in Modena. The comment by Achille Starace revealed his moral bankruptcy and cynicism: "He really died like a Jew: he jumped from a tower so as not to waste a bullet."[884] Italians worthy of their name, Jews and "Aryans" alike, understood, even though Fascist propaganda did everything it could to hide its real motivations, the meaning of that desperate and at the same time heroic gesture: that "discrimination," whatever Mussolini and his minions may say, was persecution, the most barbaric and unjust that Italy had seen in centuries, and Formiggini, by his extreme action, had flung it in the face of Fascism. The Italians, the Fascists themselves, had to draw the only possible conclusion. As Formiggini wrote to his wife a few days before:

> I cannot turn my back on what I consider to be my duty, I must show the absurd meanness of the racist measures by drawing atten-

tion to my case, which seems to be the most typical of all. I belong to a family with many Catholic branches from generations far removed; my immediate and direct forebears were not baptized, but were given by the government of the Popes, before the French Revolution, patents of "discrimination" for their honesty, which freed them of those humiliating signs of recognition and from all the other limitations common in those sad times, and are now resurfacing more ominous and more evil.

In doing away with myself, I liberate my beloved daughter from the harassment that could come from my presence: she becomes a pure Aryan and will not be harmed. The things I most cherish, my work, my offspring, rather than disappear can be reborn to a new life. I selfishly would like them to die with me. But they are not only mine and they can still be useful and honorable to my Homeland.[885]

Even more symbolic perhaps, is the suicide of Lieutenant Colonel Giorgio Morpurgo. Formiggini had anti-Fascist ideas and believed that his duty as a Jew and an Italian was to condemn the measures enacted by the Fascist government against the Jews as strongly as possible, as well as the moral drama they had forced upon so many Jews. Morpurgo, on the other hand, was a military man, whose main points of reference were patriotism and his career serving the homeland, the King, and his government. His indignation, his disillusionment, his pain could only take the shape of a drastic but silent and understated rejection. The racial measures came while he was in Spain. Having been told by his commander that, consequently, he would have to return to Italy and leave the army, he wanted to take part in one last attack. Before it took place he discarded his cover and went toward enemy positions, walking slowly and ignoring the calls to halt coming from the other side; though wounded, he continued to advance until he was shot through the heart.[886]

To mention only these cases would be incomplete because sometimes the extraordinary gesture meant as an "example," the taking of one's life, can be even easier than to live one's own tragedy in silence. At the individual level reactions varied, as well as within the more integrated and professionally established traditional circles of the state bureaucracy, but no less traumatic. The memory of these events has been either lost or kept jealously hidden within family circles so that many times these reactions can only be guessed at. We are thinking about cases we shall revisit, such as navy engineer General Umberto Pugliese and Cesare Sacerdoti who, after having been dismissed from the service because they were Jews, agreed to return during the war to help since there was no one else capable of solving certain technical problems; or that are only vaguely accounted for, as in the typical case of Guido Jung who, according to a witness we feel is truthful,[887] shortly after the start of the racial campaign, appears to have written to a Jewish friend living in New York that "the duty of Italian Jews is to come to Italy and suffer."

27.

International Reaction

In 1938 Italian diplomatic offices overseas and Fascist propaganda attempted to play down the initial anti-Semitic measures. They were given more importance only in Arab countries where Fascist Italy had every interest to appear decidedly against the Jews. Italy was worried about the sympathies Germany found in those countries because of its violent and open anti-Semitism. Italy, most of all, was concerned about relations it secretly maintained for a number of years, parallel to those with the Zionist movement, with Nationalist and Muslim pan-Arab organizations in order to create problems for the French and, most of all, the British and bring pressure on the latter to reach a "general agreement" between Italy and England in the Mediterranean.[888] In all other countries, Italian diplomacy tried to minimize the issue, or rather to focus not so much on the anti-Semitic aspect as on the racial one and to present the measures as part of colonial policy. This line was clearly followed by the Foreign Ministry itself. When Starace met with the signatories of the racist manifesto, Ciano cabled all the diplomatic and consular posts overseas, communicating the "basis of Fascist racism." The rest of this cable clearly shows how the Palazzo Chigi wanted to stress the colonial motivations of Italian racism.[889] As for the Jews, it was pointed out that, "despite the tolerant policy of the Regime, the Jews in every nation represent, with their men and their assets, the anti-Fascist high command."

The overseas Fascist press, whether or not it was influenced by the Italian government, attempted at first to maintain this line, minimizing in some ways the measures that were being adopted, praising the "humanity" of Fascism and speculating about the restrictions and obstacles to Jewish emigration enacted and in effect in many democratic countries. A more markedly anti-Semitic tone was taken by pro-Fascist newspapers in Argentina and countries where anti-Semitic agitation was stronger.

Fascist propaganda had previously attempted to minimize the first symptoms of the anti-Semitic campaign by recalling Mussolini's many statements about the absence of a Jewish question in Italy and pointing to the "racist" character of certain measures adopted in other countries. In May 1938, when Hitler came to Italy, many foreign newspapers pointed out that the Fascist government had ordered the arrest of all German Jews residing in Italy;[890] the pro-Fascist press immediately answered that this was only a temporary measure to be considered normal in such circumstances and that it not only concerned the Jews but all anti-Nazi refugees. The May 6 reply by *La gazzetta italiana* in Washington D.C. typifies this position:

> It is no mystery that many German and Austrian political refugees are Jews; it may therefore be presumed that they have been placed under temporary special surveillance. But they are not the only ones. All anti-Nazis living in Italy, whatever their faith may be, whatever race they may belong to, have been subjected to the same precautionary measures.
>
> There is no point in screaming against an anti-Semitic Italy that doesn't exist. The Jews in Italy are free and equal in every possible way to other Italian citizens. And Italy's doors have stayed open, even recently, to Jewish refugees from Germany and Austria or other countries where anti-Semitism is a harsh reality.

The manifesto of the "scientists" itself was at first presented as concerned only with the Jews from the scientific point of view—

L'Italo-Australiano in Sydney on July 23, wrote that Italian Jews "will not be subjected to any discrimination"—or placed more or less on the same level of measures adopted in other countries. *Il Progresso Italo-Americano* on July 31, for instance, referring to an article by Virginio Gayda, wrote that the American immigration law of 1924 and Roosevelt's proclamation of April 28, 1938 were typically racist. Much importance was given to *Informazione diplomatica* n. 18: *Il mattino d'Italia* in Buenos Aires—even though it often published attacks on the Jews[891]—when it proclaimed on an entire page on August 6: "The Fascist government has no plans to persecute the Jews." An article in *Il Progresso Italo-Americano* of August 28, entitled "Italiani ed ebrei d'America" [Italians and Jews of America], Generoso Pope attempted to present the *Informazione diplomatica* in the most innocent manner possible:

> There is no need for me to repeat what Mussolini told me last year concerning the Jews of Italy…Has the Italian situation regarding the Jews changed substantially?… In reality what has simply happened is the establishment of a proportionate distribution of public positions to the Jews, who represent one per thousand of the national population…Not persecution, therefore, and full respect for the Jews who, removed from the political fights of anti-Fascism, perform useful services to the country.

In the course of the same article, Pope began to soften the blow: in America there had never been any racism, nothing should trouble the friendship between the six million Italian-Americans and the four million American Jews. As for him personally, he had never thought of "any act of discrimination or persecution": "in my industrial companies I have faithful and good employees of every nationality, I even have Jews occupying important positions." These admissions explain how, a few weeks later, when Fascist anti-Semitic legislation became a reality, even many pro-Fascist papers overseas could not defend it vigorously. Only a few remained in the front line of anti-Semitism: *Il mattino d'Italia* in Buenos Aires,[892] *Il grido della stirpe* in New York,[893] *L'idea nazionale* in Lugano.[894] Even *La tribuna d'Italia,* yet another endless reincarnation of Giannini's *Il merlo,* did not feel it could completely adopt the positions of the

Fascist government when it came to anti-Semitism; Massimo Rocca, Arturo Labriola and Giannini himself did not withhold their criticism.[895]

It was certainly not with these few discredited voices that Fascism could oppose the wave of indignation prompted by the manifesto of the "scientists," followed by the legal decrees, in those parts of the world that were not under direct Fascist and Nazi influence. The huge dimensions of this wave were truly exceptional, with everyone from Moscow to London and Cape Town to Oslo being in agreement. The most well-respected voices of the world press certainly did not hold back their criticism and condemnation, as well as a good portion of public opinion and the Italian communities overseas.[897] Even in Japan, a country politically very close to Italy, the new Fascist policy on race caused some preoccupation and malaise. On August 7, 1938 the Italian embassy in Tokyo informed the Palazzo Chigi that the manifesto of the "scientists" and the Fascist propaganda campaign had met with much resistance. Ambassador Auriti himself joined in:[898]

> I would like to draw the attention of the Royal government to the fact that it is preferable not to use expressions which might clash with Japanese pride in formulating our principles on the question of race. One of the biggest difficulties for westerners in gaining Japanese confidence is their feeling of being considered an inferior race while they feel, instead, they belong to a superior race …The Japanese do not comprehend the Jewish question because there are no Japanese Jews and they tend to confuse this question with their own. News of our measures against the Jews as they reach this country do not make a good impression on its public opinion.[899]

In many countries numerous democratic, trade, and anti-Fascist organizations quickly joined in with the press protests. Several Jewish organizations even proclaimed, without much success, the collective and individual boycott of Italian goods.[900] There were also many individual protests. Among them, playwright Henry Bernstein and pianist Artur Rubinstein both turned in the decorations of Officer of Saints Maurizio e Lazzaro and of Knight of the Crown of Italy they had respectively been awarded.[901]

Once the initial moment of indignation had passed, world press attention focused mostly on the relations between the Fascist government and the Holy See[902] and the possibility of creating in Ethiopia a center for Jewish emigration from Italy, and from Europe in general.[903] The large influential newspapers, such as *The New York Times*, whose initial reaction to the Fascist measures had in a certain sense attempted to minimize them (perhaps in order to avoid losing Italian advertising or perhaps for even less honorable reasons) for the most part let the matter drop.

International diplomatic repercussions were few and not particularly violent. The expulsion of foreign Jews and the withdrawal of Italian citizenship to the Jews who had obtained it after January 1, 1919 did give rise to protests from the United States,[904] Holland,[905] Greece,[906] Turkey[907] and a few other countries; faced with Fascist intransigence and Rome's tendency to examine and settle in a favorable manner the few administrative cases pending—the great majority of foreign Jews were Germans, Austrians, and stateless—most did not persist with their protests, limiting themselves to asking for clarification on individual aspects of the new legislation and trying to obtain favorable treatment for their own citizens.[908] The only country that took a clear and hard position was Turkey, threatening to initiate measures against Italian Jews in Turkey similar to those taken by the Italian government toward the Turkish Jews in Italy if a special agreement was not reached; and so it obtained the suspension of the Italian measures.

On a broader political level, the only initiative of significant weight came from Roosevelt's message to Mussolini, delivered by the United States ambassador to Rome, William Phillips, on January 3, 1939. The president of the United States attempted, unsuccessfully, to persuade the Duce to begin enacting his project of allowing a mass Jewish emigration to Ethiopia. From Ciano's diary we know that Mussolini rejected the suggestion, saying that only Russia, the United States and Brazil had the necessary potential to resolve the Jewish question by giving the Jews the necessary territory.[909] Although Chamberlain discussed the Jewish question with Mussolini and Ciano on January 13, 1939,[910] he appears not to have exerted any pressure to obtain the reversal or the softening of the measures taken by Italy, not even those pertaining to foreign Jews.

VII.

Fascist Persecution

28.

Anti-Semitic
Legislation and Fascist Policy

The Royal Legal Decree (R.D.L.) of November 17, 1938 n. 1728 has been referred to as the "Magna Carta" of Italian racism. Actually, it only provided the basis for turning the decisions of the Grand Council of Fascism of October 6, 1938 into laws of the state. The racism, in its purely anti-Semitic manifestation, which is our concern, took shape and developed through a series of laws, rules, and regulations that only vaguely followed the decisions of the Grand Council and, in many instances, actually went far beyond the letter and the spirit of those decisions. To discover the reasons for the development of the legislation, and of Fascist anti-Semitic policy in general, is not a simple matter. Some of the reasons are obvious: the text issued by the Grand Council, in spite of its long gestation, was far from being complete, and when put into practice, it quickly proved to be another of the many products of Mussolini's slipshod approach. First, it had been written with very little knowledge of Italian Jewish life; second, in order to mark the difference between Fascist and Nazi racism and put in practice the formula of "discriminate, but do not persecute," it eschewed the "biological" path, the only one possible for anyone seeking to create a real anti-Semitism, and instead remained on a somewhat hybrid terrain at once a bit biological, a bit religious, and a bit political that, actually, created a whole series of obstacles and contradictions; for all those who had to write the laws and apply the resulting legislation, finally, the third point is that, due to the mostly "political" nature of the text approved by the Grand Council, it quickly became obsolete because of the dynamics of Fascist anti-Semitism. A few months to a year, at most, were enough to convince the decision makers that, once a course had been set, to discriminate meant either to fail to solve the problem or to persecute. Mussolini, as usual, was not receiving advice from his entourage and was instead being encouraged to "act" by those who were solely inspired by absolute anti-Semitism and, because of the alliance with Germany, he quickly found himself trapped in a dead end. A cold-blooded general persecution was certainly far removed from his natural inclinations and political intentions, which actually still tended generally to differentiate Fascism from Nazism so that the superiority of the former would stand out by comparison. Nor was it possible for him to consider a blatant persecution; even though he had little regard for public opinion and the political maturity of the Italian people, and despite the enormous propaganda bombardment, it was clear that the initial measures and their underlying idea had been rejected by the overwhelming majority of Italians with such unanimity as to be, for once, truly "totalitarian." It was equally impossible for Mussolini to turn back; that would have meant a political defeat with unforeseeable consequences, a real debacle which, beyond international repercussions, would have destroyed any confidence in Fascism in Germany—where there already were innumerable skeptics and critics—and would have shaken the very foundations of Fascism in Italy, handing a victory to the "bourgeoisie" and the "pietists." For the first time, Mussolini found himself trapped between a rock and a hard place just as the international situation worsened and the possibility of world conflict, which appeared to be five or six years removed when he began the racial campaign, tied his hands by making any other initiative impossible, such as, for example, finding an international solution for the entire issue. While we have no documents to support our viewpoint, with the exception of a few rumors filtering through Fascist circles at the time—that are confirmed by his interest in having Central European Jews settle in Italian East Africa, and by a number of leaks that appeared in foreign newspapers—as well as his own repeated mentions of a Jewish state that would not be in Palestine, we still feel that Mussolini thought it possible in 1938 and perhaps even during the first few months of 1939, to propose a grand international solution to solve the Jewish question—a kind of Munich for the Jews—that would allow him to play, once again, the role of mediator and major international problem solver, while at the same time "brilliantly" resolving even the otherwise insoluble problem of the Italian Jews.

The Fascist anti-Semitic laws were developed in 1939 against this general background as well as the related projects of 1939 and of the first few months of 1940 in the files of Demography and Race and other sources. The first impulse was to enact the resolutions of the Grand Council. However, seeing that this was impossible without turning to persecution, and once it became clear that a comprehensive international solution to the Jewish question was impossible, a proposition was made to break out of the dead end the Fascists had driven themselves into: switch to expelling all the Jews out of metropolitan Italy over a number of years under economic conditions that were not too unfavorable to them. This project was also shelved, certainly because of the worsening international situation and possibly due to economic and internal difficulties.

All the well-known laws and regulations which constituted Fascist anti-Semitic legislation until 1942 (when civilian regulations went into effect) belong to the first of these three moments up to July 25, 1943. The laws and regulations were clearly inspired by the declaration of the Grand Council and the D.L. of November 17, 1938 (in the report to the Senate before passage of the law,[911] reference was explicitly made to its impending passage) even though, as we have mentioned earlier, they already went much further in certain areas.

The first law enacted was the D. L. of February 9, 1939 n. 126, relating to the rules of enactment and the integration of the measures contained in article 10 of the R. D. L. of November 17, 1938-XVII, n. 1728, pertaining to the limits placed on Italian Jews to own real property and engage in industrial and commercial activity.[912] This law minutely regulated Jewish property;[913] it established that the portion of any estate exceeding the limits allowed by the law of the previous November must be transferred to a special government office to manage and liquidate real estate, the EGELI,[914] that was to pay the former property owners the equivalent amount in thirty-year certificates at a 4% annual rate; a special declaration of all real estate held by Jews was to be submitted within ninety days of the passage of the law; and, finally, it ordered that within six months all corporations working for national defense and those employing over one hundred people were to be divested and the resulting funds reinvested in nominal stock certificates.[915]

Three more laws, in June and July, were to follow this first law of application. The law of June 29, 1939 n. 1054 regulated the right of Jews to engage in the professions.[916] In practical terms, through this law Fascism prohibited all Jews, without exception, from being notaries, and to those who were not discriminated, from being journalists—private teaching had already been allowed only if administered to students of "the Jewish race"; the professions of medical doctor, surgeon, pharmacist, veterinarian, midwife, lawyer, district attorney, defense counsel, consultant for business and trade, accountant, engineer, architect, chemist, agronomist, land surveyor, agricultural expert, and industrial expert were regulated according to the following criteria:[917]

a. exclusion from the related professional rolls;

b. creation of "adjunct lists" for those discriminated and of "special lists" for those not discriminated;

c. those included in the special lists were excluded from the trade associations of that category, while still subject to the regulations of collective work relations;

d. those belonging to the special lists were excluded, "except for cases of proven need and urgency," from exercising their profession in favor of persons who did not belong to the "Jewish race"; none, without exception, could be placed in important positions having the function of a public official or similar assignments;

e. any form of association or collaboration between Jewish and non-Jewish professionals was forbidden.[918]

The law of July 13, 1939 n. 1055 set the rules for wills and successions (any condition that was placed upon an inheritance or a gift tying the recipient to the Jewish religion was declared null and void) and for last names (the authorization to change or not change typically Jewish surnames).[919]

The most important new law was n. 1024, also dated July 13, 1939.[920] Presented as a simple "additional rule" to the D. L. of November 17, 1938, it actually introduced into the Fascist anti-Semitic legislation, against any logic, whether racist, religious, or political, a new category of legal person, those who were "Aryanized." The law established that it was the prerogative of the Ministry of the Interior to declare, following an identical opinion issued by a commission of three magistrates and two functionaries from the Ministry itself—the race court—"those as not belonging to the Jewish race even when in contradiction with the evidence of civil status of record." If all anti-Semitic legislation was immoral and incompatible with the law, this law certainly was even more so. The ruling was actually based on entirely arbitrary decisions, and its purpose was only to favor, not even from a strictly Fascist point of view, those who had the credentials to be discriminated and even giving them privileged status compared to the discriminated persons themselves. Having begun under the guidance of the highest "moral and spiritual values" of Fascist Italy, in less than one year Fascist anti-Semitism became—like just about everything during those tragic and grotesque years—the source of immorality, corruption, favoritism, and graft. And all this while the rigorous aspect of the law[921] and the innumerable regulations connected to it weighed more and more heavily on those Jews who did not want or could not accept oppression and blackmail. This conclusion is not altered by the fact that the Aryanization procedure was intended to resolve situations that could not otherwise find a solution and to reward, in a manner of speaking, a few exceptionally deserving Jews. The numbers, and even more the history—the very sad history—of the Aryanizations demonstrate that in practice they only served to reward a group of corrupt individuals and a large number of persons who used the immorality these regulations represented to acquire a personal fortune.[922] The fact that the favoritism and corruption caused by instituting Aryanization cannot be attributed to the "race court," which had to make judgments based on the facts presented and, in general, tried to fulfill its mission and help those who petitioned it as much as possible doesn't mitigate the end result. This may sound like praise for the magistrates who sat on the court, but it does not justify the principle that led to its creation.

Many regulations were quickly added regarding the practical enactment of the laws, in particular the first one dated November 17, 1938. The maze of regulations, often ridiculous and always extremely damaging to the rights and dignity of those they were applied to—forbidding them to go to certain vacation spots, to have "Aryan" domestic servants, to place advertisements and death notices in the press, to own a radio, to be granted agricultural loans, to publish books,[923] to be published in the newspapers under a pseudonym, to give public lectures, to have their names listed in the phone book, to be allowed entry into public buildings, etc.—attracted the sarcasm and indignation of the Italians and the press that, after the fall of Fascism, published articles about those years. In reality the majority of those rules and regulations were consistent with racist logic and law—if one can call them that—and demonstrate that it was impossible to discriminate without persecuting. It should be noted that the "discrimination," as it was enacted, never reached the extreme consequences that some would have wished. In the files of Demography and Race there is a trail of various regulations that were suggested or placed under consideration that were, thankfully, never enacted. We do not know whether it was due to a sudden surge in morality or because of Mussolini's own opposition. It will suffice to say that in 1941 Demography and Race and the Ministry for Popular Culture considered the possible introduction of the infamous "yellow star" in Italy and that the issue did reach the Duce's desk.[924]

It is much more important to study, even in general terms, what the image of the Jew was according to Fascist legislation because to enter into the details of each issue, as documented by Demography and Race, would be almost impossible. Only after such a survey will it become possible to fully grasp all the contradictions within anti-Semitic legislation, even from the Fascist viewpoint, and understand its evolution and the projects under consideration to radically transform it.

According to the Grand Council, those who were born of two Jewish parents, those who had a Jewish father and a non-Italian mother, and the "mixed," who practiced the Jewish religion as of October 1, 1938, were all considered as belonging to the "Jewish race."

The D. L. of November 17, 1938 article 8, further specified that "the person born of parents where one was the Jewish and the other of foreign nationality" belonged to the "Jewish race"; added to the positive cases were those of the children of a Jewish mother and an unknown father; as for the "mixed," it considered Jewish even those who were on the lists of a Community and those who "in any way had demonstrated that they were Jewish."

The enactment of the D. L. of November 17, 1938 was accompanied by a confidential memorandum from Demography and Race (n.9270 dated December 22, 1938) stating, with reference to article 8:

> The criteria of this article to determine whether one belongs to the Jewish race are of a fundamental nature and consequently go beyond the present measure in scope; it is therefore necessary to reference them when applying any regulation of the law that presupposes belonging to the Jewish race.

This was followed by the explanation of the article itself:

> For para. a.) the person who is born of parents who are both Jewish is himself Jewish, whatever the religion he follows may be; in this case, therefore, the religious factor will not modify the racial origin.
>
> For para. b.) the child of a Jewish parent (Italian or foreign) is always considered Jewish. Also in this case, despite the religion followed, if the other non-Jewish parent is of foreign nationality. In this case, therefore, it is necessary for the investigation to establish the nationality of the parents, even though they may have acquired Italian nationality later on, through matrimony or naturalization.
>
> For para. d.) the person with parents of Italian nationality, of whom only one is Jewish, is considered Jewish if he practices the Jewish religion or is found to be listed in a Jewish community, or has

given evidence of being Jewish. Signs of being Jewish are to be understood as any concrete activity that reveals feelings and tendencies which are clearly Jewish.

The person born of Italian parents where only one parent is Jewish is not considered Jewish if, as of October 1, 1938-XVI, he belonged to a religion other than the Jewish religion; if, on the other hand, as of October 1, 1938-XVI, he did not belong to any religion, he must be considered Jewish.

The rules for "race ascertainments" established by the Ministry of the Interior during the first half of 1939, for those who had to resolve disputed and doubtful cases, established, finally, a series of cases that extended even more the number of those who were to be considered Jewish [925]

In less than ten to twelve months, as we can see, the image of the "Jew" began flowing beyond its original boundaries and included categories of citizens who had not initially been considered as such. At the same time the number of Jews who, according to the declaration of October 6, could have been discriminated was reduced. The Grand Council had generically referred to "families." Article 14 of the D. L. of November 17, 1938 still referred to families only for the war dead and for those who died for the Fascist cause; for other categories of persons who could be discriminated, it referred only to those directly concerned, adding that "the benefit may be extended to family members" of the discriminated person even when he was already deceased. The benefit "could" therefore be extended to family members, and not "must," as it appeared in the original declaration of October 6. And still, in article 15, besides the spouse, only the lateral relatives and progeny, up to the second level of family relationship, were considered family members.

From this rapid examination of Fascist legislation it is clear therefore that, while not adopting rigidly racist criteria and considering religious and political elements, the most common tendency among those responsible for anti-Semitic policy was to broaden to the maximum the description of the "Jew" that was to be separated from the national population while at the same time reducing to the minimum the number of discriminated Jews, meaning those somehow reintegrated to the national population. There is no doubt that this tendency had been personally set forth by Mussolini, as evidenced by a memorandum from Buffarini-Guidi at the beginning of October 1938 regarding the definition of the "family," where it was proposed that those who were to be included were "all relatives in direct line and kinsmen of the second degree (brothers and sisters), to the eventual and respective couple and their descendants" and which was returned by the Duce's secretariat with the second part crossed out by hand.[926] As knowledge of Jewish reality deepened and Fascist anti-Semitic legislation entered the implementation phase, it became increasingly clear to Mussolini, Buffarini-Guidi and Le Pera, etc., how difficult it was to translate this idea into practice. Italian Jewry soon appeared to them as it was in reality, not the fictionalized version that the anti-Semitic and anti-Zionist theoreticians had argued against, but, in fact, deeply assimilated morally and materially to the rest of the Italian population, so that a sheer cut meant to separate the Jews from the non-Jews was absolutely unattainable. Not only was such a surgical separation impossible, it showed that "separation" and "discrimination" ran, in practical terms, through thousands of "mixed" families, causing extremely serious injury to their moral and material structure, with grave consequences for their "Aryan" members. Therefore, in practice, Mussolini's initial tendency to insist on extreme rigor and a precise separation quickly clashed with another very clear tendency that was deeply felt in the entire country, warmly supported by the Holy See and Catholic circles in general, and also fully in line with Fascist policy to reinforce the family and its values: preserving the moral, spiritual, and material unity of the many "mixed" families.

The weight of this second tendency was such that in a short time, on July 2, 1939, Demography and Race felt it necessary to make it the subject of a memorandum to the Duce:[927]

> We have assembled comments [in Rome] that indicate the ordinances on race have created unsettling situations within families of Italian citizens of the Jewish race who are married to Aryan women of the Catholic religion. We have found that the foundations of these family units have been shaken because of conditions of inequality as

to rights and duties that have appeared among married couples, and the children who can claim a privileged condition over the father, especially in cases where the parent is unable to provide for his wife and children through his work.

After the enactment of the Nuremberg laws, the government of the Reich, realizing the impossibility in such cases of requiring that the couple continue living together, has allowed the Aryan member to request the annulment of the marriage. The Hungarian government, seeking to avoid similar situations, wanted to prevent their occurrence by recognizing the "baptized" Jewish spouse as being Aryan.

There is no doubt, we conclude, that it would be fair to treat favorably those spouses who:

a. contracted the mixed marriage within the Catholic Church;
b. according to the accepted rules baptized their children in the Catholic Church;
c. converted to the Catholic religion before October 1, 1938.

The undersigned requests such timely provisions of the Duce's high sense of justice.

During the following months pressure in this direction became so massive as to force a decision in the short term. A memorandum (probably to Buffarini-Guidi) from Demography and Race dated October 4, 1939[928] indicates that at this time the head office had also settled upon the Aryanization of the Italian spouse who had originally been Jewish, but had converted before the announcement of a law to be enacted, as the need arises and was married to an "Aryan" Italian Catholic with Catholic children as well, or at least was leaning in the direction of Aryanization of those who were discriminated under such conditions. Other undated documents of Demography and Race, almost certainly from the final months of 1939 or the beginning of 1940, demonstrate that the Ministry of the Interior carefully considered that memorandum, studying it in detail and ordering a "general revision" of "doubtful racial positions, especially in cases of the descendants of mixed marriages."[929] At the end of all this work it appears that Buffarini-Guidi and Mussolini were now considering a radical revision of the entire anti-Semitic policy enacted up to that time. The clash between the two tendencies we have outlined was too deep to be resolved through piecemeal ordinances. One interpretation could only be adopted through the suppression of the other. To opt for the first one would mean to worsen a situation that was already extremely serious and that was being increasingly opposed by public opinion—at a time when the international situation demanded the maximum degree of unity on the part of the Italian people around the regime—and was clearly opposed by the Holy See, with whom, especially in those circumstances, Mussolini wished to avoid a new and worse crisis after he had overcome the problems during the second half of 1938, to his advantage. To opt for the second interpretation would mean, in the eyes of the world, to admit a mistake and to lose a popular consensus, as well as to turn away from a policy of confrontation with the Holy See and give new life to the Catholic Action and to those Catholic groups in general who were opposed to Fascist policy more or less openly.

At first Mussolini attempted, as usual, to avoid the obstacle and resolve the matter without much fuss. On February 9, 1940 Bocchini, the chief of police, called the new president of the Union of the Jewish Communities, former prefect Dante Almansi,[930] and told him Mussolini had decided that "since time was now running short" the Italian Jews were to leave Italy. Almansi, caught by surprise and deeply hurt, immediately answered that it was impossible to forbid the Italian Jews, who had been living in the country for centuries, earning an honest living and fighting and dying for it on many occasions, from continuing to live in Italy. "What wrong have they done" he asked Bocchini, "to deserve such unjust treatment?" He then pointed out that while he was being given this order, police stations had been refusing, for the past few weeks, to give passports to Jews and withdrawing those already distributed. Furthermore, the ordinances of the year before concerning estates had barred the Jews, when it would have been possible for them to emigrate, from access to the required minimum to begin a new life overseas. Finally, the desire to emigrate did not mean that one could do so, because securing entry visas into another country was notoriously difficult. Faced with these reactions, Bocchini, answered that he would speak with Mussolini, and asked Almansi to come back on the 16th. Upon returning to the Palazzo Viminale, the president of the Union was told that the order was confirmed: instructions would be given regarding the passports; as for property, its exportation could only be allowed within the strict limitations of the balance of trade. Concerning the terms of emigration, Bocchini told him that Mussolini expected it to be ten units per day.

During the next few months thousands of Jews, especially youths, took advantage of Mussolini's order. At the rate of ten per day emigration would have lasted between ten to fifteen years, and it is not obvious that it could have taken place without difficulties. Those willing to leave were young people seeking a new life, ready to start from scratch or close to it, as well as those who had been able to salvage part of their estate[931] in time or who had relatives, friends, or some point of reference overseas; but it cannot be assumed that the masses would have been ready to follow them freely, abandoning what property and sentimental ties they had in Italy to face a future that would certainly not be promising. Further, considering the slowness of the exodus, this was certainly not the way to find solutions to dramatically urgent problems, such as those of mixed marriages. Mussolini and his staff must have understood this rather quickly, especially after Italy declared war on France and England and "spontaneous" emigration became more difficult while the internal situation in Italy worsened.

From the files of Demography and Race it appears clearly that around August 1940 — the exact date cannot be ascertained, but an approximate date can be based on a letter from Father Tacchi-Venturi to Buffarini-Guidi regarding mixed families that Buffarini-Guidi refers to in the draft of a note to the Duce[932] — the Ministry of the Interior was already thinking of proposing a complete revision of anti-Semitic policy and legislation. Two elements appear in the draft of the note to the Duce: 1. The gravity of the problem of "mixed" families made "a more determined racial policy aimed at the clear separation between Jews and Aryans more difficult, if not impossible," and in general the application of anti-Semitic laws had brought other problems to the surface that were no less important in other areas (trade, insurance, large industry, etc.); 2. In order to overcome these problems and contradictions, "which almost cancel out the racial directives and often interfere with many nationally productive areas," there could be for Buffarini-Guidi and Demography and Race only one solution: Aryanize those who were assimilated, meaning Jews mixed with Catholics, and expel all the others from the territory of the Kingdom.[933] Such a project was presented by Buffarini-Guidi to Mussolini in October [1940], accompanied by a comprehensive memorandum,[934] which is the clearest admission of the complete failure of the Fascist policy regarding race. Attached to the report was the text of the law that Demography and Race proposed in order to carry forward its projects. According to this draft of a legal decree,[935] the nondiscriminated Jews would be required to leave Italian territory within five years and those discriminated within ten. To accelerate the exodus, the draft also provided that those who left sooner would benefit from economic incentives proportionate to the speed with which they fulfilled the expulsion decree, while those who delayed their departure would be penalized through tax charges proportionate to the length of their stay. As a secondary solution, the Buffarini-Guidi project proposed that, should this solution not be deemed suitable, all existing ordinances were to be made more stringent.

According to a document of the following year from Demography and Race it appears that Mussolini had accepted the solution of expulsion he had been presented with. However, as we know, it did not become law, probably because of the worsening international situation and the opposition of the economic ministries.[936] The thought of expelling the majority of the Jews and Aryanizing the others was kept for another year, then simply shelved in expectation of more favorable circumstances.[937] In the end, since circumstances making it possible did not materialize, it was permanently dropped, possibly at the beginning of 1942.

Once the idea of this Italian-style "Final Solution" had been cancelled, Fascist anti-Semitic legislation remained unchanged until July 25, 1943, with the exception of the introduction in May 1942 of the draft for civilian labor. The contradiction between the two different solutions described above did not suddenly disappear, but what had not been possible in the fall of 1940, when the military-political situation of Italy and the Axis was generally more

343

favorable, became even less likely during the following years, when the political, military, and economic situation worstened, making such an undertaking more remote with each passing day. From the point of view of prestige it was impossible; on one hand, if in 1940 expulsion could still be presented as an act of generosity, and on the other hand, complete assimilation was to remain the official resolution of the Jewish question in Italy, this was no longer the case in the following years. It was impossible from the economic standpoint; in the worsening military situation it would have been unthinkable to have even a minimal loss of capital. It was impossible from the standpoint of relations with the Germans because, as they became more involved in Italian affairs, they would certainly not have allowed it to happen. It was impossible, finally, for the countries that would have welcomed, at a very difficult time, thousands of individuals who had previously refused to emigrate, and could reasonably be considered suspicious, not to mention the fear that such a mass emigration could be used by Fascism to infiltrate its agents and spies overseas, disguised as reluctant émigrés.

Having embarked irresponsibly on the adventure of anti-Semitic policy, Fascism ended up bearing the consequences. What appeared to Mussolini in 1938 to be a minor issue that could be quickly resolved, became for Fascism a huge insoluble question generating both domestic and foreign problems, and alienating public opinion more and more. Fortunately for itself and for the dignity of the Italian people, Fascism was unable to find a way out of the dead end it had entered by adopting a Nazi-type solution. Fascism resisted German pressure in that direction and tried to prevent Nazi horrors within the territories occupied by Italian troops as long as possible, at least until July 25, 1943. Mussolini could only make an apparent show of force from that point on. In 1942 he tightened the racial requirements for Aryanizations and discriminations and increased administrative pressure on the Jews, who were increasingly taking anti-Fascist positions; at the same time, he surreptitiously favored legal emigration as long as it was possible, and even clandestine emigration, since Italy was at war with practically all the countries of potential emigration or transit for the Jews.

29.

The Implementation of the
Anti-Semitic Laws

T he implementation of the anti-Semitic laws can be divided into two periods, 1938-1941 and 1942-1943, and into various subjects: political, technical-administrative, foreign Jews, and finally those relating to the developments of the war. Each of these has its own underpinnings, even while remaining connected, sometimes in important ways, to the others. Both levels will be taken into account in examining the key moments and the issues involved.

On the political side, the fundamental problem is the relationship with the Nazis and their influence on Fascist anti-Semitic policy. Nothing indicates that Mussolini had decided upon the persecution under direct German pressure and, on the contrary, we must conclude that the decision was spontaneously and exclusively his. For many years, even with respect to the enforcement of the anti-Semitic laws, Nazi influence was not a factor. In a confidential report from Dr. Carltheo Zeitschel of the SS to the chief of police and the German SD at the end of March 1943 we even read that:

> The German embassy in Rome has been receiving for years the most stringent instructions from Berlin to avoid doing anything that might compromise the friendly relations between Italy and Germany. It is absolutely not appropriate, it seems, for the German embassy in Rome to touch upon a sensitive subject such as the Jewish question in Italy. Cautious investigations by political leaders of the embassy have reached the same conclusion.[938]

Beginning in 1938 there were contacts and exchanges of information between the offices responsible for anti-Semitic policy in the two countries. A Nazi party delegation from the race office led by Dr. Gross[939] visited Milan and Genoa in June 1938; the visit was returned at the end of the year by the director and deputy director (Prof. Guido Landra and Dr. Lino Businco) of the Office of Racial Studies of the Ministry of Popular Culture, who visited various

German racial institutions (among these, the concentration camp at Sachsenhausen) and had meetings with many high-level Nazi leaders.[940] From March 6-11, 1939 a large delegation of Italian jurists, led by the president of the Corte di Cassazione [Supreme Court], Salvatore Messina, participated in the second congress of the German-Italian Juridical Collaboration Committee in Vienna, which approved, among others, a resolution on the common theme "Razza e diritto"[941] [Race and Law]. Each one of these cases, as well as others, were only formal events and friendly exchanges of courtesies and information between offices and personalities and their counterparts, normal occurrences in the climate of alliance of those years but without any direct bearing on the anti-Semitic policy pursued by Rome and Berlin. Some overzealous functionary perhaps attempted to establish tighter relations, but these were shunned in responsible Fascist circles. A typical episode from the archives of the Interior Ministry: as soon as Italy declared war, a few technical staff members in the Italian general directorate of PS [Public Security] contacted the Germans to obtain more information about the Nazi concentration camp organization. Heydrich quickly and personally wrote to Bocchini, sending him the "regulations" of German camps and stating that he would be very pleased to welcome a delegation of Italian functionaries for study purposes.[942] Bocchini—who probably knew nothing about the initiative taken by his "technicians"—did not follow up on the invitation, saying that the state of war and the demands of the service did not allow him to spare employees on a fact-finding mission.[943]

During the first months of the racial campaign the Italian government requested permission from the German government to transfer the estates of Italian Jews residing in Germany and Austria, noting that Italy could not accept discriminations of its own citizens.[944]

The first clear moves by Berlin upon Rome took place only during the second half of 1942.[945] The Germans maintained that some Axis defeats, such as the sinking of the *D'Annunzio*,[946] could be attributed to Jewish espionage, which was very active in southern France;[947] they were also outraged by the protection that Italian army units in France, Croatia, Slovenia, Dalmatia, and Greece were giving to Jews who escaped into the Italian zones of occupation. The first step to end this state of affairs was taken regarding the case of Jewish refugees in the Italian zone in Yugoslavia by the German embassy in Rome on August 17, 1942. Others were to follow, such as a particularly strong protest on February 3, 1943 regarding Jewish refugees in the Italian zone in France, which elicited no more than a general commitment from the Palazzo Chigi.[948] Berlin then decided that the entire matter would be handled personally during the meeting that was to be held a few weeks later with Mussolini and Bastianini, who at that time had replaced Ciano as head of the Foreign Ministry, with the title of Undersecretary.

The general directives issued by Demography and Race to enact anti-Semitic policy were part of the political aspects of the enforcement of the anti-Semitic laws. It is impossible to trace here the hundreds and hundreds of memoranda and instructions issued by Demography and Race itself, and, on its instructions, by the other general directorates of the Interior Ministry and various other ministries. We shall limit ourselves to a broad picture derived from the annual reports prepared by Demography and Race for the discussion of the Interior Ministry's budget,[949] a few other important documents, and some typical cases.

Demography and Race was always very strict in the interpretation and application of its own policies, which tended to become even more restrictive as the failure of the persecution became increasingly obvious, or rather, as the failure of its original plans for rapid and radical enactment faced mounting popular opposition.[950] This severity, however, did not prevent there appearing and prospering in Rome, within the entourage of Demography and Race, the most sensational cases of favoritism and corruption. The discriminations and, even more, the aryanizations became the material of what amounted to an open market. The issue became so scandalous and notorious to the general public that the work of Demography and Race was violently criticized within the party itself despite the Fascist leadership's widely practiced policy of silence at that time. From the memoirs of Carmine Senise we learn that at an assembly of party leaders, the Fascist federal secretary of Padua, in the presence of Mussolini, criticized various cases of corruption connected to aryanization procedures.[951] Various other cases are in the personal files of major Fascist leaders held by Mussolini's secretariat. In a few cases we even know the names, besides the person aryanized, of those who facilitated the aryanization and even the price (from half a million to one million lire, but there are many cases in which the decree cost up to two million lire). Some of these cases were so sensational that in order to avoid further scandal the aryanization had to be revoked. The most infamous one involved a wealthy Jew who had been aryanized because "his mother had betrayed matrimonial fidelity with an Aryan, apparently during a New Year's Eve celebration"; his aryanization was revoked after a year and a half because of "public demonstrations of Judaism," but shortly thereafter he was once again aryanized,[952] which, in any case, did not save him from being deported to Germany after September 8, 1943. While taking into account the known and honorable exceptions, we can agree with Senise that, at least with respect to aryanizations and discriminations, racial policy quickly became a way for a corrupt gang "to feed at the trough."[953]

While local authorities had a tendency to avoid pursuing the Jews too much and to not apply the letter of the regulations coming from the top, Demography and Race always maintained a line of extreme inflexibility and, to better ensure this position, attempted very quickly to centralize the application of anti-Semitic policy within its office.[954] The cases in point were those of "race ascertainment": at first these were left to the various central and local offices, depending upon the precinct or the relationship between offices, but later (toward the end of 1940) they were sent exclusively to Demography and Race. The official justification for the measure was to ensure that the manner in which the investigation was conducted and the evaluation of the demonstrations of Judaism were undertaken without varying criteria and in the same spirit of application; in reality, the intention was to put an end to the more liberal decisions made by many local offices. In 1942 especially, the line taken by Demography and Race became extremely oppressive. Not only did it attempt to eliminate Jewish activity in every area where it still existed,[955] until it even provoked an adverse opinion by the Council of State, which found that some decisions by Demography and Race went beyond its mandate;[956] not only did it revoke some discriminations that had already been granted;[957] but it also proceeded, in fact, to freeze all the open files for race ascertainment and discrimination cases yet to be decided. During a meeting of the general directors of the Interior Ministry that took place on February 18, 1942, chaired by Buffarini-Guidi and in the presence of the president of the race court, Gaetano Azzariti, and Senator Stefano De Ruggiero, the following were decided:

a. *Discriminations.*

I. Give a negative decision to discrimination requests for exceptionally deserving cases still open and review those already granted. (As the examination of the requests to be rejected is undertaken, some may be considered that can be justified as exceptionally deserving cases.)

II. Accept discrimination requests according to the law only when accompanied by the double favorable opinion of the Prefect and the Fascist federal secretary. (On the other hand, a negative opinion by the Fascist federal secretary will not be considered when not supported by specific reasons.)

III. Maintain in the undecided category requests to extend to family members the benefit of discrimination limiting its concession to the direct recipient alone.

IV. Not adopt the suspending effect of discrimination requests, inform the Finance Ministry as to estate limits that the estates of those requesting discrimination may be taken in custody but not confiscated, pending the ministerial decision on discrimination requests.

V. Reopen discriminations already granted by law in view of a possible revocation, to be decided based on the same reasons as the revocation allowed by the civil code of procedure (article 395).

b. *Race ascertainment*

I. Initiate race ascertainment procedures only if requested by public offices or organizations for reasons relating to the public interest.

II. Automatically review the racial position of mixed race cases, except to penalize those who are ascertained as being Jews and have not made the declaration as required by article 19 of the racial law.

III. In harmony with the letter and spirit of the law, to not act upon requests for race ascertainment made by the interested parties themselves, nor accept any new ones that may be submitted.[958]

It is clear from the notes prepared for the discussion of the 1943-1944 budget what Demography and Race wanted to accomplish had Fascism not been toppled in the meantime. The paragraph entitled *Racial Legislation* states:

RACIAL LEGISLATION. Racial legislation has certain loopholes that it may be necessary to close. Large areas are completely outside any legal controls. For instance, the stock market, wholesale trade, shipping, Jewish-owned corporations, etc. As for inheritances, no limits have been placed on Jews inheriting from Aryans, just as in the area of estates, no limits have been placed on the right of stateless Jews to own real property.

In the family area no penalty has been set for cases of extramarital relations between Jews and Aryans so that we reach the absurd situation of declaring Aryan the baptized children of a Jew who has lived in a common-law situation, who has married an Aryan only in a religious ceremony, in violation of the racial law forbidding matrimony between Aryans and Jews. The same can be said for sexual relations. A recent court decision acquitted a Jew who had compromised an eighteen-year old Aryan girl.[959]

In order to enforce its policies Demography and Race did not shy away from any obstacle. When in 1939 it was decided that all "Aryan" domestic servants must stop working for Jewish families, it was completely oblivious to the serious consequences this decision could have in many special cases (the great mathematician Levi-Civita died without the assistance of a nurse), or even the more general ones, such as the possibility of finding work for the 2,500 domestic servants who were suddenly in difficult financial straits. Even more typical is what happened following the decision to withdraw the licenses of Jewish rag merchants and rag-and-bone vendors. In some towns they represented the great majority of those engaged in this activity; in Rome they were 75%, and included the best ones. Shortly after the regulation went into effect various complaints reached Demography and Race asking fearful questions; once the Jews had been eliminated the entire business sector was in decline, with serious local and national consequences. The interprovincial secretary of the National Fascist Organization for Cooperation and even the prefect himself got involved in Rome. In a letter to Demography and Race dated June 1, 1942 he wrote:

> Right now, therefore, only Aryan rag merchants and shopkeepers are active in Rome, they are new at this, without the uncommonly specialized experience required for such work, motivated only by quick and easy profits. The brutal and unconscionable competition among them, added to the arrival of speculators and monopolists, is driving domestic garbage prices to unheard-of levels, to the point where factories are refusing to buy them. By eliminating the Jews from gathering and selling this garbage we have encountered a very damaging reduction in the pick-up of garbage, with the related negative effect on autarchy that one may imagine.

The prefect concluded by proposing to mobilize Jewish rag merchants as civilians and get around the obstacle posed by the law.[960] But not even this proposal appeared to be acceptable. Senise had to handle the matter and it reached Mussolini's desk requesting a decision by July 19.

This abundantly illustrates the general political enactment of the anti-Semitic laws[961] and highlights the technical and administrative aspects of their application.[962]

Census. The 1938 census was, especially in 1941, continuously updated and revised, based upon the declarations that all Jews were required to make. The report regarding the discussion of the 1942-1943 budget of the Interior Ministry indicates that as of February 12, 1942 the 1938 census had been updated for 79 provinces, while data for 18 others was still missing, and this new count had led to the "discovery" of an additional 2,633 Jews. Based upon this revision Demography and Race created what amounted to a complete card file of all Italian Jews.[963]

Race ascertainment. Connected to the census were the examinations of doubtful and disputed cases. As of February 9, 1940 Demography and Race had received 2,139 examination requests; of these 1,646 were still under consideration, 244 had been decided favorably (Aryanization), and 249 unfavorably. With all examinations being centralized in Rome, at the same date, a year later, Demography and Race had received 7,721 requests; of these, as of February 9, 1941, 5,024 were still under examination, but we do not know how many of the remaining 2,697 had been decided favorably. The requests had increased to 9,647 as of February 1, 1942; of these 4,394 were still under examination at that date, while of those examined 3,466 had been ruled to belong to the "Jewish race" and 1,787 to the "Aryan race." Around October of the same year the requests being examined were still 4,230, with 460 of these at an "advanced stage of approval"; the "positive" rulings (Aryanization) included 1,884 cases, for a total of 3,371 persons, and the "negative" ones included 3,497 cases, for a total of 3,839 persons.

Last name changes. As of October 1942 Demography and Race had authorized 241.

Aryanizations. There were 74 requests as of February 9, 1940, 148 as of October 28, 1941, and 163 as of October 1942. Of the 163 cases in October 1942, 16 were still under consideration at that date and 43 had been rejected, thus confirming the "Jewish race" of those making the request. Among the cases resolved favorably (Aryanization), 5 concerned Jews Aryanized due to "superior orders"; of the other 99 cases (regarding 140 persons), 26 were concerned with the paternal recognition of individuals who were shown to be of fathers unknown according to the registry office, 18 concerned maternal recognition, and 55 the recognition of bastardization in spite of the actual civil registry.

Assignment of real property in land and buildings to the EGELI. In 1940 about 10,000 declarations were made; in 1941 30,000. The total amounts that were over the authorized property limits set by Fascist legislation were of 113,973,137.60 lire for land and 179,407,065.80 lire for buildings. The report for the discussion of the Interior Ministry's budget for 1941-1942 stated:

While these numbers will not increase appreciably on the basis of information that may still come from the Land Technical Offices, they will have significant reductions due to the elimination of quotas belonging to Jews still awaiting discrimination, whose landed estates remain intact.

In any case we shall remain far short of the numbers that were part of the projected confiscated real estate discussed during the enactment of racial legislation.

And this not just for the exceptions within art. 3 of R.D.L. 9.2.1939 n.126 and exceptions allowed by art. 6 of the same R.D.L., but more due to the avoidance of large, often massive, real estate owned by corporations not subject to limitations and declarations beyond the aryanization of the managers and administrators.

It is well known that prior to February 11, 1939 private estates consisting of real property have hidden under the corporate veil, thus escaping the racial obligations.[964]

According to a report dated May 1945 from the EGELI to the CLNAI (Committee of National Liberation for Northern Italy)[965] it appears that for the entire year 1943 the value of real property exceeding the allowed limits was about 726,000,000 lire; only 55,600,000 had been attributed to the EGELI at the same date (it had sold only 9,794,122.80, with a net income of 29,500,000 lire). The rest of the real property in excess, not attributed to the EGELI, was administered by nineteen banks and credit institutions.

Discriminations. According to available statistics from the secret census of 1938[966] the families that could be eligible for discrimination were 3,502, as follows:

Families of:

war dead	406
war volunteers	721
decorated with the War Cross	1,597
died for the Fascist cause	3

Fascists of 1919-1922 and second
half of 1924	724
Fiume legionnaires	51

According to the same statistics there were also 834 Jews, in part within the preceding category, who could claim special merit: 453 in the economic and social fields, 328 due to positions held within the PNF and the MVSN, 43 for having initiated and financed activities of the Fascist party, and 10 for having founded and financed non-Jewish cultural or charitable non-profit organizations. This was a large group in proportion to the total Italian Jewish population. An approximate calculation estimates those who could be discriminated at 11,000-12,000. This number is not excessive, and this is borne out by the fact that, despite emigration, as of June 1, 1942 there had been 8,171 discrimination requests for 15,339 persons. According to article 14 of D.L. November 17, 1938 discriminations could be awarded for specific reasons (paragraphs *a* and *b* of the article itself) and for exceptional merit (paragraph *c*). Many made requests for exceptional merit, but many of these were relegated to the lower category due to lack of supporting material and insufficient merit. This explains why the various reports and statistics and the daily reports of Demography and Race at first seem to have contradictory numbers.[967] In sum, as of June 1, 1942 there had been presented and filed 3,319 requests (for 5,526 persons) for exceptional merit and 4,852 requests (for 9,813 persons) for specific reasons. It is interesting to note that of these requests, 207 (for 283 persons) had been presented (116 for exceptional merit and 91 for specific reasons) by Italians overseas, excluding Tunisia. The Italian Jews in Tunisia who, especially after Italian military occupation, made requests for discrimination numbered another 44 (for 111 persons), 22 for exceptional merit, and as many for other reasons.

Out of all these discrimination requests, as of January 15, 1943 Demography and Race had examined only 5,870, rejecting 3,384 and accepting 2,486. A total of 6,494 persons were granted discrimination. The following chart shows the details of these discriminations by category, as of that date.

The progressive tightening of Demography and Race, especially following the decisions of February 18, 1942, can be seen in the fact that as of February 9, 1940 1,358 requests had been accepted and 219 had been rejected; as of December 31, 1941 the accepted requests had been 2,479 and those rejected 1,692; and that finally, as of January 15, 1943 those accepted were 2,486 and rejected 3,384, meaning that in 1942 Demography and Race rejected 1,692 and accepted only 7, without counting the thousands who went unregistered.

Emigration of Italian Jews. As of October 28, 1941 5,966 Jews of Italian nationality were known to have permanently left the Kingdom.[968]

	Single	By Extension	Total
Paragraph A (members of families of war dead: Libya, World War, Ethiopia, Spain, and dead for the Fascist cause)	239	-	239
Paragraph B, n. 1 (disabled, wounded, invalids, volunteers, decorated for military valor at war)	267	749	1,016
Paragraph B, n. 2 (veterans who had at least been awarded the War Merit Cross)	739	1,237	1,976
Paragraph B, n. 3 (disabled, wounded, invalids for the Fascist cause)	3	3	6
Paragraph B, n. 4 (members of the PNF during the years 1919-1922 and second half of 1924)	442	746	1,188
Paragraph B, n. 5 (Fiume legionaries)	24	35	59
Various (having more than the merits for ordinary discrimination)	538	912	1,450
Total	2,252	3,682	5,934

Paragraph B, n. 6 (for exceptional merit):			
	234	326	560
Grand total	2,486	4,008	6,494
Rejected discrimination requests			
Ordinary		3,265	
For exceptional merit		119	
Total		3,384	

Foreign Jews. The problem of foreign Jews in Italy was one of the most difficult and delicate aspects of the entire anti-Semitic policy.[969] At the time of the enactment of the first regulations they numbered about 10,000 (including Italians who had seen their citizenship revoked); those over 65 years of age before October 1, 1938 and those who, during the same period, had married Italian citizens and were allowed to remain in Italy; all others were to leave Italy, Libya, and the Aegean by March 22, 1939.[970] At that date 3,720 had left by choice. Of the others, 933 had the right to remain in Italy, 3,190 had requested an extension to their stay, and 964 were still present even though they were not allowed to be and had not requested any extension; another 300-400 had probably escaped notice.[971] As of September 20 of the same year the number of departed had risen to 6,480, those allowed to remain had increased, after several counts, to 2,444, and those who were supposed to leave numbered 2,360. Within six months, under various guises (tourism, health, business, transit, etc.), another 2,486 foreign Jews had entered Italy.[972] In order to stem this new influx of Jews, the General Directorate of Public Security, on August 19, 1939, officially forbade entry to German, Polish, Hungarian, and Romanian Jews, as well as to those coming directly from Germany.[973] The influx continued in spite of this rule during the following months until Italy declared war, and even after that it was surreptitiously tolerated by the government and favored by the border authorities, who on many occasions pretended not to notice. As of October 28,

1941 there were 7,000 foreign Jews present: 2,950 had the right to stay in Italy, about 1,000 were left over from the initial 10,000 who were present in 1938, and 3,000 came into Italy later on.[974] As of June 10, 1940, the date of Italy's entry into the war, about 800 had left.[975] Until then the circumstances of these Jews were in a sense better that those of their Italian co-religionists, that is, even though they too had to accept the various professional restrictions being progressively introduced,[976] they were not subjected to the estate and commercial restrictions.[977]

Regulations related to the state of war. Italy's declaration of war was accompanied by a series of administrative regulations that seriously worsened the situation of Italian and foreign Jews.

On June 4, 1940, with the declaration of war only six days away, the Interior Ministry (general directorate of PS) cabled all prefects to find out if, among the foreign Jews residing in the respective precincts, there were "elements with the capacity for defeatist propaganda and espionage activity that can be the cause for internment in case of emergency," and ordering them to make up related lists, while keeping at the same time "discreet but constant vigilance."[978] The results of this first census of "subversives" were not what Rome expected. Many prefects delayed responding, while others answered that "dangerous" Jews could not be found within their provinces; the lists that were sent back were few and contained little information. The longest list—69 names—was the one from Rome. Another cable was sent from Rome on June 6 asking the prefects to reexamine the issue more rigorously. On June 10 Demography and Race produced a list of 85 names of Jews whose discrimination requests had been rejected "for reasons of unworthiness." Following new investigations about 200 Italian Jews were arrested, 36 of whom came from the list produced by Demography and Race.[979] The largest groups were from Rome (42 persons interned in remote locations and 26 in concentration camps), from Turin (15, including Leone Ginzburg, interned in remote locations), from Trieste (11), and from Padua (10). To understand the criteria used by the local authorities to proceed with internment, Padua is a case in point: among the ten internees, seven were characterized as "vocal defeatists" (one had been expelled from the PNF in 1934), one had been suspected in the past of espionage activity, another had returned home from Egypt and led a "mysterious life," and only one, Guido Jaffe, was characterized simply as an anti-Fascist. An eleventh name had been proposed but was rejected by Rome because it was the sister-in-law of a high-ranking staff member of the Foreign Ministry. During the following years various other Jews were sent to concentration camps or interned in small towns of central and southern Italy, reaching a maximum number of over one thousand in 1943, almost always on the basis of extremely subjective and contradictory criteria reflecting the different attitudes of local police authorities. In some cities (such as Leghorn, Genoa, and Rome) they proceeded quite harshly, interning aged persons, in others with leniency, while in others still no Jew was subjected to internment.[980]

The number of foreign Jews interned was much more significant. With D. L. of September 4, 1940, the concentration and internment of all enemy aliens was established.[981] In reality, through administrative and discretionary procedures, most foreign Jews were progressively concentrated and interned. The report for the discussion of the Interior Ministry's budget of 1941-1942 states:

> As for the expulsion of foreign Jews, their exodus, which had already been accelerated, has necessarily been interrupted by the international conflict, as almost all exit itineraries were closed. It has therefore become necessary to increase surveillance through internment measures in locations and zones of concentration chosen in advance.

And for the following year:

> ...due to the difficulties at this time for travel out of the country, the presence of these Jews is temporarily tolerated within the Kingdom, even though they are not authorized to reside in Italy, not having attracted any special notice because of their attitude toward the host country. Many of them are confined to specific municipalities or sent to concentration camps.

At first, internment and confinement took place without any guidelines except to spread the foreign Jews in small groups within little towns in the interior of the country. One specific case will be enough to illustrate this situation. The Frankel family had lived in Milan since 1912; Arthur, the head of the family, became an Italian citizen in 1923; internment was ordered on July 19, 1940. Arthur Frankel was sent to Cosenza, his wife to Potenza, two other relatives to Avellino, while his three-year-old daughter was left in Milan.[982] Fifteen internment camps already existed in September 1940; the numbers were to increase constantly in the years to come. They were located at Alberobello (Bari), Atleta (Aquila), Campagna (Salerno), Agnone (Campobasso), Carana (Cosenza), Ferramonti Tarsia (Cosenza), Gioia di Colle (Bari), Marsiconuovo (Potenza), Montefiascone (Viterbo), Osimo, Sforzacosta (Macerata), Terranova di Polino (Potenza), Tortoreto (Teramo), Tuscania (Viterbo), and Valentano (Viterbo). The most important ones were those of Campagna and Ferramonti, where at that date there were already about four hundred internees in each camp. Within a few years there were about four hundred remote exile locations in all, mostly in central and southern Italy and the Veneto region. From January to March 1943 in the Vicenza area alone there were twenty-seven remote locations and internment areas with about four hundred internees and exiles, mostly Yugoslavs and Hungarians.[983] Along with the foreigners, stateless Italians (Jews who had lost their Italian nationality) were also interned.

Those in internal exile were given a two-week subsidy of eight lire for the head of the household, four lire for his wife, and three lire for each child, with an additional allowance of fifty lire per month for accommodations; from time to time there were brief periods of leave to go to larger towns to take care of personal business.

Civilian labor draft. The civilian labor draft was ordered by the Interior Ministry, with the approval of the Ministry of Corporations, on May 6, 1942. Those "belonging to the Jewish race" were subject to the call, even those who, from the ages of eighteen to fifty-five, benefited from discrimination. According to the ministerial regulations those who refused to serve would be judged by military courts.[984]

The decision was made by Demography and Race to fulfill two purposes: use all available manpower to attain victory and to end popular discontent against the "favorable status" the Jews enjoyed because of the persecution; "free from military service obligations, they could dedicate their time to business and leisure, leading a kind of life that was obviously insulting to the masses of Italians who were working and fighting to achieve victory."[985]

There were shrill protests against forcing foreign Jews to participate in civilian labor, even from the Spanish government through a verbal note on the subject from its embassy in Rome. The Foreign Ministry then issued an opinion making an exception for these Jews. Among the various reasons given, the Palazzo Chigi significantly pointed to reciprocity regarding Italian Jews overseas:

> We must keep in mind the special situation of our nationals in various Mediterranean countries (Tunisia, Morocco, Bulgaria, Greece, etc.) where Italian Jews represent positions that it is in our main political and even economic interest to salvage. Regarding those countries we have recently maintained the non-applicability to Italian Jews of some measures that under the guise of applying the racial laws would have endangered the position of our citizens. Consequently we would be unable to uphold our viewpoint if we were to apply those same measures against foreign Jews in Italy.[986]

Demography and Race then issued new instructions excluding foreign Jews from civilian labor, only to go back on this decision less than a year later.[987]

According to the ministry's instructions, those drafted into labor service had to make a special declaration. This new census proceeded very slowly and many people avoided it, and for many months in many locations the draft was only nominal. From a report by Demography and Race dated May 26, 1943 it appears that, as of that date, eleven prefectures had not yet submitted to Rome precise data on Jews subject to the draft. The most complete report we have found, dated July 31, 1943—the date is significant—is still missing much data. It does state that those drafted were 15,517, of whom 2,410 had been temporarily excused and 1,301 permanently excused for health or other reasons; of the 11,806 drafted, only 2,038 had actually been put to work: 1,335 within their province and 703 in another province.[988] It should be noted that, at the time this report was issued, a new regulation had been circulated for one-and-a-half months to all the prefects, in which the new head of the Ministry of the Interior, Umberto Albini, who had replaced Buffarini-Guidi in February, had ordered on June 17:

> By higher order, prepare rapid mobilization for complete work service of physically able Jews of both sexes, including those discriminated, Jews belonging to mixed families, and foreign Jews, ages eighteen to thirty, sending them to the assembly points that will be communicated by the Ministry of Corporations. Women in an advanced state of pregnancy and those having small children will be excluded.[989]

In practical terms, thanks mostly to the fall of Fascism, but also to the lack of diligence by the prefectures in carrying out the orders sent from Rome, few Jews were actually sent to labor service and then only for short periods. Most of them proved very unproductive and not capable of functioning as manual laborers, so that few companies and organizations requested their services (in some provinces such as Pescara, as of October 1942 no requests had yet been made); sometimes military authorities were against using them (for example the Littorio airport in Rome).[990] Commenting sarcastically on April 10, 1943, the Ancona daily, *Corriere adriatico* said:

> The labor service [in Ancona], as it affects the Jews, is working magnificently well. Of thirty-two Jews called, only three actually go to work, but…they do very little work. In fifteen days one of them worked for some 34½ hours. Something like two hours per day on average!

Except for a few women employed in paper and textile mills, and food packing companies, most of the Jews sent to work were employed by agricultural concerns or to do road and sanitation work in cities. In Rome, for example, one of the first cities to send a group to work (on June 3, 1942), the Jews were made to dig up and clean the banks of the Tiber and do general road repair; at the end of November 1942, 176 were at work.[991]

The statistics of Demography and Race for the work parties in 1943 (February-July) can be summed up as follows:

Work by up to ten persons per month in the provinces of: Bolzano, Brescia, Cremona, Cuneo, Lucca, Macerata, Modena, Novara, Palermo, Perugia, Pola, Ragusa, Ravenna, Varese, and Viterbo.

Work by up to thirty persons per month in the provinces of: Ancona, Asti, Belluno, Bologna, Como, Gorizia, Grosseto, Livorno, Padova, Pisa, La Spezia, Vercelli, and Verona.

Work by up to one hundred persons per month in the provinces of: Ferrara, Firenze, and Fiume.

Work by over one hundred persons per month in the provinces of: Milan (179), Rome (393) and Turin (123).[992]

In other provinces (information is missing for Naples and Treviso) the work assignment either did not take place at all or employed a small number of people for a few days up to July 25, 1943.

Measures taken regarding Libyan Jews. Up to 1942 the anti-Semitic measures taken by the Fascist government had no significant impact on the local Jewish minority. The D. L. of April 19, 1937-XV, n. 800, regarding penalties for marital relations between citizens and natives, and the laws of June 29, 1939-XVII, n. 1004, regarding penalties in the defense of the prestige of the race in dealing with the natives of the Italian colonies in Africa, and of May 13, 1940-XVIII, n.822, concerning race mixing, all concerned the relationship of Aryan Italian citizens and natives in general and made no mention of the indigenous Jews. During the first years, racial legislation was enforced only with respect to Italian Jews in Libya.

Immediately following the introduction of racial legislation in Italy, many in Rome and Tripoli wanted to extend it to the Libyan Jews. Strong opposition by Italo Balbo had succeeded in thwarting the biggest danger for the moment.[993] Using a whole series of local economic and political reasons, the Governor had succeeded in January 1939 in getting Mussolini to authorize the application of the racial laws in Libya "with the criteria appropriate to the very special local situation," meaning with some fundamental mitigation. Following a series of preliminary contacts, Balbo sent Mussolini the following long letter from Tripoli on January 19, 1939:

My Leader,

The laws for the defense of the race are being enacted in Libya; we have dismissed government functionaries and officers of the Jewish race, and pupils of the Jewish race have been excluded from secondary schools. For the enactment of the regulations according to the law a review has been undertaken within the commissions of banking institutions, the board of directors of state and state-affiliated entities and within municipal councils.

The thorough examination that I wanted to make, under the circumstances, of the entire local Jewish problem has yielded situations and aspects that deserve careful scrutiny and that I recommend to Your high attention.

The Jewish population of this region has special characteristics, both in quality and quantity. It is a significant ethnic group; in the city of Tripoli it includes one-fifth of the entire population. The presence of strong Jewish groups in Libya can be traced back to time immemorial; since the period of Augustus they were given protection by the Romans. Even before Italian occupation they considered themselves protected by Italy, they founded schools and spread the use of our language. The overwhelming majority live in very backward social conditions and are not involved in any political activity at all. These are for the most part quiet and fearful persons, who live in their small shops as little artisans and modest merchants, interested only in making a profit from their activity.

A few dozen wealthy Jews stand out of this mass and control almost all local industries and trade; they are the main customers of the banks, and finance most of the Moslem initiatives.

The sudden end of their activity, before they can be replaced by Catholic merchants and entrepreneurs, would almost certainly throw Libyan economic life off balance.

A more specific investigation of the local situation leads me to underscore some special cases that do appear to have an easy and immediate solution:

a. Libyan hospitals have many bedridden patients of the Jewish race who are assisted by Jewish personnel. This is an essential condition, because they cannot possibly be assisted by Moslems. Even the assistance of female Moslem sections is fulfilled by

Jewish women due to the lack of Moslem female nurses. Since replacing this personnel with employees coming from Italy is impossible, besides being unacceptable, because of the Decree of November 17, 1938-XVII, which clearly forbids it, it is obvious that the rigid application of the law would end all hospital assistance to the Jews.

b. For the most part, state monopolies that have most of their factories in Tripoli use Jewish women specialized in the manufacture of cigars and cigarettes. These persons would not be able to remain as employees of the Government Administration. It is impossible to find Italians here with that experience and at the same time ready to accept the same modest compensation. A forced substitution would damage production, with related consequences for the revenues of the monopoly.

c. The Government and the municipalities employ Jewish personnel of exemplary conduct who have, for a long time, functioned as interpreters of the Arabic and Hebrew languages; their dismissal would require replacements, which, while easy for Arabic within a reasonable period, is totally impossible for Hebrew, since that language is known only among persons of the Jewish religion.

I have already pointed out all these problems to the Ministry requesting instructions but until now I have received no answer. I have also had no precise answer to the following question: ought the rules for Jews having full Italian nationality also to be applied to Jews with Libyan citizenship? In a country such as this one, which has always proudly upheld the most peaceful coexistence between Arabs and Jews, it would be wise, in my opinion, not to engage in a bitter struggle for the defense of the race. The Jews are already dead; there is no need to attack them, especially since the Arabs, the traditional enemies of the Jews, now appear to feel compassion toward them.

I cannot be accused of weakness, since, as everyone will remember, I did not hesitate two years ago to order the public flogging in the marketplace of Jews, even for those of high social status, guilty of having an attitude of passive indifference toward specific Government decrees. However, I must give an accurate picture of the situation.

I take the liberty to suggest You authorize the Libyan Government to apply the racial laws "with the criteria appropriate to the very special local situation."
  With devoted respect,
  Always at Your orders!

(Signed) Balbo

Confronted by so many issues and, no doubt, wishing to avoid discussions and arguments with Balbo, Mussolini finally accepted the proposal of the quadrumvir. The clearly argumentative tone of the closing lines of his answer, cabled on January 23, lead us to believe that the decision had not been to his liking:

> 60870. I am answering your letter regarding Libyan Jews. No changes for the cases you indicate in paragraphs a., b., c. Regarding non-indigenous Jews, meaning of Italian nationality, they must be treated in the same manner as in Italy under the recent laws. I therefore authorize you to apply the racial laws as understood above, reminding you that the Jews may seem, but never really are, completely dead.
>
> MUSSOLINI

Thanks to Balbo's initiative the Libyan Jews were able for a few years to have a less harsh treatment than that meted out to their Italian co-religionists.[994] The first stringent measures against them were enacted at the beginning of 1942 on Mussolini's specific orders. As Giuseppe Gorla noted in his memoirs, during the Italian retreat from Cirenaica the year before some Libyan Jews had joined the Senussi, destroying and looting a few Italian agricultural villages.[995] This prompted Mussolini's orders to intern the Libyan Jews and later, when the lost territories were reoccupied by Axis troops, to severely punish those responsible for the destruction and looting. The reoccupation of Cirenaica was followed in June 1942 by a series of indictments and sentences against various local Jews held responsible for the violence of the year before. Besides many sentences from six to thirty years in prison, three death sentences were handed down and carried out.

According to Mussolini's orders, Libyan Jews, both local and Italian, and in particular those in Cirenaica, which was closest to the front, were to be concentrated in Tripolitania—at Giado and Garian—while those of other nationalities, especially French and Tunisians, were to be expelled and repatriated. From the monthly reports of the PAI (Polizia dell'Africa Italiana) sent to the Ministry for Italian Africa, it appears that these orders were carried out very slowly, in part because of the difficulty of effecting the transfer and in part due to the lack of equipment and supplies necessary, as well as the resistance of the interested parties, who immediately filed large numbers of exemption requests.[996] In December 1942 in the camps of Giado and Garian there were some cases of what appeared to be typhus, and therefore, fearing an epidemic, many of those interned were freed and allowed back into Tripolitania. In all, only a minority of Jews from Tripoli were interned; those from Cirenaica were more numerous; from the Benghazi region in June 1942 refugees going west numbered 2,537 Libyan Jews and 47 Italians, while there remained 552 others, plus one Italian family that had been allowed to stay behind. As for the French Jews or those under French protection, toward the second half of 1942 about one thousand had been returned to Tunisia, while 176 had been allowed to remain in Tripolitania.

During this double refugee "exodus" toward the west, the government of Libya enacted two other measures. A decree of May 30, 1942 regulated (meaning that it actually prohibited) the transfer of real estate and economic activity belonging to Jews and limited the freedom of trade of Libyan Jews; another decree of June 28, 1942 extended to Libyan Jews and Italian Jews in Libya the regulations for civilian draft already in effect in Italy since May 6. In both cases these regulations had only very limited effect due to the precarious military situation. The same can be said for the law of October 9, 1942-XX, n. 1420 which, not even four months before Tripoli was lost, extended to Libya the full measure of the anti-Semitic laws of 1938.[997]

30.
Fascist Propaganda and
Public Opinion

T he enactment of anti-Semitic legislation did not put an end to attacks against Jews and Judaism. The failure of the psychological preparation that had accompanied the start of the last phase of the anti-Semitic campaign in 1938 prompted the need to keep the issue in the forefront in order to reverse the dominant mood of the public. Once war had been declared, anti-Jewish propaganda became a convenient diversion from other more pressing problems affecting all Italians. The first military defeats, and the war itself, were blamed on the Jews. The overwhelming majority of the journalists and writers, in their extreme slavishness,[998] had found in anti-Semitism an easy and almost endless source of material.[999] For all these reasons anti-Semitic propaganda was practically constant from 1939 to 1943. In four and one-half years it changed its themes and intensity but never stopped. By the first half of 1939 it no longer appeared on the front pages of the daily press, which were focused mostly on international and war news, giving anti-Semitism less space; but it remained contemptuously active and operating—especially in politically extreme newspapers that had a special interest in it, such as *Il Tevere, Il regime fascista*, etc., or that were published in cities where there were more Jews, such as Trieste, Ancona, and others. In some ways it was distributed better. The dailies and magazines limited themselves to accusations, background articles, and propaganda agitation, while the technical, political, and "scientific" side was taken on by more "serious" magazines, and first and foremost being the infamous *La difesa della razza*. Some new "specialized" magazines were to appear within this category starting in May-June 1939, such as *Il diritto razzista*, edited by Stefano Maria Cutelli, also editor of *La nobiltà della stirpe*.[1000] Its advisory board included the most respected names in jurisprudence at the time, from Santi Romano to Arrigo Solmi, from Pier Silverio Leicht to Fulvio Maroi, and from Pietro Fedele to Antonio Azara.[1001] *Razza e civiltà*, a monthly magazine edited by Le Pera of the superior council and the leadership of Demography and Race, began in April 1940. These culturally more "advanced" initiatives and the reactions of the Italian cultural establishment to state-sponsored anti-Semitism need to be examined, starting with the main themes of anti-Semitic propaganda in major daily newspapers.

An important and favorite subject was to illustrate the anti-Semitic actions taken by other European countries, Germany, Hungary, Romania, etc., as well as the anti-Semitic positions or comments in the press of the democratic countries. The crux of this theme was summed up by Virginio Gayda in an article in *Il giornale d'Italia* dated February 4, 1940 entitled "Razzismo Italiano" [Italian Racism]:

> The race problem exists in every country in Europe. If it is not acknowledged in the same way everywhere, the only reason is the delay of national consciousness of many peoples and regimes. If it is part of the political and spiritual foundations of Fascism and National Socialism, it is because the two regimes are, in this case as well, in advance of European changes since they stem from the popular depth of both nations. The identical racial policies of Italy and Germany can only be explained by the affinity between their two ideologies and their autonomous regimes.

The logical consequence, therefore, was the struggle against the "pietists," those who, among other things, did not accept Fascism's mission with respect to anti-Semitism. The controversy against "pietism" began to lose its importance during the second, rather than the first, half of 1939 compared to all of 1938; it remained alive but was de-emphasized to avoid creating the impression that there were a large number of "pietists" and was directed mainly against the Catholics and the Vatican.[1002] The most active daily in this area was Farinacci's *Il regime fascista*, which even published an article by the notoriously rabid anti-Semite, Julius Streicher, "Il Vaticano e gli Ebrei" [The Vatican and the Jews], on January 21, 1939, which recounted every single anti-Jewish position taken by the Catholics and repeated over and over again the traditional anti-Semitic Catholic positions.[1003] These types of articles appeared in almost the entire press. A typical example is the article "Ancora del giudaismo e filogiudaismo" [More on Judaism and Pro-Judaism], published in *Calabria fascista* by Domenico Vanelli on September 20, 1942.

A new theme in the anti-Semitic repertoire that came to the forefront in 1939-1940 was that of Jewish responsibility for the outbreak of the war. It was a way to manipulate the popular aversion for war and indirectly to exonerate Fascism and the Axis. This topic began appearing in the front pages in February-March 1939 and was to remain there practically for the duration of the war. Farinacci also became a forceful propagandist for these ideas, which were not only featured in his newspaper but were also the theme of a lecture—"Come Israele ha preparato la guerra" [How Israel Prepared the War]—held in Naples on February 29, 1940. In March 1942 the Ministry of Popular Culture published a booklet provocatively entitled *Gli ebrei hanno voluto la guerra* [The Jews Wanted the War], stating, among other things, that the war had been decided on August 3, 1939 at Cap d'Antibes by Grand Rabbi Stephen Wise and the Jews Henry Morgenthau and Bernard Baruch.[1004]

These were the main editorial themes, and any excuse to engage in anti-Semitism was welcome. For instance, it will suffice to say that when, at the end of December 1939, a large fire broke out in the palace of the Cancelleria, *Il Tevere* even suggested the possible responsibility of "the Jewish element that festers near the Cancelleria" and *La provincia di Vercelli* published an "outraged" letter from a subscriber complaining that another newspaper had accepted "four Jews" among the supporters of the "Christmas of the orphans…" Some newspapers, and not always the most notoriously anti-Semitic ones, published letters and editorial notes mentioning some "scandalous" cases—the Jews hoard "our" best flour to make unleavened bread, the Jews "have a good time" in the best holiday spots, the Jews still sell from pushcarts, etc.—and every abject act of violence against them was approved. During this "hunting down of the Jews" some were even more anti-Semitic than official anti-Semitism. The discrimination principle had many opponents, such as *Il popolo di Trieste*, which warned, on May 25, 1939, that "those discriminated in any case were still Jews." And if Preziosi asked in

369

La vita italiana in April 1939 that the Jews be shipped out of Rome, the *Sentinella fascista* of October 3, 1942 in the article "Il problema ebraico in Italia oggi" [The Jewish Problem in Italy Today] demanded that Italian Jews be considered as enemies and expelled from the country. In addition, campaigns began from time to time. For instance, when the rumor spread through Milan that some Jewish families had hired domestic servants in Switzerland and among the city's Chinese residents, it was made to appear almost as an attack on state sovereignty. In cases of Jews who had transferred their estates into the names of Aryans or attempted to take them overseas, it was suggested that this would cause a massive crisis in the Italian economy. All the campaigns, together with the lies that were periodically repeated to shock naïve readers (such as the one in *Rassegna nazionale* claiming that Caporetto was engineered by the Jewish international),[1005] were used to periodically repeat their calls for new measures against the Jews, or at least the tightening of those already in existence, and when such new measures were actually taken, to present them as absolutely necessary and unanimously demanded by all Italians.[1006] *Il regime fascista* wrote, for example, on June 25, 1940, fifteen days after Italy declared war, an editorial entitled "Occhio agli ebrei!" [Keep your Eye on the Jews!]:

> It is high time to draw the line with the Jews! They do not have, and will never again have, the honor of bearing arms. Today they only think of making money by the truckload on the backs of the fighting men of Italy. Can this go on much longer? They are traitors to the Homeland, the agitators in every latitude, who have willed the war knowing they would not have to fight in it.
>
> The Italian and Fascist press should single out these odious enemies, who have forgotten our disciplined fighting men. The good that will result from this will be great.

The EIAR was not to be outdone by the press. The most absurd "news items" were transmitted daily over the airwaves, and there were even some real "cycles" of a clearly anti-Semitic nature, such as the one sponsored by the Ministry of Popular Culture, which began broadcasting on October 15, 1941, and every Wednesday evening thereafter at 7:30 p.m., five programs of ten minutes each on the *Protocols of Zion*.[1007] Another cycle of ten programs was being prepared when Fascism was overthrown.[1008] In addition, there were the continuous references to Jewish "schemes" that were included in the various comments on the day's events, and in particular those of Mario Appelius.[1009]

Beyond the press and the radio, anti-Semitic propaganda was carried on with increasing intensity from 1939 to 1943 by the many Fascist organizations. The PNF and the Ministry for Popular Culture—which in 1941 approved a proposal by the Committee for War and Political Cinema to produce a great anti-Jewish historical film[1010]—made a grand effort certainly worthy of a better cause. For almost four and one-half years there was not a single town of importance where the National Institute for Fascist Culture (INFC), the GUF, the CAUR, or the local party federations did not organize more or less regularly a lecture or a lesson on one or another aspect of the Jewish problem. These lectures and lessons were given generally by younger people and low-level functionaries, but even well-known politicians participated actively, such as Farinacci, university professors and even the deans of the universities of Rome (Pietro De Francisci) of Bologna (Alessandro Ghigi) of Perugia, and (Orano), as well as popular writers like Beonio Brocchieri and Ugo D'Andrea. Usually all the important political, military, and administrative authorities of the town attended, and often members of the Royal House, such as the Count of Turin and the Duke of Bergamo, were present and gave their approval.[1011] Today it is extremely difficult, if not impossible, to find evidence of this massive activity, but a necessarily superficial and incomplete examination of the press can still provide some elements of understanding. For example, from mid-January to mid-April 1939 there were anti-Semitic lectures and lessons in Milan, Trent, Rome, Lanciano, Arezzo, Turin, Pavia, Venice, Bologna, Naples, Ferrara, Bari, Trapani, and Catanzaro. Basically in 1939, but also during the following years, many Fascist institutes dedicated much of their energy to racist propaganda. In Milan, for instance, the local section of the INFC organized two courses from January to May 1939, one in two and the other in three lessons, on "The Scientific and Social Problem of Race and Racial Consciousness and Colonization," and four popular lectures held in workers' recreational facilities.[1012] During the same year, also in Milan, the Sandro Italico Mussolini School of Fascist Mysticism—which had created a study section on imperial and racial policy directed by Renzo Sertoli Salis, also published bimonthly publications,[1013] and organized a competition on the theme "Mysticism of Fascist Racism," in which twenty-four contestants participated. It offered private lessons for middle-school students, girls in the fourth year of teacher training school, high-school students, and elementary school teachers, as well as public meetings every two weeks and six meetings between May 10 and June 7 on specific issues of racist policy.[1014] The Ministry of Popular Culture, also in 1939, created a center for racial questions.[1015] The following year this center set up, in various cities, political preparation centers for the study of the Jewish problem in close cooperation with the prefectures and the Fascist Party federations.[1016] The most active were those in Rome, Milan, Florence, Trieste, and Ancona.[1017] The propaganda effort was also very strong, even though in part taken up by that of INFC, GUF, and CAUR.[1018]

What were the actual results of this massive campaign? Some historians—such as Eucardio Momigliano and Antonio Spinosa[1019]—using the official records of Popular Culture regarding the centers answered this question rather quickly by noting that, when Fascism was overthrown, out of 4,000,000 card-carrying PNF members there were only 864 listed as members of the Centers themselves; in Milan, out of 100,000 Fascists only 65. That answer is too simple and, in our opinion, far from the truth. If we go beneath the surface, Italian reality during those years appears quite different and somewhat less rosy. There is no doubt that, even in 1939-1943, the great majority of Italians remained aloof and opposed to racism and anti-Semitism. No one disputes this, not even today's most ardent defenders of Fascism, not even those who played a key role in these matters and who knew, as few others did, what the real attitude of the Italian people was. The memoirs of Guido Leto are essential to understand this issue. If statistics must prove how much the Fascists were deluding themselves into believing that the Italian people were supporting them, even on the issue of anti-Semitism, the best numbers are those of the circulation of *La difesa*

della razza. Interlandi's magazine had been launched with an imposing publicity campaign; there was enormous curiosity around the
country about the first issues, which found tens of thousands of
readers. There were 140,500 copies of the first issue in two print-
ings (a second printing became necessary), of the second 140,000,
of the third 130,000, and of the fourth 150,000—numbers that
were truly very high for Italy during those years. After initial curiosity, the circulation of *La difesa della razza* fell quickly and abysmally.
From a statement sent by one of the editors to the deputy of the
Minister of Popular Culture[1020] we know that by August 1940 the
circulation had fallen to 20,000 copies, 5,000 of which were sub-
scriptions—mostly more or less automatic—and the others had huge
returns, so much so that they were thinking of replacing Interlandi
with another editor-in-chief—Acerbo and Visco were even being
mentioned.

None of these statements is wrong,[1021] but there is also no doubt
that racial policy and anti-Semitism did have many supporters in
the country, certainly more than the 864 listed at the Centers for
the study of the Jewish problem. We must have the courage to
admit that, in at least two segments of the Italian people, anti-
Semitism found significant support; just as it must be said that once
anti-Semitism had become a permanent feature of Italian life within
those years, many Italians—even though they did not consent to
it—ended up accepting it as just one more bizarre trait of the regime. After the initial reactions of puzzlement and indignation, too
many Italians, having concluded that Fascism "fundamentally was
not serious about this" and that the Jews, one way or another, were
adapting to their new situation, ended up as accomplices, covering
the persecution with a veil of silence out of a sense of "loyalty to
their homeland." It became the subject of their more or less joking
"grumbling" in private and limited themselves to helping this or
that Jew who was a personal friend or relative. The war brought
other worries more concrete and personal, drawing the attention
of many more Italians away from the Jewish question. There is no
doubt a sad amount of truth to the rumors referred back to Demography and Race, and in turn relayed to Mussolini, of popular
resentment against the Jews for not having to bear some of the

burdens of the war—first and foremost, military service. The never-ending, oppressive Fascist anti-Semitic propaganda did succeed here and there, almost inadvertently, spreading small cracks that were negligible in and of themselves, but that could widen dangerously, eroding the initial revulsion toward anti-Semitism. By hitting incessantly on the same themes, some drops of poison were taken even by those who, in good faith, thought they were immune. In order to recreate the initial atmosphere of indignation and solidarity with the Jews, it will be necessary, after September 8, 1943, to rebuild a new feeling and solidarity among Italians around new values, after living through the savage mopping-up operations and the horrible atrocities of the Nazis and the Black Brigades.

It is necessary to have the courage to recognize and say this because each one must assume his own responsibility; if the initial overwhelming blame for the persecution belongs to Fascism, it is also true that some must be apportioned to important segments of the Italian people. They somehow became accustomed to the persecution and allowed their sensibilities to be blunted by "what was bigger than them," by the routine of daily life, by the fear of having problems with the regime and even, among the upper classes, by greed for positions vacated by the Jews. Real, conscious opposition to the persecution remained, in many cases, the province of only part of the Italian people, probably a minority: anti-Fascists, "honest people," Catholics who were aware and were opposed to the persecution. For them, taking such a stance was made more difficult by the fact that important leaders of the Catholic hierarchy, both lay and clerical, did not support them and, most of all, they did not hear—as François Mauriac expressed it so aptly—the strong and clearly inspiring voice "of Peter's successor." Two groups in particular espoused anti-Semitism in significant numbers: the cultural world and the youth. The matter is too important and must be brought to light.

It is no mystery that the Italian cultural elite, whether Fascist or pro-Fascist, supported anti-Semitism on a very large scale.[1022] Antonio Spinosa has pointed this out very well in 1952, and others have reexamined the problem.[1023] Few intellectuals, even among those who enjoyed positions of such prestige as to have nothing to gain, were able to avoid the uproar of those years. Giovanni Gentile was possibly the only one able to do so among the "great ones." As for the others, men such as Massimo Bontempelli, who dared blame Bottai for his support of anti-Semitism,[1024] G. E. Barié, who at Milan University publicly came out against those who took Spinoza's philosophy to be proof of "Judaic perversion,"[1025] and Marinetti, were to remain isolated cases. Similarly isolated were the small groups of militant Catholics:[1026] the strong and clear opposition of the groups from Florence, for instance, led by Giorgio La Pira and the magazine *Principî*, while other militant Catholics, such as Teresio Olivelli, the future gold medalist of the Resistance who was to die in the Nazi concentration camp at Hersbruck, still condemned anti-Semitism, agreed to join the Fascist Institute of Culture and even the Superior Council of Demography and Race.[1027] The blame for such abject behavior should not rest solely with the regime. Those who did not want to join the pack of hounds did not have to do so; true, it meant giving up salaries and honors, but it also meant saving one's honor and integrity as a man of culture. The famous "guidelines" of Popular Culture, trotted out many times on many occasions in the history of the twenty-year Fascist rule, only represented an "orientation," an "overall directive"; their interpretation and enactment was up to the individual writers according to their conscience and dignity (the innumerable reprimands and the monthly "censures" by Popular Culture, as well as the various seizures, prove that these guidelines were not really binding). The truth is that many "men of culture" accepted state-sponsored anti-Semitism as a vehicle to fame, to further their careers, to make money, to vent their jealousy and their envy of one colleague or another. Even an important historian like Gioacchino Volpe, in his *Storia del movimento fascista* (Milan, 1939) [History of the Fascist Movement]—while being more honest than others in pointing out the uneasiness and resistance encountered by Fascist racism—was unable to oppose the tide of events, and placed racial policy on the same level as autarchy and the "enhancement of military spirit in youth" as a milestone toward building a "truly compact and united" Europe as a geographic entity "but, even more, of a spiritual entity." This is indeed a distressing illustration of Fascist "culture" being irresponsible about its real duties, not toward the regime but to itself, and explains why the theoreticians of anti-Semitism did not hide their dislike for culture, "because it is by definition the result of decadence" and "doesn't work at getting things done."[1028]

A study of anti-Semitic literature between 1938 and 1943—vast as it may be imagined[1029]—would be useless and completely uninteresting, unless it is meant to engage in a reverse witch hunt, which is not our purpose at all. A few essays taken at random among the many give a fairly complete picture, should that still be necessary, of the level of this type of literature. There can be only minimal variations of opinion in these texts, due mainly to the cultural orientation and political-ideological origins of the various authors. For Mario Ramperti, the Jews can be identified by the savagery of their eyes:

> Sallow cheeks, mouths of wild animals, eyes like blowtorches, insidious and penetrating you from the bottom up. If they could they would start a slaughter...Untie the Jew's hands, you get usury. Once you tie them up again and then untie them a second time, you get a massacre.[1030]

According to Francesco Coppola, "Jewish plutocracy" was one of Bolshevism's most enthusiastic allies, part of the "anti-Europe": "the ancient anti-Roman hatred has cemented the new alliance between Anglicanism and Bolshevism, between Judaism and Bolshevism."[1031]

For Carlo Cecchelli, the Jewish goal was world domination; to reach this goal any means was good enough: "from extreme pacifism to fomenting disputes between nations so that, following a universal conflict, the Jews may rise and take charge of a dispossessed and flattened humanity."[1032]

As for Italy, its entire existence was being subverted by Judaism; were it not for the Fascist laws, it would have been choked in a few years:

> Because this is what happened: once one got in, he made his way and prepared the arrival of another. This is how the links in the

chain were tightened. This chain would someday block anyone not belonging to the Jewish race or who was not at least pro-Jewish. Since Freemasonry is…an essentially Jewish organization, once it was kicked out the window it would come back through the front door. Then not only would the Fascist regime be locked in its jaws, but the Catholic Church would also experience the shift of an element that sees only itself and its own tyrannical preeminence in the world.

According to Guido Piovene, Interlandi's *Contra judaeos* was an important book: "the most important aspect of Interlandi's book is to have reduced the Jewish question to the bare-bones minimum, and to the simple realization of unimpeachable facts that are enough to win the argument."[1033]

For Amintore Fanfani, Fascist racial policy was only "the separation of the Semites from the national demographic group" and he added that "for the strength and future of the nation, Italians must be racially pure."[1034]

Not to mention the "shabby products of Judaism." According to Nino Petrucci, one of these was the positive school of jurisprudence: "a school, as everyone knows, of purely Jewish inspiration, designed to ensure the greatest impunity to the criminal activity of the Jew, to whom one can only apply the description of a born criminal."[1035] Domenico Paolella attacked psychoanalysis, the symbolism of signs, the Freudian libido: "this is no longer the scientist or psychologist speaking in the wake of what has been said for centuries and perhaps with some new concepts, it is the Jew judging others by the standards of his own race"; and therefore the conclusion is psychoanalysis as the ally of Judaism.[1036] And, finally, an essay of literary criticism by Francesco Biondolillo:

> The greatest danger is probably in narrative prose, where, from Italo Svevo, who is super-Jewish, to Alberto Moravia, an extra-super-Jew, there is a miserable net being cast to fish off the murky bottom of society disgusting images of men who are not "men" but spineless beings, stuck in the slime of a low and revolting sexuality, morally and physically sick, inactive, even incapable of real crimes because they were incapable of any strong action…

The Masters of all these narrators are those pathological speci-
mens called Marcel Proust and James Joyce, foreign and Jewish names
down to the marrow and defeatists to the core.[1037]

The picture does not change in the arts—this is confirmed by
two debates organized by *Quadrivio* at the end of 1938 and the beginning of 1939, and by *Il Perseo* around the same time—or within
any part of Fascist culture.

Having investigated these pronouncements, we must admit that
the racist true believers end up looking better somehow among the
cultural elite, similar to what we found among the politicians. Clearly
not those such as Guido Landra and Giulio Cogni, the pale and
slavish vestals of Nazi racism, but Julius Evola and Giacomo Acerbo,
those who, having chosen a path, presevered consistently with dignity and even seriousness compared to so many who chose lies,
insults, and the complete obfuscation of every cultural and moral
value. Acerbo,[1038] for example, did not hesitate to reject the absurdity of the manifesto of the "scientists" that was being parroted by
so many others about Italians belonging to the Nordic-Aryan race.[1039]
Evola[1040] rejected any racist theory that was exclusively biological,
enough to provoke the sarcasm and attacks of the likes of Landra.[1041]
We do not imply that the "spiritualistic" theory of race was acceptable,[1042] but it did have the merit of not completely ignoring some
values and of rejecting the German and German-style aberrations
by attempting to maintain racism on the level of a reasonable cultural discussion—which beyond its political importance, from
Boulainvilliers to Gobineau and Renan, from Herder and Kant to
Nietzsche, from Fichte to Vacher de Lapouge, did have a murky
and questionable cultural and ethical significance. Obviously on this
level and in such a political atmosphere, accepting racism did not
lose its very precise meaning of giving support to a policy that was
the antithesis and even the denial of morality and culture, but it
allowed those willing to engage in such a debate inside the "Fascist
system" a way of criticizing its most serious tangible manifestation,
which was in fact anti-Semitism. The most significant product of
this kind of internal criticism is the short volume by Vincenzo
Mazzei, *Razza e Nazione* (Rome, 1942) [Race and Nation]. Going

beyond Evola, whom he criticized profusely, and other "spiritual racists,"[1043] Mazzei not only clearly condemned Nazi racism and placed the entire issue within its historical-cultural context, but also analyzed the fundamental problem of anti-Semitism: if the Jews are not an inferior race, "one cannot combine the Jewish question with a fight against race mixing"; the struggle against the Jews was therefore a political decision, targeting not so much Italian Jews as those foreigners who were taking anti-Fascist positions (Mazzei speaks of "retaliation"); "had this been simply a problem of anti-Semitism based upon biological differences—as in Germany—there would not be any possibility for discrimination..." The conclusion, not stated but easily inferred, was that once the political situation changed—meaning once the war had been won—the anti-Semitic laws would have to be revised. This would explain the attacks leveled against Mazzei's little book[1044] by *Il Tevere*, *La vita italiana* and *La difesa della razza*, which can be summed up in the closing words of the article in Interlandi's daily: "[Mazzei] did not want to write a racist book. He wanted to make a little *Thesaurus* of dictums and ideas that are clearly the opposite of the idea of race and are used as a guide by those opposed to it."

As for the support given by many youths to racism and anti-Semitism—greater than one is led to believe—the question is more complex.

Racism and anti-Semitism had always been condemned by the younger generation and were the main reason for their criticism of Nazism and their belief in the greater superiority of Fascism. It is a fact that the anti-Jewish policy of 1938—as the Fascists themselves recognized[1045]—brought about strong opposition on the part of many youths and persuaded them to turn their backs on Fascism. It is also true that for many others, the majority of younger Fascists, this was not a crisis nor a reason to break with the party, and many sincerely supported the policy in spite of the reluctance and even the hostility displayed by the majority of Italians and many Fascists themselves.[1046] It is the historian's duty to analyze rather than condemn, since condemnation prevents us from understanding. The support of racism and anti-Semitism displayed by many youths—often in the name of a real "moral" stance and a search for renewal—cannot be summarily explained away using typical anti-Fascist arguments.

For the older generation of Fascists, there were three important motivations to support, and sometimes demand, that Italy also introduce, anti-Semitism: the desire to conform, personal interest, and fear. For some it was the conviction that this was a decisive move toward greater and ever closer relations with Germany, which they felt were required in order to create a united front opposed to England and France, to make the regime more totalitarian, to relaunch an uncompromising policy within the party and the country. For others, those often but not always from a Catholic background, the adoption of an anti-Semitic policy was seen as necessary to protect traditional Catholic culture from what was perceived as the negative impact of modern culture. To attack Judaism and cast it aside meant to sever the roots of modern culture, which denied all traditional values. To those who did not see within the "Jewish mentality" and the "guilt" of the Jews (meaning deicide), the origins of such a culture, it was simple to justify a myth that, for better or worse, had a very old history and could be revived through the Catholic tradition. There are typical cases that, while different, can be logically considered together—the Center for anti-Communist Studies, in particular its section on literature, which in 1936-1937 had been strongly anti-Semitic, was demanding the "clean-up of books," the most extreme solutions, and blamed on the "influx of Judaism" even "the pro-Bolshevik mentality" that, according to them, had a corrupting effect on some circles and personalities of the world of Fascist culture and journalism, in particular the "Fascist left wing."[1047] For Carlo Costamagna, for instance:

> from the day Baruch Spinoza appeared on the philosophical scene, the destructive work against traditional ethics, God-fearing and positive, which had for thousands of years sustained the fabric of European nations took a great leap forward. The mathematical morality of the Jewish-Dutch thinker opened the door to the formal morality of idealism that still today Benedetto Croce and Giovanni Gentile want to preach to the Italian youth of the Lictors.[1048]

For some members of the Fascist left wing, just as for those in the other group, anti-Semitic policy had an exclusively political connotation; looking at it differently than from a pro-German and extremist viewpoint, this group saw its positive value in the beginnings of an anti-bourgeois policy, a sort of litmus test by which to judge the bourgeoisie. Luigi Fontanelli wrote in *Il lavoro fascista* of September 4, 1938:

> The race problem, and particularly the resulting, indispensable anti-Semitic attitude of Fascism, is an excellent reactive agent to isolate not only the Jews but all those gray areas where—under the cover of the most "petit bourgeois spirit"—those representatives of the old ruling classes were hiding, whose motto could be: "I have changed my badge because it was convenient, but nothing else"… It is very well, therefore, that through the problem of race, revolutionary Fascism doubles its uncompromising vigilance over those elements that nurture the most deleterious and corrosive individualistic spirit, which is anti-Fascist. It has been written, and rightly so, that the friends of the Jews are no less dangerous than the Jews themselves…The circles that show little sensitivity toward the race problem will identify closely with those who are insensitive to the collective spirit imposed by a superior civilization, who do not believe in corporatism, reducing it to a system thought up to avoid or delay the solution of the biggest social problems of our times… The revolution gives no pause to these elements and gray areas representing the vestiges of that extremely ingrained mentality of the old conceited, empty, intellectualistic, and underhanded Italy that was useful to everyone and didn't scare anyone…Now they will find out that it wasn't just a flash of lightning: it's raining and it will continue to rain…

If we now focus on the positions taken by Fascist youth, this will appear similar to the above but with an added dual hope. The first was that of turning racism—taken in a much more spiritualistic than biological sense[1049]—into the catalyst of the national, but also possibly the universal, community, a goal these youths were searching for more than anything and felt was necessary in order to create roots for Fascism within the people. The June 30, 1939 issue of the GUF bulletin published in Catanzaro entitled *Razzismo* [Racism] states:

Racism, besides being a biological problem, is essentially a superior ethic, reaching out to the conscience and sharpening the sense of nationhood, a feeling for this human community drawn close together by language, religion, common history, but that discovers the strongest element of cohesion in a similar way of thinking and acting that is the result of the psychological makeup of a unified race.

The second was the hope of explaining, through the absence of any racial consciousness within the Italian people until then, why Fascist culture had not adequately fulfilled their spiritual needs and, in general, why Italian society had failed to become truly Fascist.

The "discovery of race" was for these youths an immensely important cultural factor, providing them, finally, with the pivotal reason for understanding why, until then, Fascist culture had been unable to give birth to a new Fascism, more socially conscious, more moral, more just, to react in the name of new values.[1050] This aspect appears clearly in the letters to the editor of *La difesa della razza*, in a section called "Questionario." Until the end of 1940 and the beginning of 1941, in this feature of the magazine (which later disappeared because of the war and the maturing of the youths themselves), a number of young high-school and university students and even some workers and employees (among whom we regularly encounter the names of many journalists, writers, and politicians who are well known today and are not all members of neo-Fascist movements) discussed a myriad of issues, giving a racist angle to all aspects of Italian culture of those years, criticizing and questioning everything, including religious values. For these youths racism was a way of finally understanding and criticizing all of Italian history, mounting a frontal attack on bourgeois corruption with a view of reaching at last a religious concept of life. Anti-Semitism in this context was no more than a pretense to test the Italian people, the bourgeoisie especially, and Fascism itself. Sometimes the truly anti-Semitic aspect was so far removed from the interests of these youths that they overlooked any resulting ostracism faced by those Jewish writers to whom they felt emotionally and culturally closer.[1051] The consequence was anti-Semitic violence (and not just of the verbal variety, as we shall see) by these youths on the one hand, and, on the other hand, after the initial expectations, their disappointment in realizing that once again Fascism was proving unable to renew Italy and the Italians, even after discovering the root causes of the "Italian sickness" and seeking new cultural solutions to cure that "sickness" by lumping together and criticizing both the bourgeoisie *and* Fascism. It is easy to imagine the shock of these youths as they saw the support garnered by Fascism, even on the race issue, from the most typical representatives of bourgeois anti-Fascism—representatives who had converted to Fascism, such as Mario Missiroli[1052]—and witnessing these same individuals putting forth theories on the nature of racism and offering an interpretation of "extreme moderation," meaning—from the point of view of the younger generation—its emasculation and dilution into bourgeois values.[1053]

The attitude of Italian public opinion toward anti-Semitism in 1939-1943 must be measured against this reality and the public's state of mind underlying it. It was an attitude that was both qualitatively and quantitatively different from that of 1938 and of the preceding years. It cannot be denied that state-sponsored anti-Semitism, having overcome the initial strong resistance of the Italian people, was then accepted by the great majority, "in the face of reality," as something less serious than they thought at first and somehow reabsorbed into the system; while a minority, which was not as small as some have argued, embraced it, not only out of opportunism but also by personal choice.

Prior to September 8, 1943 Italy had seen relatively few incidents of anti-Jewish demonstrations and violence. It is important to discover, therefore, whether the demonstrations and violence were provoked by the leadership or were the spontaneous result of anti-Semitic agitation within some Fascist youth organizations. It becomes immediately clear that no demonstration was organized by officials of the PNF. These were either the result of initiatives by local party leaders seeking to gain attention or the schemes of local Fascist groups that were directed not so much against the Jews—who were just an excuse—as against another faction within Fascism itself, or spontaneous actions by Fascist youth who were protesting against the weakness of Fascism and attempting to force it into a more "revolutionary" stance.

The first category, fortunately, covers only some incidents of little consequence—beatings and castor oil—perpetrated against isolated Jews in 1941-1942 in various towns, including Rome. The episodes in Rome are fairly typical: in September 1941 the infamous commander of the Fascist action squads in the capital, Guglielmo Pollastrini, threatened to "get tough" if Jewish pushcart merchants were allowed to work once again. The threat was quickly short-circuited by Senise's rapid intercession with Mussolini,[1054] but this did not prevent isolated cases of violence from taking place repeatedly, sometimes possibly motivated by personal reasons. Similar incidents also took place at Ancona and Leghorn.

The incidents in Trieste in 1941 fall within the second category. Two causes were at the origin of the situation within the city, as we have seen. On the one hand, Farinacci and Preziosi kept anti-Semitic agitation alive, via their local agents, through specific attacks in *Il regime fascista* against the Jews of Trieste, who in 1940 had been accused of arousing public opinion against the Germans,[1055] scheming to sabotage the economy and subvert public order, and setting up a real "fifth column" connected to the "Anglo-Communist-Jewish international."[1056] On the other hand, there was the continuing struggle between the two major local Fascist groups, that of Giunta and Cobolli-Gigli, to seize control of the city.[1057] A confidential note to PNF Secretary Adelchi Serena in October 1941 clearly proves that the incidents which occurred in Trieste that year, such as "the ransacking of cafés patronized by Jews, with related beatings, the distribution of anti-Jewish leaflets printed in Capodistria, desecration of the Synagogue, etc.," were the result of the double play of rivalries and external influence. The informer further wrote to Serena that the Jews played no visible political role:

> The Fascists complain that, following the racial laws, the position of the Jews in Trieste is unchanged and bitterly criticize the fact that their top echelons in the financial and economic area have succeeded in securing either aryanizations or discriminations or holding on to their privileged positions with the support of well-known individu-

als, among whom the names of their excellencies Host-Venturi and Count Volpi di Misurata are mentioned.

As for the incidents that took place, they had no political or Fascist underpinnings:

> . . . these cover up the background of a renewed fight between the supporters of his excellency Giunta and those of his excellency Cobolli-Gigli. Giunta is therefore intent on using the squad members to attack the friends of Cobolli-Gigli.

On the other hand, the squad members were using Giunta for their own personal ends. The origins of the incidents and the anti-Semitic violence could be attributed solely to a local conflict among Fascists:

> There are those who think that the aforementioned anti-Jewish demonstrations were inspired by Farinacci's friends in Trieste in order to force the Duce's hand into taking tougher measures against the Jews.[1058]

There were even rumors that they planned to set fire to the synagogue "so that Farinacci, on the 29th of this month, would see the smoking ruins" and that the prefect had dared them not to go ahead with it.

There were other serious incidents in Trieste on July 18, 1942; in the course of these incidents the Orthodox school, the Synagogue, and the offices of the Committee to assist Jewish emigrants were seriously damaged.[1059]

The incidents at Ferrara in 1940-1941 are part of the third category. In July and September 1940 violently anti-Semitic flyers were distributed in the city, signed "Black Shirt" and "The Comrade."[1060] The ultra-Fascist character of these flyers is obvious. The one signed "Black Shirt" stated:

Italians!

While our glorious soldiers valorously fight perfidious ALBION, the enemy of the HOMELAND and of European civilization, in the sea, on the ground, and in the sky, the malevolent likes of the accursed Jewish race is attempting to extend its deadly conspiracy to our cities, our towns, and among our people.

CAREFUL! The espionage carried out by the Jews and their anti-Fascist mercenaries has led to the bombing of our open cities: Turin, Genoa, Milan, Palermo, etc.

Women, old people, children killed by English bombs cry out for revenge!

Italians!

Fight the Jews by every possible means.

Keep watch on their actions and intrigues and especially those refugees in the service of Jewish and English gold.

The hour has come to liberate our Italy and all of Europe from this dirty sect, which has fomented and wanted the war against the totalitarian powers of the AXIS, against civilization, and the Christian religion.

FIGHT the infernal triple-headed snake: Judaism, Masonry, Bolshevism![1061]

The police became worried and immediately started to investigate, arresting one of the distributors, an employee of the National Patronage for Social Assistance, and discovered that the matrix of the movement was in Bologna, inside the GUF, but was unable to find the prime movers in the case. The incident appeared isolated at the time; however, there is no doubt that the attack on the Synagogue of the German-Jewish rite and on the "Fanese oratorio," resulting in the devastation of both structures, and the assault on Rabbi Leone Leoni that took place one year later—the last flyers were distributed on September 16, 1940 and the two sacred places were ransacked on September 21, 1941—originated within the same Fascist youth groups who were tired of the "weakness" displayed by Fascism toward the Jews and its "inability" to bring to full fruition its own anti-Semitic policy.[1062]

Certainly these episodes cannot be compared to what was happening in those same years in other European countries, but they do show the inroads made by anti-Semitism, especially within Italian youth. This explains why there are still anti-Semites in Italy today: because the poison was spread so liberally during those years—during the Italian Social Republic racism was part of the curriculum of the officer-trainees of the GNR — National Republican

Guard[1063]—there is no doubt that, unfortunately, consciously or not, it did spread its roots in many minds and that in the atmosphere of defeat, it was reawakened causing the savage and violent incidents that continue to disturb us.

31.

The Foreign Ministry
and the Armed Forces Overseas

A very important chapter and—at last—a very honorable one in the history of the relationship between Fascism and the Jews during the years of persecution, is the position of the Foreign Ministry toward Italian Jews overseas and that of the Italian Armed Forces from 1940 to 1943 toward the Jews in occupied France, Yugoslavia, and Greece. A vast documentation is now available regarding this attitude, including many detailed studies of local situations and innumerable eyewitness accounts.[1064] Information and testimony of great interest appeared during the trial of Adolf Eichmann in Jerusalem and during various recent congresses and symposia in the United States sponsored by Jewish associations and universities. We shall examine the most relevant themes.

We have mentioned the protection of Italian Jews overseas within the political context of the application of Fascist anti-Semitic laws. In practical terms, until September 1942, the Foreign Ministry had always insisted that Italian citizens of the "Jewish race" residing in Germany and other countries with anti-Semitic legislation should be considered "citizens with full equality of rights." It protested several times to those governments that were making it difficult for Italian Jews to return to Italy or attempting to subject them to discriminatory practices.[1065] In September 1942 the German government informed Rome that it could no longer tolerate the "privileged situation" of Italian citizens of the "Jewish race" residing within the occupied territories both east and west (France, Belgium, Holland, Norway, the Baltic states, Poland, and Greece) and that starting in January 1943 they should either be repatriated or deported to Poland. The Palazzo Chigi, realizing that any protest would be useless, proceeded with immediate repatriation. The relevant Foreign Ministry report on the problem states:

> By cable dated February 3, 1943 the Foreign Ministry ordered all relevant diplomatic and consular offices to proceed to contact Jewish fellow citizens and ask them if they wished to repatriate, having informed them of the existing danger and the consequences they would face should they refuse and no longer be under our protection. This decision was also extended to former Yugoslav Jews who originally came from territories annexed by Italy and were to receive temporary passports. With respect to real and personal property that could not be transferred back to the Kingdom, as well as corporate entities, they were to be considered as belonging to Italian citizens, and the Royal Offices, in expectation of an appropriate financial convention, were required to nominate, with the agreement of the interested parties, reliable trustees to administer their estates. The Jews were authorized to take with them possessions and valuables without any limitation, exception made for the logistics of transportation.[1066]

Another memorandum dated March 21, 1943 from the Palazzo Chigi, with the agreement of the Interior Ministry, extended Italian protection and repatriation to the close foreign relatives of Italian Jews. Acting on a proposal from the repatriation commission in Nice, the benefit was extended to Jews of Italian origin who had acquired French nationality. Through this initiative some 4,000 Jews were able to avoid deportation and return to Italy.[1067]

The same protection was given to Albanian Jews. Between 1941 and 1943 Albania became a haven for hundreds of Yugoslav and Bulgarian Jews.[1068] In Tunisia the Foreign Ministry worked intensely to protect Italian Jews and their possessions after the Beylical government, following the example of Vichy, introduced anti-Semitic policies on November 30, 1940. This effort continued even after November 1942, when Tunisia was occupied by Italian and German forces (in practical, administrative terms, only by the Germans).[1069]

Some Italian Jews residing in countries under Nazi occupation were arrested and deported along with local Jews. Even in these cases, as shown at the Eichmann trial, Italian diplomacy did everything possible to obtain information about them and obtain their release, even managing to succeed in several cases.

The Palazzo Chigi did not limit itself to helping Jews of Italian nationality. As mentioned earlier, the Interior Ministry never prevented foreign Jews who were fleeing for their lives from entering Italy. The Foreign Ministry acted in the same manner: instructions were sent to the Governorship of Libya at the end of 1940 to allow entry into the colony for a number of Tunisian and French Jews residing in Tunisia.[1070] The demand for extradition presented by Berlin for a few German Jews accused of anti-Nazi activity, now refugees in Italy, was rejected.[1071]

The largest number of lives saved by far, at least until September 8, 1943, was due to the intervention of both the Foreign Ministry and the Italian military commands in the territories occupied by Italian troops in France, Yugoslavia, and Greece. In all these territories the occupation authorities, supported by the Palazzo Chigi, helped and protected the Jews as much as possible. In a short time they became a haven for tens of thousands of Jews who arrived however they could from the adjacent German zones and from those under the control of collaborationist authorities. The situation took on such huge proportions as to create serious disputes between Italian and German commands and collaborationist governments, enough to draw a series of official protests by the Nazis in Rome. The fact is well known to historians. M. R. Marrus and Robert O. Paxton in their essential *Vichy France and the Jews* clearly state that, contrary to the general attitude of other European governments that were part of the Axis system, "the Italians defended foreign as well as Italian Jews, not only inside their own country, but also in France, Tunisia, Croatia and Greece."[1072]

In Greece, Italian military authorities, from General Carlo Geloso, commander of the Second Army, down, not only took no measures against the Jews within their zone of occupation, but in Athens they even protected the Synagogue and the headquarters of the Community with armed sentries to avoid violence by pro-Nazi Greek students who were members of ESPA. When in September 1942, ESPA headquarters were bombed and the Germans blamed the Jews, the Italian command conducted a rigorous investigation and once the Jews were found to be innocent, forbade any reprisals. In Salonica, which had a Jewish community of 55,000 persons who were almost entirely deported and exterminated by the Nazis, Italian consular authorities were able to save hundreds of Jews.

> The most distant family relations with an Italian citizen were reason enough to produce certificates of Italian nationality. It was even enough to have an Italian sounding first name. Often certificates were given to Jews just because they were being sought by the Gestapo... Some Italian officers would go to the [Nazi concentration] camp and swear that certain Jewish women were their wives.

At Larissa it was enough to go to the Italian command and say you were Jewish to be given immediate permission to travel on a military train to Athens.[1073]

The same took place in Yugoslavia. The Italian zone of occupation—about half of Croatia, Dalmatia, and Montenegro—became a safe haven for the Jews. In 1941 and during the first months of 1942, the help and rescue action took place more or less silently, on an individual basis, by the local Italian commands, with the tacit approval of the highest military authorities, who were thus reacting to the unspeakable horrors perpetrated by the Ustashi, which, if such a thing were possible, were even worse than those committed by the Germans. In this way hundreds of Jews were saved from death. As recounted by Jacques Sabille, during the summer of 1941 an Italian unit in Croatia simulated a nonexistent mopping-up operation against partisans to reach a group of Jews trapped inland and save them with their tanks. The incident caused the most violent reactions among the Croats, so much so that the Italian command had to court-martial the "guilty" officers, who were punished with a few days in the stockade. In the summer of 1942, when the Germans and the Croats decided to deport all the Jews, they immediately encountered stiff Italian opposition on the part of the local and high commands, as well as the Foreign Ministry. There were about five thousand Jewish refugees in the Italian zone at the time. A German report published by Sabille states that the

Italian commander told a high functionary of the Todt organization that "it was not compatible with the honor of the Italian army to take such measures against the Jews." After various German complaints, in March 1943—when a large number of Jews had been transferred to Italy—the Jews still in the Italian zone of occupation were concentrated on Arbe [Rab] Island, in the Gulf of Carnaro [Kvarner]. That was all the Germans were able to achieve after endless negotiations, which, from their point of view, were a dismal failure.[1074]

Events took a similar turn in France.[1075] Just as in Yugoslavia and Greece, at first, up to early December 1942, the Italians gave only passive help, which was to allow the Jews to seek refuge in their zone of occupation—its normal population of about fifteen to twenty thousand very quickly rose to fifty thousand—and to prevent French authorities, under various pretenses, from transferring them to other locations outside the Italian zone. But when on December 20, 1942 the Vichy government's prefect of the department of the Alpes Maritimes ordered all foreign Jews be transferred into forced residence in the departments of the Drôme and the Ardèche—the latter being in the German zone—Italian occupation authorities referred the matter back to Rome, informing the Foreign Ministry. The immediate response was "it is not possible within the zone of occupation of Italian troops to allow French authorities to force foreign Jews, including those of Italian nationality, to move into the zone occupied by German troops." Rome confirmed these guidelines on March 18, 1943—over the protests of Laval—with two cables to the embassies in Paris and Vichy that reiterated: "the arrest and internment of Jews, regardless of their nationality, who reside in French territory occupied by our troops are within the control of our military authorities."

In a short time a paradoxical situation was created within the Italian zone, Vichy authorities, responding to German pressure, wanted to arrest the Jews, while the Italians were forbidding them to do so. In Nice things even went so far that the Synagogue and the Jewish relief center were protected by the Carabinieri with orders, should it become necessary, to arrest French policemen. On February 12, 1943 Helmut Knochen, the head of the Nazi SD in

France, described this absurd situation to the infamous Office IV of the Gestapo:

> The utmost harmony exists between Italian troops and the Jewish population. The Italians live in Jewish homes. The Jews invite them and pay for them. The criteria followed by the Italians and the Germans appear to be completely at odds with one another. We have been informed through French sources that Jewish influence has already planted the seeds of pacifist and communist discord in the minds of Italian soldiers, including even pro-American ideas. Jewish intermediaries are doing everything they can to establish good relations between Italian soldiers and the French population.

It becomes clear why, under these conditions the Germans — who still had not complained officially to Rome, in order to avoid any acrimony with Mussolini—decided to undertake a strong approach with the Palazzo Chigi and Mussolini himself. The initiative failed even though it was made by Ribbentrop in person. The only result they could achieve was for Rome to send the Inspector General of Public Security, Guido Lospinoso, with the mission of overseeing "Jewish affairs" within the Italian zone of occupation. At first the Germans thought that Lospinoso was going to the French Riviera with the mission of "positioning the problem according to German criteria and in the closest collaboration with the German police and possibly also the French police." The presence of this high functionary, in the end, changed nothing to the existing situation: according to instructions he received in Rome, Lospinoso limited his action to transferring—in order to formally satisfy the Germans and their military worries—part of the Jewish refugees in the Italian zone from the coast to Haute-Savoie (requisitioning hotels in Mégève, Chambéry, and the environs), being careful not to deliver any of them to the Germans—as the latter would have preferred—and leaving much of the transfer logistics to Jewish relief organizations.[1076]

On the eve of the fall of Fascism, on July 21, 1943, one of the highest SS officials in France, Wilhelm Roethke, angrily summed up the situation within the Italian zone:

The Italian attitude is and has been incomprehensible.

Italian military authorities and the Italian police are protecting the Jews by any means within their power. The Italian zone of influence, in particular the Riviera, has become the Promised Land for Jews residing in France. In the last few months there has been a mass exodus of Jews who have gone from our zone of occupation to the Italian one. The flight of the Jews has been facilitated by the existence of thousands of secondary roads, by the assistance they receive from the French population, by the sympathy of the authorities, by false identity cards, and the large size of the area, which makes it impossible to cordon off the zone of influence tightly enough.

Regarding the Italian attitude towards the Jewish question, about 20 reports have already been sent to the RSHA. Up to now there has been no sign of a change in the behavior of the Italians. This problem creates considerable difficulties in Italian-German political relations, because the French and the diplomatic representatives of other countries are very clever at taking advantage of the differences in conduct toward the Jews by Italy and Germany. The Italians have transferred from the Riviera to the spas of the departments of Isère and Savoie about 1,000 poor Jews. The Jews are living very well because they are under no restrictions; on the contrary, they have accommodations in the best hotels.[1077]

The picture does not change when we look at the situation in Tunisia. Here as well, Italian troops, despite the anti-Semitic measures taken by the Beylical government in agreement with Vichy and also, despite the presence of the Germans, who dominated the entire political and military situation, never lost their natural sense of humanity, and there were many cases of protection given to local Jews, not only Italians but French and Tunisians as well. It reached the point that when on April 25, 1943 the Allies began their final and decisive attack, the camp commander at Djouggar gave Jewish workers "leave until further notice" and even provided them with trucks so that they could get back to Tunis and save their own lives.[1078]

At this point a question must be answered: who was responsible for such a firm and humane attitude in defense of thousands of Jews—not limited to Italians—in various parts of Europe? It is obvious that in large measure such an attitude comes from the Italian people, as many have stated, because by nature they were opposed to any form of anti-Semitism and were therefore decidedly against the monstrous plans for total annihilation of the Nazis and of many of their collaborators in other countries. But such an explanation is insufficient. It may explain the help and protection extended by individual soldiers and officers to individual Jews; it may also explain a few initiatives of a broader type (such as the pro-Jewish "mopping-up" by Italian tank crews in Croatia in 1941) and individual actions by commanders and consulates. However, it still cannot explain why this attitude was so widespread, since it included high officials of the Interior and Foreign ministries, generals commanding army corps, and the Head of the General Staff himself. However strong the aversion to the racial laws may have been, even though everyone was filled with horror when faced with the reality of the German "Jewish policy," no matter how strong—especially in 1942—was the growing opposition to the German-Italian alliance and to the war, such a vast occurrence cannot be explained so simply, especially if one considers the servility and fear that were so pervasive within the Italian ruling class of that time and the sense of discipline that was still strong among many in the military. Without attempting to diminish the merits of the Italian people, we must recognize that an equally important part was played by the highest Italian political personalities of the time, who are just as worthy of mention as the humanity and spontaneity of individual soldiers and functionaries. Leon Poliakov, in his *La condition des juifs en France sous l'occupation italienne* [The Life of the Jews in France under Italian Occupation], has identified this key to the problem:

> There must have been a whole series of motivations behind the action of the government in Rome. What is called "permanent national interest," some far-reaching calculations, a vague craving for reassurance, even latent Germanophobia, all must have played their part.
>
> The attitude of the Italian people as a whole clearly influenced the position taken by the government. It created a mindset in which

the action of those in positions of responsibility forced...Mussolini himself to oppose German requests.[1079]

He identifies in the different Italian and German positions on the Jewish problem "a deep incompatibility between the two Axis partners."

The Palazzo Chigi, besides being motivated by a sense of humanity, was also influenced—as is clearly shown in the correspondence with its representatives overseas—by the desire to maintain within the Mediterranean, even before any military and political advantages, those Italian moral positions so deeply threatened by German policy. It is no coincidence that since the summer of 1938 the Germans had sent their own agents into Algeria, Tunisia, and Libya to "study" those ethnic groups "that were the descendants of the Vandals and the Goths,"[1080] thus indicating early on what their true intentions were, even within a sector that was supposed to be "naturally" Italian. The protection of the Jews within the Mediterranean zone took on therefore a precise political dimension to acquire their friendship while at the same time reducing the prestige of the Germans and their local collaborators. Another worry at the Palazzo Chigi, the high command, and among those politicians who thought that Italy would now inevitably leave the conflict (it is symptomatic that Vichy[1081] and Nazi[1082] documents present Galeazzo Ciano as the deus ex machina, the "moving inspiration" of the policy of protecting the Jews) was certainly to avoid exciting international public opinion against Italy and to accept the requests of the Holy See—which by 1942 had decidedly taken a position against the horrors of the Nazis.[1083] The Palazzo Chigi also sought to cultivate good relations with the Holy See, in case its mediation for a possible armistice became necessary, and in at least some cases, to create some positive merits for oneself. Nazi documents are quite clear on this as well; in one such document regarding the Italian attitude in Yugoslavia, it appears that Italian commanders were discussing the consequences that the acceptance of German demands would have among American Jews.[1084]

Mussolini's own attitude cannot be called favorable to German demands. We have several eyewitness accounts, such as those of

"Mussolini himself, we must recall, did not thwart but actually encouraged the humane behavior of our soldiers, even risking at times some bitter reprimands by the Germans."[1087] These accounts are confirmed by a dispassionate examination of the facts and related documents, especially those regarding the February-March 1943 meeting with von Ribbentrop, von Mackensen, and Müller. With respect to these meetings, it was confirmed at Eichmann's trial that von Ribbentrop, in order to secure the transfer of Italian Jews to Germany, had told Mussolini that they would be usefully employed in German armaments plants.[1088] This shows that even at this time the Germans knew they could not come right out and simply ask the Duce to exterminate the Italian Jews. A few sentences uttered by Mussolini to Ribbentrop have been used to deny that he wanted to oppose the German demands, for instance the one about some Italian generals[1089] "being of a different intellectual background." During the first meeting with von Mackensen he repeated this opinion and accepted the "need" to take strong measures against the Jews, British, and American nationals who were still located within the occupied territories, and he appeared ready to accede to the demands that von Mackensen had put forth. So much so that the latter cabled that same day, March 18, 1943, to Berlin: "I formed the clear impression that the Duce had chosen the solution contained in our proposal n. 1."[1090] Only later, it is said, once Mussolini was confronted by his own functionaries at the Palazzo Chigi with complete documents, including "a report that had just been delivered to Italy describing for the first time the horrible massacres perpetrated by the SS in Poland," did he change his attitude and accept their modified plan to move the Jews from the French coastal zone to the Alps, but not hand them over to the Germans.[1091] Another fact used to deny that Mussolini wanted to oppose German demands, is that in 1943, under German pressure, he accepted the presence in Italy of a number of Nazi officers specializing in Jewish matters. Their presence did not affect the position of the Italian authorities in charge of anti-Semitic policy, who retained their autonomy from any real German influence until July 25, 1943. The influence of these specialists (which, at the time it was agreed to, was actually a way of satisfying Berlin to make up it was agreed to, was actually a way of satisfying Berlin to make up for the many refusals, delays, and changes of mind threatening to poison the difficult relations between the two allies) was in fact to be felt after September 8, 1943, because it allowed the Germans to quickly extend to Italy their extermination plans using first-hand information and precise documents. To fully understand and evaluate the real attitude and decisions made by Mussolini during the final months of the regime, when German pressure became stronger and more insistent, it is necessary to view the problem in broader terms, keeping in mind how the "Jewish policy" aspect fit into the bigger picture of Mussolini's vision of Italian relations with Germany at that time.

According to the documents, there is no evidence that the Germans, particularly prior to July 25, 1943, ever informed Rome of their intentions regarding the Final Solution. It is significant that in a long secret report dated February 3, 1943 sent by Alfieri to Ciano, in discussing the "Jewish problem" in Germany from November 1938—the assassination of von Rath—onward, and how it had been handled and "solved," Alfieri writes in detail about deportations from Germany and the occupied territories, the creation of ghettos in Nisko, Lublin, and Warsaw, the inhumane living conditions within these ghettos, and "mass executions."[1092] He does so, however, using only information gathered by himself and his staff or from public statements such as those of Rosenberg at the congress of the Worker's Front at the end of the previous year, according to whom the total extermination of the Jews should be considered a "humanitarian action," "in order to cleanse the people of Europe." Even before receiving this report, Rome had a rather precise idea of the policy of extermination of the Jews enacted by the Germans, even though it did not know all the details or its monstrous dimensions. Embassies, legations, military commands, individuals who had been in contact with the reality of German occupation since 1941, had all informed the Palazzo Chigi and Mussolini himself. For example, the secretary of the PNF, Aldo Vidussoni, who during the last ten days of September 1942 had led a party delegation to visit the Russian front and the troops of the 8th Army, wrote in his report to the Duce:

Complete harshness is meted out to the Jews, who are treated severely and undergo restrictions of all kinds, even though there is no lack of people who work. I have been told by Italians who live in those territories, and even by some Germans confidentially, that shootings are carried out daily against large numbers of individuals of every age and sex. In Minsk at the Opera theater we saw the belongings of thousands and thousands of Jews piled up in order, it appears, to be distributed to the population. They are using, they say, only those who are able to work until they are totally exhausted.

What has mostly shocked the Italians is the way people are killed and the apparent resignation of the victims.

Entire cities and villages have been reduced by up to one-third, due especially to the elimination of the Jews.[1093]

On November 6, 1942 Alberto Pirelli submitted a report following a trip to Paris, Brussels, and Berlin pointing out "the negative effect of German policy on occupied countries and the allies," contradicting the logic of a war of attrition, making "a lasting postwar settlement in Europe" impossible and inciting "feelings of hatred and revolt in all the populations of the occupied countries."[1094] As Pirelli began speaking about the "inhuman excesses against the Jews" and "the forced mass migrations" of the Jews by the Germans, Mussolini interrupted him with a comment showing he was already informed of the fate that was in store for them: "They force them to emigrate … into the other world."

Even though the Germans had not informed Rome of the Final Solution, they had pressured the Italians since 1941 to carry out a less "lax" and more coherent policy regarding the question of "racial policy" toward the Jews, and certainly not to protect them. The initial friction during the first half of 1941 was caused by "the lack of responsiveness" on the part of the Italians in failing to repatriate their Jewish citizens from Germany—the matter dragged on until the beginning of 1943, when Berlin threatened deportation if they were not repatriated—and with the strong requests made by Rome to free Jews of Italian nationality arrested in France or elsewhere if there was nothing "unfavorable" "besides the question of race." The Germans had escalated to protests, increasing their pressure regarding the actions of many military commands, even at the level of entire armies and Italian occupation troops in France, Yugoslavia, and Greece. Between the end of 1942 and July 1943, in the Italian zone of occupation, there were serious clashes between Vichy authorities and the Italians, who, to prevent the arrest and transfer to the Germans of Jewish refugees, had decided to arrest and hold all the Jews in the zone "regardless of their nationality."

By the summer of 1942 the pressure became heavier and more insistent. On August 17 the German embassy in Rome suggested a joint action against the three thousand Jews who were refugees in the Italian zone in Yugoslavia—which simply meant handing them over. At this point, neither willing nor able to refuse, but understanding the seriousness of the demand and pressured by many to uphold the honor of the Italian army from such shame, Mussolini used a bureaucratic ruse allowing him to avoid opposing the Germans while playing for time and watching how the situation developed. This was not a morally uplifting solution, but one that, until September 8, 1943, would contribute to saving the lives of thousands of Jews. On August 24 Ambassador von Mackensen was officially informed that the Duce had given his "permission." To give "permission" in the bureaucratic sense without any accompanying instructions meant only that the issue would be taken into consideration by those who would have to carry it out, namely the central and local military authorities, leaving all decisions, positive or negative, up to them.[1095] Therefore, the High Command, after consulting with the Foreign Ministry, began studying the problem giving the command of the Italian Second Army orders limited to taking a count of the Jews and determining their nationality. Meanwhile, the Palazzo Chigi had its legal experts establish the basis upon which the Jews were to be "pertinent" to their presence within the territories annexed to Italy. Since those who were determined "pertinent" would not be part of the group to be turned over, the interpretation was broadened as much as possible so that it included not only those born in the annexed territories but also long-time residents, those who had third-degree relatives or real estate, and those who had been helpful to Italy and to the occupying forces.

The Germans quickly understood that all this was nothing but a device intended to delay and not effect the transfer. On October 3 and again on October 21, the German embassy in Rome twice requested that Italy live up to its commitments of August 24. The only tangible result was that Italian military authorities, in order to avoid the exaggerated but possible claim that the Jews were engaged in espionage activities for the enemy, decided to concentrate them in camps from where they were transferred in March 1943 to Arbe [Rab] Island, which had been annexed by Italy, in order to avoid being caught up in any possible modification of the borders between the Italian and German zones of occupation. The German proposal of December 9, to transfer the Jews assembled in concentration camps by the Italians by ship to Trieste and from there to Germany, was also denied. Rome rejected it, answering that there was no available shipping to effect the operation. At this point Berlin's patience reached its limit. The Italian sleight of hand was demonstrated by the fact that the same attitude of delay and obstruction that was used in Yugoslavia could be found everywhere else, in France, in Tunisia, and in Greece. Ribbentrop, therefore, came to Rome at the end of February 1943 to hand Mussolini a letter written by Hitler on February 16 to solve the Mihailovic problem, meaning the relationship between the Italian occupying forces in Yugoslavia and the Cetniks, as well as the problem of the Jews.

Mussolini at this time was aiming for a strategy to end the conflict in the East: to bring about an agreement between Hitler and Stalin, or at least a defensive stabilization of the Russian front—the "Oriental wall"—that would allow the massive transfer of German troops to the Mediterranean and a victory over the Anglo-Americans. Any other issue was secondary or subordinated to this strategy. To make an issue of the Mihailovic problem had some merit, a way of showing Berlin that Italy did not intend to give up its position or the defense of its interests. Regarding the Jewish problem it was impossible to draw the line: it meant a break with Hitler, who was absolutely intransigent on this issue—a paragraph from the letter delivered by von Ribbentrop confirms this beyond the shadow of a doubt—and to have no further possibility of convincing him, and almost certainly to incur his wrath and be exposed to his fanatical determination to "do justice" to all the "traitors" and "pro-Semites." It must also be underscored that if Mussolini had until then agreed with the attitude of the military commanders, beyond that minimal sense of humanity hiding at the bottom of his conscience, it was for two purely political reasons, which in view of the way things were going were losing their importance, and in any case were insufficient to make him defy Hitler. First, he was fully aware that a passive alignment on Nazi positions for violent persecution of the Jews would cause strong adverse reactions among the Italian people and would make the regime and the war even more unpopular, bringing about a further erosion of his own prestige. The second reason was that by opting for a different anti-Jewish and racist policy for Italy, compared to Germany, he wished to make Italy a beacon for all those who feared German hegemony in Europe—governments, populations, smaller ethnic groups, and others. As long as the war was favorable to the Axis Mussolini hoped to be able in some way to reduce the power of Germany after the war.

If we keep all these elements in mind, it becomes clear why, faced with von Ribbentrop's insistence, Mussolini now drew the line on the problem of Mihailovic but did not do so regarding the Jews in Yugoslavia. As he is said to have told General Robotti a few days later:

> Minister Ribbentrop was in Rome for three days and harassed me relentlessly; he absolutely wants the Yugoslav Jews to be turned over. I beat around the bush, but since he didn't want to leave, to get him to go I had to agree. We have to bring the Jews to Trieste and hand them over to the Germans.[1096]

But once Ribbentrop had left, faced with the dissent of Bastianini, Ambrosio, Robotti, and others, Mussolini changed his mind, attempting to repeat the same game of a few months before. As he told General Robotti:

> ...I had to agree to the transfer, but you can invent all the excuses you wish to avoid handing over even one Jew. Tell them we have

absolutely no transportation to take them to Trieste by sea, since it is impossible to do so by land.

The same situation recurred one month later, when von Mackensen discussed the problem of the Jews within the zone of occupation in France, openly accusing the Italian military authorities of obstructionism. At first, Mussolini said he would issue orders to stop opposing the mopping-up operations conducted by the Vichy police on behalf of the Germans; then, faced with the arguments of Bastianini, who revealed to him that the Jews were "all being gassed, without any quarter, old people, women, children" by the Germans, he let Bastianini give von Mackensen the "real interpretation" of what he had said before: the Italian army would no longer oversee the Jews, the Italian police would from then on be responsible for their internment. Bastianini explained to the ambassador:

> The French police must not handle the mopping up of the Jews because it is secretly plotting with them; it warns them a few hours before and lets them flee after getting paid off. *Elle se fait graisser la patte* [They take bribes]…you understand? We shall place them in concentration camps and keep them under surveillance.[1097]

And so, for the time being at least, the Jews within the French zone were safe.

We do not think, based upon these facts, that Mussolini was in agreement with the Nazis; we can say that his position was absurd: between the constant need to avoid a crisis with Hitler[1098] and the desire not to order a monstrous crime, even though the executioners would be German. He was only able to play for time and find temporary solutions which discredited him in the eyes of the Germans. In any case, the fact that this was the only position the Duce was able to take is confirmed by events during the Italian Social Republic. Even then the top leadership of the RSI tried to find a middle ground between the need to demonstrate humanity, to placate public opinion, and avoid friction with the German ally.

32.
The Jews, the Union
of the Communities, and the DELASEM

F ollowing the first storm in 1938, the years that followed, up to the fall of Fascism, were to be for Italian Jews years of long and difficult adaptation to their new condition as second-class citizens. A few thousand left Italy during these years, especially before June 1940, but also after that date. Those who stayed behind slowly adjusted to a new way of life; those who were discriminated had an easier time—at least at first; and the others had greater difficulties. All of them were supported by the solidarity and often the tangible help of the overwhelming majority of the population. This was, if not a competition, at least a grand plebiscite, enabling many Jews to find new private activity. It also meant a moral, more than a practical, benefit for many of them, making up for the ostracism that Fascism had subjected them to, and the thousands of little humiliations that Fascism itself, the press, and a certain number of unconscionable fanatics inflicted upon them on a daily basis. All social classes and categories were to take part in this plebiscite, from the most humble to the most highly placed. There were many cases when help came from the Fascist ranks, from the top—for instance the aid Balbo gave to some his Jewish staff members—as well as the lower levels: as we have mentioned, over a thousand party cards were withdrawn as well as reprimands for "pietism." Beyond the practical aspects of life, the years 1938-1943 also meant a moral and psychological adaptation. Many of the wounds that had divided and placed Italian Jewry in crisis during the preceding years were patched up, and a new sense of unity, deeper and more tangible than the one Fascism had broken, slowly reconstituted itself. The old divisions between assimilated and nonassimilated, between those who believed and those who did not, between Zionists and non-Zionists or even anti-Zionists, between Fascists and anti-Fascists, all disappeared, and those who resisted the storm without giving in to compromise or flight—even among the newly converted and those Aryanized there were cases of repentance—gave birth to a new reality that was deeply united and homogeneous. There is a good example of this grand occurrence: around the end of 1942, as shown in the documents of the Union of the Communities, fortunately saved from destruction,[1099] men such as Ettore Ovazza and Aldo Finzi, who had never participated before then or had left under duress, drew closer to Italian Judaism and community life. The practical obstacles to the reconstruction of this unity were obviously gigantic. Hatred, anger, misunderstandings, moral and political prejudices of all kinds, were seemingly formidable barriers that were eventually overcome. The firm serenity with which some Jewish families were able to live through those sad and difficult years—the picture drawn by the Artom diaries is typical—had an underside of doubts, uncertainties, fears, crises that cannot even be clearly described for many other Jewish families.[1100] Besides their own particular situation [as Jews], life for all Italians was becoming more difficult by the day in the midst of war and its horrors. The Jews lived through the war — and this is a fundamental characteristic of the Jewish tragedy during those years — not simply by enduring it like all other Italians but also by participating in its developments with the same passionate interest and the same moral dilemmas. Compared to most Italians, the Jews came to this experience having a much clearer and well-defined history behind them. They saw the alliance with the Nazis in all its negative implications long before most other Italians. This did not mean the Jews were insensitive to the very serious dilemma and responsibility created by the war itself. The "homeland at war" was one more reason for the soul-searching drama of the clash between their Jewish and Italian identities, in the knowledge of what a Nazi victory would mean to them and the rest of humanity and their attachment to the homeland and its fate. Some were able to make an immediate choice, while others debated with uncertainty for a long time. If doubts linger regarding some public demonstrations and speeches, even by rabbis in certain political and military circumstances, we can conclude that these were necessary to avoid any suspicion on the part of the Fascists and the desire to blunt anti-Semitic arguments; there can be no doubts about other facts and occurrences. It is a fact—and an undeniable one that can be understood only in one way—that when Italy declared war in 1940, there were Jewish former military officers and youths—even eight who were studying in Lausanne—who asked to join and be allowed to fight.[1101] In November 1940, when the British torpedoed three battleships at Taranto, the Fascists, for whom this was completely shameful, had to ask Umberto Pugliese, a Jew and a general of the naval engineers, to help lift the ships to back to the surface. The general agreed and answered the question of what he would like in exchange by requesting a round-trip ticket and permission to wear his uniform.[1102] When, at the end of 1942, naval communications between Italy and North Africa had become practically impossible and there was a plan to build twelve cargo submarines, Cesare Sacerdoti, a Jew and the only engineer who could have designed them, also answered positively to the question put to him by General Cavallero, saying only that he agreed "in the interest of the country, and after many lost illusions in the past."[1103] Nor can the words of the Chief Rabbi of Rome in the synagogue be considered insincere during the civilian labor draft:

> The two-thousand-year history of the Italian Jews bears the permanent mark of the strongest devotion to the Homeland…Each Italian war means, for the Jews, a sacred cause in which they offer their possessions, their arms, their blood, their life. I hope no one thinks of us as privileged if, because of reasons beyond our control, we cannot fight for Italy even in this appalling war. I can declare, without fear of being contradicted, that hundreds and hundreds of our co-religionists have asked for permission to volunteer. Officers were ready to give up their ranks just to be able to fight at the front, even, I should say, in the very front lines.
>
> Our exclusion remains a wound for us that doesn't know how to heal. A sorrow that will not disappear. So we have welcomed with satisfaction the news of the call of Jewish citizens to civilian labor service. Each one of us will provide his contribution to increase the country's production, upon which today as always we call for the benediction of the Lord.[1104]

These words illustrate one of the most dramatic aspects of the life of the Jews between 1939 and 1943, just as does the poem by Angiolo Orvieto, the bard of those who are excluded:

Wandering through Florence,
uncertain exile of fortune,
while it grows ever darker
and you are deserted by your friends,
cast from your learned chair,
    you, swept away with the swept-away Jews
    expert in the pain that relentlessly burns,
    even though, in silence, you meditated
    thoughtfully about two worlds locked in struggle.

If this was the relatively easy life of Italian Jews—at least in the material sense—from 1939 to the fall of Fascism, with its problems, its difficulties, its occasional tragedies; the life of those, after June 1940, who were interned by the Fascists and the foreign Jews in general who had found refuge in Italy and were waiting to leave for more hospitable and secure countries, was more severe.

The living conditions of the free internees, meaning those in internal exile, were not too harsh, except for the fact that they were confined to small more or less isolated towns, almost always inland in central and southern Italy. It was fairly tolerable and similar, to a certain degree, to that described by Carlo Levi in his novel *Cristo si è fermato a Eboli* [Christ Stopped at Eboli] relating to the situation a few years before [1935]. A key factor in making it more or less tolerable was the adaptability of the internees themselves to the weather, with water often scarce, and the degree of humanity or zeal of the local police. If the internees ran into a police chief, or even a regular policeman who was a bit humane their life usually would quickly be organized in a rather normal way, and it was not even difficult for them to find some kind of activity to make enough money to increase the allowance the government gave them, and not even need the help provided by Jewish organizations. In many cases they adapted so well and drew the sympathy of the local population and the authorities so much as to provoke the anger of those who favored a tougher approach. We can trace these complaints in the files of the Central State Archives. In Montereale, in the province of L'Aquila, during the summer of 1942 there were five Jewish internees, Italian and foreign. They had settled in rather quickly; one, with relatives in Rome, received regular visits, while another, a doctor of German origin, had been hired by the local pharmacy, which, thanks to his presence, kept on functioning even when the owner was drafted into the army. Two anonymous letters protesting this "idyllic" state of affairs were sent to the Fascist party federation in Rome and the Interior Ministry, claiming that the Jews were having a good time in Montereale and were even disturbing the peace. In this case the matter fizzled out; the prefecture of L'Aquila quickly reported back to Rome that there was nothing abnormal in the little village. The unsigned letters must have been sent by someone who felt hurt by the hiring of the Jewish doctor and that he would be dismissed from the pharmacy once he could be replaced by someone else.[1105] In other cases the accusations brought about much tougher reactions, as in Asti in early 1943, from which many Jews were transferred to the vicinity of Frosinone after a report by Farinacci to Mussolini in which he claimed that the Jewish internees were living in excellent conditions in Piedmont, with accommodations in the best hotels, often going to the cinema in the company of the police chief, and "made a constant play for Aryan women."[1106]

Life in real concentration camps was much harder. The only camp that has been well documented was the largest and most important, at Ferramonti Tarsia in Calabria.[1107]

Treatment in these camps was not particularly harsh. Kalk writes that a gentleman's agreement was quickly established between internees and guards—"Do whatever you want as long as appearances are safeguarded and we don't get warnings or other problems." The internees organized themselves in almost perfect order, draining the land, growing crops, undertaking waterworks and plumbing, and sometimes creating miniature cities, with a social assistance program, polyclinic, public bath, work center, maternity and day care center, school, cultural commission, music section, theater group, fine arts academy, chess players' circle, sports club, religious organization (at Ferramonti there were three synagogues for the various rites), ambulance service, arbitration committee, and a sort of parliament administering the camp along democratic lines. The difficulties in these camps were caused by overcrowding and the poor locations they were in, far from main communications, far from towns, in damp or arid regions, often with little water, the accommodations being shacks or other temporary buildings. In September 1941 in the camp at Agnone, near Isernia, life in these shacks was very difficult. In an appeal to Cardinal Borgongini-Duca—who had visited it a few months before—one reads:

> A large cinema is the dormitory for all 46 of us. There are only 40 centimeters of space between beds and one can barely get through. There is no way to heat the hall because a stove would make the air impossible to breathe. In winter and fall, when we will have to close the side doors, it will stay cold and dark, without ventilation.
>
> Due to the food, the weather and the water, 20 percent of us suffer from a typhoid-like stomach infection and two of us are in the hospital at Isernia with high fever.
>
> Because the camp at Isernia is absolutely full and the crowding in our room makes even crude hygienic conditions impossible, the efforts of the camp doctors and the director appear to be useless.[1108]

Despite these difficulties the morale of the internees—especially those in the best-organized camps, such as Ferramonti and Urbisaglia—was always high, because of the hope of obtaining at any moment an entry visa into another country and therefore being able to leave the camp and Italy; but also knowing that they were, in the final analysis, privileged by comparison to millions of other Jewish internees all over Europe. Israele Kalk, in speaking to the Ferramonti internees in August 1942, could say:

> I don't think anyone will contradict me if I say that fate has been good to you and that your condition as internees in Italy is probably better than that of other brothers of ours who are still free in other European countries.

This was the general situation in which the Union of the Communities, the unified organization of Italian Jewry, had to operate.

During most of 1939 the Union was struggling with the problems we have mentioned earlier. There was the anger of a new secessionist movement led by a colonel from Florence, who was also proposing reforms on the religious level, as was observed during the meeting of the council on January 18, 1939 "of such a nature as to lead us to conclude that all of Judaism would be placed in jeopardy." There were attempts to revive the magazine *Davar*. Abjurations continued and there were many resignations from community organizations. The crisis involved the Communities in Alessandria, Ancona, Florence, Mantua, and Trieste. The Union had strong ties only with the Communities of Rome, Ferrara, and Milan.[1109] The situation was problematic from the religious point of view as well, various Communities were without a rabbi, because many positions had been filled by foreigners who had since been expelled, and some were discussing the creation of "regional rabbinates."[1110]

For a short time at the end of 1938, even the Rome Community was without a rabbi, because David Prato had been forced to leave Italy following the attacks by *Il Tevere* and other Fascist publications accusing him of being anti-Fascist and the prototype of the Jew who was the enemy of Italy. After some uncertainty Prato, in order to avoid creating additional tension in a very explosive situation and involving all of Italian Jewry in his personal plight, preferred leaving his post of his own free will.[1111]

There was a positive side to all these negatives, however. Individuals and groups were trying to cope with the most pressing problems everywhere, assisting foreign refugees,[1112] instructing children and youths who had been expelled from public schools, and above all, whenever possible, helping them go to Palestine.[1113] Not only was much being done to solve the problem of elementary and secondary schooling provided by law, there were also higher-level projects to allow young people to train for those positions not completely closed to the Jews. There was, for instance, a plan to transform the seaside summer camp Lazzaro Levi, in Castiglioncello near Leghorn, into an agricultural school for the technical preparation of youths to become farmers in Italy or within the Empire and for those who wanted some agricultural experience before emigrating.[1114] Professor Adolfo Ravà and other academics, who had been excluded from the teaching profession, were planning a free Jewish university to teach economics and business.[1115]

The role played by the Union in all these initiatives was minimal, if not totally absent. For practical purposes, separated from most of Jewry and the Communities in Italy, the Union was in limbo for all of 1939, albeit with good intentions, but fearful of provoking Fascist authorities, full of uncertainty, and unable to define a policy other than living day by day showing Fascist and patriotic zeal. The many local initiatives, such as the educational ones, were only "paper shuffling" exercises with government offices, since the Union was the only organization that could deal with them. While there were many pressing fundamental problems, the most important one, according to the files of Union correspondence with the many ministries and the reports of the meetings between attorney Ascoli and Le Pera, appears to have been that of military volunteers. This was a real problem many people were concerned about, but it was not the most important one and it affected only a minority of Italian Jewry. The issue is of rather small significance in itself, but it illustrates the policy, or rather the tactics, of the Union during the first months of persecution: to obey and show that they were zealous Fascists and Italians. The four memoranda presented during these months, which were actually the most important initiatives taken by the Union until mid-November 1939, did not go beyond a few weak general requests that appealed to the "benevolence" of the government. These appeals continuously repeated that neither the Union nor the Italian Jews wanted to issue a protest but only to point out, with increasingly troubled dignity, some aspects of the new situation they found themselves in. The first such memo was general, addressed to Buffarini-Guidi on February 21, and illustrated the moral and material situation of the Italian Jews after the first legislative measures.[1117] The second, dated May 23, to the presidents of the Chamber of Deputies, Costanzo Ciano, and of the Senate, Giacomo Suardo, illustrated some details regarding the law on professional activities.[1118] The third, dated October 30, to the Interior Ministry, dealt with the threatened revocation of Italian citizenship of the Jews of Trent and the Venezia Giulia region, who had been naturalized based on the treaty of Saint Germain.[1119] The fourth, dated November 9, was addressed to Bottai and regarded the school situation.[1120]

Most of these initiatives were less reflections of Union policy than of the personal relations between some of its officials and important Fascist leaders; these personal relationships, on the one hand, allowed the Union to voice its opinion regarding the laws the government was preparing and try to obtain some mitigation; but on the other hand, due to their personal nature, they also made it more difficult for the Union to attempt to face up to the government. Besides the trip by Vice President Ascoli in February 1939 to all the Communities to reestablish contact, the two most significant initiatives the Union took—by a small group of board members— were of an extremely confidential nature, and no trace of them can be found within the archives.[1121] The first was the creation of a special commission—including General Liuzzi, attorney Aldo R. Ascoli, General Angelo Di Nola, Commendatore Max Ravà—and of a special secret fund for "confidential distribution" to those "ready to help" the Jewish cause, to bring about certain contacts, to focus attention on broad cases, etc. The second, in July 1939, was a meeting between attorney Ascoli and Father Tacchi-Venturi to express to him and to the Holy See "the emotional feelings" of the Jewish community for the words of understanding pronounced by Pope Pius XI during his speech to the students of Propaganda Fide and, in general, for what had been done by the Holy See afterwards. During the meeting Father Tacchi-Venturi, while showing "much understanding" for what was said, was of the opinion that it would not be convenient to publicize the event "in order to avoid erroneous interpretations and reprisals," but he was ready to transmit personally to the Pope the opinions and feelings that Ascoli expressed. The result of the conversation that took place at Tacchi-Venturi's residence (and lasted a long time, touching almost every aspect of the situation, along with a few subsequent meetings between them), was that on August 3, having conferred with the Pope, Tacchi-Venturi wrote the following note to attorney Ascoli:

Illustrious Commedatore,

I am duty bound to inform you that yesterday I followed up on the task you gave me last week.

The information, as I thought and have already told you, was greeted more than benevolently, requiring me to inform you, as I am now doing, how much it was welcomed and appreciated.

With pious devotion I remain

Of Your Illustrious Excellency your most Devoted

Pietro Tacchi-Venturi S.J.

Despite some immediate advantages, it was obviously impossible to maintain such a policy. To follow this route would have quickly reduced the Union to an organization without effective functions, divorced from the real problems facing Italian Judaism. In addition, some of its members were suspected of having too cordial relations with this or that Fascist leader, to the point that other members would meet among themselves, outside the offices of the Union, to make the most important decisions. As a result we understand how much dissatisfaction existed toward the Union itself and how it was decimated by multiple resignations.

What made the cup run over was the shutting down by the government in August of the Committee of Assistance to the Jews of Italy, which created extremely difficult conditions for thousands of refugees in Italy and against which the Union had lodged only a timid protest. The management of the Union survived this blow only for a few months. Continuous resignations, even those of President Jarach, whose excuses were constant commitments in Milan, offered those backing a more radical renewal of the Union the impetus to put their plans to work. This was the opportunity for the first collaboration between the healthier part of the older generation of Jewish leaders and the anti-Fascists—represented by Raffaele Cantoni—who until then had been excluded or kept away from the leadership of Italian Jewry. Once the coup d'état had been decided, a man had to be picked for the presidency of the Union without creating undue suspicion among the government and Fascist circles in general, and who could actually inspire their confidence. After a series of harrowing searches and negotiations, former prefect and former councilor to the Court of Accounts, Dante Almansi agreed. He was an older man, rather short, looking almost insignificant, who until then had no involvement with the administration and moral life of Italian Jewry. It was because of his firmness and wisdom that the Union became once again the catalyst for the Jews from the end of 1939 until the liberation of Rome on June 4, 1944. All Italian Jews had a proud, dignified and active representation, and thousands of foreign Jews could be effectively helped to live in Italy or emigrate overseas.[1122] Once the man had been found, during a dramatic meeting of the board on November 13, 1939 in Rome, the leadership structure of the Union was completely overhauled. Almansi was named president with attorney Lelio Vittorio Valobra as vice president and board members Lionello Alatri, Mario Falco, Marco Segre, and Alfredo Sabato Toaff. Those appointed and confirmed as council members were Aldo R. Ascoli, Arturo Carpi, Marco de Parente, Salvatore Donati, Federico Jarach, Bruno Jesi, Goffredo Passigli, Mario Tedeschi, Benvenuto Terracini, and Angelo Treves.[1123]

Dawn was quick to rise. Casting away the old methods, Almansi took the initiative and visited the chief of police, Bocchini, whom he knew from years before, asking one pointed question: what do you intend to do about the Italian Jews and the Jewish refugees? As happens in such cases, the firm and dignified attitude of the new president produced a result that had never been reached by his predecessors, who had dispalyed a humble and weak attitude. The limits of the activity and the powers of the Union were finally precisely defined, and while avoiding any unacceptable compromise with the government, a kind of working collaboration began. There had been a meeting, mentioned earlier, in February 1940 between Almansi and Bocchini and the foreign Jewish refugees regarding emigration. The results of this collaboration were truly remarkable. Passports, which had become more and more difficult to obtain, were easily reissued to Italian Jews wishing to emigrate. For foreign Jews, also thanks to requests by the U.S. embassy in Rome at that time, assurances were obtained that the German Jews would not be "repatriated" and that generally the entry of refugees would not be blocked at the Italian border.[1124] The most noteworthy success was to secure permission to replace the defunct Committee for the Assistance of Jews in Italy with the Union-sponsored Delegation for the Assistance of Jewish Emigrants—the famous DELASEM—which, with government approval and help, was able during the following years to save many thousands of Jews. To get permission Almansi and Valobra, the president and vice president of the Union, divided their tasks: Almansi, in Rome, took care of Union affairs, while Valobra, in Genoa, managed the DELASEM. They used essentially two arguments: the DELASEM would relieve the government of the serious financial and organizational burden and handle the difficult problem of so many refugees crowding into Italy; also, since the DELASEM could count on the help of several important international Jewish organizations such as HICEM and the Joint Committee, the arrival into Italy of large quantities of foreign currency would be, in that moment of scarcity, extremely useful to the national economy and the government. There is no doubt that this last reason weighed heavily with the Fascists, for until the fall of Fascism the DELASEM, possibly the only such organization in Italy, had a favorable rate of exchange with the dollar of 15% over the official rate granted by the Ministry of Currency and Exchange.

Given this new situation, the years from 1940 to 1943, up to the fall of Fascism, were years of useful and productive work for the Union. It quickly returned to its mission of being the moral guide and the engine of Italian Jewry. The memory of Almansi has remained—in spite of the attacks he was subjected to right after the liberation of Rome by some newly returned exiles who had not lived through the harsh realities of Italy during those years—for all Italian Jews and for all those who were in Italy during that time, that of one of the purest and most splendid persons of those extremely sad years. The demonstrations of "patriotism" and Fascism were reduced to a minimum in order not to antagonize the Fascists and create suspicion—which did not prevent *Il Tevere* and other more extremist newspapers from attacking Almansi and the Union several times, calling it a den of anti-Fascists and its president a false Fascist, "well known to comrade Preziosi."[1125] Contacts with the government, while always carried out with dignity and firmness, were reduced to the strict minimum necessary to obtain delays in the enactment of the various laws and, when possible, their mitigation,[1126] to encourage the Interior Ministry to expedite discriminations, to protest against acts of violence that were perpetrated from time to time against Jews, and gather information regarding the direction of Fascist anti-Semitic policies. The rest of the Union's effort was concentrated mostly on coordinating, helping, and stimulating local initiatives with respect to assistance, religion, and instruction.[1127]

From 1940 onward, the most important focus for the energy of the Union as well as the Communities was on education and assistance. As soon as some students appeared classes were organized in various locations.[1128] Jewish elementary classes were being held in 1943 in Alessandria, Ancona, Bologna, Ferrara, Florence, Fiume, Genoa, Leghorn, Mantua, Milan, Modena, Naples, Padua, Pisa, Parma, Rome, Turin, Trieste, Venice, Vercelli, Verona, Viareggio, and Rhodes.[1129] Secondary and commercial state schools or community sections operated in Bologna, Ferrara, Florence, Genoa, Leghorn, Milan, Modena, Padua, Rome, Turin, Trieste, Venice, Vercelli, and Rhodes. There were private courses in many of these locations for young Jews at both the secondary and high-school levels. In Milan and Turin there were, during the years 1941-1942 and 1942-1943, even higher education classes for cultural subjects—in Milan economic and commercial subjects and chemistry; in Turin only economic and commercial subjects—given by many first-class professors such as Edoardo Volterra, Gustavo del Vecchio, Professor Marco Fanno and Professor Guido Castelnuovo. In 1942 these courses had twenty five students in Milan. An engineering course was offered in Rome. One hundred other youths were studying in Switzerland at the same time.[1130]

The assistance effort by the Communities, individual organizations—such as that of Israele Kalk, a Milan engineer—and above all the DELASEM, was truly extraordinary. The accomplishments of this last organization deserve a study of their own. Two works about it were published a few years ago, a historical study and a documentary memoir, which are complementary and can be consulted by the reader seeking more detailed information.[1131] We can safely state that by mid-1942 the DELASEM was as-

sisting over 9,000 Jews—3,500 in concentration camps, 5,000 in
internal exile scattered in 250 localities, and 500 who were free—
and extended its work not only within the territory of Italy but also
to the occupied territories in Yugoslavia. By "assistance" we mean
not just material help, subsidies, blankets, clothing, medicine, but
religious help as well, prayer books, matzos, religious vestments,
etc, and moral support, searches for relatives, communication with
them, and even specialized assistance according to religious rituals
and age groups. Browsing through the memoranda from the
DELASEM to its local offices—there were twenty-seven by January 1942[1132]—and its correspondents in various concentration camps
and internal-exile locations—170 at that same date—that have
reached us after the storm of those years, we can only be moved to
witness how attorney Valobra and his handful of assistants were
always able to find words of comfort for everyone, how they never
let a religious holiday go by without remembering it in words accessible to everyone, how they even thought of maintaining a correspondence with children and youths, attempting to bring some pleasure into their sad lives with a short story or a little poem.[1133]

During its first seven months of activity, until Italy entered the
war, the DELASEM, just as Almansi and Valobra had agreed with
Bocchini and Le Pera, was mostly trying to find ways for foreign
Jews to emigrate and assist them effectively as long as they could
do so. About two thousand Jews left Italy during that period thanks
to the DELASEM, and nine thousand others—with a continuous
rotation of three thousand persons—were under assistance. According to the report dated July 22, 1940,[1134] sent to the head office
of Public Security, about eight million lire were spent on emigration and three and one-half million for assistance. This truly imposing effort was made possible by contributions from the American Joint Distribution Committee, about $15,000 per month for
assistance, and from HICEM—the Hias-Ica Emigration Association—for emigration. The balance of the necessary funds (over
two and one-half million) was collected among volunteers in Italy.

The situation became much worse with Italy's declaration of
war. Emigration became more difficult because of the interruption
of relations with many European and non-European countries and

416

the interruption of Italian maritime services and of any transportation from Italy in general. The DELASEM, therefore, had to officially limit its activity for emigration to special trains to Lisbon through France and Spain and the airline *Ala Littoria*. Assistance itself became extremely difficult because of the ever-increasing number of refugees, their growing needs, and the fact that they were scattered in hundreds of small localities within the country. Despite these problems, during the second half of 1940 the DELASEM was able to send out 647 persons and provide assistance to over six thousand. Once the United States also entered the war the situation became even more difficult. The American Joint Distribution Committee continued to provide assistance through Mr. Sally Mayer in Switzerland and through the U.S. representative to the Holy See, Harold Tittmann; the possibilities for emigration were further reduced. This did not stop Valobra from continuing his work; hundreds of Jews traveled to safety by air to Spain and Portugal, and he even reached a transportation agreement with a smuggler from Liguria—with the knowledge of the police—who ferried up to two thousand persons into the French free zone, from which they could reach the Iberian peninsula and even North Africa. From 1939 to September 1943 the DELASEM was able to help five thousand Jews emigrate. Two thousand emigrated to Spain and Portugal, 800 to North America until 1941, 600 to Shanghai until 1940, 500 to Tangiers until 1940, 400 to France and England until 1940, 200 to Argentina until 1943, 200 to Cuba until 1942, 200 to Paraguay in 1942-1943, and 100 to Palestine until 1940. The center for emigration, up to September 8, 1943, was in Rome, where Settimo Sorani handled the relations with foreign consulates (with Father Anton Weber for the Jews who had converted to Catholicism), with the airlines and government authorities.[1135] On the eve of the fall of Fascism negotiations were taking place between Valobra and the Holy See—through Cardinal Boetto, archbishop of Genoa—for the transfer of six hundred children to Turkey.[1136]

During the second half of 1941 the DELASEM assisted about 6,700 refugees: 1,500 in internal exile, 1,200 in concentration camps, 900 free within Italian cities, almost 500 in Rhodes, 200 in Albania, and about 2,500 in Slovenia and Dalmatia.[1137] When the bombing of Italian cities became more intense, the DELASEM also organized where it was possible, in Milan, for instance, the evacuation of poor Jews.

The DELASEM also took care of Jewish refugees within the zones occupied by Italian armed forces. Valobra visited Dalmatia and Slovenia three times,[1138] having various contacts with Italian military and political authorities—in particular at the end of 1941 with General Emilio Grazioli, high commissioner for the region of Ljubljana, and one year later with General Roatta's chief of staff—securing a guarantee that they would not send Jewish refugees into Croatia. He also obtained the suspension of their internment and organized during the summer of 1942, with the Slovenian Red Cross, the transfer into the Italian zone of over fifty children and adults who had been in the no-man's-land at Lesno Brdo.[1139] It is certainly thanks to the personal contact of Valobra with the military commanders and Chief of Police Carmine Senise as well as the continuous interest by local DELASEM correspondents and workers that the conditions of the refugees in these regions were brought to the attention of Italian military authorities and they, in turn, could effectively petition Rome.

The DELASEM was not directly responsible for the occupation zone in France, but only cooperated with local Jewish assistance groups that were under an Italian director, Angelo Donati, another selfless worker who gave himself completely during those years to helping his co-religionists as they were being hunted down by the Nazis and their Vichy collaborators.

33.

The Jews and Anti-Fascism

We have already mentioned the arrests of anti-Fascist Jews by the police and the OVRA—the "mop-up" in Turin of March 1934, the arrest of Eugenio Colorni and Dino Philipson in 1938, etc.—the statements made by anti-Fascists on the Jewish question, regarding the policy followed by Mussolini and Fascism toward the

Jews, and in general, the changing attitude of Italian Jewry toward Fascism. The issue of "Jewish anti-Fascism" needs to be addressed. It is impossible, in our view, to speak of "Jewish anti-Fascism" before the anti-Semitic measures of 1938, and we think this expression should be used cautiously for the years after 1938 in measuring the political positions of many Italian Jews.[1140]

From the beginning there were, no doubt, many Jews who were anti-Fascist. Jews were active in all political parties and all major organizations struggling against Fascism from its initial appearance on the Italian political scene: in the Socialist Party with Treves, Modigliani, and others; in the Communist Party with Terracini, Sereni, etc.; in the Republican Party with Levi and Donati, among others; in the Unione Democratica of Momigliano, as well as in Freemasonry, the trade unions, and trade associations. After Fascism came to power, among those who openly took a position against it—the "Croce manifesto," for example, included about thirty Jewish signers—there were those who wrote for the last free newspapers, *La rivoluzione liberale, Il mondo, Rinascita liberale, Quarto Stato,* and *Il caffè,* and the first underground publication inside Italy, *Non mollare,* that refused to swear allegiance to Fascism. One of the first and most biting pamphlets against Fascism, *La ficozza filosofica del fascismo e la marcia sulla Leonardo,* Rome 1923 [Fascism's Philosophical Game and the March on the Leonardo] was written by Angelo Formiggini, a Jew. Once the center of anti-Fascism moved to Paris, many Jews either became its leaders or were active within the Anti-Fascist Concentration that was organized in the French capital in April 1927. From 1929 up to the tragic day at Bagnoles-de-l'Orne on June 9, 1937, the leader and moving spirit of the entire non-Communist anti-Fascist movement was Carlo Rosselli, the founder of "Giustizia e Libertà."[1141] During those years many Jews who were active in the anti-Fascist movement in Italy and were in contact with him wound up in front of the special court, in jail, or sent into internal exile on the islands and the many villages where Fascism isolated its enemies. The names of Sion and Marco Segre, Carlo and Leo Levi, Nello Rosselli, Raffaele Cantoni, Vittorio Foà, Emilio Sereni, Leone Ginzburg, Umberto Terracini, and many others, prove this commitment many times over. Young and old, early anti-Fascists and more recent ones, sons of families with deep democratic roots and of families, if not really Fascist, at least close to Fascism, men of culture and of the bourgeoisie, for all of them we can repeat what Carlo Rosselli wrote in "Giustizia e Libertà" on March 26, 1936 regarding Vittorio Foà, who had been sentenced to 15 years in jail, "He witnessed, in the act, the injustice done to the worker. He saw the regime's machine function in detail, with eyes that, in Italy, it is so difficult to keep open." Our list could go on with the Jews fighting in Spain; we shall remember Piero Jacchia from Trieste, who was in favor of the war against Austria [in 1915], became a Fascist, left the PNF in protest after the murder of Giacomo Matteotti, was then forced to emigrate, and was finally killed in Spain fighting for the defense of Madrid.

The Jewish contribution to anti-Fascism was numerically and qualitatively imposing. Yet we must be cautious in speaking of "Jewish anti-Fascism." Even when it came to Fascism the Jews took the same positions as most Italians. Their aversion to Fascism, like their approval, was dictated by motivations that had nothing to do with their being Jewish. Like all Italians they were both Fascists and anti-Fascists—sometimes starting out as Fascists and becoming anti-Fascists—either because they were living within Italy's reality, because they lived one way rather than another, because they had a certain type of family and cultural background, or had certain moral and material interests that needed to be defended. Judaism no doubt did have a liberal and democratic bent that may have induced a particular kind of political commitment, but we do not believe it was a vital factor, and had it been it would have become a commitment to Zionism, rather than anti-Fascism. Even in this area it is best to be wary of generalizations. Enzo Sereni became a Zionist, but his brother Emilio—who had the same cultural background, lived through the same experiences, and was influenced by them in the same manner—became a Communist. We can even say that, for many, at a certain time, to become Zionists, even for the younger generation, did not really mean that they were completely and actively anti-Fascists, but that it was rather a way to escape one kind of reality and its national problems for another reality and higher ideals. Ideals that were just as high as those of the anti-Fascists, but a form of escape from Italian reality, and it required a certain amount of naïveté and immaturity to think that the tragedy of Israel could be solved by ignoring the tragedy of Italy and of international Fascism. Only later—when the picture changed completely and became clear—did Zionism and anti-Fascism coincide. During this first period, Italian Zionists, especially among the youth, were still relatively few. Confronting Italian reality and its problems, many who, at first, had become Zionists, and believed in Zionism's ideals, discovering those values that Fascism denied, wound up leaving the movement and becoming decidedly anti-Fascist, like Eugenio Colorni or Enzo Tagliacozzo. Therefore, we should speak of anti-Fascists who were Jews rather than "Jewish anti-Fascism."

The problem changes radically with 1938. Not that the Jews, now persecuted by Fascism, simply became anti-Fascists. Many were to remain Fascists for a long time, and many, once the war was declared, were more "a-Fascists" than anti-Fascists. The fact is that with 1938, for the first time, the persecution itself was setting them apart not as Italians but as Jews. Both Mussolini's alliance with Hitler at first followed by the persecution, accelerated the process in a short time. Significantly, the Fascists themselves understood that something had changed. Up to 1938-1939, the Fascists, who were keen on suppressing any kind of dissent, refrained from persecuting the Zionists, limiting themselves to increased vigilance of the more active Jews within organizations and rescue committees for foreign Jews, who were arriving from countries, especially Germany, where the persecution was now underway. With 1938-1939 and, even more, with Italy's entry into the war, they immediately proceeded to get rid of them. For instance, the *reason* for the arrest of Nino Contini in Ferrara on June 13, 1940—and along with him many others throughout Italy—was typical: "Known in Ferrara for his anti-Fascism, we believe he helped the Reds in Spain. He is guilty of having helped and taken the side of the anti-Hitler Jews."[1142]

By 1938 the issues themselves had dramatically changed. While many social groups in Italy were beginning to revise their opinions on Fascism because of the new anti-Semitic policy, among the Jews that same kind of revision was to take place even faster.[1143] This was of paramount importance for the Jews, who, contrary to the

421

anti-Fascists until then, no longer felt isolated, not only on the human level and as citizens, but also because of their more or less rapid political evolution. Many who remained in Italy became anti-Fascists, or at least became vocal about being cut off from the political life of the regime, and quickly found contacts with militant anti-Fascism. Even those who did not break with Fascism right away, stuck in the quagmire of ill-conceived patriotic ideals, wound up taking such clear and strong anti-German and anti-war positions that became part of the criticism and the need for clarity within Italian society. Characteristically, police reports and reports from the Fascist federations identify, from 1938 onward, the Jews as determined enemies of the alliance with Germany, then of the war and, once both became a reality, as "rumor mongers," "pacifists," and "defeatists." This explains why, following July 25, 1943, there were so many Jews within the reconstituted anti-Fascist parties and during the struggle for liberation they became a strong element in the leadership of both.

Among the few thousand who emigrated, anti-Fascism was almost a rule, even though not all Jewish emigrants became active anti-Fascists. The anti-Fascist movement all over the world, and especially in the United States, was greatly energized by these exiled militants. This was not just a mass emigration—given the size of the political émigré world—but one of culturally advanced persons, who quickly became the key leadership cadre within the new political spectrum, especially inside the bourgeois movements, taking upper echelon positions and bringing new ideas to the anti-Fascist movement, a new mentality that was more modern and more representative of the current Italian scene. On this specific issue the conclusions of Aldo Garosci in his *Storia dei fuorusciti*[1144] [History of the Émigrés] are very appropriate:

> The Italian racist campaign brought a new element to the political émigré movement. It changed the situation in two ways: it created a new suspicion on the part of bourgeois circles toward Fascism and new emigrants on the one hand; on the other, a deep change in the relationship between Fascism and Vatican Catholicism. The racial campaign was unleashed in July 1938; the first Jewish emigration be-

gan at the end of that year or during the first months of 1939 and continued to a lesser degree into the first months of the war during the tenuous Italian neutrality. Naturally, not all those among the racial refugees, nor those connected to racial emigration as blood relations, or for similar reasons, took an active part in the political struggle; many had been too intensely Fascist or still were—Mrs. Sarfatti for instance, who had emigrated to Argentina; others had only private interests and blended into the new country that welcomed them without having any relations with anti-Fascist emigrants—like university professor Enrico Fermi, whose Jewish wife contributed to his emigrating, along with several others from his institute. The nucleus of racial refugees brought renewed contact with the Italian situation to the other émigrés—for instance, only anti-Fascist newspapers published the news of the publisher Formiggini's suicide as a result of the racial laws—and a growing contribution, as time progressed, in intellectual and organizational capabilities. The presence overseas, even in far away countries such as Brazil and Argentina, of men like Rodolfo Mondolfo, Renato Treves, and Tullio Ascarelli undoubtedly enhanced the prestige of exiled anti-Fascism. Others, especially younger people, drew closer to the émigré groups and political parties.

It must be pointed out that those who joined the organized anti-Fascist movement after emigrating—like those who slowly joined it within Italy—did so as Italians and not as Jews. It is significant that in exile the Italian Jews did not start their own anti-Fascist movement but spread into the parties and movements already created by Italian political émigrés. As Garosci notes, the parties and movements that most benefited from Jewish emigration were the Communist Party and Giustizia e Libertà.[1145]

The Communists, both in France and in the United States, attracted various young scientists who did not want to follow Fermi's example[1146] and were influenced instead by Joliot-Curie; the best known example of this group was Bruno Pontecorvo. Giustizia e Libertà also attracted many young Jewish intellectuals who quickly became its driving force—for example, Bruno Zevi, who during the war years created the *Quaderni Italiani* in the United States—but through them came exposure to the liberal-socialism that had appeared in Italy during those years. As Garosci points out: "People who had been in contact with it during the times of its creation returned to GL and renewed these contacts in emigration, as Gentili did." Besides the Communist Party and Giustizia e Libertà, all anti-Fascist movements and parties more or less attracted an influx of Jewish emigrants to their ranks, and with them various radical and anarchist groups close to Gaetano Salvemini in America, like Enzo Tagliacozzo, Mario Carrara, Lamberto Borghi, etc.

The only example of a more targeted Jewish anti-Fascist organization appeared in Tunis. Even though this group quickly dissolved into a wider anti-Fascist organization, its creation is explained by the existence of a large number of Jews in Tunisia and the importance of the Italian contingent, as well as the local situation, which for many years was dominated by Freemasonry, where Jews were in the majority. Since the time of the Congress of Masonic Lodges of North Africa, which took place in Tunis in April 1930, a nucleus of anti-Fascist Jews of Italian origin had been active in the city and were openly antagonistic in 1930-1931 to the Fascist consulate because of some local problems, mostly tied to the administration of the orphanage *Principe di Piemonte*.[1147] It stands to reason that the first exiles of 1938 would join this group. Despite its characteristics, it is significant that this Tunisian group immediately adopted within its anti-Fascism, not what could be called a "Jewish line," but, rather, a clearly Italian identity. In a pamphlet written by Andrea Mortara and published at the end of 1938, entitled *Ebrei italiani di fronte al "Razzismo"* [Italian Jews Face "Racism"] this position is already very clear. The diagnosis is typically "national" "The Fascist government is striving to create ideological connections between the Italian people and German Hitlerism in every way possible to consolidate the Rome-Berlin Axis"; Italian Jews have been, contrary to Mussolini's statements in Trieste, anything but anti-Fascists, they helped Fascism at the beginning by financing the March on Rome through Toeplitz, "and today one can find among the strongest supporters of the regime Italian industrialists of Semitic origin"; "all of this amply proves that the attempt to justify anti-Semitism with the excuse of the anti-Fascism of the Jews is absolutely ridiculous."

With the anti-Semitic action Mussolini believes he can: 1. Reinforce the non-existent ideological basis for the alliance with Hitler at the level of racist barbarism; 2. Channel popular discontent into blaming the Jewish minority; 3. Prepare the country for a new world war that Hitlerism is about to embark on and that today's Fascist government wants to drag Italy into, against the unanimous wishes of the Italian people.[1148]

The therapy must also be "national": we must be Italians and fight against Fascism. It is an identical diagnosis and therapy that the various anti-Fascist Italian groups were pursuing in their own name as well as through the many anti-Fascist and anti-Nazi international organizations.[1149]

Only the Zionists maintained a critical stance based exclusively on Jewish terms, but on the level of practical action they found themselves taking the same positions as general anti-Fascism. The most typical document of this position is the pamphlet *La questione ebraica* [The Jewish Question] which we have mentioned before, published in Tel Aviv in 1939 under the pen name Immanuel Romano, but actually authored by Enzo Sereni, which was not distributed in Italy because the few copies shipped in were intercepted by the police. The rigid Zionist position was confirmed: "to prepare through the understanding of the causes of anti-Semitism a positive solution of the Jewish question." The very inflexibility of this stance explains, in our opinion, the reasons for the practical failure of Zionism in the years of persecution, both in Italy and among the émigrés overseas. The overwhelming majority of Italian Jews felt, during those years, that it was more anti-Fascist than pro-Zionist. It is no accident that Sereni and the Zionists came to the same conclusion once the war broke out, while never abandoning their ideals and their Zionist objectives, in recognizing that the struggle was first and foremost against Fascism and Nazism.[1150] Within the anti-Fascist movement, the Jews participated actively in its struggle in Europe, the Americas, Australia,[1151] and North Africa. Some played an important role in the press: in *La controcorrente, L'Italia libera, Nazioni Unite, L'unità del popolo, Corriere d'Italia.* In the United States many joined the Mazzini Society, founded in 1941 by

Max Ascoli, which was the most important Italian anti-Fascist organization in America. Some worked for the propaganda services of the Allied Forces, in delicate political and military missions:[1152] Enzo Sereni participated in propaganda actions among Italian prisoners of war in Egypt;[1153] Dino Gentili was the one who, for the anti-Fascists, negotiated with Undersecretary Adolf A. Berle and other important persons within Roosevelt's entourage the question of recognizing the integrity of Italian national territory and the precise commitment that the peace would not be punitive toward Italy.[1154] Aldo Cassuto with Bruno Foà, then later alone, was the author of the over 1,100 radio conversations Colonel Harold Stevens broadcast to the Italian people from the BBC in London.

The work done by various relief organizations was also significant: in 1940 the Italian Emergency Committee (a branch of the Mazzini Society), whose treasurer was Roberto Bolaffio, was even able to save some Jews in France.[1155] The help given by American Jewish relief organizations and the unions, where Jews were particularly strong, to Italian anti-Fascist groups was considerable, and helped save many comrades who would otherwise have fallen into the hands of the Nazis and French collaborators by managing to move people from one location to another.

VIII.

The Last Act of the Tragedy:
Nazi Extermination

34.
The Badoglio Government

T he fall of Fascism on July 25, 1943 was welcomed by the Jews with greater elation than by other Italians: for them it meant a double liberation from Fascist tyranny and from persecution. This was how they saw it, with exaggerated optimism. The director of Demography and Race, Antonio Le Pera, was arrested and taken to the Regina Coeli prison, from which he was freed on September 13, 1943.[1156] After this initial act of reparation, everything remained unchanged. Even without its director, Demography and Race continued to function and, more importantly, so did the racial legislation that went with it. Badoglio, who had previously been unable to resist being swept into the racial campaign and had voiced his support for "Racist law,"[1157] wrote in his memoirs about those years:

> It was impossible, at that time, to bring about the overt termination of the racial laws without causing a violent clash with the Germans or, to be precise, with Hitler, who had not only proposed them but had actually imposed them on Mussolini, who had declared to the Senate a few months earlier that the Jewish problem did not exist in Italy.
>
> I called several Jewish leaders and told them that, even though we could not, for the moment, radically abolish the laws, they would not be enforced.[1158]

The threat represented by the Germans with their armed presence throughout Italy and being on edge as to any action taken by the new Italian "ally," is an undeniable fact. However, Badoglio's statement does not quite describe the situation accurately enough; besides, as we have seen earlier, the idea that the persecution was "imposed" by Hitler is mistaken. There were various contacts between the Union and the government from July to September 1943, but it does not appear that Badoglio or his ministers made the specific commitments stated by the marshal in his memoirs. From documents in the Union archives[1159] it appears that, as of August 31:

> there had been only a few changes and administrative decisions, such as the lifting of the prohibition on vacation travel to certain spots and spas; the return, upon request of the interested parties, of radios that had been previously confiscated; complete equality of the Jews with other citizens in the issuing of passports for foreign travel.[1160]

Negotiations were taking place as of September 8, 1943 with the Finance Ministry to avoid any new expropriations of Jewish-owned property and the sale of property already transferred to the EGELI,[1161] and, following an investigation by Professor Guido Castelnuovo through Guido de Ruggiero at the National Education Ministry, to find a formula allowing young Jews to go back to school during the 1943-1944 school year.[1162] There is nothing besides these facts and the following point, in the report to the Finance Ministry:

> The Union hopes that in the new climate created by the return to statutory freedoms, the Government led by His Excellency Marshal Badoglio will want, at the appropriate time, to proceed with the abolition of the racial laws enacted by the former Fascist Government.

This notation does not lead us to believe that by then the Union had been given assurances as Badoglio claims.[1163] There is no memorandum from the Interior Ministry to the prefectures and police stations regarding the Jews that could, even with all due caution, be understood to request a softening of the Fascist laws. There are, on the contrary, some symptomatic cables to prefects, especially in southern Italy, showing that local authorities were asking about the problem of the Jews and were requesting instructions from Rome.

For example, the prefect of Naples on August 2 informed Demography and Race that in his province there were 29 civilian labor workers and asked if "in anticipation of new measures depending on new laws," Rome agreed that "these Jews, or only the most deserving ones, should be granted a period of leave..."[1164]

The government, which was much too intimidated to really make any decisions, took no other initiative in favor of the Jews, only individual prefects and the few newly appointed functionaries who, here and there, had replaced the old Fascist leaders. The new commissioner for the Blue Ribbon Institute, General Achille Martelli, for example, gave orders to readmit as members those Jews who had previously been members of the Institute.[1165]

Despite the extremely delicate political and military situation, the press already showed clear signs of the Italian intolerance of anti-Semitism, which was still officially the law of the state.[1166] The most open position on the subject was taken by Guido de Ruggiero. Under the title "Una nostra intervista" [One of our Interviews], *Il resto del carlino*, on August 1, 1943, reported a declaration from the day before in which de Ruggiero discussed whether or not one should collaborate with the Badoglio government, stating clearly: "The announcement of a labor revision opens a vast area. We can hope that the racial laws, which weigh so heavily on Italy, will also be quickly done away with." De Ruggiero's position followed another, a few days earlier, by Antonio Banfi, Gianfranco Mattei, Giovanna Pagliani, Giorgio Peyronel, and Mario Alberto Rollier, who on July 26 had distributed semi-clandestinely—and this was the reason for their having a smaller audience than de Ruggiero—a leaflet demanding the immediate abolition of all religious, political, and racial discrimination in the universities and asking other professors to join them, "convinced, as we are, that only once this shame is washed away can Italian universities hope to be readmitted among the universities of civilized countries."

The immediate Nazi reaction to the announcement, on September 8, 1943, that an armistice had been signed between Italy and the Allies, unfortunately did not allow the Union or those in the country specifically requesting the abolition of racial legislation, to bring about changes by the government.[1167] Actually, September 8, 1943 was the beginning of the final act in the immense tragedy of the Italian Jews.

The quick retreat and the lack of sizable numbers of troops in southern Italy did not allow the Germans to enact their extermination plans.[1168] However, tens of thousands of Jews in the Aegean Islands and the Italian occupation zones were unable to escape at that time.[1169]

Up to July 25, 1943 the anti-Semitic laws had been enforced very lightly in Rhodes. After 1938, of the almost ten thousand local Jews there were about 3,000 left, the others having emigrated in groups, for the most part to Palestine. The Germans arrived on the island of Rhodes in February 1944. Between July 20 and 21 all the Jews were concentrated at the air force command headquarters while the Greeks and the Germans ransacked their homes. Protests by the bishop were useless; only the Turkish consul was able to obtain the release of Jews of Turkish nationality, foreigners, and those who had married Turkish citizens. The others, 2,780 of them, were shipped to Greece at the end of July and from there taken to the extermination camps at Auschwitz and Buchenwald. At war's end only 140 returned.

The only attempt by the Badoglio government to save many thousands of victims of German savagery was directed at those within the Italian zone of occupation in France. The Badoglio government limited its efforts for the Jews in Yugoslavia to a cable to the commander of the Second Army on August 19, 1943:

> We must avoid abandoning the Croatian Jews or leaving them at the mercy of foreigners, deprived of all protection or exposed to the danger of reprisals, unless they wish to be set free outside our zone of occupation.[1171]

Badoglio authorized the army to "examine benevolently" individual cases and give every Jew the opportunity to "decide his position according to his own personal situation within the limitations of present conditions" and asked military authorities on the spot to study, as soon as possible, the transfer to Italian territory of the Jews interned at Arbe [Rab]. In practical terms this order meant that on September 8, 1943 the Jews who were interned were set

430

free to try and save themselves by linking up, as many were, in fact, able to do, with Tito's partisan forces.

Attempts to save the Jews in the Italian zone in France were more extensive. The measures taken since the end of 1942 were for the most part the initiative of Angelo Donati. Originally from Modena, he had been a liaison officer with the French army during the First World War; he moved to France after that war, where he had been one of the founders of the French-Italian bank. Since 1933 he had been active in assisting refugees from Germany. Donati dedicated himself completely to this activity in 1940, giving it all his resources and energies. When the Vichy government decided, as we have shown, to follow German orders even within the Italian zone of occupation, Donati, along with the Capuchin monk Benoît-Marie (Father Benedetto), was given permission from Italian civilian and military authorities to request the rapid intervention of the Italian government. During the months that followed, Donati collaborated closely with Commissioner Lospinoso for the transfer of part of the refugees from the coastal area to the Alps. After July 25, 1943 he traveled to Rome several times to negotiate with the Italian government, the Vatican, the British and American representatives to the Holy See, to permanently save the thousands of his co-religionists who were crowding the Italian zone. The Foreign Ministry examined three possibilities of providing help: either transfer all the Jewish refugees to Corsica, or transfer them to Italy, or to not oppose their entry into Italy if they arrived on their own. Of the three, the first possibility was discarded because it would certainly have brought about the opposition of Vichy, and the second because it would provoke the Germans; the third was finally agreed to.[1172] This decision, taken on August 28, was transmitted to the Italian civilian and military authorities in France on September 7, informing them that they could "send to Italy those persons who can justifiably be given Italian nationality, even though it is not certifiably the case"; "as to the others…it would be desirable for them to be transferred into the zone of occupation of our troops [therefore, given the Italian-German agreement of those days, to the east of the Tinea-Var line], giving them every possible assistance."[1173]

While he was taking these steps with the Palazzo Chigi, that would not, in any case, have resolved the fate of the refugees, Angelo Donati attempted a three-party agreement in Rome between the Allies, Italy, and the Vatican, to save their lives. During a series of meetings in the Vatican with the British Minister, Sir Francis Osborne and U. S. representative Harold Tittmann, Donati arranged for four Italian ships to transfer the Jews in the Italian zone to North Africa during the second half of September—the original armistice agreements with Italy stipulated that the armistice would be made public in October.[1174] On the morning of September 8, 1943, having successfully concluded the agreements with the Italian government, Donati left Rome to return to Nice, where the influx of Jews toward the coast had started. Unfortunately, late in the afternoon of that same day the headquarters of General Eisenhower suddenly announced the signing of the armistice with Italy. For the Jews in the Italian zone of occupation tragedy was about to strike. Some followed retreating Italian troops; a group of a few hundred was able to cross the Alps and seek refuge in Italy, many of whom were to be captured by the Germans in Florence; the great majority were to become the victims of Nazi savagery. "The 'manhunt' on the French Riviera in the autumn of 1943," wrote Leon Poliakov, "went, in horror and savagery, beyond anything that was known until then, at least in Western Europe."[1175]

35.
The Italian Social Republic–RSI

The anti-Semitic policies of the RSI, like most of the workings of the reborn Fascist regime in northern Italy, were, in practical terms, either dictated directly by the Germans or through their agent, Giovanni Preziosi.

The convention of the republican Fascist party that met in Verona and approved the program manifesto that had been written, as we know,[1176] by Mussolini, with the help of Nicola Bombacci and Alessandro Pavolini, handled the Jewish problem in a very brief

The Synagogue at Ferrara was ransacked during the incidents of October 1941.

Jews being arrested by SS units in Varese, May 1944.

The guard tower at Fossoli concentration camp.

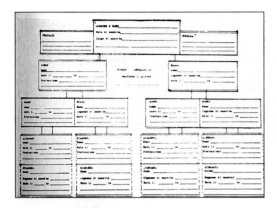

left

The "Genealogical File" Giovanni Preziosi planned to introduce, establishing the racial classification of Italians, May 1944. *(Central State Archives. Rome.)*

below

Anti-Semitism at a Rome clothing store, 1938. The sign says "Aryan store," meaning Aryan-owned.

above

Monsignor Borgongini-Duca, the Vatican's Nunzio to the Fascist government in 1938.

left

The *Gazzetta del Popolo* announces in October 1938, that Jewish teachers and pupils are barred from Italian schools.

Gazzetta del Popolo

Insegnanti e alunni ebrei esclusi dalle scuole italiane

Sospensione in data 16 ottobre XVI degli insegnanti giudei attualmente in servizio - Gli universitari ebrei potranno ultimare gli studi - I membri di razza ebraica di Accademie e Istituti culturali cesseranno di farne parte

Il Gran Consiglio preciserà la posizione degli ebrei nella Nazione

Giuseppe Bottai, Minister of National Education and
zealous enforcer of anti-Semitic regulations.

Enrico Fermi emigrated to the United States in 1938.

The most widely distributed anti-Semitic magazine of the Fascist period: *La Difesa della Razza*.

Achille Starace, Fascist Party Secretary
and main organizer of the government's
anti-Semitic propaganda campaign.

left
Pope Pius XII in 1939

right
Pope Pius XI

Alfredo Oriani, the ultra nationalist writer and journalist who inspired Fascist ideology.

right
Guido Buffarini-Guidi, Undersecretary of the
Ministry of the Interior and main enforcer
of Fascist anti-Semitic policy.

below
Ambassador Raffaele Guariglia (at right)
headed Italian policy in the Middle East and
Palestine during the 1930s.

right
Italo Balbo, one of the few top Fascist leaders
to oppose the anti-Semitic policy.

below
SS Reichsführer Heinrich Himmler and
Arturo Bocchini, head of the Italian police
meet in Rome in 1938.

above
SS Major Herbert Kappler at his trial in Rome
for the Ardeatine Caves massacre of 1944.

right
Stella Di Porto, known as "black panther",
who betrayed many Roman Jews
in hiding to the Nazis.

left
Cardinal Ildefonso Schuster of Milan.

below
Mussolini, Ciano and von Ribbentrop at the
Palazzo Venezia in 1939.

statement. Point seven stated: "Those belonging to the Jewish race are foreigners. For the duration of this war they belong to an enemy nationality."

This was a very serious statement and a moral and historical aberration, but one that, examined closely, did not really alter the position taken by Mussolini and Buffarini-Guidi during the years before and their plans to expel all "pure" and non-assimilated Jews. Characteristically, the Verona assembly, which was vibrant and given to extreme self-criticism,[1177] practically did not even discuss the point, proof that the Jewish question was not considered essential by the majority of republican Fascists, nor is there any indication that Mussolini had adopted Nazi extermination policies. Mussolini's idea, which was also shared by the "moderates," was no doubt to concentrate all the Jews and delay any solution of the problem until the end of the war—as was actually ordered by then Interior Minister Buffarini-Guidi on November 30, 1943.[1178] In their biography of Mussolini, Giorgio Pini and Duilio Susmel accurately write that the race-related principles approved at Verona "were still influenced by the war situation" and that "a later revision process would have to take place."[1179] The absurdity of the solution adopted is obvious: anyone with any common sense could clearly see that, due to the unstable conditions of the actual power of the RSI and with armed Germans in the country and in total control of the situation, to concentrate the Jews really meant allowing the Nazis to take them whenever they chose and therefore to exterminate them. Even regarding this particular problem the RSI was clearly not a viable regime and the claim made by those who created and supported it, not just to salvage Italian "honor" but also to safeguard certain Italian interests that would otherwise have been left at the discretion of the occupying power, and its anger for the "betrayal" of September 8, 1943, made little sense. What they were able to secure does not justify, even for those who were sincere in their motivations, the fact that, in practical terms, they placed themselves at the service of the Nazis and therefore endorsed their regime of terror. This being said, it must be pointed out that the Fascist measures taken against the Jews at the end of 1943 and during the first months of 1944 were not simply motivated by the need to satisfy the Germans and their most vocal anti-Semitic supporters on this issue, among others, but also by the precarious financial and economic conditions of the RSI. The confiscation of Jewish property—beyond proclaiming that the proceeds would be used to indemnify those who had lost everything during Allied bombings, amounted to a Fascist propaganda law!— was also a device to inject some oxygen into the empty vaults of the exhausted RSI. Police Order number 5 of November 30, 1943 was quickly followed by the D. L. of January 4, 1944 n. 2, paving the way for the basis for ownership of real and other property by Jews; in fact, establishing their complete expropriation.[1180] With this legal decree all Jews, both foreign and Italian, were forbidden:

   a. to own entirely or partially or to manage in any capacity any type of company, or be the director of such companies, or be their administrator or auditor;
   b. to own any land or buildings or anything related to them;
   c. to own stocks, bonds, credits, and participatory rights of any kind, or to own any other property of any kind.

The expropriated property, along with the decree issued by the relevant provincial leader and its publication in the *Gazzetta Ufficiale* was thus placed under the administration of the EGELI,[1181] so that after paying any potential creditors—including the state for taxes, contributions and registration fees—it would proceed with its sale.[1182] In order to make the complete expropriation effective, the same decree, along with a special order from the Interior Ministry, dated January 17,[1183] authorized the opening of safety deposit boxes and locked deposits at banks.[1184] These initial orders were followed on March 2 by those for the seizure of works of art belonging to Jews and Jewish institutions of any type.[1185] Using methods amounting to robbery, by December 31, 1944 the republican administration had taken possession of property, buildings, stocks, credits, cash, etc., valued at over 1,900,000,000 lire. Expropriations had not yet been completed in many provinces and could not take place in the zones of the Pre-Alps and the Adriatic coast—including Trieste— where the Germans had their own administration and prevented the application of Fascist laws. A note to the Duce from the Finance Minister, dated March 12, 1945,[1186] states that as of December 31, 1944, 5,768 expropriation decrees had been sent to the EGELI—by the Liberation the number of decrees had increased to about 8,000—on the basis of which the RSI had taken possession of land for 855,000,000 lire, buildings for over 198,000,000 lire—the values were calculated on the basis of average selling prices of 1940—industrial and other stock certificates for over 731,000,000 lire, state bonds for over 36,000,000 lire, and 75,089,047.90 lire in cash, besides other stocks of indeterminate value, 182 industrial and commercial companies which had not yet been appraised, and a huge mass of possessions—furniture, jewelry, household linens, general merchandise—the value of which could only be determined at the time of sale by the Finance Ministry.[1187] This mass of possessions obviously went far beyond the 1,900,000,000 lire specified in the note, especially when one considers that the EGELI was often unable or only partially able to take possession of the expropriated property due to the more or less artificial difficulties created by local authorities.[1188]

Besides the economic motivation, during the first few months following the issuance of Police Order Number 5, the anti-Semitic policy of the RSI remained somewhat moderate. There were relatively few acts of violence against individual Jews or groups by regular republican forces. The violence and massacres against both were perpetrated for the most part by the Germans and the many autonomous Fascist irregular formations—often organized within the German army, like the SS Italiana—over which the Fascist government had, for the most part, only nominal authority. The concentration of the Jews themselves was conducted by the prefectures and was—given the times, naturally—relatively humane and incomplete as the order of November 30, 1943 would lead us to believe. The concentration—often taking place in schools and public buildings belonging to the Communities or to Jewish institutions—did not include persons over seventy and the very sick, Aryanized and "mixed" Jews (not considered racially pure and belonging to mixed families.)[1189] Besides this, on January 20, 1944, Buffarini-Guidi, having learned that in many towns the Germans were demanding the transfer of the Jews who had been concentrated, gave instructions to take the necessary steps with the "central German authorities" that "in accordance with the criteria that had been stated, orders be issued for the Jews to remain in Italian camps."[1190] Orders to not hand over the concentrated Jews to the Germans were then transmitted to the local authorities: the commander of the Fossoli camp near Modena, the largest concentration camp organized by the Fascists, often repeated to the Jews in the camp that should the Germans come to Fossoli to demand their being turned over, he would shut down the camp—something he obviously did not do when the Germans actually did show up. In the various local internment sites and at Fossoli, life for the Jews—given the general conditions of those months—was not, comparatively, too hard. Food was slightly worse than outside the camp, but almost everyone received packages from friends and family and therefore had enough to eat. Several former detainees at the Fossoli camp do not have completely unpleasant memories of the place—there were even some preparing for state examinations and hoping to obtain a pass to take them.[1191]

The practical steps taken with the German government and following Buffarini-Guidi's instructions to province heads (this was the name given to the prefects by the RSI) to concentrate the Jews but not hand them over to Germans remained inoperative. Berlin ignored the requests, and the German commands in Italy completely disregarded all the decisions taken by the Fascist government on the issue. On October 16, 1944 Eugenio Cerrutti, the head of the RSI police, made the following observation on the matter in a letter to the Interior Ministry:

> It is a fact that, with few exceptions, German authorities proceed with the arrest and transfer to concentration camps in Germany or camps located in Italy, but under the complete control of German military authorities, of all Jews, including those gravely ill and over seventy years of age and those belonging to mixed families.[1192]

In some cases the Foreign Ministry of the RSI attempted to obtain, through its German counterpart, news concerning the fate of some of those deported. These steps inevitably yielded nothing, only provoking the anger of Eichmann's office, which oversaw the extermination of the Jews throughout Europe. At Eichmann's trial in Israel a very telling document was exhibited on this issue. The Italian embassy in Berlin had asked the Wilhelmstrasse about the fate of an Italian Jew deported to Poland; informed of the matter, Eichmann's office, the infamous IVB4, immediately reacted with indignation:

> We refrain from following up on the request from the Italian embassy to research the location where the Jew Taubert is residing at this time. It will be advisable to inform Italian diplomacy to never again put through any such requests. We require time and energy to dedicate ourselves to vital matters in the general interest. Five years after the beginning of the war, this German organization has undertaken much more important missions than that of investigating what fate befell a Jew. We regret to see the embassy of a Fascist republic continue to interpose its offices in favor of the Jews.[1193]

In conclusion we can say that during the first months of the ephemeral existence of the RSI, Fascist authorities gave anti-Semitic persecution more of an economic and financial character, while attempting to maintain a relatively humane attitude towards other matters, and trying to avoid deportation outside of Italy.[1194] Things were to change radically after the creation on March 15, 1944[1195] of the race office,[1196] attached to the Presidency of the Council of Ministers, headed by Giovanni Preziosi.[1197]

Preziosi, even though he had seen his policies succeed and had been the driving force behind Farinacci regarding anti-Semitism,[1198] had never been able to overcome, up to July 25, 1943, strong suspicion and antipathy on the part of Mussolini. He had played the role of instigator and intransigent accuser, rather than effective leader, during the racial campaign.[1199] Immediately following July 25, 1943, he had traveled to Germany and already during the night of September 8–9, with Farinacci and Pavolini, had begun Fascist broadcasts from Radio Munich. These broadcasts were to continue for a long time, even after Mussolini's liberation and the birth of the RSI, and the Duce demanded unsuccessfully for several months that they be stopped. Filippo Anfuso wrote: "Every evening this radio taught him [Mussolini] very respectfully, and the public very vigorously, what a Mussolini who wanted to avoid being betrayed a second time should do, taking his cue from German 'absolute' reality."[1200] In Germany, Preziosi strengthened his connections with the Nazis, particularly with their most extreme elements, and with Hitler himself, whom he visited and who invited him to his headquarters as a guest; so much so that until Mussolini was liberated he was Rosenberg's (who accused Mussolini of having protected the Jews)[1201] candidate to preside over a new Fascist government.[1202] Preziosi maintained that since December 1942 there had been contacts in Switzerland for a separate peace and that he had informed Mussolini in time of this "crime" being perpetrated against the Duce personally to take Italy out of the war, but to no avail.[1203] He also accused Buffarini-Guidi and Pavolini of conniving with Masonic and Jewish elements. Once Mussolini had been liberated and the neo-Fascist government had been formed in the north, Preziosi did not immediately return to Italy. He continued to speak from Radio Munich and denounce Mussolini to the Nazis for "unconscionable tolerance" toward Jews and Freemasons.[1204] It was only on December 5, 1943, having been informed that Mussolini was extremely displeased with his attitude,[1205] that he returned to Italy to meet with the Duce. Four days later he sent him three articles in six installments that he had published in October in the *Volkischer Beobachter* aiming at "explaining to the Germans how the incredible collapse could have taken place" and blaming the Jews and the Freemasons. In an accompanying letter he observed: "On this issue I feel that if we do not take the path of a deep purge of Freemasonry and the complete solution of the Jewish question, we shall have disappointments."[1206] The result of the meeting and of the two letters was what Preziosi had hoped for. A few days later he returned to Germany and resumed his intrigues, succeeding in convincing General Karl Wolff, supreme commander of German police in Italy, and Ambassador Rudolf Rahn of the need to eliminate Buffarini-Guidi from the Salò government, who according to Preziosi, was a Freemason, much too soft on the Jews, and too corrupt, as well as the secretary of the party, Pavolini, because he had a Jewish sister-in-law.[1207] Initially Preziosi's initiatives had no tangible results because Rahn had secretly informed Buffarini-Guidi and Pavolini of his maneuvers.[1208] Preziosi then decided to bring pressure on the source of absolute power itself. On January 31, 1944 he sent Mussolini a long memorandum on the part played by Judeo-Masonry in Italian life over the previous thirty years and the urgent need for a radical fight to the finish against the Jews and the Freemasons. After a detailed explanation of how they had arrived at the events of July 25, 1943, the conclusion was that the real causes for the anti-Mussolini coup d'état were in fact: "a. the failure to resolve the Jewish question; and b. the failure to resolve the problem of Freemasonry within the state and party." The Preziosi memorandum also proposed future action to be taken. Quoting from *Mein Kampf* he wrote:

> The first task is not to create a national constitution of the state, but to eliminate the Jews. As it often happens in history, the main difficulty is not in creating a new state of affairs, but to make room for them.

Preziosi continued in his own words:

> The first task is not the so-called "national harmony" that others are blabbering about along with Gentile,* but the total elimination of the Jews, beginning with those, and they are many, who revealed themselves during the census of August 1938, which was never published. Then weed out the others more or less baptized or Aryanized. Then exclude from every key area of national life, the army, the judiciary, the central and local party leadership, the half-breeds, the husbands of the Jewesses, and all those with drops of Jewish blood. The same must be done for those who belong to Freemasonry.

And in conclusion:

> I wish to tell you that there is only one way to recapture our honor: absolute loyalty towards our betrayed Ally. Therefore, to eliminate all unconscious anti-German tendencies, whatever form they may take, always keep in mind that what is being built must be for an Aryan European unity that can best be achieved through the German racial

---

* Philosopher Giovanni Gentile. [NDT]

laws. To apply these laws, men who are capable of inspiring confidence are required and not those compromised by their notorious past, which is quite difficult to forget.[1209]

A serious attack, obviously, of a kind that Mussolini had rarely had to endure and that did not even spare the Duce's actions since his liberation from the Gran Sasso; everything Mussolini had done during those months was useless, according to Preziosi, if it also did not include a ruthless fight against the Jews and Freemasonry; a fight that—the call for German racial laws and the attack on "unconscious anti-German tendencies" are more than telling—could only be engaged using Nazi methods; a fight, in the end, for which Preziosi clearly proposed his own candidacy. Besides being extreme, the attack was also blackmail in the form of an ultimatum. Preziosi sent a copy of his memorandum to Hitler, so that Mussolini—Dolfin said that when the Duce found out he became indignant and furious[1210]—after some hesitation was forced to capitulate, not wishing to break with the Führer. On March 15, 1944, Preziosi was named Chief Inspector for Race, reporting directly to the Presidency of the Council of Ministers—a last desperate attempt by Mussolini to avoid losing complete control of anti-Semitic policy.[1211]

Preziosi set up his office as Inspector at Desenzano. Appointed in mid-March, after two months he was already recommending to Mussolini the first measures to be taken. The daily *Brescia repubblicana* of March 23, 1944 announced that a few days earlier there had been "a series of meetings presided over by the Duce at headquarters, with reports by the Inspector General for Race, the Justice Minister, and Judge Carlo Alliney," in the course of which had been discussed "measures of a racial nature that innovate and update the legislation in force today." The Brescia newspaper then briefly indicated the substance of the new measures: rules to determine and differentiate races; legal status of half-breeds; creation of a race commission. According to the documents that have reached us it appears that the meetings mentioned by *Brescia repubblicana* were not very calm. Preziosi proposed various drafts of new laws: one defining and differentiating race, another regarding the civil and estate limitations to be imposed on Italian citizens of foreign blood and mixed race, a third on the makeup of a race commission, and a fourth on civil limitations to be placed on all current and former Freemasons. The most important of these laws, for our purposes, is certainly the first. It generated most of the disagreements; it was in effect an "Italian translation" of the infamous Nazi Nuremberg race laws. A first draft was modified extensively; in particular, the reference to a so-called "white Caucasian race," of which Italians were purportedly a part, was changed to the more vague "Aryan race" (articles 1 and 2), and it was defined as a "crime against the race" to procreate children between individuals of Italian blood and individuals of foreign blood or half-breeds, while it had been extended in the first draft to simply mean any "carnal contact out of wedlock." The modified text[1212]—which Preziosi called necessary to enhance the "Nation's racial qualities and provide a rigorous defense against any new influx that would contaminate it physically and spiritually"[1213]—established that those to be considered of Italian blood were only "Italian citizens whose forebears have resided in Italy since January 1, 1800, of the Aryan race and not contaminated by mixing with Jews or other external races"; it established who should be considered of blood compatible with the Italian, of foreign blood, mixed and mixed assimilated to persons of foreign blood, etc.; it forbade marriage between citizens of Italian blood and persons of foreign blood or half-breeds; it introduced the crime "against the race," canceled all surname changes authorized to the Jews in the preceding years, subjected all aryanizations to review, and introduced a "genealogical file" to establish the racial category of Italians. The second law proposed by Preziosi established the exclusion of all citizens who were not of Italian blood and half-breeds from any public activity, professional and artistic, the confiscation of their real as well as industrial and commercial property, and the creation of a race commission that would establish, case by case, the non-application of these norms to the categories that had already been considered for discrimination by the declaration of the Grand Council of 1938.[1214] Despite the many changes, Preziosi's proposals were very much criticized. In Mussolini's files there are also "Some observations on the new racial law" written by Buffarini-Guidi himself during the night of May 16–17 in preparation for

441

the meeting of May 18, when Preziosi was to ask Mussolini for his approval of the decrees on race and the Jews.[1215] These "observations" are quite typical and shed light on the disagreements that must have taken place between Preziosi and the other participants. The opening note of these observations shows these differences of opinion and how far apart the positions of Preziosi and Mussolini were, in fact. It states:

> Rather than the need, we must examine the political propitiousness of issuing new decrees regarding the issue of race. It remains doubtful whether these decrees should be part of a new and real "Race Charter" or if it is not more expedient to issue regulations that would cancel some stipulations of the existing Law and integrate it to others, thereby reaching the same and possibly more concrete goals.[1216]

This preamble is followed by an analysis of various articles of the draft that is actually a refutation of the draft and the criteria underlying the information it contains; some of its passages are clearly called "aberrations." Despite the "positive" note published by *Brescia repubblicana* and the announcement of the early adoption of the measures under discussion, the meetings at Mussolini's headquarters in the middle of May ended practically in a serious rebuff for Preziosi.[1217]

Setting aside, for the moment, the idea of taking new legislative initiatives, Preziosi worked in two directions during the following months—from now on he took the attitude of someone who was being persecuted,[1218] which did not prevent him from resuming publication of *La vita italiana* in September and writing articles that were increasingly virulent against "the men within the ranks of Freemasonry for the benefit of Judaism" who, according to him, held many key positions in the RSI.[1219] On the one hand, he demanded more rigorous application of existing laws, and on the other hand he wanted to transform the Inspector's office into a super-police modeled on the Gestapo. The orders issued by the Interior Ministry in October 1944 came in response to an earlier demand that not only pure Jews should be sent to concentration camps, as had been the case until then, but also "those who were of mixed origin who have been considered as belonging to the Jewish race."[1220] In July, he brought some pressure to bear on Mussolini to persuade him—claiming that the coffers of the republic could take in three or even five billion lire in property values—to authorize the confiscation of the property of Aryanized Jews.[1221] Preziosi also sent innumerable requests to Mussolini to be given all the files and documents of the old "Direzione Generale per la Demografia e la Razza," the EGELI, the Jewish Communities, and the synagogues.[1222] A truly impressive document on the second part of these intrigues is the long fifteen page memorandum sent to Mussolini at the end of June by a certain Luigi Renoldi, who was part of Preziosi's entourage at Desenzano, regarding the tasks and the organization of the Inspector General's office for race. This memorandum was the blueprint for the immediate and implacable repression of all "the unmentionable injustices that were being perpetrated with impunity on the territory of the Republic" and in order to bring about this repression, the granting of full power to Preziosi's Inspector General's office, enabling it to have "a police activity of a very profound nature in *any* sector of national life" and to "strike at any citizen of the Italian Social Republic, without exceptions."[1223] To reach this goal, Renoldi's memorandum proposed the creation of regional sections of the inspector's office having the broadest powers and to which all authorities, military formations and police, would grant, without discussion, every form of collaboration.[1224]

The RSI took the initiative of new anti-Semitic legislation only when it was in its death throes. During the final meeting of the Council of Ministers on April 16, 1945, ten days before the insurrection for liberation, it approved a Law Decree setting forth stricter anti-Semitic laws. Once again it only concerned economic and financial measures: the closing of the Union of the Communities, and of the individual Communities, and the suppression of all public Jewish charitable and assistance organizations (article 1) were only the pretexts to order the confiscation of all their possessions (article 2).[1225] With yet another act of robbery, the curtain fell on the RSI and with it, on Fascist persecution. During the days that followed, most of those responsible for the persecution itself were to be executed by popular justice. Only Preziosi was able to avoid retribution by committing suicide along with his wife.

We have dedicated much time to the history of the attitude of the RSI, which has remained secret until now, since we consider this an aspect of the persecution and of the history of Fascism and because it completes, in a certain sense, the description we have made in the preceding chapters. Before reaching the conclusion of our narrative we must make an important point. Besides the position of major individuals during this final act of the Fascist tragedy, and besides the position of a Mussolini or a Preziosi, if in fact the RSI did have toward the Jews an attitude different from that of the Germans, in that it was without a doubt more humane and far from adopting mass extermination, it is also true that, in practice, the RSI was forced to not only tolerate and assist in the indiscriminate arrests, the massacres, and the deportations undertaken by the Germans in defiance of its laws, but in countless cases to collaborate with them. After September 8, 1943 the Nazis—the Gestapo as well as the Foreign Ministry (the order to deport the Roman Jews, whom some Nazi leaders in Rome would have preferred to use to build fortifications, was confirmed on October 9, 1943 by the Wilhelmstrasse)[1226]—decided to include Italy in the Final Solution.[1227] Fascist authorities, in words rather than deeds, held up "their" legislation in the face of the hunt for Jews that was quickly set in motion in the entire country by German occupying forces, but in practical terms they were willing to passively accept it, becoming therefore de facto accomplices in an unforgivable way. Local authorities, civilian and military, both regular and, most of all, the semi-official ones, participated in the hunt for the Jews on a vast scale, even though this went beyond the laws and instructions of the republican government and the fact that the Germans had only one fate in store for those captured: death. Some prefectures and commanders executed the orders from the Germans with an almost incredible zeal made up of fanaticism, lust for violence, greed (the Germans paid a "premium" for every captured Jew, and in the confusion of the arrests and searches, some of the valuables found often became the booty of those who made the arrests)[1228] and the desire to look good. There are similar cases among civilians as well; if the overwhelming majority of the Italians in the north gave the Jews who were being hunted every kind of assistance at the risk of their own lives, many would be imprisoned and shot for these "crimes";[1229] there were also cases of the most abject denunciations and of participation of civilians in the hunt for Jews initiated by the Germans. At Adolf Eichmann's trial in Jerusalem it was stated: "every Italian Jew who survived owes his life to the Italians." This statement can only fill us with joy and satisfaction and lead us to better measure the abyss into which the Nazis and the Fascists would have thrown Italy. It will not make us forget that there was, in 1944, in Venice, a center for the study of the Jewish problem in line with Preziosi, that a magazine like *Italia e Civiltà* was published in Florence in which, despite its pseudo-Christian name, anti-Semitism was very much present,[1230] that anti-Semitism had many supporters within the RSI, and that the Germans found a whole series of collaborators in Italy, voluntary and not, to carry out their extermination plans. Even when there was not enthusiastic collaboration it is a fact that the police, the carabinieri, and the army, except in a few cases, were to passively execute the orders issued by the German commands, making arrests, participating in mop-up operations, and handing over Jews. The traces of this collaboration are many and remain in the memory of the survivors and of those who witnessed them, but also in hundreds of documents indicating without a doubt or justification that soldiers and functionaries of the RSI collaborated on a huge scale in the hunting down and, therefore, in the extermination of thousands of Jews. What is particularly noteworthy are the dozens and dozens of transfer papers showing how the Germans used the carabinieri and the Italian police on a regular basis to transfer the Jews into the various concentration camps, especially to Fossoli, which became, after the Germans took over its control at the beginning of 1944, the most important assembly point before transfer to the extermination camps in Germany and Poland. According to the recorded testimony of Herbert Kappler in Rome, made for the Eichmann trial, after October 1943 all the arrests of Jews were carried out not by Germans but by Italians.

Having taken the path of the alliance with Germany and of war, Fascism went all the way, from one degradation to another and from one crime to the next. Given the premises, as absurd and monstrous even for some top Fascist leaders, could the tragic epilogue, the bloody outcome couldn't have been any different. Anti-Semitic persecution was but one, even though it was the most horribly obvious, aspect of the tragedy. To say that up to July 25, 1943 the persecution was "benign" at least by comparison to what was happening in other countries, to say the government of the RSI itself tried to keep it from worsening, to say that the violence and exterminations were perpetrated or at least ordered by the Germans, to say that the great majority of Italians always deplored this violence and these exterminations—all of this is true. But these truths do not make the persecution any less heinous, and in a certain sense they increase its moral more than material significance and demonstrate how Fascism threw Italy into a moral and material abyss from which there was no exit, except through still worse degradation; a darkness into which Fascism pushed Italy not only because of the irresponsibility and unconscionable behavior of its leaders, as some would say, nor, as others say, because every other path had been closed due to the egoism and myopia of the democracies. The democracies do have a responsibility for what happened in Europe and the world between the two world wars, just as precise responsibility must be laid on their doorstep for the extermination of over six million Jews by the Nazis.[1231] Fascism's tragic end was contained in very origins and its own logic, within its anti-democratic tendencies and the suppression of freedom, its lack of respect for the most elementary values of humanity, its conviction of being the sole and unique representative of the destiny and true will of the Italian people. From such foundations Fascism could have one end result in responding to the appeal of Nazism, which also had its roots in anti-democratic and anti-liberal ideas as well as the conviction of representing the only truth. In a certain sense it can be said that, starting from such origins, the tragedy of the Italian Jews originated from the beginning within Fascism itself, not because there was in Fascism at the start some elementary anti-Semitism (and there were anti-Semites among its leaders), but because Fascism had no respect whatsoever for anything not identified to it, even morally. Mussolini sacrificed the Italian Jews on the altar of the alliance with Hitler without giving it much thought, even though he did not really believe in their guilt, committing a crime perhaps even more morally revolting than that committed by the Nazis, who at least believed in the guilt of the Jews; he sacrificed the Jews to Hitler and he would have sacrificed something else had he become Stalin's ally. As Hitler's ally he played the role of the anti-Semite:

> had circumstances taken me to a Rome-Moscow axis rather than a Rome-Berlin axis, I probably would have prepared the Italian workers, dedicated to their work as they are with such briskness and yet with a detachment that the racists would call Mediterranean, for the same joke of Stakhanovite ethics and the happiness they represent. And in this case as well they would have been an obvious but inexpensive pawn...[1232]

Is it not difficult to imagine how, coming from a man capable of thinking up such colossal madness, Italy survived anti-Semitic persecution and everything else? The tragic epilogue of Fascism was, we repeat, contained in its very origins. Piero Caleffi, in thinking about the inhuman horror of the Nazi extermination camps has written very perceptively:

> It was as if the satanic inventors of this world, which was cut off from the real world, were the instruments of superhuman logic, answering to a pitiless god intent on thinning out a guilty and unhappy humanity, too populous to still be obedient and resigned to its fate. But never before had the connection between my first sentencing and the humiliating beatings in Italy in 1923 during the initial Fascist reaction and the frightening world I was now living in appeared so close.
>
> Consciously or not, the Fascists had been ahead of their time as far as extermination camps were concerned.[1233]

36.

Hunting Down the Jews

After the initial moments of chaos and confusion caused by the armistice of September 8, 1943 and once the front had stabilized to the south of Rome, the Germans began immediately, between September and October, to hunt down the Jews. Undertaken with typical German thoroughness and in many locations with the help of the lists of Jews that had been established after 1938 by the police precincts and periodically brought up to date by requests from Demography and Race, this hunt at once took on characteristics of extreme cruelty and sealed the fate of thousands of Jews. In many towns the Germans did the hunting themselves, in others they used Fascist units, in still others they simply "took custody" of Jews who had been interned by the Fascists and who in many cases had presented themselves on their own in response to the orders posted by the Germans, the posting being among the most typical and dramatic occurrences of those first months following September 8, 1943. Many Jews continued to believe, even after the armistice, that the kind of excesses done to them in other countries would never take place in Italy. "Such things just don't happen in Italy" was the statement that went around in those days. The manner in which the persecution had taken place until then, the presence of the Vatican, and the new laws and those reconfirmed by the RSI with their many exceptions and their apparent humanity, gave hundreds and hundreds of Jews an initial moment of illusion. The testimony of an Italian witness at the Eichmann trial is typical. Answering the question if in September 1943 she had any idea as to the fate of the Jews under the Germans and what her reactions were to the news of deportations being broadcast by Radio London, she said:

> We still hoped that this was mostly propaganda, and at the same time we thought that the position of the Jews in Italy was unique and that certain things could not happen here. Actually we had already seen how, during the Fascist regime, in spite of anti-Jewish legislation, we

could find a way of living and hoped that this would continue afterwards. Not only that: some of us thought that due to the various discriminations we had benefited from under Fascism, we would continue to benefit from the same discriminations under the German regime.[1234]

Until they actually saw proof of what the Germans intended to do, many hundreds of Jews remained confidently at home, disbelieving even the advance signals of the tragedy to come. Having seen that the Germans, and in some cases the Fascists, at Ancona for example,[1235] were demanding ransoms in exchange for immunity—the case of Rome was only the most glaring among many—a lot of Jews believed that all one had to do was pay to save one's life. Today, years later and knowing how events were to unfold, it is inconceivable that so many Jews were seized by the Germans when they had many opportunities to save themselves or at least attempt to do so. A few extreme, but no less significant, cases will illustrate how confident so many were at the beginning. At Ferrara the Fascists concentrated the "pure" Jews in one wing of the prison, those falling into the category to be interned by the RSI. During a bombing raid the building was damaged and the Jews left, but once the raid was over they all returned to the prison and reported back to the Fascists, so that a modus vivendi was established: when the Allies were bombing the Jews could seek refuge where they wished, and afterwards they would come back. Very few took advantage of this situation to escape; most of them were careful to respect the "agreement" and were later interned at Fossoli. As long as Fossoli was managed by the Fascists it did not have such a bad reputation; at Ferrara, when it was known that the Jews were being transferred there, some "mixed race" persons who had been excluded from internment by the laws of the RSI did everything they could to be taken to Fossoli, where things were better and there was no risk of bombing.

Panic and terror struck everyone only after the first large-scale raids and the first massacres.[1236] But it was much too late. In Rome alone those taken in raids were over two thousand (2,091). Venice, Genoa, Fiume, and Florence each gave over two hundred victims to the Nazi concentration camps. The total number of those deported from Italy between 1943 and 1945 was 7,495.[1237] Of these only 610 were able to return from the hell of the Lager; 6,885 died in captivity.

To these 6,885 victims of Nazi savagery must be added the 75 Jews murdered in cold blood at the Ardeatine Caves in Rome on March 24, 1944, who represented every social class and condition, sex and age, young boys and old men, and many other victims of the executions undertaken by the Nazis and the Fascists during those years.[1238] Many others were murdered during raids not because they tried to escape but out of sheer cruelty. The most horrible instances were those of September-October 1943 on Lake Maggiore and Val d'Aosta. Many Jews had sought shelter there simply as refugees, as well as to escape from the Nazis and the Fascists. Having been informed, the Germans organized a series of raids. Many Jews were captured. Nazi butchery reached its peak in the areas of Arona, Meina and Intra: the Jews captured were not even deported, but with hands and feet tied were drowned in the lake. In the following days about twenty bodies were recovered that could not all be identified because many of the Jews in hiding were Greeks with no family in Italy, and those who could escape the massacre scattered out into the area—among these victims were the writer Sabatino Lopez and Commander Federico Jarach.[1239] A similar and possibly even more horrible case took place at Gressoney. The family of Ettore Ovazza was in hiding, consisting of the former editor of _La nostra bandiera_, his wife, and his fifteen-year-old daughter—another son had been killed and robbed by a guide who was supposed to get the boy into Switzerland and seems to have tipped off the Germans about the hiding place of the whole family. On October 9, 1943 the Germans surprised the Ovazza family, arresting them and locking them up in the local schoolhouse where they were murdered two days later, their still-live bodies incinerated in the boiler of the heating system. These were, we repeat, only some of the more sensational among many such cases. We could also mention the massacre of the "Pardo house" on August 1, 1944 at Pisa, in which the Germans murdered seven other Jews.

The largest such raid, at least in number of victims, was the well-known action in Rome described by Giacomo De Benedetti in a short book appropriately entitled *October 16, 1943*. Besides being the largest, it is for our study quite typical and illustrates Nazi methods applied to a single situation that was to be repeated in many smaller towns: first, trick the Jews into believing that by paying they could save their own lives, then deport them while at the same time grabbing all their valuables.[1240]

From September 8-25, 1943 the Jews of Rome were not harmed. As Ugo Foà wrote: "They were beginning to secretly hope that the excesses the Germans had engaged in against their brothers in faith in other countries previously invaded would not be repeated in Rome." Suddenly, on September 26, Union President Almansi and the president of the Community Foà were summoned to the German embassy by the police commander, the infamous SS Major Herbert Kappler, "for communications." Kappler received the two personally; at first he was friendly, then he became tougher and said:

> You and your co-religionists are Italian nationals, but that is of no consequence to me. We Germans consider you only as Jews and therefore as our enemy. Rather, to be more precise, we consider you a distinct group, but not completely apart from the worst enemies against whom we are fighting. And this is how we shall treat you. But we shall not take your lives nor your children if you agree to our requests. It is your gold that we want, to buy more weapons for our country. Within 36 hours you must pay 50 kilograms to me. If you deliver it, no harm shall come to you. If you don't, 200 among you will be taken and deported to Germany to the Russian border or otherwise be rendered harmless.

Any attempt at discussion by Almansi and Foà was useless. They asked whether the threatened measures applied only to the Jews who were listed as members of the Community or also those dissociated, baptized, those of "mixed race"; Kappler answered unhesitatingly: "I make no differences between one Jew and another. Whether they are on the Community lists or dissociated, baptized, or mixed, all those with a drop of Jewish blood are the same to me. They are all enemies."

The only concession he agreed to was about the payment: besides gold he would be ready to accept sterling and dollars, but not Italian lire: "I don't know what to do with your currency, I can print as much of it as I want." After the meeting with Kappler, the two presidents attempted to convince the Italian police authorities to step in and mediate, but neither the general director of Public Security, police headquarters, nor Demography and Race wanted to handle the matter. The collection of the gold began immediately.

They tried to inform as many Jews as possible, and the news was spread by word of mouth throughout the city. At first, fearing they could not assemble the entire amount of gold demanded, it was decided to buy part of it—this was the only form of cooperation given by Italian authorities, who authorized the purchase of gold even though it was forbidden—and one of the organizers of the gathering of the gold, Renzo Levi, asked the vice abbot of the Sacred Heart, Father Borsarelli, to find out, if time made it impossible to deliver the full amount, whether the Holy See would be amenable to lending the difference. The Holy See answered that it would be ready to give the balance of gold required and that the Community should not worry about repayment, which could take place at a later date when it was able do so. In the end there would be no need for the help of the Holy See. Hundreds of Jews and even non-Jews, among them some priests, answered the call of the Community without hesitation. At the end of the time limit set by the Nazis, almost eighty kilograms of gold—the difference was hidden and used after the war to help create the State of Israel—had been collected, mostly consisting of rings, necklaces, and other small gold objects that were everything the poor families of the Roman ghetto owned, but there were also some very large donations. The gold was then taken to Via Tasso on September 28. The Italian police provided an escort for the transportation upon request from the Union, and Police Commissioner Cappa of Demography and Race was also present at the delivery, in civilian clothes, among the workmen who were carrying boxes full of gold. When the time came to weigh the gold, five kilos at a time, a Captain Schutz, on the German side, attempted to cheat on the weight, saying that the gold totaled 45 kilograms and 300 grams rather than 50 kilograms and 300 grams; only because of complaints from Almansi and Foà did they finally acknowledge that the amount was correct, but they refused to issue any kind of receipt for the delivery.

Once in possession of the gold the Germans began enacting the second part of their criminal plans. On the morning of September 29, the day after the gold was delivered, they blocked the entrance to the Community and a group of officers who were experts in the Hebrew language began a detailed search of the premises. They removed 2,021,540 lire from the safe, as well as all the documents it contained. During the following days and until October 13, the Germans came back to the synagogue and to the Community several times, attempting to gather information regarding the wealthiest Jews and looking over the extremely valuable library collection. Fearing with good reason that the Germans wanted to take the books, a collection of immense historical and commercial value, the president of the Union, Almansi, warned the General Director of Libraries and the Ministry of the Interior, the Director of Religious Affairs, the Director General of Public Security, and the Director of Civilian Administration on October 11 that this danger existed but no one came forward to save the treasure. And so on October 13 the Germans—having returned in strength—were able to take, completely undisturbed, all the books belonging to the Community and the Rabbinical College. After plundering these valuables the Germans began the last phase of their plan, which was not to be carried out by Kappler and the army, who it appears were against it, but by three special police units sent to Rome for this purpose under the direct command of Captain Theodor Dannecker, one of Eichmann's most brutal lieutenants.

At dawn on October 16, German police surrounded the ghetto and systematically grabbed all the Jews living there, sparing no one.[1241] "Neither sex, nor age, nor poor health, nor honorary titles of any kind were of any protection against such barbaric actions: old people, children, the seriously ill, people who were near death, pregnant women or women who had just given birth, all were taken away indiscriminately." With guns drawn and on the basis of detailed lists of names, the Germans searched all the houses within the ghetto, while others broke into many residential buildings outside the ghetto area all around the city. "All morning the wave of terror covered all of Rome with the anguish that followed the black and sinister vehicles of plunder." This is how the plunder was described in the official report signed by Kappler from Rome via radio to SS General Karl Wolff:

> Today we started and concluded the anti-Jewish action, following the plan prepared in this office allowing us to take advantage of the situation. We have used all the units of the security and special police at our disposal. Due to our complete lack of confidence in the Italian police for such an action, it was not possible to have it participate. We could therefore only undertake individual arrests through 26 neighborhood actions in immediate succession. It was not possible to completely isolate some streets, both due to the requirement to maintain the status of Open City, and, most of all, due to the insufficient number of German policemen, totaling 365. In spite of this, during the action that lasted from 05:30 to 14:00 arrests were made in Jewish residences of 1,259 individuals who were taken to the assembly point at the Military School. After having freed the persons of mixed race and foreigners, including one citizen of the Vatican, the families of mixed marriages, including the Jewish spouse, Aryan domestic servants and those who were subletting, we were left with 1,007 Jews. The transport is scheduled for Monday, October 18 at 9.
>
> They will be accompanied by 30 men of the special police. The Italian population clearly displayed an attitude of passive resistance, which in many individual cases turned into active help.
>
> For example, in one case the policemen were stopped at the door of one residence by a Fascist in his black shirt, with an official document, who had most certainly substituted himself for the Jewish occupants claiming he had requisitioned the house one hour before the arrival of the German forces.
>
> We could also clearly see attempts to hide the Jews in nearby residences as the German forces suddenly appeared, and it is understandable that in many cases these attempts were successful. No appearance was made by the anti-Semitic part of the population during

the action: only a passive mass that in some cases even tried to separate the forces from the Jews.

In no instance was it necessary to use firearms.[1242]

The raid continued for several days, but many Jews who had been informed were able to save themselves in time. Some took their own lives to avoid arrest, and some of those who were sick died from fear. Within a few days over eight thousand Jews under arrest were sent north and from there to the extermination camps, especially at Birkenau. At war's end, out of this mass of unfortunate people only fifteen were to return, fourteen men and one woman. Once the raid on people was completed, the raid on their possessions continued; homes were ransacked, stores and warehouses—over forty in November-December—were forced open and emptied.

What took place in Rome was only one case among many, though probably the most dramatic of all given the number of victims. Ransoms like the one imposed on the Roman Jews on September 26 were imposed in many other Communities, and the same can be said for the raid on the Venice ghetto, which took place in two stages on December 31, 1943 and August 17, 1944, even though it was to have fewer consequences because the Jews were now on the alert and many were in hiding and because of the heroic sacrifice of an official of the Community, Professor Giuseppe Jona. When asked by the Germans to produce the lists of his co-religionists he told them to come back the next day, and during the night he was able to destroy the records and warn the others of the impending danger, after which he committed suicide. The other cruel raid was that of January 20, 1944 at Trieste, attacking the old and sick residents of the Gentilomo nursing home. Here as well[1243] Nazi efforts did not fully succeed because of one man's sacrifice: Community secretary, Carlo Morpurgo, who perished tragically at Auschwitz.[1244]

The large-scale raids stopped after the first months of 1944, but the plight of the hunted Jews did not, as the search for them continued within the territory under German occupation.[1245] The fate of those who fell into the hands of the Nazis or the Fascists was almost always a foregone conclusion: assembled at Regina Coeli, at San Vittore, at Marassi, at San Saba, if they were lucky and were not placed on the lists of those executed during the periodic reprisals ordered by the Germans, such as the Ardeatine Caves, they were taken to various local camps,[1246] and from there to Fossoli,[1247] Verona or Bolzano[1248] for the journey to the extermination camps. Sometimes the search did not spare sacred places and even extraterritorial ones: in Rome a group of Jews was captured in February inside the San Paolo basilica.[1249] The most fortunate were those who, due to a local need or poor communications, could not be sent to the transit camps and remained in prison or the smaller local internment camps and were sent, especially in Liguria, to work on fortifications or road repair; for them the departure for the terrible camps to the north was avoided or at least delayed, and there was always the hope of liberation or escape. For some small groups of Jews in the region near Cuneo this form of survival worked all the way up to the Liberation; however, at Cuneo six Jews who had taken refuge in Italy from France were executed by the fleeing Black Brigades on April 25, 1945. It must also be said that if the most fortunate were those who were able to stay under the control of the Fascists, even for those in German hands living conditions and the possibility of survival varied according to whether their jailers were part of the SS, the army or, above all, the navy. German sailors in Liguria, for example, were often very humane. From the unpublished diary of two Jews from Genoa arrested in June 1944 and detailed for a few days to doing digging work near Voltri, it appears that during the absence of the SS sergeant commanding the group, the sailors, who were part of the escort, said words of sympathy to the prisoners and even did part of the work that the poor exhausted men were supposed to do:

> One of them stood guard to warn us in time of the return of his superior. We smoked and talked with them: they said some comforting words to us; we had to admit that not all Germans live up to their reputation as being cruel and mean.

Despite this pitiless manhunt, thousands of Jews were able to save their own lives. A few hundred were able to find refuge in

Switzerland. Here too there were dramatic episodes: Swiss authorities allowed entry only to the aged and those with children; often the border guards closed their eyes and let some youths in as well, but there were many cases where the Jews reached the border and were implacably turned away.[1250] The mass of Italian Jews and those who were refugees in Italy owed their survival mostly to the solidarity of the Italian population. Despite the ransoms and the reprisals by the Germans and the Fascists, after September 8 it can really be said that every Jew owed his life to an Italian. The president of the Union of the Jewish Communities, Sergio Piperno, acknowledged this fact at the Capitol in Rome on December 14, 1956, during an important ceremony in which the Jews gave thanks to their Christian fellow citizens who helped them during the persecutions:

> Everyone helped; all those who in some way could follow the moves of the occupying power and its collaborators were quick to warn their innocent and marked victims; all the friends, the acquaintances, the neighbors were quick to take them in, hide them and help them; everyone labored at procuring false documents for the Jews and derailing the searches.

A few cases of denunciations, out of greed or fear, out of exasperated Nazism[1251] or Fascism took place among the Jews themselves. One example will suffice, that of the famous "Black Panther," who did so much harm to her Roman co-religionists. These few cases of denunciation were countered by the thousands of cases of concrete and, almost always, disinterested help given to the Jews by Italians of every social class and condition. Most of these cases were anonymous, but they live on in the memory of those who received help during those terrible days when even with false documents it was extremely dangerous for most Jews to wander onto the streets, with the fear that the capture of one could lead to the capture of others, so that any contact with the outside world was reduced to the strictest minimum. Those were days when, to avoid being seen and in order not to cause too much danger for those who were extending hospitality, the Jews had to constantly change their hiding places, and in some towns of northern Italy where raids were more frequent and the search was more thorough, to retreat more and more into the mountains, to isolated areas with little means of survival. Every town had its cases of solidarity and unfortunately also its victims. This human solidarity included people of all walks of life, social and financial condition, civilian and military, often holding public office and using their influence to help Jews and partisans, and who were of every political and religious faith.[1252] The twenty-three gold medals and the hundreds and hundreds of diplomas for merit given after the war by the Union of the Jewish Communities and by the various Communities to those who in 1943-1945 helped the Jews, often at the cost of their own lives—seven of the gold medals are posthumous—are there to illustrate these cases of human solidarity. Since it is impossible to mention all these episodes we shall describe only a few. In Rome the president of the association for assistance to those in prison, Amedeo Strazzera Perniciani, taking advantage of his important position was able to save many Jews imprisoned at Regina Coeli, succeeding under various pretenses in avoiding their transfer to the north and giving them information that could comfort them and help them defend themselves.[1253] In Milan, as in Rome and many other cities, false documents and food cards were given to the Jews by municipal employees and in some cases even by police headquarters; many Jews in Rome were saved by the commissioner of the office of foreigners, Angelo De Fiore, who not only always interpreted the orders given to him with human sensibility, but also collaborated with Jewish organizations; in Milan false documents were prepared for dozens and dozens of Jews by an Egyptian, Antonio Ingeme, who had an important position at the municipality and was to disappear in an extermination camp once he was found out; in Genoa, when at the end of 1943 the internment order came from Salò, two local leaders of DELASEM were called to the police station for some "communications" and an absent-minded functionary forgot, since he was "distracted," the cable that had just arrived from the Interior Ministry on the table; in Abbazia, Public Security Commissioner Olindo Cellurale, having received the order to arrest the Jews in the area, warned all those he could, allowing them to save themselves. In Turin, Dr. Domenico Coggiola organized a section for "infectious diseases" whose only purpose was to hold many Jews at the Mauriziano Hospital. Also in Turin, Judge Emilio Germano saved many Jews from deportation by naming them as witnesses in various trials and holding them as such at the disposal of the court. Help given by the peasants and the mountaineers was even broader. Hundreds of families found shelter with the simplicity and altruism that can only come from the most humble citizens. A typical episode is recounted by Augusto Segre in his memoirs, about a brave Piedmontese partisan whose family was given shelter by a peasant family of the Langhe. Having approached this family with some fear, since he knew the risks they would be taking, to request hospitality for his family, not only did they accept immediately but, when he asked to pay for it, they answered to not even think about it: "for us it is a manner of restitution"; many years before, a Jew from Asti had preferred to sell his land in installments to that poor peasant rather than sell it for immediate cash to someone else, and remembering that gesture the peasant now wished to help another Jew.[1254] What the help from the local peasant population meant is well summed up in this portion of a report written immediately following the Liberation by the Jewish Assistance Committee of Cuneo:

> It is not difficult to imagine the conditions of refugees in the mountains. These poor people, with no equipment, no blankets, no roof during the two winters they had to spend in the mountains, would have certainly died of cold and hunger without the assistance of the local Alpine population who with admirable generosity shared their meager resources with them. The most tragic time was when the order came to declare the tenants and indicate on the door of each house the information identifying each person living there. Because of this order many had to leave the houses where they were living and hide in remote lodges, often without doors or windows, spending two winters in those conditions. The population, in this circumstance as well, gave the best possible assistance and if, for security reasons, it could no longer offer any hospitality, it helped by providing the tools and supplies to avoid death through hunger and cold to these poor refugees.

To evaluate the help given by the Italian population to the Jews during the period of the Italian Social Republic (RSI) and German occupation in Italy it is best to look at the statistics. According to the best estimates by the Center of Contemporary Jewish Documentation in Milan, at that time there were 1,000 Jews active in the Resistance, 5,000 to 6,000 had been able to enter Switzerland, almost 4,000 were already present in or had succeeded in reaching the southern regions that had been liberated by the Allies, and 7,000 were either deported or killed in Italy. The number of Jews whose lives were saved in the areas under RSI or German control was therefore about 27,000. Not a high number in itself, but a significant one, especially compared to other countries, and it can only be adequately explained by the solidarity shown toward the Jews, Italian and foreign, by the Italian population.

The peasant population of central and northern Italy made a significant contribution to this rescue operation. While there were many pro-Fascist elements among them, and many were fearful of the harsh punishment that was meted out to those who helped or gave shelter to the Jews, the solidarity of the rural populations, especially in mountain areas of the Alps and Apennines, was fundamental, because the Jews who had taken refuge in those areas were able to escape persecution and overcome the difficulties of the location.

Despite written and oral testimony and memoirs by Jews, no investigation has yet been undertaken to analyze and study the reasons for this attitude, to go beyond generic explanations of humanitarianism and Christian solidarity, constant and typical values of peasant culture, and other characteristics dependent upon traditions and memories that were particular and/or local. An initial assessment of the reasons that were at the root of this attitude emerges from the testimony by two Italian Jews, Augusto Segre[1255] and Giancarlo Sacerdoti,[1256] quite different in their attitude toward Judaism because of their ages and origins and the environments in which they found refuge. One in the Langhe in Piedmont, an area marked by much penetration among the peasants of partisan fighters, and the other in the Apennine Mountains near Bologna, where this interaction was much less frequent, allows us to identify within the behavior of rural populations the result of a cultural heritage that brought about the recognition, with shades of truly religious feeling and inspired by an elementary sense of justice, of common human values that had been trampled upon by the persecutors. The persecuted Jew was perceived as being without any guilt, and therefore deserving of their help. The only limitation, many times difficult to overcome, to putting this feeling of solidarity into practice was the need to defend their own possessions: the house, the cattle, the fields, the only true reasons for living, suggested caution and to compromise oneself the least bit possible, by giving immediate help without extending it to lasting hospitality. This was given more easily in areas where partisan groups were at the same time a guarantee and a warning. A second reason for peasant solidarity can be found in the growing intrusion of the war and a heightened feeling of remoteness from the conflict, of hostility toward those who had started it, of nostalgia and worry for the children and relatives who had been scattered after the collapse of the Italian army; all this encouraged them to help the Jews who had been reduced to the condition of desperate runaways. It must also be remembered that there was a traditional anti-German hostility, especially among the population in the Alps, stemming from the experiences of the First World War and the recent dramatic plight of the ARMIR, the Italian Army in Russia. How much weight could be attributed to a positive image of the Jew is a matter still open to research; a significant example is found in the *Memorie di vita ebraica* by Augusto Segre, regarding the countryside in the region of Monferrato, where the memory of the honesty of one Jew represented for the local peasants an example of honorable behavior that deserved to be rewarded with the same standards of human solidarity.

Based upon available information we can conclude that the number of Jews hidden within cities was much smaller than that of the Jews who were in hiding in the countryside. This comes as no surprise if we consider the greater risks incurred by the Jews and their potential hosts in the urban centers and also helps explain that in the towns those who gave shelter to the Jews had been in contact with them beforehand, knew them personally or through friends and relatives they could trust, or were connected to the resistance movement. In the countryside, on the contrary, the Jews were for the most part unknown to those giving help and a place to hide. In the cities the help given by the Church was much more important, mostly through hospitality within monasteries.

Rescue work by the various churches was truly imposing, from the smallest, such as the Quakers, to the Catholics. The Waldenses— who as long as it remained possible, had worked hard to secure through relatives and friends overseas the required affidavits for many Jews to leave the country—gave shelter in their buildings to dozens and dozens of Jewish families, and it can be said that in 1943-1945 there was not a single one of their temples that did not hide a Jew. During the regular searches by the Fascists in Rome, Professor Ugo della Seta would hide in the bellows of the church organ. More than one pastor had to run to the hills himself because he was being sought for having helped Jews and creating false documents for them. A young evangelical pastor from Florence, Luigi Santini, helped some Jews cross the lines in Abruzzo several times and from there reach the south.

The Catholics provided by far the most important contribution.

We have seen how, in 1938, the Holy See had taken a moderate attitude in the face of the Fascist racial laws, attempting to avoid appearing as a fellow traveler of Fascist policy on race in the eyes of public opinion and to be clear regarding its aversion to any form of racism, such as the Nazi variety, which could take on "pagan" and anti-Christian characteristics, and finally to defend the Concordat and the rights it guaranteed to the Church from any possible manipulation. Once Mussolini decided to pursue his policy and violated the Concordat through the racial laws, the Holy See protested against this violation, but fearful of provoking an anti-clerical attitude in Mussolini, thus causing an open break, kept its protests in very moderate terms and strictly on the legal level of the Concordat. The more extreme opinions within the Church had certainly greatly influenced this attitude, both the pro-Fascists and those who followed the traditional policies of the Church, who did not altogether disapprove of a moderate persecution of the Jews, limited to the loss of a few civil rights. Once Pius XII became the pontiff, and with the steady worsening of the international situation, the Holy See was engaged in attempting to avoid the conflict. With the outbreak of war there had been many calls and appeals, some of them quite energetic, to the belligerents and the Nazis in particular, to refrain from cruelty, injustice, and indiscriminate slaughter; the attitude of the Holy See was to avoid public condemnation and transmit its calls and appeals through traditional diplomatic channels.[1257] As Father Cavalli wrote in *La civiltà cattolica*, Pius XII had attempted "mostly to use the moral authority of the Holy See" and avoid through his firm but not public appeals conducted through the "discreet language of diplomacy," of "being accused of partiality by one of the belligerents" and "offering a new hook for the one-sided propaganda of the other [belligerent]," so that he could prevent "his words…from provoking against innocents without the ability to defend themselves, the reprisals of the angered persecutor."[1258] It is not the purpose of this study to examine whether this attitude was correct and how it ended up helping only one of the belligerents—the Holy See pursued this line of conduct even after September 8, 1943, when the Germans took control of central and northern Italy. It continued even when Nazi violence became more pervasive in Italy, reaching the city of Rome, and through the violation of the extraterritorial nature of the Basilica of San Paolo, also directly involving the Vatican itself. The Holy See persevered in its policy during the massive raid on the Jews of Rome on October 16, 1943. As soon as it was informed of the raid, the Holy See took two semi-official initiatives with the Germans, one by Monsignor Luigi Hudal, rector of Santa Maria dell'Anima, and the other by Father Pancrazio Pfeiffer, of the Society of the Divine Savior, pointing out—as in father Hudal's letter to General Rainer Stahel—that "in the interest of peaceful relations between the Vatican and the German military command" the arrests should be immediately stopped, hinting that it could not be excluded "that the Pope would take an official position against these arrests."[1259] According to a document published by Paul Duclos, both initiatives were successful: on October 17 Monsignor Hudal was informed by the German military commander in Rome that Himmler, having been informed of the Vatican's position, had given orders to suspend the arrests.[1260]

Pius XII refused to go beyond these two semi-official initiatives, to the amazement of the Nazis themselves. On October 17, von Weizsäcker, German ambassador to the Holy See, informed Berlin of the consternation the events of the day before had created within the Vatican and gave information regarding the pressure placed on the Pope to force him out of his reserve, not ruling out the possibility that Pius XII could take a strong position.[1261] But on October 28 the same von Weizsäcker could definitely reassure the Foreign Ministry in Berlin:

> While pressured by many, the Pope has not allowed himself to be dragged into any open disapproval regarding the deportation of the Jews of Rome. Even though he must expect that such an attitude may be held against him by our enemies and can be used by Protestants in Anglo-Saxon countries in their anti-Catholic propaganda, he has done his utmost, regarding this delicate problem, to avoid upsetting relations with the German government and German representatives in Rome. Since, no doubt, there is no reason to expect further German actions against the Jews in Rome, we may consider that this problem, which is unpleasant for the relations between Germany and the Vatican, is now eliminated.
>
> In any case, a sign of this state of affairs is noticeable in the Vatican's attitude. *L'osservatore romano* has emphasized a non-official communiqué concerning the charitable activity of the Pope in its issue dated October 25-26. This communiqué is written in the typical Vatican style, somewhat contorted and nebulous, declaring that the Pope helps everyone regardless of nationality, race or religion, through his paternal solicitude. The multiple and continuous activity of Pius XII has appeared to increase in recent times because the suffering of so many people is so much greater.
>
> There is little to object to in the wording of this message, in that only a small number of persons can recognize a special mention of the Jewish problem.[1262]

According to leading Catholic writers—the Jesuit Father R. Leiber, a close aide to Pius XII, among them—the fact that even on this occasion the Holy See remained committed to the same line of conduct it had taken since the beginning of the war, in spite of all the pressures the Pope was subjected to, was due to the knowledge of "the damage that would have ensued [from taking a position against the persecution of the Jews], upon the Church and the Catholics, upon Rome itself and throughout the territory that was then under Hitler's control." Rather than incurring such a risk, "for the persecution of the Jews, as in similar cases, the fundamental principle followed by Pius XII was the following: to save lives";[1263] therefore to extend to the Jews being persecuted a practical helping hand without being backed into a dangerous position that could anger the Nazis and end up provoking their savagery. There is some truth to this explanation, as it remains also true that given its universal character, the Catholic Church had the duty to help all mankind and not only a portion of it, even though only one part was the most persecuted; some doubt lingers—going beyond the human regret, so eloquently proclaimed by François Mauriac, on the part of the Catholics, of not having had the official support of Rome in their efforts to help the persecuted Jews—that, even after the methods Hitler was using to solve the Jewish question became known, and beyond the motives stated earlier, the attitude of the Holy See may have been influenced by the traditional stance taken by some Catholic groups toward the Jews.[1264] In the name of human solidarity and Catholic piety, the Jews could be and had to be helped as oppressed people; it was, however, not for them alone that the person of the Pope himself could be placed at risk (his firm attitude in general leaves no doubts on this subject) far more important were, as Weizsäcker noted, the relations between Germany and the Vatican, and therefore a possible mediation by the Vatican to shorten the war and its horrors.[1265]

The growing help, which was very important and constantly increasing, given, beyond just individual Catholics, by almost all Catholic institutes and many priests to Jews who were being hunted by the Germans after September 8, 1943, is fully within the position taken by the Holy See. This kind of help had already been extended for years in countries under Nazi occupation, such as France, Romania, Belgium, and Hungary. Beyond simply material help and the saving of individuals being persecuted, the Church had intervened, at least since 1941, through approaches made by

Father Tacchi-Venturi and Monsignor Borgongini-Duca toward the Fascist government in favor of the Jews within the territories occupied by Italian troops. In September 1941 there had been contacts on this subject even between the DELASEM and Father Tacchi-Venturi to help the Yugoslav Jews.[1266]

Prior to September 8, 1943, the Holy See, through the works of San Raffaele, which during the war was to help about 25,000 persons in need, both Jews and non-Jews, helped about 1,500 Jews emigrate by providing the required visas—Brazil alone provided 3,000 visas for Jews who had converted to Catholicism.[1267] After September 8, 1943, thousands of Jews took refuge in convents, parishes, and religious institutes in Rome, even inside the Vatican, and in other extraterritorial places (the basilicas of San Paolo, of the Lateran, etc.). There were 4,000 Jews in Rome who benefited from this help. Of these, 680 were accommodated in buildings owned by churches and religious institutes for a few days while they waited for more secure locations, while 3,700 others were to find shelter for many months in over 100 religious congregations for women and 55 parishes, institutes, houses and religious convents for men.[1268] The Franciscans of San Bartolomeo in the Isola Tiberina gave shelter to 400 persons. Beyond this imposing chain of institutes and religious homes and parishes, the Jews of Rome and those who had taken refuge in Rome were also rescued by the assistance works of San Raffaele—under the leadership of Father Antonio Weber—and by the assistance works of Ruppen-Ambord (named after Colonel Ulrico Ruppen and the Jesuit Father Beato Ambord). The same took place in almost every city, small and large, of central and northern Italy where there were Jews. Unfortunately for these other cities beyond Rome we lack detailed statistical information. We shall therefore only cite a few cases as examples. The parish of Sormano di Santa Valeria near Canzo was a long-time refuge for many Jews in 1943-1944; the seminary of Nonantola, as well, sheltered part of the refugees held until September 8 at Villa Emma;[1269] in Turin the archbishop's offices, through the archbishop's secretary, Monsignor Vincenzo Barale, helped and hid all the Jews who asked for aid; and in Trieste Bishop Antonio Santin had been very active since 1938, when he had helped the Jews and was decidedly opposed to the racist policy of Fascism, approaching General Roatta in 1942 many times in favor of the Jews in Croatia.[1270]

Until September 8, the DELASEM was intensely active in helping refugees; after the armistice its work became much more difficult, confronting insurmountable odds.[1271] Forced to go underground, the DELASEM continued its work until it became impossible, especially through its two main offices in Rome and Genoa, which also had to face the influx of a few thousand refugees from France and Yugoslavia (about 1,000 arrived in Rome in 1944). The leaders and staff of the DELASEM worked hard to assist their co-religionists and avoid losing contact with other offices. DELASEM workers provided identity documents and food cards by the thousands, either doctored or manufactured, to the Jews who were in hiding in the cities or the countryside. The Rome head of the DELASEM office, Settimo Sorani—who was in contact with the Vatican and with Dr. Cyril Kotnik, on the staff of the Yugoslav legation to the Holy See, who was giving all his energies to helping the Jews—was captured by the Germans in October 1943 and succeeded in escaping through a stroke of good fortune. Mario Finzi, the head of the DELASEM in Emilia, had no such luck: arrested in Bologna at the end of March 1944 he ended tragically in a Nazi extermination camp. At one point the Nazi-Fascist surveillance became so efficient that the majority of the leaders of DELASEM offices everywhere had either been captured, forced into hiding in the mountains, or escaped to Switzerland.[1272] From this moment until the end of the German occupation, the DELASEM was managed by a group of heroic priests and friars who kept in contact with those in hiding and continued to give them the material assistance that was still coming in from abroad.[1273] Thanks to these members of religious orders thousands of hunted Jews could still count on the assistance and care provided by the DELASEM (in Rome by the middle of May 1944 there were 2,532 persons being helped).[1274] In Rome, at the end of 1943, Father Benedetto, who had already worked very hard on the French Riviera, centralized the entire assistance operation into his own hands: the headquarters of the Capuchin monks in the via Sicilia became his headquarters; the other important locations through which he was able to pursue the work of the DELASEM were the home of the Franciscan Poor Clares nuns in the via Vicenza, the parish of the Sacred Heart in the via Marsala and that of Santa Maria degli Angeli. For his work, Father Benedetto was awarded the gold medal of gratitude by the Union of Italian Jewish Communities after the war, and many thousands of Jews have given him a place in their hearts, no less important than the one they had for relatives and friends who had been exterminated.[1275] The equivalent of Father Benedetto in Genoa was the secretary of the archbishop, Don Francesco Repetto; he also kept the DELASEM going even though his activity was known to the Nazi-Fascists, who issued more than one order for his arrest. At war's end he was also awarded the gold medal of Jewish gratitude. Besides Father Benedetto and Don Francesco Repetto, we must also mention Don Paolo Liggeri and Father Giannantonio in Milan, Don Paolo Caresama and Don Giovanni Brossa in Rome, and many, many others who cannot all be mentioned here as they should be, and with them the hundreds of humble parishioners and Catholics who in those very hard months between September 1943 and April 1945 demonstrated by their deeds and without mental reservations, what being Christian really means.

Nor can we conclude without mentioning the activity—in rather difficult circumstances because of the ambiguous and cautious attitude of the Swiss authorities as well as the hostile to non-collaborative attitude of large sectors of the population[1276]—in Switzerland, where there were five to six thousand refugees, of the committee to rescue political and racial deportees set up within the Free Italian Community of Lausanne in July 1944 by Luigi Zuppelli, Franco Panza De Maria, and Angelo Donati[1277] and most of all by the DELASEM, managed by attorney Valorba and Raffaele Cantoni out of its headquarters in Zurich. The latest research has shown how the Swiss delegation of the DELASEM, which was in close contact with the World Jewish Congress and the American Joint Committee, did not limit its activities to helping Jewish refugees within Switzerland but also helped those who were still in Italy. It was in contact with the Italian legation in Bern for this purpose and also with military authorities in Rome and the CLNAI (National

Liberation Committee of Upper Italy)—which was to receive over 25,000 Swiss francs to help the resistance movement—in order to elicit actions "by the resistance front ...for the liberation of Jews from the concentration camps" in northern Italy and obtain the help of the partisan movement to assist and rescue Jews in hiding in Italy.[1278]

The price exacted in blood by the Nazis from the Italian Jews in 1943-1945 was enormous; if it did not reach the terrifying percentages of other countries in Europe it was certainly because of this wave of solidarity, which was truly national and saw the overwhelming majority of Italians helping their Jewish compatriots and anyone else seeking refuge from Nazi barbarism in Italy, every way they could. One of the more graphic poems by Angelo Orvieto, "Il fuggiasco" [The Runaway], laments the tragic destiny of the Jews from times past, forced to flee full of pain and tears, "stunned at becoming slaves once again." An image by Orvieto effectively sums up in two verses the terror of the precursors of his own Jewish contemporaries:

> They look with empty eyes at the horror of the day gone by,
> With glassy eyes they gaze at the horror of the new day
> beginning.

And he sings the solidarity of those more fortunate Jews with their unfortunate co-religionists:

> The runaway cries. I cry and welcome him with a fraternal
> kiss,
> I mend his wounds, and ease his pain.
> I want him to stay in my home, that he rest with me in the
> greenery;
> that the olive trees and vine leaves may console him while he
> is with me.

The Jews found this same solidarity in Italy in 1943-1945, not just among their co-religionists but among all real Italians. Thanks to this solidarity the Jews could not only welcome the new dawn without horror, but just as they had felt in their flesh and soul the Nazi-Fascist persecution, they could understand how foreign it was to the Italians and could, once again, be confirmed in their identity as Italians among other Italians and see, even before the curtain fell on the curse of Nazism, the promise of a new and more fruitful life for them as Italians and as Jews. "I was born in the fervent love of Italy, I die with the certainty of hope in the destiny of Israel." These words written by one of the many victims of those dark and yet so luminous years aptly sum up the entire tragedy of the Italian Jews persecuted by Fascism, their suffering and their solace.

The Jews were to demonstrate this faith in Italy and the Italians through their extraordinary contribution to the partisan struggle. The last week of April 1945 not only uncovered a few hundred poor, brutalized and suffering bodies in the extermination camps in Germany and Poland and a few thousand refugees in the mountains, in ramshackle barns lost in the countryside, in convents and hospices, in homes and underground hiding places of old and new friends; it also witnessed the hundreds of Jews who with weapons had been fighting for months with the best of their compatriots against the Germans and the Fascists.

In many cases some of the Jews had been among the first ones to fight, right after the armistice, against the Germans and give rise to the first groups of partisans.[1279] And all this while their identity as Jews would have allowed them to easily find shelter and wait, with some security, for the epilogue of the immense tragedy and despite the knowledge that, while fighting was a risk for everyone, it was even more so for them. If for other freedom fighters to fall as prisoners of the Germans and Fascists meant almost certain death, for the Jews it was absolutely guaranteed. A whole series of tragic cases will confirm it, first and foremost that of Emmanuele Artom, brave partisan and political commissar of the V division Giustizia e Libertà, who, having been taken prisoner by the Germans and recognized as an important Resistance leader in Piedmont, was well treated—in view of a potential exchange—and murdered after horrible torture only once the Germans discovered his Jewish identity.[1280] Ada Gobetti in her *Diario partigiano*, in referring to Giulio Bolaffi (Aldo Laghi), who had created, immediately after September 8, in the Val di Lanzo and then in the Val di Susa what was to be the IV Division Giustizia e Libertà, wrote:

In the end his only crime was to be a Jew, and he could have, like thousands of others, hidden in some quiet corner, which with his money he certainly was able to do. Instead, he chose to place himself in harm's way, to organize a partisan group in Val di Lanzo.[1281]

These words could certainly apply to most of the Jews who took part in the Resistance. In their simple way they are the best praise for the over two thousand Jews who fought in the struggle for liberation. These included not only veteran and "marked" anti-Fascists (like Eugenio Colorni, organizer of the military center of the underground Socialist Party, who was to die in Rome a few days before the liberation of the capital, and Leone Ginzburg, the director of the underground newspaper *Italia Libera*, who died following beatings at Regina Coeli prison) not only active militants (such as Eugenio Curiel, one of the promising young leaders of the PCI and organizer of the underground *Fronte della gioventù* [Youth Front], who also died fighting) but a mass of men and women of all social origins and ages (the youngest partisan to die was the fourteen-year-old Franco Cesana, a runner for the Scarabello group within the Garibaldi division) many of whom had been until 1938 and later "good Italians," "men of order" who felt, like many dozens of other youths and older men, the real significance of the renewal promised by the Resistance. There were also many among the partisans and patriots who had been militant Fascists a few years before and to whom the harsh school of Fascism had taught where their true place should be. Here as well, one name will be enough to demonstrate how, in the struggle for liberation, the Jews behaved neither more nor less than any other Italians. Aldo Finzi, former Fascist undersecretary of the Interior and a member of the Grand Council, who had been arrested a few days before for having helped and sheltered in his villa on the Castelli Romani a group of partisans, was also murdered, along with many others, at the Ardeatine Caves.[1282] Once the time for decision came within the struggle, everyone found his place.

To reduce to statistics the Jewish contribution to the Resistance—besides being a difficult task because Jewish partisans and patriots were just about everywhere, in every formation and underground group, and their stories, mixed in with those of the formations and groups, would only be dry descriptions of actions and executions—would be to reduce the meaning of such a contribution by free Italians to the liberation of Italy. We shall therefore only recall that there were about 2,700 Jewish patriots and partisans, of whom one-tenth died in combat or were massacred by the Nazi-Fascists in Piedmont alone[1283]—and that five have been awarded the posthumous gold medal in memory: Eugenio Colorni, Eugenio Curiel, Eugenio Calò, Mario Jacchia and Rita Rosani. We can only quote the words written by Ferruccio Valobra (Capitano Rossi) before his execution: "I hope my sacrifice, like that of my companions, will give you a better tomorrow, in a more beautiful Italy, as you and I always dreamed of in the deepest parts of our soul."[1284]

These words need no comment and at the same time they bring us back to what we have already said about the Jews and anti-Fascism. They prove very well how in a historical study it is not possible to speak for Italy either of a "Jewish anti-Fascism" or of "Jewish resistance." As Leo Valiani has stated:

> The Jews as such had good reasons to join the partisan ranks but in spite of this they always had—in the great majority of cases—the feeling that they were fighting for the freedom of the Italian homeland… Therefore just as there had been no specifically Jewish anti-Fascism, there also was no specifically Jewish partisan struggle. Everyone fought for the common future of the Italian homeland, knowing that the destiny of the Jews was tied to that of a free and democratic Italy.[1285]

Notes

1. G. L. Mosse, "Razzismo," in *Enciclopedia del novecento*, V, p.1057.

2. G. L. Mosse, *Il razzismo in Europa dalle origini all'olocausto*, Bari 1980, p. 215.

3. See G. Modiano, "Razza" in *Enciclopedia del novecento*, V, p. 1050.

4. G. L. Mosse, "Razzismo," cit., p. 1057.

5. *Ibid.*, p. 1052.

6. Z. Sternhell, *Maurice Barrès et le nationalisme français*, Paris 1972; *La droite révolutionnaire. Les origins françaises du fascisme*, Paris 1978; *Nè destra nè sinistra. La nascita dell'ideologia fascista*, Naples 1985.

7. G. L. Mosse, "Razzismo," cit., p. 1062.

8. For an introduction to the French situation see F. Furet, *Gli ebrei e la democrazia francese: qualche libro recente* (1981), in *Ibid., Il laboratorio della storia*, Milan 1982, p. 263.

9. For an overall view, see K. J. Bade, "Stranieri nativi" and "tedeschi stranieri." *La nuova situazione nella republica federale tedesca: problemi, prospettive* in *L'esilio nella storia del movimento operaio e l'emigrazione economica*, M. Degl'Innocenti, Manduria 1992, p. 273.

10. For a general picture, see P. Hyman, *From Dreyfus to Vichy: The Making of a French Jewry, 1906-1939*, New York 1979; P. J. Kingston, *Anti-Semitism in France during the 1930s*, Hull 1938; R. Schor, *L'Antisémitisme en France pendant les années trente*, Brussels 1992; D. H. Weinberg, *A community on trial: the Jews of Paris in the 1930s*, Chicago 1977.

11. See W. Laqueur, *The Terrible Secret: Suppression of the Truth About Hitler's Final Solution*, Boston: Little, Brown, 1980.

12. See Bernard Lewis, *Semites and Anti-Semites: An Inquiry into Conflict and Prejudice*, New York, 1986.

13. G. Preziosi, "Centomila?," in *La difesa della razza*, October 5, 1938, p. 8.

14. In 1932 there were 45,410 Jews listed in the Community Registers.

15. R. Bachi, "La distribuzione geografica e professionale degli ebrei secondo il censimento italiano 1931," in *Israel*, September 13, 1934, correctly wrote that "convenient refuge was to be found in the two categories of people without a declared religion for the many Jews unwilling to declare themselves as such."

16. The general data, both regional and local, taken from the census of August 22, 1938, and the subsequent updates and statistics based upon it, is to be found in ACS, Ministry of Internal Affairs, Demography and Race (1938-43), folder n. 14, file n. 47. (These do not appear to have been published by the Fascists.) After the publication of the first edition of this book, several studies on the data from the 1938 census have been at-

tempted; particularly worth consulting are those of S. Della Pergola and E. F. Sabatello, extracts of which have been published in *Genius*, vol. XXIV, Nos. 1-4, 1968, and in the miscellaneous volumes of *Scritti in memoria di Enzo Sereni. Saggi sull'ebraismo romano*, edit., D. Carpi, A. Milano, and U. Nahon, Jerusalem 1970.

17. See R. Bachi, *La distribuzione geografica e professionale ecc*. Cit.

18. For further notes and facts see, as well as the useful L. Livi *Gli ebrei alla luce della statistica*, Florence 1918-20, 2 vols., R. Bachi, "La demografia degli ebrei italiani negli ultimi cento anni," in *Atti del congresso internazionale, di studi sulla popolazione*, Rome 1934, VI, pp. 79-157 and Idem., "La demografia dell'ebraismo italiano prima della emancipazione," in *Scritti in onore di Dante Lattes*, Citta di Castello 1938, pp. 256-320.

19. The most important groups were in the Eastern Mediterranean, Salonika, Turkey, Alexandria and in Tunisia. From a dispatch of December 19, 1938 from the ambassador to Ankara, De Peppo, to the Ministry of Foreign Affairs (ASAE, Turchia, p. 19, 1938) there were around 1,400 Italian Jews in Turkey (700 of which had acquired Italian citizenship after 1919), who held important economic positions. In a dispatch of August 20, 1937 from the legation in Egypt to the Ministry of Foreign Affairs (ASAE, *Palestina*, p. 19, 1937) there were more than 5,700 Italian Jews in Egypt.

20. R. Bachi, *La demografia dell'ebraismo italiano ecc*. Cit., estimated, on the basis of the 1931 census, that around 5,400 foreign Jews were permanently residing in Italy. Also according to the 1931 census, there were around 2,000 foreign Jews in the Italian colonies; 694 in Libya, 10 in Eritrea, 2 in Somalia and the rest in the Aegean Islands.

21. According to the 1938 census, there were 2,985 Jews that had taken up Italian citizenship after their birth, divided as follows according to their origin:

Austria	734	Tunisia	18	Cuba	2
Hungary	640	Spain	16	Japan	2
Turkey (Europe)	253	Argentina	13	Norway	1
Greece	182	Bulgaria	12	Arabia	1
Czechoslovakia	164	Latvia	11	British colonies	
Germany	149	USA	9	In Africa	1
Poland	147	Lithuania	7	In the Pacific	1
European Russia	124	Netherlands	7	In Asia	1
Romania	106	Belgium	7	Chile	1
Egypt	77	Albania	5	Costa Rica	1
Turkey (Asia)	61	Portugal	4	Afghanistan, Iran, Nepal, Siam	1
Yugoslavia	61	French colonies		Syria	1

France	58	In Africa	4	Stateless	39
Great Britain	34	In the Pacific	3		
Switzerland	27	Uruguay	2		

22. On the basis of the 1938 census, there appear to have been 1,424 foreign Jews out of 10,173 in Italy since birth; 980 for twenty years or more; 2,010 for nineteen years; 736 from six to nine years; 699 for five years; 579 for four years; 537 for three years; 919 for two years; 1,031 for a year and 1,039 for less than a year. The Ministry of Internal Affairs did not have information regarding the other 219.

23. See R. Bachi, "Gli ebrei delle colonie italiane. Note statistiche sul censimento 1931," in *Rassegna mensile di Israel*, January-February 1936, pp. 385-96.

24. The Libyan Jews, who were mainly concentrated in Tripoli and Benghazi, were the elite of the local population. Economically, they played a significant role in industry, commerce, and transport; socially and culturally they were closest to the Italians. Regarding this last point, it is sufficient to note that 43.8% of Jewish males and 29.7% of Jewish females in Tripoli spoke Italian. In Benghazi, 67.1% of Jewish males and 40.8% of Jewish females were Italian speaking. Whereas, of the Arab males, only 29.2% in Tripoli and 34.5% in Benghazi spoke the Italian language, whilst of Arab females only 2.6% in Tripoli and 1.6% in Benghazi spoke Italian. See R. De Felice, *Ebrei in un paese arabo. Gli ebrei nella Libia contemporanea fra colonialismo, nazionalismo arabo e sionismo (1835-1970)*, Bologna 1978. On the whole, the Jewish element in Libya made up for 3.57% of the population.

25. G. Preziosi, *Giudaismo-bolscevismo-plutocrazia-massoneria*, 3rd. ed. Milan, 1944 pp. 46-47.

26. G. Preziosi (*Ibid.*, pp. 49-52) reproduces (based upon an examination of Jewish surnames from the *Annuario generale del Regno d'Italia*) according to him, what the "presence" of the Jews would have meant in the administration of the State in 1920.

27. *Corriere istriano*, September 7, 1938.

28. *La Stampa*, September 10, 11, 14, 15, 17, 27, 1938.

29. A typical example of the kind of errors made with such information gathering criteria is offered by the national statistics of university professors, published by *Il Tevere* and republished by almost all of the other newspapers during the first days of September 1938: according to these statistics, Jewish university professors were 174 (out of 1,632); in reality, according to the official list of teachers that had to leave the teaching profession because they were Jewish (to be found in *Vita Universitaria*, October 5, 1938) there were only 97.

30. *Il telegrafo*, September 1, 1938.

31. In Rome, the real estate assets of the Jews amounted to around 1,200,000,000 lire; in Milan and Turin they amounted to 1,000,000,000; in Trieste and Genoa to 500,000,000; in Ferrara, to 250,000,000; in Padova, to 125,000,000; in Bologna, to 64,000,000; in Ancona, to 50,000,000; in Alessandria, to 42,000,000; in Pisa, to 37,000,000; in Mantova, to 21,000,000; in Gorizia, Treviso and Livorno, to 15,000,000; in Rovigo, to 9,000,000, etc.

32. *Il resto del carlino*, September 9, 1938.

33. A. Momigliano, *Gli Ebrei d'Italia*, in *Ibid.*, *Pagine ebraiche*, edited by S. Berti, Torino 1987, p. 138.

34. See A. Momigliano, *Pagine ebraiche* cit., p. 237.

35. See R. De Felice "Per una storia del problema ebraico in Italia alla fine del XVIII secolo e all'inizio el XIX," in *Italia giacobina*, Naples 1965, p. 317.

36. S. Foà, *Gli ebrei nel Risorgimento*, in *Israel*, 16 November 1922.

37. Regarding the "Mortara Case," see G. Volli, *Il caso Mortara nel primo centenario*, Rome 1960.

38. For an overall view see A. Milano, *Storia degli ebrei in Italia*, Turin 1963.

39. Regarding the same, see A. Momigliano, *Pagine ebraiche* cit., p. 133.

40. The number of Jews who enlisted in the colonial wars, and particularly the First World War, was remarkable. As was their bloodshed (on the 1915-1918 war, see *Gli israeliti italiani nella guerra 1915-1918*, edited by F. Tedeschi, Florence 1921). Many Jews, especially in Trieste, were irredentists. It is significant to recall that 261 Jews died during the course of the First World War and that 2 were decorated with gold medals, 207 with silver, 238 with bronze, while 28 received an *encomio solenne*.

41. This psychological attitude gave rise to heated protests amongst both practicing and foreign Jews. It seems that even those who were not Jewish were unpleasantly shocked. Regarding this issue see, N. Goldmann, D. Lattes, U. Nahon, G. Romano, *Nel centenario della nascita di Teodoro Herzl*, Venice-Rome 1961, *passim* and particularly pp. 77-82.

42. No Italian representative was present at the first Zionist congress (1897). Rabbi Sonino, of Naples, who participated in the second (1898), was strongly criticized for this participation by all of the Rabbis and leaders of the Italian community. For many years the majority of Italian Jews considered that Zionism only concerned Jews in countries where discrimination and civil injustice ruled. This opinion was even shared amongst the first Italian Zionists, who believed that their support was out of duty "in the name of solidarity, uniting the *happy* with the *anguished*, the *prosperous* with the *deprived*." See A. Fano, "L'alijàh dall'Italia dal 1928 al 1955," in *Rassegna mensile di Israel*, July 1955, pp. 264-65; D. Lattes, "Il sionismo di Herzl in Italia," in N. Goldmann, D. Lattes, U. Nahon, G. Romano, *Nel centenario della nascita di Teodoro Herzl* cit., pp. 15-25.

43. A worthy example will prove this: according to *La difesa della razza*, October 20, 1938, p. 25, in 1936, 175 mixed marriages took place (92 where the man was Jewish and 83 where the woman was Jewish) and just as many between Jews; according to the figures of the Sant'Offizio (kindly supplied by Father Angelo Martini S. J.) exemptions were actually only 44. The only analysis of a scientific nature is by S. Della Pergola, *Jews and Mixed Marriages in Milan 1901-1968*, Jerusalem 1972.

44. For the Jewish side, see A. Ruppin, "L'importanza della Palestina per l'avvenire degli ebrei," in *Rassegna di studi dedicati alla memoria di Ugo Hirsch dai soci del gruppo sionistico di Ferrara*, Ferrara 5691, p. 9.

45. ACS, *Min. Int., Dir. Gen. Demografia e Razza (1938-43)*, b. 113, folder 44.

46. *Ibid.*

47. D. Lattes, "Coloro che non son partiti," in *Rassegna mensile di Israel*, August-September 1960, p. 348.

48. The higher numbers of 1933, 1934, and 1935 can certainly be explained by the enforcement of the *Norme sulle Comunità israelitiche* that rendered the separation from the community legally possible (with the revocation of all related costs).

49. A. Milano, "Un secolo di stampa in Italia," in *Scritti in onore di Dante Lattes,* cit., p. III.

50. I. Romano, *La questione ebraica*, Tel Aviv 1939, p. 73.

51. A. Fano, *L'alijàh dall'Italia etc.*, cit., p. 264.

52. D. Prato, *Dal Pergamo della Comunità di Roma*, Rome 1950, p. 73.

53. A. Milano, "Un secolo di stampa perodica ecc.," cit., pp. 107-8.

54. I. Romano, *La questione ebraica* cit. p. 8.

55. M. Toscano, "Gli ebrei in Italia dall'emancipazione alle persecuzioni," in *Storia contemporanea*, October 1986, pp. 913-14, and more over pp. 905-16, where the most informative Italian and foreign contributions on the subject are discussed, of which H. Stuart Hughes, *Prisoners of Hope. The Silver Age of the Italian Jews, 1924-1974*. Cambridge, MA, 1983; L. Allegra, "La communità ebraica di Torino attraverso gli archivi di famiglia," in *Ebrei a Torino. Richerche per il centenario della sinagoga 1884-1984,* Torino 1984, pp. 31-36; A. Boralevi, "Angiolo Orvieto, *Il Marzocco*, La società colta ebraica," in *Il Marzocco. Atti del seminario di studi,* edited by C. Del Vivo, Florence 1985, pp. 213-33; id. "La costruzione della Sinagoga di Firenze" in *Il Centenario del Tempio Israelitico di Firenze*, Firenze 1985, pp. 50-72. Apart from these contributions of a scientific nature there are also those of a historical-memorial nature by A. Segre, *Memorie di vita ebraica*, Rome 1979, and *Racconti di vita ebraica*, Rome 1986.

56. It is significant that the assimilated Jew only felt Jewish when confronted by anti-Semites; everyone knows Luigi Luzzatti's famous phrase on this topic: "I was born Jewish and I remember it proudly every time that I am

criticized for being one, and when it puts me in danger . . . the day anti-Semitism should cease, this [Christianity] is what I would openly declare."

57. On Zionism see D. Lattes, *Il Sionismo*, Rome 1928, 2 vol.; I. Cohen, *Le mouvement sioniste*, Paris 1946; as well as, from an extremely critical point of view, N. Weinstock, *Storia del sionismo*, Rome 1970, 2 vol.

58. According to D. Lattes, "Il paradosso del sionismo," in *Annuario del movimento sionista*, I (1905-1906), now republished in N. Goldmann, D. Lattes, U. Nahon, G. Romano, *Nel centenario della nascita di Teodoro Herzl* cit., p. 21, "Zionism came to resurrect, to nourish, to guide towards freedom this nationality that the Orientals [Jews] sanctified and protected with their sacrifice and with their hearts even before Zionism, and that the westerners suffocated with all of their ignorance, so pointlessly. Therefore Zionism had to lead the lost children back to Judaism; rebuild the wholeness of the soul and of the Jewish social system; resume—after the vision of oblivion, of cowardice, appearing in one night and vanishing in one night—the story of our doctrine and of our lives. Here then is the truth that once seemed a paradox: the free Jews of France, Germany, Austria, Italy and all countries which call themselves civilized, had more need of this call to Judaism than the poor slaves of Russia."

59. On the origins of Italian Zionism see D. Lattes, "Le prime albe del sionismo italiano," in *Scritti in memoria di Leone Carpi. Saggi sull'ebraismo italiano*, edited by D. Carpi, A. Milano and A. Rofè, Jerusalem 1967, pp. 208-18; for a general view see F. Del Canuto, *Il movimento sionistico in Italia dalle origini al 1924*, Milan, n.d. [but 1972], and above all A. Segre, "Sionismo e sionisti in Italia (1933-1943)," in *Scritti in memoria di Nathon Cassuto*, Jerusalem 1986, pp. 176-208.

60. The opinion is of C. Weizmann, *La mia vita per Israele*, Milan 1950, p. 314.

61. On the Jewish press in general in the 19th and 20th centuries and, in particular, the Zionist press see the article by A. Milano, "Un secolo di stampa periodica, ecc. " cit.

62. A. Milano, "Gli enti culturali ebraici in Italia nell'ultimo trentennio (1907-37)," in *Rassegna mensile di Israel* February-March 1938, pp. 253-69; as well as M. Toscano, "Fermenti culturali ed esperienze organizzative della gioventú ebraica italiana (1911-1925)," in *Storia contemporanea*, December 1982, pp. 915-61.

63. A. Milano, "Un secolo di stampa perodica, ecc." cit., pp. 112-12, 121-25. On D. Lattes, see the special edition of *Rassegna mensile di Israel*, September-October 1976, *Nel primo centenario della nascita di Dante Lattes*, edited by A. Segre.

64. A. Milano, "Un secolo di stampa periodica, ecc." cit., pp. 112-13.

65. On this see *Ibid.*, pp. 127-28.

66. R. De Felice, *Ebrei in un paese arabo* cit., pp. 47-52.

67. M. Toscano, "Ebrei ed ebraismo nell'Italia della Grande Guerra. Note su una inchiesta del Comitato delle comunità israelitiche italiane del maggio 1917," in _Israel—Saggi sull'Ebraismo italiano_, edited by F. Del Canuto, Rome 1984, pp. 340-92.

68. A. Fano, _L'alijàh dall'Italia ecc._, cit., _passim_ and especially p. 266.

69. As a comparison it may be useful to know that—according to the _Statistics of Jews_—in the same period the number of Italian Jews emigrating to the USA was ten to fifteen persons per year.

70. In-depth studies on the Italian Zionist movement and its various components during the twenties and thirties are somewhat lacking; for a basic reconstruction on this, there is T. Eckert, _Il movimento sionistico chalutzistico in Italia nella prima metà del XX secolo_, Città di Castello 1970.

71. One must not believe, though, that Zionism was the expression of anti-Fascism by the Jews. They behaved, towards Fascism and anti-Fascism, as did all other Italians; Zionism was the political alternative for some, whereas for others it was Socialism, or Liberalism or some other party. If Enzo Sereni's case is typical from one side (Zionism as a form of anti-Fascism) it is also from another: within the same practicing Jewish family, one brother (Enzo) became a Zionist, another (Emilio) a Communist. On Enzo Sereni, see R. Bachi, "Il sognatore del ghetto: Enzo Sereni," in _Rassegna mensile di Israel_, July 1951, and more importantly, the first part of _Scritti in memoria di Enzo Sereni_ cit. Enzo Sereni does not fit very well, neither in the first category of Italian Zionists, who became Zionists before Fascism, nor in the second group where anti-Fascism played a large part coupled with Zionism: in a certain sense he was part of both one and the other. Which does not take away the fact that, in our opinion, the response to Fascism played an important role also for him.

72. On racism in general, see T. Simar, _Etude critique sur la formation de la doctrine des races_, Brussels 1922; J. Comas, _Les mythes raciaux_, Paris 1951 and above all, G. L. Mosse, _Toward the Final Solution: A History of European Racism_, Madison, WI, 1985.

73. On German racism, also see G. L. Mosse, _The Crisis of German Ideology: Intellectual Origins of the Third Reich_, New York, 1964.

74. For an example, see G. Papini, _La Pietra Infernale_, Brescia 1934, pp. 231-45; B. Croce, "La Germania che abbiamo amata," in _La Critica_ November 20, 1936, pp. 461-66.

75. G. Sera, entry "Razza," in _Enciclopedia Italiana_, XXXVIII, p. 925.

76. See _Piccola bibliografia razziale_, edited by G. Landra and G. Cogni, Rome 1939; G. Cogni, _Il razzismo_, Turin 1937.

77. F. Petruccelli Della Gattina, _La storia dell'idea italiana_, Naples 1882.

78. For an example, see F. Montefredini, _Studi critici_, Naples 1878; _Ibid._, _Rivoluzione francese: nazione socialistica_, Rome 1889; G. Trezza, _Studi critici_,

Verona-Padova 1878; P. Mantegazza, "Il preteso pregiudizio delle razze," in *Rivista d'Italia*, January 1906; L. Ratto, "Il pregiudizio contro la razza," in *Rivista d'Italia*, February 1916; G. A. Cesareo, "La coscienza storica," in *Rivista filosofia*, III, 1918; L. Valli, "Lo spirito filosofico delle grandi stirpi umane," in *Atti del IV Congresso della Società filosofica italiana*, Bologna 1922.

79. A. Rocco, *Scritti e discorsi politici*, Rome 1938, I, pp. 71, 88.

80. A. Viviani, *Il poeta Marinetti e il futurismo*, Turin 1940, p. 57.

81. Other mentions, equally vague and confused, of an Italian race can easily be found in all of the main nationalist magazines of the period (*Leonardo, Hermes, Il Regno*). See *La cultura italiana del'900 attraverso le riviste*, I, Turin 1960, *passim* and particularly pp. 422-24 (G. Papini) and 455-56 (G. Prezzolini).

82. Commenting on some racial interpretations of artistic activity, A. Farinelli, in December 1907, from his university post in Turin, said, "There is a lot of talk about races, it is daunting and continues to grow. There is a crying disgrace to some and glory to others, to the living and to the dead, in the name of race, without any judgment, with the same security of the infallible and the solemnity of the prophets, of art, of all the arts, of all nations, of all ages, also and mostly those who are without any gift or knowledge of art. And all historical events, the most intricate, victories and defeats, the blossoming and withering of civilizations, covered in layer upon layer of ruin. Every brave and every weak man, every noble and every ignoble man acting as separate individuals and of entire nations, in short and vast periods of time, everything is explained by the fetish of race, and with startling quickness. In conclusion, masked in the name of science, such an insane school of ignorance and presumption, it is astonishing that there are not more frequent uprisings of protest to condemn the infamy, and put this misleading wisdom back on its right course. (Cit. in V. Mazzei, *Razza e nazione*, Rome 1942, p. 5.) In the same period, those who also protested against Darwin's theories and its confusion between the biological element of race and the historical aspects of civilization were, N. Colajanni; for an example, see his *Razze inferiori e razze superiori o latini e anglosassoni*, Rome 1903.

83. See G. Mosca, *Cenni storici e critici sulle dottrine razziali* (1933), largely in *Storia delle dottrine politiche*, Bari 1945, pp. 318-38.

84. G. Lombroso, *L'antisemitismo e le scienze moderne,* Turin-Rome 1894, *passim* and particularly pp. 5 and 9.

85. The existence of a "Jewish race" was resolutely denied in the *Enciclopedia Italiana* (under "Ebrei," XIII, p. 329): "first of all it is necessary to state the nonexistence of a so called Jewish race or type, that is, the nonexistence of a group of physical characteristics limited to the Jewish people."

86. Among the most important statements on the Jewish Problem and anti-Semitism during the 19th century, see, V. Bani, *L'antisemitismo*, Rome 1898; G. B. Borelli, *La questione semitica e la sua possibile soluzione*, Rome 1883; L. Carpi, *La schiatta ebraica davanti all'umanità. In riposta al sen. Mantegazza*, Rome 1886; U. Dal Medico, *L'antisemitismo. Lettera a Enrico Ferri*, Rome 1893; A. G. De Marzo, *L'ebreo nel secolo XIX*, Florence 1878; G. De Stampa, *La piaga ebrea*, Treviso 1889; D. Pergola, *L'antisemitismo ed il torto degli ebrei*, Turin 1887; E. Reghini, *Antisemitismo e semitismo nell'Italia politica moderna*, Milan-Palermo 1901.

87. A. Canepa, "Emancipazione, intergrazione e antisemitismo in Italia. Il caso Pasqualigo," in *Comunità*, June 1975. pp. 166-203.

88. A. C. Jemolo, *Chiesa e Stato in Italia negli ultimi cento anni*, Turin 1949, p. 377.

89. A. Canepa, "Cattolici ed ebrei nell'Italia liberale (1870-1915)," in *Comunità*, April 1978, pp. 43-109.

90. For a general picture regarding this see, P. Pierrard, *Juifs et Catholiques français. De Drumont à Jules Isaac (1886-1945)*, Paris 1970.

91. G. Candeloro, *Il movimento cattolico in Italia*, Rome 1953, p. 167.

92. Despite the many sensational debates and public demonstrations, which had no practical outcome and of which it is sufficient to recall the inauguration of the monument to Giordano Bruno in Rome. The political consequences of this state of affairs were, in 1887, the failure of the Concordat attempt; in 1888, the dismissal of the Mayor of Rome, Torlonia, and the defeat of the clericals during the administrative elections that followed; facts which took on a distinctly political flavor, such as government measures on sacramental contributions to charitable works and articles 182-84 of the new penal code.

93. P. Scoppola, *Dal neoguelfismo alla democrazia cristiana*, Rome 1957, pp. 41-42.

94. E. Soderni, *Il Pontificato di Leone XIII*, Milan 1932, pp. 310-20.

95. On the cultural and political origins of this identification of the Jews with the revolutionaries and its developments outside of Italy, as well as the connection, antithetical but convergent, of the Jews with great industrial wealth and, above all, financial groups, which was repeated in many circles both of the left and of the right wing see J. L. Talmon, "Gli ebrei tra rivoluzione e controrivoluzione," in *Comunità*, November 1971, p. 25 ff.

96. G. Salvemini, *Mussolini diplomatico*, Bari 1952, pp. 269-70; A. Caracciolo, *Roma Capitale dal Risorgimento alla crisi dello Stato liberale*, Rome 1956, *passim* and particularly pp. 106-47.

97. A. Gramsci, *Note sul Machiavelli, sulla politica e sullo stato moderno*, Turin 1949, p. 238.

98. F. Mauriac, Introduction to L. Poliakov, *Il nazismo e lo sterminio degli ebrei*, Turin 1964.

99.   In the pamphlet *Della questione giudaica in Europa* (Prato 1891, p. 53) it is written: "To attempt to overthrow Christianity, and the Catholic religion in particular, it was necessary for the Jews to work under water, and with great stealth send others forward, and hide behind them; to not reveal the Jewish claw, abhorred by all: to bring down the fortress in the name of freedom. It was therefore necessary to undermine this solid base, and overturn the whole structure of Christianity. It is this undertaking to which they put their hand, placing themselves at the head of the occult world, using Freemasonry which they controlled." "Here we are, a century since Judaism began its emancipation in France... This emancipation was the secretly intended fruit of the revolution, which invented the famous *rights of man*, to equalize the civil rights of the Jews to those of the Christians. To this, and nothing else, the extolled freedom was being inoked for whch that formidable revolution was started."

100. R. Ballerini, "Gli ebrei perché restino ebrei," in *La civiltà cattolica*, 1892, issue n. 1004, p. 138. Ballerini was the author of the most important articles on the Jewish issue, anonymously published in *La civiltà cattolica* in the last decade of the century.

101. Interesting observations on the anti-Semitism of the Social-Christian Austrians in G. Weil, *Le pangermanisme en Autriche*, Paris 1904. p. 235.

102. "L'Avvenire," in *La civiltà cattolica*, 1888, issue n. 921, pp. 257-71 and issue n. 923, pp. 513-32: "In the transmigration of people, generally, families or races became mixed in such a way that it is difficult to distinguish between the outsiders and the natives: Not the Jew! He can always be singled out among all races, and the curse imparted for twenty centuries is as if it had been given only yesterday" (p. 258).

103. R. Ballerini, "Gli ebrei perché restino ebrei," cit., p. 136.

104. *Della questione giudaica in Europa* cit., p. 3.

105. *Ibid.*

106. "L'Avvenire" cit., p. 258.

107. The Catholic press even dug up the most absurd and fantastic stories, like those connecting the Jews to ritual homicide, infanticide, blood rituals and similar. On March 9-10, 1890 *La voce della verità*, organ of leading Roman association for Catholic interests, mentioning a request presented to the Pope by a Jewish newspaper in Magdeburg, asking that he publicly declare false and slanderous, the accusations made about the Jews using Christian blood in their rituals, wrote: "It is right to remind the Jews that in the liturgy of the Church their barbaric and superstitious practice is recognized as fact. It is sufficient to recall the cult rendered to B. Simoncino of Trento and B. Lorenzino of Marostica, both murdered by the Jews. If they have now abandoned the unholy and bloody custom, every good soul will be joyous. But, if they think to change history to suit themselves,

we must warn them that their efforts will not succeed." The same made repeated appearances, in 1913 and in 1919, in *Il Cittadino* of Genoa. *La civiltà cattolica* published, in issue n. 1023 in 1893 (pp. 269-86), an article, "La morale giudaica e il mistero del sangue," on the subject. For the truth on these "abominations" and in particular that of the blessed Simoncino, see V. Manzini, *L'omicidio rituale e i sacrifici umani,* Milan 1925.

108.   R. Ballerini, "Gli ebrei perché restino ebrei" cit., p. 137.

109.   *Della questione giudaica* in *Europa* cit.,pp. 81-82.

110.   R. Ballerini, "Gli ebrei perché restino ebrei" cit., p. 138.

111.   F. S. Rondina, "La morale giudaica," in *La civiltà cattolica,* 1892, issue n. 1022, pp. 145-56.

112.   Nothing, though, was left unmentioned even at the risk of appearing ridiculous. As, when documenting the anti-national spirit and the perpetual Jewish betrayal, they claimed that the Austrian military disasters, Magenta, Solferino, and Sadowa, were supposedly "caused by the treachery of the Jews as opposed to the strategy of the French and Prussian Armies." (*Della questione giudaica in Europa,* cit., p.47).

113.   The claim that the Risorgimento was, directly or indirectly, a Jewish undertaking, remained for a long time a trademark of Jesuit anti-Semitic political journalism. In 1938, again in "La questione giudaica e la *civiltà cattolica,*" in *La civiltà cattolica,* issue n. 2119, Jesuit Father E. Rosa, even though he makes many subtle exceptions, used it once again. As an excerpt, this brief quote is taken from *Questione giudaica in Europa* cit. (p. 60): "Mazzini had a secret love for the Synagogue, which is well known in the Capitol in Rome; the same for Garibaldi and the Synagogue, Farini and the Synagogue, De Pretis and the Synagogue; and many of those 'greats' were humble servants of the Synagogue, to whom the public's gullibility erected, and continues to erect, plaques and busts to glorify the love of 'liberty' and of the 'homeland.'"

114.   *Della questione giudaica in Europa* cit., pp. 33-47.

115.   *La voce della verità,* August 10, 1900. The same newspaper, in January 1890, when describing, in apocalyptic terms, the situation of France as victim of the Jews, gave the number of half a million.

116.   *Della questione giudaica in Europa,* cit., pp. 81-82: "Given that the age old experiment, and what we are now doing, demonstrates that equal rights with Christians, granted to them in Christian states, has had the effect of the oppression of the Christians by the Jews, or their extermination by the Christians. In conclusion, the only way to reconcile the presence of the Jews with Christian rights is to regulate them with such laws, that at the same time, will prevent the Jews from offending the well being of the Christians and of the Christians to offend that of the Jews."

117.   *Ibid.,* pp. 82, note 83.

118. "La dispersione di Israello pel mondo moderno," in *La civiltà cattolica*, 1897, issue n. 1125, pp. 267-71.

119. *La voce della verità*, February 21, March 27, April 2, 1890; *La civiltà cattolica*, 1897, issue n. 1125, *La dispersione di Israello ecc.*, cit.

120. *Della questione giudaica in Europa*, cit., p. 73.

121. *Unità cattolica*, December 14, 1889.

122. For an example, see the article by A. Frank, "La situazione morale degli Israeliti en Europa," in *Rassegna nazionale* of July 1883, and the editorial "L'ordine del giorno dell'associazione costituzionale di Milano," of January 1890.

123. Franz Graf von Kuefstein, *La questione degli Ebrei e Israele nella Società cristiana*.

124. Idem., *Israele nella Società cristiana* cit., pp. 318-19.

125. *Ibid.*, pp. 306-17.

126. *Ibid.*, p. 299: "Another thing to note is that in those countries in which there are more or less large numbers of Jews, where some Christians take advantage of the actual economic situation to grow rich rapidly, with means, that can be in contradiction with Christian morals, one finds all of the rancor of the lower social classes against what is called wealth. And in this, it is more the fact in itself that they want to destroy, than the actual individuals who are the proprietors and the manipulators of this given thing, capital."

127. F. Di Kuefstein, *Israele nella Società cristiana* cit., p. 293.

128. For some information relative to this period, see A. Zussini, *Luigi Caissotti di Chiusano e il movimento cattolico dal 1896 al 1915*, Turin 1965, pp. 22-24; L. Ganapini, *Il nazionalismo cattolico. I cattolici e la politica estera in Italia dal 1871 al 1914*, Bari 1970, pp. 121, 141-143.

129. Typical examples of this new position are articles which appeared in a Catholic weekly in the Lazio region, *La difesa del popolo*, edited by U. Tupini: "Una battaglia perduta," signed P. Campilli, July 2, 1911 and the anonymous paragraph "Patriottismo ebraico," December 8, 1912.

130. To take only one example, *La civiltà cattolica* 1922, issue n. 1736, "La Rivoluzione mondiale e gli Ebrei," published a "statistic" showing that the Bolshevik leadership, 447 Soviet state officials out of 545 and 17 People's Commissar out of 21, were Jews. From which it was concluded that it was a "Jewish Communist Republic," based on the doctrine that only "the perversion of a Semite imagination" could understand, overturning all the traditions of mankind.

131. *Acta Apostolicae Sedis*, April 2, 1928.

132. *La civiltà cattolica* (1928, issue n. 1870, "Il pericolo giudaico e gli Amici di Israele") commenting on the action and taking a position against the complaints and the uncertainties that this had provoked, explicitly stated that society had degenerated. Falling into "debauchery" and "deviations"; as

well as once again condemning anti-Semitism in its most violent and obvious aspects (and quoting, regarding this, the *Protocols*, that at this stage were already discredited internationally). And did not miss the opportunity to regret the good times of the ghettos and to restate his intolerance: "But, returning to the point the document is making, the Jewish peril, threatens the entire world with its ruinous infiltration and its evil meddling, particularly in Christian populations, and more especially still, Catholics and Latin peoples, where the folly of old liberalism has mainly favored the Jews, whilst it persecuted the Catholics and above all, the devoutly religious. The danger remains, growing each day; and it is to the credit of our magazine—we may say so in all sincerity—to have constantly reported, right from the beginning, and gradually documenting, with real proof justifying the facts, the frequent and undeniable alliance with Freemasonry, the Carbonari movement, or other sects and cliques, camouflaged in patriotic appearances, but in truth fluctuating, or dedicated to the secret purpose of overthrowing contemporary society, religious or civil."

133.   A. Rocco, *Scritti e discorsi politici* cit., I, p. 88.

134.   A. Oriani, in *Il resto del carlino* January 31, 1904, reproduced in *Fuochi di bivacco*, Bari 1918, pp. 191-95.

135.   P. Orano tried to determine and explain, from a historical point of view, these Jewish "characteristics" and prove that they were opposed to the Christian and Roman spirit, in *Il problema del Cristianesimo* (Rome 1895) more familiarly known under the new title, *Cristo e Quirino*. In these books, which were even considered pro-Jewish (Orano was even more explicitly pro-Jewish in a letter to the lawyer Raffaele Ottolenghi, published in *Il Corriere israelitico* May 31, 1905, in which he said to have understood the vital force of Judaism and to have "a burning desire to contribute to the full, and final emancipation of this marvelous race in their current struggle"), Orano "demonstrates" why the Jews were congenitally pessimistic, frightened by death, afflicted with a sense of guilt, mysticism, etc. and consequently potential democrats and socialists, and also why their contribution has been occasional and secondary. Polemical essays and articles, that were explicitly anti-Semitic, appeared frequently in the weekly publication, *La lupa*, edited by P. Orano, in 1910-11. In the issue of July 16, 1911, an aggressive piece appeared, signed "Y," in which, after once again having dug up the old accusations of ritual homicides, he declared: "Our money, often manipulated by extortion, mostly ends up in the hands of Jews; public matters, even if appearing to be under Jesuit control, are frequently handled by Jews; the universities are overrun by them, with the damage caused to young and free intellects by Jewish elements." In reply to the article by Y, *La lupa* published (see the number of July 31, 1911) an

article by R. Ottolenghi, *L'omicidio rituale e le infinite colpe del quattrino giudaico*. In 1918 ("Israele italiana e la guerra," in *Il giornale d'Italia*, March 10) Orano stressed his "psychological" interpretation of Judaism ("The Jews feel the need to inflict upon the world exactly what has been inflicted upon them, marvelous agitators of all kinds of illusions and apathy"), defining Zionism an "Israeli Eldorado," a "parody of the Messiah awaited for five thousand years" and at the same time declaring that "only in Italy, mixing in the Latin nation, has Israel fulfilled its humanitarian dream." Replying to a report on Freemasonry, promoted by *L'idea nazionale* in 1914, Orano wrote: "The Italian patriotism of the Jews of Italy is always, if you search deeply, marked by tolerance, an effort, unspoken suffering, a silent condemnation. The Jews are patriots by necessity, socialists by contrivance, subversive by tradition, absolute enemies of Latin civilization and history by nature." See *Inchiesta sulla massoneria*, edited by E. Bodrero, Rome 1925, p. 171.

136. A. Oriani, *Fuochi di bivacco* cit., p. 194.

137. E. Corradini, *L'ombra della vita*, Naples 1908, pp. 170-73.

138. Significant, in this regard, is the controversy towards the end of 1911 because of an article by Francesco Coppola published in a nationalist paper. The article ("Israele contro l'Italia," in *L'idea nazionale*, November 16, 1911) provoked the resignation of Raffaele Levi from the Nationalist Association and a vehement protest from Alberto Musatti ("Parole chiare," therein, November 23, 1911) to which F. Coppola answered with an embarrassed reply: *Il mio "antisemitismo,"* therein, November 30, 1911.

139. A. Rocco, *Scritti e discorsi politici* cit., I, p. 3.

140. R. Mazzetti, *Orientamenti antiebraici della vita e della cultura italiana. Saggi di storia religiosa politica e letteraria*, Modena 1939; Idem., *L'Antiebraismo nella cultura italiana dal 1700 al 1900. Antologia storica*, Modena 1939.

141. This mood, though, gregariously helped some to reject the discussion when they were themselves in difficulty; you find, for example, in *L'arduo* of Bologna, the debate on the failure of nationalism between Arturo Orvieto and Concetto Valente, indignantly "resolved" by the latter (C. Valente, "Critica a critici," in *L'arduo*, September-November 1914, p. 124) with the specious argument that "only merchants and Jews—I name the Jews forsakers of any patriotic feeling and stateless people—can object to the rise of a party that gathers and merges in a single bush, the most valid and virginal of forces."

142. On the anti-Semitism of Ellero, see R. Mazzetti, *Orientamenti antiebraici ecc.* cit., pp. 147-55.

143. On him, see R. De Felice, "Giovanni Preziosi e le origini del fascismo (1917-1931)," in *Rivista storica del socialismo*, September-December 1962, now in Idem., *Intellettuali di fronte al fascismo*, Rome 1985, pp. 128-89 (with

integration); M. T. Pichetto, *Alle radici dell'odio. Preziosi e Benigni antisemiti*, Milan 1983.

144. G. Preziosi, "L'internazionale ebraica," reproduced in *Giudaismo-bolscevismo-plutocrazia-massoneria* cit., pp. 83-98.

145. Above all, see M. Pantaleoni, *La fine provvisoria di un'epopea*, Bari 1919, *passim*, particularly pp. 186, 206-8, 224, 246.

146. NOI, "Una dannosa e chimerica pretesa dei sionisti," in *La vita italiana*, February 1919, p. 143.

147. For example, see the long essay by E. Beer, "Il problema sionista e l'Italia," in *La vita italiana*, October-November 1918, February, May 1919.

148. *Ibid.*, May 1919, p. 473.

149. See G. De Ruggiero, "La pensée italienne et la guerre," in *Revue de métaphysique et de morale*, September 1916, pp. 749-85, now reproduced in Idem., *Scritti politici 1912-1926*, Bologna 1963, pp. 125-65.

150. G. Preziosi, *Giudaismo-bolscevismo-plutocrazia-massoneria* cit., pp. 88-89.

151. *Ibid.*, p. 91. G. Preziosi dedicated an entire article on Bolshevism in the September issue of *La vita italiana*, reprinted integrally in G. Preziosi, *op. cit.*, pp. 99-110. The "Jewish" interpretation of Bolshevism was refuted, on several occasions, by the Jewish press; *Il Vessillo israelitico*, for example, dedicated numerous articles on the subject, of which; E. Specos, *Il bolscevismo e gli ebrei. Contro un pogrom giornalistico* (July 15-31, 1919); L. Bernstein, *Ebrei e bolscevichi. La leggenda a la realtà* (May 15-31, 1920); M. Ginzburg, *Il bolscevismo e gli ebrei* (April 15-30, 1921). *Il vessillo israelitico* also republished (January 15-31, 1920) the well-known article by M. Nordau, *Il Bolscevismo e giudaismo*.

152. G. Preziosi, *Giudaismo-bolscevismo-plutocrazia-massoneria* cit., p. 93.

153. *Ibid.*, p. 98.

154. *Ibid.*, p. 99.

155. G. Preziosi, "I principali strumenti della internazionale ebraica: la massoneria e la democrazia," in *La vita italiana* May 1921, reproduced in full in *Giudaismo-bolscevismo-plutocrazia-massoneria* cit., pp. 163-72 (the quotation is on p. 164). *Il Vessillo israelitico* replied strongly on several occasions, as it did regarding Bolshevism, towards the "Jewish" interpretation of the Freemasonry. For all of these, see the article "Ebraismo e Massoneria" by E. Specos in the issue of September 15-30, 1920.

156. The *Don Chisciotte*, a Roman nationalist periodical, edited by Filippo Tempera, was, especially by 1920, one of the most virulent anti-Semitic papers. In some respects, as in the dispute with the Banca Commerciale and Toeplitz, it violently adopted the same position as Preziosi (see the principal articles of his editor collected in one volume, F. Tempera, *La guerra e la pace d'Italia insidiate dalla Banca Commerciale di Joseph Toeplitz*, Rome 1920). As far as Tempera was concerned, all the evils of Italy where works of

international Jewish high finance, "of which the strongest champions are Rothschild in London and Toeplitz in Milan" (*Ibid.*, p. 84); in fact all of Italian life, according to him, was enslaved by the Jews (pp. 43-45). The *Don Chisciotte*, besides other things, gave ample space to a violent anti-Semitic interview with the Romanian Elena Bacaloglu (the issue of October 8, 1920) and took up the cause of a phantom "National Italian-Romanian Fascist Party" with an uniquely anti-Semitic background (for an example, see the issue of October 10, 1920). As far as he was concerned even the union of Montenegro to Yugoslavia was the work of Jewish high finance (see the issue of November 7, 1920).

157. G. Preziosi, *I Protocolli dei Savi Anziani di Sion*, Milan 1920; G. Preziosi, "Gli ebrei nelle amministrazioni dello Stato italiano," in *La vita italiana* August 1922, pp. 106-11 (almost fully reproduced in G. Preziosi, *Giudaismo-bolscevismo-plutocrazia-massoneria* cit., pp. 46-54); P. Bandini, "Gli ebrei nell'amministrazione dello stato italiano," in *La vita italiana*, October 1922, pp. 306-10.

158. The literature on the Protocols is vast; for all, see P. Charles S. J., "Les Protocoles des Sages de Sion," in *Nouvelle Revue théologique*, January 1938; G. Volli, *La vera storia dei Protocolli dei Savi Anziani di Sion*, in *Il ponte*, November 1957; and above all Norman Cohn, *Warrant for Genocide. The myth of the Jewish world-conspiracy and the* Protocols of the Elders of Zion, *History of a Forgery*, Harper & Row 1966.

159. One finds it reproduced in M. Pantaleoni, *Bolscevismo italiano*, Bari 1922, pp. 207-19.

160. See, "Per gli ebrei non esiste in Italia la proporzionale?" in *La vita italiana*, April 1922, p. 360.

161. In the July 1922 issue of *La vita italiana* you find G. Preziosi, "Walther Rathenau fu assassinato perché ebreo" (pp. 72-76); in the August issue you find P. Praemunitus, "Come l'alta banca internazionale ebraica continua a rivoluzionare il mondo" (pp. 91-96); G. Preziosi, "Gli ebrei nelle amministrazioni dello Stato italiano," cit.; in the September issue G. Filalete, "Le origini dell'antisemitismo negli Stati Uniti" (pp. 209-17); P. Praemunitus, "Gli ebrei e la massoneria" (pp. 218-23); in the October issue A. Palmieri, "La questione ebraica nella Polonia" (pp. 299-305); G. Preziosi, "Medaglione: l'on. Gino Olivetti" (pp. 336-37).

162. The article that appeared on pp. 97-105 has been reprinted in G. Preziosi, *Giudaismo-bolscevismo-plutocrazia-massoneria* cit., pp. 179-89.

163. *Ibid.*, p. 54; G. Trevisonno, "Indici per autori e materia de *La vita italiana* dal 1913 al 1938," Cremona 1940, p. XVIII.

164. M. Missiroli, *Opinioni*, Florence 1921, pp. 20, 174.

165. For an example, see the article by G. Prezzolini, "Un romanzo storico antisemita," in *Il resto del carlino*, 8 May 1921, which so provoked G. Preziosi

("L'autenticità dei *Protocolli dei Savi Anziani di Sion* e il plagio di Giuseppe Prezzolini," in *La vita italiana*, June 1921, pp. 519-25).

166. For an example, see G. Forte, *Abbasso gli ebrei!*, Rome 1923.

167. M. Missiroli, *Opinioni* cit., pp. 176-78.

168. See what *Israel* wrote on January 11, 1923 in dispute with Modigliani and *La giustizia*.

169. In *L'Unità*, edited by G. Salvemini, the attacks on the "Jewish" Banca Commerciale actually go way back to 1912 (see, in the number of 28 September, "Un anno dopo," and in the number of October 12, the reply of S. Foa, in "La posta dell'*Unità*").

170. See R. Romeo, *Breve storia della grande industria in Italia*, San Casciano 1961, pp. 71-72, 88-91.

171. To have an idea of what was, ultimately, "popular" anti-Semitism in Italy before the First World War and the importance that clerical propaganda had upon it, see R. Ascoli, "L'antisemitismo in Italia. Cause e rimedi," in *L'idea sionistica*, March-April 1904.

172. See *Pagine scelte dai diari di T. Herzl*, edited by D. Lattes, Rome 1958, pp. 305-10; N. Goldmann, D. Lattes, U. Nahon, G. Romano, *Nel centenario della nascita di Teodoro Herzl* cit., *passim*.

173. See *Il Corriere israelitico* from those years (in particular the articles by R. Curiel, "Tripoli," in October 15, 1911, by "A Young Jew," in the same number and in that in 15 May 1912, and by A. Orvieto, "Gli ebrei e il nazionalismo," in June 15, 1912).

174. F. Coppola, "Israele contro l'Italia" cit. in *L'idea nazionale*, November 28, 1911. Attacking Coppola *Il Corriere israelitico* replied with the leading article of December 15, with the title of "Inconsulte manifestazioni antisemite."

175. On Orano, see in particular the article of August 7, 1913 in *L'idea nazionale*.

176. See *Il Parlamento Italiano e la Questione Ebraica*, Milan n.d. (but 1916); A. Pacifici, *La questione nazionale ebraica e la guerra europea*, Florence 1917; also, for an overall view, U. Nahon, "Gli echi della Dichiarazione Balfour in Italia e la Dichiarzione Imperiale del maggio 1918," in *La rassegna mensile di Israel*, June 1968.

177. R. Ruffini, *Sionismo e Società delle Nazioni*, Bologna 1919, p. 6.

178. Almost all their names appear amongst those who, after the war, gave life to, and adhered to, the Pro-Israel Association, the leading figures, above all, were G. A. Colonna di Cesarò, F. Ruffini, G. Amendola. See the pamphlets *Il Risorgimento Nazionale d'Israele in Palestina*, Rome 1919, in which there are copies of the speeches and agreements from a pro-Zionist meeting held in Rome on December 8, 1918; and *I pogrom contro gli Ebrei in Russia e in Ungheria nell'anno 1919*, Rome 1920 (the formulation of this pamphlet denotes the democratic-radical movement of the Pro-Israel

Society). On the demonstration in Rome on December 8, 1918 and on a similar one held in Florence February 2, 1919, see A. Segre, "Quaranta anni or sono," in *Israel*, January 22, 1959. G. Restivo-Alessi dedicated an article to the "Pro-Israele," *Il popolo d'Italia* January 30, 1917, the article, even if cautious, was not opposed to the Jewish cause. A position of sympathy and support of Zionism was held during the entire period in which Umberto Zanotti Bianco's *La voce dei popoli* was released in 1918-19; other than the section "Israeliti" in the regular column "Per le libertà nazionali," see the report on the Roman demonstration of December 8, 1918 (in the issue of the same month, pp. 180-83) and the note by A. Caffi-U. Zanotti Bianco, *Ebrei e sionismo* (in the March-May issue of 1919, pp. 446-51).

179.   M. Missiroli, *Opinioni*, cit., p. 20.

180.   For an example, see the brief article, "La bandiera di Sionne," signed "Cantachiaro," in *Epoca*, October 28, 1920. In this piece, dedicated to the Trieste Zionist Convention of that time, one reads: "The Zionist movement for the reconstitution of a country for the Jews, is full of interest, and we send them all our best wishes. In Italy it has found goodwill amongst the liberal element in which the tradition of Jewish emancipation goes back to the beginnings of the Risorgimento, and has Lambruschini and Cavour as its original supporters. The rebuilding of the temple of Israel in Palestine could be a good thing and beneficial to the interests of European peace. The Jews in anti-Semitic countries have the absolute right to escape oppressive laws and a public opinion, even more oppressive than these laws.

"But this movement is not understood in Italy where, not only do the Jews benefit from every right, as all citizens, but public tolerance is such that they can occupy whichever post and position in political, scientific and financial life, to which their merits give them right. Anti-Semitism does not exist here. It has never stepped over the line farther than a joke or a literary import.

"If the Zionist movement, which thinks to turn the Jew into a man with another nationality, wishes to work in Italy and stir up this national separatist awareness amongst the Jews who are, at this point, well adapted, they would run the risk of giving rise to a faction of serious anti-Semitism. It is a danger that we point out to the leaders of the Zionist movement, among whom there are persons of undisputed scientific and apostolic value.

"To us a Jewish Italian is simply an Italian. We consider such an achievement a merit of our culture." Also see G. Rocchi, "La questione sionista e un vecchio opuscolo di un israelita," in *Il raccoglitore*, February 1920.

181.   See E. Beer, *Il problema sionista e l'Italia* cit.; D. Lattes, *Gli interessi italiani nei confronti della Sede nazionale ebraica in Palestina*, Trieste 1922 (participation in

the first Italo-Oriental-Colonial congress, held in Trieste from September 12-15, 1922); and also O. Pedrazzi, "Il problema d'Israele e l'espansione italiana in Levante," in *Rivista coloniale*, January-February 1918. On the Italian policy towards Palestine immediately after the war, see S. I. Minerbi, *L'Italie et la Palestine (1914-1920)*, Paris 1970.

182. F. Lampertico, *Il protettorato in Oriente*, Torino 1913, p. 79.

183. A brief illustration of the activity of the National Association is in *L'Italia e la Palestina*, San Benigno Canavese 1917, pp. 65-87.

184. See P. Baldi, *Nei luoghi santi*, Florence 1912. In 1918-19, Baldi also published a whole series of booklets in Turin on the various aspects of the problem of the Holy Places and on the custody of the Holy Land by the Franciscans.

185. *L'Italia e la Palestina* cit., p. V, see also pp. 61-62.

186. See C. Weizmann, *La mia vita per Israele* cit., *passim* and particularly pp. 310 - 12; A. Besozzi, *Italia e Palestina*, Milan 1930, pp. 93-104. For direct records see S. Minerbi, "Il Vaticano e la Palestina durante la prima guerra mondiale," in *Clio*, July-September 1967; as well as U. Nahon, "Il viaggio di Sokolov a Roma nel 1917," in *La rassegna mensile di Israel*, May 1968.

187. All of the main newspapers of the time, in one way or another, participated in the dispute between *L'osservatore romano* and *Israel*. The papers *Corriere d'Italia, L'avvenire d'Italia, Il corriere di Romagna, Il Momento, La Stampa, L'idea nazionale,* and *Il popolo d'Italia* sided in favor of the Catholic theory. In favor of the Zionist theory (or rather, against the sectarian position of its adversaries) were *Epoca, Il Mondo, La voce repubblicana, Ora nuova, Il Secolo, La Giustizia,* and *Il Paese.*

188. See G. De Rosa, *Rufo Ruffo della Scaletta e Luigi Sturzo*, Rome 1961, pp. 125-127.

189. See, particularly, *L'osservatore romano* April 8, 1921, May 13, 1922.

190. See "L'agitazione antisionista in Palestina," in *Corriere d'Italia*, 19 April 1923. The *Corriere d'Italia* in 1922-23, also published some articles on Palestine, of decidedly pro-Arab tendency by Don Giulio de Rossi, head of the studies office of the Partito Popolare.

191. See R. Tritoni, *Come va risolta la questione dei Luoghi Santi*, Rome 1925, pp. 5-6.

192. *Ibid.*, p. 6. On R. Tritoni, also see *Il sionismo e le sue difficoltà politiche in Palestina*, Rome 1924.

193. R. Tritoni, *Come va risolta ecc*, cit., pp. 329-70. Though it is not for this reason that the position of Tritoni can be considered pro-English; like the majority of Catholics, he saw the presence of Anglicans in Palestine as a grave danger to Catholicism, and blamed their presence, holding them partially responsible, for Jewish penetration.

194. See A. Corsaro, "La Palestina italiana," in *Corriere d'Italia*, June 28, 1923.

195. See, in *Israel*, October 30, 1924, the reply from the Zionistic Organization's Roman office.

196. On the position of F. Meda, one finds, for example, his article on Zionism published by Palermo's *L'Ora*, August 28, 1924. Of the main Catholic figures, Vercesi showed more understanding for Zionism, and recognized the "subjective sincerity" of the Zionists admiring their ebullient faith. Although, he too believed that England reaped the benefits of Zionism and he saw methods in Palestinian Zionism that "dangerously" recalled those of the Third International.

197. The Catholic papers and the same *L'osservatore romano* (see the issue of April 21, 1922) did not miss the opportunity to openly accuse the Zionists of having a "dual nationality," thus turning the dispute into a nationalistic matter. Tritoni's entire argument moved explicitly on Catholic-nationalistic grounds.

198. See F. Coppola, "L'equivoco sionista," in *La tribuna*, October 20, 1926.

199. See, for example, the opinion held by L. Federzoni in June 1922 in the name of the nationalists in Parliament (as well as the parallel stance taken by *L'idea nazionale*); the article by G. Genocchi, "La questione dei luoghi santi studiata in occasione del Congresso della Pace," in *La vita italiana*, July-August 1919, also the numerous attacks on Zionism that periodically appeared in the same magazine from 1919-20 onwards (already apparent in the February issue of 1919 was the editor's note *Una dannosa e chimerica pretesa dei sionisti*); the articles by F. Coppola in *La tribuna* (especially the two of October 13 and 20, 1926).

200. A. Besozzi, *Italia e Palestina*, cit., *passim* and particularly pp. 10-11, 115, 130, 134-35, 265-66, 271.

201. On the other hand, even in the beginning, the nationalists did not entirely ignore the possibility of an agreement with Zionism as long as they would have been prepared to "collaborate" with Italy. Mentions of this are to be found in 1918-19 in *La vita italiana* (especially in the articles by E. Beer, already mentioned), which is indicative, given that it is Preziosi's magazine, even if he was not yet the torchbearer of anti-Semitism. Also A. Besozzi, *Italia e Palestina* cit., pp. 136-37, did not fail to mention it, even if timidly.

202. G. Provenzal, "Il Sionismo," in *Il nuovo patto*, January-February 1919, pp. 45.

203. D'Annunzio did have a greater following, although he did not have set ideas on the Jewish question and was ready to accept, and just as easily to refuse, the various opinions and usual clichés about it, as demonstrated by the mild debate which took place in October 1919 in *Vedetta d'Italia*, in Fiume, and its later statements retracting any alleged anti-Semitism (also see *Il Vessillo israelitico*, October 15-31, 1919, pp. 418-20. The

superficiality and confusion of D'Annunzio's position clearly appear in two writings. In *Il Piacere* he describes a Jewish funeral as "cold and melancholy," as if there were such a thing as a "warm and happy" funeral; and he also says, that all of those men "with their hooked noses and greedy eyes all looked the same as if they were consanguineous." In an article published in *Il Giorno* on May 21, 1900 ("La coscienza nazionale"), it warned that Italy was "destined to fall into the hands of a Jew with a low forehead, gluttonous for his fingernails and earwax" (Sonnino), "to whom a babbling soldier would surrender like some would give an old shoe to a second-hand dealer in the ghetto" (Pelloux).

204. One of the few exceptions is *Memorie di un fascista (1919-1922)* by F. Banchelli, Florence 1922, where there are frequent hints of anti-Semitism (see pp. 3, 137, 138, 139, 143, 176, 179, 200-1). Jewish capitalism is identified with Communism and Fascism is explicitly opposed to the Jewish-Germanic culture, that, according to Banchelli, for fifty years had brought Italy to ruin, and that international Jewish capitalism, after having triggered the war, "dictated the peace" by tricking Italy with the aid of Italian industrialists, of "Jewish and anti-Fascist" ministers Schanzer and Alessio and of their "mediators" Nitti and Orlando. In spite of this "anti-Semitic consciousness," it is significant that Banchelli, an exponent—with A. Dumini—of those most identified with extremist Fascism and Florentine Fascist action squads, did not make any attempt to transfer his loathing of Jews onto a political level or even into action with the Fascist squads.

205. The *Storia del fascismo* was really the work of Professor Giorgio Masi (see L. Cabrini, *Il potere segreto*, Cremona 1951, p. 351); obviously the point, for our purpose, clearly has no value other than to reflect the position of its author. On Farinacci, see H. Fornari, *Mussolini's Gadfly: Roberto Farinacci*, Nashville 1971 (on his attitude towards the Jews see, above all, pp. 212-26).

206. In 1932, when Mussolini named Guido Jung as Minister of Finance, it appears that he said to his close friends that a Jew was what was needed in the Ministry of Finance. According to F. Suvich, *Memorie 1932-1936*, Milan 1984, pp. 6 and 17, amongst Mussolini's "Aegeria," in economic matters, were, in the twenties (especially in occasion of the *quota novanta*), the senators Ugo Ancona and Achille Loria and, later, Teodoro Mayer, "perhaps his most esteemed financial consultant."

207. Mussolini was known to say to his friends, when discussing various nationalities and their contribution to civilization, that the Jews had given a God to humanity.

208. Mussolini's main references to race and racism, in November-December 1908, before the March on Rome, were in the essay "La filosofia della forza," which appeared in *Il pensiero romagnolo* (see B. Mussolini, *Opera Omnia*,

edited by E. and D. Susmel, Florence 1951, I, pp. 174-84); in 1911, "Il Trentino veduto da un socialista" (see *Opera Omnia* cit., XXXIII, pp. 151-213), there are rumors in the little book of a decidedly pan-German, antiracist character; in November 1921, in occasion of the Rome's Augusteo congress (see *Ibid.*, XVII, p. 219), when, for the first time, he stated (without, though, in our opinion, giving a truly racist meaning to his words, but only eugenic and of "physical soundness" in a broad sense): "the racial question is of great importance to Fascism; the Fascists must concern themselves with the health of the race, because the race is the material with which we intend to build history." Regarding the interpretation to give to this last statement of Mussolini, see D. Monari, "Il miglioramento della razza e il Fascismo," in *Gerarchia*, October 1922, pp. 592-96.

209. See A. Spinosa, "Le persecuzioni razziali in Italia, I: Le origini," in *Il ponte*, July 1952, pp. 964-66; M. Michaelis, "On the Jewish Question in Fascist Italy. The Attitude of Fascist Regime to the Jews in Italy," in *Yad Vashem Studies*, IV, Jerusalem 1960, p. 8; *Idem.*, "I rapporti italo-tedeschi e il problema degli ebrei in Italia" (1922-38), in *Rivista di studi politici internazionali*, April-June 1961, pp. 239-41, and above all in *Idem.*, *Mussolini e la questione ebraica*, Milan 1982, pp. 33.

210. For an overall view of anti-Semitic political writings immediately after the war, and to get an idea of both their "arguments" and of how they occasionally appeared in papers that were not suspected of an anti-Semitic bias, see A. Nicolau, *L'allarme. Accuso! Il bolscevismo visto alla sua sorgente e nel suo fine. Gli ebrei nel conflitto mondiale*, Milan 1920. The little book is made up of a collection of information and press comments, with an essay as a preface. Nicolau, a Romanian, was clearly a fervent supporter of Mussolini (whom he thinks deserves the credit for Italy's participation in the war), but regarding Mussolini's attitude, and that of his paper, towards the Jews, he was not entirely satisfied. "Even in *Il popolo d'Italia*" — he writes (p. 188) — "we find Mr. and Mrs. Sarfatti hidden, whilst poor Mussolini writhes about like a damned soul in the Styx!"

211. See B. Mussolini, *Opera Omnia* cit., XIII, pp. 168-70.

212. See B. Mussolini, *Opera Omnia* cit., XV, pp. 269-71.

213. See G. Pini-D. Susmel, *Mussolini ecc.* cit. m II, pp. 132, 137, 140, 147-51.

214. D. Bachi and the editor of *Giovane Israele*, Gino Corinaldi, replied to Mussolini's article with two "letters" to *Il popolo d'Italia* (see issues of October 22 and 26, 1920). Specifically on the Zionist question, Corinaldi wrote: "He is alarmed by the words 'specific problems,' contained in the Zionist Congress program. I am more than happy to explain, but it would have been sufficient to read the working agenda. The problems of the Jewish Italians are simply the following: (1) cultural revival (conferences, books and magazines, schools); (2) community redevelopment; (3) assis-

tance and organization of Jewish emigrants from eastern Europe; (4) contribution to the central organization (individual quotes or Shekalim, Keren kajemeth or funds for the acquisition of land in Palestine, Keren ha-jesod or funds for the reconstruction).

"There is certainly no Bolshevism in Trieste, but only celebration for its liberation and for the greatness and generosity of Italy.

"But as much as we Italian Jews adore Italy, this cannot be the new Zion, because it cannot certainly accommodate nine million Oriental Jews impatient to abandon the place of their martyrdom."

Also the first article by Mussolini, in 1919, provoked a reaction; see, above all, the article by Leone Carpi, June 5, 1919, in *L'Italia del popolo*.

215. See B. Mussolini, "Rappresaglia," in *Il popolo d'Italia*, June 25, 1922, now in *Opera Omnia* cit., XVIII, pp. 256-57.

216. A few days later (November 5) *Il resto del carlino* reproduced the well-known article *Sionismo* by G. Sorel.

217. See Camera dei Deputati, "Atti Parlamentari," session of June 21, 1921, pp. 93-94; *Il popolo d'Italia*, September 1, 1921 (both against Zionism) and June 16, 1922. Also see, G. Pini-D. Susmel, *Mussolini ecc.* cit., II, p. 186.

218. To all of these positions taken by Mussolini and the *Il popolo d'Italia*, the Jewish press generally replied sharply, countering and rectifying. See, for example, in *Il Vessillo israelitico* of 1921, the notes of the June 15-30 issues ("Mussolini antisionista," pp. 180-90) and of the 15-30 September ("Antisemitismo," pp. 272-77) and in *Israel* of September 8, 1921 "Una risposta al *Popolo d'Italia*." Also see, G. Preziosi, "Mussolini e l'ebraismo prima della Marcia," in *La vita italiana*, September 1940.

219. This "national" behavior of the Italian Jews is recognizable even amongst the Zionists. At the already mentioned Trieste Zionist congress of 1920, there were violent disagreements between the participants, many of whom wanted the congress to unequivocally proclaim the "loyalty" and "national sentiment" of the Italian Zionists. The very violent debate, for a moment, seemed as if it would degenerate into a brawl (see *Piccolo della sera*, Trieste, 19 October 1920).

220. See Y. De Begnac, *Vita di Benito Mussolini*, Milan 1939, III, appendix, pp. 603-9; A. Tamaro, *Venti anni di storia 1922-1943*, Rome 1954, pp. 304-5; and also G. Pini-D. Susmel, *Mussolini ecc*, cit., I, p. 280.

221. G. Bassani, "Gli ultimi anni di Clelia Trotti," in *Paragone*, April 1950, pp. 69-72; R.B., "Gli ebrei a Ferrara dal fascismo alla liberazione," in *Competizione Democratica*, April 1955, p.14.

222. See E. Kuhn Amendola, *Vita con Giovanni Amendola*, Florence 1960, pp. 539-40, 568-69.

223. L. Gasparotto, *Diario di un deputato*, Milan 1945, pp. 116-17, speaking about the presence of various Jews in the first Milanese Fascism, he wrote: "the tendency is purely anticlerical and many Jews enter."

224. At the political elections of May 15, 1921 nine Jewish deputies were elected (see *Il Vessillo israelitico*, May 15-31, 1921, p.155), of those only one (A. Finzi) was a Fascist. Also, none of the eighteen Jewish senators (see *Il Vassillo israelitico*, October 15-31, 1919, p. 413) was a Fascist.

225. E. R. Papa, *Storia di due manifesti*, Milan 1958; *La scure*, Piacenza, August 12, 1938.

226. See "Un esempio," in *Israel*, April 19, 1923.

227. Even Zionist supporters, though, were not lacking in accepting Fascism in power. This was the case, for example, with the Rabbi of Genoa, G. Sonino, who, shortly after the "March on Rome," sent his congratulations to Mussolini. The fact, on its own is of little importance, but is made interesting by the fact that Mussolini replied to Sonino with a handwritten letter (not dated, but with a postage stamp of November 13, 1922): "Distinguished Rabbi, I received your letter and reply to express my gratitude and positive feelings. I count upon all those who really love Italy. Consider me devoted to you." (Kindly shown to us by F. Sonnino) This is indeed further confirmation—in our opinion—of Mussolini's new policies towards the Jews during these years. They go so far as to accept the support, even if only formal, of well-known Zionist leaders for Fascism.

228. See B. Mussolini, *Opera Omnia* cit., XVI, p. 439.

229. On the position of General E. Pugliese, commanding officer for the protection of Rome during the March on Rome, an important study was dedicated by M. Michaelis, "Il generale Pugliese e la difesa di Roma," in *La rassegna mensile di Israel*, June-July 1962.

230. Regarding this campaign see, above all, the issues of the *Don Chisciotte* published between November 16, 1922 and February 1, 1923. The common thread of these issues was to ask Mussolini to "liberate" Italy of the "Jewish Holofernes" and in particular of Toeplitz. "Jewish high finance that has in its international strong box, red and black," wrote the *Don Chisciotte* on January 16, 1923, "it controls diplomacy, the press, justice and schools and for this reason Versailles was a disaster and Italy was punished for having won the world war! For an incorrect calculation she applauded Fascism yesterday, today she doggedly fights it with the most dark and vile means so that it assumes a purely Italian character, of overall reform. Honorable Mussolini, before you lose your head to the venomous snakes in Italy who serve you, and whom you serve, why don't you conclude the great task that you set out to do!"

231. *Fascismo e antisemitismo*, in *Israel*, December 6, 1923; and also Comunità Israelitica di Roma, *In memoria di Angelo Sacerdoti*, Rome 1936, pp. 15-16.

232. The news of the meeting between Mussolini and Sacerdoti and the related press release greatly contributed to determine in various Fascist circles

an attitude of criticism towards certain obscure hints of anti-Semitism. Indicative of this is the case of *Critica fascista*, the magazine of G. Bottai: on February 1, 1924 it published an article by an ex-serviceman, Herz Joffe (*Il Fascismo e gli Ebrei*), against all anti-Semitism and he preceded it with an editorial note in which it was stated that it was exactly "the declarations made by Benito Mussolini to the Rabbi of Rome" that made the editorial department of the magazine overcome "the hesitation in publishing writings permeated by a very noble spirit, but such as to arouse malicious disputes."

233. See, for example, R. Farinacci, "Un periodo aureo del Partito Nazionale Fascista," Foligno 1927, *passim* and particularly pp. 166-67; in these speeches R. Farinacci, at the time national secretary of the PNF, even though frequently violently attacking Freemasonry and high finance, never mentions the Jews and their presumed role in these organizations (a role that was instead addressed in *Cremona nuova*).

234. Of the various positions taken by *La vita italiana* during these years those that are noteworthy are the articles by G. Zoppola, "La trasformazione dei valori" (September 1929), and "Ebrei che si dànno la zappa sui piedi" (January 1930), and by G. Sommi Picenardi, *Israele contro Roma?* (April 1932). As for G. Preziosi, see his main positions in the already mentioned collection *Giudaismo-bolscevismo-plutocrazia-massoneria*, pp. 205-45. In 1928 G. Zoppola published a volume: *Imperialismo spirituale e Imperialismo materiale— Cattolicesimo e fascismo—Giudaismo e Massoneria*, from a Catholic-Fascist anti-Semitic point of view.

235. When introducing the bill in Parliament Mussolini did not raise the question of the Jews being members of Freemasonry (see *Opera Omnia* cit., XXI, pp. 309-11). Interesting is the comparison of the various positions taken on the subject: see Mussolini-Nathan-Torrigiani, *La Massoneria*, Rome 1925 (the more significant positions taken by the main political newspapers are to be found in the appendix). Some clerical writers joined the national Fascist choir against the Jewish Masons; for example, see P. Maraglia, *Massoneria ed ebraismo nella vita e nella storia contemporanea*, Pistoia 1926: "Freemasonry and Judaism united, just as the knife is united to the hand of the murderer that brandishes it, like the torch to the fist of the arsonist that clenches it." (p.47)

236. *Israel* periodically gave an account of the worst of these attacks in its column dedicated to the Italian press.

237. R. De Felice, *Ebrei in un paese arabo* cit., pp. 188-92.

238. "Che succede a Tripoli?" in *Israel*, October 4, 1923; also in *Israel* see "La crisi rabbinica a Tripoli" (October 18, 1923), "Dopo i fatti di Tripoli" (November 1, 1923), "Echi della crisi rabbinica a Tripoli" (November 8).

239. See *Israel* February 28, 1924 and April 8 and 22, 1926.

240. With a certain severity, the December 20, 1923 issue of *Israel*, taking the idea from a December 11 article in *Il Piemonte*, wrote: "Reacting against Judaism because there are some Jews who are not congenial to a party or government, detrimental to the nation, or dishonest, is anti-Semitism."

241. See *Israel*, January 31, 1924 (regarding a visit to G. Gentile by a delegation of the Hungarian committee to thank him for how much the Italian government had done for the Hungarian students); September 16, 1926 (regarding the denial of "Il Fascio"), etc.

242. For example, the typical positions taken by the *Israel* on the occasion of the two attacks on Mussolini, by Violet Gibson ("crazy criminal act of the mad Irish woman") and of Lucetti ("he did not avoid to arouse a deep-felt resentment, along with satisfaction for the danger avoided, in the widest circles of the Jewish population"); see the issues of April 8 and September 16, 1926.

243. D. Lattes, *Gli interessi italiani ecc.* cit., pp. 1-2.

244. Other than the news periodically published by *Israel* on the activities of this committee see, in particular, its periodic accounts to the Royal General Commissariat of Emigration (particularly important those dated April 17 and May 14, 1924), especially the two comprehensive files for the years 1920-24 and 1924-27.
    In the report of the April 17, 1924 (Comitato Italiano Di Assistenza Agli Emigranti Ebrei-Trieste, *Relazione al R. Commissariato Gen. dell'Emigrazione - L'opera del Com. It. Ass. Em. Ebrei—1920-23*) one reads of the assistance given to the students (pp. 11-12): "It seemed to us rather positive to attract Jewish students to the Italian Universities, who, up until now, have been attending universities in Switzerland, Germany, France, and England. So that they may absorb from the sources of science and the Italian spirit and could then take that influence and knowledge to their homeland." From the same report it emerges that, during the school year of 1923-24, more than three hundred foreign Jewish students came to study in Italian universities, taking advantage of the easy admissions established by the Ministry of Education. A general picture on international Jewish emigration and transit through Italy, is found in the report for the years 1924-27. On Jewish organizations of assistance and their activity, see M. Leone, *Le organizzazioni di soccorso ebraiche in età fascista*, Rome 1983, pp. 21 sgg.

245. Typical, even if published a few years later, is a long article by R. Bachi, "La Palestina ebraica," in *La riforma sociale*, March-April 1929.

246. See I. Zoller, "L'Italia Cattolica ed il divorzio fra acattolici in Italia," in *Israel*, May 17, 1923; C. Morpurgo, 'Per la conservazione del diritto al divorzio degli ebrei delle nuove provincie," in *Israel*, May 5, 1923; *Idem.*, "Sulla questione del divorzio degli ebrei dopo la recente discussione parlamentare," in *Israel*, June 28, 1923.

247. The most complete and in-depth theory, in an ideological and religious vein, of the Zionist revival during these years was written by D. Lattes in the volume *Apologia dell'ebraismo*, Rome 1923 (3rd edition, amplified, with the title *L'Idea d'Israele*, Rome 1951).

248. The leading article of the February 26, 1926 *Israel*, "Il problema della scuola ebraica in Italia." It is typical in this respect when it writes: "Italian Judaism... has not seriously considered the new awareness that these minority rights imply: and this happens, whilst in Italy the philosophic and cultural changes of the last twenty years prepared, with idealistic reaction, a greater understanding of the essentially spiritual nature of the nation, and a virile conception of the efficiency of the nation considered as 'personality,' as active 'individuality,' in which it finds the more serious ideological base, the new theory of minority rights... There is no alternative for us: either deny in this new life one's own personality, with a suicide we can't tell whether it is more dishonorable or...impossible; or to bring the contribution of historical personality, by means of a renewal of our own historical conscience, a close examination of the distinctive values of Judaism... Our school problem, on the positive side, comes from this fundamental need; and whichever solution we attempt we must seek inspiration from this, if we want to work, seriously, for the future."
    Still on the problem of the Jewish school, see *Israel*: D. Lattes, "Il problema della scuola ebraica e i provvedimenti del Ministro Gentile" (March 1, 1923); *Idem*, "Ancora sulla istruzione religiosa nelle scuole" (May 17, 1923); E. Sereni, "Di qua del ponte" (December 27, 1923); F. Bassani, "Un altro pericolo per l'ebraismo" (January 24, 1924); G. Castelbolognesi, "Compiti e figura del rabbinato in Italia" (March 12, 1925); "La necessità della scuola secondaria" (March 12, 1925), as well as the report (*Israel*, November 5, 1925) of the fifth congress of the Italian Jewish Community.

249. Even if less explicitly, the same needs are suggested in a speech made at Passover in 1925, held in the main temple of Leghorn by that rabbi and reproduced in the booklet: A. Toaff, *Libertà*, Leghorn 1925.

250. The convention's report was published in the November 20, 1924 issue of *Israel*. On the precedents and the quite modest developments (the convention of Jewish students held in Florence in April 1925) M. Toscano, *Fermenti culturali ed esperienze organizzative* cit., pp. 947-61.

251. N. Rosselli published some of his "impressions" of the Leghorn convention in the November 27, 1924 issue of *Israel*. In the same paper G. Bedarida continued the debate between the Zionists and Rosselli ("In difesa dei vigliacchi," December 18, 1924), eliciting a new reply by those concerned (January 15, 1925). The substantially liberal position of Rosselli was well understood by G. Prezzolini who made mention of it in *Il resto del carlino*.

On the ethical-political context, from which arose the intervention of N. Rosselli, see G. Belardelli, *Nello Rosselli uno storico antifascista*, Florence 1982.

252. *Tre vite dall'ultimo '800 alla metà del '900. Studi e memorie di Emilio, Emmanuele, Ennio Artom*, edited by B. Treves, Florence 1954, pp. 10-13.

253. See L. Salvatorelli–G. Mira, *Storia d'Italia nel periodo fascista*, Turin 1957, pp. 357-87.

254. See the memoirs of A. Theodoli, *A cavallo di due secoli*, Rome 1950, *passim* and particularly pp. 135-38. The work of Theodoli, as president of the Commission of Mandates, was generally much criticized by the Zionists. C. Weizmann, for example (*La mia vita per Israele* cit., pp. 367, 408-9), defined him as a "definite adversary of the Zionist movement" and tied— through the Arab relatives of his wife—to the position and interests of the Arabs in Palestine.

255. See *Israel*, May 24, 1926.

256. *Ibid.*, September 22-29, 1926 and above all C. Weizmann, *La mia vita per Israele* cit., pp. 405-7.

257. On this first meeting, see M. Michaelis, *Mussolini e la questione ebraica* cit., pp. 46-48.

258. Mussolini tended to recall that not all Jews were Zionists; Weizmann replied, reminding him that not all Italians were Fascists.

259. See *Israel*, May 12, 1927.

260. *Ibid.*, June 9, 1927; and also D. Carpi, "Il problema ebraico nella politica italiana fra le due guerre mondiali," in *Rivista di studi politici internazionali*, January-March 1961, pp. 35-36 (Jacobson's account on his meeting with Mussolini is cited on pp. 47-48).

261. See *Israel*, 3 November 1927; as well as U. Nahon, "La visita di Sokolov a Livorno e in Italia nel 1927," in *La rassegna mensile di Israel*, July-August 1972, pp. 147-66.

262. The president of the Italy-Palestine Commission was Prince Pietro Lanza di Scalea, Alberto de Stefani was vice president, Dante Lattes was secretary, and Angelo Sacerdoti was treasurer; among its members were Roberto Cantalupo, Antonio Cippico, Alfredo Baccelli, Roberto Almagià, Ugo d'Ancona, Giacinto Motta, Gino Olivetti, Nicola Vacchelli and Gioacchino Volpe. Bottai and Bodrero, among others, attended the reception in honor of its creation (see *Il Messaggero*, March 8, 1928).

263. The idea of authorizing the commission's creation was suggested to Mussolini by Raffaele Guariglia, in charge of the Ministry of Foreign Affairs' oriental office. "Given the great Jewish interests that Italy had in the Mediterranean and given the obvious benefit in closely monitoring the developments of Zionism and to not leave this movement completely in the hands of Britain, but to 'follow it from inside,' as is good political practice, I proposed to Mussolini to create, also in Rome, a pro-Zionist

Association that would be completely private" (R. Guariglia, *Ricordi*, Naples 1949, p. 183).

264. See G. Bedarida, *Ebrei d'Italia*, Livorno 1950, pp. 10, 20. Almost at the same time, the Italian Embassy in Washington issued a declaration on the situation of the Jews in Italy, to deny all accusations of anti-Semitism: "Italy has been, and is still, the classic land of Jewish liberty, and the Jewish people are well aware of this." (see *Israel*, March 29, 1928)

265. In a short book published by the PNF for political preparation courses inside the Party, *L'Italia nel Mediterraneo* (Rome, the year XIV [1936], p. 44), it is explicitly stated: "Italy's behavior towards Zionism is different when it concerns Zionism in Palestine and the participation of Italian citizens in the Zionist movement. The latter is unacceptable. The Zionist movement in Palestine is followed by Italy with great attention."

266. R. Guariglia, *Ricordi* cit., pp. 183-84, writes that the attack by *Il popolo di Roma* was personally written by Mussolini. But he confuses *Il popolo di Roma* with *Il popolo d'Italia*. The same point is made in U. Nahon, "*La polemica antisionista del* Popolo di Roma *nel 1928*," in *Scritti in memoria di Enzo Sereni* cit., pp. 216 *ff* that offers a detailed reconstruction of the whole event.

267. See *Israel*, November 6, 12, 22, 29, 1928.

268. See *Popolo di Roma*, December 3, 5, 7, 9, 12, 1928; also *Israel*, December 9, 20-27, 1928.

269. See, regarding this, U. Nahon, *La polemica antisionista del "Popolo di Roma" nel 1928* cit., pp. 251.

270. ACS, *Min. Int., Gabinetto, Ufficio cifra - Telegrammi in arrivo e in partenza (1922-41), 1929, Telegrammi in partenza*, vol. VI, Bocchini, to the prefect of Turin, February 11, 1929.

271. See *Il Progresso Italo-Americano*, New York, May 16, 1929.

272. The bulletin *Italia* (organ of the Italian Anti-Fascist Concentration) published on June 1, 1929 a note titled "Gli ebrei in Italia," in which it was said that *Israel* had been suppressed by the government because of the article by Pacifici. Commenting on the news, the *Italia* wrote: "The Fascist era, now reinforced by Roman clericalism, is not at all favorable to the Italian Jews. The religious revival observed amongst the Jews in recent times finds more and more difficulties that were more grave and totally unheard of up until now, at the time of the liberal regime." To belie the news, the Rabbi of Rome, Angelo Sacerdoti, immediately cabled Filippo Turati [Socialist Party leader in exile] in Paris. In the issue of June 13, Claudio Treves replied, specifying that what was published at the time was not the *Israel* but the *Rassegna mensile di Israel*; to this reply another followed by Sacerdoti, dated June 21 and, finally, a violently argumentative letter (dated July 9), from Turati to Sacerdoti (see A. Schiavi, *Esilio e morte di*

Filippo Turati, 1926-1932, Rome 1956, pp. 271-77). The news of the suppression of *Israel* was also gathered by other foreign papers, see the polemical article "Fantasie macabre," in *Israel*, July 18, 1929.

273. See Atti Parlamentari, *Camera dei Deputati*, session of April 30, 1929. On the new religious laws, a careful and favorable article was published by M. Falco, "Il nuovo decreto sui culti," in *Israel*, April 25, 1930.

274. In the papers of the PNF the heaviest attack, and most unwarranted, was perhaps established by two articles by C. Pelizzari, "La finanza internazionale ebreo-massonica e la crisi economica," in *Il popolo di Brescia*, July 28, August 6, 1932. (*Il popolo di Brescia* was the organ of Augusto Turati [Fascist party leader and party secretary].)

275. E. Ludwig, *Colloqui con Mussolini*, Milan 1950 (photographic edition of the draft of 1932 with handwritten corrections made by Mussolini and with a "brief chronicle of the origins of the first and second editions of the *meetings* with Mussolini" edited by A. Mondadori), pp. 71-73. Preziosi understood the seriousness and importance of the statements made by Mussolini to Ludwig and, in a quibbling note in *La vita italiana* (August 1932, p. 222) tried to dilute them by using the pretence "different conceptions of the homeland" which supposedly were "all of the antithesis" between Mussolini and his interviewer.

276. Having declared the nonexistence of an Italian anti-Semitism, Mussolini lost interest in foreign initiatives, alien to Fascism and set on fighting it. Particularly unpopular with the Fascists was the International Alliance against anti-Semitism, who considered it to be, and not mistakenly, anti-Fascist (see, in the papers of January 1930, the violent attacks made towards the Alliance and F. S. Nitti who had attended its national congress in Paris). Also initiatives that did not come from anti-Fascist organizations, like Professor Guido Tedeschi's project for an international convention under the protection of the League of the Nations (1932), did not find favor within the government nor the party (see the polemical article "Minoranza nazionale o ghetto?" in *Il telegrafo*, August 5, 1932).

277. See R. Frau, "Appunti sul regime giuridico delle Comunità Israelitiche in Italia dallo Statuto sino al R.D. 30 Ottobre 1930, n. 1731," in *Studi economico-giuridici* by Cagliari University, 1969; also G. Fubini, *La condizione giuridica dell'ebraismo italiano*, Florence 1974 and A. Calo, "La genesi della legge del 1930," in *Rassegna mensile di Israel*, September-December 1985, pp. 334-439.

278. See ACIR, p. 45, *Carte del rabbino Angelo Sacerdoti, Relazione presentata al Comitato delle Comunità isr. it. dalla Commissione rabbinica consultiva (5683-1923)*, f.7.

279. For a documented historical profile of the Italian Jewish congresses, see A. Segre, *1861-1961, I Congressi delle Comunità israelitiche italiane*, text dupli-

cated by the Department of Education and Culture of the Union of Italian Jewish Communities, Rome 1961.

280. Comunità Israelitica di Roma, *In memoria di Angelo Sacerdoti* cit., pp. 35-36.

281. Unione delle Comunità Israelitiche Italiane, *Primo Congresso delle Comunità (1933-XI). Relazione del Commissario governativo Avv. Felice di L. Ravenna*, Rome 1933, p. 2.

282. M. Falco, "Comunità israelitiche," in *Novissimo Digesto Italiano*, Turin 1959, p. 8 of the extract; also *Il corriere della sera*, November 25, 1929.

283. See ACS, *Presidenza del Consiglio dei ministri, Gabinetto, Provvedimenti sottoposti all'esame del Consiglio dei ministri (1921-45)*, the year 1930-Ministry of Justice, file 34 (therein the correspondence of the Ministry of Internal Affairs Cabinet and of the Accounts department of the Ministry of Finance); *Ibid.*, year 1931, Ministry of Justice, file 41.

284. See *Document I: Relazione allo schema di decreto legislativo sulle Comunità Israelitiche e sulla Unione delle Comunità medesime.*

285. See *Document 2.*

286. See Unione delle Comunità Israelitiche Italiane, *Primo Congresso delle Comunità* cit., pp. 4-5; also "Dieci anni fa. Come Alfredo Rocco sventò il tentativo ebraico di far riconoscere il Talmud quale religione ufficiale," in *Il popolo di Trieste*, November 20, 1938.

287. See Unione delle Comunità Israelitiche Italiane, *Primo Congresso delle Comunità* cit., pp. 2-3.

288. For its legal significance and more details, see M. Piacentini, *I culti ammessi nello Stato italiano*, Milan 1934, *passim* and particularly pp. 113-216; also M. Falco, *Comunità Israelitiche* cit.; A. C. Jemolo, "Alcune considerazioni sul R.D. 30 Ottobre 1930 n. 1731 sulle Comunità Israelitiche," in *Il diritto ecclesiastico*, 1931, II.

289. Twenty-six metropolitan communities were established: Abbazia, Alessandria, Ancona, Bologna, Casale Monferrato, Ferrara, Florence, Fiume, Genoa, Gorizia, Leghorn, Mantua, Milan, Modena, Naples, Padova, Palermo, Parma, Pisa, Rome, Turin, Trieste, Venice, Vercelli, and Verona. Through other laws other communities were established in Tripoli and Benghazi, Rhodes, Asmara, and in Mogadishu. At the first Union Congress, this total of thirty-one communities amounted to 12,410 dues-paying members.

290. If from the reactions of that time, one goes on to those of thirty years later, the evaluation of those approving obviously changes greatly. The most balanced and convincing historical assessment of the laws on the Communities in 1930 appears to us to be that of F. Pitigliani, "Rielaborazione della cronaca di una infamia," in *La rassegna mensile di Israel*, November 1969, pp. 519-22.

291. See *Israel*, 21 October 1930.

292. See, for example, *La Riforma delle Comunità,* therein, June 12, 1929.

293. A. Revere, "Rabbinato e Comunità," in *L'idea sionistica,* April 1932, pp. 12-13.

294. See "Il giornale d'Oriente," Alexandria, Egypt, October 19, 1930.

295. Unione delle Comunità Israelitiche Italiane, *Primo Congresso delle Comunità* cit., p. 14.

296. See, for example, the *Bollettino della Sera,* September 22, 1929 and *Il Corriere d'America* October 5, 1929 and October 23, 1930, both from New York.

297. Y. Colombo, "Legislazione fascista. Il nuovo ordinamento dell Comunità israelitiche," in *Corriere padano,* December 17, 1931.

298. Various Fascist papers declared themselves violently against this interpretation; see, for example, *Il popolo d'Italia,* October 21, 1930.

299. A. Schiavi, *Esilio e morte di Filippo Turati* cit., p. 276.

300. See *Israel,* February 5, 1931 and, more widely, Unione delle Comunità Israelitiche Italiane, *Primo Congresso delle Comunità* cit., pp. 35-38.

301. See *Israel,* April 30, 1931.

302. Also see A. Pacifici, *La reconquista del Sciabat,* Rhodes 1931.

303. See *Israel,* December 9, 1930 and January 12, 1933. For a general idea on the Tripoli community in this period, see *Relazione finale del commissario straordinario governativo comm. dott. Alberto Monastero sulla gestione della Comunità israelitica della Tripolitania dall'agosto 1929 al maggio 1931-IX,* Tripoli 1931.

304. Confronted with government resistance, the Union tried to "get around" it by connecting the Sabbath day of rest to the forty hour work week reduction, established by the government (see Unione delle Comunità Israelitiche Italiane, *Primo Congresso delle Comunità* cit., p. 10).

305. See I. Cohen, *Le Mouvement Sioniste* cit., pp. 190-213.

306. G. M. Sangiorgi, "I 'pogroms' in Palestina," in *Il resto del carlino,* August 30, 1929.

307. See P. Orano, "Il decimosesto congresso sionista e Dall'Aja a Ginevra," in *La Nazione* August 13 and 29, 1929.

308. See, for example, *Il popolo d'Italia,* August 30, 1929 and *Telegrafo sera,* September 3, 1929.

309. V. Gayda, "Sangue in Palestina. Gli Arabi contro gli Ebrei," in *Gerarchia,* September 1929, p. 758. In the same issue, Ausonio, *I recenti avvenimenti in Palestina,* appeared to be almost certain that "the Zionist experiment" in Palestine could have reached its full realization.

310. "Ordinaria amministrazione dei mandati," in *Il Tevere,* August 30, 1929.

311. Against this chorus, Alfonso Pacifici protested, in *Israel* March 11, 1930, with a heartfelt article entitled "Lasceranno continuare questo i cattolici di tutto il mondo?"

312. *L'osservatore romano,* August 29, 1929.

313. See C. E. Barduzzi, "La rivolta degli arabi palestinesi," in *L'avvenire d'Italia*, 4 September 1929. By Barduzzi, see also the pamphlet *La Palestina agricola e industriale, il Sionismo ed i luoghi Santi*, Faenza 1930.

314. E. Vercesi, "Palestina e Sionismo," in *Cultura moderna*, January 1930, p. 49. By Vercesi, see also the pamphlet *Palestina di ieri e di oggi: una piaga sempre aperta*, Rome-Milan 1930.

315. R. F. Michetti, "Cristiani, musulmani ed ebrei in Palestina. Bilancio: Un decennio di dominio inglese," in *Palestina*, January 1930, p. 4.

316. C. Barduzzi, *La rivolta ecc.* cit. The mandate to Italy was requested by many Catholic columnists. See, for example, also "L'Italia in Palestina," in *Palestina*, February 1930.

317. It is interesting to note how, in the anti-Zionist debate, Catholic propaganda accepted points, even coming from Slav journalists; see A. Soviè, *Il Vaticano e la Palestina o la Chiesa romana e il Zionismo giudaico*, Zagreb 1929 (this regards two articles of April 1929 of *"Katolièki list"* di Zagabria).

318. G. Preziosi, "Il segretario di Gog," in *La vita italiana*, January 1931, pp. 5-7.

319. J. Billig, *Le commissariat général aux questions juives (1941-44)*, Paris 1957, II, p. 326.

320. F. M. Tinti, "L'offensiva ebraica contro il Trono e l'Altare," in *La stella di san Domenico*, August 1931, p. 383.

321. F. M. Tinti, "Il sionismo ebraico e la cristianità," in *Luce*, 4 April 1930.

322. See "I torbidi in Palestina," September 14, 1929; "Il mandato sulla Palestina," November 29, 1930; "Benedetto XV contro l'egemonia ebraica sionista massonica in Palestina," December 17 and 24, 1932.

323. The importance of the effects of the Fascist press abroad, is indirectly confirmed by the fact that the Anti-Fascist Concentration in Paris, itself, felt the need to take a position on the Palestinian events. In the bulletin *Italia*, September 6, 1929, Filippo Turati published a letter, "I proscritti italiani agli ebrei della Palestina" (see A. Schiavi, *Esilio e morte ecc.* cit., pp. 277-79), of complete solidarity with the cause and the suffering of the Palestinian colonists.

324. See, for example, G. Engely, "Il mandato in Palestina," in *Opinione*, Philadelphia, October 11, 1930.

325. "La questione dei mandati," in *Italia*, Montreal, September 26, 1931.

326. See, for all, "La beffa palestinese,' in *Corriere padano*, April 2, 1932: the anonymous article was directly inspired by Jabotinsky, through his trustworthy colleague in Italy, Leone Carpi; see L. Carpi, "Lettere di Jabotinsky," in *Scritti in memoria di Leone Carpi* cit., pp. 48-49; the entire essay, pp. 35-36, is worth consulting, in order to evaluate Jabotinsky's position towards Italy; on the same subject, see also C. L. Ottino, " Jabotinsky e l'Italia," in *Gli ebrei in Italia durante il Fascismo*, III, Milan 1963, pp. 51-81.

327. On the beginnings and the development of the Zionist-revisionist movement in Italy, see E. Levi, "Episodi di vita ebraica milanese fra le due guerre mondiali," in *Scritti in memoria di Leone Carpi* cit., pp. 228-40.

328. Some of the communities in the north had added to the prayer for the prosperity and glory of the King, that had been recited every Saturday for centuries, the reference to Mussolini "head of government and Duce of Fascism." (See E. Toaff, *Perfidi giudei fratelli maggiori*, Milan 1987, p. 16.)

329. D. Lattes, *"Angiolo Orvieto, poeta ebreo,"* preface to A. Orvieto, *Il vento di Sion* e i *Canti dell'escluso*, Rome 1961, p. 12.

330. The activity of the Zionists-Revisionists began to gain some importance in Italy around 1927. Though even before the "March on Rome" the head of international revisionism, Jabotinsky, had already first written to Mussolini. In a letter dated July 16, 1922 (see Z. Jabotinsky, *Verso lo Stato*, Florence 1960, pp. 27-31) he tried to cultivate the sympathies of the future Duce by demonstrating the precariousness of the pro-Arab stand for Italy, and proposing, instead, a sort of Italian-Jewish Mediterranean collaboration. The first action of which, should have been "a gesture of the Mediterranean Jews to restore the dominion of the Italian language."
    In 1930, as has already been said, the Zionist-Revisionist movement began publication of one of its newspapers, *L'idea sionistica*, in Milan, edited by Leone Carpi. In the first issue of this publication (Number 1, May, p. 2.) the revisionists openly professed faith in Italy and hoped for close Italian-Jewish cooperation ("Italy and Israel will be great, and will together mark the new century. The path to the future will be theirs, and they will walk along it side by side."). In February 1932, the first Italian Zionist-Revisionist conference was held in Milan (see *L'idea sionistica*, April 1932). The importance that the movement attributed to its success amongst Italian Jews (and, consequently, to good relations with the government) is amply proven by the fact that, Jabotinsky, in occasion of the Eighteenth World Zionistic Congress, wanted to present himself as candidate of the Italian Revisionists (see, in Z. Jabotinsky, *Verso lo Stato* cit., pp. 167-68, his appeal "To the Zionists of Italy" in July 1933). The revisionists underlined, above all, three aspects of their propaganda organization: their strong dislike of English policy, and Weizmann's policies as well, too favorable to the British (see any issue of *L'idea sionistica*); their just as strong anti-Communism (see Z. Jabotinsky, *Verso lo Stato* cit., pp. 190-95); the identity of their position compared to Palestine with Italian interests in the Mediterranean and particularly in the Near East (see *"Ordine italiano in Oriente,"* in *L'idea sionistica*, May 1932, pp. 1-3.).

331. On February 16, 1933 Mussolini once again received N. Sokolov.

332. Typical are the three articles, on "Il problema della razza," which appeared in the *Gazzetta del Popolo* of Turin in January-February 1933. The third, in

particular (N. Pende, "I vivai umani del Fascismo," February 3, 1933) is proof of what we claimed. Everything revolves around the "physical robustness, moral soundness, and demonstrated fertility," also the "simplicity of rural and artisan life, the sobriety, the industriousness, the fertility" as opposed to the "physical degeneration" of urban life.

333. M. Michaelis, *Mussolini e la questione ebraica* cit., p. 54, mentions an article ("Il regno di Geova"), most likely written by Mussolini himself, in *Il popolo d'Italia*, March 17, 1932 against high finance. The incident by itself does not seem to be enough to prove active anti-Semitism by Mussolini during that period. As Michaelis correctly notes (pp. 242-43), the theme of high finance was commonplace not only in Italy but also in democratic countries.

334. *Italia*, September 21, 1931, p. 10.

335. Still in November 1933, many exiled anti-Fascists did not believe in a Fascist anti-Semitism. At this time the *Quaderni di 'Giustizia e Libertà,'* where many Jews were publishing, in addition to Carlo Rosselli who was the editor (Max Ascoli, Vittorio Foà, Leone Ginzburg, Carlo Levi, Mario Levi, Riccardo Levi, Gino Luzzatto were contributors), printed an article by H. E. Kaminsky, *Fascismo tedesco e fascismo italiano* (pp. 33-36), in which one of the very few differences between Hitlerism and Fascism was identified by the different attitude regarding the Jews.

336. On the Fascist attitude towards National Socialism and the relations between the two parties until 1933, see R. De Felice, *Mussolini e Hitler. I rapporti segreti (1922-1933)*, Florence 1983, and K. P. Hoepke, *La destra tedesca e il fascismo*, Bologna 1971.

337. A typical initiative is the inquiry into National Socialism, organized (at Mussolini's request) by *Antieuropa*, March-September 1931 and later assembled in the volume *Inchiesta su Hitler*, Rome 1932.

338. Among the most explicit, see "Croce uncinata," in *Il Tevere*, June 13, 1931. In 1933, "Il padre dei razzismi," *Il Tevere* (May 11-12) reached the point of accusing the Jews of being the originators of racism ("All racism is nothing but a derivation of Semitic racism or a defense against it") and that because they refused assimilation and made themselves upholders of their own nationalism of, the "most closed and narrow-minded" kind.

339. See C. Pavolini, "Germania 1935, XI: Il sogno dell' 'unità germanica,'" in *Il Tevere*, October 13, 1930. Pavolini, on his return from Germany, repeated his thoughts in a lecture, published in *Il bargello* of Florence. In the same magazine, Lodovico di Caporiacco, harshly criticized him, defending Nazi racism and the myth of blood and race: "In such terms it seems to me that the racism of the German right-wing party is an indication of awareness and adherence to reality, not prejudice" (L. Di Caporiacco, "Ancora sulla Germania hitleriana," in *Il bargello*, March 27, 1932).

340. See, for example, G. Sommi Picenardi, "Hitler e gli Ebrei," in *Il regime fascista*, October 30, 1932 and "Dura legge," in *Il regime fascista*, October 10, 1931.

341. B. Mussolini, *La dottrina del fascismo*, Florence 1937, pp. 19-20: "A nation is the union of those who, from nature and from history, ethnically find reason to form it, setting off on the same lines of development and spiritual formation, as if conscience and will were one. Not race, nor different geographical region, but lineage, historically perpetuating itself, multitudes unified by one idea, that is, the will to existence and power: self consciousness, personality." In the 1937 edition, to which we refer, the antiracist direction of this definition of a nation was already confirmed, in a note, by a clear reference to the *Colloqui* with Ludwig.

342. We owe the knowledge of this letter to the kindness of Mrs. Sarah Fano.

343. See, regarding this, R. De Felice, *Mussolini e Hitler* cit.

344. See, also, M. Michaelis, *Mussolini e la questione ebraica* cit., pp. 66-69.

345. The case of Giovanni Gentile is typical. On May 15, 1933, K. Vossler asked for his intercession in favor of professor Richard Honigswald, professor of philosophy at the University of Munich and "a true proponent of critical idealism," who, as a Jew, ran the risk of losing his professorship, despite the fact that he was held in high consideration by all and that his colleagues wished for him to stay. Gentile, before intervening, wanted an authorization, granted July 5, from the Ministry of Foreign Affairs. See ASAE, *Germania*, p. 14, *1933*, sub file *Antisemitismo tedesco - 3° trimestre 1933*.

346. See *Il popolo d'Italia*, July-August 1933.

347. *Israel* systematically gave an account of these viewpoints; see, for example, the issues from June 8, September 12-20, October 19, December 21, 1933 and March 15-22, 1934.

348. See "Fallacia ariana" and "Razze e razzismo," in *Il popolo d'Italia* August 4 and September 8, 1934. By November 4, 1933 the article entitled "Non una, ma cinque" in *Il popolo d'Italia* had criticized Nazi racism.

349. G. Piazza, "Il ratto d'Apollo e altre cose buffe," in *La Stampa*, March 29, 1934.

350. L. Salemi, "Universalità del fascismo e razzismo nazional-socialista," in *L'Ora*, April 2, 1934.

351. M. Rivore, "La razza contro la storia," in *Il popolo di Lombardia*, September 1, 1934.

352. February 4 1933, an editor's note, entitled "Hitler nominato cancelliere," in *Liguria del popolo*, commented on the rise to power of Nazism with these words:

"Although we have never shared the opinion, nor can we sympathize with all of Hitler's program, especially from a religious point of view, nevertheless we have followed, with courageous sympathy, the gigantic fight undertaken against the formidable Jewish-Masonic sectarianism with whom other parties in Germany, the Center not excluded, for political opportunity, appear to come to terms with. The present victory, however, is also a bit of a victory for the *Liguria del popolo*, the only Catholic paper who, in contrast with the growing hostility of those Catholic tendencies in the habit of blindly believing the politics of the Center to be the cure for all of the actual disgraces afflicting Germany, has placed in a correct light the high social and patriotic judgment of the new chancellor." Other openly anti-Semitic attitudes appear in the issues of January 21 and 28, 1933.

353. The accusation of ritual homicide, other than by the *Liguria del popolo* of February 25, 1933 ("Noi e gli ebrei," by V. F.), was repeated in 1935 by the *Gazzettino* of Venice (January 25 and 26, signed by Eugenio Bellati). Some readers protested against the articles of the Venetian papers (see issues January 21 and 22 and February 7, 1935 of the *Gazzettino*), as did the Union of the Communities, with two official initiatives, dated January 15 and 29, 1935, in the presence of the undersecretary for Press and Propaganda, G. Ciano. The latter, on February 1, replied, assuring of having given the prefect of Venice the order that these attacks were not to be repeated. See AUCII, *1934-35, Manifestaz. pubbliche e della stampa sugli ebrei e sull'ebraismo*, subtitled *Rapporti con le autorità*.

354. See, for all, G. Papini, "Razzia di razzisti," in *Il frontespizio*, December 1934.

355. Card. Faulhaber, *Giudaismo-Cristianesimo-Germanesimo*, Brescia 1934; H. Belloc, *Gli ebrei*, Milan 1934. On Cardinal Faulhaber's sermons, see R. Paoli, "Il Cardinale e i Germani," in *Il frontespizio*, May 1934. During these years, P. Bargellini's magazine frequently and pointedly criticized racism, Nazi anti-Semitism, and their Italian supporters. In its issue of December 1934, going into battle against racism, among others, was also G. Papini (*Razzia dei razzisti*), defining it "the latest German battle against Rome" and Catholicism.

356. E. Rosa, "La questione giudaica e l'antisemitismo nazional socialista," in *La civiltà cattolica*, 1934, issues 2024 and 2025.

357. E. Rosa, *La questione giudaica* cit., pp. 126 sgg.

358. t.t., "Pro-Iudaeis," in *Rassegna romana*, May-June 1933, p. 336.

359. P. Perali, "Dalla razza alla 'ecclesia.' L'Italia madre di popoli," in *Rassegna romana*, September-October 1934.

360. Also, the Italian language papers abroad took different positions, some openly in favor of the Jews and against Hitler (for an example, see G. Pope, "Hitler e gli ebrei," in *Il Progresso Italo-Americano*, New York, March 25, 1933); others, the majority perhaps, tried to keep an equidistant stance, criticizing Nazism, but not sparing criticism towards the Jews (for an example, see the *Bollettino italo-canadese* and *L'unione*, of San Francisco,

of April 7, 1933). A decidedly anti-Jewish position was assumed by *Il mattino d'Italia*, of Buenos Aires (see the issues of March 31 and April 4, 1933) and *Il Lazio*, of New York (see the issue of April 1933).

361. See *Israel*, April 27, 1933.

362. See "Giudaismo e Fascismo. Un'intervista di Angelo Sacerdoti con *l'Echo de Paris* e un commento del *Popolo d'Italia*," in *Israel*, October 19, 1933. The comment by *Il popolo d'Italia* in the interview by Angelo Sacerdoti, "Giudaismo e Fascismo," appeared, signed "Farinata," (Ottavio Dinale) in the issue of October 15 (that "Farinata" was Dinale is actually said by O. Dinale, *Quarant'anni di colloqui con lui*, Milan 1953, p. 73). Sacerdoti's interview even caused a stir abroad; see, for example, *La Turquie* November 18, 1933.

363. L. Poliakov, *Il nazismo e lo sterminio degli ebrei* cit.

364. ASAE, *Carte recuperate nel 1945 (fondo Lancellotti), Gabinetto, Antinazismo (1933)*; all of the telegrams cited for the period of March 29–April 4, 1933 are filed in this box. On March 26 Mussolini cabled Cerruti to send information on "the true evaluation of the widespread news in the press all around the world, regarding anti-Semitic violence committed in Germany after March 5." From the same telegram it emerges that on March 25 the British ambassador to Rome had exchanged opinions with Mussolini on the subject. In his telegram of the 29th, Cerruti harshly condemned the German actions, blaming Göring and Goebbels above all. From another of Cerruti's cables, on the 30th, it also emerged that he had met at a reception in honor of the Vatican with von Papen who had insistently asked him to speak with Goebbels. The conversation did not achieve any results.

365. Just before going to see Hitler, Cerruti had been given a draft in Rome of a declaration to suggest, if necessary, to Hitler, to allow him to elegantly get out of the situation in which he found himself with the Party's proclamation. The plan was as follows: "The Cabinet of the Reich having reviewed the proclamation launched by the Directorate of the Nazi Party regarding the measures to be adopted against the Jews living in Germany to begin April 1, orders the Nazi Party not to initiate the aforesaid measures, claiming that the government of the Reich, through the means at its disposal, has not reestablished the truth of the facts, and certifies that no repression has been carried out against Jews residing in Germany."

366. Recalling those days in "Mussolini e gli ebrei" [Mussolini and the Jews] (published in *La Stampa*, September 12, 1945), V. Cerruti referred to that meeting more extensively, using slightly different terms, especially with regard to the second part, following from the end of the reading of Mussolini's message. According to Cerruti's account, "Hitler could not manage to control his irritation, at first he was calm, then became more

and more excited until he was shouting like a mad man and saying precisely:

'You know how great my admiration is for Mussolini, whom I consider to be the spiritual head of my "movement" since, if he had not been able to assume power in Italy, national socialism would have had no chance of success in Germany. For more than three years the bust of Mussolini has been in my office at the Brown House in Munich, in front of my desk. This being said, allow me to state that Mussolini understands nothing of the Jewish problem, whereas I know it in depth, having studied it for years, from every angle, like no other. In Italy you have, it seems, the good fortune of having few Jews. I am happy for you, but it is no reason for you to ignore the danger that Judaism represents, being closely tied to Bolshevism all over the world. I am in possession of recent and correct information according to which the United States will have to face this grave problem in order to liberate themselves from the Marxist danger. In America, they will have to take recourse to methods far more energetic than mine, and I predict, in a short while, there will be pogroms on an unprecedented scale. Anyway, I ask you to tell Mussolini that I appreciate his concern, but that I believe I must persevere in doing what I set out to do, the result of profound reflection, in conformity with the necessity to perform the task that I have imposed upon myself. Also tell him that I don't know that if in two or three hundred years my name will be held in high esteem for what I ardently hope to do for my people, but of one thing I am certain: that in five or six hundred years the name of Hitler will be glorified everywhere as the name of the man who once and for all extirpated the plague of the Jews from the world.'

"The diplomatic initiative could not have been more unsuccessful.

"Nevertheless I still wished to make two points: that commercial relations would have fatally suffered, because foreign countries traded with Germany without distinguishing between Christians and Jews; that the Nazi government could derive great moral effect from an act of clemency. His strength was already considered as awesome; therefore the revocation of the ordered measures would not have been judged as a sign of weakness, but of magnanimity.

"Hitler replied: 'The boycott will last, as I told you, such a short time, that it will not damage foreign commercial trade. Regarding the second comment, he who is my friend would consider an act of strength the revocation of the measures, but certainly none of my many enemies.'"

367. From one of Cerruti's telegrams, April 4, it emerges that von Neurath, to this date, still hoped to pry from Hitler the revocation of the decisions.

368. The instructions were given on April 4, with a circular cable signed by Mussolini, worded as follows:

"It appears that notably exaggerated information is being disseminated abroad, that is nothing short of false, regarding the behavior of leading associations towards the Jewish community.

"I pray that Your Excellency would, when the occasion presents itself in conversations when the issue is raised, to warn, on his own initiative, against such extreme verbal abuse, using arguments that will induce a more serene valuation of the needs and difficulties of the present German situation."

369. ACS, *Segr. part. del Duce, Carteggio riservato*, file n.442/R, *Hitler*.

370. ASAE, *Germania*, p. 14, *1933*, sub-file "Antisemitismo tedesco-1° semestre 1933." Other than to Jarach, the reply was announced April 13 at the embassy in Berlin: "The Royal Government is not opposed in principle to German Jews coming to reside in Italy, naturally as long as they have not actively taken part in political parties opposed to Fascism, and in no uncertain terms would the Royal Government tolerate any political activity whatsoever against the German regime by them."

371. Various professional organizations, worried about the competition that might harm their members by an authorization given to German Jews to reside and exercise their professions in Italy, tried to prevent, if not the entry of the refugees, at least the authorization to allow them to practice. At first, the oppositions mainly came from the National Medical Doctor's Union. Professor E. Morelli, union secretary, wrote, in May, to Bodrero, of the National Confederation Fascist Union of Professionals and Artists, regarding the issue:

"I believe it my duty to make you aware of a major danger threatening the medical professionat this time. Since the expulsion of the Jews from Germany, a great number of doctors have requested permission to come to Italy. Numerous letters have been sent both to myself and other colleagues. They are from university professors, of great renown, who wish to join our institutes in any position, and they are medical practitioners in search of a position... I fear that there is something being contrived similar to that of the unauthorized dentists who used a doctor's name as a figurehead. Since the problem is also political, I pray you to ask for instructions." (ASAE, *Germania*, p. 14, 1933, under the file "Antisemitismo tedesco-1° semestre 1933," attached to a letter of May 31, 1933 from E. Bodrero to Bruno Biagi, undersecretary to the Ministry of Corporations).

Despite resistance to the influx of Jewish professionals, it was not really forbidden (for doctors, veterinary surgeons, and pharmacists, professional practice was regulated with D. L. n. 184 of March 5, 1935; see *Gazzetta ufficiale*, n. 64, March 16 1935). In November 1934 the PNF published in its "Bulletin" the "wishes" of some professional categories that would have liked to limit the professional practice of Jewish refugees in Italy and also students who took their degrees in Italy (see ACS, *Min. Int., Dir. gen. Demografia e Razza [1915-44]*, 2, file 16, *Pratiche riguardanti il ministero delle Corporazioni*, Alessandro Pavolini to the Ministry of Corporations and the Ministry of Justice, August 23, 1938).

372. In the copy of the agenda sent to Mussolini, the words from "Nations" to "solemn" are underlined in Mussolini's own hand and checked with an exclamation mark. (See ASAE, *Germania*, p. 14. *1933*, under the file "Antisemitismo tedesco–1° semestre 1933.")

373. ASAE, *Germania*, p. 14, 1933, under the file "Antisemitismo tedesco-1° semestre 1933," legation of Riga to the Ministry of Foreign Affairs, May 13, 1933.

374. Of the various reports by V. Cerruti to the Ministry of Foreign Affairs and to the "Duce," we refer to the one that is truly dramatic, Document 3, to Mussolini, May 5, 1933 (ASAE, *Germania*, p. 14, 1933, under the file "Antisemitismo tedesco-1° semestre 1933)."

375. This happened in any case without any difficulty or commotion. In a confidential report of the Director General for Public Security, General Affairs and Reserved Affairs divisions (signed by C. Senise) to the Ministry of Foreign Affairs, Political Affairs, Office I, July 7, 1933, one reads: "Serious conflicts between Jews and anti-Semites never having occurred in Italy, the arrival of political refugees in our territory has passed almost unobserved and it has not been necessary to adopt special measures." In the same report it was said that more than 800 German Jews had embarked in Naples, on the *Vulcania,* sailing to Palestine. In another, similar, report of August 29, it is shown that until that date, since January 1, 380 German Jews had remained in Italy (250 in Milan, 45 in Naples, 31 in Rome, and 26 in Turin). The only disturbances were (Ministry of Internal Affairs, Director General for Public Security to the Ministry of Foreign Affairs, Political Affairs, Office I, July 7, 1933) near Bolzano, the work of Nazis who, in Merano, had struck two Italian Jews and written anti-Semitic graffiti on the walls. Only the prefect of Carnaro expressed any perplexity on the prospect of receiving German refugees in that border area. In spite of these misgivings and the dissatisfaction of the "local Fascist element" the government also authorized the area of Fiume (see ASAE, *Germania*, p. 14, 1933, under the file "Antisemitismo tedesco - 3° and 4° trimestre 1933)."

376. The British embassy in Rome verbally asked the Ministry of Foreign Affairs, May 27, 1933, for news regarding the influx of German refugees in Italy. On July 15, still verbally, the Palazzo Chigi replied that the government, given the irrelevance of their numbers, "had not felt it advisable to adopt special measures and provisions." See ASAE, *Germania*, p.14. 1933, under the file "Antisemitismo tedesco–3° trimestre 1933."

377. In a memorandum by Suvich, it emerges that Weizmann insisted above all on his project to emigrate 50,000 young Jews from Germany to Palestine and regarding the problem of the liquidation of Jewish possessions in Germany; he promised to keep Mussolini informed on both matters, who, it appears, listened "with interest and goodwill" (see ASAE, *Palestina*, p. 5, 1933, *Colloquio fra il Capo del Governo e il Signor Weitzmann* [sic]. From Rome, Weizmann went to London where he spoke very well about Italy, "The only country which has widely opened the doors of its schools to Jewish students, which demonstrates the generosity of the Fascist government." On the meeting, its preparations, and the direct and indirect consequences, see S. Minerbi, "Gli ultimi due incontri Weizmann-Mussolini (1933-1934)," in *Storia contemporanea*. September 1974, pp. 431-66.

378. ASAE, *Germania*, p. 14, 1933, under the file "Antisemitismo tedesco–3° trimestre 1933," in Document 4.

379. ASAE, *Germania*, p. 14, 1933, under the file "Antisemitismo tedesco–3° trimestre 1933, Appunto per S.E. il Capo del Governo" (August 21, 1933), "Appunto per il Sottosegretario di Stato" (August 31, 1933).

380. ASAE, *Germania*, p. 14, 1933, under the file "Antisemitismo tedesco-4° trimestre 1933," Italian Jewish Community Union to the Ministry of Foreign Affairs, September 14 1933; ASAE, *Archivio di Gabinetto del Ministro*, p. 1368, 1933-36, under the file "Conferenza Ebraica Mondiale di Ginevra, La seconda conferenza ebraica mondiale di Ginevra" (report dated September 12, 1933, with three attachments). According to this report, if the conference approved a final resolution that was "weak" and "pale" it was due to the Italian delegates who avoided the approval of the first project which was "clear-cut," "formal," "resolute," "unequivocal." The proceedings regarding Italy, in Geneva, were also followed by the Dutch A. Pelt, of the League of Nations. In his opinion, the Italian delegates wanted to dissuade the congress from resorting to violent demonstrations and extreme solutions, like the German economic boycott. See ASAE, *Palestina*, p. 5, 1933.

381. In spite of the discretion with which Sacerdoti and Lattes carried out their mission, something still leaked to the press. See *Le Petit Parisien*, September 6 1933; *L'Ami du Peuple*, September 1933 and *La Liberté* September 7 1933. These last two newspapers emphasized that Sacerdoti, "ami personnel" (*Ami du Peuple*) and "intime" (*Liberté*) of Mussolini, had strongly denounced Nazi anti-Semitism and promised the German Jews support from the Italian Jews.

382. The authorization was granted by the Ministry of Foreign Affairs on September 25 1933. See ASAE, *Germania*, p. 14, 1933, under the file "Antisemitismo tedesco–4° semestre 1933, Appunto per il Sottosegretario di Stato" (September 25 1933). At the same time though, the ministry

prohibited the publication of a statement by the Union of the Communities, which was strongly critical of Germany. On the same day, Mussolini, worried about the developments and repercussions that the resolutions of Geneva could have on public opinion, and perhaps to see if his "recommendations" had been considered, telegraphed all of the embassies and legations of Europe (excluding Berlin) and America, asking them to keep him informed of all "the demonstrations against Hitler staged by the Jews."

383. The aid and assistance for the refugees in transit, or to those coming to reside in Italy by Jewish Italian organizations (on June 15 1935 the latter were estimated by the "Haut-Commisariat pour les Refugiés [israélites et autres] provenant d'Allemagne" to be around 1,100; see the *Rapport du Haut-Commissaire*, M. J. G. Mcdonald, London 1935, p. 10), continued until June 1940. For this purpose, the Commission of Assistance for Jews in Italy was created in 1933, funded by the charity of Jews, and those not Jewish, and with the help of the Italian Commission of Assistance to the Jewish emigrants of Trieste (a rich documentation on the activity of this commission, chiefly relating to the period of persecution, was published in the *Rassegna mensile d'Israel*, October-November 1965). Considerable help was also provided by various international Jewish aid organizations (see AUCII, *1932-33* and *1934-35, Assistenza profughi dalla Germania; 1934-35, Istituzioni temporanee di soccorso*). To give an idea of the truly meritorious work achieved, it is sufficient to mention that the Trieste Commission, in 1933, assisted 526 "wayfarers" and in 1934, 438 (confronted with the 127 in 1931 and the 212 in 1932); see COM. IT. ASS. EM. EBREI, *Relazione sull'attività del Comitato negli anni 1931-34*, Trieste 1935. With the authorization of the Italian Government, and the economical aid of the industrialist from Prato, Giulio Forti, three farms were bought in Tuscany for the agricultural preparation of the Jews who were to establish themselves in Palestine (see ASAE, *Palestina*, p. 9, *1934*, under the file *Acquisto di una fattoria in Toscana per avviarvi gli ebrei tedeschi; Germania*, p. 27, *1935*, under the file *Anitsemitismo tedesco*). The three farms were in Castellina in Chianti, Iolo and Firenze-Castello. The prefect of Florence established a service of "understated surveillance" around their inhabitants. Lesser initiatives of the kind were taken up in other localities. It is extremely difficult to establish the number of Jewish refugees in transit in Italy. In 1933 alone 21,183 went through Trieste (out of 74,898 from 1920 to 1933). Of these 21,183 people, 6,095 appeared as "tourists" and 1,931 as "capitalists" (that is, those who had a regular entry permit for Palestine, demonstrating to be in possession of at least one thousand pounds). Yet, of these 21,183; 6,000 were German (10,747 were Polish and 1,615 were Baltic). From Trieste, the emigrants traveled on the ships of the Lloyd Triestino, that

offered them considerable discounts (up to 75%). An official report, of March 3, 1934, from the Royal Inspectorate of Emigration of Trieste to the Ministry of Foreign Affairs, estimated that two thirds of all the traffic for Palestine passed through Trieste. The Lloyd had drawn up an agreement with the Jewish Agency, the basis of which was to undertake the transportation via Trieste of 45% of the emigration from Poland and 75% of that of Germany and neighboring countries. (See ASAE, *Palestina*, p. 8, 1934.)

Operating in Switzerland, to aid German Jews, was the anti-Fascist Matteotti Foundation. Eric Allatini, a decorated former volunteer in the war, was part of the French Commission for the protection of persecuted Jewish intellectuals. Angelo Donati was also very active in France.

384. ASAE, *Germania*, p. 38, 1937, *Colloquio Duce–von Neurath* (May 3, 1937).

385. See C. Weizmann, *La mia vita per Israele* cit., pp. 409-10 and above all the two reports on this, compiled by V. Jacobson (see Document 5) and L. Kohn, kindly provided by the Weizmann Institute of Rehovoth, as well as S. Minerbi, *Gli ultimi due incontri Weizmann-Mussolini* cit., pp. 466-77.

386. Of the advice that Mussolini gave to Dollfuss regarding this, there was not to forget—if necessary to maintain oneself in power—a certain amount of anti-Semitism (see *Geheimer Briefwechsel Mussolini–Dollfuss*, Wein 1949, p. 53) but later, with other incentives, he would suggest going in the opposite direction. As is clear, the pro-Jewish politics of the Duce during these years were chiefly opportunistic.

387. A. Theodoli, *A cavallo di due secoli* cit., pp. 170-71.

388. A. Theodoli, *A cavallo di due secoli* cit., p. 171; C. Weizmann, *La mia vita per Israele* cit., p. 410.

389. A. Theodoli, *A cavallo di due secoli* cit., p. 171. Another 2,000 German Jews were to be authorized entry into Italy in 1936 (see *La nostra bandiera*, March 15, 1936).

390. See G. Pini–D. Susmel, *Mussolini ecc.* cit., III, pp. 299 and 459. See also, K. Heiden, *Der Führer*, New York 1944, p. 585.

391. *Documents on German Foreign Policy 1918-45*, series C. (*1933-37*), III, London 1959, pp. 12, 18.

392. See *Protocole de la troisième Conférence Juive Mondiale. Genève, 20-23 août 1934*, Paris 1934, pp. 108-9 (comments by Angelo Sacerdoti).

393. *Ibid.*, pp. 87 and 89.

394. J. Draenger, *Nahoum Goldmann*, Paris 1956, II, pp. 214-36. The pages in question have been partially reproduced by *Israel*, July 12 1956: *Una pagina dimenticata di storia. L'incontro Goldmann-Mussolini, 13 Novembre 1934*. Given their importance and the difficulty of gaining access to Draenger's book in Italy (which reports the meeting from the unpublished memoirs of Goldmann), we offer them in Document 6 herein. Goldmann's memoirs,

later published (*Memories. The Autobiography of Nahum Goldmann*, London 1970), reproduce the meeting with variants of little importance, see pp. 134 and 153.

395. See ASAE, *Archivio del Gabinetto del Ministro, 1934-35, Sarre*, p. 364; J. Draenger, *Nahoum Goldmann*, cit., II, pp. 234-37 (on p. 235 appears the letter from von Neurath to P. Aloisi, with which Germany undertook to allow the eventual free exodus of the Jews from the Sarre).

396. Regarding the problem of the refugees after the coming to power of Nazism, see M. Leone, *Le organizzaioni di soccorso ebraiche in età fascista* cit., pp. 77; S. Soriani, *L'assistenza ai profughi ebrei in Italia (1933-1947). Contributo alla storia della "Delasem,"* Rome 1983, p. 29. No study exists on the Jewish intellectual emigration from Germany to Italy, which is by no means insignificant and also concerns personalities who were to play significant roles; for example, Karl Löwith and George L. Mosse.

397. AUCII, *1934-35, Manifestazioni pubbliche e della stampa sugli ebrei e l'ebraismo*, under the file "Communità," Community of Genoa to the Union, January 18, 1934.

398. *Corriere padano*, March 2, 1934.

399. According to M. Michaelis, *Mussolini e la questione ebraica* cit., p. 76, the campaign was started by Mussolini. The claim is not only unproven (the reference to *Il Tevere* is worthless, because if it were true that Mussolini wanted its creation in 1924, and if it sometimes served for taking positions and unofficial attacks, it is just as true that Interlandi directed it according to his own understanding of Fascism, and for years did not avoid making periodic anti-Semitic and pro-Nazi quips, so much so that since 1926 he earned the smug attention of Alfred Rosenberg), but profoundly reflects the marked tendency of Michaelis in minimizing and frequently ignoring the internal political ramifications of Mussolini's Jewish policy, of Mussolini, and Fascist policy in general, and the changes and movements within his various positions. Regarding this, see the correct observations of Mario Toscano, *Gli ebrei in Italia dall'emancipazione alle persecuzioni* cit., p. 921.

400. See *Il Tevere*, April 7 and 9, 1934.

401. Therein, February 28, 1934; see the violent attack on the *Corriere padano*, in an article by Leo Cappa on Judaism.

402. See *Il Tevere*, August 28, 1934; *Ottobre*, August 29, 1934; *La scure*, Piacenza, August 30, 1934.

403. See *Il Tevere*, March 20, 1934.

404. See *Il Tevere*, February 7, 1934 (attorney Rubens Samaia), February 8, 1934 (Dr. Mario Rossi). The comment of M. Rossi was a real article of more than a column and was, besides others, printed integrally by the *Piccolo della sera* February 10.

405. See *Israel*, February 15-22, 1934.

406. The letter insisted, above all, on the concept that Zionism was the Jewish answer to the tragedy that had fallen upon them:

    "Who states that being Zionist cannot be compatible with being a good Italian demonstrates an ignorance of what Zionism is in Italy. It is not lack of love for Italy that pushes us Jewish Italians to work together for the reconstruction of a Jewish Palestine, but the heartfelt conviction that, as Jews, we cannot remain insensitive to the inhumane tragedy that weighs upon a great part of Judaism. Must we remember the hundreds of thousands massacred in Russia, Ukraine, and Poland, the *numerus clausus* at universities in many countries, the present persecution of the Jews and their descendants in Germany? The only light for those millions of Jews, who struggle today in such an extremely sad situation, is that shone by Zionism, which has achieved, and continues to carry out, a high work of social redemption to the advantage of both the Jewish and non-Jewish, transforming thousands of fugitives into productive men, giving them the possibility to live in Palestine with dignity and to make the Jewish name honorable, which in many countries, let's not forget, is still, to inevitable disgrace also to us Italian Jews, insulted and mocked.

    "There is no doubt that we, who feel ourselves the children of Italy, and who participate in Italian life in the most complete and intimate ways, could ever easily forget the history and misfortune of the Jews. All that is good in us, our dignity, our sense of duty, will not allow us to do so.

    "Participating in the rebirth of that land, where God almighty revealed himself, where the light of the Bible first shone, and where we have faith that the spiritual values of Judaism can once again blossom, we are certain that we are contributing to a very noble work of justice and civility, and certain that we are not doing anything that is incompatible with our patriotism."

407. Of all of the most significant positions taken, it is worth remembering the debate that took place in *L'universale* of Florence, in which Giacomo Lumbroso, Mario Luzzatto, Adriano Ghiron, Berto Ricci and Alberto Luchini participated, and which also caused comment in *Il bargello* (March 4); as well as that which appeared in *Vent'anni*, of Turin.

408. On the episode, see also B. Allason, *Memorie di un antifascista*, Florence 1946, pp. 157-80; L. Levi, "Antifascismo e Sionismo: convergenze e contrasti (note e ricordi sui 'fermi' e sui fermenti torinesi del 1934)," in *Gli ebrei in Italia durante il fascismo*, I, Turin 1961, pp. 49-62; S. Segre Amar, "Sopra alcune inesattezze storiche intorno alle passate vicende degli Ebrei in Italia," in *La rassegna mensile di Israel*, May 1961; ID., "Sui 'fatti' di Torino del 1934," in *Gli ebrei in Italia durante il fascismo*, II, Milan 1962, pp. 125-34.

409. See Davide Nissim's letter, "Ebrei...ed ebrei," to _Il popolo biellese_, April 9 1934.

410. Even within the leadership of the PNF, with the onset of 1934, some started to speak in more or less explicitly anti-Semitic terms. Typical of this are the notes of July 30, 1934 by Starace for a letter to the provincial party secretary of Trieste: "Certain small groups, accustomed to exercising uncontrolled influence upon the local situation, are not able to conceal their intolerance for the discipline which has recently grown stronger in Trieste. Senators Segre-Sartorio, Banelli, Pitacco, Hon. Coceani, Dr. Guido Segre, the lawyer Dr. Cuzzi, and other lesser figures, have this tendency. It is the old situation of Trieste that is based on factions and local combinations, upheld by the Jewish Levantine congregations, which have the economy and local finance in their grip. It is therefore necessary that these gray areas be done away with and that Fascism assume its position of authority and command." See ACS, _PNF, Situazione politica delle provincie (1923-43), Trieste._

411. G. Salvemini, "The Jews," in _Racial Minorities Under Fascism in Italy_ (published by the Women's International League for Peace and Freedom), Chapter VI, Chicago 1934.
The essay was republished with slight variations in 1937.
In America the campaign of _Il Tevere_ and _Il regime fascista_ and other papers during the period of January-April, 1934, caused a great stir. In December at City College in New York, a protest demonstration was held in occasion of the arrival of a group of Italian university students; not to mention various attacks by the press, in particular the Jewish press. Angelo Sacerdoti protested with a harsh letter on December 14, 1934, to Dr. Stephen Wise, president of the American Jewish Congress, in which he expounded the Italian Government's policy of goodwill towards the Jews (see, ACIR, p. 37, _Carte del rabbino A.Sacerdoti_). Similar protests appeared, under the name of I. C. Falbo, "L'Italia e gli ebrei," in the December 20, 1934 issue of _Il progresso italo-americano_ of New York.

412. The cited passages are taken from the agenda approved by the representatives of various European Fascist parties and movements, gathered in Montreux in December 1934. Firmly against this agenda, was E. Garibaldi, "Il congresso di Montreux e la questione ebraica," in _La nostra bandiera_, May 1935.
For further information, see M. A. Ledeen, _L'Internazionale fascista_, Bari 1973.

413. AUCII, _1934-35, Manifestazioni pubbliche e private della stampa sugli ebrei e sull'ebraismo_, under the file _Privati_, L. Carpi, G. Ottolenghi, R. Segre, to Felice Ravenna, Milan, February 8, 1934.
The three signatories, "reserve officers, war veterans and decorated servicemen," asked for the intervention of the Union that cleared "in an

unequivocal way, that Zionism had never given the Jews the slightest moral doubt on the priorities of Italian spirit and Judaism. And proof is that the argument was never raised again, having been already resolved in a precise manner, whilst the Zionists themselves, who represented the better part of Judaism, are and feel one hundred percent Italian"; and that it rejected "proudly the accusation that there could exist, amongst the Italian Jews, persons without the highest feelings of Italian solidarity."

The initiative, even if personal, is attributed to the Zionist-Revisionist group.

414. See AUCII, *Libro dei verbali, Giunta*, February 21 and March 22, 1934.

415. AUCII, *1934-35, Manifestazioni pubbliche e della stampa sugli ebrei e sull'ebraismo*, under the file *Privati* (insert *Torino*) and *Comunità* (inserts *Milano, Torino, Verona*).

416. "Triste episodio," in *Israel*, April 12, 1934.

417. AUCII, *1934-35, Enti mondiali*, Augusto Levi and Felice Ravenna, Florence, April 23, 1934.

418. AUCII, *Libro dei verbali, Consiglio*, April 24, 1934. There were protests against these, verbally by D. Lattes, the FACE (Federazione associazioni culturali ebraiche) and the *Israel*, also, in general, the Zionists who appear to not have been advised of any measures taken by the Union.

419. The most important articles by Ovazza in 1934 were republished in one volume: E. Ovazza, *Sionismo bifronte*, Rome 1935.

420. *La nostra bandiera*, May 1, 1934, republished in E. Ovazza, *Sionismo bifronte* cit., pp. 27-35.

421. G. Ciano, for example, appears to have been opposed to the initiative. See ACIR, p. 46, *Carte del rabbino Sacerdoti*, A. Sereni to Felice Ravenna, Rome, December 15, 1934.

422. Keeping in mind what would become the executive Committee of Jewish Italians, which was to be established in 1936 by Ovazza and company, it is striking that on March 27, 1933 the Ministry of Foreign Affairs wanted to be informed by the embassy in Berlin on the Federation of German citizens of Mosaic faith. See ASAE, *Germania*, p. 14, *1933*, under the file *Antisemitismo tedesco–1° semestre 1933*.

423. AUCII, *Libro dei verbali, Giunta*, May 10, 1934.

424. AUCII, *1934-35, Presidenza*, Felice Ravenna to the members of the committee, Rome, May 15, 1934. Almost at the same time, Mussolini, through a Jewish professor later converted to Catholicism and very close to the magazine *Gerarchia*, sent a request to D. Lattes, to dissolve the FSI and liquidate the movement. Lattes, though, resisted such pressure. Mussolini carried out similar steps, most likely through Angelo Sacerdoti with Weizmann. The matter was discussed at a meeting,

held in Merano, between Weizmann, Lattes, and Sacerdoti, and once again rejected.

425. See *La nostra bandiera*, May 24, 1934, republished in E. Ovazza, *Sionismo bifronte* cit., pp. 75-77. The Turin Community elections gave 733 votes out of 741 (57 % of those assigned the right to vote) in favor of the list of General Liuzzi (see *La nostra bandiera*, June 21, 1934). The June 21, 1934 issue of *Israel* insinuated that the success of the list had been ensured, apart from the very energetic propaganda, by ample recourse to the delegation system. On June 17 in Milan the head Italian rabbis met, approving the two agendas, one which maintained that "it is groundless and incorrect to believe that a Jew, because he is such, can be less Italian than someone who is not Jewish" and another which maintained that "no motive exists wherefore Jewish Italians can be differentiated for national and political purposes by their fellow citizens." Furthermore, the rabbis united in Milan, expressed their solidarity towards the union (see *La nostra bandiera*, June 28, 1934, republished in E. Ovazza, *Sionismo bifronte* cit., pp. 113-15).

426. AUCII, *Libro dei verbali, Giunta*, June 7, July 4, September 27, 1934.

427. The text says: "The Union of Italian Jewish Communities, whilst it believes that the fact of having the Government ratify the Balfour declaration, obliging Italian Jews to support, as far as possible, and in a way that can be accepted by the Italian Government, the Jewish Palestinian rebirth of which the highly religious significance is recognized, declares that this and nothing else must be the correct attitude towards Zionism and fervently reaffirms to be Italian and faithful to the regime equally for all of the communities, that it, with vigilant conscience, associates and represents."

428. AUCII, *Libro dei verbali, Giunta*, November 14, 1934.

429. AUCII, *1934-35, Presidenza*, Felice Ravenna to the members of Council, Rome, July 11, 1934.

430. ACIR, P. 37, *Carte del rabbino Sacerdoti*, Angelo Sacerdoti to the rabbi of Gorizia, Rome, December 1934; *Ibid.*, p. 46, A. Sereni to Felice Ravenna, Rome, December 15, 1934; E. Ovazza to Angelo Sacerdoti, Turin, December 1934.

431. R. Guariglia, *Ricordi* cit., pp. 181-83.

432. D. Lattes, "Angiolo Orvieto, poeta ebreo" cit., p. 12.

433. C. Weizmann, *La mia vita per Israele* cit., p. 410.

434. For a clear view of the Palestinian question, see E. Anchieri, *La questione palestinese, 1915-1939*, Milan-Messina 1940; for the years until approximately 1930 see, more in detail, A. Giannini, *L'ultima fase della questione orientale (1913-1932)*, Rome 1933 and Ibidem *Documenti per la storia della pace orientale (1915-1932)*, Rome 1933.

435. A. Theodoli, *A cavallo di due secoli* cit., p. 135: "I thought that Jewish emigration in Palestine should have not only been checked, but controlled, held back, and kept within its natural limits, for motives of social and political order, of which it does not appear to me that they took into proper consideration."

436. C. Weizmann, *La mia vita per Israele* cit., p. 408.

437. See G. Salvemini, *Mussolini diplomatico* cit., pp. 146-56; L. Salvatorelli–G. Mira, *Storia d'Italia ecc* cit., pp. 652-53, 666-71; R. Guariglia, *Ricordi* cit., p. 141.

438. The outcome of trade between Italy and Palestine, during the entire Fascist period, showed a decidedly favorable balance in Italy's favor. Italian purchases, which were mostly made up of potassium salts, grain, scrap iron, rawhides, and animal offal, in 1937 reached the sum of 78,000 Palestinian lira. Whereas exportation, in the same year, reached 320,000 Palestinian lira; the most significant items were yarn and fabric of rayon and mixed fibers, carpets, ropes, hats, berets, manufactured metal products, machinery, electrical appliances, tires and inner tubes, marble, paper, cardboard, pasta, preserved fruits and vegetables, and marc oil. Although increasing in total, Italian exports diminished in proportion: from 4.9% in all of Palestine in 1928, to little more than 2% in 1937. See, also "I rapporti economici fra l'Italia e la Palestina in uno studio dell'Istituto Nazionale per l'esportazione," in *Israel*, June 1, 1934. Also papers such as *Il regime fascista* ("Trecentomila ebrei in Palestina," January 29, 1935) supported the expediency of increasing trade relations between Italy and Palestine. In 1935 Lloyd's of Trieste published a special issue, in both Italian and Hebrew, on the maritime traffic for Palestine via Trieste. For the following period, see "Il commercio estero della Palestina con particulare riguardo agli scambi con l'Italia," in *Israel*, April 22, 1937.

439. Typical of this new direction, in Italy, is the article "Problemi sionisti" which appeared, signed "Italicus," in the January 1933 issue of Mussolini's magazine *Gerarchia*. In this article, Zionism was criticized, but also taken seriously and not subjected to any final judgement; it showed a new interest in what Zionism meant to Palestine. More explicit was *Il popolo d'Italia*, September 8, 1933, in a paragraph titled "Saggezza," on the Prague Zionist congress: "All things considered, there can only be one solution to the problem of the Jews: a Jewish state in Palestine. The declarations of Prague, in which assimilation is condemned and clearly proclaim that Judaism is not a religion but a race, drive further towards this complete and final solution."
These Fascist opinions where echoed by the Zionists on November 20, 1933, Professor Sokolski, of the Zionist Organization, who in Warsaw, in a dispute with the association because of the propaganda in favor of the

mandate on Palestine, stressed the "wise, just, and well-balanced" policy of Mussolini towards Italian Jews and his cordial interest in the Palestinian problem.

440. See U. Nahon, "Incontri e rapporti con Weizmann," in *La rassegna mensile di Israel*, January-April 1985, pp. 143-47. At the end of 1933, Weizmann sent his own envoy to Italy, Eliahu Golomb, to examine the possibility of buying arms for the Hagana. See *Ibid.*, p. 147.

441. In March 1933 Weizmann, thinking that Mussolini might do something "to restrain Hitler," wrote to the British Premier Ramsay MacDonald, who, with the Minister of Foreign Affairs, Sir John Simon, was about to meet Mussolini in Rome, asking him to suggest to the Duce a move in that direction. See *Ibid.*, pp. 147-48.

442. In 1933-34 other attacks, towards hints of Italian anti-Semitism, appeared in the *Haaretz* of Tel Aviv, September 24 ("Antisemitismo in Italia?"), October 17, 1934 ("La verità circa l'antisemitismo in Italia—divergenze di opinioni nel Partito fascista riguardo la questione ebraica"), and in the *Doar Hayóm*, of Jerusalem, July 29, 1934 ("Posizione degli ebrei in Italia. Ostile atteggiamento del fascismo nei riguardi del sionismo").

443. ASAE, *Palestina*, p. 5, *1933*, Polverelli to De Angelis, July 28, 1933. Probably following the denial of the consulate in Jerusalem, October 13, 1933 the *Doar Hayóm* published an article in favor of Mussolini's policy ("La differenza di razza tra il Fascismo e il Nazismo").

444. The meeting between Mussolini and Weizmann was prepared on the Italian behalf, by P. Quaroni and by Victor Jacobson on behalf of the Zionists; see D. Carpi, *Il problema ebraico nella politica italiana ecc.* cit., p. 53.

445. In the previous months, Mussolini had received some Arab chiefs (the last, in order of time, a few days before, was the Emir Scekib Arslan). In Palestine, from 1933, two papers, the *Meraat Ashark* of Jerusalem and the *Falastin* of Jaffa, had begun to push for the constitution of an Arab Fascist party, undoubtedly inspired by Rome. For Mussolini's Arab policy, see R. De Felice, "Arabi e Medio Oriente nella strategia politica di guerra di Mussolini (1940-1943)," in *Storia contemporanea*, December 1986, pp. 1255-359.

446. ASAE, *Palestina*, p. 8, *1934*, under the file "Articolo de *Il popolo d'Italia* sulla soluzione del problema ebraico," Aloisi to De Angelis, February 24, 1934.

447. See *Adiffà* of Jaffa, April 9, 1935 (against the facilitation granted by the Lloyd Triestino to the Jewish emigrants in Palestine), and *Giamia al Islamia*, also of Jaffa, July 22, 1935 (explicitly denouncing Italy's goodwill towards Zionism). The latter, in particular, attacked an interview released in Salonika by the director of Italians abroad, Pietro Parini, in which he had denied the existence of Italian anti-Semitism and separated the position of Fascism from that of Nazism, and also against the *Doar Hayóm* who, on March

15, had favorably commented on this interview ("Il fascismo italiano è ben lungi dall'antisemitismo").

448. The article went on to note that since 1925 there had been a certain evolution in Mussolini, in a favorable sense towards Zionism, and how in certain "semi-official" Italian circles there were even those who would have liked an Italian mandate on Palestine.

449. ASAE, *Palestina*, p. 8, *1934*, W. Gross to B. Mussolini, April 25, 1934.

450. ASAE, *Palestina*, p. 10, *1935*, the Italian Consulate in New York to the Ministry of Foreign Affairs, January 1935 and the Ministry of Foreign Affairs to the Italian Consulate in New York, March 15, 1935.
On another project, still on March 22, 1936, D. Prato would turn to Mussolini to ask his intervention with the Polish Government regarding the controversial question of the authorization of the Jews, in that country, to slaughter their cattle according to Mosaic custom. (See ASAE, *Palestina*, p. 13, *1936*.)

451. ASAE, *Palestina*, p. 10, *1935, Relazione a S.E. il Sottosegretario di Stato*, November 4, 1935; as well as, for clarification, E. Levi, *Episodi di vita ebraica milanese ecc.* cit., pp. 238-39.

452. In 1935 Jabotinsky found himself under pressure to publicly deny more and more frequent accusations of Fascism that greatly compromised his party in the eyes of the majority of international public opinion. See Z. Jabotinsky, *Verso lo Stato* cit., pp. 213-18 and particularly pp. 215-16. Jabotinsky's position was, with regard to his disagreements with Weizmann and both his opinions on Fascism and his relations with the Italian Government, at the center of a violent controversy, which frequently passed from a purely political line to a historical one. Regarding his opposition to Weizmann, F. Furet understood them best (*Il laboratorio della storia*, Milan 1985, p. 295) who described them as follows: "Weizmann is Cavour, and Jabotinsky reincarnates both Mazzini and Garibaldi; the first, a diplomatic visionary, but gifted as a tactitian, keeps to the official program on the home front, with an attentive eye on the international scene; the second, romantic, dazzling, always in a rush, seeks a short cut that leads to the state of Israel." Put in these terms, it is also easy to understand their relationship with Rome and their respective attitudes towards Fascism. Relationships and attitudes that must be placed in the specific climate in which, between two wars and during the Second World War, sparked the movements for national liberation and independence of North Africa and various Asian countries. In a certain sense, one could say that Weizmann was the Zionist Nehru, whilst Jabotinsky was, until the eve of the war, Bose. And, not by chance, if the "winners" in the end, were Weizmann and Nehru, both Jabotinsky and Bose are today placed amongst the "fathers" of Israel and India, even if their extreme anti-English attitude proved mistaken and self-defeating.

453. This was also the opinion of De Angelis. In a confidential telegram on October 2, 1934, to the Ministry of Foreign Affairs and to the Undersecretary for Press and Publicity, regarding the request forwarded to him in Jerusalem by a member of the Revisionist Party, Doctor Wolfgang von Weisl of Vienna, to admit "as assistants in Fascist institutes of any kind, for the entire period necessary, four young Zionists, the Revisionist Party would send to the Kingdom at its own expense, with the intention of having them understand the spirit and learn in detail the mechanisms of Fascist organization," and if the experiment worked, others that "would then become the instructors of the Revisionist masses." De Angelis, giving his favorable opinion (confirmed by G. Ciano, then Undersecretary for Press and Publicity as of October 13, 1934), emphasized "If a comparison was allowed, one could say, with considerable realism, that revisionism has in Zionism the parallel position that Fascism had in Italian life before the March on Rome. The revisionists actually consider themselves, and are considered, a little like 'the Fascists' of Zionism." See ASAE, *Palestina*, p. 5, *1933*, under the file *Ammissione di giovani sionisti del Partito revisionista in istituti fascisti*. It must be remembered that the Palazzo Chigi intended to make a real Fascist party out of revisionism, and it is no coincidence that, amongst the documents at the Palazzo Chigi at the time, there was a real "programmatic base of Jewish, Palestinian, and international Fascism" (see ASAE, *Palestina*, p. 10, 1935).

454. In light of Guariglia's report it is of great interest to reread the opening article "Ordine italiano" in *Oriente* in the May 1932 issue of *L'idea sionistica*, which appears as a clever paraphrase of Jabotinsky's thesis.

455. For the programmatic base of the New Zionist Organization, see Z. Jabotinsky, *Verso lo Stato* cit., pp. 231-36.

456. On the school in Civitavecchia, see I. Halpern, *Techiath ha-yamauth ha'-ivrit* (*La rinascita della marina ebraica*), Tel Aviv 5721 (1961). Halpern offers an extremely valuable documentation; although it appears that he tends to greatly underestimate the political significance of the school. The same limitations, in our opinion, can be found in L. Carpi, *Come e dove rinaque la marina d'Israele. La Scuola Marittima del "Bethar" a Civitavecchia*, Rome 1965, but still of great documentary importance.

457. The courses lasting one year, included the curriculum normally taught in Italian Naval Schools (the students could specialize in navigation, fishing, naval mechanics, and shipbuilding). Other than these subjects, the students had to study physical education and certain Jewish subjects (Hebrew, Palestinian geography, etc.). The qualification obtained, through exams in naval theory and practice, was the same as normal Italian naval schools. The students had to pay a fee of 200 lire per month. All other expenses were met by the Tel-Hai Foundation, which also provided an annual grant for those who could not afford the fee.

The school always remained a prerogative of the revisionists (Jabotinsky often went to visit it) and a request on behalf of the Zionist officials to send their own students there was apparently refused. (See *La nostra bandiera*, April 15, 1936.) For information on the ideological fundamentals of Bethar (the youth organization of the revisionists), see Z. Jabotinsky, *Verso lo Stato* cit., pp. 140-50.

458. See ASAE, *Palestina*, p. 10, *1935*, under the file *Scuola professionale marittima di Civitavecchia. Iscrizione di giovani ebrei.* Useful information can also be found in a pamphlet distributed by Bethar in 1936, *La section juive de l'Ecole Maritime de Civitavecchia (Italie)*.

The foreign press also took interest in the school of Civitavecchia and the cruises of the *Sara*; see, for example, "La navigation juive," in *Ere Nouvelle* of Paris, November 17, 1935. On the other hand the Italian Jewish press often gave ample space to articles, news, and photograph of the school (see, for example, *Davar*, April 4, 1935).

459. ASAE, *Palestina*, p. 19, *1937*, under the file *Scuola professionale marittima di Civitavecchia (1936)*.

460. ASAE, *Palestina*, p. 18, *1937*, in the file "Scuola professionale marittima di Civitavecchia (1937)". On the matter of the changing of the flag, see I. Halpern, *Techiath ha-yamauth ha'-ivrit* cit., p. 125.

461. When Hitler visited Rome, during his trip to Italy, the Fascist government had wanted the *Sara* to go to sea along with all of the students. Halpern, who had an undefined function at the school—but similar to that of Jabotinsky's "political advisor"—obtained though, that they could remain, confined to barracks, on the school's premises. See I. Halpern, *Teciath ha-yamouth ha'-ivrit* cit., p. 214.

462. Typical of this opinion is what the Italian Consul General in Tunis cabled Rome, December 31, 1937, local Jews, who were not favorable to Italy, were very impressed by the visit of the *Sara*: "The stopover of the ship in Tunisia constituted a useful instrument of Fascist publicity." See ASAE, *Palestina*, p. 27, *1938*, under the file *Scuola professionale marittima di Civitavecchia.* Still in Tunisia, there were considerable reactions, obviously unfavorable, from within Arab circles. See the *Gazzetta del popolo* and *Corriere della sera* January 4, 1938. It is not clear if the *Sara* was sabotaged or not; see *Il nuovo cittadino*, January 14, 1938 and *Il giornale di Sicilia*, January 15, 1938.

463. See the *Corriere padano*, February 15, 1938.

464. The advertising campaign for the subscription of "The Sea of Israel" was decided in a meeting held in London in February 1938 under the chairmanship of Jabotinsky with the intervention of financiers and those with major interests in the venture.

465. A request in this direction was made again by two revisionist agents to Mazzolini, the Italian Consul in Jerusalem, in July 1938. From his report

to G. B. Guarnaschelli of the Ministry of Foreign Affairs, July 23, 1938 (ASAE, *Palestina*, p. 27, *1938*, under the file *Scuola professionale marittima di Civitavecchia*), it emerges that the two had asked to send approximately twenty people to Italy to study infantry command, explosive works, aeronautics, radiotelegraphy, and telephony.

466.   It is demonstrated that these plans were correct, for example, in the book published in 1936 in Tel Aviv by an ex-student of the school in Civitavecchia, K. Zwi, *Mussolini ishiato vetorato (Mussolini la sua personalità e il suo insegnamento)*. On some preliminary events relating to this book, see I. Halpern, *Techiath hayamauth ha'-ivrit* cit., p. 91.

467.   See "Italian propaganda in Palestine," in *The Times*, October 12, 1935. Also see *La nostra bandiera*, December 1935 ("Propaganda italiana"), in debate.

468.   See C. Weizmann, *La mia vita per Israele* cit., p. 431; for the relations between Italy and the great Mufti of Jerusalem, see R. De Felice, *Arabi e Medio Oriente* cit.; L. Goglia, "Il Mufti e Mussolini: alcuni documenti sui rapporti tra nazionalismo palestinese e fascismo negli anni trenta," in *Storia contemporanea*, December 1986, pp. 1201-53.

469.   If we wish to establish the period in which this orientation became the norm in the Italian attitude towards Palestine and Zionism, one can assume, more or less, as the starting date, early 1937, that is, when the Ministry of Foreign Affairs–now in Ciano's hands–ordered the various Mediterranean representations to gather precise political-statistical facts on the Jews in general and on the Italians in particular in their respective countries (see ASAE, *Palestina*, p. 19, *1937*, under the file *Sionismo*).

A hardening of Italy's attitude towards Palestine can already be observed in October 1936, when the new Consul General was sent to Jerusalem, Q. Mazzolini, a Fascist diplomat certainly not well disposed towards the Jews (as it clearly appears right from one of his first dispatches to Rome, October 27, in which he refers to the visits he made, upon arriving, to various local authorities). See ASAE, *Palestina*, p. 13, *1936*. On Mussolini's projects for a "general accord" with England, see R. De Felice, *Mussolini il duce*, 2, *Lo Stato totalitario (1936-1940)*, Turin 1981, *passim*.

470.   The Ministry of Foreign Affairs had one of its functionaries from the Vienna delegation (to which the three Italian delegates, Leone Carpi, Angelo di Nola and Isacco Sciaky, participated) follow the NOS Association Congress in Vienna from September 1935 (see ASAE, *Palestina*, p. 10, *1935*, under the file "Congressi sionistici di Vienna e di Lucerna"). The ministry refused–on personal orders from Mussolini–to authorize a congress in Trieste the following year. See ASAE, *Palestina*, p. 13, *1936*, under the file *Partito sionista revisionista*. In this same period the SIM watched over the revisionists in Italy, which is evidenced in a letter intercepted on May 27, 1936 from I. Sciaky to Jabotinsky (*Ibid.*).

In December 1935 the revisionists approached the Italian consulate in Haifa to see if they could send some youths to train with the Italian air force; the request was made again in April 1937. In October 1937 the revisionists made other moves proposing the creation of their own Palestinian naval operation (fishing in particular); the following month one of their papers, the *Palestine Flames*, asked the Italian Consulate in New York for financial aid in the form of publicity (ASAE, *Palestina*, p. 19, 1937). In July 1938, as previously mentioned, two revisionist agents again proposed to send youths from their party to Italian military schools.

471. See ASAE, *Palestina*, p. 13, *1936*, under the file "Partito sionista revisionista."

472. ASAE, *Palestina*, under the file "Agitazione ebraica in Palestina per i provvedimenti del governo in Libia."

473. Z. Jabotinsky, *Verso lo Stato* cit., p. 392.

474. In a brief biographical note by Weizmann, sent to Rome in early January 1938 by the General Consul in Jerusalem, the Zionist leader had defined himself quite simply "pro-British" and it was said "His sentiments towards Italy certainly do not err for an excess of benevolence, as can be noted from some of his official declarations during the recent Abyssinian conflict." (See ASAE, *Palestina*, p. 19, *1937*, under the file "Sionismo").

475. See ASAE, *Palestina*, p. 10, *1935*, under the file "Sionismo."

476. ASAE, p. 10, *1935*, under the file "Partito sionista revisionista"; p. 13, *1936*, under the file "Partito sionista revisionista." The "Tedeschi mission" is documented in three reports by Tedeschi himself, two from Palestine (Tel Aviv, February 6, 1936; Jerusalem, February 10, 1936) and one upon returning home (Florence, March 12, 1936), all to Raffaele Guariglia. These reports are a clear confirmation of the kind of *penetration* that Fascism wanted to make in Palestine and of the arguments used by Guariglia to achieve this goal. They are fully reproduced in Document 8 herein.

477. Despite Italy's efforts, Jewish public opinion in Palestine in 1936 was largely anti-Italian. The ever-tightening relationship between the Italian Government and some Arab countries and chiefs, the pro-Arab propaganda by Radio Bari (who until then had maintained a neutral position of goodwill towards the Jews) and English propaganda, in the spring and summer, provoked an outcry against Italy, enough to prompt an official protest by the Consul General in Jerusalem to the Palestinian Government on May 14 and 18, 1936. Italy was accused of fomenting disorder in the mandate and of helping the Arabs (see ASAE, *Palestina*, p. 13, *1936* under the file "Agenzia Palcor"). Towards the end of the year the attacks concentrated instead on Italian anti-Semitism. See, for example, M. Carmon, "Il fascismo e gli ebrei," in *Hadashot Ahronot*, of Jerusalem, October 28, 1936; "Ondata di antisemitismo in Italia," in *Haaretz*, of Tel Aviv, November 10, 1936; "Un atteggiamento collettivo da parte dei governi tedesco, italiano, austriaco

e ungherese di fronte alla questione ebraica," in *Haaretz*, November 25, 1936.

478. Grandi's position regarding this kind of scheming with the Zionists was always extremely cautious for fear of unnecessary complications with England. A cable from him to the Minister of the Colonies, Lanza di Scalea, November 5, 1926, illustrates this very well: "With regard to the question in general, I inform Your Excellency that the National Government sees no reason nor any special Italian interest to develop a decidedly pro-Zionist policy and to decidedly favor this religious-political movement. Seeing that, especially in the Mediterranean colonies there are numerous and influential Jewish elements, who, besides helping Italian institutions, and our expansion, in most cases, have generally demonstrated up until now a commendable loyalty towards the National Government and strong feelings of Italian spirit, we can not, and must not ignore such factors, and still less be opposed to their aspirations when they are not in contrast with Italian interests. On the other hand Zionism is a movement from which we cannot remain absent nor renounce exercising a vigilant control upon it that is required by the need to protect and develop our interests. We must, therefore, endeavor as far as possible to have in its ranks persons of Italian character, so that such a movement does not become favorable to other powers that have conflicting interests with ours in the Mediterranean. And for this reason, without openly favoring it, we must not hinder it when there are no particularly unpropitious reasons; on the contrary, we must see that Italian interests are strongly represented within the Zionist movement." In 1929, to transform this caution into actual hostility, it must have hardly helped that David Prato, when writing to Mussolini on September 18, made it clear that the costs for the activity of the Federation of Sephardic Communities, proposed by him together with the office of Jewish Affairs (that had a photograph of the person who was supposed to be the director, which resembled Prato himself), would not have been borne by the Italian Government, but by the Italian Jews. In a note to Mussolini eight days later, Grandi actually stated, with annoyance, that it was not possible to "accept money from these people." See DDI, s. VI, voll. IV, pp. 369-70 and VIII, p. 41.

479. On the entire matter, see S. Minerbi, "L'azione diplomatica italiana nei confronti degli ebrei sefarditi durante e dopo la 1° guerra mondiale" *(1915-1929)*, in *La rassegna mensile di Israel*, July-December 1981, pp. 86-119; S. Della Seta, "Gli ebrei del Mediterraneo nella strategia politica fascista sino al 1938: il caso di Rodi," in *Storia contemporanea*, December 1986, pp. 997-1032; A. Scarantino, "La comunità ebraica in Egitto fra le due guerre mondiali," therein, pp. 1033-82.

480. On the Italian-Ethiopian conflict and its capital aspects, see A. Cohen, *La Société des Nations devant le conflit Italo-Ethiopien*, Geneva-Paris 1960.

481. The application of the sanctions by Palestine, other than being a serious diplomatic checkmate, was damaging to Italy economically. If, in 1937, Italian exports to that country amounted to 320,000 Palestinian lire, in 1936, precisely because of the sanctions, they reached only 86,000.

482. There was some debate for and against the sanctions even amongst the Palestinian Jews: see, for example, the *Palestine Post* of Jerusalem in November-December 1935 and in particular the issues of November 15 and December 5. The theory of "absolute neutrality" was upheld by the president of the Jewish University of Jerusalem, Judah Magnes, among others. As for the Zionist-Revisionists, they provided the Palazzo Chigi with the "Legal-Constitutional" notes to oppose them. (See ASAE, *Etiopia, 1936*.)

483. ASAE, *Etiopia, 1936,* under the file "Atteggiamento della Palestina."
This telegram was brought to the attention of the Italian Embassy in London by the Ministry, October 22, with the following note: "This Royal Ministry lets Your Excellency dwell upon the above-mentioned matter, until Your Excellency decides to meet initially with Dr. Weizmann, then, eventually, with the Foreign Office."

484. ASAE, *Carte recuperate nel 1945 (fondo Lancellotti)*, chapter 62 (p. 37). *Etiopia–affari politici 11-12 (Sanzioni), 1935*: "I inform Your Excellency that the chief rabbi, Dr. Angiolo Orvieto, is going there on a mission of trust and to create propaganda in these Jewish circles. I ask Your Excellency to discreetly support him in the best way possible."

485. ASAE, *Carte recuperate ecc.* cit.

486. ASAE, *Carte recuperate ecc.* cit., D. Lattes to R. Guariglia, Rome, November 12, 1935.

487. See P. Aloisi, *Journal (25 Juillet 1932–14 juin 1936)*, Paris 1957, pp. 326 (November 28 and 30, 1935), 330 (December 14, 1935), 332 (December 20, 1935).

488. P. Aloisi, *Journal* cit., p. 330.
Aloisi also discussed the matter with the German Ambassador, Ulrich Von Hassel (P. Aloisi, *Journal* cit., p. 326).
The campaign probably should not have been approved by Suvich. In a telephone conversation with Aloisi on September 6, 1935, Suvich had asked him not to dramatize the Jèze incident: see ASAE, *Carte recuperate nel 1945 (fondo Lancellotti)*, n. 109, *Etiopia*, under the file 6. *Appunti per il Duce: Suvich*, a note for the Duce September 7, 1935. On the Jèze case, see A. Cohen, *La Société des Nations* cit., pp. 114-16.

489. P. Aloisi, *Journal* cit., p. 364.

490. While the Italian Fascists and their supporters accused "international Judaism" of having triggered the war against Italy, boycotting the recognition of their "God-given" rights, in England the Imperial Fascist League accused the Jews of…arming the hand of Mussolini (see Document 9).

From this it is clear that the peculiarity of anti-Semitism was good for all causes and all propaganda. In the attack by the Imperial Fascist League there is more than likely Nazi influence. In 1924 the Nazi biographer of Mussolini, A. Dresler (*Mussolini*, Leipzig 1924, p. 58), had defined Fascism as a Jewish capitalist movement. Parallel accusations, still before the rise to power of Hitler, were repeated by Rosenberg and Streicher.

491. G. Preziosi, *Giudaismo-bolcevismo-plutocrazia-massoneria* cit., pp. 264, 405-6.

492. Of all the Jewish communities in the Mediterranean basin, that of Tunisia was the most decidedly Fascist, as we will see in more detail further. The community of Alexandria was, at least while D. Prato was rabbi (for this period, see D. Prato, *Cinque anni di rabbinato*, Alexandria, Egypt 1933), for the most part under the spiritual and moral influence of Italian Judaism (this was then partly undermined by French Judaism); many Jews of Italian origin had supported Fascism, many others were anti-Fascists and Freemasons and even among the Fascists "even though very determined to submit *laudabiliter* to the new political order, have conserved ancient ties which in the past united them to anti-Fascist institutions and particularly Freemasonry"; they were all anti-German. The community of Cairo was, especially amongst its oldest members, inclined towards Zionism; it was not lacking in Fascists, although not completely "pure." The community of Port Said, perhaps because of the presence of the activity of the Union Internationale pour la Paix, of a decidedly anti-Fascist nature, was the least tied to Italy and to Fascism (see ASAE, *Palestina*, p. 19, *1937* Royal Legation of Italy in Egypt to the Minister of Foreign Affairs, Bulkeley, August 20, 1937). As for Palestine, the majority of the Jews established there were ("except in the circles that surrounded Italian institutions") clearly anti-Fascist and often anti-Italian (ASAE, *Palestina*, p. 19, *1937*, Royal Consulate General in Jerusalem to the Ministry of Foreign Affairs, Jerusalem, March 1937).

493. See ASAE, *Palestina*, p. 13, *1936*, under the file "Sionismo," Felice Ravenna to B. Mussolini, Rome, March 3, 1936.

494. ASAE, *Palestina*, p. 13, *1936*, under the file "Sionismo," Report of the Italian Institute Commercial Union to the Ministry of Foreign Affairs, August 1936.

495. ASAE, *Palestina*, p. 13, *1936*, under the file "Sionismo, Appunto per il Sottosegretario–18 febbraio 1936."

496. ASAE, *Carte recuperate nel 1945 (fondo Lancellotti)*, n. 109, *Etiopia*, under the file b. "Appunti per il duce: Suvich, Per Sua Eccellenza il Capo del Governo, 7 febbraio 1936."

497. R. Guariglia, *Ricordi* cit., p. 328.

498. ASAE, *Carte recuperate nel 1945 (fondo Lancellotti)*, n. 109, *Etiopia*, under the file *Appunti per il duce: Ciano, Appunto per il duce, 26 settembre 1936* (Ciano-

Drummond meeting); n. 187, *Gran Bretagna*, 11/12, *1930-38*, under the file a. *Trattative italo-inglesi 1937*; G. Ciano, *Diario, 1937-38*, Milan 1948, pp. 40, 60, 136, 142; ID., *L'Europa verso la catastrofe*, Milan 1948, pp. 287, 293-94.

499. ASAE, *Carte recuperate nel 1945 (fondo Lancellotti)*, n. 187, *Gran Bretagna*, 11/12, *1930-38*, under the file *Trattative italo-inglesi 1937*; see, in particular, the telegram from Grandi to Ciano, July 27, 1937, regarding his meeting of the same day with Chamberlain. Grandi had assured him that Mussolini had personally intervened to stop anti-British propaganda by Radio Bari. G. Ciano, *Diario, 1937-38* cit., pp. 99-100. On the broadcasts of Radio Bari, see also "Le trasmissioni in ebraico dalla Radio Bari," in *Israel*, December 19-26, 1935.

500. ASAE, *Carte recuperate nel 1945 (fondo Lancellotti)*, n. 187, *Gran Bretagna*, 11/12, *1930-38*, under the file d. "Accordo italo-inglese; note pubbliche; assicurazioni verbali per la Palestina e note riservate."

501. ASAE, *Palestina*, p. 13, *1936*.

502. ASAE, *Palestina*, p. 19, *1937*, under the file "Finanze ebraiche ed arabe. Proposta di costituzione di una banca ipotecaria in Palestina con capitali italiani."

503. ASAE, *Palestina*, p. 19, *1937*, under the file "Colloquio S. E. Ciano con il dottore N. Goldmann e pubblicazioni antiebraiche in Italia."

504. Before leaving Jerusalem, Goldmann had already expressed to the Consul General Mazzolini, his preoccupations regarding the anti-Semitic campaign that was being orchestrated in Italy. The latter replied by bringing up the negative behavior towards Italy of the *Davar*, of Tel Aviv (ASAE, *Palestina*, p. 19, *1937*, Mazzolini to the Cabinet, April 28, 1937). After the meeting with Ciano, Goldmann, continuing the campaign, protested in a letter from Geneva, May 27 (which never received a direct reply) to Guarnaschelli of the Ministry of Foreign Affairs: "We can only profoundly deplore this anti-Zionist campaign which, in reality, has no justification and moreover is likely to damage feelings of deeply felt sympathy and friendship that the Jewish people and the Zionist movement have always felt towards Italy" (ASAE, *Palestina*, p. 19, *1937*). For some retrospective memories of Goldmann and on his meeting with Ciano on May 4, see U. Nahon, *Rapporto confidenziale all'esecutivo sionistico* cit., p. 265 n.

505. A letter from Eucardio Momigliano, January 4, 1937, to Sommi Picenardi (and forwarded to Farinacci) must be interpreted that way. Momigliano, taking his cue from the first cases of the already openly tortuous anti-Semitic campaign in Italy, wrote: "And now? I beg you to consider these facts: the revision of the colonial mandates is imminent. The only victorious country without mandates is Italy. For more than ten years in Palestine there has been a growing tendency favorable to the transfer of the Palestinian mandate to Italy. England has proven to be negative; their

necessity of a pro-Arab policy has clashed with the Balfour declaration. The Jewish faction has been united by the strong Catholic tendency, represented by the monastic orders to see the Holy Places entrusted to a Catholic Power. The government is aware of this situation and has ably exploited it: at least initially... Direct steamship routes with ships bearing Jewish names and ritual food on board, generous hospitality at the Levantine fair for Palestinian Jewish Industries, Jewish broadcasts by Radio Bari, etc." And therefore proceeded, advancing the idea that anti-Semitism in Italy was perhaps artfully promoted by the English to damage Italy in the eyes of the Jews and to derail the transfer of the mandate from London to Rome: "I feel that the truth is far more clear and obvious; in London they want Italy to appear geared towards an anti-Semitic attitude to cut all Palestinian Jewish aspirations to support an eventual mandate to us... You see then, how the strange campaign, while by some is engaged without doubt in good faith, coincides in a surprising way with the interests of the Intelligence Service." (See ACS, *Roberto Farinacci [1921-45]*, b. 69.)

506. G. Ciano, *Diario* cit., *1937-38*, p. 113. Some papers (for example *Le Temps*, February 19, 1938) and even some governments (for example that of Poland) made suppositions on where the "Jewish State," foretold by Mussolini (usually it was thought to be in the AOI), was to rise, and they even asked the Palazzo Chigi. (See ASAE, *Palestina*, p. 27, *1938*.)

507. As often happened to Mussolini in his dealings with Hitler, the Führer immediately denied the statement of his ally regarding the Jewish state. To the note of *Informazione Diplomatica*, on March 22, the German Embassy in Rome replied with a note in which it was written:
"The attitude of different governments faced with the possibility of founding a Jewish State in Palestine, has not always been clear until today. The German point of view regarding the problem of the formation of a Jewish State in Palestine has been reviewed in recent times. Until now the goal of the German policy concerning the Jews has been that of possibly favoring the emigration of the Jews from Germany. This German attitude, dictated by internal political motives, which practically favored the consolidation of the Jews in Palestine and thus accelerated the construction of a Jewish State in Palestine, should have shown that Germany was clearly favorable to the formation of a Jewish state in Palestine. In reality, Germany has a major interest in maintaining the splitting up of the Jewish race. More particularly, a Jewish state in Palestine would not absorb the Jews but would create a new power base for them founded on the rights of the people, which would not be in the interests of German foreign policy." See ASAE, *Palestina*, p. 27, *1938*.

508. ASAE, *Palestina*, p. 27, *1938*.

509. ASAE, *Palestina*, p. 27, *1938*, under the file "Professor Wardi."
To give a more precise idea of these last contacts, reproduced in *Document 10*, is the report of the meeting between Azkin and Mazzolini, April 28, 1938, transmitted to Rome by Mazzolini on the 30th of the same month, and a memorandum presented to Mazzolini, June 14, 1938, by Professor Wardi, before leaving for Rome for his last initiative at the Palazzo Chigi.

510. ASAE, *Palestina*, from a note by Guarnaschelli, July 8, 1938.

511. G. Leto, *OVRA. Fascismo-Antifascismo*, Bologna 1952, p. 139.

512. L. Salvatorelli–G. Mira, *Storia d'Italia ecc.* cit., pp. 795-98; A. Garosci, *La vita di Carlo Rosselli*, Florence n.d., II, pp. 115-50.

513. G. Galli, *Storia del Partito Comunista Italiano*, Milan 1958, pp. 172-75.

514. G. Leto, *OVRA*, cit., pp. 203-13.

515. See ASAE, *Palestina*, p. 13, *1936*; Germania, p. 36, *1937*, under the file "Rapporti politici." Though, still in 1938, there were Italian diplomats in Germany who did not hide in their reports to Rome, their disapproval of what was happening in that country, under their very eyes. See ASAE, *Germania*, p. 48, *1938*.

516. See *Il popolo d'Italia*, October 29, 1937.

517. See *L'Italia in Africa*, historical-military study, *L'opera dell'esercito (1885-1943)*,I: M. A. Vitale, *Ordinamento e reclutamento*, Rome 1960, pp. 43 and 50.

518. See *Israel*, December 12, 19-26, 1935; January 2, 9, 1936. *La nostra bandiera*, January 15 and 31, February 15 and 29, 1936. *El boletín* (monthly organ of the Community of Rodi), November, December 1935; February 1936.
In occasion of Yom Kippur of 1935, the rabbi invoked the divine protection "in this historical hour" upon Italy, "on those who hold its destinies in their hands and on the gallant Italian soldiers." (see *Israel*, October 10, 1935.)

519. See *El boletín*, February-March, 1936.

520. See "Vittoria italiana," in *Israel*, May 7-14, 1936; M. Da Fano, "La proclamazione dell'Impero fascista," in *Davar*, May-June, 1936; "A proposito de la victoria italiana," in *El boletín*, April-May, 1936; *La nostra bandiera*, May 31, 1936.

521. Of the many articles, see, particularly that of C. A. Viterbo, "I Falascià," in *Israel*, May 7-14, 1936; and also "Con l'occupazione di Gondar si pone agli ebrei italiani problema dei falascià," in *La nostra bandiera*, April 15, 1936.

522. See *Israel*, June 18, 1936.

523. Therein, August 27, 1936.

524. Other than the news periodically published by *Israel* (particularly the issue of September 30, 1937), see *L'attività delle Comunità israeitiche italiane nel quinquennio 1933-XI–1938-XVI. Relazione del Presidente al II Congresso delle Comunità (1938-XVI)*, Rome 1938, pp. 22-26 and also "La presa di contatto con i Falascià," in *La nostra bandiera*, December 16-31, 1937; *Notiziario per le*

Comunità Israelitiche italiane, n. 3, September 1937 and above all the long report drawn up by Viterbo for the Italian Ministry of Africa and for the Communities Union at the end of his mission, recently published by F. Del Canuto, in *Israel–Saggi sull'Ebraismo italiano* cit., pp. 47-113 with a preface by the same Del Canuto, "Come si giunse alla missione in Etiopia presso i Falascià," pp. 23-45, as well as the integration by M. Toscano, "Gli ebrei in Italia dall'emancipazione alle persecuzioni" cit., pp. 927-31; less useful instead, is E. Trevisan Semi, *Allo specchio dei falascià. Ebrei ed etnologi durante il colonialismo fascista,* Florence 1987.

525. As usual Preziosi did not pass up, even this time, the opportunity of attacking the Jews; see *La vita italiana,* September 1937, p. 340.

526. See *Israel,* August 22, 1935.

527. R. Forges Davanzati, *Cronache del Regime,* Milan 1936, I, pp. 165-66; also in the two later volumes there are no explicit anti-Semitic attacks yet; the debate only revolves around Freemasonry, Bolshevism and Anglicanism, not against the Jews.

528. See *Israel,* March 4, 1937.

529. See *Il Corriere d'America,* July 4, 1937.

530. See *Comunità Israelitiche italiane ecc.* cit., pp. 8-9.

531. See "Italo Balbo, ebreo!," in *La nostra bandiera,* June 30, 1936.

532. A. Aniante, *Italo Balbo maréchal de l'Air,* Paris 1933, p. 104.
Mussolini's copy of this book is stored in the Central State Archive ("Mussolini Collection"). In it there are three paragraphs underlined in Mussolini's hand, one which we have reproduced here, and another (p. 241) that mentions the "conscience scrupuleuse [de Balbo] qui le rend inébranlable" [the scrupulous conscience (of Balbo) that makes him unshakable].

533. See N. d'Aroma, *Vent'anni insieme. Vittorio Emmanuele e Mussolini,* Bologna 1957, pp. 266-67.

534. G. Ciano, *Diario, 1937-38* cit., p. 190 (dated June 18, 1938).

535. For a more complete update, see R. De Felice, *Ebrei in un paese arabo* cit., 193 *sgg.*

536. ASAE, *Palestina,* p. 5, *1933.*

537. See "Le scuole della Tripolitania alla settimana fiera di Tripoli," in *Agenzia di Libia,* February 4, 1933. From *La tribuna* February 15, 1933, one gathers that in Tripolitania there regularly took place a soccer championship between Jewish teams.

538. ACIR, p. 45, *Carte del rabbino Angelo Sacerdoti.*

539. AUCII, *1934-35, Legislazione sulle Comunità israelitiche delle Colonie.*

540. For a more complete view that takes into account both the preceding as well as the developments of the situation, see R. De Felice, *Ebrei in un paese arabo* cit., pp. 206.

541. See AUCII, *1934-35, Tripoli*, under the file "Missione Castelbolognesi," G. Castelbolognesi to Felice Ravenna, Tripoli, February 19, 1934, reproduced in *Document 11*.

542. See AUCII, *1934-35, Tripoli*, under the file "Missione Castelbolognesi," G. Calò to Felice Ravenna, Tripoli, December 6, 1934; Felice Ravenna to the Jewish Administrative Commercial Commission in Tripoli, December 10, 1934 and Felice Ravenna to G. Castelbolognesi, December 31, 1934.

543. See N. d'Aroma, *Vent'anni insieme* cit., p. 267.

544. See AUCII, *1934-35, Tripoli*, under the file "Missione Castelbolognesi," Felice Ravenna to G. Castelbolognesi, February 8, 1935. Mussolini declared to Sacerdoti "that he would have ordered both that it were conceded to Jewish students not to write [!!] on the Sabbath nor on the high holidays, and that the school problem in Tripoli was considered with special benevolence and sympathy."

545. AUCII, *1934-35, Tripoli*, under the file "Missione Castelbolognesi," G. Castelbolognesi, *Relazione dell'attività svolta in Tripoli dal novembre 1934 a tutto maggio 1935, passim* and particularly ff. 1-10. All of the information, not otherwise marked, is taken from this report.

546. AUCII, *1934-35, Tripoli*, under the file "Missione Castelbolognesi," G. Castelbolognesi to Felice Ravenna, November 13, 1934.

547. The government's decision was presented, by some papers in Jerusalem and Cairo, as a transformation of Italian colonial policy and in particular, as an approval of the Sabbath as a day of rest in Tripoli. The matter much indisposed Balbo who gave a "lecture" to Castelbolognesi. See AUCII, *1934-35, Tripoli*, under the file "Missione Castelbolognesi," Relazione *ecc.* cit., ff 11-12 and G. Castelbolognesi to Felice Ravenna, Adar 10, II 5695.

548. On the opinion of Italian Zionist circles regarding the whole matter, see *Israel*, January 24, 1935.

549. AUCII, *1934-35, Tripoli*, under the file "Missione Castelbolognesi," Felice Ravenna to G. Castelbolognesi, May 31, 1935.

550. On the entire matter, see the report to the Union by G. Castelbolognesi, *Relazione del caso Nemni-Hassan*, in AUCII, *1934-35, Tripoli*, under the file *Missione Castelbolognesi*.

551. AUCII, *1934-35, Tripoli*, under the file "Missione Castelbolognesi," Felice Ravenna to G. Castelbolognesi, May 31, 1935 cit.

552. See in AUCII, *1934-35, Tripoli*, under the file "Missione Castelbolognesi," the report by Felice Ravenna on the meeting and the attached documents regarding the final communication.

553. The text of the statement was initially suggested by N. Quilici, instead of the sentence "The governor... overseas," it read that the governor was sure that "the community of Tripoli would know how to be worthy through their own merit of the ever growing praise that is given by such a high authority."

554. See "La giusta punizione applicata ieri ad alcuni ebrei recalcitranti," in *L'avvenire di Tripoli*, December 3, 1936.

555. See ASAE, *Palestina*, p. 13, *1936*, under the file "Agitazione ebraica in Palestina per i provvedimenti del governo in Libia."
The protests by the Aschenazy Rabbi of Jerusalem, and his incitements to the Jews of Tripoli to take a stand against Balbo's law, pushed the Italian Government to protest to the Rabbi himself. See ASAE, *Palestina*, p. 16, *1937*, under the file "Agitazione ebraica in Palestina per i provvedimenti del governo in Libia," G. Ciano to the Consul General in Jerusalem, January 1937.

556. See "Cronaca nera ebraica," in *L'avvenire di Tripoli*, December 7, 1936 and, above all, two telegrams from Italo Balbo to the Ministry of the Colonies on December 6 and 15, 1936 (ASAE, *Palestina*, p. 13, *1936*, under the file "Agitazione ebraica in Palestina per i provvedimenti del governo in Libia," reproduced in *Documents 12*).

557. For greater detail, see R. De Felice, *Ebrei in un paese arabo* cit., pp. 233 *sgg*.

558. See "Le Maréchal Balbo et le Grand Rabbin," in *La Presse*, Tunisia, January 21, 1937.

559. See B. Fattori, "I purosangue," in *Il telegrafo*, January 22, 1935; G. Sommi Picenardi, "Le nuove Valchirie," in *Il regime fascista*, January 31, 1935.

560. P. Bargagli, "Società delle Nazioni," in *L'azione coloniale*, December 19, 1935.

561. "La questione giudaica," in *La civiltà cattolica*, 1936, issue 2071.

562. Amongst others the archbishop of Genoa cardinal Minoretti and the bishop of Terni and Narni, Boccoleri. See A. Romanini, *Ebrei-Cristianismo-Fascismo*, 2nd edition Empoli 1939, p. 6.

563. *Il regime fascista*, February 5, 1936 had already (C. Longo, *Fascismo ed ebraismo*) explicitly condemned international Judaism, distinctly classifying Jewish Fascist politics according to whether they were internal or international matters. Along the same lines, G. Pistello, "Il problema ebraico in Italia," in *La vita italiana*, August 1936.

564. Still in *Il regime fascista*, see also the paragraphs, "Replichiamo" and "Un discorso chiaro," respectively, September 17 and 22, 1936.

565. See Documents 13.

566. Regarding this, see also "Delineata offensiva di pressioni straniere per suscitare l'antisemitsmo in Italia," in *La nostra bandiera*, August 1, 1936.

567. On August 28, the telegraphic agency, Oriente, circulated a note with the eloquent title of "Una razza inferocita contro il Fascismo: l'ebraica."

568. This coincidence was emphasized also by certain foreign papers and magazines, for example the American *The Jewish Advocate* and the Arab-English *Palestine and Transjordan*.

569. ACS, *Segretaria particolare del Duce, Carteggio Riservato (1922-1943)*, file 242/R *Gran Consiglio*, under the file 14; insert C, November 1936.

570. On January 15, 1937, in replying T. Salvotti, published an article in the *Wille und Macht* titled "Das faschistische Italien und die Juden." Salvotti belonged to the group of Farinacci and Preziosi.

571. See ASAE, *Germania*, p. 32, *1936*.

572. For the months from April to June the report, that U. Nahon, *Rapporto confidenziale ecc.*, cit., pp. 263-76, made to the Zionistic Executive, is extremely revealing. But, see also A. Calò, "Stampa e propoganda antisemita del regime fascista prima delle leggi razziali (1936-1938)," in *Israel–Saggi sull'Ebraismo italiano cit., pp. 115-63*.

573. A. Spinosa, "Le persecuzioni razziali in Italia. I. Origini," in *Il ponte*, July 1952, p. 975.

574. D. Lattes immediately wrote with insight that Orano wanted the Italian Jews to become either Atheists or Christians, in *Israel*, April 15, 1937 (*Un libro sugli ebrei in Italia*): "Is it possible that the Italian Government desires what Paolo Orano believes to be the ideal goal, that is, that Jewish give up all religious belief and become hostile, as he says, to the Communities? Is it possible, since Jewish worship is permitted and is granted a respectful regulation of its ideals, is it possible, today, in Italy, to ask all Jews to become atheists or to convert directly to Catholicism, or indirectly through mixed marriages, that in a few years would eliminate any trace of the Jewish religion in Italy? And what would become of the respect that the Italian government has towards Jewish tradition if it were intent on keeping Italy's Jews away from Judaism?"

575. For *Israel*, apart from the already mentioned article of April 15, see that of June 4, 1937, "Il problema ebraico e il sionismo." The article stressed that "in Italy Zionism is a permitted and legal activity: not an underground secret activity"; that also Italy had subscribed to the "Zionist reestablishment"; that Italian Zionists had always been very good Italians and "that with their most modest of capabilities they have always taken part in the opposition against every attempt by England to benefit from its position of mandatory power." On *L'idea sionistica*, see L. Carpi, *Sionismo e Italianità*, June 1937, that, in a revisionist vein, repeated the same ideas and above all pointed out that Palestinian independence would have made English influence disappear, or diminish, in that region, and that Zionism, instead of being a means of anti-Fascist propaganda was mainly national, and therefore, anti-socialist and anticommunist. On the group of *La nostra bandiera*, see, instead, the volume by E. Ovazza, *Il problema ebraico. Risposta a Paolo Orano*, Rome 1938. Ovazza also published a long letter in the *Gazzetta del Popolo* April 8, 1937. For a complete picture, see also A. Levi, *Noi ebrei italiani*, in *Noi ebrei. In risposta a Paolo Orano*, Rome 1937, pp. 9-24; ID, "Ebraismo e Cattolicesimo," in the *Universalità fascista*, June 1937 (for a kind of humanitarian Zionism).

576. A. Nosari, "Gli ebrei in Italia," in *Il giornale d'Italia*, April 20, 1937.

577. Radius, "Gli ebrei in Italia," in *Il giornale d'Italia*, May 18, 1937.

578. Victor, "Gli ebrei in Italia," in *La Stampa*, May 27, 28, 29, 1937.

579. The attacks on "Jewish culture" then became more explicit and violent. In August, the *Meridiano di Roma* harshly attacked the *Ebrei in Sardegna* by Guido Bedarida (see the issues of August 29 and September 14 and 19, 1937). Still in August, A. Ghislanzoni, "Il discorso del cancelliere Hitler sull'arte moderna," in *Il Musicista*, official organ of the Nazi Fascist Union of Musicians, reported extensive passages of Hitler's ridiculous speech (mostly dedicated to anti-Semitic accusations) saying that "the German chancellor, with extraordinary intuition and vigor, had plunged the knife into the most painful wounds of the artistic world."

580. A. Fratelli, "O Roma o Sion," in *La tribuna*, May 26, 1937.

581. O. Gregorio, "Gli ebrei in Italia," in *Il popolo d'Italia*, May 25, 1937.

582. See *Il popolo d'Italia*, June 1, 3, 5, 10, 1937 (also reproduced in *Noi ebrei ecc.* cit., pp. 37-64).

583. G. Pini, *Filo diretto con palazzo Venezia*, Bologna 1950, p. 104 (at the date of June 8, 1937).

584. See "Sionismo e Fascismo," in *Regime Fascista*, June 8, 1937 and also *La vita italiana*, August 1937, pp. 218-20.

585. The following day, Mussolini, to whom the general direction of the press had asked instructions on how to develop the press campaign "on the Jewish problem in Italy," gave instructions to reduce the attacks. On the same occasion, the Duce rejected the proposal to suppress all of the Jewish press. See ACS, *Ministero della Cultura Popolare*, b. 130.

586. Pressure mounted, though, on government units by groups and spokesmen who were most aggressively anti-Semitic, interested in drawing attention towards the "mischief" of the Jews and constantly suggesting measures and anti-Semitic attacks. Particularly active in this area was the Center of Anticommunist Studies of Rome (not coincidentally connected to the Nazis). See ACS, *Cultura popolare*, b. 126, file "Centro studi anticomunisti."

587. *Il Tevere* was, above all, furious at the presence of Jews in the arts, perhaps hoping to attract to its crusade the sympathies of various artists, of little worth and without scruples, interested in furthering their careers in the Fascist unions and of succeeding through their participation in exhibitions, competitions, and the like. Another prerogative of *Il Tevere* was that of continuously publishing letters, true or false from people who *denounced* and *documented* Jewish intrigues and intrusiveness, invoking measures and discriminations. Also in *Il Tevere* there was no shortage of letters by anti-Zionist Jews. With the obvious aim at creating mass hysteria aiming at "hunting down the Jews," *Il Tevere*, just like *Quadrivio*, published a list of the Italian Jewish surnames, taking it from the Schaerf.

588. Preziosi, in "Dieci punti fondamentali del problema ebraico," in the August issue of *La vita italiana* (pp. 210-12) engaged in an argument with P. Orano (as also did *Il Tevere* on November 21)—who was too "soft" on the Jews for his liking—made himself the advocate of the existence of a super-Jewish racism, which had at its foundations, so to speak, not so much a biological factor as much in Jewish *essence*:
"The Jews agree in affirming the immutability and inalterability of this 'essence.' The Jew remains a Jew regardless of his nationality. The Jew remains a Jew regardless of his political beliefs. The Jew remains a Jew even when he becomes a Christian. While on the other hand, the Christian or the Moslem who takes on the Jewish faith could never become, or consider himself, Jewish. All of this is explicitly declared by the spokesman of Judaism, and even recently I produced unequivocal Jewish documents regarding this issue. Race, in the Jew, is far from being a pure biological and anthropological factor. Race is the law. This, intended as a molding force from the inside and in a certain sense even from above, in the Jew everything is based on that." The conclusion that Preziosi drew from this, his "discovery," was that the Jews were always "Jews," even when they did not want to be: "A Jewish International does exist and operate. To recognize the existence of this International it is not necessary to recognize that all Jews are directed by an actual world organization and that all of their acts consciously follow a plan. The connection mostly exists already because of essence and instinct. It is a fact that from the work of the Jews in the most disparate fields—from science to finance, from the letter [sic] to literature to psychology and to sociology—arise disintegrating and subversive results, that always converge and singularly produce the same effects." Therefore, obviously, arises the need to fight *all* Jews indiscriminately.

589. Other than the book by Sottochiesa, also worth mentioning are those by H. De Vries De Heekelingen, *Israele, il suo passato, il suo avvenire* and by G. Natti Dubois, *Ebrei e cattolici*. Even if dated 1938 they were already circulating in 1937 in the editorial office of major newspapers and had already been reviewed. The volume by De Vries de Heekelingen had already frequently been mentioned by *La vita italiana* of August, just released in France. Some French Fascist groups, though, did not approve of the translation of this last work, defining it pro-Zionist (see, for example, B. Ricci, "Precisazioni su un problema," in *Il bargello*, December 26, 1937). Still in 1937, Preziosi edited the publication of a new edition of the *Protocols*, which was received with great commendation by *Il regime fascista* (G. Sommi Picenardi, *Un libro boicottato*, November 20, 1937). See also Arthos, *La volontà di potenza ebraica e l'autenticità dei Protocolli*, in *La vita italiana*, December 1937.

590. G. Cogni, *Il razzismo*, 2nd edition Milan 1937; ID, *I valori della Stirpe italiana*, Milan 1937.

591. G. Evola, *Il mito del sangue*, Milan 1937.

592. See, for example, M. Bendiscioli, *Neopaganesimo razzista*, Brescia 1937; L. Pollini, "Idee correnti e controcorrente," in *Alleanza nazionale del libro*, November 1937; and for certain aspects at least, even R. Pavese, "Il mito del sangue," in *La nobiltà della Stirpe*, July 1937; D. Lischi, "Parate e a fondo," in *Costruire*, July 1937.

593. Also reproduced in "Segnalazioni," in *La nostra bandiera*, July 16, 1937.

594. A. Tilgher, "I Protocolli dei Savi Anziani di Sion," in *Il lavoro*, November 17, 1937. See also the reply by G. Preziosi, "Gratta gratta e riviene fuori il firmatario," in *La vita italiana*, December 1937, pp. 740-41.

595. "Ma perché?" in *Il regime fascista*, December 25, 1937.

596. See *Il giornale d'Italia*, September 15, 1937.

597. See A. Garosci, *Storia dei fuorusciti*, Bari 1953, p. 238 and above all A. Giannini, *Io, spia dell'Ovra!*, Rome, I.

598. See F. Cundari, "Il sionismo e l'Italia," in *Il merlo*, July 25, 1937. In the article the pro-Nazi significance of the anti-Semitic campaign was explicitly stated: "It appears that a Jewish question has never existed in Italy. And yet, right now, there is an editorial uprising against the insignificant number of Jews residing within the national territory. What is the advantage of all this? Is it the expressed desire, of a danger actually perceived aiming at undermining national companies in their economical-political aspect, that Zionism supposedly represents? Or is it not, instead, apelike behavior for the ways imported from beyond the Alps and precisely from Germany? It appears to us to be the latter factor."

599. AUCII, *Libro dei verbali, Consiglio*, January 9, 1935; See also *La nostra bandiera*, February 5, 1935, reproduced in E. Ovazza, *Il problema ebraico* cit., pp. 211-13.

600. Aucci, *Libro dei verbali, Giunta*, February 10 and April 3, 1935.

601. Aucci, *Libro dei verbali, Consiglio*, May 2, 1935.

602. Aucci, *Libro dei verbali*, July 17, 1935.

603. See AUCII, *1938, Presidenza*, memorandum from General G. Liuzzi to the general aide-de-camp of H.M. The King Emperor, reproduced in *Documents 14*.

604. The proof is in the contacts that the editorial office of *La nostra bandiera* kept with the Undersecretary for Press and Propaganda and with the Ministry of Foreign Affairs, to which they submitted, before publication, the most important articles regarding foreign political matters. See ASAE, *Palestina*, p. 10, 1935.

605. The sympathies held by *La nostra bandiera* for the Zionist-Revisionists of Jabotinsky are significant (of whom they also published two articles). See,

in particular, *La nuova Organizzazione Sionista,* in the December issue of 1935.

606. See Aucci, *Libro dei verbali, Giunta,* February 25, 1936; *La nostra bandiera,* February 26, 1936.

607. F. G., "A proposito dei tributi," in *La nostra bandiera,* February 15, 1936; "Una relazione sull'opera dell'Unione delle Communità," therein, March 31, 1936; "Largo alla giovinezza!," therein, April 15, 1936; A.M.F., "I gravi problemi dell'ebraismo italiano esigono un serio programma di sistematica soluzione," therein, May 15, 1936; A.M.F., "Aspetti del problema ebraico italiano per il quale urge un programma organico di soluzione," therein, May 31, 1936.

608. See also the interview with G. Liuzzi, published in *La nostra bandiera* June 15, 1936 entitled "Il compimento del dovere ebraico nell'Italia fascista" (Fulfilling one's Jewish duty in Fascist Italy).

609. The following is the summary of the "questions" presented in the pamphlet:
The question of organization: the reform should first be enacted and then legalized, and not vice versa; "the authority responsible should first prepare the consolidation and regular operation and then, only following this, prepare the gradual legalization of the means advantageously adopted and experimented" (which in other words meant the demand for full and absolute power). Instruments and organs of the reform should be the Union and the Community (with few "new" counselors chosen through "methods of a Fascist nature") and the rabbinate (headed by a Grand Rabbi of Italy). *The religious spiritual question:* the rabbis (only Italians) should be hierarchically organized and their economic situation improved in a way that would benefit from actual autonomy; the rabbinical title should be given only to those holding a degree from the rabbinical college of Rome. *The administrative question:* the Union should be allowed to have a "direct impact upon the administration of the Communities with regard to the compulsory part of religious practices"; there is the need to try to "shift to the Unions, which today have insufficient authority, the excess autonomy of the Communities, which appears harmful to discipline and impartiality." *The religious question in the schools:* the Jewish religious teachings (to be entrusted to the rabbis and to teachers who have been trained in a modern manner) should be performed in the Jewish primary schools and as after school activities for students in junior high school; the schools "should follow the curriculum of all the other Italian schools, answering to the regular state school authorities," religious teachings should "absolutely" not interfere with other teachings. *The question of social life:* the Jews should not avoid the social life common to all Italians, and neither should they be intrusive; it is absurd that there were those who preferred to carry

out their business in a purely Jewish environment. *International Jewish questions*: "strictly speaking we do not know of any, seeing that we can not even consider that the Zionists are a purely Jewish concern: Palestinian colonization has a uniquely political character, economical and social, whilst Jewish concern must essentially revolve around religious affairs." The circumstances of life and the mentality of the various Jewish groups were so different that congresses and international meetings were useless. Some problems relating to historical and religious culture could have been raised at international rabbinical congresses. *The economic question*: charitable works should be set up under the direction of one exclusive organization directly under the control of the Union. *Moral and disciplinary questions*: the communities should be freed from all of the "complications" imposed by the Union and dedicate themselves to cultural and charitable activities. *Colonial questions*: the Union should seriously and actively be involved with the "progressive elevation" of the Jews in the colonies, "in perfect harmony with the government."

610.   During the discussion within the council, the pamphlet by General Liuzzi was called a declaration of "ignorance" and demonstrated a "lack of discipline," someone proposed to ask for the dismissal of Liuzzi from the position of president of the Community of Turin, by "superior authorities." In the end it was decided to defer this proposal and to reject and deplore it instead, without starting any disputes regarding the statements in General Liuzzi's pamphlet. This was expressed in the following motion: "… [the Union] in refraining from revealing the errors of a religious and civil nature, notes with distressing amazement, that in it he refuses to acknowledge the work of dedicated Italian spirit carried out by the Union, principally in this epic hour for the homeland, and he ignores that all of the work done abroad, by the Union itself, has always been undertaken by, with the full approval and the consent of, the Fascist government. [The Union] disdainfully rejects any suspicion of old Masonic roots and international bonds and regrets that a leader of the Community, through an act of indiscipline, censures the legal system given by the Fascist government to Italian Judaism." (see AUCII, *Libro dei verbali, Giunta*, June 11, 1936)

611.   The August 27, 1936 issue of *Israel* criticized the Union for its response to the pamphlet of General Liuzzi. Repeating all that he had written at the beginning of the year, for *Israel*, the Union, in doing so had attributed too much importance to the pamphlet.

612.   Aucci, *1936, Presidenza*.

613.   See, above all, "Per intendere," in *La nostra bandiera*, October 16, 1936; "Italiani e Fascisti," therein, November 1, 1936; "L'anti-antisemitismo," therein, December 16, 1936; "Fuori di ogni equivoco," therein, March 16, 1937; "Chiarificazione opportuna," therein, June 1, 1937.

614. Aucci, *Libro dei verbali, Giunta,* September 15, 1936; *Document 14.*

615. See "Penosa situazione a Tripoli," in *La nostra bandiera,* December 16, 1936; "Smentite e esagerazioni sui fatti di Tripoli," therein, January 1, 1937. The position of *La nostra bandiera* was made the object of a brief exam by G. Valabrega, "Prima notizie su *La nostra bandiera (1934-38),* in *Gli ebrei in Italia durante il fascismo* cit., I, pp. 21-33. We have already spoken of the unacceptability of the interpretations of Valabrega in our introduction to the first edition of this book.

616. See G. Preziosi, *Eccola integralmente la lettera dell'ex direttore di "Davar,"* in *La vita italiana,* August 1937, pp. 218-20.

617. See Aucci, *Libro dei verbali, Giunta,* July 1, 1937; ASAE, *Palestina,* p. 19, *1937,* the Italian Legation in Egypt to the Ministry of Foreign Affairs, July 10, 1937; *La nostra bandiera, passim* and particularly June 1, 1937 (the elections of the Community of Florence).

618. See Aucci, *Libro dei verbali, Consiglio,* April 6, 1937.

619. Aucci, *Libro dei verbali, Consiglio,* June 10, 1937; as well as U. Nahon, *Rapportio confidenziale ecc,* cit., pp. 272-74, where, besides the statement by Buffarini-Guidi, there is also mention of an interview–June 3–of Rabbi Prato at the Palazzo Chigi, during which Ciano stated that "Italian politics had not undergone any changes and that the newspaper articles are not official opinions" and proclaimed himself as personally not being an anti-Semite, on the contrary, a very good friend of numerous Jews.

620. See *Israel,* June 17-24, 1937.

621. A declaration dated May 30, 1937, on the occasion of the first positions taken by *Il popolo d'Italia* regarding the book by P. Orano, caused a great stir throughout the press. In this declaration (see *Il corriere della sera,* June 5, 1937) among other things, contained the following statement: "The Committee of Italians of Jewish religion, founded in Rome, January 24, 1937-XV, in coordination with the preceding initiatives originating in the various Italian Communities, having seen the article published in *Il popolo d'Italia* on May 25, 1937-XV, as a review of the book by the Hon. Paolo Orano, and of various publications on the subject, in full awareness of the purpose of its publication, responds precisely that Italians of Jewish religion are, and declare themselves to be, decided enemies of any International, whether Jewish or non-Jewish, Masonic, subversive or dedicated to subversion and above all anti-Fascist. They consider Judaism as a purely religious matter; declare having nothing in common with whoever professes Zionist doctrine; and they refuse to acknowledge the newspaper *Israel,* whose ideas and programs are clearly opposed to their convictions and to their character." The following participated in the meeting, during which the above declaration was approved: Gaddo Belelli (Rome), Angelo di Nola (Rome), Enrico Foá (Parma), Enzo Zevi (Mantua), Guido Liuzzi

(Turin), Attilio Morpurgo (Gorizia), Silvio Ottolenghi (Rome), Mario Ottolenghi (Leghorn), Goffredo Passigli (Florence), Guido Poggi (Genoa), Max Ravà (Venice), Giacomo Russi (Ancona), Guglielmo Vita (Florence), Gino Zabban (Bologna), Ettore Ovazza (Turin), and Mario Ravà (Rome).

622. See "Verso il Congresso delle Comunità Israelitiche Italiane," in *La nostra bandiera*, October 16-31, 1937; "Verità," therein, November 16-30, 1937.

623. On December 5, 1937, the Committee voted an agenda against the nomination to the Rabbinical Chair of Rome of D. Prato, whom *Il Tevere* had accused of anti-Fascism. The council of the Community of Rome, following this agenda, was on the verge of revoking the appointment of Prato, when the General Directorate of Religious Affairs intervened. (See Document 14)

624. As an example: in July the Union asked the Ministry of Foreign Affairs for the authorization to send one of its delegates to Zurich in August for the meeting of the Jewish Agency. The authorization was granted only verbally but not in writing as on other occasions. The Union then decided not to send anyone to Zurich (see AUCII, *Libro dei verbali, Giunta*, July 21 and October 21, 1937).

625. See for example, "Esame di coscienza," in *La nostra bandiera*, September 16-30, 1937. The news of E. Ovazza's withdrawal (see *La nostra bandiera*, September 1, 1937) caused much sensation (also a comment in *La nostra bandiera*, September 16-30). To get a better idea of Ovazza's position, the reading of his *Il problema ebraico* cit., is indispensable.

626. In 1937 the "dissociations" were little less than half of the preceding year, 65 against 37.

627. See *I rabbini d'Italia ai loro fratelli*, Rome 5698-1938, *passim* and particularly pp. 6-7: "If one of us has lost, or is weakening in his conscience, if one of us refuses the task, or denies the race, or ignores history, or abandons the doctrine, he cannot drag all of Judaism down to his own likeness. His aberrations cannot cover the facts, modify our existence, and the opinion that those who are reasonable have of it. The *tesciuvà* to which we are called by the sound of the *shofàr* must bring those who have been lead astray to recognize their mistakes. The preoccupation of relationships with non-Hebrews must not be an obstacle to such recognition. There is no reason to be preoccupied. It is not about disclosing something that is not well known, instead we are right to believe what is, for some non-Jews, reason for astonishment and suspicion, the spectacle of certain attempts to withdraw from clear evidence that does not allow denial or from a sacred heritage that does not allow rejection."

628. Episodes such as the duel with Treves in 1915 should be viewed from this angle (on the subject of which one can hardly speak of anti-Semitism, see C. Rossi, *Trentatre vicende Mussoliniane*, Milan 1958, pp. 64-66) and the ob-

jection to the idea of a marriage between his daughter and a Jew. Regarding the subject of Mussolini's attitude towards the Jews in general, anti-Semitism and Zionism, see A. Segre, *Sionismo e sionisti in Italia* cit., pp. 184 (which reveals a different position to some extent).

629. Against the statement made in the *Colloqui* by Ludwig, see U. Ojetti, *I Taccuini*, Florence 1954, p. 391.

630. G. Preziosi, "Die geheimen Mächte in Italien," in *Völkischer Beobachter*, October 31, 1943 (also mentioned by M. Michaelis, *I rapporti italo-tedeschi ecc.*, cit., pp. 248-49), stated that in March, 1933, Mussolini intended to eliminate Jews and Freemasons from "positions of command." Either it was a misprint (1933 for 1923) or a forgery. The Grand Council of Fascism discussed the proposal (not Mussolini's but that of Preziosi, who had been asked to study an eventual reform of the bureaucracy) in March-April 1923, without reaching a decision. See Document 35 and L. Cabrini, *Il Potere segreto* cit., p. 70.

631. On this aspect of "ideology" and Fascist politics until 1937, see L. Salvatorelli–G. Mira, *Storia d'Italia ecc.* cit., pp. 877-81.

632. For those of France, which caused much sensation in Rome (even if it concerned above all Jewish refugees from Central Europe and not French Jews), see D. H. Weinberg, *Les Juifs à Paris de 1933 à 1939*, Paris 1974, pp. 95.

633. See Y. De Begnac, *Palazzo Venezia–Storia di un regime*, Rome 1950, p. 643.

634. Regarding all, see the report presented to Mussolini by Farinacci upon returning from his trip to Italian East Africa, and dated Cremona April 24, 1938. The two sentences quoted are on pages 1 and 14 (ACS, *Segreteria particolare del Duce, Carteggio riservato*, file 242/R, "Farinacci, avvocato Roberto," under the file 39, dossier D). In his report, Farinacci wrote: "Italian nationals are not being policed that much, and therefore do not offer a very imperial spectacle to the natives. The episodes provoked by their vulgar, disgusting or offensive ways, are numerous. The following is a list of some, among the most serious that were reported:

a)   total lack of comprehension and respect for the customs and traditions of the population;

b)   Terrible behavior by Italian civilians and military toward native women;

c)   Demanding loans from wealthy locals;

d)   Uncouth ways of living and dressing, which is in jarring contrast to the ways in which the locals behave and dress etc."

635. See the declarations of Mussolini to von Bülow in September 1937, in *Documents on German Foreign Policy 1918-1945*, s. D. (*1937-45*), I, London 1949, p. 2. During the same conversation, Mussolini said that at present the problem of relations between blacks and whites, according to him, was basic. According to Farinacci (cited report, p. 4) 90% of the Italian

girls in Italian East Africa were pregnant; though he did not specify if this was the work of Italian nationals or the natives.

With D. L. April 19, 1937 the relationships "of a conjugal nature" with the subjects of the Italian East Africa were punished by imprisonment of one to five years.

636. G. Ciano, *Diario, 1937-38* cit., pp. 94 and 216.

637. "To require in the *harshest* of ways, from all Italians residing in Ethiopia, that which is called racial dignity or, dignity of the Italian people. Moral composure is the external uniform of Italians–especially officers and soldiers–it must be absolutely faultless. The natives must be convinced a) of our superiority and consequently of our right to govern; and b) that the government will raise the standards of living. Our *lack of racial preparedness* is at the root of the bitter Scioana insurrection. Too many Italians have given several serious motives of scandal and inadequacy... No familiarity with the natives, but also no brutality. Understanding and justice. Schools, no further than grade level and a number which are of a professional character; welfare services and medical treatment of a systematic and general nature; accustom the natives to regular work which is regularly paid; punished harshly, when necessary, but after due process. Consent, respect and devotion must rise up together with force. This will be achieved *if all the Italians* in Ethiopia, adapt their actions and their entire lives to *the style that I shall call the Style of the Fascist Empire.*" We owe access to these instructions to the kindness of the present Duke of Aosta.

638. B. Mussolini, *Opera omnia* cit., XXXIX, pp. 190-91.

639. All around it has been said–though without really getting down to the crux of the matter–that economic interests influenced Mussolini's decision to begin the persecution. That some fascist leader or business welcomed the racial campaign, intending to draw advantage from it (taking the place of the expelled Jews or eliminating a rival or similar) is certain, and proof of this is not lacking. As numerous as these episodes were, they basically only vaguely influenced Mussolini's decision, which was uniquely political.

640. The role of the entourage has been much played down M. Michaelis, *Mussolini e la questione ebraica* cit., pp. 189-90; and easily criticized, D. L. Germino, *The Italian Fascist Party in Power. A study in totalitarian rule*, Oxford 1959, pp. 28, 85, in which there are numerous inaccuracies on the origins of the anti-Jewish actions of October 1938.

641. N. d'Aroma, *Vent'anni insieme* cit., pp. 266-67.

642. *Ibid.*, p. 274; G. Ciano, *Diario, 1937-38* cit., p. 300.

643. ACS, *Emilio De Bono (diari)*, q. 43, September 4, 1938.

644. G. Ciano, *Diario, 1937-38* cit., p. 78.

645. *Ibid.*, p. 15.

646. *Ibid.*, p. 157.

647. *Ibid.*, p. 62.

648. Y. De Begnac, *Palazzo Venezia ecc.* cit., p. 643.

649. G. Ciano, *Diario, 1937-38* cit., 264.

650. Y. De Begnac, *Palazzo Venezia ecc.* cit., p. 643.

651. See G. Ciano, *Diario, 1937-38* cit., p. 78.

652. See "In casa Farinacci," in *Il caffè.* November 1, 1924.

653. See ACS, *Segreteria particolare del Duce, Carteggio riservato*, file 242/R, *Farinacci avvocato Roberto*, under the file 26, dossier F.

654. See G. Ciano, *Diario, 1937-38* cit., p. 186.

655. See ACS, *Segreteria particolare del Duce, Carteggio riservato*, file 242/R, *Farinacci avvocato Roberto*, under the file 2, dossier B.

656. C. Senise, *Quando ero capo della polizia*, Rome 1946, pp. 112-13.

657. ACS, *Segreteria particolare del Duce, Carteggio riservato*, file 242/R, "Farinacci avvocato Roberto," under the file 39, dossier D.

658. R. De Felice, *Mussolini il duce. 2. Lo Stato totalitario (1936- 1940)*, Turin 1981, chapter three.

659. See G. Bottai, *Diario 1935-1944* cit., p. 129.

660. Critica fascista, "Politica fascista della razza," in *Critica fascista*, August 1, 1938, pp. 290-91. In the following issues, Bottai's magazine often returned to the theme of racism, trying to reassert the theories presented in the first leading article (see, for example, "Il razzismo fascista" in *Critica fascista*, September 1, 1938, pp. 322-23; B. Ricci, *Codreanu*, December 15, 1938, p. 62; G. A. Longo, *Il "punto" del razzismo fascista*, October 1, 1939, pp. 367-68), but also more frequently publishing articles not "spiritually" formulated, and even lenient towards German racism.

661. See *Diorama. Problemi dello spirito nell'etica fascista. Antologia della pagina speciale di "Regime Fascista" diretta da Julius Evola*, edited by M. Tarchi, Rome 1974.

662. See *Julius Evola nei documenti segreti del Terzo Reich*, edited by N. Cospito and H. W. Neulen, Rome 1986. The volume is also interesting for the information given regarding two projects, both aborted, to found an Italian-German Academy for race and for a magazine, *Sangue e Spirito*, written in both Italian and German, the former shortly after the adoption of the race policy, and the latter in 1942.

663. J. Evola, *Il cammino del Cinabro*, Milan 1963, p. 169.

664. It is significant that even in the days immediately following September 8, [1943] when the attacks by the Nazis against Italy, and the "traitors" to Fascism, were at their most violent, German propaganda never even mentioned the fact that the policy of race had been imposed upon Italy by Germany in 1938. The only hint, in reality quite vague, and in any case not referring to "order" but of quid pro quo, that we were able to find is in Nazi propaganda amongst the Germans residing in the Alto Adige to-

wards the end of 1938. Such propaganda, extolling German military power, maintained that Germany "protected" Italy which, "in compensation has for the moment adopted the race policy, and later will surrender the Alto Adige." (See ASAE, *Carte recuperate nel 1945 [fondo Lancellotti]*, *Gabinetto*, p. 136, *Germania [1938]*, under the file *Note fiduciarie dal 29 luglio al 5 dicembre 1938*, the Inspector General of Public Security Peruzzi [?] to the Director General of P.S., Milan, December 5, 1938). This is clearly not much in the way of proving an "order" of Hitler.

665. G. Ciano, *Diario, 1937-38* cit., pp. 61-62. A further confirmation may be found in the aforementioned meeting between Mussolini and Bülow. Two months before, during which the Duce stated that the Jewish question was not a problem for him since there were only 70 thousand Jews in Italy. Instead, there was a *racial question* for Italy, limited to colonial populations. See *Documents on German Foreign Policy* cit., s. D., I, p. 2; and also H. Frank, *Im Angesicht des Galgens*, Munich 1955, p. 222.

666. A. Tamaro, *Venti anni di storia* cit., pp. 305-6. See also, M. Magistrati, *L'Italia a Berlino (1937-1939)*, Milan 1956, pp. 99-100.

667. See ACS, *Min. Culturale popolare, Gabinetto*, p. 35, file *Germania*, G. Ciano to all of the ministers, November 23, 1936.

668. E. Mussolini, *Mio fratello Benito*, Florence 1957, p. 178.

669. G. Ciano, *L'Europa verso la catastrofe* cit., p. 220.

670. See ACS, *Min. Int., Dir. Gen. P.S., Div. Aff. Gen. E ris. (1903-1949)*, cat. RG, year 1936, b. 429, file 42; year 1937, b. 430, file 42.

In the first case (November 1936) it is a request for information, before disclosing the matter to the Gestapo, regarding a Milanese business man, suspected of having had contacts in Nuremberg with "Jewish groups" and having proceeded on to Stockholm to meet with Trotsky. The second case (December 1936 and June 1937) concerns information about property bought in Italy by Jewish emigrants from Germany and mostly about the eventual "permutation" of such property.

671. G. Leto, *OVRA cit., pp. 161-63.*

672. ACS, *Min. Int., Dir. Gen. P.S., Segreteria del capo della polizia*, file *Visita del Capo della Polizia in Germania (1936)*, reproduced in *Document 15*.

673. See, for example, "L'esodo degli ebrei dall'Italia," in *Kölnische Zeitung* of September 9, 1938.

674. ACS, *Roberto Farinacci (1921-45)*, file 68.

In another letter from Pauler to Farinacci (ACS, *Roberto Farinacci [1921-45]*, file 71) on May 8, 1938, on the occasion of Farinacci being decorated with the Great Cross of the Order of the German Eagle, one reads: "If the official policy of Fascism for tactical reasons, satisfactory to me, has until now not dealt with the Jewish question, nor reached a solution with the desired clarity, nevertheless, your heroic fight against the world wide

Jewish plague is well remembered in Germany, and this fight has been awarded the highest decoration of the new Germany, its esteem and gratitude [sic]."

675. ASAE, *Germania*, p. 47, *1938*, M. Magistrati to the Ministry of Popular Culture and the Ministry of Foreign Affairs, Berlin, December 23, 1938; see reproduction in *Document 29*.

676. P. Aloisi, *Journal* cit., p. 365.

677. G. Pini, *Filo diretto con palazzo Venezia* cit., p. 58 and also pp. 72-73 (January 1937).

678. *Ibid.*, p. 88.

679. G. Ciano, *Diario, 1937-38* cit., p. 78.

680. See *Il popolo d'Italia*, June 4, 1938; *Annali del fascismo*, June 1938, p. 47.

681. G. Pini, *Filo diretto con palazzo Venezia* cit., pp. 169-70.

682. F. Charles-Roux, *Huit ans au Vatican 1932-40*, Paris 1947, p. 163, perceptively wrote that "comme médusé par la puissance du Reich, le fascisme italien se mit à l'unisson du nazisme allemand" [as if mesmerized by the power of the Reich, Italian Fascism marched in unison with German Nazism]. In the same sense, E. Conti, *Dal taccuino di un borghese*, Cremona 1946, pp. 612-13.

683. The entirely manipulative and political character that the measures on race represented for Mussolini, clearly emerges from an episode referred by G. Acerbo, *Fra due plotoni di esecuzione. Avvenimenti e problemi dell'epoca fascista*, Bologna 1968, pp. 297-99. In the first months of Italian non-belligerency, precisely in December 1939–January 1940 (that is, when Mussolini was hesitating the most about partcipating in the new war, and he strongly resented the fact that Hitler had entered into the alliance with the USSR and had "accelerated" the conflict itself with respect to the date that had initially been agreed upon), Acerbo–whose racial theories decidedly contrasted with those of the Nazis–was asked by Ettore Muti, then secretary of the PNF, to hold a lecture to illustrate his own point of view and in this way stress the difference between Fascist racism and that of the Nazis. The lecture took place in Florence, at the Palazzo Vecchio, January 27, 1940, with the participation of Muti and many other members of the government. And, as if that were not enough, the Minister of the Popular Culture, on explicit orders from Mussolini, decided to publish the expanded text of the lecture in many thousands of copies, which, when they were ready, were never distributed, because the success of the Germans in Denmark and Norway had meanwhile altered Mussolini's plans once again, and therefore made any initiative that marked a change in attitude between the "allies," useless, or rather, politically dangerous. See, also ACS, *Min. Cultura popolare*, b. 113, file I.

684. On the period 1938-39, see T. Staderini, *Legislazione per la difesa della razza*,

Rome 1940. For a comparison with that of the Nazis, see *Le leggi razziali tedesche*, special issue of *Dottrina fascista*, April 1940.

685. See G. Ciano, *L'Europa verso la catastrofe* cit., p. 171; Y. De Begnac, *Palazzo Venezia ecc.* cit., pp. 642-43; E. Mussolini, *Mio fratello Benito* cit., p. 223; B. Spampanato, *Contromemoriale*, Rome 1952, II, p. 132.

686. G. Ciano, *Diario, 1939-43* cit., II, pp. 174-75.

687. See J. Billig, *Le commissariat général aux questions juives* cit.; *La persécution des Juifs en France et dans les autres pays de l'Ouest présentée par la France à Nuremberg*, edited by H. Monneray, Paris 1947.

688. B. Spampanato, *Contomemoriale* cit., II, pp. 130-32.

689. Y. De Begnac, *Palazzo Venezia ecc.* cit., p. 642.

690. Y. De Begnac, *Palazzo Venezia ecc.* cit., p. 643.

691. See G. Ciano, *Diario, 1939-43* cit., *passim.*

692. *Ibid.*, p. 211.

693. G. Ciano, *Diario, 1937-38* cit., p. 207; see also G. Gorla, *L'Italia nella seconda guerra mondiale*, Milan 1959, pp. 378, 393.

694. Y. De Begnac, *Palazzo Venezia ecc.* cit., p. 643.

695. G. Bastianini, *Uomini Cose Fatti, Memorie di un ambasciatore*, Milan 1959, p. 54.

696. A. Tamaro, *Venti anni di storia* cit., III, p. 310.

697. A rapid profile of the man has been drawn by the articulate A. Spinosa, *Le persecuzioni razziali in Italia* cit., I, p. 975: "This half-pseudo-literary critic— half revolutionary, acted in cynical bad faith. The race issue was, for him, a card just like any another. He bet on it heavily, convinced that he had sensed the right moment at the wheel of good fortune. Interlandi did not believe in the venture that he lead with cynicism at all. One of the strong points in defense of race, in his propaganda, was the military education that the youth of the Littorio received on Saturday afternoon in the gyms of the GIL, but nevertheless he made sure his son, Cesarino, was ex- empted from every exercise, or disturbance in general, because in private he considered them to be useless, ridiculous and stupid."

698. See B. Spampanato, *Contromemoriale* cit., I, p. 180: Preziosi "had filed thou- sands of names with their past activities, and had minutely followed their political moves."

699. ACS, *Emilio De Bono (Diari)*, q. 43 at the date of September 13, 1938.

700. See *Corriere mercantile*, of Genoa, March 1, 1938.

701. See, for example, Arianus, "Inchiesta degli ebrei a Torino. Quanti sono— Cosa fanno," in *Il popolo*, Turin, January 26, 1938; M. Cosimelli, "Antiroma," in *Acciaio*, Terni, June 18, 1938.

702. See *Il Tevere*, February 9, 1938.

703. Therein, January 11, 1938.

704. *La vita italiana*, January 1938, p. 106.

705. At the same time, one Francesco Consoli sent, on January 23, 1938, a long report to Mussolini, which claimed that *Il piccolo* was an instrument of national and international Judaism. Similar accusations had already been made, since 1933, about *Il piccolo* and R. Alessi by a group of "Fascist action squad" members from Trieste. Rino Alessi objected to these accusations and to the campaign of Farinacci, with a letter to Mussolini on August 8, 1938, in which the director of the Trieste daily defined his accusers as "dubious suspicious characters who gather around a discredited politician," and explicitly stated: "they abuse the racist question hoping to extract the progress that they have never managed to achieve due to the squalid poverty of their moral makeup." See ACS, *Segreteria particolare del Duce, Carteggio riservato*, file 242/R, *Rino Alessi*.

706. *La vita italiana*, January 1938, p. 107 (against Alessi); *Il regime fascista*, January 19 and 22, 1938; *Il giornalissimo*, February 11, 1938.

   Il piccolo in Rome replied with two articles by Bac (Alessandro Bacchioni). January 14 (*Amicus Plato*) and 21, 1938 (*L'intruglio moscovita dei Savi di Sion*). At the beginning of February, *Il giornale d'Italia*, of which *Il piccolo* was the midday edition, changed ownership (see G. Ciano, *Diario, 1937-38* cit., p. 105): therefore the probable cause of his withdrawal from the debate. This, regarding the *Protocols*, immediately had an indirect consequence: in the second half of January the *Protocols* were widely reviewed by *La Stampa* (January 16), by *Il Brennero* (January 20), by *Il resto del carlino* (January 21) and by *La tribuna* (January 26), as well as various other minor newspapers. Not all the reviewers, though, were unconditionally favorable. *La Stampa* got out of it by stating that "true or apocryphal, they emerge to be undeniably the faithful reflection of Jewish essence and will"; R. Muzzi, in *Il resto del carlino*, made some veiled objection, warning against "unjust generalizations" and limited himself to writing that, of the reader one asks only to "seriously reflect."

   On the authenticity of the *Protocols* see also, *Il Tevere*, February 8, 1938. For the official position of Fascism, see A. Casolo Ginelli, "I Protocolli di Sion," in *Gerarchia*, April 1938, pp. 295-96.

707. On *Il piccolo*, see S. Benco, *"Il piccolo di Trieste." Mezzo secolo di giornalismo*, Milan-Rome 1931.

708. ACS, *PNF, Situazione politica delle provincie (1923-43), Trieste*.

709. Proof of the level of excitement the anti-Semites of Trieste were able to spread in certain circles of the city like this obscene statement from a recorded telephone conversation between a member of the National Confederation Fascist Union for Industry and a naval captain (ACS, *PNF, Situazione politica delle provincie [1923-43], Trieste*, March 24, 1938), commenting on the first official positions taken by the government against the Jews: "I would like to see the [...] of the Jews in Trieste at this moment."

710. See *Il regime fascista*, March 8, 1938.

711. See, in particular, "Radio cronaca," in *Il regime fascista*, February 13, 1938; "Cose riservate," therein, April 19, 1938.

712. See G. Ciano, *Diario, 1937-38* cit., p. 214.

713. A strong position taken against anti-Semitism appears also by F. Sebastiani, "Problemi di attualità," in *Rivoluzione fascista*, of Siena, January 30, 1938. In it, anti-Semitism ("born under other skies") was decidedly rejected as being alien to Fascism. For the author of the article, this had a universal value, and "therefore one must not falsify it, or diminish it by attributing policies which are absolutely foreign to it."

714. See, for example, N. P. Romualdi, "Noi e gli ebrei," in *Il popolo di Romagna*, Forlí, January 29, 1938; "Gli studenti ebrei," in *Corriere adriatico*, Ancona, February 9, 1938; "Studenti Ebrei," in *Eccoci*, Cremona, February 16, 1938.

715. G. Ciano, *Diario, 1937-38* cit., p. 215.

716. The debate against such "universalist" interpretations was taken up by many commentators; see, for example, F. Chilanti, "La coscienza di razza nel popolo lavoratore," in *L'ordine corporativo*, July 1938, pp. 615-17; A. Gravelli, "Il razzismo italiano tra l'universalismo astratto e l'universalità concreta," in *Il messaggero di Rodi*, August 22, 1938.

717. As to how this news was presented and distorted, it is clear even from a small episode such as a political discussion, in Dijon, between two Jews on the opportunity or not of a war against the Nazis, that degenerated into a commotion during which the shop of one of the two was ransacked by some of those present at the discussion. The news was reported by many newspapers between October 3 and 5, with the following titles: "A Jew who wanted war assaulted and knocked down by the crowd" (*La gazzetta del lunedí*, Messina); "The shop of a warmongering Jew devastated by the crowds in Dijon" (*Il popolo di Roma*); "The shops of two Jews, supporters of the war, devastated in Dijon" (*Il messaggero*, Rome); "Insurrections caused by a Jew in the center of Dijon" (*Il Veneto*, Padova); "Episodes of hostility towards the Jews in France" (*Il popolo di Sicilia*, Catania); "In France they kill Jews" (*L'isola*, Sassari).

718. See the press, above all that of Rome, of October, as well as *Il resto del carlino*, December 9, 1938, for the conclusion of the whole affair. For further information on other developments, see the anti-Fascist *Corriere d'Italia*, *Il Cairo*, April 11, 1941: "At leisure n Capri."

719. See "Editori e libri," in *Il corriere della sera*, September 11, 1938.

720. See *Corriere adriatico*, Ancona, August 11; *Il regime fascista*, August 24; *Il giornalissimo*, Rome; *Gazzetta*, Messina; *Il popolo*, Trieste, August 26; *Gazzettino*, Venice, September 6, 1938.

721. *Il regime fascista*, October 5, 1938.

722. See *Il popolo d'Italia*, August 30 (accountants), August 31 (lawyers), September 7 (credit institutes), September 8 (insurance agencies), September

11 (periodical editors), September 13 (representatives), September 14 (artisans), September 17, 1938 (antique dealers).

723.　See, for example, "Non oltre i confini delle direttive segnate per l'esaltazione e la difesa della razza," in *La sera*, Milan, September 8, 1938. The article invited to "not overstep the boundaries of the directives set for race policy" and wrote explicitly: "Instead we now witness an exasperating straying beyond the indicated lines which reveals an irrational evaluation of the problem and can lead to dangerous distortions, in the fight that the Regime has initiated against the contamination, against every danger, to the purity of the Italian race. We agree to uncompromising action, but this must be disciplined and exclusively follow the directives which have until now been laid out and that the regime intends to continue to issue. The problem has been presented by Fascism in its correct terms, aiming at strengthening the purest virtues of the race, it is necessary to look at it without distortions, as it has been presented and not misinterpret its essence. Yesterday we deplored the hurried heedlessness in naming names and positions. Today we reconfirm our disapproval, echoing the displeasure of those important people who found themselves named as belonging to the Jewish race." More explicit was perhaps *Il popolo Biellese*. October 13, this newspaper published a short article (*Razzismo e dignità*) which violently attacked these aberrations: "Racism is one thing: anti-Semitism is another. To be racist, one can become an anti-Semite; but it is unacceptable to become an anti-Semite, to prove that we are good racists. Therefore, it is not a matter of defending the Jews. But of defending ourselves, our dignity as Italians and our dignity as Fascists. The system of spreading about rumors regarding authentic Aryan Christian Italians saying that they are Jews is wretched and vulgar. The behavior of those who participate in this game is cowardly, encouraged by the usual agents provocateurs of the small desperate opposition party of those in tow, the misfits, those "put out to pasture," the disillusioned, the skeptics and the weak."

724.　See, for example, G. Sommi Picenardi, "La 'guerra promessa,'" in *Il regime fascista*, October 21, 1938; A. Luchini, "Guerra giudaica," in *Il bargello*, October 23, 1938.

725.　See *Il popolo di Trieste del lunedí*, October 24, 1938.

726.　Much space was given to the discussion of the problems of race by the *Cronache del regime* (held by Aldo Valori, Ezio M. Gray, F. S. Grazioli, A. Pavolini, G. Bottai and V. Gayda). See also, in the *Radiocorriere* of July 21-27, 1938 (p. 3), the article by U. D'Andrea, *Coscienza della razza* in which racism was defined "the crowning achievement of the new conscience of Fascist Italy, the realization necessary to confirm and consecrate the transition from the national cycle to that of the Imperial cycle of the third Italy."

727. See *L'avvenire d'Italia*, Bologna, September 4, 1938; *Il Tevere*, September 6, 1938.

728. See *Il corriere della sera*, November 21, 1938; *Il Tevere*, November 22, 1938.

729. See *Il popolo del Friuli*, of Udine, October 19, 1938.

730. (I) *The characteristics of Roman civilization*; (II) *From Rome to us, the unity of history, the unity of the population*; (III) *How to defend the race*; (IV) *The problem of crossbreeding*; (V) *The demographic problem: purity, quantity, quality*; (VI) *The conscience of race and colonization*; (VII) *Aspects of the Jewish problem: from emancipation to Zionism*; (VIII) *Aspects of the Jewish problem: the Jews and the Nation*; (IX) *Aspects of the Jewish problem: Jewish culture and Modern culture.*

731. (I) *The characteristics of civilization*; (II) *The problem of race*; (III) *The Regime for the defense of race*; (IV) *The "problem of problems"*; (V) *Colonization and the problem of race*; (VI) *The Jewish question in the modern world.*

732. See the interview granted by President E. Coleschi to R. M. Moretti, "Il razzismo Italiano nei Rapporti dei CAUR," in *L'Ambrosiano*, September 7, 1938.

733. See ACS, *Min. Int. Dir. Gen. Demografia e Razza (1915-44)*, b. I, file 2, *Notiziario Antibolscevico (Roma)*.

734. See G. Insolera, "I giovani e la razza," in *La verità*, September 1938, pp. 552-54; M. Marioli, "Impero Autarchia Razza," in *Il Bò*, Padova, September 24, 1938; B. Giannetti, "I Guf di Catanzaro per La difesa della razza," in *Roma fascista*, October 5, 1938.

735. Cfr. ACS, *Min. Int. Dir. Gen. Demografia e Razza (1915-44)*, b. I, file 4, *Notiziario "Razzismo" (Catanzaro)* and also "Il GUF di Catanzaro per La difesa della razza," in *Il giornale d'Italia* (provincial edition), October 16, 1938.

736. The winner of the competition in 1939, held in Trieste, was Mario Fausti (Rome), followed by Luigi Piacentini (Florence) and Giorgio Maggioni (Padua); that of 1940, held in Bologna, was won by Giuseppe Altini (Bologna), followed by Nicola Galdo (Naples) and Alfassio Grimaldi (Pavia). For the names of the other winners see G. S. Spinetti, *Difesa di una generazione*, Rome 1948, pp. 158 (1939) and 164 (1940).

737. See G. Pini, *Filo diretto con palazzo Venezia* cit., pp. 93, 102, 104 (April 7-June 2, 1937); G. Ciano, *Diario, 1937-38* cit., p.13 (at the date of September 6, 1937).

738. See G. Pini, *Filo diretto con palazzo Venezia* cit., p. 134; G. Ciano, *Diario, 1937-38* cit., p. 113 (at the date of February 15, 1938).

739. See G. Ciano, *Diario, 1937-38* cit., p. 113.

740. Beginning in March 1937, the office of the Italian press service, at the Ministry of Popular Culture, wrote out a monthly report on the development of the demographic and racist policy in Italy. See ACS, *Min. Cultura popolare, Gabinetto*, file 424, *Dir, gen. per la stampa italiana (1937-38)*.

741. ACS, *Presidenza del Consiglio, Gabinetto (1937-43)*, *Atti amministrativi (1937-39)*, b. 118, file 3/2-2, n. 5441/14.

742. G. Ciano, *Diario, 1937-38* cit., p. 214.

743. ACS, *Roberto Farinacci (1921-45)*, file 64.

744. ACS, *Presidenza del Consiglio, Gabinetto (1937-43)*, *Atti amministrativi (1937-39)*, b. 117, file 3/2-2, nn. 5111-16, under the file 14/3.

745. See Document 16.

746. See Document 17.

747. See G. Ciano, *Diario, 1937-38* cit., p. 209 (at the date of July 14, 1938).

748. ACS, *Min. Cultura popolare, Gabinetto*, b.3, file 43. August 1, Pende cabled from Chianciano-Terme to Sebastiani, Mussolini's secretary: "Please repeat need to issue new declaration to the press by commission race submitted to chief." August 3, Alfieri telegraphed Pende: "By superior order I inform you that it is not believed important for the moment to publish such declaration." ACS, *Min. Cultura popolare, Gabinetto*, b. 4, file 43.

749. See "Canovaccio per commedia," in *Il Tevere*, October 17, 1938. ACS, *Min. Cultura popolare, Gabinetto*, b. 3, file 43, *Appunto per S. E il ministro* of September 14, 1938 (seen by Mussolini on the 19th). In this *note* it said that the work of Pende "appears more and more in contradiction with the principles of racism, which have been officially imposed by the Regime" and it is defined "dangerous" and "pernicious." Attached to the *note* was a *report* on the attendance decided upon by Pende at the seventeenth congress of the Italian Association for the progress of Science at Bologna, September 7, in which the "dangerous" statements, made by Pende himself, were disapproved. An extensive summary of the report by Pende in Bologna is in *Il popolo di Trieste*, September 9, 1938.

750. See "Processo a Pende," in *Israel*, January 13, 1949 (therein, a long letter by N. Pende with a reply by C. A. V[iterbo].

751. See ACS, *Min. Cultura popolare, Gabinetto*, b.4, file 43. The order to keep silence on all that concerned Pende was given on October 16 and revoked on the 20th after a letter of the 19th from Pende to Alfieri.

752. The report on the census data was completed by the beginning of September. See ACS, *Presidenza del Consiglio, Gabinetto (1937-43)*, *Atti amministrativi (1937-39)*, b. 117, file 3/2-2, n. 5441, under the file 4, *Dir. gen. Demografia e Razza* to *Presidenza del Consiglio*, September 8, 1938. On the way the census was taken, its standards, results and limits, see F. Sabatello, "Il censimento degli ebrei del 1938 (note metodologiche sulla preparazione, la sua realizzazione ed i suoi risultati)," in *La Rassegna mensile di Israel*, January-February, 1976, pp. 25-55; S. Della Pergola, "Appunti sulla demografia della persecuzione antiebraica in Italia," therein, January-June, 1981, pp. 120-37.

753. See Document 18.

754. The replies from all the ministries and bureaus are in ACS, *Min. Int., Dir. gen. Demografia e Razza (1938-43)*, b. 4, file 15, *Direttive dei ministeri in materia di razza*.

755. The list of Jewish authors (114) was published by the press October 7, 1938; see, for example, *Il telegrafo* of that date.

756. ACS, *Min. Int., Dir. gen. Demografia e Razza (1938-43)*,b. 4, file 15, *Direttive dei ministeri in materia di razza.*

757. ACS, *Min. Int., Dir. gen. Demografia e Razza (1938-43)*, under the file *Ministero dell'Interno.*

758. ACS, *Min. Int., Dir. gen. Demografia e Razza (1938-43)*, b. 2, file 16, *Pratiche riguardanti il ministero delle Corporazioni.*

759. F. Guarneri, *Battaglie economiche*, II, Milan 1953, pp. 374-75; P. Grifone, *Il capitale finanziario in Italia*, Turin 1945, pp. 169-70.

760. See R. D. L. September 7, 1938 n. 1381, in T. Staderini, *Legislazione per la difesa della razza* cit., pp. 16-17.

761. See R. D. L. September 7, 1938 n. 1390, integrated and coordinated with R. D. L. November 15, 1938 n. 1779 in T. Staderini, *Legislazione per la difesa della razza* cit., pp. 22-27.

762. G. Ciano, *Diario, 1937-38* cit., p. 227.

763. *Ibid.*, pp. 230-31.

764. News of the event and extensive excerpts of Colonel Adami's diary were published in the *Gazzettino del lunedì* on May 11, 1970. The letter, signed T. Corradino, was widely reprinted by *Israel* on June 4, 1970. Of another similar project, which Mussolini had Vincenzo Tecchio study towards the end of 1937, S. Maurano writes, "Mussolini voleva dare una 'terra promessa' agli Ebrei," in *La settimana Incom illustrata*, April 24-May 1, 1959.

765. See J. Billig, *Introduzione a Dossier Eichmann*, Rome 1961, pp. 1-45, *passim*; L. Poliakov, *Il nazismo e lo sterminio degli ebrei* cit., pp. 70-75.

766. G. Ciano, *Diario, 1939-43* cit., I, p. 280; P. Schmidt, *Da Versaglia a Norimberga*, Rome 1951, p. 435.

767. S. Minerbi, "Il progetto di un insediamento ebraico in Etiopia *(1936-1943)*," in *Storia contemporanea*, December 1986, pp. 1083-1137. Useful information is also in R. Pankhurst, "Plans for Mass Jewish Settlement in Ethiopia (1936-1943)," in *Ethiopia Observer*, 1973, n. 4, pp. 235-45; M. Michaelis, *Mussolini e la questione ebraica* cit., pp. 193-212.

768. Various documents (see S. Minerbi, *Il progetto di un insediamento ebraico in Etiopia* cit., pp. 1113-15) prove that the project of settlement in Italian East Africa was viewed with suspicion by Italian Judaism and Zionism and some of their executives took steps to make sure it would fail with Italian authorities and during the visit of Chamberlain and Halifax to the British Embassy in Rome. According to R. Pankhurst, (*Plans for Mass Jewish Settlement* cit., p. 242) it was actually their opposition that prevented an agreement between Rome and Washington. This hypothesis is not sustainable; although it is very likely that the attitude of Italian Jewish executives must have contributed to Mussolini's loss of interest in an even lim-

ited settlement, that would have avoided political problems only if the
Italian Jewish leadership had been in agreement and the *leadership* of foreign immigrants had been in the hands of "good" Italian Jews.

769. G. Ciano, *Diario, 1939-43* cit., I, p. 22.

770. W. Laqueur, *Il terribile segreto. La congiura del silenzio sulla "soluzione finale,"*
Florence 1983; also M. Gilbert, *Auschwitz and the allies*, London 1981; B.
Wasserstein, *Britain and the Jews of Europe (1939-1945)*, London 1979; D.
Wyman, *Paper Walls*, Amherst 1968; H. Freingold, *The Politics of Rescue*,
New Brunswick 1970; B. Wasserstein, "Alliés et neutres face à la politique
nazie," in *L'Allemagne nazie et le génocide juif*, Paris 1985, pp. 356-72; M. R.
Marrus-R. O. Paxton, *Vichy et les juifs*, Paris 1981, pp. 53-76.

771. S. Minerbi, *Il progetto di un insediamento ebraico in Etiopia* cit., pp. 1129-36.

772. The list of university professors excluded from teaching because they
were Jews (96) was published in *Vita universitaria*, October 5, 1938; that of
high school professors (174) was published by *Il giornale della scuola media*,
February 1, 1939; that of qualified university teachers (195) by the same
paper, June 11, 1939.

773. ACS, *RSI, Segretaria particolare del Duce, Carteggio riservato (1943-45)*, file
Buffarini-Guidi avvocato Guido. See also G. Ciano, *Diario, 1937-38* cit., pp.
235 and 300; also the speech of Victor Emmanuel III at the opening of
the XXX Legislature of the Chamber of Deputies in March 1939.

774. See A. Spinosa, "Le persecuzioni razziali in Italia" cit., II, "L'attegiamento
della Chiesa," in *Il Ponte*, August 1952, pp. 1078-96; E. Rossi, *Il manganello
e l'aspersorio*, Florence 1958, pp. 365-93; A. Martini, "L'ultima battaglia di
Pio XI," in *La civiltà cattolica*, June 20 (file 2616) and September 19 (file
2622) 1959, pp. 574-91, 572-90; ID., "Gli ultimi giorni di Pio XI," in *La
civiltà cattolica*, November 7, 1959 (file 2625), pp. 236-50: the essays have
been combined in A. Martini, *Studi sulla questione romana e la Conciliazione*,
Rome 1963, pp. 175 sgg.; D. Carpi, "The Catholic Church and Italian
Jewry under Fascists (to the death of Pius XI)," in *Yad Vashem Studies*, IV,
Jerusalem 1960, pp. 43-56.

775. See *Le encicliche sociali dei papi da Pio IX a Pio XII (1864-1946)*, edited by I.
Giordani, Rome 1946, pp. 501-26.

776. *La civiltà cattolica*, 1938, issue 2115, pp. 277-78.

777. The article by the Jesuit A. Brucculeri began:
"Italian scholars have taken up a firm and precise position regarding racism, which, from a philosophical point of view, is not objectionable. While
on the notion of race every kind of vagueness, gross misunderstandings,
enormous stupidity, has abounded, Fascist teachers in our universities have
enounced in few and transparent thesis' the whole content of racism, in
which a perfunctory justice is made of all of that irrational garbage, with
which a theory of race has been built, that documents the disorientation

and the decadence of contemporary thought. 'The concept of race,' our scientists proclaim, 'is a purely biological concept.' In this declaration, which can only be shared by scholars of every school and every belief, one of the main causes of the present day confusion on racist theories is rejected."

778. A. Martini, *Studi sulla questione romana e la Conciliazione* cit., p. 178.

779. ACS, *Segreteria particolare del Duce, Carteggio riservato*, file 242/R *Farinacci avvocato Roberto*, under the file 39, dossier D, R. Farincacci to B. Mussolini, August 3, 1938; see copy in Document 19.

780. ACS, *Segreteria particolare del Duce, Carteggio riservato.*

781. ACS, *Presidenza del Consiglio, Gabinetto (1937-43)*, *Atti amministrativi (1937-39)*, b. 117, file 3/2-2, n. 5441/2 and also *Min. Int., Dir, gen, Demografia e Razza (1938-43)*, b.4, file 17. See copy in Document 20.

782. ACS, *Presidenza del Consiglio, Gabinetto (1937-43)*, *Atti amministrativi (1937-39)*, b. 117, file 3/2-2, n. 5441/2, the prefect of Trieste to the Cabinet of the Ministry of Internal Affairs, October 12, 1938; the prefect of Padua to the Cabinet of the Ministry of Internal Affairs, October 12, 1938.

783. See A. Giovannetti, "Pio XI e un appello," in *L'osservatore romano,* January 26, 1961.

784. Mussolini's most violent public statement against the Pope was expressed during the speech in Trieste, September 19, 1938. See B. Mussolini, *Opera Omnia* cit., XXIX, p. 146.

785. From a note (n. 6480) of the Apostolic Nunciature dated October 21, 1938, filed in its original text among the papers of Buffarini-Guidi, it appears that the Holy See immediately tried to obtain the cancellation of the date of October 1, 1938, used as the limit by the declaration of the Grand Council, to consider as belonging or not the the Jewish race the children of mixed marriages not practicing the Jewish religion. The note emphasized the necessity that "those converted to Catholicism, those who had the courage and heroism to tear away definitively from their country of origin, abjuring the Mosaic religion, were not confused with the Jews." For the text of the note in its entirety, see G. Buffarini-Guidi, *La vera verità. I documenti dell'archivio segreto del ministro degli Interni Guido Buffarini-Guidi dal 1938 al 1945*, Milan 1970, pp. 25-26.

786. The banned article read more or less like this: "Concubinage is forbidden between people who cannot join in marriage due to the provisions of article 1. Violators are punished with a sentence of up to two years in prison and a fine of 5,000 to 10,000 lira." Its approval would have basically meant that even religious marriage would have been considered concubinage.

787. The draft of article 7, before the meeting between Buffarini-Guidi and Tacchi-Venturi on October 29, read more or less like the final text of D.

L. November 17, 1938, n. 1728 (art. 6), reproduced in Document 23.
The text sent to the Holy See on November 2, instead reads as follows: "A marriage not celebrated in accordance with article 1, does not have any civil validity, except if it has been celebrated according to the rules established by the law of May 27, 1929-VII, n. 847; on the point of death or, with prior dispensation by the civil authorities for the legitimization of children. Only in these cases is permission given to registration of the marriage act according to the cited law." After the counterproposal by the Holy See, if it had been accepted, article 7 should have been as follows: "A marriage not celebrated in accordance with article 1 has no civil validity, except if it has been celebrated according to the rules established by the law of May 27, 1929-VII, n. 847; in danger of death or for the legitimization of children, or also when both of the contracting parties, even if of different race, profess the Catholic religion; which in the last case, children born of such marriage may marry only Aryans. Only in these three cases is permission given to register the marriage according to the cited law. In the case of marriage for the legitimization of children, permission is not given to the register until the dispensation of the civil authorities has been received. The decision by which permission is granted or denied is issued by Decree on the motion of the Minister for Internal Affairs." The text in this last draft is part of the papers of Buffarini-Guidi (G. Buffarini-Guidi, *La vera verità* cit., p.29); that of the two preceding ones from A. Martini, *Studi sulla questione romana e la Conciliazione* cit., p. 205.

788. See Document 21. The letters of Pius XI and Victor Emmanuel III have already been published by A. Martini, *Studi sulla questione romana e la Conciliazione* cit., pp. 210-14; that of Mussolini is published here, for the first time, from a telegram from G. Ciano (confidential, n. 17870 P. R.) on November 7, 1938, to the Cabinet of the Ministry of Internal Affairs and conserved amongst the papers of Buffarini-Guidi. Extracted from these same papers is the letter written at the last minute, by Father Tacchi-Venturi, to Mussolini, November 9, 1938, on the evening before the Council of Ministers was to approve the measures "for the defense of the race" (already published in G. Buffarini-Guidi, *La vera verità* cit., p. 33).

789. For all of these incidents, see A. Martini, *Studi sulla questione romana e la Conciliazione* cit. (where the most important relevant passages of G. Ciano's diary, are reported), and E. Rossi, *Il manganello e l'aspersorio* cit., pp. 369-393. Other documents in ACS, *Min. Int. Dir. Gen. Demografia e Razza (1938-43)*, b. 3, file 14, *Appunto* by Father Tacchi-Venturi, September 10, 1938 (seen by Mussolini on September 22) on the "ex-Jewish Italian Catholics."

790. G. Ciano, *Diario*, 1937-38 cit., p. 227; G. Bottai, *Vent'anni e un giorno*, Milan 1949, p. 121.

791. G. Ciano, *Diario*, 1937-38 cit., p. 230 (at the date of September 4, 1938).

792. ACS, *Segreteria particolare del Duce, Carteggio riservato (1922-43)*, file 242/R, *Gran Consiglio*, under the file 16, dossier B.

793. ACS, *Segreteria particolare del Duce, Carteggio riservato (1922-43)*, file 242/R, *Gran Consilglio*, under the file 16, dossier B.

794. The text as is follows: "Duce, on the eve of the meeting of the Grand Council please hear the solemn reaffirmation and unanimous vote of the Council of the Union of the Italian Jewish Community, that the Italian Jews have had nothing in common with any Jewish International, Masonic, Bolshevik, or anti-Fascist. We have sworn loyalty and grateful devotion to the sovereign and to the House of Savoy that gave us freedom. We have sworn devoted obedience to yourself, Duce of Fascism, who have given us the pride of renewed greatness of our Imperial Homeland. You are not without evidence of our faith. For Italy and Fascism, we ask to be able to continue to work with dignity in peace, and to die with honor in war. We have never doubted your generosity, and in the purity of our conscience we appeal to the spirit of Roman justice and humanity from which you have inspired all of your renovating and creative works."

795. There was no lack of statements and pressure, dictated not by political reasons, but by economic interests. A telegram sent to Mussolini on October 4 is typical: "Examining Grand Council problem defeatist disintegrating Jews in science, literature, finance, etc., not to forget protect physical Italian race from medicine of Jewish manufacture." See ACS, *Presidenza del Consiglio, Gabinetto (1937-43), Atti amministrativi (1937-39)*, b. 118, file 3/2-2, n. 5441/10.

796. See H. M. Franco, *Les martyrs juifs de Rhodes et de Cos*, Elisabethville 1952, pp. 44-46.

797. See PNF, *Foglio d'ordini*, n. 214, October 26, 1938, p. 9 (session of October 18, 1938).

798. G. Ciano, *Diario, 1937-38* cit., p. 264 (at the date of October 6, 1938).

799. L. Federzoni stated, in a letter to *Il gazzettino* published in Venice, January 26, 1962, that De Stefani pushed "to improve the harsh treatment threatened upon officials, functionaries, teachers, etc., to be retired, the separation pay established for pensioners who had reached the age limit" and that Acerbo intervened in the discussion with a "very powerful and original" speech, criticizing the definition given by Mussolini to the problem, defining it inspired by "old-fashioned proposals from the German school of the nineteenth century." These two speeches do not appear in the report of the *Foglio d'ordini*; the information is however reliable, whether it is due to an omission, or whether the speeches took place during the course of the meeting of the Grand Council. G. Acerbo, *Fra due plotoni di esecuzione* cit., p. 284, speaking of the meeting of October 6-7, writes: "There were

only four members of the assembly who were ready to declare their disapproval of the serious questions: Federzoni, De Bono, Balbo and Acerbo. The objections of the first three were strictly in reference to the proposed legislative rules, respectively considering them under the legal and constitutional aspects, and in the context of recent military history and Fascist precedents; whilst my objections were focused on the ideas underlying the introductory theories." This last assertion is confirmed by documents conserved in ACS, *Min. Cultura popolare*, b. 113, file 1. Also on the session of the Grand Council, see L. Federzoni, *Italia di ieri per la storia di domani*, Milan 1967, pp. 160-61.

800.   G. Bottai, *Diario, 1935-1944*, Milan 1982, pp. 136-37 (at the date of October 6, 1938). On the events surrounding Lumbroso, see ACS, *Min. Interno, Dir. gen. PS, Casellario politico centrale*, file "Lumbroso, Giacomo." Lumbroso, an ex-nationalist turned to Fascism in 1920 and after the "March on Rome" became a leader of Tuscan dissidents, in 1930 he refused to re-enter the PNF and converted to Catholicism at the time of his marriage to an aristocratic woman (which explains why P. Tacchi-Venturi showed so much interest in him before and after his five year sentence to internal exile). With respect to Mussolini's declaration of having "practically dictated" the racial manifesto, this is not borne out by the facts, the Duce had indeed limited himself to some comments on the text prepared by the *scientists* under the aegis of the Ministry of the Peoples Culture. According to Bottai (*Ibid.*, p. 125, at the date of July 16, 1938), the group of *Il Tevere* had been "completely left out" of the preparation of the manifesto and also the party had only vaguely been informed. Guido Landra, a young anthropologist, assistant to Sergio Sergi, whom Mussolini had supposedly "entrusted with the problem" since October of the year before [1937], played an important role.

801.   ACS, *Emilio De Bono (diari)*, q. 43, at the date of October 6, 1938.

802.   See E. Romagna-Manoja, "Da Cristo a Hitler," in *Le Ore*, February 6, 1960. In the already mentioned letter of L. Federzoni to *Il gazzettino* of Venice on January 26, 1962, it is claimed that the originator of the proposal to widen the discrimination to all of the Jews decorated with the Distinguished Service Cross, was the same Federzoni, whilst Balbo had only seconded him.

803.   G. Ciano, *Diario, 1937-38* cit., p. 264.

804.   See Document 23.

805.   The original text of D. L. of November 17, 1938, n. 1728 and the relative "Report" are to be found in the papers of G. Buffarini-Guidi. The "Report" is published in G. Buffarini-Guidi, *La vera verità* cit., pp. 26-29.

806.   See T. Staderini, *Legislazione per la difesa della razza* cit., pp. 22-27.

807.   *Ibid.*, pp. 119-25.

808.   *Ibid.*, p. 126.

809. News in the press in mid-November announced that up to that date the families already discriminated amounted to 3,522, out of a total of more than 15,000.

810. G. Ciano, *Diario, 1937-38* cit., p. 289.

811. He managed this in March 1939; see "Foglio di disposizioni" of the PNF, n. 1275.

812. ACS, *Min. Int., Dir. gen. Demografia e Razza (1938-43)*, b. 4, file 15, the General Directorate of Public Security, AG division, section III to the prefects of the kingdom, to the police superintendent of Rome and the division of the frontier police, October 24, 1938.

813. ACS, *Presidenza del Consiglio, Gabinetto (1937-43)*, *Atti Amministrativi (1937-39)*, b. 118, file 3/2-2, n. 5441/25, *Fondazioni ed enti morali di origine ebraica*.

814. ACS, *Min. Int., Dir. gen. Demografia e Razza (1938-43)*, b. 9, file 34.

815. For example, at the beginning of November the ritual killing of cattle was forbidden. See the comment, "Israel vegetariano," in *Il popolo d'Italia*, November 9, 1938.

816. ACS, *Presidenza del Consiglio, Gabinetto (1937-43)*, *Atti Amministrativi (1937-39)*, b. 117, file 3/2-2, n. 5441/1-3.

817. It came to the point that when the prediction that the winner of the fourth national competition of grain and farming would have been a Jew, the Minister of Agriculture and Forests asked (October 19, 1938) the chairmanship of the Council (who obviously replied negatively) if it could have been announced publicly or not. See ACS, *Presidenza del Consiglio, Gabinetto (1937-43)*, *Atti Amministrativi (1937-39)*, b. 118, file 3/2-2, n. 5441/1-3, *Concorrenti di razza ebraica al concorso nazionale del grano e dell'azienda agraria*.

818. G. Leto, *OVRA* cit., pp. 191-92.

819. R. Zangrandi, *Il lungo viaggio*, Turin 1948, pp. 76-77, 92-93.

820. Such denunciations were often dictated by specific economic interests or by the desire to expel a Jew from a determined position in order to replace him. A specific case is that of a memo from the National Fascist Federation of factory owners (see *Il regime fascista*, November 11, 1938) where it is clear that some owners had demanded that the expulsion of Jews from Italy would not be recognized as an "act of God" with regard to the cancellation of leases.

821. See "Foglio di disposizioni" of the PNF n. 1341 of June 7, 1939.

822. See *La Sentinella d'Italia*, Cuneo, December 6, 1938; *Il regime fascista*, December 16, 1938.

823. See *La nostra bandiera*, November 1, 1936.

824. See "Un'autorevole testimonianza a carico dell'arte 'moderna' straniera, bolscevizzante e giudaica," in *Il Tevere*, January 24, 1939.

825. There were many news articles also abroad. See, for example, *Israel*, Cairo, March 30, 1939, which, clearly, attributed it to Marinetti.

826. See *Per un orecchio*, in *Il regime fascista*, January 16, 1939; E. Garibaldi, "Carte in Tavola," in *Camicia rossa*, December 1938 (the issue came out in the second half of January of 1939).

827. See, for example, C. Villani, "Dietro le quinte," in *Il Ferruccio*, Pistoia, September 3, 1938; G. De Rosa, "Disinfezione delle Università," in *Corriere d'Alessandria*, October 6, 1938.

828. See, for example, "Però, poverini," in *Corriere adraiatico*, Ancona October 6, 1938; "Borghesi ed ebrei," therein, September 7, 1938; "Giudei Onorari," in *Il regime fascista*, September 7, 1938; "Pietismo," in *Corriere adriatico*, September 8 and 10, 1938; "Pietismo fuori posto," in *La stampa*, Turin, September 10, 1938; "Troppe inutili lacrime," in *Il giornale di Genova*, September 11, 1938; "Animule tenerelle," in *Il lavoro fascista*, Rome, September 13, 1938.

829. Ardi, "Il pietismo: trappola giudaica," in *Il piccolo*, Rome, September 21, 1938.

830. "I sentimenti," in *La scure*, Piacenza, October 6, 1938.

831. See "Il monito razziale del Segretario del Partito," in *Il resto del carlino*, November 26, 1938; "Il pietismo e gli ebrei," in *Il Tevere*, November 26, 1938; F. Scardaoni, "La dottrina della razza e il pietismo," in *La tribuna*, November 27, 1938.

832. See, for example, G. Rosso, "Giudei e Giudaizzati, ottussità dello 'spirito borghese,'" in *L'Ora*, Palermo, December 15, 1938; "Fascismo e Borghesia," in *Il regime fascista*, December 26, 1938.

833. ACS, *PNF, Situazione politica delle provincie (1923-43), Torino*.

834. *Ibid*.

835. *Ibid*.

836. ACS, *Segretaria particolare del Duce, Carteggio riservato (1922-43)*, file 242/R, *Parenti commendator Rino*.

837. In a report to the PNF directorate from the DICAT command, of the MVSN in Rome (based on information coming from Trieste) on July 26, 1938, it was stated that "if in Italy there is a Jewish problem, this problem has its roots in Trieste," and it stressed that after the *Anschluss* Trieste had become "a focal point in Italian-German interests," but that "until the situation is restored in the racist sense, this ideal atmosphere of trust cannot exist, in as much that the Jews who still occupy public positions and who are the declared enemies of Germany, can certainly not favor the desired cordial relations": see ACS *PNF, Situazione politica delle provincie (1923-43), Trieste*. On the persecution in Trieste, see S. Bon Gherardi, *La persecuzione antiebraica a Trieste (1938-1945)*, Udine 1972.

838. ACS, *PNF, Situazione politica delle provincie (1923-43)*, Trieste.

839. On the attitude of the Catholics in general, see R. A. Webster, *La Croce e i Fasci*, Milan 1964, pp. 156, 171, 216, sgg., also P. Zovato-P. A. Passolunghi,

"La reazione cattolica al razzismo fascista (1938)," in *La scuola cattolica*, 1976, n. 1, pp. 47-82.

840. ASAE, *Santa Sede, 1936-39*, p. 4, *parte politica*, Buffarini-Guidi to the Ministry of Foreign Affairs - Office V. the Holy See, August 23, 1938.

841. See, for example, R. M., "Questioni di coscienza," in *L'avvenire d'Italia*, Bologna, November 11, 1938.

842. See, for example, R. M., "Comprenderci," in *L'avvenire d'Italia*, Bologna, November 15, 1938; "Il Matrimonio e il Concordato-Divergenze," in *L'Avvenire*, Rome, November 15, 1938. For an idea on the arguments adopted against, by the Fascists, see, for example, "Punti Fermi," in *Il regime fascista*, November 15, 1938; G. Sottochiesa, "Il divieto dei matrimoni fra ariani e non ariani e il Concordato con la Chiesa," in *Il Tevere*, November 15, 1938.

843. ACS, *Min. della Cultura popolare, Gabinetto*, b. 39, *Goebbels, Giuseppe*.

844. Also in this action Preziosi was, in reality, the one who made the first move. Already in October 1937 *La vita italiana* had published an extensive document by a Polish Monsignor, S. Trzeciak, "L'antisemitismo dal punto di vista cristiano."

845. Also see Catholicus, "La Chiesa e gli ebrei," in *Il popolo d'Italia*, August 21, 1938; A. Trizzino, "La Chiesa e gli ebrei," in *Il Tevere*, August 23, 1938; C. Di Marzio, "Il volume dei loro cuori," in *Meridiano di Roma*, August 28, 1938; "I gesuiti e gli ebrei," in *Il regime fascista*, October 8, 1938; B. Damiani, "I Giudei nel Pensiero Cattolico," in *Il Tevere*, November 15, 1938; Augusto, S. Paolo, "I Giudei," in *Il regime fascista*, November 18, 1938; Erresse, "Cattolicismo e Razzismo," in *Il giornalissimo*, November 26, 1938.

846. R. Farinacci, *La Chiesa e gli Ebrei*, Rome XVII (December 1938). The lecture was also reprinted in ID., *Realtà storiche*, Cremona 1939, together with various other documents and speeches made in Italy and Germany.

847. See G. De' Rossi Dell'Arno, "Cattolici e Razzismo," in *Italia e Fede*, Rome, December 4, 1938.

848. R. Webster, *La Croce e i Fasci* cit., p. 168.

849. See *La difesa della razza*, October 20, 1938, p. 62.

850. According to G. Ciano, *Diario, 1937-38* cit., p. 216, "even the nuncio, Monsignor Borgongini-Duca, was very anti-Semitic."

851. See *La Civiltà cattolica*, 1938, issue 2113, pp. 62-71.

852. See M. Barbera, "La Questione dei Giudei in Ungheria," in *La Civiltà cattolica*, 1938, issue 2114, p. 151.

853. E. Rosa, "La Questione Giudaica e *La Civiltà cattolica*," in *La Civiltà cattolica*, 1938, issue 2119.

854. In 1940, Father A. Messineo when reviewing *I Fondamenti della Dottrina fascista della razza*, by G. Acerbo (see *La Civiltà cattolica*, 1940, issue 2169, pp. 216-19), went as far as stating: "We fully agree with A., seeing that all

historical and scientific arguments converge and confirm his theory, and we close this review, expressing the wish that other works similar to the present one, inspired by a great respect for real science and contained within the limits allowed by the progress of objective research, can clear up the issue by explaining a matter, which needs to be freed from terrific complications and resolved in a manner in keeping with the glorious cultural traditions of the Italian race, propagator of the highest achievements of the human spirit in the entire world."

855. See Italicus, "Diorama Internazionale. Il mondo davanti a Pio XI," in *Vita e pensiero*, March 1939, pp. 154-55.

856. See *Il corriere della sera*, January 11, 1939.

857. ACS, *Segreteria particolare del Duce, carteggio riservato (1922-43)*, file 242/R, *Farinacci avvocato Roberto*, under the file 39, dossier E, R. Farinacci to B. Mussolini, Cremona March 19, 1939. In the letter Farinacci expressed himself about Father Gemelli as follows: "The nomination of Father Gemelli [to the Academy] would not only make a very fine impression but would reward a worthy man whose political opinions I know very well. It would be appropriate if this happened very soon also because it is almost certain that in the next Conclave he will be made a Cardinal. And with the way things are now it would be very valuable to have a man around the successor to St. Peter who was really one of our own. It is necessary that you pull some authority with Federzoni who is more pro-Jewish than Fascist, does not show great sympathy for Gemelli. We must, dear President, make the most of those men who in every moment can be of use to us. Furthermore, I add that in Germany they spoke to me of Gemelli with great sympathy." At the bottom of Farinacci's letter, in Mussolini's own hand and strongly underscored "No, he is not ready yet."

858. See *Il regime fascista*, January 7, 1939, and also G. Cazzani, *Unità cristiana e giudaismo*, Cremona 1939.

859. "La Nota della 'Informazione Diplomatica' sulla Questione Ebraica," in *Israel*, February 24, 1938.

860. *Tre vite ecc*, cit., pp. 43-44.

861. ACS, *PNF, Situazione politica delle provincie (1923-43)*, Turin.

862. Ostracized by the "conformists" and by the group of *La nostra bandiera*, the young pro-Zionists (mostly from Rome, Florence, and Turin) were practically prevented from presenting their own names for the short-list for the new positions at the Union.

863. AUCII, *1938, Ministeri*, under the file "Min. Int.," verbal manuscript of the meeting Montecchi-Ascoli, Rome, May 18, 1938.

864. Apart from the unbiased difficulties, very few Jews publicly entered into polemics with the manifesto of the "scientists." For all, see SICOR, "Alcune Osservazioni sulle Razze," in *L'igiene e la vita*, September 1938, by a young Jew from Piedmont, Bruno Segre.

865. AUCII, *1938-39, Presidenza*, the president of the Union's councilors to the Community's president, July 29, 1938.

866. AUCII, *Libro dei verbali, Consiglio*, July 25, 1938.

867. See the letter from C. Grego to *Il grido d'Italia*, Genoa, July 30, 1938; also the polemical "Lacrime di Coccodrillo," in *Il regime fascista*, August 12, 1938, which was in a dispute regarding a letter (not published) from Professor Ruggero Ascoli to the same paper to counter the manifesto of the "scientists." See even a brief letter from the Rabbi of Mantua, Gustavo Calò, to *La voce di Mantova* September 11, 1938. As far as we can understand from *Il Tevere*, September 6, 1938, there was also no shortage of violent insulting letters to the most animated anti-Semitic papers, precisely like *Il Tevere*.

868. On July 22, for example, a Jewish farmer, Gilberto Terni, wrote to Mussolini asking "a word" for the Jews; see ACS, *Presidenza del Consiglio, Gabinetto (1937-43), Atti amministrativi (1937-39)*, b. 116, file 3/2, n. 5412.

869. "Le dichiarazioni sul problema della razza e gli ebrei d'Italia," in *Israel*, July 21, 1938.

870. "Il problema della razza e gli ebrei d'Italia," in *Israel*, August 11-18, 1938.

871. AUCII, *1938-39, Presidenza*.

872. *Ibid.*

873. The most important were, one on July 25, after the publication of the manifesto of the "scientists," one on October 4, before the meeting of the Grand Council (republished herein) and one on October 12, after the meeting of the Grand Council: "The Council of the Union of the Italian Jewish Communities, meeting after the deliberations of the Grand Council of Fascism, "reaffirms in the strongest terms the complete dedication of the Italians of Jewish religion to the Fascist Homeland, even in the moment in which superior demands require them to make painful sacrifices, hopes that the measures relating to co-religionists who have titles of obvious merit can be as extensive inasmuch as they have always served as good citizens of the Homeland and the Regime. In particular it requests that all of the youths born and bred in the climate of Mussolini be spared the utmost pain of not being able to offer a helping hand and offer their lives in combat for the Homeland."

874. See AUCII, *1938-39, Ministeri*, under the file *Min. Int., Dir. gen dei Culti*. The vice president, A. R. Ascoli, to His Excellency, Minister of Internal Affairs (Director General of Religions), Rome, September 12, 1938

875. On October 30, 1938, F. Jarach and A. R. Ascoli sent Mussolini an "address" in which they asked to be received by him to express "with disconsolate dignity and with the absolute discipline of good citizens of the homeland and sentiments of Italians of the Jewish faith" and to ask him for the authorization to "lend a most modest collaboration in the applica-

tion of some declaration that concerned them collectively." Mussolini did not grant the audience and delegated Buffarini-Guidi make a decision regarding the second request. Buffarini replied favorably to the request. The attorney Ascoli then had some meetings, in November, with Le Pera and with Bottai which in fact did not produce any concrete results. Ascoli had had a previous meeting with Bottai on October 7. Of that meeting we have an extensive verbal account by Ascoli himself, which constitutes one of the most shocking pieces of evidence of the hypocrisy and deceit of certain Fascist leaders. Indeed, with Ascoli, Bottai, who the day before had demonstrated the intolerance that we described during the Grand Council, flaunted an attitude that was more than "understanding," even going so far as "deploring" the measures decided upon a few hours earlier (see AUCII, *1938, Ministeri*, under the file *Min. Int.; 1938-39, Ministeri*, under the file *Min. Educ, naz.* and *Min. Int., Dir. gen Demografia e Razza*).

876.   The last issue of *Israel* was published on September 22, 1938. The paper was actually banned a few days later with the specious excuse that its editor was not present in Italy (the attempts to resolve the matter by appointing another editor were to no avail). Along with *Israel*, the publications of *Rassegna mensile Israel* also stopped publication; *La nostra bandiera* had stopped being published in mid-April; *L'idea sionistica* had for some time been issued with extreme irregularity; at the beginning of October the publication of *Davar* also stopped. After October only the *Notiziario* printed in ditto format in Rome by the Union was published, but by December it also had to suspend publication. The attempt to resume publication at the end of 1939 failed; the Ministry of Culture refused permission due to "lack of administration" (see AUCII, *1938-39*, "Relazioni," under the file *Notiziario*).

877.   See D. Lattes, *Coloro che son partiti* cit., p. 348.

878.   The fact that a certain number of those who abjured during the persecution returned to Judaism when it ended is common. See D. Lattes, *Coloro che son partiti* cit., p. 349.

879.   See AUCII, *1938-39*, "Manifestazioni pubbliche e della stampa sugli ebrei e sull'ebraismo," under the file *Circolari; 1938-39, Presidenza; 1938-39*, "Giunta," under the file *Max Ravà*. The first symptoms of this tendency were felt from the end of May; the most notorious cases, though, occurred between September and December of 1938.

880.   See AUCII, *1938-39, Presidenza*, the minutes of the resolutions of the Board of Directors of the Jewish Community of Turin, Turin, December 23, 1938.

881.   AUCII, "1938-39, Manifestazioni pubbliche e della stampa sugli ebrei e sull'ebraismo," under the file *Torino*; as well as Document 14.

882.   See ACS, *Emilio De Bono (Diari)*, p. 43, at the date of September 23, 1938.

883. See ACS, *PNF, Situazione politica delle provincie (1924-43), Torino, Trieste, Napoli,* etc.

884. See A. Spinosa, *Le persecuzioni razziali in Italia* cit., IV: *La legislazione,* p. 963.

885. Formiggini wrote something similar also to Mussolini, see A. F. Formiggini, *Parole in libertà,* Rome 1945, p. 129. On him, see *Angelo Fortunato Formiggini un editore del Novecento,* edited by L. Balsamo and R. Cremante, Bologna 1981, in particular the contribution of P. Treves, *Formiggini e il problema dell'ebreo in Italia,* pp. 55-72; as well as G. Turi, *Il fascismo e il consenso degli intellettuali,* Bologna 1980, pp. 151-92.

886. To hush up the "scandal" in some way, a gold medal was awarded to the memory of Morpurgo with the following motivation: "As a staff officer in charge of a special mission on the front lines, he performed with the passionate competence that he had shown unsparingly in numerous previous battles. The supreme hour of the infantry arrived, taken by his heroic spirit and won by the atmosphere of enthusiasm which had inflamed the troops, he took the lead of the most courageous ones with the war song of "Govinezza." Repeatedly injured to his arms, he insisted with the intention to get past a still intact barbed wire fence until a last gunshot pierced his heart, bringing him down on the enemy's ground. Seros bridgehead, December 23, 1938."

887. F. Suvich, *Memorie 1932-1936* cit., p. 193.

888. On this entire complicated matter, also very important for a deeper understanding of the Jewish policy of Fascism, see L. Goglia, *Il Mufti e Mussolini* cit.; R. De Felice, *Arabi e Medio Oriente nella strategia politica di guerra di Mussolini* cit.

889. ASAE, *Italia,* p. 57, *1938,* G. Ciano to all of the Royal Diplomatic representatives and career consuls, July 26, 1938.

890. On these arrests, see W. Phillips, *Ventures in Diplomacy,* London 1955, pp. 111-12.

891. See, for example, M. Intaglietta, "Gli ebrei nella rivoluzione comunista," in *Il mattino d'Italia,* July 12, 1938.

892. *Il mattino d'Italia* regularly copied the prose of *Il Tevere* and *La difesa della razza* (see "Il tentativo ebraico di acclimatare i profughi in Italia," September 2, 1938), trying to demonstrate how Fascism wanted to avoid the infiltration of the Russian bacillus through the Jews (see the issue of September 9, 1938). It was one of the very few Italian papers overseas daring to castigate the actions of those Jews, like Bernstein, who had publicly protested against the Fascist measures (see M. Intaglietta, *Il ghetto a raccolta intorno a Bernstein,* in the issue of September 8, 1938). The decisions of the Grand Council on October 6 were, according to *Il mattino d'Italia* (see the issue of October 8, 1938), "human and radical"; the following is the paper's summary: "No persecution, no seizure, no concentration camp. Simply

the command to the *ahasveri*, to the wandering Jews of the postwar period, to get out."

893.   *Il grido della stirpe* was certainly the most openly anti-Semitic paper among the pro-Fascist papers abroad. Still during the war period the exiled, G. Salvemini in particular, was often arguing with it (see, above all, *La controcorrente* and especially the issue of January 1943, American edition). The paper attributed all of humanity's evils to the Jews (see "I delitti ebraici attraverso la storia," in the issue of October 15, 1938). The editor of *Il grido della stirpe*, Domenico Trombetta, supported Fascism also on radio, on August 7, 1938, from the microphones of the WHOM, he gave a lecture on the *Problem of race in Italy* (reproduced by *Il grido della stirpe* August 20).

894.   *L'idea nazionale* was the only Swiss paper that openly supported Fascist anti-Semitism and tried to establish it also in Ticino. For many months *L'idea nazionale* published a regular feature titled "Noi ticinesi e gli ebrei." Contrary to the rest of the international pro-Fascist press, it immediately presented (see the issue of July 23, 1938) the manifesto of the "scientists" as "the awakening of anti-Semitic defense in Italy."

895.   See A. Giannini, *Io, spia dell'Ovra!* cit., I, pp. 413-15.

896.   See ASAE, *Italia*, p. 57, *1938*, under the file *Razzismo in Italia, parte generale e Razzismo fascista; La stampa*; p. 58, *1938* under the file *Razzismo.*

897.   Officially most of them supported the anti-Semitic measures, sending more or less enthusiastic reports to the respective consular representatives. There was even the support of the small community of Hong Kong (see ASAE, *Italia*, p. 57, *1938*, under the file *Razzismo fascista*).

898.   ASAE, *Italia*, p. 57, *1938*, under the file *Razzismo in Italia, parte generale.*

899.   Mussolini hastened to personally send instructions to Auriti so that he clarify "origins and objectives of Fascist racism." "Emphasize," he telegraphed on August 8, "that we await from Japan, who has admirably maintained its race pure, whom we admire for the high qualities that distinguish them, a position of friendly solidarity on this problem. Emphasize also that the set of rules of Fascist scholars exclude subdivisions of races as superior and inferior. Our policy aims at defending the purity of our stock and to strengthen in the Italians, who have conquered an empire in Africa, that deep racial consciousness which is essential to great colonizing nations" (see ASAE, *Italia*, p. 57, *1938* under the file *Razzismo in Italia, parte generale*).

900.   See F. Guarneri, *Battaglie economiche* cit., II, pp. 373-74.

901.   See ACS, *Presidenza del Consiglio, Gabinetto (1937-43), Atti amministrativi (1937-39)*, b. 117, file 3/2-2, n. 5441/7, *Restituzione decorazioni da parte di ebrei stranieri*. The Fascist press reacted to these returns with extreme violence and vulgarity. See the papers from September 9-12, 1938.

902. See, for example, F. Gervasi, "Italy violates marriage pact, Vatican charge," in *The Washington Times*, November 14, 1938; "Pope Pius Fights Italy's New Racial marriage controls," in *The Washington Evening Star*, November 15, 1938; "Pope appeals to Duce and King against ban on mixed marriages," in *The New York Herald Tribune*, November 15, 1938; "King assures Pope on marriage laws," in *The New York Times*, November 16, 1938.

903. See, for example, "M. Mussolini projette-t-il de créer un état juif en Afrique Orientale?," in *Le Temps*, Paris, February 19, 1938; "Ein Judenstaat in Aethiopien?," in the *Neue Zürcher Zeitung*, February 21, 1938; "L'Etiopia rifugio per gli ebrei?," in *Il Progresso Italo-Americano*, September 7, 1938; "L'Italie et le problème juif," in *Le Temps*, Paris, January 13, 1939.

904. See *Documents on American Foreign Relations (January 1938-June 1939)*, Boston 1939, pp. 332-33. The note was presented on September 5, 1938, the Palazzo Chigi replied on October 17. Officially the Italian reply was characterized in Washington as "satisfactory" (see *Il mattino d'Italia*, October 18, 1938). Some explanations were previously requested (September 6) by the U.S. Embassy's advisor, Edward Reed (see *Il Progresso Italo-Americano*, September 7, 1938).

905. See G. Ciano, *Diario, 1939-43*, I, p. 40 (at the date of February 14, 1939).

906. ASAE, "Grecia, 1938," under the file *Miscellanea*.

907. ASAE, *Turchia, p. 19, 1938, Rapporti politici - 2° semestre*; p. 26, *1939, Rapporti politici*.

908. Towards the end of 1938, the Palazzo Chigi compiled in a single report, for internal purposes, all of the "queries addressed to this Ministry on behalf of representative organizations abroad, diplomatic representatives, and foreign consuls in Italy, with regard to the application of measures relevant to the Jews." (See ASAE, *Italia*, p. 58, *1938*.)

909. G. Ciano, *Diario, 1939-43* cit., I, pp. 14-15.

910. *Ibid.*, p. 22.

911. See T. Staderini, *Legislazione per la difesa della razza* cit., pp.54-58.
     The active nature of the Grand Council's declaration was stressed also by Buffarini-Guidi on the occasion of the Ministry of Internal Affairs Budget meeting, 1939 (May 11) and 1940 (April 26). It is significant that in 1940 Buffarini-Guidi mentioned—even if negatively and caustically—those who "await Fascism at the moment of its inevitable repentance."

912. The law was drawn up on the basis of three drafts prepared by the Ministries of Internal Affairs, of Finance, and of Justice and elaborated by a special committee (Giaquinto, Sirovich, De Ruggiero, Le Pera, Migliori, Letona). At the suggestion of the Ministry of Finance it was not extended, provisionally as was initially thought, to Libya and the Aegean. See ACS, *Min. Int., Dir. gen. Demografia e Razza*, b. 2, file 10; *Presidenza del Consiglio, Gabinetto, Provvedimenti Legislativi (1938-39), Interno*, b. 20.

913. See T. Staderini, *Legislazione per la difesa della razza* cit., pp.64-118.

914. The statute of the EGELI was then established by R. D. L. of March 27, 1939, n. 665. See *Ibid.*, pp. 127-35. As soon as the legislative decree was published on November 17, 1938, the president of the National Fascist Federation of Savings Banks asked (December 12, 1938) the head of the government that Jewish property held in trust exceeding the limits foreseen by article 10 of the legislative decree was entrusted to the Savings Banks: see *Presidenza del Consiglio, Gabinetto (1937-43), Atti amministrativi (1937-43)*, b. 117, file 3/2-2, n. 5441/1-8.

915. For the list of industries that enter in these categories, see *Gazzetta Ufficiale*, 1939, numbers 184, 189, 266, 273, 276-77, 287, 293-94, 298.

916. See T. Staderini, *Legislazione per la difesa della razza* cit., pp.139-42.

917. At the time of its approval in the Chamber [of Deputies] and the Senate the law underwent various modifications, becoming more restrictive each time. Other proposals of this kind were not accepted by the government. See the session of May 26, 1939, XXX legislation, Legislative Commission files, *Atti*, pp. 37-48.

918. Up until the end of February 1940 the law established that Jewish professionals could continue to practice their activity without any limitations; another temporary regulation even established that Jews who were authorized to pursue graduate studies, could, upon graduation, be registered on the two lists that had just been created.

919. See T. Staderini, *Legislazione per la difesa della razza* cit., pp.139-42.

920. *Ibid.*, pp. 136-38.

921. During the first ten months of 1939 the nomination of the various organs created by the anti-Semitic legislation proceeded. Document 24 contained the make up of the high council for Demography and Race, of the race tribunal and of the board of directors of EGELI.

922. The matter was clearly discussed even by G. Preziosi in *La vita italiana*, September 1941, pp. 304-7, who went as far as writing that it demonstrated that "our racial laws were prepared by Jews behind the scenes!" On the same theme see also *Il regime fascista*, August 21, 1941.

923. See Ministero dell'Educazione Nazionale, *Elenchi di opere la cui pubblicazione, diffusione o ristampa nel Regno è stata vietata dal ministero della Cultura popolare*, Rome 1940. Not even the works of the "deserving" Fascists were exempt from such suppression, such as Pitigrilli (Dino Segre) who, even in 1935, had worked for the Fascist police against the antifascists in Turin. See L. Salvatorelli-G. Mira, *Storia d'Italia ecc.* cit., p. 775; D. Zucaro, *Lettere all'OVRA di Pitigrilli*, Milan 1961.

924. ACS, *Min. Int., Dir. gen. Demografia e Razza (1938-43)*, b. 2, file 10; b. file 42.

925. ACS, *Min Int., Dir. gen. Demografia e Razza (1938-43)*,b. 2, file 10, reproduced in *Document 10*.

926. ACS, *Min Int., Dir. gen. Demografia e Razza (1938-43)*, folder *Lavori preparatori.*
927. ACS, *Min Int., Dir. gen. Demografia e Razza (1938-43)*,b. 2, file 10, folder *Famiglie miste.* The memorandum was accompanied by a note reproducing the three final points.
928. *Ibid., Promemoria. Oggetto: "L'unità familiare nei matrimoni misti."*
929. ACS, *Min Int., Dir. gen. Demografia e Razza (1938-43)*, b. 2, file 10, folder *Famiglie miste,* see, above all, *L'accertamento dell'arianità dei figli nati da matrimoni mist ed il problema delle famiglie miste* (eleven pages).
930. See D. Almansi, "La progettata espulsione. Contributo alla storia delle persecuzioni razziali in Italia," in *Israel*, October 18, 1945.
931. Regarding the attempts made by numerous Jews to secretly export at least a part of their possessions, and the attitude of various governmental bodies towards such exportations and towards monetary transfers in general by the emigrants, see F. Guarneri, *Battaglie economiche* cit., II, pp. 369-70 and 376-78.
932. ACS, *Min Int., Dir. gen. Demografia e Razza (1938-43)*, b. 2, file 10, Father Tacchi-Venturi to G. Buffarini-Guidi, Rome July 26, 1940. Father Tacchi-Venturi sent the following letter he had received the day before from Cardinal Maglione for the Secretariat of State of the Vatican:

"Most Reverend Father,

"You know, most Reverend Father, how, following the 'racial' measures, the prestige and authority of parents, and the actual family unit itself, in families of mixed marriages, were seriously damaged because one of the parents, considered of the 'Jewish race,' having had their rights limited or denied, found themselves in a position of inferiority compared to other members of the family. However, with the implementation of the 'racial' provisions concerning professionals, the situation of the aforesaid families of mixed marriages, already serious enough, has become even more distressing with regard to those who have, as the head of the family, a father who is a professional man, considered of 'Jewish race,' even more so if not 'discriminated.' Indeed, as the Reverend Father knows, professionals of the 'Jewish race' who are not discriminated, are prohibited from exercising their profession in favor of Aryans. It is easy to understand how such a situation causes desolation and ruin for many of the aforementioned families, who, except for the head, are of Aryan origin, in the sense that the head of the family has no possibility to work that even from the 'Work Charter' is considered as 'a social obligation.' In truth they cannot count, in any way, on work that comes from those from whom they are cut off. Nor is the moral damage less great, coming from the fact that the head of the family must break off all relations of association and collaboration other than mutual trust, coming from, from family ties, contracted with Aryans. The Holy See has learned with satisfaction of rumors of some amendments to the law by which 'discrimination' would be given to the head of the family of mixed marriages, even when he is without 'exceptional merit.' This would be a due and just measure, because it cannot be ignored that to have a Jew, who, at the time, was not under suspicion, in a regular mixed marriage, having given his children a Christian education, and he himself, in many cases, being baptized, is proof that can only weigh greatly in his favor. Thus Reverend Father you would carry out highly deserving and most useful work, not only for religion but also for society, if through ways which You will choose with circumspection, will do Your best to see that the rumored measures come to pass, for the comfort of many fathers and many mothers who continue to implore the help of the Holy Father in their present sad circumstances.

"I take opportunity on the occasion to renew to Your Reverend Father my sense of religious observance with which I pride myself.

"Devoted to God

(Signed) " L. Card. Maglione"

933. ACS, *Min Int., Dir. gen. Demografia e Razza (1938-43)*, b. 2, file 10, *Al Duce*.

934. *Ibid.*, b. 13, file 44, *Al Duce*, reproduced in Document 26.

935. ACS, *Min Int., Dir. gen. Demografia e Razza (1938-43)*, b. 2, file 10, reproduced in Document 27.

936. In various Fascist business circles it was feared that the drain of Jewish capital could cause serious damage to the national economy. It is significant that in Parliament in April 1939 the proposal was put forward to "exchange" the property of the Jews in Italy with that of Italians abroad who wanted to repatriate. See Legislature XXX, Legislative Commission of Foreign Affairs, session of April 25, 1939, *Atti*, p. 3 (Thaon di Revel).

937. Still in September 1941 Demography and Race requested it in a report to Buffarini-Guidi. See ACS, *Min Int., Dir. gen. Demografia e Razza (1938-43)*, b. 13, file 44, reproduced in Document 28.

938. See L. Poliakov-J. Sabille, *Gli ebrei sotto l'occupazione italiana*. Milan 1956, p. 86.

939. See *Annali del Fascismo*, June 1938, p. 47.

940. ASAE, *Germania*, p. 47, *1938*, M. Magistrati to the Ministry of Popular Culture and the Ministry of Foreign Affairs, Berlin, December 23, 1938, reproduced in Document 29.

941. See *Il Tribunale*, of Naples, March 31, 1939; *Il giornale d'Italia*, of Rome, March 12, 1939; *Il diritto razzista*, May-June, 1939, pp. 139-40. The text of the approved resolution stated: "Every nation, which is a community for living, must also resolve the problem of its identity according to its own spiritual and racial dispositions. On this basis, Fascism and National-Socialism both claim the right to defend and to improve European culture. The judicial system of the totalitarian state seeks moral integrity and soundness of body and mind of its people for coming generations. It is the

purpose of Fascism and National-Socialism to raise the level of consciousness of the national and racial nature of the nation through an intense action of moral and cultural education. The values of race must be defended particularly from Judaism by the absolute and definite separation of Jewish elements from the national community, to prevent Judaism from exercising any influence whatsoever on the lives of the two nations. The Italian and German nations oppose the universalistic and cosmopolitan ideologies of International Judaism, the principles that derive respectively from the Nuremberg laws of September 15, 1935 and from the Grand Council of Fascism of October 6, 1938-XVI." The reporters mentioned by the Italian press were C. Costamagna, L. Piccardi, F. Ruttke and W. Lasch. According to the "Zeitschrift der Akademie für Deutsches Recht" (April 1939, p. 221) the reporters were only C. Costamagna and F. Ruttke, while Piccardi and Lasch had only participated to the editing of the conclusive "theories." For the texts of the Italian and German reports, see *Lo Stato*, March 1939, pp. 135-66 (which printed them signed respectively by Costamagna and Ruttke). A rich documentation on the works of the Vienna convention is conserved in Amsterdam at the Dutch State Institute for war documentation (Papers of the Reichsführer A. Seyss-Inquart).

942. ACS, *Min. Int., Dir. gen. PS, Div. Aff. Gen. e ris. (1903-49),* cat. RG (1940), b. 434, file 33, *Corrispondenza varia con la Gestapo,* Heydrich to Bocchini, Berlin, July 22, 1940.

943. *Ibid.,* Bocchini to Heydrich, Rome, August 5, 1940.

944. ASAE, *Germania,* p. 45, *1938,* under the file *Germania ebrei* and *Questione degli ebrei austriaci e tedeschi.* The matter is confirmed also by G. Bastianini, *Uomini Cose Fatti, Memorie di un ambasciatore* cit., pp. 54-55, which states the instructions given by the Palazzo Chigi to the consuls: "Abroad, every Italian must continue to be protected, helped, defended, himself and his property, without discrimination of any kind." Still for the period of 1942-43, see also *Il messaggero di Roma,* May 9, 1961 (account of the trial of A. Eichmann). Simultaneously, the Palazzo Chigi, informed that in Austria after the Nazi occupation, some fictitious marriages took place between local Jews and Italian citizens, gave instructions to the Embassy in Berlin and to all consulates to avoid that matters of that nature be repeated. See ASAE, *Germania.* p. 48, *1938,* under the file *Matrimoni fittizi fra ebree tedesche e cittadini italiani in Austria.*

945. An extensive documentation, taken from Nazi archives, on German anti-Semitic policy in relation to Italy from 1933 to 1944 is in United Restitution Organization, *Judenverfolgung in Italien, den italianisch besetzen Gebieten und Nordafrika,* Frankfurt am Main 1962.

946. See U. Cavallero, *Comando supremo, diario 1940-43 del capo di S. M. G.,* Bologna 1948, p. 437 (at the date of January 16, 1943).

947. See *Trial of the Major War Criminals etc.* cit., *Proceeding*, X, pp. 406-8 (interrogation of Von Ribbentrop).

948. See L. Poliakov-J. Sabille, *Gli ebrei sotto l'occupazione italiana* cit., pp. 17-18.

949. See ACS, *Min. Int., Dir. gen. Demografia e Razza (1938-43)*, b. 13, file 44.

950. ACS, *Min. Int., Dir. gen. Demografia e Razza (1915-44)*, b. 1, files 2 and 6, *Quesiti a S. E. Buffarini*.

951. C. Senise, *Quando ero capo della polizia* cit., p. 165 and mostly pp. 164-68.

952. ACS, *RSI, Segreteria particolare del Duce, Carteggio riservato*, file 32, *Buffarini-Guidi Guido*, under the file 2.

953. C. Senise, *Quando ero capo della polizia* cit., pp. 164-68; G. Ciano, *Diario, 1939-43* cit., p. 158; G. Leto, *OVRA* cit., pp. 191-92.

954. ACS, *Min. Int., Dir. gen. Demografia e Razza (1938-43)*, b. 13, file 44, *Relazione per la discussione del bilancio dell'Interno 1941-42*, f. 1.

955. *Ibid., Relazione per la discussione del bilancio dell'Interno 1942-43* (February 12, 1942), f. 2.

956. ACS, *Min. Int., Dir. gen. Demografia e Razza (1938-43)*, notes for the report 1943-44.

957. *Ibid.*, f. 6.

958. *Ibid.*, b. 3, files 11 and 12. The decision was communicated by Buffarini-Guidi to all prefects by means of a very confidential memo on March 6, 1942 n. 131/30 R.

959. ACS, *Min. Int., Dir. gen. Demografia e Razza (1938-43)*, b.13, file 44.

960. ACS, *Min. Int., Dir. gen. Demografia e Razza (1938-43)*, b. 8, file 33.

961. A very special case was that of the six Jewish senators because they had been appointed for life by the King and could not be expelled without causing a huge scandal at the Palazzo Madama. The problem was solved by letting them know that their presence in the Senate was not appropriate.

962. Unless otherwise indicated the information given from here on is obtained from the annual reports for the discussion of the budget in the Ministry of Internal Affairs.

963. Many Jews who failed to register as established by art. 19 of Legislative Decree, of November 17, 1938, were denounced and brought to trial in 1939. In Milan alone there were 160, 16 in Leghorn, and 8 in Turin.

964. From a letter by the Minister of Justice, D. Grandi, to the Ministry of Finance on July 20, 1940 (with a copy to the Prime Minister and to the Ministry of Internal Affairs) it appears that, to get around these "omissions" and above all to ensure that in some way what had been initially envisaged by the drafters of the provisions covering estates, had been proposed even in June-July 1940 to modify the initial rules stated above. In particular from Grandi's letter, which was mostly negative towards every change that could "give the impression that the Government intended to reverse itself on the treatment given to the Jews" and at the same time,

deprive the Jews of the use of their property without receiving any revenue, it seems that the modifications proposed concerned above all a deferment to a later date of payment on behalf of EGELI for the equivalent of the confiscated property and of the interest of 4% provided by the law. See ACS, *Presidenza del Consiglio, Gabinetto (1937-43), Atti amministrativi (1940-43)*, b. 117, file 3/2-2, n. 5441/1-8. The Keeper of the Seal at the Ministry of Finance, Rome, July 20, 1940.

965. A. Scalpelli, *L'Ente di gestione e liquidazione immobiliare: note sulle conseguenze economiche della persecuzione razziale*, in *Gli ebrei in Italia durante il fascismo* cit., II, pp. 95-96.

966. ACS, *Min. Int., Dir. gen. Demografia e Razza (1938-43)*, folder 14, file 47.

967. ACS, *Min. Int., Dir. gen. Demografia e Razza (1938-43)*, b. 13, file 45; see also b. 6, file 27.

968. ACS, *Min. Int., Dir. gen. Demografia e Razza (1938-43)*, b. 13, file 44, *Situazione ebraica al 28 Ottobre 1941*. With a circular of March 19, 1939, to the prefects, to the Police Commissioner of Rome and to the frontier precincts, A. Bocchini communicated that "by superior order" it had been decided that "the exodus of elements of the Jewish race, not allowed to leave the Kingdom and who intended to transfer abroad permanently should be facilitated to the utmost."

969. On this, see K. Voigt, *Gli emigrati in Italia dai paesi sotto la dominazione nazista: tollerati e perseguitati (1933-1940)*, in *Storia contemporanea*, February 1985, pp. 45-87 and particularly pp. 72 sgg. (the essay is to be kept in mind also for the years preceding the persecution).

970. For the events of the Aegean Jews, see H. M. Franco, *Les martyrs juifs de Rhodes et de Cos* cit.

971. ACS, *Min. Int., Dir. gen. Demografia e Razza (1915-44)*, b. 2, file 20, *Ebrei stranieri, appunto per il Duce* by Buffarini-Guidi.

972. *Ibid.*, another *Appunto per il Duce* also by Buffarini-Guidi.

973. *Ibid.*, b. 2, file 20, *Ebrei stranieri*. The measure was probably caused by the arrest on August 4, in San Remo, of a group of 43 Jewish "tourists" (41 Germans, 1 Russian, and 1 Pole) who wanted to cross the border into France illegally. The Ministry of Foreign Affairs gave a favorable opinion to the measure. See ACS, *Min. Int., Dir. gen. Demografia e Razza (1938-43)*, b. 4, file 18. The most conspicuous "contribution" was made by 814 Jews, bound for Palestine, who on July 3 shipwrecked with the *Rim* (flying the Panamanian flag) on a tiny island near Rhodes. See *La stampa* of Turin, July 7, 1939.

974. ACS, *Min. Int., Dir. gen. Demografia e Razza (1938-43)*, b.13, file 44, *Situazione ebraica al 28 Ottobre 1941*.

975. The Lloyd Triestino handled the transfer of most of these emigrants until June 10, 1940, generally to Shanghai, obtaining for them the necessary

transit visas. See ACS, *Min. Int., Dir. gen. Demografia e Razza (1938-43)*, b. 4, file 18, Lloyd's of Trieste to the Ministry of Foreign Affairs and to the Ministry of Internal Affairs, Trieste, September 4, 1940.

976. This does not mean that some did not manage to find work. *Il popolo d'Italia* April 6, 1939 referred, for example, with great scandal, that a certain Doctor Roisenzwit "collaborated" in the dental office of Dr. Bruno Faleschini.

977. ACS, *Min. Int., Dir. gen. Demografia e Razza (1938-43)*, b.13, file 44, *Relazione al bilancio 1940-41*, f. 9.

978. ACS, *Min. Int., Dir. gen. PS, Div. Aff. Gen. e ris. (1903-49)*, category. E/c; E/i, b. 479.

979. Of these 36 names, the following were defined as anti-Fascist: Camillo Artom (Italia Libera), Mario Artom (anti-Fascist), Giorgio Ascoli (relations with A. Cianca), Giuseppe Bachi (anti-Fascist), Giorgio Bloch (anti-Fascist), Angelo Cassuto (subversive), Raffaele Cantoni (Italia Libera, Freemason, deferred in 1930 to the special tribunal), Arturo Coen (Zionist), Strolego Dello (Freemason, ex-radical), Odoardo Della Torre (Socialist), Vito Fano (republican), Dino Jacchia (Freemason), Dino Lattes (Italia Libera), Giusto Levi (Freemason, anti-Fascist), Giacomo Lumbroso (anti-Fascist, already interned in 1938), Alfredo Morpurgo (republican), Attilio Orvieto (socialist, already interned in 1939), Giovanni Sermoneta (anarchist), Carlo Alberto Viterbo (Zionist).

980. See ANPPIA, *"Pericolosi nelle contingenze belliche." Gli internati dal 1940 al 1943*, Rome 1987, pp. 19-20.

981. On August 1, 1942, the ascertainment of the *race* of all foreigners residing in the Kingdom. See ACS, *Min. Int., Dir. gen. Demografia e Razza (1938-43)*, b.3, file 14.

982. AUCII, *1940, Assistenza rapporti con i Comitati locali.*

983. ACS, *Min. Int., Dir. gen. PS, Div. Aff. gen. e ris (1903-49)*, category E/c; E/i, b. 478.

984. With a memorandum sent the day before to the prefects, Demography and Race had established the general lines and time of the mobilization. See ACS, *Min. Int., Dir. gen. PS, Div. Aff. gen. e ris (1920-45)*, category A 5 G, b. 57, file 160, *Ebrei. Mobilitazione civile.*

985. ACS, *Min. Int., Dir. gen. Demografia e Razza (1938-43)*, b.13, file 44, notes for the report for the discussion of the Internal budget 1943-44.

986. ACS, *Min. Int., Dir. gen. Demografia e Razza (1938-43)*, b.9, file 38.

987. ACS, *Min. Int., Dir. gen. PS, Div. Aff. gen. e ris (1920-45)*, category A 5 G, b. 57, file 160, *Ebrei. Mobilitazione civile*, reproduced in Document 30 a.

988. ACS, *Min. Int., Dir. gen. Demografia e Razza (1938-43)*, b. 9, file 38, and also b. 11, file 41.

989. See ACS, *Min. Int., Dir. gen. PS, Div. Aff. gen. e ris (1920-45)*, category A 5 G, b. 57, file 160, *Ebrei. Mobilitazione civile.* A memorandum of Demography

and Race, dated July 15, 1943, reproduced in Document 30 b, transmitted the instructions for the implementation of this order sent by cable.

990. Moreover, the Ministry of Public Works itself could not foresee, in October 1942, being able to immediately employ more than 1,500-1,600 Jews in all of Italy. ACS, *Min. Int., Dir. gen. Demografia e Razza (1938-43)*, b.13, file 44.

991. There was no shortage of cases where business, with the excuse that the Jews drafted "did not produce," arbitrarily reduced their compensation. In October 1942 a business in Rome reduced their pay from 2.87 lire per hour to 46 centimes per hour. See ACS, *Min. Int., Dir. gen. PS, Div. Aff. gen. e ris (1920-45)*, category A 5 G, b. 57, file 160, *Ebrei. Mobilitazione civile*.

992. ACS, *Min. Int., Dir. gen. Demografia e Razza (1938-43)*, b.9, file 39.

993. ASMAI, Gabinetto, 1939.

994. For more information, see R. De Felice, *Ebrei in un paese arabo* cit., pp. 259 *sgg.*

995. G. Gorla, *L'Italia nella seconda guerra mondiale* cit., p. 286, at the date of February 7, 1942.

996. ASMAI, *Gabinetto*, Reports of the PAI.

997. R. De Felice, *Ebrei in un paese arabo* cit., pp. 265-79.

998. See G. S. Spinetti, *Difesa di una generazione* cit., pp. 46-49.

999. Some newspapers did not miss the opportunity to repeat, more or less verbatim, the "arguments" of Nazi anti-Semitism. The *Italia* of Rome, for example, at the end of 1941 and above all in 1942, systematically published the translation of short articles from the "Stürmer" in the section *orientamenti*.

1000. S. M. Cutelli was received by the Duce on two occasions, in February and November of 1940; in February to present him with a study of his on the "improvement of the organization of the PNF," and in November with the members of the editorial board of *Il diritto razzista* (see ACS, *Presidenza del Consiglio, Gabinetto [1937-43], Atti amministrativi [1940-43]*, b. 118, file 3/2-2, n. 5441/13, *Pubblicazioni riguardanti i provvedimenti adottati a tutela della razza*). On August 14, 1938, at a ceremony, G. Preziosi presented to Mussolini the collection of *La vita italiana* (see *La vita italiana*, September 1938, p. 374).

1001. The Italian courts, in general, did not behave much better. A selection of typical sentences during those years has been put together by A. Spinosa, *Le persecuzioni razziali in Italia* cit., IV: *La legislazione*, pp. 964-68; see also I. Tambaro, "Le leggi per La difesa della razza nella giurisprudenza dello Consiglio di Stato," in *Rassegna di legislazione per i Comuni*, October 15, 1942, pp. 863-67; and, more generally, U. Montefusco, "Razzismo nel diritto," in *La vita italiana*, February 1939, pp. 164-70. Although, there were also judges who, even within the range of Fascist laws which they had to follow, judged according to their conscience trying to uphold the rights of the Jews. See, for example, the sentence of the III division of the Court of Appeal in Turin (President Peretti-Griva, Drafter Bozzi) in the Rosso-Artom case (*Gazzetta del Popolo*, Turin, May 19, 1939). Also worth mentioning is the behavior of the Court of Trieste, headed by the presiding judge of the Appeal Court, Paolo Gaetano, who, notwithstanding the opposition of the PNF, established that Jews with professions could offer their services to foreigners, without regard to whether these were Jews or not. Also significant is a passage from the presentation (*Ai lettori*) by Cutelli of his "Il diritto razzista"; in it (p. 7), after having mentioned the support given until then, Cutelli complained about the "abstention of some politicians and jurists who, even though officially racist ("racists by discipline!"), obviously do not want to contribute to the development and dissemination of the new legal specialization if not within the close limits set for them, out of "interest" and "obedience," so that they could then confidentially justify themselves with their democratic associates, whispering to their chaste ears: "I did just that little bit, which I could not avoid.""

1002. There was no shortage of attacks even upon Italian Protestants whose marked aversion to racism and anti-Semitism was well known. *Il Tevere* argued with them on various occasions, speaking of "half caste religions" and more or less obscurely hinting at anti-Italian intrigues of Anglican and Jewish Internationals. The most personal attack, though, was that by *Il regime fascista* on August 4, 1938, "Anch'essi," openly opposed to the Evangelical publication *Luce*. On the attitude of Italian Protestants regarding the persecution, see S. Sarti, "Il mondo protestante e la questione razziale: note sulla rivista 'Gioventú cristiana'" (1933-40), in *Gli ebrei in Italia durante il fascismo* cit., II, pp. 86-91.

1003. See, for example, *Il regime fascista* of January 17 and 25 and March 11, 1939.

1004. A classic example of this course is the volume by G. Mastrojanni, *Marte e Israele. Perché si combatte*, Bologna 1943.

1005. See, for example, in 1939-40, the column, "Ebrei: peste delle nazioni" in *Il popolo di Brescia*.

1006. The way that the civil draft was presented is typical. See *Il messaggero*, June 7, 1942; *La stampa*, October 6, 1942; *Corriere d'Alessandria*, October 10, 1942; as well as, more generally, V. Gayda, "Il servizio del lavoro," in *Il giornale d'Italia*, June 6, 1942.

1007. ACS, *Min. Cult. Pop., Gabinetto*, b. 13, file 281, *Propaganda razziale*. The five conversations were also collected in a small volume.

1008. *Ibid.*

1009. See M. Appelius, *Parole dure e chiare*, Milan 1942, *passim* and particularly pp. 172-78, *Israele, traditore del mondo*. In some cases, the "comments of the day's events" by Appelius were so violent as to arouse criticism even within the circles of the Popular Culture. For example, his comment on March 21, 1942 stirred lively criticism: his attack on the Jews, who have filled the registers of the grand hotels of Italy and the most elegant resorts, drew a counterproductive description of the Italian economic situation. See ACS, *Min. Cult. Pop., Gabinetto*, b. 2, file 11, *Mario Appelius*.

1010. See *Il messaggero*, May 15, 1941.

1011. See *Il corriere della sera*, January 14, 1939 and *Il piccolo*, Trieste, of January 19, 1939.

1012. ACS, *Min. Cult. Pop., Gabinetto*, b. 28, file *Ist. Naz. di cultura fascista–Sez. di Milano*.

1013. Of those, N. Giani, *Perché siamo antisemiti* and R. Sertoli Salis *Le leggi razziali italiane*. In 1940 the Milan division of the INFC published another two books of the kind: G. C. Ballarati, *Le leggi razziali tedesche* and E. Leoni, *Mistica del razzismo fascista*.

1014. ACS, *Min. Cult. Pop., Gabinetto*, b. 28, file *Scuola di mistica fascista Sandro Italico Mussolini–Milano*.

1015. The Ministry of Popular Culture and Demography and Race tried, especially after Italy's entry into the war, would completely take over the coordination and direction of racist action, avoiding initiatives not directly under their control. So that, in December 1940, a proposal by the National Council for research to create a commission to study the problems of race did not get a favorable reaction. See ACS, *Min. Int., Dir. gen. Demografia e Razza (1938-43)*, b. 4, file 15.

1016. See "Possibilità del centro di preparazione politica per lo studio del problema ebraico," in *Rassegna italiana*, May 1940.

1017. As examples of the kind of propaganda generated by these centers, see *Corriere adriatico*, Ancona, November 29, 1941 and *Il popolo delle Alpi*, Turin, January 17, 1942 (for the center in Ancona); and *La Nazione*, Florence, November 1, 1942 (for the center in Florence).

1018. The president of CAUR, Eugenio Coselschi, participated at the end of 1938 with a report read by Alberto Luchini, director of the institute of Fascist Culture in Fiume and then head of the Race Office at the Ministry of Popular Culture who also gave a report at the International anti-Jewish Convention in Erfurt. See Arthos, "Il nuovo convegno internazionale antiebraico di Erfurt," in *La vita italiana*, January 1939, pp. 45-48.

1019. E. Momigliano, *Storia tragica e grottesca del razzismo fascista*, Milan 1946, p. 135; A. Spinosa, *Le persecuzioni razziali in Italia* cit., III: *L'azione della stampa*, p. 1607.

1020. ACS, *Min. Cult. Pop., Gabinetto*, b. 14, file 314. From the same complaint it emerges that among the main editorial staff and contributors there were various persons who were not Fascist, and even one from the Alto Adige, who had opted for Germany.

1021. To judge just how far removed anti-Semitism was from the majority of
Italians, it is significant that from 1938 to 1943 more than one thousand
membership cards were withdrawn from those belonging to the PNF for
"pietism." Likewise, in January 1940, five national councilors were officially reprimanded (see *Il messaggero*, January 7, 1940). Even amongst the
Federal party secretaries there were those who opposed the anti-Semitic
policy. In March 1939, Mussolini received the following "anonymous"
letter from one of them:

The latest mockery!

The discriminated!

That rogue who reigns in Italy and dominates the will of the Duce, that
ignoble charlatan in a recent statement of provisional party secretaries,
said:

"Yes…the discriminated! Those who will be must in all cases be considered the worst, the last elements that need to be endured."

Poor Italy! In whose hands we are!

ONE OF THE PRESENT PARTY SECRETARIES
in the name of 44,000,000 Italians

Rome, March 7, 1939.

See ACS, *Presidenza del Consiglio, Gabinetto (1937-43), Atti amministrativi
(1937-39)*, b. 118, file 3/2-2, n. 5441/10, *Esposti anonimi ed altro riguardanti
le disposizioni sulla razza.*

1022. For the position of the only anti-Fascist group in Italy which had some
influence on official cultural life, see the article by B. Croce, in the *American Hebrew and Jewish Tribune* of December 7, 1934 (now in P*agine sparse*,
Naples 1943, II, pp. 409-10) and above all his letter during the second
half of 1938 in reply to an appeal which appeared in the Swedish press in
favor of the persecuted German Jews. In his letter *(ibid., pp. 410-11)* Croce
wrote:

"You must believe that it is not only the result of my philosophical and
historical work, but simply as a civilized man and as a liberal that I have
rebelled against the atrocious persecutions of the Jews which take place in
Germany and Austria. I have been writing in their defense for five years,
again and again, in essays and in protests, and I have demonstrated what
kind of interest and affection I really have for my Jewish friends in Germany. Following a declaration, I dedicated one of my books (*Nuovi saggi su
Goethe* dedicated to Leo Spitzer) to an excellent philosopher, who has been
forced into exile.

"Here is how someone who shares your ideas and your sympathies speaks.
Now, unfortunately, anti-Jewish racial action has suddenly also begun in
Italy. One does not yet know what will be the actual effect of this legisla-
tion, but, in any case, I fervently hope that it does not last long.

"These events which occur in front of our terrified eyes in so many parts of the world, exceed all limits of emotion and tradition in which my generation grew up and which has always been considered sacred.

"The accumulation of horrors and the impossibility to effectively oppose them induces a resignation of the spirit which is akin to numbness and indifference. It appears to me that this is one of the worst aspects of the situation, and has struck me with sadness. I hope that you will be in a position to carry out, entirely or in part, the generous noble mission proposed in Sweden."

See also the most violent reply by *Il Tevere* on December 21, 1938, *Il chassidismo di Benedetto Croce*.

1023. A. Spinosa, *Le persecuzioni razziali in italia* cit., III: "L'azione della stampa," pp. 1611-17; A. Benini, "Il contributo italiano alla storia del razzismo," in *Il Paradosso*, January-March 1960, pp. 53-57; on the Catholics, see R. Webster, *La croce e i fasci* cit., pp. 208 *sgg.*

1024. E. Momigliano, *Storia tragica e grottesca* cit., p. 133.

1025. A. Benini, *Il contributo italiano alla storia del razzismo* cit., p. 53.

1026. Of the very rare positions taken against Fascist anti-Semitic policy by authoritative priests and men of culture, the most significant is perhaps a letter that Father Giuseppe De Luca sent on April 13, 1942 to G. Bottai (amongst whose private papers it is filed). It reads:

"The first topic, which I cannot remove from my mind, is this: that we, in Italy, have taken in as our own, a way of thinking and action that can never be ours: the race debate. That underneath this debate lays a reason, and not a pretext, is certain: no one can doubt, especially in some countries and under certain aspects, of the legitimacy of measures that the state can and must take regarding particular categories of situations and even men: in the circumstance of the Jews and their (as God called them in the Old Testament) fornication. But it is one thing to watch over them and, when they break the law, crush their action; but it is another to give as reason for their conviction, not their behavior, but their race. Already now one does not convict he who is not guilty: who can regard himself to be guilty of being born of one or another race? This is Human, it is Roman, and Christian: condemn the crime or offence, not the bloodline. Secondly, to establish repression because of race, means to have accepted their very own preaching: and that is to make their racism burn again in faith and martyrdom, between mourning and admiration of the civil world. Thirdly, the Jews are too close to Christianity and have, with the church, promised continuity: a Catholic nation, like ours, understands that they can never be destroyed, and therefore the action that aims to destroy them is, not only unjust, but in vain. In case we, instead of accepting a preordained, well-founded dispute rather than an ugly and poorly executed one, had allowed ourselves to settle the grave problem, but finding our own solution, we would have acted with far more national dignity, besides being truthful and charitable. With Roman and Catholic tradition, we could have, and still can say, that no race is outside mankind if it is human. Even less can be a race to which mankind owes so much. Without saying that to condemn a race, means condemning them all outside of our own: which one shall we admire? The German race? And so let's condemn ours. Ours? And so then let's condemn the German, the Balkan, etc., etc. "Faced with the awakening of the Far East, we who are racists, how shall we act? Shall we condemn them? And in the Middle East, Islam which is recovering and reassembling itself, will it be condemned by us? It has not been considered that the Arabs are, far more so than the Jews, Semites: and so, why is our anti-Semitism not consistent?

"The foundation of this racial discrimination is not only uncertain, fit for men of no culture or civility, not only unjust, but brings frightful consequences if applied; and if not applied, makes us appear incompetent.

"Could we not have, and can we not still, point out to M[ussolini] that an Italian custom is to resolve problems in the Italian way? And it would end this way—because the truth ends up attracting—attracting to our concept of friends, and commanding respect from our enemies. Is it possible that we Italians must participate in gross mistakes of basely socialistic origins, which stink of working class universities and vulgar materialism? And would not this be the way to show, not only with cannons, but with real intelligence, that we are great, valid and capable of lighting up the world? Would a legislation which is respectful of all humanity, which aims only at punishing wrongdoings with extreme severity, not be sufficient (in fact more useful) to defend the nation? And would it not mark the beginning of a new concept in the world, between the two extremes of Semitism and anti-Semitism: and that is, determine the wrongdoings, but not incriminate a bloodline?

"Lastly, the debate which we have ignorantly accepted, aims (not openly, but surely) at offending and damaging Christianity. We who declare ourselves Catholics, have we no reason for laughter to have accepted it like this? Neither is it said, as it has been stupidly said, that Catholicism is something apart from Christianity, and that it is something Italian. They are two fatal errors: first of all it takes from Catholicism nothing less than its Christian substance, and then what does it become? In the second place, even granting for the sake of argument that Catholicism is something other than Christianity, this is, historically, more due to France (from Charlemagne to the 19th Century) than to us Italians: I say this theoretically and as an opinion. Also the French, such as Franks and Gauls, are Germans: and we? We usually applaud the one who slaps us.

"Why must no one say these things to M[ussolini]; and whilst he has so many worries, leave him to make such grave decisions without advice, only contenting ourselves to clumsily echo him, making, if possible, both he and ourselves appear ridiculous?"

1027. On La Pira, see C. Francovich, *La resistenza a Firenze*, Florence 1961, pp. 10-13; on Olivelli, see F. Magri, *La democrazia cristiana in Italia*, I, Milan 1954, pp. 264-70, as well as A. Caracciolo, *Teresio Olivelli*, Brescia 1947. Regarding La Pira it is particularly worth reaching the very harsh attack ("Giú la maschera!") published against him by *Il Bargello*, January 4, 1942. In it the Florentine Fascist Federation's weekly accused the "Jewish" couple, La Pira-Enrico Finzi, and their "gray" friends P. Calamandrei, S. Cugia, F. Calasso, A. Zoli and A. Paganelli, of anti-Fascism and pro-Judaism.

1028. *La difesa della razza*, November 20, 1939, pp. 43-44.

1029. For the earliest '"bibliography" there are to be found in *La difesa della razza* the columns "Razzismo in libreria" and "Hanno scritto articoli su…"

1030. M. Ramperti, "Piú che dalla stella gialla gli ebrei si riconoscono dalla ferocia dello sguardo," in *Il popolo di Roma*, December 1941, cit. by A. Spinosa, *Le persecuzioni razziali in Italia* cit., p. 1614.

1031. F. Coppola, *Fascismo e bolscevismo*, Rome 1938, pp. 19-20.

1032. C. Cecchelli, *La questione ebraica e il sionismo*, Rome 1939, pp. 25 and 37.

1033. *Il corriere della sera*, November 1, 1938. For his subsequent position, see G. Piovene, *La coda di paglia*, Milan 1962.

1034. A. Fanfani, "L'impulso politico all'economia,' in *Rivista internazionale di scienze sociali*, May 1939, p. 256.

1035. N. Petrucci, "Razza e diritto penale," in *L'appello*, Palermo, February 18, 1939.

1036. D. Paolella, "Gli alleati del giudaismo. La psicanalisi," in *Fronte unico*, Rome, January 25, 1939.

1037. F. Biondolillo, "Giudaismo letterario," in *L'unione sarda*, Cagliari, April 14, 1939.

1038. G. Acerbo, *I fondamenti della dottrina fascista della razza*, Rome 1940. Acerbo was violently attacked by *La vita italiana* in July and August of 1940 and had a harsh debate with Farinacci and Preziosi; see, above all, the August issue "Per la serietà degli studi italiani sulla razza." For Preziosi, the position of Acerbo and nationalists in general (see "Nazionalismo–Fascismo–Razzismo," in *La vita italiana*, February 1941) was slave to the "Jewish-Masonic School of Anthropology" of the end of the nineteenth and beginning of the twentieth century. Acerbo had wanted to reply to the attacks of *La vita italiana* with a dignified article in *Il giornale d'Italia*; but Mussolini was against it. ACS, *Min. Cultura popolare*, b. 111, file 1.

1039. The scientific weakness of the Manifesto of July 14, 1938, soon became very clear to those responsible for racial policy. Around 1940 the office of

Demography and Race worked intensely to prepare a text on the "Italian Race" which, probably, was supposed to substitute the Manifesto. Various laborious drafts exist of this text: ACS, *Min. Int., Dir. gen. Demografia e Razza (1915-44)*, b. 1, file 1, *Rapporto settimanale del ministero della Cultura popolare*; and *(1938-43)*, b. 3, file 13, *Definizione di razza italiana*, which are reproduced in Document 31 which is, probably, the last. In 1942 the Superior Council of Demography and Race then studied the possibility of adding a "scientific and historical" *definition* of the "Italian Race"; but even this time no conclusion was reached, even if at least two extensive texts of the *definition* were drawn up. ACS, *Segreteria part. del Duce, Carteggio ord.*, file 500014, "Min. Interno."

1040. See, above all, J. Evola, *Sintesi della dottrina della razza*, Milan 1941; as well as, for a further autobiographical judgment (and for some unpublished particulars) ID., *Il cammino del Cinabro*, Milan 1963, pp. 160.

1041. See, for example, G. Landra, "Razzismo biologico e scientismo. Per la scienza e contro i melanconici assertori di un nebuloso spiritualismo," in *La difesa della razza*, November 5, 1942, pp. 9-11.

1042. The following passage from his *Sintesi* (pp. 3-4), accurately summarizes Evola's position: "The racial doctrine certainly has its special aspects, that are strictly biological and anthropological; but, these aspects, given the way in which, above all, the problem of race must be presented in Italy, do not acquire their real value other than as a concept and a broader doctrine. With racial doctrine one vision of the world is substituted to another, from which derive, for a whole group of special disciplines, particular and very precise methodological principles. In its highest form, racial doctrine effectively has the value of a revolutionary idea, spiritually and culturally. It can have the value of a myth in the Sorelian sense, that is, as a power-idea, a crystallization center for creative energies and instincts of a specific time."

1043. See, for example, M. Scaligero, *La razza di Roma*, Tivoli 1939.

1044. See *Il Tevere*, September 11, 1942; J. Evola, "In alto mare," in *La vita italiana*, November 1942; *La difesa della razza*, September 20, 1942, p. 22.

1045. For admissions in this direction, see G. Landra, "Il razzismo e la gioventú italiana," in *La difesa della razza*, December 5, 1942.

1046. See the observations of J. Evola, "Razzismo e gioventú," in *Roma fascista*, December 11, 1940.

1047. On the activity of the center, see ACS, *Min. Int., Dir. gen. PS, Div. Aff. gen. e ris.(1903-49)*, b. 432; as well as *Min. Cult. Pop.*, b. 126, file "Centro Studi Anticomunisti."

1048. La Direzione, "Professori ebrei e dottrina ebraica," in *Lo Stato*, August-September 1938, p. 490.

1049. Regarding biological racism, it is worth noting that the Fascist youth press published, even after 1938, a number of direct and indirect opinions critical of it, emphasizing the spiritualistic "superiority" of Italian racism, with respect to that of the Germans which was biological, precisely.

1050. This need is clearly shown, to use just one example, in the letters to *La difesa della razza* from a young student, Enzo Santarelli, who became a collaborator of *La vita italiana* in 1942. For him "racism is above all a cultural movement." (See E. Santarelli, "Razzismo. Sociologia e Storiografia," in *La vita italiana*, January 1942, p. 32.)

1051. A typical case (which provoked vehement protests by G. Preziosi in the December 1942 issue of *La vita italiana*) was the initiative, announced by the paper of the GUF in Forlí, *Pattuglia*, in November 1942 to publish a selection of writers from Venezia Giulia, that included Svevo and Saba.

1052. We refer in particular to the article by Mario Missiroli, "Razza e cultura," in *Circoli*, July-August 1939, pp. 981-89. In this article—most probably, as Y. De Begnac noted, it is what Mussolini referred to in his already mentioned description of his point of view regarding racial policy—Missiroli wrote:

"It is impossible to find one's bearings in a problem extremely complex such as that of race, if one does not use principles of extreme caution. Scientific anthropology is scarcely a century old. The position assumed by Fascism is that of extreme moderation. It draws from those conclusions more accurately ascertained by scientific research and it is absolutely alien to the polemical premise of a religious or political nature. It upholds the existence of races in general theories; but seeing that tracing the nature of the original races would take us back to remote times with all the uncertainties of an impenetrable night, one stops to consider those which are called the 'small races,' which, from a biological point of view, make up the 'real' present races, the existence of which no one can deny, because they fall under experimental observation. These races are historical formations based on a natural primitive fact that is easily verifiable. Biological diversities do not allow, scientifically different values, any sort of reference to 'superior' or 'inferior' human races. One can only speak of 'different' races.

"A position of absolute objectivity, which should be placed in the correct light, such as the one that eliminates the materialistic presupposition from the Fascist conception, which was the spark of the first racial conceptions and clashed with invincible prejudices of a philosophical and moral order. The highest spiritual values are an achievement of our conscience, the result of effort and perpetual selection and, as such, are not tied to any form of nature, because, in this case, nature would take second place to the spirit, which is manifestly contrary to the ethics of Fascism, entirely founded upon the absolute supremacy of the will and of moral responsibility. No pessimistic fatalism pollutes this conception, which does not, in any way, weaken faith in life."

1053. In *Roma fascista*, the organ of the GUF in the capital, a debate took place between December 1940 and April 1941 regarding two years of racism in Italy which is, in fact, extremely revealing because it indicates how, in two years, much enthusiasm for racist politics had evaporated under the observation that, once again, the regime was not able to control the situation and those who had prevailed were the "pro-Jewish," the "Pietists" (the theory of the failure of Fascist racism was upheld, often with similar arguments, but denounced by G. Preziosi in "La battaglia antiebraica è fallita?!" in *La vita italiana* of February 1942), and because the conclusion of the debate, attempting to reconcile the various trends that emerged, was very much contested by a group of young Fascists who claimed that racism should have been considered only as "antagonism of conscience" with respect to other races. See "O razzismo o nazionalismo o antirazzismo," in *Roma fascista*, April 2, 1941.

1054. C. Senise, *Quando ero capo della polizia* cit., pp. 130-31.

1055. A confidential note to the secretary of the PNF in January 1940 clearly maintained that the anti-Jewish campaign was made up of Farinacci-type constituents, in contact with Cremona and with Preziosi. "They want us to believe," one reads, that the "natural repugnance of the people of Trieste to tie themselves with the Germans" is a result of scheming by the Jews. See ACS, *PNF, Situazione politica delle provincie (1923-43), Trieste.*

The pro-Farinacci elements also controlled the racist section of the GUF of Trieste who published its own bulletin and on November 18, 1939 also printed a pamphlet, *Razzismo fascista*, of a particularly violent tone.

1056. See, for example, G. G. Bonifacio, "Cammina Asvahero," in *Il regime fascista*, October 24, 1941. From a confidential note in October 1941 it seems that the attacks of *Il regime fascista* were also determined by the desire to "create trouble" for the existing Prefect, His Excellency Tamburini, who had apparently clashed with the collaborator of Preziosi's paper." See ACS, *PNF, Situazione politica delle provincie (1923-43)*, Trieste.

1057. From a classified report by the German Consul General in Trieste on November 23, 1942, it appears that even then the fight against the Jews of Trieste was an excuse for the various Fascist factions which sought the post of podestà of the city. See C. Ventura, "Il centro fascista di Trieste per lo studio del problema ebraico," in *Trieste*, May-June 1961, p. 22. In the same report it was said that the national vice-secretary of the PNF, Farnesi, was a supporter of the Jews and that in Trieste, on the initiative of the local Center, the filing of all of those of "mixed" background had begun. The Trieste Center for the study of the Jewish problem was, since July 25, 1943, particularly active and in constant contact with G. Preziosi. In December of 1942 a forty-page report was sent to Mussolini, bearing the title "Enemy propaganda–Judaism–Internal Front," written by the Center on November 16, aimed at demonstrating how the "Jewish Central of Trieste" was one of the major instruments of enemy espionage and how it had managed to install numerous members in the highest of hierarchies of the PNF "carried out by the innocent Vidussoni". See Document 35 and L. Cabrini, *Il potere segreto* cit., p. 211.

1058. ACS, *PNF, Situazione politica delle provincie (1923-43), Trieste.*

1059. See the denunciation of the president of the Community to the King's attorney in Trieste on July 20, 1942, in L. Morpurgo, *Caccia all'uomo!,* Rome 1946, p. 333-35. Other incidents occurred on May 19, 1943; during the funerals of some Fascist militiamen, various shops in the city that were run by Jews were ransacked and raided by Fascist groups.

1060. ACS, *Min. Int., Dir. gen. PS, Div. Aff. gen. e ris. (1920-45),* category A 5 G, b. 48, file 58, *Propaganda antisemita.*

At about the same time similar anti-Semitic unrest also appeared in Florence. On July 17, 1940 the prefect of the city sent to the Ministry of Internal Affairs an anonymous letter which had been circulated in Florence a few days earlier. This letter "denounced" a "pack of shitty Jews" who gorged and delighted themselves while the Italians were fighting. It also wrote: "It is deplorable that our regime doesn't ever fully carry out its intentions. Everything fizzles out along the way… Why don't you give us orders to ram a bullet in those heads covered in sebaceous crimped hair. It's about time. This state of things is revolting. Let's pray to God that another 1919 does not occur."

1061. In another leaflet Italians were incited to completely isolate the Jews: "ITALIANS–do not go near the Jews. There is no distinction between the discriminated and the non-discriminated. Beware of those baptized at the last minute, they are the most dangerous because they are the most cowardly. Those who protect them and who help them are neither Fascists nor Italians, but one of their sect,"

1062. See R. B., *Gli ebrei a Ferrara dal fascismo alla liberazione,* in "Competizione democratica," April 25, 1955 (special issue dedicated to the resistance of Ferrara), pp. 16-17. Almost at the same time as the serious events in Ferrara, there was also some anti-Jewish unrest: placards were put up and on the night of October 14–15, 1941 there was also an attempt to set the Synagogue on fire. See *Tre vite ecc.* cit., pp. 174-76.

1063. See ACS, *RSI, Segretaria particolare del Duce, Carteggio riservato (1943-45),* b. 29, file 498, *GNR. Corso di Cultura politico razziale.*

1064. *Relazione sull'opera svolta dal ministero degli Affari esteri per la tutela delle comunità ebraiche (1938-1943),* Rome n.d.; L. Poliakov-J. Saville, *Gli ebrei sotto l'occupazione italiana* cit.; A. Cavaglion, *Nella notte straniera. Gli ebrei di S. Martin Vésubie e il campo di Borgo S. Dalmazzo. 8 settembre–21 novembre 1943,* Cuneo 1981; R. De Felice, *Un nuovo documento sulla condizione degli ebrei nella zona d'occupazione italiana in Francia durante la seconda guerra mondiale*, in *Israel– Saggi sull'Ebraismo italiano* cit., pp. 179-84; J. Sabille, *Les juifs de Tunisie sous Vichy et l'occupation*, Paris 1954; D. Carpi, "The Rescue of Jews in the Italian Zone of Occupied Croatia," in *Rescue Attempts During the Holocaust Proceedings of the Second Yad Vashem International Historical Conference–April 1974*, Jerusalem 1977, pp. 465-525; ID., *Notes on the history of the Jews in Greece during the holocaust period.* "The Attitude of the Italians (1941-1943)," in *Festchrift in Honor of Dr. George S. Wise*, Tel Aviv 1981, pp. 25-62; ID., *Nuovi documenti per la storia dell'olocausto in Grecia. L'atteggiamento degli italiani (1941-1943)*, in "Michael," VII, 1981, pp. 119-200; S. Loi, "L'esercito italiano di fronte alle persecuzioni razziali," in *Revue internationale d'histoire militaire*, 1978, n. 39, pp. 276-87; R. Pommerin, "Le controversie di politica razziale nei rapporti dell'Asse Roma-Berlino (1938-1943)," in *Storia contemporanea*, October 1979, pp. 925-40; M. Michaelis, *Mussolini e la questione ebraica* cit., pp. 291-304; *Gli ebrei e l'Italia durante la guerra 1940-45*, edited by N. Caracciolo, Rome 1986.

1065. *Relazione ecc.* cit., *passim* and particularly pp. 10-18, 23-28.

1066. *Relazione ecc.* cit., p. 6.

1067. *Ibid.*, pp. 6-8.

1068. *Ibid.*, p. 17.

1069. *Ibid.*, pp. 36-41.

1070. *Relazione ecc.* cit., p. 41.

1071. *Ibid.*, p. 3.

1072. M. R. Marrus-R. O. Paxton, *Vichy et les juifs* cit., p. 332.

1073. *Relazione ecc.* cit., pp. 42-59; L. Poliakov-J. Sabille, *Gli ebrei sotto l'occupazione italiana* cit., pp. 159-68. Italian diplomatic authorities also made every effort to try to save hundreds of Spanish Jews in Greece, granting them permission to transit into the Italian zone and to Italy; if rescue was not possible it was due only to the slowness and uncertainty of the Spanish authorities who gave their approval only when it was too late (see *Relazione ecc.* cit., pp. 57-59). Thanks to Italian involvement, Swiss, Turkish, Portuguese, and Argentinian Jews were saved.

1074. *Relazione ecc.* cit., pp. 18-22; L. Poliakov-J. Sabille, *Gli ebrei sotto l'occupazione italiana* cit., pp.133-55 and 169-87.

1075. *Relazione ecc.* cit., pp. 22-36; L. Poliakov-J. Sabille, *Gli ebrei sotto l'occupazione italiana* cit., pp. 3-129; M. R. Marrus-R. O. Paxton, *Vichy et les juifs* cit., pp. 290-95.

1076. G. Bastianini, *Uomini Cose Fatti, Memorie di un ambasciatore* cit., pp. 86-88; V. Statera, "L'ex questore Lospinoso ci racconta come aiutò quarantamila israeliti," in *La stampa*, Turin, April 5, 1961.

1077. L. Poliakov-J. Sabille, *Gli ebrei sotto l'occupazione italiana* cit., pp.104-5.

1078. J. Sabille, *Les juifs de Tunisie sous Vichy et l'occupation* cit., *passim* and particularly pp. 111-15, 141-45, 186-88.

1079. L. Poliakov, *La condition des juifs en France sous l'occupation italienne* cit., pp. 18 and 42-43.

1080. ACS, *Min. Cult. Pop.*, b. 35, file *Germania*, telegraph Ministry of Foreign Affairs to the Ministry of Popular Culture, Rome, September 5, 1938.

1081. L. Poliakov-J. Sabille, *Gli ebrei sotto l'occupazione italiana* cit., p.46.

1082. *Ibid.*, p. 94.

1083. The Holy See intervened, for example, on several occasions *in loco* and in Rome (through Monsignor Borgongini-Duca) in favor of the Jews in the Italian zone in France. See L. Poliakov-J. Sabille, *Gli ebrei sotto l'occupazione italiana* cit., p. 22; G. Bastianini, *Uomini Cose Fatti, Memorie di un ambasciatore* cit., pp.86-88.

1084. L. Poliakov-J. Sabille, *Gli ebrei sotto l'occupazione italiana* cit., p. 186 (the document is from November 20, 1942).

1085. G. Bastianini, *Uomini Cose Fatti, Memorie di un ambasciatore* cit., pp. 54-55.

1086. C. Senise, *Quando ero capo della polizia* cit., pp. 102-3.

1087. R. Guariglia, *Ricordi* cit., p. 182.

1088. See *Il messaggero*, of Rome, April 19, 1961.

1089. *La persécution des juifs ecc.* cit., pp. 292-93.

1090. L. Poliakov-J. Sabille, *Gli ebrei sotto l'occupazione italiana* cit., p. 65.

1091. L. Poliakov-J. Sabille, *Gli ebrei sotto l'occupazione italiana* cit., pp. 18-20, 63-68; and also *Dossier Eichmann* cit., pp. 168-69.

1092. ASAE, *Uffico coordinamento*, b. 36, *Germania (1943)*, file 1, reproduced in *Document 32*.

1093. ACS, *Segretaria particolare del Duce, Carteggio riservato (1922-43)*, file 242/R., *Aldo Vidussoni*, "Visit to the Eastern Front, to the Führer's headquarters and to Munich by the PNF led by the Secretary of the PNF", Rome October 24, 1942.

1094. See A. Pirelli, *Taccuini 1922/1943*, Bologna 1984, pp. 364 *sgg.* and in particular p. 365.

1095. R. Ducci, in *Gli ebrei e l'Italia durante la guerra 1940-45* cit., pp. 112 *sgg.*; but also see Verax [R. Ducci], "Italiani ed ebrei in Jugoslavia," in *Politica estera*, October 1944, pp. 21 *sgg.*

1096. L. Poliakov-J. Sabille, *Gli ebrei sotto l'occupazione italiana* cit., pp. 152-53 (the words of Mussolini cited by us are taken from the original source, the report by Col. Vincenzo Carlà, head of office "I" of the command of the 2nd army, transmitted on March 6, 1945 to the General Staff of the Army–Information Office, in Archives of the Historical Office of the General Staff–Army, Rac. 185/6).

1097. G. Bastianini, *Uomini Cose Fatti, Memorie di un ambasciatore* cit., pp. 86 *sgg.*; L. Pietromarchi, *Diario*, March 31, 1943 (the passage is published in "La difesa degli ebrei nel'43. Frammenti delle Memorie dell'ambasciatore Luca Pietromarchi," in *Nuova antologia*, January-March 1987, pp. 245-46).

1098. The Nazis brought up the issue again at the Feltre Conference (on July 19, 1943); at least this is what can be inferred from a memorandum from the German Ministry of Foreign Affairs to Himmler, published in United Restitution Organization, _Dokumente über Methoden der Judenverfolgung im Ausland_, Frankfurt am Main 1959, pp. 89-90, translated in Document 33.

1099. AUCII, _1942-43, Precettazione civile._

1100. Among the most graphic and vivid direct memoirs of those years are S. Lombroso, _Si può stampare. Pagine vissute 1938-45_, Rome 1945; L. Morpurgo, _Caccia all'uomo!_, cit.

1101. ACS, _Presidenza del Consiglio, Gabinetto (1937-43)_, Administrative acts _(1940-43)_, b. 118, file 3/2-2, n. 5441/39.

1102. E. Momigliano, _Storia tragica e grottesca_, pp. 90-91.

1103. U. Cavallero, _Comando supremo_ cit., pp. 357, 362.

1104. ACIR, p. 44, _Persecuzioni razziali_, under the file _Precettazioni._

1105. ACS, _Min. Int., Dir. gen. PS, Div. Aff. gen. e ris. (1903-49)_, category E/c; E/i, b. 479, under the file _L'Aquila._

1106. ACS, _Segreteria particolare del Duce, Carteggio riservato_, file 242/R, _Farinacci, avvocato Roberto_, under the file 40.

1107. I. Kalk, "I campi di concentramento italiani per gli ebrei profughi: Ferramonti Tarsia (Calabria)," in _Gli ebrei in Italia durante il fascismo_ cit., I, pp. 63-71; R. Pacufucu, "Il 'campo' di Ferramonti negli ultimi tempi del regime fascista," in _Quaderni del Centro di studi sulla deportazione e l'internamento_, n. 6 (1969-71), pp. 89-91 and above all F. Folino, _Ferramonti. Un lager di Mussolini_, Cosenza 1985 and C. S. Capogreco, _Ferramonti. La vita e gli uomini del più grande campo d'internamento fascista (1940-1945)_, Florence 1987.

1108. AUCII, _1941, pos._ 4434, file _Corrispondenza dell'avvocato Valobra._

1109. AUCII, _Libro dei verbali, Consiglio_, January 18, 1939.

1110. _Ibid._, May 22, 1939.

1111. See D. Prato, _Dal Pergamo della Comunità di Roma_ cit., pp. XXIV-XXV. For an assessment of Prato's position towards Fascism, see, in _La Comunità Israelitica_, March 1937, pp. 6-16, the text of his speech on the occasion of his inaugural as Rabbi of Rome.

1112. At the end of 1938 in Milan, a committee of assistance for Jews in Italy (COMASEBIT) was established, a derivation of the old assistance committee for Jewish refugees. R. Cantoni was the moving force within the committee, although due to his anti-Fascist past he did not appear as its leader. The presidency was formally given to Renzo Luisada, a painter who has now emigrated to Israel, and Umberto Nahon, an active Zionist, was named head of the committee. In six months the committee managed to expatriate as many as 600 Jews and organized an extensive assistance service in many regions. In Milan it organized two canteens. For its work, it used voluntary donations and grants from various international

Jewish organizations. It had relations with some consular representations in Italy and with the German and Austrian Communities with which it tried to coordinate the influx of refugees into Italy. On Cantoni, see S. Minerbi, *Raffaele Cantoni un ebreo anticonformista*, Assisi-Rome 1978.

1113. Almost until the end of June 1940, the transfer of young Italian and foreign Jews to Palestine was supervised by the Aliàth Honòar, directed by Augusto Segre, Berti Eckert, and Franca Muggia. The last departure for Palestine (22) was January 1940. See Aliàth Honòar, *Presente e futuro d'Israele*, Busto Arsizio 1953, *passim* and particularly pp. 61-65; also A. Segre, "Movimenti giovanili ebraici in Italia durante il periodo razziale," in *La rassegna mensile d'Israel*, August-September 1965 (important also to understand the nature of "resistance" that in certain circles of young Jews, Zionists or Zionist influenced, took the form of assistance and transfer of the refugees to Palestine) and T. Eckert, *Il movimento sionistico-chalutzistico in Italia fra le due guerre mondiali* cit.

1114. AUCII, *1938-39, Varie*, under the file *Scuole agricole*. The formula used with the Italians had already been extensively experimented in 1937-39 with foreigners who had to emigrate to Palestine (in 1938 there were forty or so small agricultural centers), to readapt the Jews, who had been excluded from every other activity, to agriculture.

1115. AUCII, *1938-39, Varie*, under the file *Corsi universitari*.
The project was submitted to the Ministry of Education which, with a letter from Bottai, dated November 2, 1939, refused the authorization: "With all due consideration, I must point out that a private institute of university instruction does not exist in Italy, at least not one which is entitled, directly or indirectly, to any legal recognition and, besides, the authorization of a request of that kind cannot be granted."

1116. AUCII, *1938-39*, under the file *Min. Int., Dir. gen. Demografia e Razza*, minutes of the meetings of December 22, 1938, April 25, 1939 and September 16, 1939.

1117. AUCII, *1938-39*, under the file *Min. Int., Dir. gen. Demografia e Razza*. The memorandum, which was very long and wordy, requested: (a) the regulation of expatriates allowing those who wanted to leave Italy to be able to transfer "a significant sum of personal property" abroad; (b) to not increase the legislation, especially with regard to professional activities, already established; (c) to avoid minor harassment, local minor arbitrary acts and the slanderous attacks by the press; (d) to authorize Jewish immigration in the AOI.

1118. AUCII, *1938-39*, file *Varie*, under the file *Professionisti*. The memorandum (of which the Senate was informed through its spokesman, Senator Celesia, on the related law) asked to reduce the number of professions granted to the Jews to a minimum, to take seniority into consideration in active professional practice, and to consent that the discriminated be listed in the new registers instead of the special lists.

1119. AUCII, *1938-39,* file *Varie,* under the file *Problema della cittadinanza.* The memorandum stated that it had to take into consideration the Jews from Trentino and Venezia Giulia to benefit from the full rights of Italian citizenship and that this could not be revoked. The point was accepted by the Ministry of Internal Affairs.

1120. AUCII, *1938-39,* file *Varie,* under the file *Ministero dell'Educazione nazionale.* The petition summarized all of the school-related problems still pending, on which the ministry had not yet expressed its opinion.

1121. All of the information related here has been kindly supplied by the lawyer Aldo R. Ascoli.

1122. R. J. Almansi, "Mio padre, Dante Almansi," in *La Rassegna mensile di Israel,* May-June 1976, pp. 234-55.

1123. AUCII, *Libro dei verbali, Consiglio,* November 13, 1939.

1124. *Ibid.,* February 26, 1940.

1125. See "Gli ebrei," in *Il popolo di Roma,* June 7, 1941; and above all "Gran mondo giudaico in maschera," in *Il Tevere,* September 26-27, 1941. In this second article, among other things, one reads: "The most suspicious and questionable characters have, recently, resurfaced as leaders of the Jewish communities of Italy, their organizations and institutions, the most blatant agents of a Zionism which was attacked and exposed just in time in this very paper. These leaders naturally influence the mass of the members which they direct, more and more decidedly, towards their unchanged objectives." D. Almansi was defined as a "cover," "rising with the votes of the Zionist brigade," who "spreading honeyed words everywhere, and deceptively availing himself of his past as a functionary, has been able to obtain all kinds of clever loopholes for his followers." The columnist then examined the various members of the Union Council defining them "official spokespersons for anti-Axis and anti-Fascist propaganda." There was also direct exposure of the relations existing between the Union and notorious antifascists such as Cantoni. "In short," concluded the article, "a clean sweep is due... The practice of a cult which can still be tolerated must not become an alibi for anti-national activity, clearly defined by the law and pursued with just severity with regard to everyone, with merciless rigor with regard to the Jews, whom we are still obliged to accommodate, hidden behind the masks that they don."

1126. In particular, the Union managed to obtain that tenure was recognized for university professors who had been expelled from teaching, and therefore were to be given the appropriate salary reinstatement; and that the confiscated equipment of the Jewish foundations and institutes would be passed on to the schools instituted by the communities; an adjournment was also obtained on the withdrawal of the street trader's licenses, also various eractionsmm =cribed

other concessions and adjournments of lesser account (of which, the exclusion of rabbis from civilian draft). See AUCII, *1940-43, Libro dei verbali, Giunta.* At the beginning of 1940 the Union even had unofficial contacts regarding eventual permission for Jewish Italians and refugees in Italy to settle in the AOI, in Gimma. See AUCII, *1940-41, Presidenza,* A. R. Ascoli to D. Almansi, Rome, January 15, 1940.

1127. The Fascists were closely watching the Union's activity. The mail, especially that of the DELASEM and coming from overseas, was regularly opened, photographed and sometimes intercepted. See ACS, *Min. Int., Dir. gen. Ps, Div. Aff. gen. e ris. (1920-45),* cat. A 5 G, b. 10, file 3, *Attività degli ebrei;* and *Comitato assistenza agli ebrei;* b. 57, file 160, *Ebrei mobilitazione civile.*

1128. AUCII, *Libro dei verbali, Giunta,* May 18 and December 21, 1941.

1129. Detailed lists of Jewish schools operating in the years 1940-43 can be found in the *Lunario ebraico,* the years 5702 (1941-42) and 5703 (1942-43) published by the Jewish Community Union. For a particular experience, see Y. Colombo, "Il problema scolastico per gli ebrei d'Italia nel'38. La scuola di Milano," in *Rassegna mensile di Israel,* June 1965, pp. 259-72.

1130. AUCII, *1940-43, Manifestazioni pubbliche e della stampa sugli ebrei e sull'ebraismo,* file *Studenti in Svizzera; Scuole agricole, professionali, artigane; Corsi superiori; 1940-43, Scuole.*

1131. M. Leone, *Le organizzazioni di soccorso ebraiche in età fascista* cit., pp. 167 sgg; S. Sorani, *L'assistenza ai profughi ebrei in Italia* cit., pp. 53 *sgg.*

1132. From a circular, dated January 24, 1942 it appears that the operating agencies at that time were those of Alessandria, Ancona, Bologna, Casale Monferrato, Durazzo (Albania), Ferrara, Florence, Fiume, Gorizia, Leghorn, Lubiana, Mantua, Milan, Modena, Naples, Padua, Parma, Pisa, Prishtina (Albania), Rodi, Rome, Spoleto, Turin, Trieste, Venice, Vercelli, Verona. See AUCII, *Delasem.*

1133. See Document 34.

1134. AUCII, *Delasem.*

1135. There are no studies on emigration from Italy, on emigration in general and on the countries of emigration. In the US (a total from 1938 onwards of around two thousand persons) it has been studied, based on the archives of some American organizations for Jewish assistance, by G. Prezzolini, *America in pantofole,* Florence 1950, pp. 341-75. From this study it appears that emigration to the US had some very definite characteristics. The emigrating Jews were above all wealthy merchants, entrepreneurs, professionals, intellectuals, who mostly settled (generally without turning to local aid organizations) in New York and in the large cities on the east coast, securing, except in unusual circumstances, living conditions and work a little more modest than what they had at home. These emigrants did not generally mix neither with their co-religionists nor with the Italian-Americans and lived somewhat isolated. For the emigration to Palestine, see S. Della Pergola-A. Tagliacozzo, *Gli italiani in Israele*, Rome 1978.

1136. AUCII, *Corrispondenza dell'avvocato Valobra*, file 1942, *Lavoro internati.*

1137. See *Due anni di Delasem*, Genoa 1942, *passim* and particularly pp. 24-35.

1138. The travels of Valobra occurred in complete agreement with Chief of Police Senise and the Ministry of War and sometimes took place with seaplanes placed at their disposal by the army.

1139. AUCII, *Libro dei verbali, Giunta,* December 21, 1941; *Delasem: Croazia—Slovenia—Dalmazia*; I. Vaccari, *Villa Emma*, Modena 1960, pp. 17-20.
The Union and the DELASEM managed to take care of the conditions of the Jews in the Italian occupied zone of Yugoslavia, and in August 1941, the Secretary of State of the Vatican also took interest in the case.

1140. Regarding this problem, see P. Treves, "Antifascisti ebrei od antifascismo ebraico?," in *La rassegna mensile di Israel*, January-June 1981, pp. 138-49.

1141. On Carlo Rossi, see A. Garosci, *La vita di Carlo Rossi*, 2 vol. Rome-Florence-Milan s.d. (ma 1946).

1142. See *Tre lettere di Riccardo Bauer a Nino Contini*, in *Gli ebrei in Italia durante il fascismo* cit., I, p. 90.

1143. A vivid memoir about this is the diary of G. Douro [R. Bianchi-Brandinelli], *Dal diario di un borghese*, in "Società," January-June 1945, pp. 46-47; another, also significant, *Dall'Italia e sull'Italia*, in the second of the "Quaderni italiani," Boston, August 1942, p. 109.

1144. A. Garosci, *Storia dei fuorusciti* cit., pp. 192-93.

1145. *Ibid.*, p. 153.

1146. On the Fermi case, see E. Segrè, *Enrico Fermi, fisico*, Bologna 1987, pp. 98 sgg. and 249 sgg.

1147. ACS, *Min., Int., Dir. gen. PS, Div. Aff. gen. e ris. (1930-31)*, categ. K 3, *Massoneri*, bb. 48 and 49.

1148. [E. Mortara], *Ebrei italiani di fronte al "Razzismo,"* Tunisia 1938, p. 22.

1149. Italian antifascists were, among other things, particularly active in the Ligue internationale contre l'antisémitisme, of which the Italian section was presided by Lionello Venturi. The Italian section of the Ligue, amongst other things, made a "spoken newspaper" recorded on discs in Italian. When Mussolini discovered this from *Il regime fascista*, he demanded a copy of the discs. See ACS, *Min. Cult. Pop., Gabinetto*, b. 13, file 294, *Professor Venturi*; and also *La vita italiana*, June 1939, p. 768.

1150. *Enzo Sereni–Vita e brani scelti*, Milan 1947, p. 40 (letter to his children, December 27, 1942). On E. Sereni, see the wonderful essay by C. L. Ottino, "Cenni sull'esperienza sionista e antifascista di Enzo Sereni," in *Gli ebrei in Italia durante il fascismo* cit., II, pp. 67-85.

1151. See M. Montagna, "I rifugiati ebrei in Australia e il movimento antifascista "Italia libera (1942-1946)," in *Notiziario dell'istituto storico della resistenza in Cuneo e provincia*, January-June 1987, pp. 5 sgg.

1152. U. Limentani, "Radio Londra durante la guerra," in *Inghilterra e Italia nel'900*, Florence 1973, pp. 201 sgg.; *Radio Londra 1940-1945. Inventario delle trasmissioni per l'Italia*, edited by M. Piccioluti Caprioli, Rome 1976, I, pp, XIV sgg.; G. Padovano, "Appunti sulle origini, gli sviluppi dell'O. W. I and of the "Voce dell'America," in *L'antifascismo italiano negli Stati Uniti durante la seconda guerra mondiale*, edited by A. Varsori, Rome 1984, pp. 69 sgg.; T. Zevi, *L'emigrazione razziale*, therein, pp. 75 sgg..

1153. *Enzo Sereni–Vita ecc.* cit., pp. 15-16.

1154. A. Garosci, *Storia dei fuorusciti* it., pp. 224-28; 289-93.

1155. Archivio di GL, section VI, *Mazzini society*, file 3, *Rifugiati*.

1156. A. Strazzera Perniciani, *Umanità ed eroismo nella vita segreta di Regina Coeli–Roma 1943-44*, Rome 1959, pp. 22, 25; also T. Interlandi was arrested and held in custody at the Forte Boccea, from which he was freed by the Germans after September 8; see Eugen Dollman, *Roma nazista*, Milan 1951, p. 261.

1157. *Il diritto razzista*, May-June 1939, p. 5.

1158. P. Badoglio, *L'Italia nella seconda guerra mondiale*, Milan 1946, p.92.

1159. AUCII, *1943, Abolizione decreti razziali*.

1160. *Ibid.,* circular signed by D. Almansi, dated August 31, 1943, to the Community of Ancona, Turin and Trieste.

1161. *Ibid.,* memorandum addressed to the Ministry of Finance on August 30, 1943.

1162. *Ibid.,* the Union to the Rabbi of Turin, September 3, 1943.

1163. Various private appeals were sent to Badoglio to have the racial laws revoked. On July 29, even the Argentinian Jewish associations cabled him about it. See ACS, *Presidenza del Consiglio, Gabinetto (1937-43), Atti amministrativi (1940-43)*, b. 118, file 3/2-2, n. 5441/10, *Esposti anonimi ed altro riguardanti le disposizioni sulla razza*.

1164. ACS, *Min. Int., Dir. gen. Demografia e Razza (1938-43)*, b. 9, file 38.

1165. AUCII, *1943, Abolizione decreti razziali*. The Union made a request on September 6, via General Martelli, to readmit, "in this grave hour that has come," the Jews into the army.

1166. See, for example, S. D'A. (Silvio D'Amico?), "Teatro politico?," in *Il giornale d'Italia*, August 22, 1943.

1167. The Badoglio Government passed the first Legislative Decree of abrogation of racial legislation on January 20, 1944 in Brindisi (see *Gazzetta Ufficiale*, n. 5, February 9, 1944).

1168. Even though they had to quickly withdraw towards the north the Germans, when it was possible, still tried to grab the many Jews (keeping in mind the thousands of foreigners who were confined and interned in the south by the Fascists) who were on their path. On September 12, for example, they tried to scour the famous community of San Nicandro in

Puglie (see P. E. Lapide, *Mosè in Puglie*, Milan 1958, pp. 186-91). Luckily the overwhelming majority of those confined and interned had scattered in the countryside, immediately after September 8, and, with the help of the population, managed to escape capture.

1169. For a general picture of what was done by the Germans in Greece and Yugoslavia after September 8, 1943, see *La persécution des juifs dans les pays de l'Est présentée à Nuremberg. Recueil de documents publié sous la direction de H. Monneray*, Paris 1949; for Corfú see, in particular, G. Volli, "La tragedia degli Ebrei di Corfú," in *Israel*, November 14, 1946.

1170. See G. Volli, "Rodi, una comunità che piú non esiste," in *Israel*, July 25, 1947; H. M. Franco, *Les martyres juifs de Rhodes et de Cos* cit., pp. 93 sgg. and above all E. Fino, *La tragedia di Rodi e dell'Egeo*, Rome 1957, pp. 249-57.

1171. L. Poliakov-J. Sabille, *Gli ebrei sotto l'occupazione italiana* cit., pp.154-55.

1172. *Relazione ecc.* cit., p. 35.

1173. L. Poliakov-J. Sabille, *Gli ebrei sotto l'occupazione italiana* cit., pp. 23-24; R. Guariglia, *Ricordi* cit., p. 699.

1174. L. Poliakov-J. Sabille, *Gli ebrei sotto l'occupazione italiana* cit., pp. 24-27; "Una lettera di Padre Benedetto," in *La Comunità Israelitica* July 1955.

1175. L. Poliakov-J. Sabille, *Gli ebrei sotto l'occupazione italiana* cit., pp. 27-29; see also "Una perdita dolorosa, Angelo Donati," in *Israel*, January 12, 1961.

1176. G. Pini, *Itinerario tragico (1943-45)*, Milan 1950, pp. 40, 272.

1177. G. Pini-D. Susmel, *Mussolini ecc.* it., IV, pp. 361-65.

1178. ACS, *RSI, Presidenza del Consiglio, Gabinetto, Provvedimenti legislativi sottoposto all'esame del Consiglio dei ministri (1943-45)*, b. 33, file 3/2-2, under the file 13, the Minister for Internal Affairs to all heads of provinces, Police Order n. 5. "1. All Jews, even if discriminated, of whichever nationality, and in any case residing within the national territory must be sent to the relevant concentration camps. All of their personal possessions and property must be submitted to be immediately sequestered, before being confiscated in the interest of the RSI, that will assign them to benefit poverty-stricken victims of invasions in enemy zones. 2. All those, born of mixed marriages, who have, in application of the current Italian racial laws, the certainty of belonging to the Aryan race, must be placed under special surveillance by the police. The Jews are, in the meantime, placed in provincial concentration camps before being gathered in special concentration camps established for this purpose."

1179. G. Pini-D. Susmel, *Mussolini ecc.* cit., IV, pp. 363-64.

1180. See *Gli ebrei in Italia durante il fascismo*, I, cit., pp. 117-23. The rules for implementation were then established by the Ministry of Finance through circular n. 4032 B, issued in Brescia on February 12, 1944. If the measures had been carried out to the letter, there would not have remained even enough for the Jews to live on. The Ministry of Internal Affairs, aware of this, cabled on March 19, 1944, informing the heads of the provinces that from the confiscation, "amounts of money, valuables and property in general, indispensable for the life of the aforementioned persons and those living under their care" should be excluded and in particular "in consideration of their essentially alimentary nature" pensions, compensation for work injuries, invalid and old age pensions and, in general, all monthly checks. The Ministry of Finance, though, protested against this memo from Buffarini-Guidi, having preferred a literal application of the Legislative Decree of January 4. In the end, the Head of State, with a note by F. Barracu on October 9, 1944, established that "the execution of the provisions can be reached making adjustments for individual cases," and arranged an agreement between the Ministry of Internal Affairs and the Ministry of Finance. See ACS, *RSI, Presidenza del Consiglio, Gabinetto, Provvedimenti legislativi sottoposti all'esame del Consiglio dei ministri (1943-45)*, b. 38, file 3/2-2, under the file 5/2.

1181. It is interesting and significant that, in October 1943, before moving the offices of the EGELI to the north, its commissioner had contacted the Minister of Switzerland in Rome to inform him of the coming move and to reassure him in a sense, that this way the EGELI would have been better able to safeguard the entrusted property, once belonging to the Jews and to enemy citizens. See A. Scalpelli, *L'ente di gestione e liquidazione immobiliare* cit., pp. 97-98.

1182. The expropriations—once the Ministry of Internal Affairs and the Ministry of Finance discussed its limits—were generally carried out with extreme rigor, as stated in the related decrees published by the *Gazzetta Ufficiale d'Italia*, April 8 1944, p. 445):

"Confiscated in favor of the State, the movable property belonging to Mr. Sommer Antonio of the Jewish race.

THE HEAD OF THE PROVINCE OF VICENZA

Considering the legislative decree of the Duce n. 2, dated 4-1-1944-XXII:

Considering the declaration of the property possessed by the Jew Sommer, Antonio of Montecchio Maggiore;

Decree:

The property belonging to the Jew Sommer Antonio is confiscated:

10 ladies' hats	2 pillow cases
5 used pairs of ladies' shoes	4 small cotton towels of which one toweling
1 used pair of men's house slippers	1 ladies' cotton night dress
1 single cotton sheet	1 apron
1 girdle	2 feather cushions
2 bathrobes	5 coat hangers
1 dressing gown	1 rubber shopping bag

1 men's shirt	3 small aluminum pots
2 used pairs of men's socks	1 bowl
1 ladies' slip	3 shoe brushes
4 ties	1 packet of medicinal cotton
3 used ladies' silk dresses	1 bedside mat
3 silk shirts	4 suitcases
1 used ladies' suit	

The said property passes into the trusteeship of Ente Gestione and Liquidazione immobiliare."

At a certain point, on May 21, 1944, the Ministry of National Education ended up protesting with Undersecretary Barracu. In a memorandum of the same date it was noted that the lists published by the "Gazzetta Ufficiale" offended "propaganda" and "historic documentation." "Such lists, that could have other significance and other consequences if they consisted of descriptions of vast properties, of precious collections, etc., are often boiled down, quite pitifully, to arouse only negative judgment. It reads, for example, that from Jew X 'two pairs of used socks' were confiscated in favor of the State, from Jew Y, 'a national flag, a bidet, an enema syringe,' from Jew Z, 'an outdated wool sweater, three dirty pairs of used underpants', etc." Following this memorandum, the lists of confiscated property were only published in specially provided supplements of the *Gazzetta Ufficiale*. See ACS, RSI, Presidenza del Consiglio, Gabinetto, Provvedimenti legislativi sottoposti all'esame del Consiglio dei ministri (1943-45), b. 38, file 3/2-2, under the file 5/2.

1183. ACS, *Min. Int., Dir. gen. PS, Div. Aff. gen. e ris. (1920-45)*, category A5G, b. 63, file 230, *Ebrei, sequestro beni*.

1184. Some banks attempted to oppose this decree, with the excuse of not knowing the names of their Jewish clients. The prefect of Rome, on February 16, 1944, gave this information to the Ministry of Finance, which was preparing a list of 18 thousand names of Jews residing in Rome and its province, to distribute to the banks. See ACS, *Min. Int., Dir. gen. PS, Div. Aff. gen. e ris. (1920-45)*, category A5G, b. 63, file 230, *Ebrei, sequestro beni*.

1185. ACS, *RSI, Presidenza del Consiglio, Gabinetto, Atti amministrativi (1943-45)*, b. 38, file 3/2-2, under the file 5/2.

1186. ACS, *RSI, Segreteria particolare del Duce, Carteggio riservato (1943-45)*, file 653, reproduced in Document 35.

1187. A part of these possessions (gold coins, valuables, hard currency, checks and money orders for around one billion lire) was recuperated in 1954 from the vaults of the Banca d'Italia in Vicenza, where the authorities of the RSI had deposited it. See *Il messaggero di Roma*, February 11, 1954.

1188. See A. Scalpelli, *L'ente di gestione e liquidazione immobiliare* cit., pp. 99-101.

1189. ACS, *Min. Int., Dir. gen. PS, Div. Aff. gen. e ris. (1920-45)*, category A5G, b. 63, file 230, *Ebrei, sequestro beni*, the Chief of Police, to the heads of the provinces and to the police commissioners, December 10, 1943; Ministry of Internal Affairs, Director General. Demography and Race, division AG I to the chief of police, January 27, 1944 and to the Cabinet Minister, February 1, 1944.

1190. *Ibid., Promemoria per l'Eccellenza Pagnozzi*, dated January 21, 1944 signed by the deputy chief of police.

1191. Information kindly provided by Dr. Luciana Nissim Momigliano. Nissim was deported from Fossoli on February 22, 1944 to Auschwitz. See L. Nissim, "Ricordi della casa dei morti," in *Donne contro il mostro*, Turin 1946, pp. 19-58.

1192. ACS, *Min. Int., Dir. gen. PS, Div. Aff. gen. e ris. (1920-45)*, category A5G, b. 63, file 230, *Ebrei, sequestro beni*.

1193. *Il messaggero di Roma*, April 19, 1961.

1194. It seems that Hitler had given the order that the Italian Jews were to be interned in Austria as "hostages" and that their deportation to extermination camps in Germany and Poland occurred because of Eichmann's "zeal." See *Il messaggero di Roma*, May 12, 1961.

1195. The decree for the establishment of the inspectorate and the appointment of Preziosi were only approved by the Council of Ministers on April 18. See B. Mussolini, *Opera Omnia* cit., XXXII, p. 76.

1196. The office for Demography and Race on April 16, 1944, was transformed into the General Directorate for Demography, also assigning it duties relative to the large families and, to maternity and childhood. In the beginning it was thought to also give it duties for statistics; the project was abandoned because of opposition from the commissioner at the National Institute of Statistics. See ACS, *RSI, Presidenza del Consiglio, Gabinetto, Provvedimenti sottoposti all'esame del Consiglio dei ministri (1943-45)*, b. 34, file 3/2-2, under the file 28.

1197. In mid-May G. Preziosi chose as principal collaborators, a magistrate, Dr. Carlo Alliney, as head of his Cabinet, and the provincial party secretary Giovanni Pestalozza as special secretary. See the announcement of the agency Stefani, n. 34, on May 17, 1944. In the post war period there was unfortunately no lack of extollers of Preziosi; see L. Cabrini, *Il potere segreto* cit., a messy anti-Masonic and anti-Jewish pamphlet, where G. Preziosi is actually called as "the most celebrated" Italian political writer. In 1944-45 Cabrini was very close to Preziosi and was part of his press office.

1198. On October 14, 1938, Farinacci turned to Mussolini to obtain a "position" for Preziosi, pushing for a place for him in a temporary role in diplomacy or the nomination as senator (see ACS, *Segreteria particolare dell Duce, Carteggio riservato*, file 242/R, *Farinacci, avvocato Roberto*, under the file

39, dossier D, R. Farinacci to B. Mussolini, Cremona, October 14, 1938). Mussolini nominated Preziosi as State Minister in 1942; the nomination, though, more than being a "reward" was, probably an "insult" to the Vatican, given that the editor of *La vita italiana* was an ex-priest and that he continuously attacked the Vatican and the Pontiff (see R. Guariglia, *Ricordi* cit., p. 504). This nomination was harshly criticized by the anti-Fascists. "Nazioni unite" on December 24, 1942, after having defined Preziosi as "one of the shady characters of Italian journalism," interpreted it as the beginning of "a new wave of racist rage against the Jews."

1199. In a telegram from Von Mackensen on February 15, 1943, Preziosi was named "the propelling force of Italian anti-Semitism." See M. Michaelis, *I rapporti italo-tedeschi ecc* cit., p. 274. Especially in 1942, Preziosi requested, with insistence and truly Catonian fanaticism, that the pages of his magazine print the complete text of the current anti-Semitic legislation and the coming of an integral racism. See, for example, M. Scaligero, "Per un razzismo integrale," in *La vita italiana*, May 1942; G. Preziosi, "Per la soluzione del problema ebraico," therein, September 1942; G. Landra, "La guerra e il razzismo italiano," therein, May 1943; A. Capasso, "Per un razzismo italiano," therein, July 1943.

1200. F. Anfuso, *Da palazzo Venezia al lago di Garda (1936-1945)*, Bologna 1957, p. 348.

1201. *Ibid.*, p. 321.

1202. G. Pini-D. Susmel, *Mussolini ecc.* cit., IV, p. 326.

1203. *Ibid.*, pp. 270-71.

1204. G. Goebbels, *Diario intimo*, Milan 1948, p. 688.

1205. ACS, *RSI, Segreteria particolare del Duce, Carteggio riservato (1943-45)*, file 166, *Preziosi Giovanni*, under the file 2, G. Preziosi to B. Mussolini, December 3, 1943.

1206. *Ibid.*

1207. G. Pini-D. Susmel, *Mussolini ecc.* cit., IV, p. 386.

1208. *Ibid.*, p. 396.

1209. ACS, *RSI, Segreteria particolare del Duce, Carteggio riservato*, under the file 2, G. Preziosi to B. Mussolini, Munich, January 31, 1944, reproduced in Document 36.

1210. G. Dolfin, *Con Mussolini nella tragedia*, Milan 1950, pp. 264-69.

1211. For a study of Mussolini's position in the context of the anti-Semitic debate, it is significant that, even during the months of June and July of 1944, Mussolini was personally very moderate with attacks on the Jews. In his famous *Il tempo del bastone e della carota* (Milan 1944) he limited himself to writing that the vast middle classes, Freemasonry and Judaism during the Fascist period were "loyal" and that "the tutor of the Prince was the

Jew, Professor Polacco" (p. 40). Very little, especially compared to what others were writing, not only Preziosi but also almost all of the major political commentators of the RSI (see, for example, *La repubblica fascista*, February 18, 1944; *La stampa*, February 19, 1944; *La gazzetta di Parma*, February 26, 1944; *Il regime fascista*, March 1, 1944; *La nazione*, March 1, 1944).

1212. ACS, *RSI, Segreteria particolare del Duce, Carteggio riservato (1943-45)*, file 385, *Provvedimenti razziali*, file 166, *Preziosi, Giovanni*, under the file 3, reproduced in Document 37.

1213. *Ibid.*, file 166, *Preziosi, Giovanni*, under the file 3, accompanying note to the Duce from G. Preziosi.

1214. ACS, *RSI, Segreteria particolare del Duce, Carteggio riservato (1943-45)*, file 166, *Preziosi, Giovanni*, reproduced in Document 38.

1215. Buffarini-Guidi wrote to Mussolini, with his "observations," on the morning of May 17: "Duce, allow me to submit some observations hurriedly formulated last night, on the new racial law. I ask you, Duce, to be so kind as to give them your valuable attention, to point out, in my opinion, some inadequacies in the laws that require indispensable modifications. Minister Buffarini." See G. Buffarini-Guidi, *La vera verità* cit., p. 56.

1216. ACS, *RSI, Segreteria particolare del Duce, Carteggio riservato (1943-45)*, file 385, *Provvedimenti razziali*, reproduced in Document 39.

1217. In all of these events and in general on the baleful role of Preziosi in the RSI, see E. F. Moellhausen, *La carta perdente*, Rome 1948, pp. 311-16, and R. Rahn, *Ambasciatore di Hitler a Vichy e a Salò*, Milan 1950, p. 287. For Moellhausen, Preziosi was "the real incarnation of hate," capable, if they opposed him, to "write to Hitler and denounce everyone, Mussolini and Rahn to begin with, as traitors, pro-Jewish and pro-Masonic."

1218. ACS, *RSI, Segreteria particolare del Duce, Carteggio riservato (1943-45)*, file 166, *Preziosi Giovanni*; for example, after he was denied special indemnity for the members of his inspectorate. Notwithstanding this presumed "persecution," Preziosi managed to have himself granted a "subsidy" of 100,000 lire for damages sustained when he abandoned his properties in Rome and Naples and, in December 1944, managed to have himself appointed ambassador.

1219. The following letter from Preziosi to Mussolini on February 26, 1945 is typical:

"Duce, exactly five days after my return from Germany—or has it been a year?—a Fascist who knew and whom you know, told me: You will never establish the Inspectorate. And he gave me ample and precise details regarding this decision.

"For an entire year I have split my personality, and I have been actor and observer at the same time. Actor, in the sense that I tried to overcome all the maneuvers on a daily basis; and as an observer, who studied, these maneuvers and saw that they were part of a plan.

"Today I can only tell you that the close examination of this "episode" of the Inspectorate will allow you to understand the power, the means, and the system that Freemasonry still commands, whether its agents are conscious or not.

"It is enough for me to tell you that since the March [on Rome], except for the Council, the Head of State has always had a Freemason as his secretary, and a Freemason has always been head of the Presidential Cabinet.

"For Freemasonry, the Inspectorate, given its aims and the person called by you to establish it, is enemy number one. Devotedly, Giovanni Preziosi." See ACS, *RSI, Segreteria particolare del Duce, Carteggio riservato (1943-45)*, file 166, *Preziosi, Giovanni*, under the file 3.

1220. ACS, *Min. Int., dir. gen. PS, Div. Aff. gen. e ris. (1920-45)*, category A5G, b. 63, file 230, *Ebrei, sequestro beni*.

1221. ACS, *RSI, Segreteria particolare del Duce, Carteggio riservato (1943-45)*, file 385, *Provvedimenti razziali, Appunti per il Duce*, by G. Preziosi, July 1, 1944, point I.

1222. See the *memoranda* "for the Duce" by G. Preziosi, October 7, 1944 (two) and February 9, 1945 (in G. Buffarini-Guidi, *La vera verità* cit., pp. 60-62). In the first of these memorandums Preziosi, after having protested because "notwithstanding repeated solicitations" the Ministry of Internal Affairs had only given him 50 cases out of 120 from Demography and Race, he hysterically wrote: "Now it is a question of "placing into safe-keeping" all of this documentation, otherwise tomorrow it will not be known who is a Jew in Italy and who is not. This documentation will end up like the Masonic documentation."

1223. ACS, *RSI, Segreteria particolare del Duce, Carteggio riservato (1943-45)*, file 385, *Provvedimenti razziali*, memprandum and accompanying letter dated Milan, June 28, 1944.

1224. During the same period G. Preziosi worked on preparing a report, on the theme "La parte del giudaismo nella massoneria, specialmente in relazione ai recenti avvenimenti italiani," for an important international anti-Jewish congress that the Nazis were preparing, and to which they had invited, besides Preziosi, also Farinacci (from whom, though, Preziosi had distanced himself and who, instead, passionately fought as a defender of the Freemasons). Preziosi's report should, according to what he had been explicitly requested by Rosenberg, "stand for the comprehensive position held by the congress and constitute part of the final communication to be circulated through the press." See ACS, *RSI, Segreteria particolare del Duce, Carteggio riservato (1943-45)*, file 385, *Provvedimenti razziali, Appunti per il Duce*, by G. Preziosi, July 1, 1944, point II; as well as (on the preparation of the congress) *La persécution des juifs en France ecc.* cit., p. 287.

1225. ACS, *RSI, Presidenza del Consiglio, Gabinetto, Atti amministrativi (1943-45)*, b. 64, sitting of April 16, 1945.

1226. The *Frankfurter Allgemeine* published the relevant documents. See "La deportazione di ottomila ebrei romani fu ordinata personalmente da von Ribbentrop," in *Il tempo*, April 6, 1961.

1227. On October 29, 1943, the headquarters of the SS and of the German Police in Italy communicated to General Tamburini, chief of the Fascist Police, the list of the Italian "staff liaison to the police and the Militia." See ACS, *Min. Int., Dir. gen. PS, Div. Aff. gen. e ris. (1920-45)*, category A5G, b. 63, file 229, *Ufficiali di collegamento della polizia tedesca con la polizia italiana.*

1228. See, for example, *Il processo alla Muti*, edited by L. Pestalozza, Milan 1956, pp. 82-86.

1229. The case of the Troiani family in Rieti is typical, three members were shot for having helped the Jews. For the same crime others were deported, very often never to return from the terrible German and Polish extermination camps. The case of the administrator of *L'avvenire d'Italia*, Odoardo Focherini, is typical; he was arrested and deported to Flossenburg, from where he never returned.

1230. See C. Francovich, *La resistenza a Firenze* cit., p. 116 (for other aspects of anti-Semitism in Florence, p. 112).

1231. See H. Morgenthau, Jr., "La responsabilità dei governi americano e inglese nella tragedia degli ebrei d'Europa," in *Rassegna mensile di Israel*, June 1948, pp. 105-15.

1232. E. Mussolini, *Mio fratello Benito* cit., p. 175.

1233. P. Caleffi, *Si fa presto a dire fame*, Milan-Rome 1955, p. 135.

1234. See G. Romano, "Una testimonianza sul 'capitolo' italiano al processo di Eichmann," *in La rassegna mensile di Israel*, March-April 1962, p. 243.

1235. Comunità Israelitica di Ancona, *Relazione del Consiglio d'amministrazione 10 marzo 1940–11 maggio 1946,* p. 6.

1236. On the German organization in charge of capture and deportation see L. Piccioto Fargion, "Polizia tedesca ed ebrei nell'Italia occupata," in *Rivista di storia contemporanea*, July 1984, pp. 456-73.

1237. It is impossible to establish precisely, the community from which this mass of deportees, belonged to both because of the loss or damage to some community archives, and because many of the deportees were raided in localities other than their original community or in some cases they were not registered in any community, also because the lists drawn up immediately after the Liberation, are sometimes incomplete without personal data indispensable to solve uncertain, or homonymous cases and Italian Jews are not always separated from foreign Jews. The numbers reported in the following table (compiled by Dr. Eloisa Ravenna of the Center of Contemporary Jewish Documentation of Milan, whom we wish to thank for her patient work) can only be a broad statistic:

Community	Deported	Returned
Alessandria (with Acqui and Asti)	31	1
Ancona	10	1
Bologna	86	2
Casale Monferrato	16	-
Ferrara	87	5
Florence (with Siena)	263	9
Fiume	258	22
Genoa (with La Spezia)	244	12
Gorizia	45	-
Livorno	93	15
Mantua	39	1
Merano	58	-
Milan	896	50
Modena (with Reggio Emilia)	14	-
Naples	12	-
Padova	50	3
Parma	23	-
Pisa	9	1
Rhodes	1,667	?
Rome	1,727	105
Turin (with Carmagnola, Cherasco, Chieri, Cuneo, Fossano, Ivrea, Mondoví, Saluzzo, Savigliano)	407	31
Trieste	620	17
Udine	4	-
Venice	212	15
Vercelli	24	-
Verona	30	-

1238. See A. Ascarelli, *Le Fosse Adreatine*, Bologna 1965.

1239. N. G., "Il 'pogrom' degli ebrei del lago Maggiore," in *Il momento*, Rome, December 28, 29, 1945, January 1, 5, 1946.

1240. See "Relazione del Presidente della Comunità Israelitica di Roma Ugo Foà, circa le misure adottate" in *Roma dopo l'8 settembre 1943 (data dell'armistizio Badoglio) a diretta opera delle autorità tedesche di occupazione*, reproduced in L. Morpurgo, *Caccia all'uomo!* Cit., pp. 110-29; and also in *La voce della Comunità Israelitica di Roma*, September-December 1952; as well as in *Comunità Israelitica di Roma, Ottobre 1943: cronaca di un'infamia*, Rome 1961, pp. 9-29 (in the same pp. 35-43, *Dal diario di R. Sorani, impiegata della Comunità di Roma nel periodo dell'occupazione tedesca*); as well as the autobiography of the then Rabbi of Rome (converted to Catholicism in February 1945) E. Zolli, *Before the dawn*, New York 1954, pp. 132-63 (very critical of the direction of the community) and, more generally, L. Picciotto-Fargion, *L'occupazione tedesca e gli ebrei di Roma*, Rome 1979.

1241. The most extensive reconstruction of the tragic episode is by M. Tagliacozzo, "La comunità di Roma sotto l'incubo della svastica. La grande razzia del 16 ottobre 1943," in *Gli Ebrei in Italia durante il fascismo* cit., III, pp. 8-37 and ID., *La responsibilità di Kappler nella tragedia degli ebrei di Roma*, in *Scritti in memoria di Attilio Milano*, Milan-Rome 1970, pp. 389-414. Unreliable, because of the factious polemic against the leaders of Rome's Jewish Community, is instead Robert Katz, *Black Sabbath. A Journey Through a Crime Against Humanity*, Toronto 1969.

1242. The document was introduced by the prosecution at the trial against Eichmann.

1243. In Trieste, in the building of the Risiera of San Sabba, from June 1944 until the eve of the liberation, operated the only crematorium known to exist on Italian territory. See C. Schiffrer, *La risiera*, Trieste s.d. (but 1966) and Ferruccio Fölkel, *La risiera di San Sabba*, Milan 1979.

1244. On the period of the Nazi occupation of Trieste, see S. Bon Gherardi, *La persecuzione antiebraica a Trieste* cit., pp. 187 sgg.

1245. For an overall view, see G. Mayda, *Ebrei sotto Salò. La persecuzione antisemita 1943-1945*, Milan 1978. Among the many studies of a local nature see, above all, other than those already cited by L. Picciotto-Fargion on Rome and of S. Bon Gherardi on Trieste, D. Di Vita, "Gli ebrei a Milano sotto l'occupazione nazista," in *Quaderni del Centro studi sulla deportazione e l'internamento*, n. 6 (1969-71), pp. 16-72; N. Irico-A. Mancinelli, "Vittime della speranza. Gli ebrei a Saluzzo dal 1938 al 1945," in *Notiziario dell'Istituto storico della Resistenza in Cuneo e provincia*, December 1985, pp. 90 sgg.; P. Pandolfi, "Ebrei a Firenze nel 1943. Persecuzione e deportazione," in *Argomenti storici*, n. 5 (1980), pp. 1-113; P. Sereni, "Della Comunità ebraica a Venezia durante il fascismo," in *La resistenza nel veneziano*, Venice 1985, I, pp. 529 sgg.

1246. On the life in one of these camps, that of San Dalmazzo, see A. Cavaglion, "La deportazione dall'Italia. Fossoli di Carpi," in *Spostamenti di popolazione e deportazioni in Europa 1939-1945*, Bologna 1987, pp. 356 sgg.

1247. On the camp of Fossoli, see L. Casali, *La deportazione dall'Italia. Fossoli di Carpi*, in *Spostamenti di popolazione e deportazioni* cit., pp. 382 sgg.

1248. On the camp of Bolzano, see G. Ottani, *Un popolo piange*, Milan 1945, pp. 109-13.

1249. See "Il racconto di uno scampato," in *Israel*, May 31, 1945 (by one of those arrested in the raids in the basilica of San Paolo).

1250. The "Colonia italiana libera di Losanna" and the relief Commission for the Italian political and racial deportees, greatly contributed to the relief work for the refugees in Switzerland. The Commission was headed by Luigi Zappelli and Angelo Donati also participated, who tirelessly continued his benevolent work in Switzerland. See Colonia Italiana Libera–Losanna, *Relazione sull'attività svolta (1944-45)*, s. l. nord., and also I. Silone, "Le 'Nuove edizioni di Capolago' e gli anni della guerra," in *Egidio Reale e il suo tempo*, Florence 1961, pp. 162-65.

1251. The life of the Jews was particularly hard in Merano (they were sixty or so on September 8, 1943) even if they could benefit from the humane attitude and the solidarity of the Italian population, had to, suffer that of the fanatical Nazi Germans, who actively collaborated in hunting down the Jews. Around fifty Jews were deported from Merano, only one whose life was to be spared from the Nazi camps.

1252. For one case, among many, that saw, apart from the local municipal authorities, also the carabinieri who were in charge of transportation to Fossoli, cooperate in the rescue of a group of Jewish children, see G. Funaro, *Vicende dell'orfanatrofio israelitico di Livorno dopo l'otto settembre 1943*, in *Gli ebrei in Italia durante il fascismo* cit., I, pp. 72-77.

1253. A. Strazzera Permociani, *Umanità ed eroismo nella vita segreta di Regina Coeli* cit., *passim* and particularly p. 211.

1254. A. Segre, *Memorie di vita ebraica* cit., pp.312-14.

1255. A. Segre, *Memorie di vita ebraica* cit., pp. 315 sgg.

1256. G. Sacerdoti, *Ricordi di un ebreo bolognese. Illusioni e delusioni 1929-1945*, Rome 1983.

1257. See D. Tardini, *Pio XII,* Rome 1960, p. 164.

1258. F. Cavalli, "Il Vaticano e la guerra: 1939-1940," in *La civiltà cattolica*, 1960, issue 2651, pp. 513-14; ID., "Pio XII visto da vicino," in *La civiltà cattolica*, 1960, issue 2636, p. 166.

1259. See P. Duclos, *Le Vatican et la seconde guerre mondiale. Action doctrinale et diplomatique en faveur de la paix*, Paris 1955, pp. 189-90; the most important passages regarding our case have been reproduced under the title of "La razzia degli ebrei del 16 ottobre a Roma," in *Israel*, October 29, 1959.

1260. P. Duclos, *Le Vatican et la seconde guerre mondiale* cit., p. 190.

1261. L. Poliakov, *Il nazismo e lo sterminio degli ebrei* cit., p. 385.

1262. *Ibid.*; Weizsäcker's telegram is reproduced also in (in original text) G. Schoenberner, *Der gelbe Stern*, Hamburg 1960, p. 108.

1263. R. Leiber, "Pio XII e gli ebrei di Roma 1943-44," in *La civiltà cattolica*, 1961, issue 2657, pp. 454-55 and above all, the recent R. A. Graham, "Il Vaticano e gli ebrei profughi in Italia durante la guerra," in *La civiltà cattolica*, March 7, 1987, pp. 429-43, which is based on an examination of the documentation published by the Holy See.

1264. This doubt is confirmed by the already famous report by the ambassador of Vichy, Léon Bérard, to Marshal Pétain in 1941 (reproduced in L. Poliakov, *Il nazismo e lo sterminio degli ebrei* cit., pp. 387-89) on the Vatican's reactions to the anti-Semitic provisions adopted by the French collaborationist government in June of that year. In this report Ambassador Bérard reaffirmed the Church's complete aversion to racist theories, but, when speaking of the behavior of the same towards the Jews, noted that, even though stating that one should be tolerant towards the Jews as far as the practice of their religion was concerned and even having frequently protected them against the violence and injustice of their persecutors, the Church, from the mouth of Saint Thomas, recommended appropriate measures to limit their political influence: "It would not be reasonable to allow them to run the government in a Christian state, and have Catholics under their authority. It is, therefore, legitimate to forbid their access to public administration as well as to proportionately limit their attendance at universities (numerus clausus) and in the professions." In conclusion, Bérard stated: "As an authorized person told me in the Vatican, we will not be criticized because of the Jewish charter"; it was enough that the legislation of Vichy did not contemplate any provision "touchant au mariage" [concerning marriage] and that in the application of anti-Semitic laws, principles of justice and charity were taken into account.

1265. M. Michaelis, *Mussolini e la questione ebraica* cit., pp. 347 sgg., reconstructs and discusses the behavior of the Holy See in general, and in relation to the ghetto of Rome.

1266. AUCII, DELASEM, note dated September 12, 1941.

1267. See R. Leiber, *Pio XII e gli ebrei di Roma* cit., pp. 451-52.

1268. See in Document 40, the list, kindly procured by Father R. Leiber, of the houses and Roman religious institutes in which the Jews took refuge in 1944 (R. Leiber in his article, p. 451, mentions this list says that it was relative to 1945; it is, obviously, a *lapsus calami*).

1269. I. Viccari *Villa Emma* cit., pp. 28-34.

1270. See P. Zovatto, in *Il vescovo Antonio Santin e il razzismo nazifascista a Trieste (1938-1945)*, Quarto d'Altino 1977.

1271. See M. Leone, *Le organizzazioni di soccorso ebraiche in età fascista* cit., pp. 244 sgg.; S. Sorani, *L'assistenza ai profughi ebrei in Italia* cit., pp. 117 sgg.

1272. Notwithstanding this very precarious situation, in certain localities some small relief organizations to aid the Jews continued to function and even some new ones appeared, which carried out, within limits, an untiring activity. We mention the Jewish Assistance Commission created in Turin, in agreement with the CLNAI thanks to Raffaele Jona, Lia Corinaldi, Gino Giuganino, and Bruno and Giorgina Segre.

1273. Father R. Leiber, in his article cited pp. 452-53, justly recognized the great economic strain sustained by the Holy See and by the Catholic Refugees

Committee to rescue the Jews in Italy in 1943-45. Without wanting to diminish this effort, it must be said that the activity of the DELASEM, even when this was directed by Father Benedetto and other priests who, like him assumed the task of assuring the operation, was always paid for from the contributions of international Jewish organizations (above all the Joint and Sally Mayer), partly paid out in Genoa and in Rome by the old managers of the DELASEM to the new, and in part continuously flowing through American and neutral representations to the Holy See. See *Una lettera di padre Benedetto* cit., in which it is explicitly said that the money distributed was "all from Jewish sources."

1274. AUCII, DELASEM, *Attività della "Delasem" dopo l'8 settembre 1943.*

1275. See the complete list with the explanations of the twenty-three who were decorated with a gold medal in *Il popolo del lunedì*, April 18, 1955, as well as, for the activity of the DELASEM, the report by Father Benedetto kindly supplied by Dr. S. Sorani, in Document 41.

1276. See M. Sarfatti, "Dopo l'8 settembre: gli ebrei e la rete confinaria italo-svizzera," in *La rassegna mensile di Israele*, January-June 1981, pp. 150-73.

1277. M. Sarfatti, "Il 'Comitato di soccorso per i deportati politici e razziali' di Losanna (1944-1945), in *Ricerche storiche*, May-December 1979, pp. 463-83.

1278. E. Signori, *La Svizzera e i fuorusciti italiani. Aspetti e problemi dell'emigrazione politica 1943-1945*, Milan 1983; M. Toscano, *Gli ebrei in Italia dall'emancipazione alle persecuzioni* cit., pp. 937-43.

1279. See L. Picciotto-Fargion, "Sul contributo degli ebrei alla Resistenza italiana," in *La rassegna mensile di Israel*, March-April 1980, pp. 132-46.

1280. E. Soave, *Partigiani ebrei in Piemonte*, in "Ha-tikwà," January 1961.

1281. A. Gobetti, *Diario partigiano*, Turin 1956, p. 186.

1282. See P. Levi Cavaglione, *Guerriglia nei Castelli Romani*, Turin 1945, *passim* and particularly pp. 144-45.

1283. On the contribution of the Jews to the Resistance in Piedmont, see the articles by E. Soave, in "Ha-tikwà," November 1960-March 1961.

1284. *Lettere di condannati a morte della Resistenza italiana*, edited by P. Malvezzi and G. Pirelli, 11th ed. Turin 1966, p. 376.

1285. Cit. in M. Michaelis, "La resistenza israelita in Italia," in *Nouva Antologia*, October-December 1986, p. 243. Essentially in agreement with Valiani A. Segre, *Sionismo e sionisti in Italia* cit., pp. 207-8.

Documents

1.

Report on the draft of the legal decree on the
Jewish Communities and on the Union of Jewish Communities

The changes in the legal system of non-Catholic faiths, which article 14 of the law, dated June 24, 1929-VII, n. 1159, authorized the King's Government to execute, is especially necessary for the Jewish Communities, which are regulated in entirely different ways in the various regions of Italy, in that some of them are territorial corporations subject to public law, empowered with the right to levy taxes upon their members, others are non-profit organizations, others are simply associations.

The legislation now in force regulates in many different ways the organization of each community and its functions, because, while the Sardinian law of July 4, 1857, n. 2325, limits the Jewish Communities to worship and religious education—with the exception of the supervision of charitable institutions founded for the benefit of the Communities—while many other statutes attribute the responsibility of charitable activities to the Community.

There are therefore differences in oversight; since the communities subject to Sardinian law undergo almost the same set of controls exerted in the municipalities, the others are subject to the regulations of charitable institutions, and those set up as non-profit organizations, or lacking official recognition, are not subjected to any form of supervision whatsoever.

The proposed draft of the legal decree accounts for the integration of the legislation on Jewish communities, establishing a uniform regulations and control system for them, in compliance with modern public law which provides that all forms of activities, especially those that are of a collective nature, are subject to the authority and strict supervision of the State.

The legal system chosen is essentially based on the Sardinian law of 1857, which regulates the Jewish communities with a criterion of thoroughness, roughly based on municipal and provincial laws regulating municipalities. It has been decided not to adopt the Austrian legal system, enforced in the new provinces, which is restricted to the fundamental laws, thus allowing the communities, broad autonomy to set up their own statute.

The proposed draft of the legal decree maintains the basic autonomy of the single communities that only recently adopted a voluntary Consortium incorporated as a non-profit organization by the Royal decree of May 6, 1920, n. 611. It was decided not to adopt the legal system in force in other countries such as

France, according to which, all the Jews of the state form a single corporation that includes the local Communities with limited autonomy.

Furthermore, without prejudice to the legal autonomy of each Community, which is in line with Italian tradition, the recognition of the Union of Italy's Jewish Communities as a compulsory Federation was suggested, thus complying with the general interests of Italian Jewry and at the same time allowing it to be the sole representative to the Government. This provision also takes into account the penetration in the Eastern basin of the Mediterranean, which gives access to a large number of Jewish groups.

Concerning the administrative bodies of the communities, having adopted the criteria of concentrating executive and decision-making power in the hands of few persons, it was decided not to completely abandon the electoral system, since the activity of Community representatives mainly lies in the administration of contributions, a task with no political implications.

Recognizing the *necessary* character of individual communities, in the sense that all local Jews must become members, the question of belonging to the Jewish faith still had to be resolved. The accepted principle is that it is not possible to profess to be a Jew for civil purposes, and not wish to become a member of the community, thus refusing the financial contribution to the recognized body, which represents the supreme interest of the Community. Furthermore, as a token to the reaffirmed freedom of conscience, regarding the decision to cease belonging to Judaism, Jews have been granted the right to renounce their ancestral religion, not only by converting to another, but also by simply stating their will to no longer be a Jew.

According to the proposed legal system, the task of the Jewish Communities is to fulfill the religious needs of their members. These are: the practice of worship and religious education. The communities are allowed to make offerings aimed at charity for religious practices. They will also be responsible for administering charitable institutions, and all other institutions created for the exclusive benefit of the members of those communities, which do not have their own organization, as well as the supervision of those which have their own administration.

The draft of the proposed legal decree extends to all communities the power to tax the Jews, as prescribed by the Sardinian law dated 1857. This extension cannot raise objections as the desired ends justify the means. Facts show that not all Jews benefiting from the Community are willing to support its financial needs.

An important innovation is undoubtedly the obligation of all Communities to confederate into a union, which encompasses and represents the interests of all Italian Jewry. The transition from the present optional Consortium to the compulsory Union is in compliance with the modern trend, which supports the grouping of interests and corresponds to the State's preference for a collective organization. Of course, having recognized the compulsory Union of all Jewish

Communities, it is necessary to grant it, as was done for the individual universities, the right to collect taxes. The difference lies in the fact that while for the communities the taxpayers are individual Jews, for the Union the taxpayers are the communities.

An organization connected to the Union is the rabbinical Committee, which generally has the power of consultation and limited power of deliberation, within strictly necessary limits, to ensure the education of future rabbis. The rabbinical Committee has no power, not even disciplinary power, over the rabbis of the Communities. The reason lies in the preference to avoid a unified organization of religious components of Judaism headed by the Rabbis of the Committee.

The King's Government is confident that, through the proposed draft of the legal decree, the Italian Jewish groups subject to the same legal system under the control of state bodies, while preserving their Jewish religious traditions, will also be able to preserve their noteworthy artistic and cultural heritage and be active in compliance with Italian interests.

2.
Regulations of the Jewish Communities and the Union of Jewish Communities. R. decree October 30, 1930, n. 1731
(Official Gazette n.11. dated 15-1-1931)

Title I.
On the Communities.
First chapter. On the Constitution of the Communities.
Art. 1. The Jewish Communities are *non-profit institutions,* which fulfill the religious needs of the Jews according to Jewish law and traditions. They ensure the practice of worship, religious education, they promote Jewish culture, administer Jewish charitable and assistance institutions and of any other nature, which do not have their own organizations, supervise all those institutions having their own administration and safeguard local interests of the Jews in general.
Art. 2. The new law recognizes as Jewish Communities the Universities, Communities, Fellowships, Fraternal Associations, Jewish Associations and Societies, which will be included in a specific list to be approved by Royal decree, on the proposal of the Minister of Justice and Religious Affairs, in agreement with the Minister of the Interior, having heard the State Council and the Council of Ministers. The same decree will establish the territorial district of each community.
Art. 3. The creation of new communities will be established by Royal decree following the proposal of the Minister of Justice and Religious Affairs, in agreement with the Minister of the Interior, having heard the Union of the Communi-

ties in reference to Art. 35 and having heard the Council of State and the Council of Ministers. The same provisions apply to the union of two or more Communities and to the modification of the districts. In all cases, the Royal decree provides for the succession brought about by the modification or the closing of the Communities. The decree itself can prescribe that the property of the closed communities be devoted entirely or in part to matters of general interest to the Italian Jews.

Art. 4. All Jews residing in the territory of a Community have the right to become its members.

Art. 5. The Jew who converts to another religion or who claims he no longer wishes to be considered a Jew according to the present decree, ceases to be a member of the Community. Such statement must be filed with the president of the Community or with the Chief Rabbi, in person or by a legal document. The Jew who ceases to be a member of the Community according to the first clause, loses the right to benefit from the Jewish institutions of any community. In particular, he loses the right to ritual acts and to burial in Jewish cemeteries.

Second chapter. On the administration of the Communities.
Section I. On the Council.

Art. 6. The council consists of:

3 members for the Communities not exceeding 500 Jews.

6 members for the Communities not exceeding 1,000 Jews.

9 members for the Communities not exceeding 5,000 Jews.

12 members for the Communities not exceeding 10,000 Jews.

15 members for the Communities exceeding 10,000 Jews.

The function of counselor is held on a voluntary basis.

Art. 7. The right to vote for the election of members of Council is granted to all Jewish taxpayers who are of age and who have completed the cycle of compulsory education, or to those who, although not taxpayers, have obtained a rabbinical certificate.

Art. 8. The right to vote is denied to those who do not comply with the conditions provided for in art. 25 of the municipal and provincial law, the only text, approved by Royal Decree on February 4, 1915, n. 148

Art. 9. All male voters who are over 25 years of age, who have passed their junior high school examinations, or similar diploma, or have a rabbinical title and regularly practice their religion may be candidates to the council. Voters who are not Italian citizens become eligible only after having lived in the Kingdom for at least three years. The number of counselors who are not Italian citizens cannot exceed by one third those assigned to the council.

Art. 10. The following cannot be part of the Council: those who receive a salary from the Community or from the institutions which it administers or subsidizes;

their relatives up to a third-degree of relationship, those who receive—or those whose third-degree relatives receive—charitable subsidies from the Community or from its institutions; those who handle Community funds, who have pending litigation with it, who directly or indirectly participate in services, purveyance, or contracts in the interests of the Community.

Art. 11. Those who are directly related, or are second-degree relatives, cannot be members of the same Council. In case these are elected, the member who obtains the lower number of votes is eliminated by the one who has the higher number, and in case of a draw, the older candidate has priority over the younger.

Art. 12. Counselors are elected for six years. Every two years the Council is renewed by one-third. After the first and second two-year period following the general elections, the counselor or counselors leaving office, are appointed by blind vote. Outgoing counselors are re-eligible. If, due to a vacancy, the number of counselors is reduced to less than two thirds, the entire council will be renewed.

Art. 13. For assemblies to be valid, the presence of two out of three members Councils is required, and of half-plus-one members in other Councils.

Art. 14. From its members the Council elects the president and the other members of the Committee.

Art. 15. The Council has the following duties:

a) approve regulations concerning the various services of the Community and its dependent bodies;

b) approve regulations concerning the discipline of employees and workmen of the community, as well as its organization chart;

c) determine the tax-rate;

d) fix the taxes for religious services;

e) approve the tax roll and election-lists;

f) examine and approve the budget, the account statement and the proposals of transfers and withdrawals from the reserve fund presented by the Committee;

g) appoint, confirm and revoke the chief rabbi;

h) appoint, confirm and dismiss from service the secretary and the treasurer, when there is one;

i) appoint the member of the arbitration Commission referred to in art. 27;

l) elect the delegates of the sections, the administrators of the institutions that are part of the Community and do not have their own organization and the delegates of the Community to the Congress as referred to in art. 39, and in the Councils of those institutions in which it must be represented;

m) discuss all matters submitted by the Committee.

Section II. The Committee

Art. 16. The Committee consists of a President and a number of councilors equal to a third of the members of the Council. In those Communities with a three-member Council, the Council also takes on the tasks of the Committee. The Committee elects its vice president.

Art. 17. The tasks of the Committee are:

a) to file the entries in the tax-rolls and in electoral lists;

b) to establish the aggregate income, the taxable income and the amount due by each taxpayer;

c) to prepare the balance sheet and the statement of account;

d) to propose changes of in the capital account and the withdrawal from the reserve funds;

e) to appoint and dismiss religious ministers, teachers of religion, and all other employees with exception made for the secretary and the treasurer;

f) to supervise the institutions referred to in art. 1 and propose reforms and changes of purpose of such institutions;

g) to examine the statutes of public assistance and Jewish charitable institutions, and their financial statements;

h) to elect special Commissions;

i) to take all the resolutions aimed at pursuing the goals of the Community which are not among the Council's duties.

The Committee, in case of emergency, also decides matters, which are the province of the Council, provided that the latter is informed for approval, at the first meeting.

Section III. On the President and the Vice-President

Art. 18. The President of the Committee is also the President of the Council. Only Italian citizens are eligible for the presidency. The election of the President is subject to approval by the Minister of Justice and Religious Affairs, after having consuleted with the Union.

Art. 19. The President is the head of the Community and he represents it. The duties of the President are:

a) to summon the Council and the Committee and implement its resolutions;

b) to sign the money orders, the tax-rolls and the collection orders;

c) to control the revenues, the expenses and all the services;

d) to exert disciplinary power over the employees;

e) to appoint and dismiss employees;

The President, when necessary, makes the decisions which are within the province of the Committee, which benefit the Communities' interests, provided that the latter is informed of its approval, at the first meeting. In case of absence or impediment, the President is replaced by the Vice-President to whom he may delegate some of his duties permanently, or all of them temporarily.

Section IV. On assets, finance, and accounting.

Art. 20. The property belonging to the Community consists of the synagogues, the cemeteries, and the other personal property and real estate belonging to the Community. The synagogues and houses of worship which are not private property with their related ornaments are part of the possessions of the Community under whose jurisdiction they lie. In order to record the Community's possessions in the public as well as in the mortgage and land office registers, a tax-exemption over business transactions is granted, including land office dues and mortgage payments registrations for the relative documents.

Art. 21. The financial year begins on January 1st and ends on December 31st each year.

Art. 22. The revenue of the Community consists of:
  a) revenue from assets;
  b) income deriving from taxes and dues;
  c) the overall compulsory contributions of the members of the Community.

Art.23. The expenses of the Community include charges for assets and the necessary expenses for the achievement of its mission.

Art. 24. The contribution is due by all members of the Community according to their individual overall income, wherever it originates. The income of the wife is combined with that of the husband. The evaluation of incomes is based on the the assessment of direct taxation as well as from estimated income deriving from lifestyles or other external evidence. In establishing the income liable to taxation, the social condition of the taxpayer's family is taken into account.

Art. 25. Every year the Council of the Community establishes the rate of taxation to be applied to the taxpayers' incomes. A lower rate of taxation can be applied to those taxpayers who live in a different municipality than the Community's office. These taxpayers are therefore unable to enjoy all the facilities offered.

Art. 26. The evaluation of the overall revenue of each taxpayer, the assessment of the income liable to taxation and contribution, are to be decided by the Committee.

Art.27. The tax-roll, drawn up by the Committee, is published and deposited for fifteen days running in the Community secretary's office. Its publication will be posted on the billboard of the secretary's office and of the main synagogue. In case of a first enrollment or change, each taxpayer will receive written communication of the amount recorded on the tax roll. Within twenty days of publication or communication, the taxpayer may appeal to the Council to reject the Committee's assessment of the taxable income. Within twenty days from the notification of the Council's decision it is possible to appear before a Commission of three arbitrators nominated amongst the taxpayers: one from the Council, one from the claimant and a third agreed upon by the two arbitrators or, in case the latter disapproves of the person to be nominated, by the King's Attorney General at the Court of Appeals. No appeal is to be heard against the decision of the arbitrating Commission, except for an appeal to the judicial authorities and only in cases when the law has been broken.

Art. 28. The tax roll is established by the King's Attorney General at the Court of Appeals and is published for eight days in the manner prescribed in the first part of the preceding article.

Art. 29. The collection of the amounts assessed in the tax roll, takes place in the manner and forms established for local tax-collection.

Art. 30. The taxpayer who changes his place of residence or who, according to art. 5, ceases to be a member of the Community, must continue to pay his dues for the current and the following financial years if the tax roll has already been in force. As long as the taxpayer, who has changed his place of residence, continues to pay his contribution to the Community he has left, he is exempted from paying his dues to the Community to which he has transferred his new membership.

Third Chapter. On the Institutions administered and controlled by the Community.

Art. 31. The Jewish associations whose sole or main purpose is religious, are not subject to changes and are administered by the Jewish Community in whose territorial district they are located.

Art. 32. The proposals to reform the organic statute and the administrations, mergers and changes of purpose of Jewish public institutions of assistance and charity, can also be presented by the Community in whose territorial district the institution is based or by the Union of the Communities.

Chapter Four. On the Spiritual leadership of the Communities.

Art. 33. The spiritual leadership of the Communities belongs to the Chief Rabbi. He takes part in the meetings of the Council and of the Committee with an advisory vote. He must always be heard in decisions concerning religious functionaries and teachers of religion.

Art. 34. The Chief Rabbi must preferably be an Italian citizen. The Presidency of the Union must notify the Ministry of Justice and Religious Affairs of the appointment of the Chief Rabbi for its ratification. The appointment of the Chief Rabbi becomes final at the end of a three-year period, which has been devoted to religious practice in the same Community. If the Chief Rabbi, following a summons or a state examination, moves to another Community, he maintains his seniority and the right to the position already attained.

Part II.

On the Union of the Communities.

First Chapter. On the Constitution of the Union.

Art. 35. The Jewish Communities of the Kingdom, of the Colonies and of the Dominions constitute a compulsory Union that goes under the name of Union of Italian Jewish Communities. It is a non-profit organization which has its main seat in Rome.

Art. 36. The Union of the Italian Jewish Communities has the task of administrating and safeguarding the general interests of the Jews in the Kingdom, the Colonies, and the Dominions. In particular, its duties are the following:

a) represent the Community and Italian Jews before the Government and the public in all matters of Jewish concern;

b) ensure the continuity of Jewish traditions and the fulfillment of religious rites and general customs of Italian Jews;

c) ensure the preservation of historical, artistic and literary heritage of Italian Jewry, spread its knowledge and promote the development of Jewish culture;

d) exert, vis-à-vis Jewish institutions having general purposes, those functions which according to *Art.1* regarding local institutions, are to be performed by the Communities;

e) ensure the education of rabbis, religious ministers and teachers of religion, especially through the Italian Rabbinical College, which it administers, with the right to delegate this task to a Commission;

f) ensure that the Communities fulfill the tasks they have been assigned by the present decree and co-ordinate their undertakings;

g) settle the controversies of the Communities between themselves and between the Communities and their rabbis;

h) promote the authorities' provisions which are in the interest of the single Communities and of their institutions;

i) subsidize those Communities which do not have sufficient financial means, but whose activity lies in the long-lasting interest of the Jews;

j) participate in the general religious and social activities of Judaism;

k) maintain religious and cultural relations with Jewish Communities abroad; in particular with those which by tradition, have relations with Italian Jewry and with Italy.

Art. 37. The Union ensures the achievement of its goals by the following means:

a) revenues from assets;

b) contribution of the Communities.

Art. 38. The contribution of each metropolitan Community is determined by the overall taxable income of all its taxpayers, assessed by the Community of which they are members. The contribution of the Communities of the Colonies and the Dominions is determined according to the revenue of each Community.

Second Chapter. On the administration of the Union.

Section I. On the Congress

Art. 39. The Congress consists of the delegates of the Communities, elected by the respective Councils among those eligible candidates for councilor, except for the members holding office in the Council of the Union. Each Community has the right to elect a delegate; those Communities with over 300 taxpayers have the right to elect another delegate every 300 taxpayers up to a maximum of 7 delegates.

Art. 40. The Congress meets ordinarily every 5 years. Extraordinary meetings may be held whenever the Council of the Union considers it necessary or when a series of Communities representing a third of the overall number of the Communities' taxpayers demand that a meeting be held. The meetings are held in Rome. The Congress elects its President amongst the participants. The President acts as chairman of the meetings, moderates the talks, and certifies the statements.

Art. 41. Every delegate has the right to one vote; but if a Community elects a number of delegates inferior to the number it is due, the delegate or delegates actually elected have the right to as many votes as the number of delegates that are due to the Community.

Art. 42. Five Chief Rabbis, appointed with the title of Senior Rabbi, elected by the Chief Rabbis and by the Deputy-Chief Rabbis of the Communities, take part in the sessions of the Congress with advisory vote. The vote must be expressed in writing, according to the forms established by the regulations.

Art. 43. The Congress has the following duties:

a) approve the statement of financial condition over five year, taking into account the reports of the auditor on the financial statements of the Union;

b) discuss and vote on issues of paramount importance concerning Italian Judaism, which the Committee wishes to submit to its examination;

c) elect the members of the Council including the rabbis who are members of the Rabbinical Conference, as referred in art. 54, and the auditors as referred in art. 52.

Section II. On the Council.

Art. 44. Those candidates who are eligible to the post of Councilor of the Community are eligible to the post of councilor of the Union. The Council consists of fifteen members elected by the Congress and by three rabbis who are part of the Rabbinical Conference. They hold office for five years and may be re-elected. If vacancies take place during the five years, the Council is filled by co-optation. All members of the Council of the Union, including the rabbis, must be Italian citizens. The Councilor's office is filled on a voluntary basis.

Art. 45. The Council elects its own President, the vice president, and three other members, who, together with a rabbi, also elected by the Council amongst the members of the Rabbinical Conference, make up the Committee. The election of the President is subject to the approval of the Ministry of Justice and Religious Affairs.

Art. 46. The Council meets in ordinary session twice a year, and in extraordinary session each time the Committee considers it necessary or when at least 6 councilors file a request stating the reasons to do so. For meetings to be valid, the presence of at least 10 members is required.

Art 47. The Council has the following duties:

a) to approve the budget and the financial statement of the Union and of the institutions which it administers;

b) to fix the tax-rate of the Community towards the Union;

c) to appoint the secretary of the Union and fix his conditions of employment and dismissal as well as of other employees and Union staff;

d) to discuss all issues filed by the Committee.

Art. 48. The budget of the Union, approved by the Council, is communicated to the Communities. These may communicate their remarks to the Union's President within 15 days from the date of receipt. After this period, the President, having heard the Council, when necessary, sends the budget with the remarks of the Communities and the deliberations of the Council to the Minister of Justice and Religious Affairs for its ratification.

Section III. On the Committee

Art. 49. The Committee meets regularly once a month, but it can be summoned by the President whenever he considers it necessary. The meetings are valid when at least four members are present.

Art. 50. The Committee has the following duties:

a) to implement the decisions of the Congress and the Council;

b) to perform the assignments referred to in points d. and f. of art. 36;

c) to express its opinion in those cases where the law provides that the Union must express itself;

d) to appoint Commissions and entrust special assignments;

e) to perform all the necessary tasks to achieve the goals of the Union;

f) to take all those steps which are not within the provinces of the Council or of the President;

g) to appoint and dismiss employees of the Union.

Section IV. On the President.

Art. 51. The President of the Council is also the President of the Committee. He is the chief leader of the Union, he represents it, ensures the implementation of the decisions taken by the Congress, by the Council and by the Committee; he chairs and moderates the meetings of the Council and of the Committee; he appoints employees of the Union and takes the necessary steps to ensure the discipline of employees and staff. In the case of necessity, he carries the resolutions belonging to the Committee when necessary to safeguard the interests of the Union. These resolutions are subject to the Committee's ratification at its next meeting. Should the President be absent or unable to attend he is replaced by the Vice-President. He may permanently delegate to the Vice-President some and all of his assignments only temporarily.

Section V. On the auditors.
Art. 52. In every ordinary session of the Congress, three auditors are elected. They must be chosen amongst those eligible to the post of councilor of the Community. The incompatibilities established in art. 10 shall also apply to the auditors. If during the five-year period, one or more of the auditors is absent, they are replaced by auditors appointed by the Minister of Justice and Religious Affairs among those eligible for the post of councilor of the Community. They will hold office until the next session of the Congress.
Art. 53. Each year the auditors must examine the Union's financial statements, which are to be filed with the respective reports to the Union's Congress.

Third Chapter. On the Rabbinical Conference
Art. 54. The Rabbinical Conference of the Union consists of three members elected by the Congress amongst the five Chief Rabbis who stand as delegates to the Congress according to art. 42. In case one or more of the elected members is absent, the Council will replace him by choosing between the other two, and in case they are absent, the rabbis having the higher number of votes, after the five elected members, will be chosen.
Art. 55. The Rabbinical Conference must be heard:
  a) on all matters of general, cultural and religious interest. In particular, on the provisions necessary to the achievement of the goals according to art. 36 notes b, c, e, and m.
  b) on the appointment, whenever it occurs by summons, of the Chief Rabbi and of the deputy Chief Rabbi; on the dismassal of the Chief Rabbi and of the Deputy-Chief Rabbi and on the disciplinary measures against them, as well as on the disputes between them and the respective Communities.

The Rabbinical Conference is in charge of the disciplinary and educational supervision of the Italian Rabbinical College and of public institutions whose purpose is the schooling of rabbis, teachers of religion, and religious ministers.

Part III

On the Government's supervision and oversight

Art. 56. The supervision and the preservation of the Union of Jewish Communities, of the Communities and of its religious institutions, is the responsibility of the Minister of Justice and Religious Affairs.

Art. 57. In case the administration of the Union of the Communities, the Communities, and their religious institutions, should be dissolved, the government's officer for their temporary management should, if possible, be a Jew.

Art. 58. The general regulations of the administration and the organic regulations of the Community and the Union must be approved by the Minister of Justice and Religious Affairs.

Part IV

Provisions concerning the Community and the Union.

Art. 59. The members of the Council and of the Committee, who, for no reason fail to take part in three consecutive sessions, are dismissed from office.

Art. 60. Decisions are made by a majority vote by those present; in case of a draw, the president decides.

Art. 61. The secretary of the Community and the secretary of the Union are in charge of the administration of the Community and the Union, they countersign the cash orders, the tax-rolls and the collection orders. They take part in the sessions of the Council, the Committee, and the Congress.

Art. 62. The Chief Rabbis, the Deputy-Chief Rabbis, the religious ministers, the teachers of religion, the employees, the laborers and their families, must be granted by the Community and by the Union upon which they depend, an equal retirement pension, which shall not be less than the amount provided by law, to employees of local government units.

Part V

General and transitional provisions

Art. 63. By the same Royal decree, which approves the list of Communities recognized in accordance with the present decree, in compliance with the last paragraph of art. 3, regarding the property belonging to the institutions referred to in art. 2, now existing, will no longer be so recognized.

Art. 64. Candidates who occupied the post of councilor before the enforcement of the present decree are eligible to be part of the Council of the Community. Also veterans who reached the rank of officer may be re-elected even if without the school diplomas required by art. 9.

Art. 65. Claims by private citizens on ornaments in synagogues and houses of worship as in art. 20, must be filed, under penalty of cancellation, within two years from the enforcement of the present decree.

Art. 66. Rabbis and, in general, officers and other employees of the Community, who at present have no right to a retirement pension, or who have the right to a

pension which is inferior to what they are due according to the rules of the present decree, are admitted, following their request, to the retirement pension of the present decree limited to the part attributed to the Community. They may obtain the entire amount if they contribute the sum they would have had to pay. *Art. 67.* The Administrations of the institutions referred to in art. 2, now existing, are dissolved. The Attorneys General of the King, in charge of the district, will appoint for each Community recognized by Royal decree, as in art. 2 of the present decree, a government official, of the Jewish religion, to perform routine work and to ensure the drawing up of electoral rolls, according to arts. 7, 8, and 24 of the present decree. It is possible to oppose the decisions of the government official by filing an appeal, within fifteen days, to the Attorneys General of the King, who will then make the final decision. The elections of the Councils of the Community must take place within six months after the enforcement of the present decree. The Councils must draw up the new tax-roll within one year from taking office. In the meantime, contributions will be determined according to the obligations taken by the Jews vis-à-vis the institutions referred to in art. 2 of the present decree or according to the tax rolls of the institutions, provided that no additional rolls are drawn up.
Art. 68. The Administration of the Consortium of the Italian Jewish Communities, incorporated as a non-profit organization by Royal decree on May 6, 1920, n. 611 is dissolved. The Minister of Justice and Religious Affairs will appoint a government official, of the Jewish religion, to perform all the routine work and to ensure that the Congress of the Union is convened. The Union of the Communities will take over the assets and liabilities of the Consortium of the Jewish Communities.
Art. 69. All the provisions which contradict the present decree are cancelled. Within two years from its enforcement, the Communities will reform their regulations so that they comply with the provisions of the present decree.

We order the present decree, provided with the State Seal, be inserted in the official body of laws and decrees of the Kingdom of Italy, proclaiming that all concerned respect it and make certain that others respect it.

Made in San Rossore on October 30, 1930-Year IX.

Vittorio Emmanuele
Mussolini-Rocco-Mosconi

3.

[The Ambassador
to Berlin's report on Nazi Anti-Semitism]

Royal Italian Embassy
Berlin
Berlin, May 5, 1933-XI

To the Head of the Government:

Anyone who has followed the National Socialist movement over the past few years is aware that one of its main components is anti-Semitism. However, the latter underwent ups and downs, especially due to tactical changes forced upon the movement in its various stages. An important element of those changes was the relationship with the "Volkischen," initially united with the National Socialists only later to become their worst enemies. Regarding this connection it is worth mentioning the disputes between Ludendorff and some of his lieutenants, who accused the National Socialists of having neglected that very element of their original program.

The fact remains that several times during the past few years, the National Socialists, when asked what they intended to do with the Jews once they came into power, never gave precise answers, nor did they answer regarding the application of other sensitive points of their program. On the other hand, they frequently mentioned the elimination and expropriation of "bank and stock exchange Princes" and often made distinctions between "Ostjuden" [Eastern Jews] and other Jews, thus stating that future legislative measures were mainly aimed at those Jews who had not arrived in the Reich before 1914, meaning, against those who migrated there, mostly from Eastern countries, during the postwar period.

That category did include some less than savory individuals. Some of them constantly took active part in all major scandals that took place during the Republican regime: it is sufficient to recall Barmat, Kutisker, and Skiarek, just to mention the most sensational events. Many German Jews were the first to approve and support the measures against them, they who had always drawn a clear line of separation between themselves and the immigrants, whose bad reputation had frequently affected them in many ways.

From January 30 to March 23 (Chancellor Hitler's declarations to Reichstag) the problem was only officially mentioned in the famous speech by Göring in Essen, in which he said, among other things, that he did not intend to allow his police to protect Jewish stores and that Germans should learn to shop at German stores. The speech caused a great stir, but, compared to Hitler's declarations, which prohibited any individual intemperance, was soon forgotten and considered as a consequence of electoral excitement.

Hitler, in his speech of March 23, soon after having highly praised the two Christian religions, added that people belonging to other religions would benefit from civil rights and state protection as long as they respected the law.

A few days later, when asked a similar question by an American agency's correspondent, Hitler replied that in Germany, the Jews were treated exactly like other German citizens as a result of their behavior towards the National Government. Towards the end of March, foreign countries began publicizing the "atrocities." I was unable to verify the extent of this campaign. Some say that it did no go beyond the communist and social democrat press, i.e., the so-called anti-German press. On the other hand, this came about after the big actions carried out after the attempted fire at the Reichstag.

However, with impressive promptness, since this lead to believe that on the German side they were waiting for an excuse, Germany reacted to that campaign by fully launching its anti-Semitic campaign. The boycott of April 1 represented a barbarous and abhorrent event for the combination of bureaucracy and brutality with which it was carried out. It is true, though, that probably as a result of influential internal interventions, the boycott lasted only one day instead of indefinitely, as previously thought. It is true that some of the most economically absurd measures were canceled before being put into action, but it is also true that day had a symbolic meaning, in the sense that it shook, probably irreparably, faith in justice and the judicial systems of this country. One of the paradoxes of the event was that the notorious "Ostjuden" suffered less than the others. As a matter of fact, all of those, and there were many, who were not naturalized German subjects, or if so also had another nationality, were not involved in the boycott for the fear of complicating foreign matters. However, some shops owned by Polish and Lithuanian Jews were streaked with mocking and insulting graffiti, but soon after the intervention of the consular authorities of the respective countries, the same people who wrote the insults were forced to remove them. Meanwhile, many ex-servicemen and decorated veterans were insulted with words such as thieves, swindlers, and traitors.

Almost at the same time as the boycott, which temporarily forced judges, lawyers, notaries, doctors, etc., to stay away from their professional activities, the legislative action against the Jews began. It regarded the most wide-ranging "reestablishment" of the professional functionary, that is the cleanup of all public functions, with no exceptions, of "undesired" elements, basically Jews.

Initially, the Jews were allowed, at best, to have a representative body proportional to their number with respect to the German population, that is, about 1%. For instance, out of about three thousand Berlin lawyers, the number of Jews who were until now about 2,400 should have been reduced to 36.

In light of this situation, and some say because of Hindenburg's intervention, the question of Jewish veterans was immediately raised. Therefore, a fundamental principle of the new legislation was the fact that "non-Aryans" can carry out their professions and be allowed to enter or keep public functions as long as: (a) they had already carried out such functions or had become officials before August 1, 1914; (b) they had fought for Germany or for its allies; (c) their father or son had died during the war; and (d) they had not been communist or social democratic party members.

The relevant laws, under the full power provisions, had been published in the Official Gazette, therefore have become State laws. Consequently, they should have been entirely enforced. Such laws would have created a relatively acceptable base, at least as a temporary solution, even without considering some of their imperfections, and, above all, the general concept of "race" which is not only much criticized and difficult to apply, but also false, since its starting point is the "religion" of the four grandparents.

Their application was completely sabotaged by executive authorities, first of all by the governments of the confederated states, despite the political unification of the Reich. It is obvious that, especially concerning the paragraph regarding the servicemen, the writers of the law, prisoners of the cliché "Jews do not fight," calculated that only several dozen Jews would have benefited from the law. To use the example of the Berlin lawyers, from a complete, and even limited application of the law, more than 1,300 people would have been allowed, once again, to carry out their profession.

In the same way, the documented claims reached the Council of the Order, but the Prussian justice minister seeking to save the action, declared that he interpreted the law differently, in precisely the same way Hitler did. Without going into details of such interpretation he issued a bulletin in which he stated that claims required a lot of time to be examined and processed, and warned people not to make demands or to appear before the courts. Meanwhile, the examination continues its course and some say it will not end before September. Not to mention the chaos that this event brought to justice and naturally to the economy, above all because nobody bothered to think about temporary arrangements. And so it is in all other sectors of national life, except the banks, where nothing has changed until now, even if some say that soon the rules will also apply to them.

The school system focused its attention on the legislation. The aim of the new organization is to forbid to as many Jews as possible access to junior and senior high schools. However, the law envisages an exception regarding those children who were born from mixed marriages between "Aryans and non-Aryans"; as long as the wedding took place before the law came into force, the children can attend schools. Such attention is explained by the fact that the German aristocracy is strongly related to the Jews. In this case, the consequence of the strict application of the four ancestors' test was that a high percentage of noble families, officers and officials, etc., could not send their children to school.

It is not necessary to mention the moral and political consequences that the action, carried out with such little moral and psychological sensibility against the

Jews, has had around the world. Many people, who during the war, refused to believe those atrocities attributed to the "Huns," the barbarians, now stop and ask themselves if those accusations were really true. Even in Germany, many people also ask themselves what would have happened to the world if the Germans had won. The French conviction that the German anti-Semitic action was for France "a second battle of the Marne" is frequently mentioned.

The economic consequences of this action are already being felt and in the future will be far more tangible. Jews who have lost, or fear to lose their economic viability, hasten to reduce as much as possible their standard of living. Notices of termination of tenancy agreements, dismissals of personnel, coworkers, and domestic servants are more and more frequent. The most affected are artists, booksellers, and suppliers of every kind of goods, that is, many Aryans whose clients were mainly Jews. It is known, but obviously even the relatively independent press only just mentions it, that the boycott towards Germany regards the cancellation of orders, concerts, tours, and exhibitions of German artists. An ironically sad aspect is that the victims of this boycott are many shopkeepers, artists, etc., Jews that are boycotted from abroad because they are Germans.

Of course, all of this cannot help but seriously affect Germany's economy; the economic situation of the country cannot allow such dangerous experiments.

It would be appropriate to examine separately the contradiction between the constant unifying and totalitarian trend of the National Socialist regime and the desire to eliminate, according to a flimsy concept of race, which contradicts the concept of nation. The aim is to eliminate from the totalitarian structure at all costs a small part of the population, which was, whether they like it or not, already part of it and had lived the life of the German nation since its foundation, by participating in its wars, taking part in loans, paying taxes, etc. On this basis and without daring to speak of religion (since all baptized Jews should then be excluded from Judaism) the point is to establish discrimination and create a pariah category by inflicting a "second-class" treatment not only upon those who had been social democrats, communists or masons, or carried out an activity under their responsibility, but upon those whose only fault is to have a grandfather who was not baptized. In other words, and we should continuously emphasize this point, since it is impossible to define a race they go back to the concept of religion that is also said to be inviolable and that is also considered with some indifference since religion is said to be a private matter.

The practical enforcement of the new legislation with all its damaging aspects for the Jews, is already being enacted: the newspapers are repaeating every day the lists of professors and and instructors who have been dismissed from universities and other institutions of learning. The dismissal of lower level personnel is not reported, nor are the firings of the relatively few employees of private companies being publicized as imposed by National Socialist "cells" with their more or less self-appointed commissars that are terrorizing management. The Jews who have been fired are then denied any form of social assistance.

The few Jewish students who still attend courses at the universities are expressly excluded from the rights awarded by the recent legislation to all students, so that in effect they only have duties. Jewish teachers who are still working are boycotted by most students. At Goettingen, a famous Jewish professor of physics, Frank who received the Nobel Prize, was a volunteer in the war who fought at the front for more than four years, had every right to be kept in service but preferred to resign on his own. The "ario" Spranger, full professor of philosophy did the same at the Univeristy of Berlin. The great economist, Professor Bonn, head of the Berlin higher school of commerce is also among those dismissed among many other representatives of world science in teaching, research and especially the medical profession.

There have been many serious proposals, that will perhaps be applied only in Bavaria, to have Jewish medical students use only the cadavers of Jews for their studies or only sick Jews to practice upon. The latter should only be assisted by Jewish nurses. Another serious proposal is that should any German Jews write a book, it must be written in Hebrew (a language almost nobody knows), so that only translations would be published in German.

A town in Baden has decided that in swimming pools and other baths, Jews may enter only at determined hours, that is when Christians are not bathing. The list of rules could go on ad infinitum as they have been adopted and proposed which are often in at least moral contradiction among themselves.

It is not just the Jewish question that is worrisome in all this, even though one should take into account the political, moral and humanitarian side. What is much more serious is the situation of virtual ananrchy that has been created and that ends up precisely with that Bolshevism that National Socilaism claims it rid the civilized world which should therefore be grateful. It can be easily guessed what consequences all this will have on capital and investments; one often hears that anti-Semitism is just the beginning and that it will be followed by pure and simple anti-capitalism, extended progressively to one category or the other.

This goes to show how even to those who are well disposed towards National Socialism, and especially to them, what a gigantic mistake it has been to unleash this movement which is called "mystical" here and to excite the lowest passions of an often brutal and unreasonable populace. What is more serious is that the Nazi leadership, as true Germans, do not wish to admit and will not admit that they have made a colossal mistake that will cost Germany dearly.

Once one takes the path of cunning, according to the German frame of mind, it should be taken to the bitter end. With *Mistik* and *Gründlichkeit* they can go very far.

The future will show what the consequences of this mistake will be. The fisrt and only big mistake made by the national government whose members will have to bear full responsibility for. The government probably hopes that the world will get used to this and forget the violence, the desperation, the innumerable suicides that have been the result of this action and which are being reported constantly, while it remains impossible for the press to report them except in certain very noteworthy cases as for the suicide of professor Jacobsohn at the Univeristy of Frankfurt.

We hope this decision is not mistaken because the consequences would be serious not just for Germany.

Kindly accept, Sir, as Head of the Government, the expression of my deepest and devoted homage.

[Signed] Vittorio Cerruti

4.
[The Sacerdoti report on contacts with International Jewish organizations]

Jewish Community of Rome
Chief Rabbi
Rome, July 10, 1933-XI

To His Excellency, Cavaliere Benito Mussolini
Prime Minister
Rome

Further to the request to be received which I submitted to His Excellency's private secretary, I have been asked by the same to write a report on the conversations I held with some representatives of Jewish organizations during a mission abroad on behalf of the Union of Italian Jewish Communities.

Even if it is not always easy to write as efficiently as it would be to explain orally, I accept the request and I shall attempt to be as accurate as possible.

During the audience of April 20, which I had the honor to be granted by His Excellency, in speaking of the serious situation of the German Jews, His Excellency, after mentioning the steps taken in favor of the Jews with deep humanitarian sense and political understanding towards the German government, I feel once more the right to express all my gratitude also on behalf of the Italian Jews, while examining the even more serious situation since it was sanctioned by the legislative measures, which are aimed at eliminating the existence of the German Jewish Community, you stated your generous intention to intervene with the German government in order to try and convince it to re-examine those measures which have already been taken and present other measures which had been planned.

At that time, if I fully understood His Excellency, it was his intention to interact between the German government and the Jewish world, so that if the former changed it's attitude, the second would engage itself in keeping a well-disposed neutral attitude towards the new Germany.

While upholding all the generosity and grandeur of His Excellency's intention, and the historic importance of a similar event, I have to point out that the Jewish world, which is often spoken of, is something inconsistent or, perhaps better defined as nebulous: it is therefore difficult to speak on behalf of the Jewish world since it is not organized and therefore lacking representative organs, and it is even more difficult for me since I feel lacking in authority and influence, that only a few men operating in this vast world, beyond effective legal authority, are sometimes able to obtain from a moral point of view.

I therefore suggested Dr. Weizmann as the man who might have obtained, not only the ordinary, but also the formal assent from Jewish bodies of various countries and of all different classes. Therefore, I asked His Excellency to grant Dr. Weizmann an audience since he would have visited Rome on April 26, and Your Excellency willingly agreed.

I was not present at the conversation between His Excellency and Dr. Weizmann, but according to what he referred to me, I gained the impression that since he was worried about a vast migration plan, aimed at sending a great number of German Jews to Palestine, he was not sure whether to accept a task of even greater responsibility.

A few weeks passed before I knew if Dr. Weizmann, who then harbored a deep feeling of distrust towards what can be called Germany's international honesty, a feeling which I realized was widespread among French and British people, had done something to prove to His Excellency that he had the necessary elements to accomplish the highly just task.

Such a state of affairs was unbearable to the Union of Jewish Communities and it strikes my feelings, since as an Italian I am a great admirer of the Prime Minister's, and of my country's genius and I was willing to see Italy capable of facing, and solving, the Jewish question, which has been shaking the world for thousands of years; still, I do not have the slightest doubt that His Excellency, on that occasion, would have found the necessary way to solve such a grievous problem, my desire to see Germany's co-religionists return to their dignified way of life was dashed.

I ask myself, if by suggesting Dr. Weizmann as the one who could accept His Excellency's proposal, I was also influenced, apart from the awareness of my reduced status and high esteem of Dr. Weizmann, by the unconscious desire to shirk an undoubtedly serious and difficult task. Therefore, after having obtained the permission given by my colleagues of the Italian Union of Jewish Communities' Council of Directors, I decided to work at obtaining the assent of Jewish representatives of various countries.

While I was in Geneva during the discussion of the problem of Jews in Upper Silesia, and in Paris in occasion of a meeting of Jewish migration Committees, I met representatives of the British Jews' Board of Deputies, of the Consistory of French Jews, of the Alliance Israélite Universelle, of the Zionist Organization, and I even approached some directors of Agudat Israel, Jewish Association, which was founded in February 1919 and whose task it was to defend Jewish orthodoxy in the world against liberal modernist trends. I finally saw Dr Weizmann.

I only opened my heart, completely, with the Grand Rabbin de France, Dr. Israel Levi, with the President of Alliance Israélite Universelle, Dr. Silvain Levi, with the representatives of the Board of Deputies of British Jews, Lasky and Bentwich, and with Dr. Jacobson of Zionist Organization.

I confidentially revealed to them what His Excellency told me during the aforementioned audience, having started by saying that I could not guarantee that His Excellency still meant to carry out the action planned for April 20 and 26. I pointed out that circumstances can change every day in politics, and I asked them whether they would agree to support an action aimed at creating a situation allowing His Excellency to intervene, as planned, with the German Government.

Everyone felt the need to express their highest approval of His Excellency's project and to show their admiration for Italy's Prime Minister. Some of them were worried about the difficulty in achieving concrete results, others would have liked to inform their Government before giving their assent, which I could not allow; however, at the end of the conversation, everyone declared to be ready to use their personal influence in order to obtain, through local organizations and the Jewish press, a different attitude towards Germany by Jews all around the world, if the situation in that country returned to normal.

While Dr. Weizmann was engaged in obtaining the assent from the governing circles of American Judaism, and I committed myself to enter into direct relations with Agudat Israel's chairman, who has great influence on Jewish circles of Western Europe, it was decided that Dr. Weizmann would have written to His Excellency whilst I would have tried to talk to you in order to inform you of the measures which had been taken and to have indications for a further action.

The problem of the Jews in Germany is becoming more and more serious from a political, as well as a human, point of view. On the one hand, the possibilities of life for German Jews are more and more reduced each day because, while legal limitations according to which Jews are considered citizens only with regard to their duties towards the State and deprived of all rights, extra legal pressures frustrate the few possibilities of life left to them by law. On the other hand, the possibility to settle, in other countries, this multitude of people who mainly belong to the intellectual bourgeoisie, is becoming more and more complex. The crisis, which is spread everywhere, limits job possibilities for citizens of each country and therefore especially for foreign people.

In the event this takes place, trade unions of various countries are beginning to worry, and paving the way for the anti-Semitic campaign, which is spreading from Germany to neighboring countries.

Even Italy, where, until now, there has been no influx of refugees, is showing signs of alarmism, and some newspapers have already mentioned the need to fix a percentage for Jews who are allowed to carry out their profession and introduce the quota at the universities.

The pan-Aryan league, which a few months ago had already started its activity in secret, (in Italy, the engineer Vassileff was one of its emissaries during the final months of last year) is working more vigorously and preparing a congress organized, as far as I am told, by Mr. Fabre Luce, who is apparently the director of the new CIT office in Paris.

However, it is logical that, after having witnessed protests from the entire civilized world against the methodical and disrespectful application of its anti-Semitic program, which is always considered aimed at defending the Aryan race, Germany is looking for support in order to avoid isolation in various countries and is helping in every way the extremists of this pro-Aryan league, whose program is to eliminate non-Aryans (i.e., Jews) from Europe.

This is why the problem of the German Jews is becoming more and more international and therefore governments of all countries are worried, because they see how feelings of agitation and division are increasing in an already too agitated and divided mankind.

By confusing the concept of citizenship with the nation, and furthermore, with that of race, the peaceful cohabitation among citizens of the same country is becoming more and more difficult and, paradoxically stated by Rosenberg, it seems as if Germans have defended the Aryan race from the legions of Varus, who, according to the aforementioned author, were not made up of Aryans.

And if today, in Germany, Roman law is rejected as a non-genuine expression of Aryan thought and civilization, tomorrow we will see how the Bible, the Old and New Testaments, is going to be rejected as a genuine expression of the Semitic soul.

All this may sound absurd and fantastic, however, no one can tell where a movement, inspired by racist theory, might lead to, especially in a period when the world is more in the grip of a moral crisis than an economic one.

I am sure these dangers do not pass unnoticed to such a farsighted mind as His Excellency's; therefore they are surely given accurate consideration.

It is necessary to re-establish a condition of equilibrium in this area, not only in the interest of the Jews, who are aware of having contributed to civilization something of great importance in the past, and are sure of contributing at present as well, of being able to offer in the future new impulses to the moral and material progress of mankind, but also to the tranquility of all countries. This is a highly dignified task for Italy, Rome's heir, for which people, of all races and religions, were considered as citizens as long as they had such qualities, and therefore it must be faced by those, who like His Excellency, knew how to reconcile the Papacy with the Italian State, and overcome, in a moment of extremely serious international tension, through the "four-party Agreement," the condition of psychological war which follows physical war.

For this reason, trusting in His Excellency's deeds, since you are predestined, like all great mankind's dominators, from Alexander to Caesar and Napoleon, to understand Israel's soul and make it the element of general well-being, I thought to start an action, the accomplishment of which I would be glad and proud to co-operate using my most modest forces, but with great enthusiasm, as soon as His Excellency will be good enough to let me know that this is not in contradiction with His plans.

I am sure His Excellency perfectly understands that I am awaiting an oral or written reply, which will allow me to inform people, whom I had already contacted, of further events.

With unwavering devotion, I pay His Excellency, my respects.

[Signed] Dr. Angelo Sacerdoti

5.

Report on the conversation between H.E. Mussolini and Prof. Weizmann at the Palazzo Venezia on February 17, 1934

After the greetings Mr. Mussolini asked Mr. Weizmann what was the subject he was most concerned about at the moment. Mr. Weizmann answered that the question of German refugees was foremost on his mind. Without being able to forecast what may happen next, Mr. Weizmann can state that this year 10,000 German Jewish refugees arrived in Palestine, out of a total of 40,000 immigrants this year.

Mr. Mussolini was very much impressed by these high numbers.

Mr. Weizmann explained that the conditions of youths were the most bothersome: they are unable to accept the poisoned atmosphere that is breaking their hearts morally even more than materially. They all want to go to Palestine. But Palestine is influenced by the world situation and is worrisome for anyone who is thinking about world political problems. Mr. Weizmann feels that Mr. Mussolini is very worried about this problem and that Austria is the focal point of these worries. The Jews are apparently the main targets, but the truth is that this is an attack on Christianity. We are the point of least resistance. Today it is us, tomorrow it will be the British, the French, etc.

Mr. Mussolini replies that this is true and asked whether Mr. Weizmann has spoken with the Germans.

Mr. Weizmann reminded Mr. Mussolini what he had told him during their previous conversation that he doesn't speak with tigers.

Mr. Mussolini: You are absolutely right. In any case I absolutely want to support Dollfuss. We want to publish a communiqué of the three powers. It is difficult. The British are very slow. I am very pessimistic regarding the world situation. We are threatened by more than war—the total destruction of European civilization. The downfall can take place even without a war, through the victory of barbarism.

Weizmann: I know that there can be …[illegible word] between an Italian and an Englishman …[illegible word] a Frenchman.

I don't wish to be involved in these problems. Yet I am convinced that saving the world and civilization is a higher task than these passing conflicts. We must create a barrier against barbarism, and that barrier is called London, Paris and Rome.

The current leadership is "slow," but the younger British statesmen are different. They understand the changes that have taken place in the world. They have the same problems. They are the men of tomorrow. They must be prepared now.

Mr. Mussolini: I find your idea excellent, but coming back to Palestine you must create a Jewish state. I have already spoken with the Arabs. I think we can reach an agreement. The difficulty is the question of Jerusalem. The Arabs say the Jews should have Tel Aviv as their capital.

Weizmann: You have just stated a great idea. To me, even a small state is Archimedes' point of departure.

Mussolini: The importance of a state lies in its recognition by other states. Those nations (that are not crystallized as sovereign states) are born and die because the others do or do not do certain things. The existence of a nation is therefore in its recognition as a state, which is of paramount importance. But what do you think of Jerusalem?

Weizmann: One thing is absolutely certain: if Jerusalem does not become a Jewish capital, it cannot in any case be an Arab capital, because there is the Christian world. Jerusalem is the "meeting point" of three religions. But you must note that the sanctity of Jerusalem for the Moslems is a rather recent invention, whereas for the Jews it is the city of David and for the Christians it is the center of the Holy Land.

Mussolini: You are right: we must find a solution that will satisfy everyone.

Weizmann: I have always been very cautious as to the question of Jerusalem. We are now the majority in Jerusalem.

Mussolini: Is that possible?

Weizmann: Absolutely, and yet I always told my friends to avoid using this information precisely because it concerns Jerusalem.

Mussolini: You are very wise.

Weizmann: When we reach the point of concrete action, may I count on your support?

Mussolini: Absolutely.

Weizmann: Mr. Theodoli asked me what we could do for Italian interests in Palestine. I answered that right now we can do very little, but as we get stronger we can remember our friends. The Jews never forget their friends or their enemies. On the other hand I feel we may be able to be of service in England and shall prepare the way for collaboration. We can still do a small thing that I thought of as a trained chemist: we could help Italy break loose of the German influence in several areas of the chemical industry.

Mussolini: That's very important, the Germans want to grab everything. We have just created a Special Committee presided by Mr. Paravano and I would like you to contact him.

Weizmann: Should I tell him that you mentioned it?

Mussolini: Absolutely.

Weizmann: I could place at your disposal a whole team of chemical scientists of the highest caliber: men who are competent, faithful and loyal who have only one desire: to help Italy and damage Germany. If necessary we can also find the required capital.

Mussolini: That's really very important.

Weizmann: My wife and I would be very honored to have one of your photographs.

Mussolini: You'll have it tomorrow during the day.

Weizmann: Stay well. You look tired. We all still need you.

Mussolini: Thank you. Like you I want to continue working for a long time.

Victor Jacobson
(Translated from the French)

6.

[Mussolini-Goldmann meeting]

In 1934 when the problem of the Saar was in the news and when it was possible to forecast a German victory in the plebiscite after fifteen years of French occupation, the Jews from the Saar appealed to the Committee of Jewish Delegations, of which I was president, asking that organization to represent their interests at the league of Nations and to obtain, in case the Saar was to return to

Germany, the authorization for the Jews of that region to leave the country taking their possessions in French currency without having to pay the so-called "fugitives from the Reich" tax and other taxes through which the Nazis were practically expropriating Jewish emigrants. During the long negotiations on this matter for many months with members of the League of Nations, I had many dealings with Italy. At that time Italy was still loyal to the spirit of the League. The Italian representative to the international organization in Geneva presided over the Commission of Three entrusted with resolving the question of the Saar. The above-mentioned negotiations made it necessary for me to have a meeting with Mussolini.

I had another reason to wish to see the Duce. The Italian government and Mussolini in particular, were at the time far from any anti-Semitic prejudice. One example among many will prove this fact: about six months before my meeting with Mussolini, I was told that Austrian Chancellor Dollfuss, who was completely under Italian influence, was about to make changes to the Austrian constitution. I wanted, among other things to change the constitutional guarantees giving equal rights to the Jews.

I contacted the Duce through Baron Aloisi, the Italian representative to the League of Nations, asking him to ask Dollfuss to not reduce the rights of the Austrian Jews. The Duce then let me know that he had sent Dollfuss a letter through Baron Suvich, who at the time was Undersecretary of State of the Ministry of Foreign Affairs and was going to Vienna on an official visit, to ask he Austrian Chancellor not to reduce the status of the Jews. This news was to be confirmed to me by my Viennese Jewish friends.

However at the time we are discussing, during the winter of 1934, the relations between Mussolini and the Italian Jews were somewhat troubled. An anti-Fascist plot was uncovered in Turin. Most of the conspirators were Jewish students. That was the reason Mussolini was temporarily irritated at the Italian Jews. He had refused to meet with the Grand Rabbi of Rome, Sacerdoti, with whom he had always had excellent relations. My friend Sacerdoti, who was a member of the Executive Committee of Jewish Delegations, asked me to take advantage of my meeting with Mussolini to try to improve his disposition towards Italian Judaism. Sacerdoti asked me also to make it possible for him to be present at the meeting with the Duce to try and reestablish contact.

I requested from the Italian representative to the League of Nations for the courtesy of a private meeting with Mussolini. Very quickly I was informed that the Duce would be pleased to see me on November 13, 1934, at 5:30 p.m. and that Sacerdoti could come with me.

Before going to the Italian capital I had to go to Poland. In Kracow I took the express train to Rome. I was practically alone in the sleeping car. I remember a typical event at the Austro-Italian border. That border is very closely patrolled. All the various political blacklists were carefully consulted for each traveler to check whether he was not on one of them. The Italian border guard came to my compartment and asked me for my destination. I answered "Rome."

"How long will you stay in Rome," the functionary asked me sternly.

"About 30 to 60 minutes."

He was very surprised by this answer and said:

"What do you mean?"

"I have to meet someone in Rome and then, right after that, I'm leaving."

"And who are you meeting with in Rome?"

I answered quite innocently:

"The Duce."

The border guard looked stricken. He excused himself, gave a military salute and disappeared. It was proof of the magical effect of certain prestigious names and indicated how easy it is to dupe people when one has enough of a straight face to use well-known names.

Sometime later I had a similar experience in Vienna when the Schuschnigg government was cracking down on Nazi emissaries. The travelers were rigorously checked. On my way to Poland I stopped in Vienna for 24 hours. I was staying at the Bristol hotel. I was in my room for just a few minutes unpacking my luggage and about to wash my hands, when a policeman brutally entered my room and began interrogating me straight away:

"What are doing in Vienna?"

"Nothing in particular."

"Why did you come?"

"To meet with some people I know."

"Who are these people you know?" The policeman screamed out this question.

"For example, the Federal Chancellor Herr Schuschnigg."

"I thank you very much," mumbled the policeman, and he disappeared.

I arrived in Rome on the morning of November 13 from Kracow. I had a talk with the heads of the Jewish Community. A few minutes before 5:30 p.m., I was at the Palazzo Venezia accompanied by Dr. Sacerdoti. The reception with Mussolini was organized like a great theatrical set according to Max Reinhardt's technique. We reached the Palazzo Venezia, which was closed. We rang the bell. An officer came out and asked what we wanted. Sacerdoti showed the invitation and said: "Summons to the President of the Council for Doctor Goldmann."

The officer, who obviously knew about the visit, opened the door wide. We went in through a phalanx of soldiers and policemen in uniform. The officer took us to the second floor. There the same ceremony was repeated: a closed door and a booth that opens up. Same question and same answer. Once again the door opens and another string of puppets in uniform appears. Another officer took us up one more flight where the same charade was repeated for the third time. On every floor the word "summons" was cried out louder. That was how we reached the third floor where the Duce's famous office was located.

We were ushered into an anteroom with its walls covered with marvelous Renaissance paintings. One of the Duce's secretaries entertained us. He told us how the Duce, who suffered from stomach problems, lived on coffee and fruit. He made a suggestion:

"When you approach the Duce, he will welcome you standing up and will not ask you to sit down right away. If he is not particularly interested in you and feels that this an official visit he will not ask you to sit down at all and will dismiss you after a few minutes. On the other hand if he is interested, he will ask you to sit down and then you will be able to have a normal conversation with him."

I answered the secretary:

"I can guarantee you that he will offer me a chair."

The secretary laughed:

"How can you be so sure?"

I smiled back:

"He will…"

We waited for about twenty minutes, then the secretary took us to another waiting room. This one was filled with valets and policemen, one of them opened the door and an usher announced us.

We then entered Mussolini's famous room, a vast room where Mussolini was standing in front of his desk at the other end. It was about 6 p.m. and was almost dark. The only lighting in the room was a reading lamp that shed its light on Mussolini and kept everything else in the shadows. When we entered the room, Mussolini raised his arm in the Fascist salute. Sacerdoti saluted him the same way while I bowed politely. There were some forty to fifty steps to reach Mussolini. The good Sacerdoti was very excited.

I found the entire thing quite funny and as I reached Mussolini I mumbled to Sacerdoti: "It's very funny around here." Sacerdoti feared that the Duce may have overheard and was so frightened that he almost fell to the floor. Finally we reached the desk. Mussolini was dressed with a sort of studied negligence: gray pants, gray field jacket, with a belt. There was bowl filled with fruit on his desk.

The Duce asked me:

"Which language do you wish to speak?"

"French."

"You have asked for a meeting. I am happy to be able to meet with you and thank you for coming. You are making this effort for your people and one must do everything for one's people."

"That's why I'm here, Your Excellency."

"Which problems do you wish to discuss with me?"

We were both standing.

"Please allow me first of all, Excellency, to analyze the situation of the Jews today."

"I know it quite well because I am very much interested in the Jewish question."

"In that case I can shorten my presentation. A few words will be sufficient: before the war, millions of Jews from Eastern Europe were denied their rights. Today they have, no doubt, all their rights on paper, even the rights of a national minority. Yet, from the economic point of view, the condition of millions of Jews in Poland, Romania, etc., is worse than it was in the worst times of Russian Tsarism."

"I knew that the condition of the Jews was sad. But I did not think it was so bad. Aren't you perhaps exaggerating a bit?" (In saying this, Mussolini was staring at Sacerdoti)

"I would like to give you a series of reports regarding the situation of the Jews in the countries of Central and Eastern Europe."

Mussolini took the documents, leafed through them, then said:

"I promise to read all this very carefully. What I promise, I keep. I see you have a chapter on the Jews in the Soviet Union. Where do get this information? Did the Russians allow you to send a representative to investigate the condition of the Russian Jews?"

"No, but from time to time we obtain information from indirect sources."

"Messages written in disappearing ink?"

"What makes you think of that, Excellency?"

"I'm an old revolutionary and I know all the tricks of secret activity. Those were the days when I was writing messages in disappearing ink myself."

Mussolini looked at me and said:

He addressed himself to me and not to Grand Rabbi Sacerdoti.

"Won't you sit down?"

"After you."

"I, he answered as if he addressing a crowd, I prefer to stand."

"Have you read Nietzsche," I asked.

"Do I know Nietzsche! He's my favorite philosopher."

"Then Your Excellency knows, no doubt, that Nietzsche writes about two sorts of thinkers: those who sit and those who stand. Your Excellency is a standing thinker…"

Mussolini felt like laughing but the role he had adopted as Caesar would not allow that. He therefore repressed a growing smile.

"I'm not a thinker, he said vigorously, I am a man of action."

"Yet I hope you do think well before you act."

The Duce smiled broadly. I finally took a chair and sat down...

"What do wish to discuss with me?" he asked.

"Of the fate of the Jews in Germany, the problem of the Saar, the Jewish question in Austria, as well as the minority treaties and how Poland is applying them."

Mussolini grabbed a piece of paper and noted these points.

"Very well. Let's begin with the Saar."

First I informed Mussolini of the conversation I had that same morning with Biancheri. Then I described the situation of the Jews in the Saar. I said that a temporary protection of the equal rights of the Jews of the Saar, in case the Saar was reunited to Germany, was not enough. What was required was a permanent guarantee. I agreed that there were legal problems on that issue. But I also told the Duce of the second legal opinion by Bourquin and Hudson. The entire problem of the Jews in the Saar was based on principle. To allow the Saar to be returned to Germany without guaranteeing the rights of the Jews meant that the League of Nations approved German anti-Jewish legislation. It was in any case necessary to add a clause in the pact with Germany regarding the Saar, whereby Germany would allow the Saar Jews who wished to emigrate to take their entire personal fortunes in French currency.

Mussolini answered me:

"You want the League of Nations to do all this? You want the League of Nations to act? Are you so naïve as to think that the League could actually carry out anything at all?"

He then went into a tirade against the League of Nations that lasted two to three minutes. This monologue included one of the best theatrical repartees I had ever heard.

"What do you think, sir?" clamored Mussolini. "The League of Nations should act? The League of Nations never acts! It's a debating society, a senate of old talkers, who discuss, discuss and rediscuss endlessly. The Jews are intelligent people. You are certainly an intelligent man as well. And yet you expect some kind of production from that academy of long-winded men? The League of Nations only knows how to talk not how to act."

That was the conclusion of his "monologue."

"Yet Your Excellency himself, as a member of the League of Nations, does take action!"

"How do you expect me to act over there in Geneva, where fifty governments are playing politics? When I act I act alone. I have proved that in the Austrian question."

I once again mentioned to Mussolini that Italy had responsibilities for this question since Baron Aloisi was president of the Commission of Three to solve the problem of the Saar.

Mussolini answered as follows:

"I shall force Germany to allow the Saar Jews to leave with their money."

He took a large block of paper and a pencil, tore off a sheet and wrote: "Saar- Jews – Emigration."

"That's it," said Mussolini, "consider it done."

After that we went on to the Austrian question. I told Mussolini that I had met with chancellor Schuschnigg in Geneva. Mussolini knew it already. He asked me:

"What was your impression? Is he an intelligent man?"

"Yes I think he's very intelligent."

"Do you think he is a sincere Catholic?"

"I have never seen him pray, Excellency, and would not pass judgment on that subject."

"I am told that he is a very sincere believer. I have the highest regard for people who are sincerely religious."

I explained to Mussolini our concerns regarding the situation in Austria. I informed him of the anti-Jewish administrative harassment by the Austrian bureaucracy that were victimizing doctors, functionaries and other professions. I told him that Jewish public opinion was very worried about the Austrian situation and that American Jewish groups were ready to protest and that I had been able to forestall them for now.

Mussolini said:

"It is very much to the point on your part. These American Jews, just like the non-Jewish Americans, are always ready to clamor and protest and get involved in European affairs they understand nothing about. It was already the case with president Wilson and it is the same today: a very bad habit."

I told Mussolini that I felt any public protest against the Austrian government would be out of place. Yet we had to face a change in attitude toward the Jews in Austria. In this matter we placed most of our hopes in Mussolini. I recalled the memorandum the Duce had sent to Dollfuss some time before, guaranteeing equal rights for the Jews. Following his initiative, Dollfuss had canceled his plans. However, the danger for the Austrian Jews remained according to information I had received in Vienna.

"Would it be possible that Your Excellency could convince Schuschnigg that it would be bad for Austria to create a Jewish question and turn the Jews of the world against Austria?"

"I shall certainly do so. It is real folly on the part of the Austrian government, a government that has trouble standing up, to look for problems with the Jews. You may rest assured, added Mussolini, I am a friend of the Jews. We cannot accept that the Jews of Austria be attacked. Next week, Mr. Schuschnigg will be here. He will sit right where you are sitting now and I will tell him that I don't want there to be a Jewish question in Austria. Don't worry. I shall talk to him very seriously, you can count on me."

The Duce once again took a piece of paper and wrote down: "Austria—Schuschnigg—Jewish Question."

"Now let's talk about Germany."

I addressed the Jewish question in Germany and explained to Mussolini the reason why I had to reject some time earlier Mussolini's proposal to find a compromise formula to reach an agreement with Hitler. (To understand this part of the conversation, we must explain the following: about one year before the meeting, Sacerdoti came to see me in Geneva, he was very emotional. He told me that the Duce had called him and told him that he wanted to avoid a hostile position against Hitler by world Judaism. Mussolini wanted to broker an agreement between Hitler and world Jewry: "Bring me the Jewish leaders, asked Mussolini of Sacerdoti. "I want to find out from them what their minimum demands are towards Hitler." Mussolini had decided to get Hitler to agree on this issue. Sacerdoti answered him: "There are no Jewish leaders, the Jews are not organized; they are divided." Mussolini thought aloud: "Still there must be someone I can negotiate with." Sacerdoti answered: "You know Dr. Weizmann; but he is concerned mainly with Palestine. It would be best to be in touch with Dr. Goldmann in Geneva, he is the president of the Committee of Jewish Delegations."

"In that case go to Geneva, ordered Mussolini, and bring back Dr. Goldmann."

I had to explain to Dr. Sacerdoti why I couldn't come back to Rome with him. There were no conceivable formulas to reach an agreement with Hitler: "Tell the Duce that what we seek for the Jews of Germany is full equality of rights. The very notion of equality of rights demonstrates that on this issue there is no compromise possible. Either we have equal rights or we don't. There cannot be equal rights at 50% or 80%. If the Jews accepted a compromise with Hitler sacrificing the principle of 100% equal rights we would compromise the equal rights of all the Jews in other countries. If we sacrifice full equality of rights in Germany, we could no longer demand it elsewhere as well. Since Hitler will never recognize equal rights for the Jews, there is no basis for an agreement between Hitler and the Jews. However should Mussolini be able to get Hitler, having denied equal rights to the Jews, to refrain from persecuting them, it could moderate a bit the struggle of world Jewry against Nazi Germany. However, we Jews cannot accept any formula that would cancel full equal rights. That's why these negotiations would be meaningless." Sacerdoti transmitted this negative answer to Mussolini who was very displeased.)

I was referring to this episode and now explained to Mussolini why I could not accept his benevolent offer to act as mediator:

"I am defending the interests of all the Jews in the world. I cannot allow the principle of equal rights for the Jews of the rest of the world be curtailed for a hypothetical improvement for the Jews inside Germany. This is, actually, a permanent principle, just as important for future generations of Jews as for those today. We are an ancient people and our policy must not sacrifice the future of the people for a few small improvements for a small part of the current Jewish generation."

Mussolini listened to me very carefully and then explained:

"When Sacerdoti gave me an account of your reaction some time ago, I was very angry. Now I understand that you are right. You are an intelligent man and you do represent a great and eternal people. Don't be afraid of 'Herr Hitler.'"

Even though we were speaking French, Mussolini said "Herr." In any case, like any good Latin, he was unable to correctly pronounce the Germanic "h"…

"I know Mr. Hitler." (A few weeks earlier, the first famous meeting between Hitler and Mussolini had taken place in Venice.) "He is an imbecile and a good-for-nothing; an endless talker. To listen to him speak is real torture. You are much stronger than Mr. Hitler. In the future there will be no remaining trace of Mr. Hitler while the Jews will still be a great people… You and we," emphasized Mussolini (I didn't know whether by "we," he meant Italy or Fascism) "are the great historical powers. As for Mr. Hitler, he is a joke that will last only a few years. Don't be afraid of him and tell your Jews they must not be afraid."

"Hitler does have a fleet, an army, and a people of 70 million organized individuals. As for us, we are scattered. We have no fleet, no army and no power."

"All this is nothing," replied Mussolini. "I can assure you that you are more powerful than Mr. Hitler. The important thing is that the Jews shouldn't fear him. We shall all bury him. But you must create a Jewish state. I am a Zionist myself. I have already told Dr. Weizmann. You must have a real state and not the ridiculous National Home the British have offered you. I will help you create a Jewish state. The most important thing is for the Jews to be confident in their future and not let themselves be scared by that idiot in Berlin."

The conversation finally turned on the subject of minorities.

"Let me tell you openly and candidly. Poland's attitude worries us very much. We are well aware that the minority rights granted to Poland's Jews don't have any real significance. These rights are mostly theoretical, but nevertheless, they a certain guarantee as the legal basis for Jewish rights."

I quoted a statement by Sir Robert Vansittart, under secretary at the Foreign Office, who had told Laski: "The difference between the position of the Eastern Jews with minority rights and without them is the difference between hell and bloody hell." And then I continued:

"Poland intends to do away with minority rights. The declaration made by the Polish minister of Foreign Affairs at Geneva on the subject means officially instituting this policy the results of which will depend upon the signatories of the Treaty of Versailles. I am sure of England's attitude and almost as sure of France's. Yet I have no assurance as to your attitude, if you allow me to say so, for two reasons: in general you are not a great supporter of minority rights and then you are not opposed, in principle, to the revision of treaties. The question of treaty revision is part of high level policy making where we Jews do not get involved. But if we must revise treaties, it must be a radical revision, including addressing the Jewish question, in order to create a firm basis for our existence."

"Don't worry, sir. I am thinking like you are. The Polish gesture was due to megalomania. Poland would like to imitate me. She wishes to play the role of a Great Power. But Poland is not a Great Power: 30 million people, Ukrainians, Russians, Germans, Jews, it is not a Great Power. I will never agree to begin the process of revising the treaties by the question of the rights of minorities. Baron Aloisi has already made a statement about this at Geneva. I shall maintain this attitude, which is mine alone. If we must revise the treaties—a revision that I feel is necessary—then it must be complete and total and address the borderlines, the Hungarian question, etc. Should the Poles come to me on the question of minorities—which they haven't done so far—I will tell them: 'No! No!' You can rest assured, sir!"

"I thank you for this statement that clears up our apprehensions as to your position. Allow me again, Excellency, after all that you have said, to express my gratitude for your understanding of Jewish questions. As President of the Committee of Jewish Delegations it was very comforting for me to have received, since the beginning of the movement for a World Jewish Congress, the support of Italian Jewry. I thank you for the expressions of sympathy you have expressed to our movement. I hope Italian Judaism will be represented at the World Congress that we intend to assemble next year based on democratic elections."

"Dr. Sacerdoti, who is present here, is witness to my deep and enduring sympathy for the World Jewish Congress."

The meeting was over on these final words from Mussolini. I was about to stand up and pay my respects. But Mussolini asked me to remain a few minutes more:

"Can you explain something to me that I don't quite understand? The Jews are an intelligent, practical and realistic people. Why are there always and everywhere fanatical supporters of formal democracy?"

It was a tricky question. I didn't wish to antagonize Mussolini. I also could not proclaim my Fascist faith:

"There is first of all an historical reason. Oppressed people are always revolutionary, liberal and democratic. Democracy brought the Jews emancipation and equal rights. All Jews are naturally very thankful for that."

"I understand very well," said Mussolini.

Since the Duce appeared to be in a good mood, I used the opportunity to establish good relations between him and Dr. Sacerdoti:

"I took the liberty of coming accompanied by the Grand rabbi. He would like to speak with you about certain questions regarding Italian Jewry, if you will give him the opportunity."

"I shall be happy to do so since you ask me. But not today."

Speaking to Sacerdoti in Italian, Mussolini said that today's interview was for me and all he had to do was request a private meeting some time later.

One month later Sacerdoti was received by the Duce and good relations between the two were reestablished.

Before paying my respects I added:

"I shall ask you for another small favor. I would very much like the Stefani Agency, the official news agency of the Italian government, to mention this meeting you have been so kind to agree to, officially."

"Why do you need this? For your prestige?"

"Excellency, my prestige depends upon the opinion the Jewish people have of me. My request is for the following reason: it is good the Jews and the anti-Semites know that you have officially received a representative of the Jews and that you have seriously discussed Jewish issues with him."

"I understand that, and it shall be done."

He took another piece of paper from his agenda and wrote down: "Doctor Goldmann—Stefani Agency." The next day the agency published an official communiqué of our meeting.

"This conversation," said Mussolini, "was very instructive on many issues. Come and see me again when you need me."

I couldn't help answering:

"I shall see you again perhaps in Geneva."

But Mussolini responded:

"Me at Geneva? I don't attend that academy of fast talkers. It's a waste of time. I'm used to taking action and not wasting days in discussion."

"Very well," I said, "if you promise me to act for the Jews every time I speak with you, I shall gladly come back."

Mussolini smiled, pressed a button and gave the Fascist salute. I bowed and a secretary walked us out.

(Translated from the French)

7.

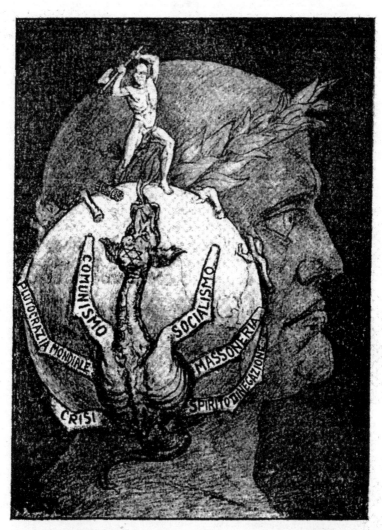

IL FASCISMO CHE SBANDA IL DISFATTISMO MONDIALE

È necessario comprendere che tutto il disfattismo mondiale degli ultimi duemila anni —
dalla decadenza dell'Impero e Spirito Romano per mezzo dello spirito di negazione, fino
alla generale degenerazione di oggi per mezzo della crisi mondiale — è un'azione dello
stesso autore, per andare alla ricerca dov'è la via della salvezza dell'umanità oppressa
spiritualmente e economicamente. Il Fascismo l'unico, l'ha trovata, e quindi vince.   S. F

8.

[Corrado Tedeschi's report on his mission in Palestine]

Tel-Aviv, February 6, 1936-XIV

His Excellency,

My mission in Palestine is off to a good start and my initiatives are being promptly carried out. This is mainly because I find the situation to be quite favorable, and also because of the good will and understanding of the people I met.

Needless to say, the group of Italian Jews that I encountered in Tel-Aviv, are enthusiastically Italian and Fascist.

I had three meetings with Mr. Meyer Dizengoff who, as His Excellency knows, is the mayor of Tel-Aviv, and a supporter of Italy, with whom I have already had good relations in the past. During these talks, I obviously kept strictly to the instructions His Excellency gave me. In brief, I told him that Italy, a country where there has never been anti-Semitism, is sympathetic to the Zionist movement. The Italian Government supports the de facto establishment of the Jewish National Center in Palestine, takes into consideration the effect of Zionism in the world, and appreciates its importance. Conversely, the Jews must logically realize that any movement in a Mediterranean country cannot neglect the importance of Italian policy: in short, not just England but also Italy is following and carefully watching all Mediterranean matters. We decided that it would be appropriate to begin with some positive articles regarding Italy, on behalf of Palestinian Jewish newspapers and hopefully also some foreign ones.

A member of the Zionist Executive was present at my second meeting with Dizengoff and we agreed that I would meet with the Zionist Executive in Jerusalem, where I shall pursue the initiative according to the plan.

I suggested to inform public opinion through Palestinian newspapers, that Italy will maintain a sympathetic attitude towards the Abyssinian Falasha and this idea was favorably received.

I had other talks with Mr. Ben Avi, a very good friend of Italy and Fascism, who told me that he personally knows His Excellency.

With Ben Avi it was agreed that he will write and publish articles favorable to Italy under his own name, and make sure that his journalist friends, Jews of various nationalities do the same, in the newspaper *Doar Hayom* and other Palestinian newspapers.

He and his colleagues would write in their articles:

1) That in Italy there have never been, and never will be, anti-Semitic movements, in order to deny biased news of Italian anti-Semitism, which has been published in Palestinian newspapers.

2) That the Italian press never sided against Jews of other nations, by accusing them of wanting to overwhelm Italy in the present situation. In this connection, a few hints were published by some newspapers (*Il Tevere?*, *Il lavoro fascista?*)—but Ben Avi and his colleagues will write that this is irrelevant and that if anything had been mentioned, it was without the Government's knowledge, since, the latter, on the contrary, makes sure that no such misunderstandings take place in the Italian press—proof is our policy sympathetic towards Jews in all of our colonies, especially in Rhodes and Tripolitania.

3) The assurance that the Italian Government will do its best to protect the Abyssinian Falasha in occupied territories and in those that shall be occupied in the future, making sure to educate them and make them good subjects. The hope, also, is to see their co-religionists, the Falasha, finally freed by a friendly power, such as Italy.

If His Excellency is not opposed to it, I would like to receive a reply on these three points. This way, without needing official or semi-official declarations, Mr. Ben Avi and his colleagues will be able to launch their favorable press campaign.

As Mr. Ben Avi and others have said, and this is a well-known fact, many native and revisionist Palestinians are potentially Fascist and could fully adopt the theory and practice of Fascism as their own, in agreement and in contact with Rome.

In this regard I suggested to wait for a quieter and more favorable atmosphere in the future; since I know that according to the indications I received from His Excellency, it could actually worsen the situation and be more negative than positive.

However, I believe it appropriate to re-confirm to His Excellency that most revisionists support Fascism.

I also had a meeting with Dr. J. Faitlovitch. As His Excellency knows, he has devoted many years and much activity to raise the levels of opportunity and culture of the Abyssinian Falasha. The meeting gave me the idea that the Italian government could do something useful by sponsoring a sort of tourist trip by a group of Italian Jews to the occupied Tigre [province] in order to convince the Falasha of the friendly Italian attitude towards its subjects of the Jewish faith. I am not making a suggestion, but only providing an indication in saying this.

Following what I have stated if we are tactful, there is suitable ground to enlist many supporters in favor of the Italian cause.

Naturally, I continue my work of approaching the various sectors of Zionism.

I hope His Excellency will let me know His opinion and His instructions in a letter addressed to me, at the Royal Italian Consulate in Jerusalem.

While awaiting Your reply, please accept, Your Excellency, my best regards.

Yours faithfully
Corrado Tedeschi

To His Excellency
Raffaele Guariglia
Rome

Jerusalem, February 10, 1936-XIV

Your Excellency,

I met Dr. Leon Cohen, secretary of the Zionist Executive's political department, at the Jewish Agency in Jerusalem.

I assured Dr. Cohen that I am certain Italy is friendly towards the Zionist movement, and that I believe that such an attitude can be very useful to Zionism.

Dr. Cohen discussed past events, mentioning a program transmitted by Radio Bari, which was pro-Islamic and not pro-Jewish, just to indicate that there had been no recent demonstration of friendliness towards Zionism on Italy's part. I asked him to not take into consideration the past, which, in many other circumstances, bears witness to my statement; but instead I urged him to look at the present and the future. Politics is made of current events, especially of today's attitudes, which will determine the transformation of the future.

I also asked him: Does Zionism feel strictly tied to England and does it intend to continue in that direction? Dr. Cohen (of the general Zionists, Weizmann, etc.) clearly admitted that it did.

Then I said that even if Zionism at this time is tied to England, one must acknowledge the fact that London's aim is not to help Zionism, but most definitely to protect its own interests.

London will eventually abandon Zionism or turn against it when it is no longer in line with its interests.

As a matter of fact, Zionists should not be intent on maintaining this or that friendship, but must seek the ultimate goal of national re-establishment. For this purpose, it would be useful to have a close relationship with Italy, without abandoning England's friendship. Currently, London holds all the trump cards regarding Zionism; a political monopoly, in effect, it may also take advantage, as it sometimes does, using a policy of equivocation and compromise. Simply stated, if England had to endure competition from Italy regarding the Zionists, it should then be much more favorable towards the Jews.

The logic of this argument convinced him. I added that the concept of a close friendship, almost a spiritual alliance, and the protection of Zionism by Italy, is, for the moment, purely a personal idea. But the fact is that a close collaboration in the future must begin with tangible facts in the present.

Italy, through its real gesture of friendship, is holding out its hand. And, on Italy's behalf, this is enough, together with the lack of any past or future hostility towards the Jews. The Zionists must know they should seize the day and hold out their hand. For this reason the Jewish Agency and the Zionist Executive must make a tangible effort by demonstrating sympathy towards Italy in the press, in all areas, including the Abyssinian matter.

Dr. Cohen attempted to retreat by saying that concerning foreign politics, local newspapers do not follow the Zionist Executive's suggestions. But I insisted that we must reach a conclusion. If journalists won't do it spontaneously, it will be necessary to urge Palestinian newspapers to publish pro-Italian articles, which the Executive itself will write and hand over. It was agreed to do it this way, by developing points in the articles, which I will gradually suggest. Finally, we agreed to activate these political lines, during a meeting between myself and some members of the Zionist Executive, among whom would be Mr. Shertok, head of the Executive's political department. I will give His Excellency all the details concerning such meeting and any further action.

I would like to assure His Excellency that my mission is being carried out with due caution, without wounding the susceptibilities of the various Zionist parties.

I would be honored if His Excellency would send me further communications, addressed to the Royal Italian Consulate in Jerusalem.

Please accept my best regards.

Yours faithfully,
Corrado Tedeschi

To His Excellency
Raffaele Guariglia
Ambassador of His Majesty the King
Ministry of Foreign Affairs
Rome

Your Excellency,

As soon as I returned to Italy on March 1st, I came to the Ministry of Foreign Affairs, without having the honor of finding His Excellency.

Further to my letters dated February 6 and 10, sent from Jerusalem, I am hereby informing His Excellency of the conclusions of my mission to Palestine.

I would like to just mention the Arab element, whose press is strongly hostile to Italy, often publishing completely unfounded articles. However, this press has a very limited influence and such little weight upon international matters that there is nothing to worry about.

Regarding the Jewish element, it remains necessary to distinguish between the various divisions of Zionism.

I had several meetings with some of the most eminent revisionists living in Palestine. I found them, in general, to be extremely cautious and worried after the painful measures of repression, imprisonment and the shutting down of newspapers imposed by the British.

They have natural affinities with Fascism and are friendly towards Italy, but as we know, are closely tied to their leader. The chances of success for the revisionists are much greater in other countries than in Palestine, where instead it is said that any action on their behalf would be easily overwhelmed by a strong reaction of the left-wing parties.

However, there are many Jews in Palestine who, even though they have contacts with revisionism, do not want to belong to that party. This includes thousands of people who are much closer to Italy and to Fascism, and who would easily and usefully support our policy of friendship.

Despite pessimistic views which I do not share and which I will later mention, if we so desire, these people could even be organized into a Jewish-Fascist movement. I, myself, would undertake the task of bringing this about.

However, even without going so far, these thousands of people could be able to carry out a series of positive actions for Italy, and their main representatives could effect a press campaign in our favor. They do not limit themselves to expressing good intentions and promises. Further to my talks, some of which I have mentioned to You from Palestine, Mr. Ben Avi published in *Doar Hayóm* February 21, a long article on the decisive Italian victory in Abyssinia. I am sure others will follow, as agreed.

Naturally, we could never reach great success in this part of Zionism if we do not operate properly: that is, without a follow up to my action of penetration and friendship.

Regarding the Palestinian left-wing parties, the so-called general Zionists, it is true that they are mostly tied to British policies, thus following its friendships and its international disagreements. And it is also true that it is necessary to carry out a clever, intelligent and active action of penetration and persuasion to make sure they draw closer to us as much as possible.

I don't share at all the pessimism, the "laissez faire" tendency that is widespread in some Italian circles, which are directly involved in the matter.

I refer to statements such as the following:

"They follow England's destiny. When England realizes that it is making a mistake towards Italy, they will also realize it and will automatically change their attitude."

"We must not give the impression that we intend to buy them at all costs."

"A mighty Power such as Italy cannot beg for the friendship of people like that. After all, it is not so important for us and we can also do without it."

As I mentioned in my letters from Palestine, I had tactfully agreed with the members of the Central Executive—who, whether we want to accept it or not, are real ministers—to start publishing a series of articles, that I would inspire, favorable to Italy, in general Zionist newspapers: *Haaretz* (liberal, Weizmann); *Haboker* (liberal but anti-socialist); *Davar* (socialist worker). Obviously, I did not want to insist and go too far without first obtaining His Excellency's approval.

Also in this context, Italian circles which are directly involved in the matter display a pessimistic attitude, believing that perhaps the typographers would suddenly get sick, or the equipment would break down at the last moment, anything to make sure that the articles would finally not be published.

I am dwelling on these details because I believe they are quite relevant.

A policy which is characterized by absenteeism, pessimism or contempt towards Zionism can still be carried out, but its results would surely be negative.

I wish to make three points:

1. Zionism is a force which is in the process of formation and continuously increasing.

2. In politics, it is necessary to identify future forces, since great results can be achieved without much expenditure, operating at a time when tomorrow's powerful forces are still weak and young.

3. The target is an effective collaboration and future alliance, or safeguard, or protection of Zionism by Italy.

Vast concepts could pass unnoticed by those who are not intellectually used to aiming so high.

"It is a diplomatic skill," His Excellency wrote, "which reveals its beauty to a few practitioners, but which is denied to common people because they do not understand the technique involved. The diplomatic technique has a special balance of the highest qualities of mind and heart and therefore may even escape the attention of those who are called to apply it."

Luckily, the high vision does not pass unnoticed to His Excellency, who has written such noble concepts.

On the other hand, the Honorable Coselschi informed me that he received orders not to get too involved in my mission, because one does not want to displease, for instance, the Germans and other Nordic groups with a policy of sympathy towards Zionism.

However, a policy of understanding and sympathy that welcomes the Zionist national reconstruction (whoever is familiar with the problem is perfectly aware of it) cannot irritate Germany and other Nordic groups. Obviously, it would be wrong to do so; we would lose the clear vision of the future and of our interests if we did not understand that any German position, or another power's positions will not stop Jewish power from growing.

Since His Excellency is such a profound expert I do not need to explain this any further.

In conclusion:

1. A policy of absenteeism and "laissez faire" cannot be fruitful. It is somehow necessary to operate to avoid being unprepared and absent from future developments.

2. Italy's friendship and eventual protection of Zionism can be extremely fruitful for Italy. English politics bears witness that England made well-known gains by protecting Zionism.

3. Such a friendship is possible, as shown by the results of my contacts in Palestine.

4. If one wants to benefit from the initiatives I have carried out up to now, it is necessary for me to return to Palestine and continue to implement, according to His Excellency's instructions, the policy that has been launched.

My respects,
Corrado Tedeschi

Via Ferdinando Paoletti, n.17
Firenze   March 12, 1936-XIV

To His Excellency
Raffaele Guariglia
Ambassador of His Majesty the King
Ministry of Foreign Affairs
Rome

9.

Anti-Semitic leaflet printed by British Fascists

Reprinted from " The Fascist," September, 1935.

The Duce and the Deuce!

What Counts in Italy

Mussolini Abandons Italian Fascism for Jewish Gangsterism.

HERE are the secrets (some of them) of Italy :—The chief financier of Mussolini's revolution was the Jew Goldmann, industrialist of Milan. His wife's two sisters, Jewesses, married the Director of the Commercial Bank of Milan, and the editor of " Secolo," respectively. An intimate of the three sisters was Signora Sarfatti, another Jewess, Mussolini's biographer and private secretary.

Signor Uceili (actually the Jew Vogel) is Director of United Co. of Italian Navigation which received concessions from the Jewish Soviet for transport in the Black Sea.

Mussolini's closest friend is Count Volpi, the Jew financier.

Mussolini's son-in-law, Count Ciano, Minister of Press and Propaganda, is an intimate friend of the Rothschilds.

Mussolini's Finance Minister is the Jew Signor Yung.

Signor Balbo's right-hand man is the Jew Major I. Levi.

"The Fascist" has frequently published instances of Jews in prominent public positions in Italy; for instance the Rector of Rome University, the Commandant at Turin, the Principal of the School of Economics at Milan and Expert on Financial Questions at Geneva, the Mayor of Trieste, and many Senators, Members of the Industrial Lower House, and Members of the Fascist Party and its Directorate.

But what counts, and what is driving Italy to war against Abyssinia in the hope that the Negro in Africa will be stirred up to rebellion against the Whites, is Jewish propaganda, and we have been in Fascism long enough to know that it is *many* which dictates policy with any political creed which is not basically racial like ours.

And perhaps the three most striking facts of all are that Baron Franchetti, who was killed in the recent aeroplane disaster on his way to Eritrea and who was Italy's chief authority on Abyssinia, was grandson of a Rothschild; that the General commanding in Italian Somaliland is the Jew Granziani; and that on his return from Geneva on the 4th August, Mr. Eden flew straight to Sir P. Sassoon's home at Hythe.

JOIN THE IMPERIAL FASCIST LEAGUE

30, CRAVEN STREET, LONDON, W.C.2.

Founded in 1928.   (A. S. Leese, Director-General).

No connection with Sir Oswald Mosley.

Subscribe to our Paper "THE FASCIST," 1d. monthly, 1½d. post free.
Annual Subscription 1/6 (post free).

Walter Whitehead, Printer, 22 Lisle Street, Leicester Square, London, W.C.2.

10.

[Final contacts between Italian diplomacy and Zionism]

Talks between Azkin and Mazzolini, April 28, 1938-XVI

Mr. Azkin, after mentioning the cordial relations he had with the Royal Embassy in London, which he praised for their hard and useful work and the kind interest shown each time he had the pleasure of meeting with the officials. He summarized, in the following list of facts and statements, the causes of the complaints regarding Italian behavior, which are widespread in the new Zionist environment.

1. The diplomatic correspondence communiqué which, although it confirmed the idea of a Jewish State, excludes the Palestinian venue.

2. The lack of any Italian gesture capable of arousing the sympathy of the Jewish world.

3. The cruise of the *Sara*, from the school of Civitavecchia, forced to fly the French flag instead of the Italian flag, which instead would have been of great propaganda value amongst the various Jewish communities around the Mediterranean landing ports.

4. Some articles published by our newspapers and the impression that an anti-Jewish movement is rising in Italy as well.

5. The decision to abolish the Sabbath by Libya's general government.

6. The campaign in favor of Palestinian Arabs on Radio Bari, considered as one of the forms of pro-Arab politics inevitably opposed to pro-Jewish politics.

7. Italian-German relations.

Mr. Azkin was told the following:

1. The communiqué of the diplomatic correspondence should have instead been the source of favorable attitudes from the Jewish world, since the need to create a Jewish State is clearly expressed for the first time. If it is true that this excludes Palestine, no other government is known to have made even unofficial declarations regarding the establishment of a Jewish State in Palestine.

On the other hand, everyone knows that much of the Jewish world is opposed to the creation of a Jewish State. Therefore, there is no reason why Italy is expected to do something that others never did.

2. What you mean by an Italian gesture, capable of arousing the sympathy of the Jewish world is far from clear. From time immemorial, Italy has been the only country in the world where Jews, although few, live in peace and at the highest levels, both material and moral. In Italy many Jews have held, and still hold, prominent positions; the Royal Senate has a Jewish representative in the person of Senator Isaia Levi in Turin; there are no poor Jews in Italy.

During the historic period Italy has recently lived through, the Jewish world made no favorable gesture towards Italy; the opposite happened with the mobilization of Jewish forces against Italy; it would be useful to see at least one, even remote expression of sympathy by the Jews towards Italy; they should be the ones making a favorable gesture towards Italy, not asking to receive one.

3. Regarding the episode of the *Sara,* one must consider Italy's needs and not just the desires of the Jews. Due to the attitude of many Jews, it was not expedient, at such an exceptionally delicate moment, to fly our flag at the risk of incidents. The fact that the *Sara* flew the French flag must not be interpreted as a gesture of hostility, but as a measure of precaution. The fact remains that if the ship was able to sail the Mediterranean, it is because of the school of Civitavecchia, which properly trained the officers and crew.

4. The articles published by the Italian press represent only a small percentage of what Jewish newspapers or Jewish representatives have written, and continue to write, against Italy without any justifiable reason. During the conflict between Italy and Ethiopia no Jewish voice was raised in favor of Italy. Even if ties with Great Britain were understandable, it was still, however, possible to remain neutral rather than taking a position against a country which has always assisted, honored and protected Italian Jews and foreign Jews residing in Italy.

It has been necessary to intervene several times in Palestine against the lies published by the only English-language Jewish newspaper, the *Palestine Post* and against the bias and slander repeatedly published by *Davar,* the voice of the Jewish community.

5. The matter of the Sabbath rest has been artificially inflated in order to foment anti-Italian sentiment. The Royal Government had to take the step of limiting the weekly rest to Sunday, in the interest of the colony and of the Jews themselves, who own numerous insurance agencies, banks, transport companies, and whatever else enters into the activity of Maritime services. But, before taking this step, it made an accurate investigation in all of North Africa, showing that in no country, Morocco, Tunisia, Algeria, Egypt, was the Sabbath rule observed. It was therefore rather curious that Italy was targeted in this case as well.

It is even more curious that no one thought of mentioning the many steps taken in favor of the Jews. In Italy, thousands of Jewish students from all over the world live and study free of charge: last year, at the Bari fair, a pavilion was created with three sections: Christian, Jewish, and Muslim, that provoked the greatest admiration; for fifteen years in Rhodes there has been a Rabbinical Sephardic college, which is still today the only one in the Mediterranean. No Jewish newspaper has ever spoken about these things.

6. The broadcasts of Radio Bari are another exaggeration. In the first place, they were not aimed only at the one million Palestinian Arabs in an anti-Jewish

manner, but to the other 399 [million] in the Arab world where Italy has important and perhaps greater interests than other nations. The Arab world never took a hostile attitude, as the Jews did; the news broadcast by Radio Bari was identical to that published in Palestinian and English papers. None of it was invented. And no one protested against radio propaganda in every country in the world during the Italian Ethiopian conflict.

7. Italian-German relations are part of general and international politics: the Jewish question is an internal German question. Germany has been close to Italy during the historic moment; while other countries tried to harm it. Italy does not forget, and knows how to demonstrate its gratitude.

These relations should instead be a lesson for the Jews and not a source of complaint. In international relations the factors that create them are multiple: the Jewish question cannot, in this particular case, dominate the others, and because of what precedes the Jews cannot demand it.

Mr. Azkin replied that he was not aware of these facts and was genuinely surprised. He asked what could be done to change this situation and to favorably influence Italian public opinion.

We replied that the Jewish world possesses men, means and instruments that already function perfectly for particular purposes and to the advantage of others. All that needs to be done is to employ them to Italy's advantage.

The preceding does not at all translate into hostile attitudes toward the Jewish world, but is only an objective explanation of the root causes of the complaints made by Mr. Azkin. It was necessary to examine such situations in detail, and not remain on the surface of isolated episodes.

Letter from Chaim Wardi to the Consul of Jerusalem

To Count Quinto Mazzolini
Royal Consul General of Italy
Jerusalem

Dear Sir,

I have the honor of presenting you a summary of what I discussed with you regarding changes in ways of thinking in recent months within the leadership of Zionism in Jerusalem.

Hostile sentiments towards Italy have practically never existed. There was a press campaign during the Ethiopian war and during the period of the Italian-British sanctions. With respect to this, the difference in attitude between Jewish newspapers and the *Palestine Post* should be highlighted. That campaign did not accurately reflect general public opinion, and even less the political opinion of the Jewish agency. The official circles of Zionism were always aware of the fact that only relations of peace between Italy and England could establish the necessary base for the continuation of their work in Palestine and for the realization of their political aspirations. Besides the escalation of the conflict between Italy and the League of Nations and the rise of dangerous Italian-British tension, the leaders of Zionism found themselves in an extremely delicate situation with the British Government. In London, it was said in some pro-Arab circles that it was perhaps necessary to give in to the requests of the Arabs, at the expense of the Jews, who, it was said, could not be relied on. Faced with such scheming, the Arabs found themselves obliged to make declarations that might lead one to believe that they had abandoned their usual position of neutrality, or constitutionality, so to speak, to take a clearly pro-British direction. Nevertheless it should be said that even in moments of extreme tension, the Zionists never committed any act which could have been considered hostile towards Italy, and the undersigned, who during the entire period, spared no efforts within the Jewish Agency for the need to maintain an attitude of absolute neutrality, often found acceptance and understanding at the political office of the Jewish Agency in Jerusalem.

There was only one moment of serious doubt: when a certain number of Italian newspapers launched an all-out anti-Semitic and anti-Zionist campaign. The Zionists, used to clearly distinguishing between the attitude of Fascism and that of Nazism towards the Jewish problem, were puzzled when they faced those apparently coordinated actions.

But very soon, once the campaign stopped, they had the opportunity to ascertain the true thoughts of the Government in Rome and, at the same time, the humanity and goodwill of Your Excellency.

The Italian-British conversations were followed by the Zionists with great interest and the agreements reached were welcomed with general satisfaction. The Zionists considered, actually, that if in an atmosphere of conflict they would have been unable to be useful to Italy, in normal conditions they would certainly been able to contribute to strengthening, and enhancing, Italian-British collaboration. Even before the agreements between the governments of Rome and London were concluded, the Zionist executives tried to reestablish contacts with the representative of the Italian Government; consequently, some meetings that took place between the Italian Consul and the heads of the Jewish Agency and the National Council, Mr. Shertok assembled all Jewish journalists to state the opinion of the Jewish Agency and invite them to abstain from any sort of comment capable of offending Italian sensibilities. Once the Italian-British agreements had been reached, the idea was raised in National Council circles to create a form of Zionist representation in Rome, to promote cultural and political relations and mutual comprehension between the two countries in contacts with the Italian government. It is certainly not without significance that, for the realization of that idea, the heads of the National Council had thought of the undersigned, noted in Zionist circles as an old friend of Italy and a firm supporter of pro-Italian trends.

The proposal has been forwarded to be studied by the political office of the Jewish Agency and in the meantime, seizing the opportunity of a trip to Italy, I have been asked to promote the idea mentioned above to the government in Rome.

With deepest respect,

Dr. Chaim Wardi
Jerusalem, 14-6-1938.

11.

(Summary of first Balbo-Castelbolognesi meeting)

The Jewish Community of Tripoli

The Chief Rabbi
Tripoli, February 19, 1934 – XII

Dear Councilor,

This morning I was invited to Government House where, receiving flattering precedence over many others, I was almost immediately received by His Excellency. During our half hour conversation, standing up, his tone was friendly and hopeful.

He told me that the attorney, Mr. Ravenna, is a friend of his just like the entire Ravenna family from the city of Ferrara, and had told him that Tripoli is among the best Italian communities, but added that they aren't Italians but rather Libyans. I answered that for that reason precisely they have been granted special rules and, since we were speaking in general, I said that I hoped to hear something regarding the question of the Sabbath. He answered me that at least for now, we have to avoid that subject. He talked about the silversmiths and his desire to encourage that art; he promised to pay a visit to the Fair at the Hara, and at this I replied that frankly, while thanking him, I was not very interested in showing him the folklore of the Jewish ghetto and recalled that the Turkish government regretfully had kept the Jews in the Ghetto right up to 1908. He added immediately: of course, that's only superficial, we are trying to delve deeper, we want to de-ghettoize.

Coming to the point of the Jews' loyalty, which I had mentioned, he said that, however, the Arabs had fought and died for Italy and that there was something rotten among the Jews and that he wants to do away with gambling; he has found out that many Jews gamble too much, that many 'failures' have been caused by gambling and that it would be best if it stopped. As soon as he said this, I replied that what is evil must always be uprooted and, as for gambling, I had already urged in two different speeches that gambling be given up entirely. We will insist on it, but legislation is needed, because I cannot do as was done in Benghazi and excommunicate gamblers, I am an Italian citizen and cannot fall back upon medieval methods; this made him smile broadly. He mentioned the possibility of granting the privilege of Italian citizenship to "upstanding heads of families" whose sons would be fit for military service and also mentioned his wish to concentrate on questions that would elevate this Jewish population, keeping, however, to general terms for the near future, without getting into any details. I seized the moment, given the tone and the general direction of the conversation, to return to the subject of the Sabbath and said that even today in Germany, school absences are permitted. He spoke out fiercely against the German persecutions and boasted to me about his mediation between Göring and the Italian Government, at which I repeated our gratitude in the name of us all.

But I added that, if I could consider myself no longer speaking to His Excellency as such but rather as one person to another, I regretted that a favorable solution could not be found for a question of such little import that would, instead, have had a most beneficial effect upon the Community and would have helped in the plan of cultural improvement. He answered that he had received orders that for now he was not to deal with this and that he is a soldier. I also told him that, in my view, the question would have had a certain political weight, since improving education in Tripoli could be useful and attractive as well as positive propaganda within in the Mediterranean colonies. He answered: Do you want to create your own school? To which I replied: Who knows? If you helped us! And he said goodbye to me very warmly asking me to come back at any time I felt it necessary.

In conclusion, therefore: a lot of sweet smoke; before we get to the roast, however, time will go by and many obstacles must be overcome, like biased attitudes, etc.

Mr. Bruno Hassan and Mr. Di Segni, to whom I described the conversation, were very satisfied...I was less so inasmuch as I would have liked to have better clarified the question of the Sabbath. Perhaps one of the *dajanim* is right and the transfer of the Headmaster should take place; he is probably the one and only cause; but who would be able to get this done?

Yesterday evening I went to the Sium Masehtà party and I must say that I did enjoy it; at the Yeshiva, which is a little on the primitive side, but is nonetheless a Talmudic Yeshiva, I received great *cavòd* and the speech, which I adlibbed, in answer to Daian Rabbi Hai Gazibon, who was the selected speaker, who made everyone very happy.

But I am awaiting the answer to yesterday's letter. H.E. leaves for Italy the day after tomorrow; I'd like to be able to do the same and to even to come back were it necessary. Shalom Ubrahà.

G. Castelbolognesi

Thank you for the copy of Mr. Ruben Hassan's letter. It is certainly too flattering. But no one here even dreams that I would abandon the community. A sudden call back to Italy with the promise to return is perhaps the best way out for everyone.

12.

[The Tripoli Incidents]

Tripoli, December 6, 1936 – XV

General Administration North Africa
to
H. E. the Minister for Colonial Affairs

Following what I have already told the Head of the Government and to Your Excellency, the ordinance which obliges Jewish-owned shops in the new city to remain open on Saturdays has been put into effect. Yesterday was the first Saturday that the new ordinance was to be applied. Several dozen shop owners were in violation of the prescribed rule, and almost all of them in the Via Gue neighborhood or nearby, where the more backward individuals have their places of trade.

Only two Jews had closed on Corso Vittorio Emmanuele, one a French subject and the other Libyan. Their licenses were revoked and the Libyan will be flogged as ordered by police regulations.

Everyone has been advised to show complete obedience to the law; there are about ten of them who have been responsible for disregarding this rule following an inquiry by the King's Attorney, and their licenses will be revoked.

The measure was totally effective from the start, considering that, with the exception of the above cases, all the shops along the main street stayed open and that most of those in violation had only shortened working hours or obstructed various commercial operations. A thorough inquiry to bring to light all those responsible continues, but I feel that I will have to substitute the Chief Rabbi since I have learned that he did not urge obedience to the regulation and that, in the past few days, he has received two telegrams from the Grand Rabbi of Jerusalem encouraging resistance and ensuring him of moral support. One can assume that without this encouragement, the episode would not have had much importance.

In any case, I will see that the ordinance is fully respected. While the most obstinate traditionalists may move to the old city and close shop on Saturdays to show respect for old religious teachings has not been undermined, the new Tripoli will appear decisively modern and Italian in accordance with our national customs.

Governor General
(signed) Balbo

****

Government of Libya
Department of A.E E and C.

Tripoli Dec. 15, 1936 - XV

Re: Working hours of shops and sales operations. Statement of the Union of Italian Jewish Communities.

To the Royal Colonial Ministry
Chief Administration for the North African Colonies
Rome

Enclosed please find a copy of the ordinance issued by the Provincial Police Commission of Tripoli n. 24558 of November 14, 1936 as requested by the above-mentioned Ministry in document n. 71117 dated Dec. 2, 1936-XV regarding the obligation of all shops without exception that are located in the new section of the city, to remain open for business every workday.

The ordinance, which this Government had adapted for Tripoli and that will be issued for Benghazi as soon as possible, is in accordance with Art. 2 of the outline of the R.D. accompanying note n. 63556 of March 21, 1936 inasmuch as said article reads that "the measure enacted by the Provincial Police Commission could take into consideration, if need be, the religious traditions and customs of Italian Libyan citizens" and therefore does not contain the obligation to respect these traditions.

In any case, it is good to emphasize that the measure, while leaving the traditions of the old city unchanged, is to be effective only in the neighborhoods of the new city, and will exclusively affect the business concern and not the people it employs.

Thus, the business concern may employ persons of a different faith from that of the owner in order to operate during days of religious observance.

What with the numerous Jewish-run shops closed on Saturdays and on the many Jewish holidays, frequently for several days in a row, the new city of Tripoli took on the aspect of a Jewish city, very similar to Tel-Aviv.

Therefore, a measure was called for to correct the situation, although it was limited to the new city, which has a prevalently metropolitan character.

It should be added as well that, before the ordinance became effective, Jewish-run shops were authorized to delay opening until 10 o'clock on Saturdays, to allow their Jewish employees to perform their religious duties.

It should be noted that the first day the ordinance was in effect, on Dec. 5, there were numerous violations making it necessary to resort to police and administrative penalties. There were two sentences of corporal punishment and twelve commercial licenses revoked. The following Saturday, instead, the ordinance was fully respected, which leads us to believe that the Jewish shop owners in new Tripoli are adapting to the living customs of their metropolitan co-religionists.

The Governor General
(signed) Balbo

13.

[Reply by the Union of the Communities to the attacks published in *Il regime fascista*]

Hon. Roberto Farinacci,
Editor, *Il regime fascista* - Cremona

As President of the Union of the Italian Jewish Communities, I have not replied until now to the articles in your highly esteemed newspaper, since I did not believe that, provoked by the "Nuremburg Indictment," which is part of the domestic policy of the German Reich and the treatment of the Jews therein, they could possibly wish to draw us into the dispute, when we have the good fortune to live in Fascist Italy with the indomitable pride of being Italian.

But since mention has been made lately of the Jewish communities, legally represented by the Union, due to a law that is of a noble Roman and Fascist stamp, may it please you to grant me the hospitality, which was in effect offered to me in your newspaper for the following, brief statements:

1) The Fascist Revolution, which is without precedent, and has no foreign precedents, was carried out and has triumphantly created the moral and millitant unification of the entire Italian people (the last test was just yesterday, before the entire world) and in this the Duce, in his great wisdom as a statesman and his indomitable zeal as an Italian, never once felt the need to distinguish between

race or religion within the living and compact unity of the people, among whom the Jews have always fulfilled their duty like everyone else.

2) It is highly unjust, besides being foolhardy, to deny this fact, under the pretext of its universal character, which the Jewish religion has in common with other organized religions and whose faithful have never been accused in this manner.

It is also an indication of complete ignorance of Jewish morality to imagine even an inclination towards tolerance of nihilistic theories that are the basis of Bolshevism and other similar madness, the negation of all human society.

3) Even more unjust would be to find reasons for an anti-Semitic campaign in Italy because of the presence of foreign Jews in one or another subversive organization and accusing us of a nonexistent co-responsibility; and in order to do this, conferring upon Italian Jews, who are fully recognized citizens and completely loyal to their country, the impulses and the animosities which might be understood in those Jews members of groups that are methodically subjected to extortion, harassed, stripped of every elementary feature of civilized life.

4) Within the limits of an assistance that becomes even more imperative as it becomes impossible to imagine it coming from elsewhere, it is intolerable that Italian Jews be blamed for offering relief and aid to their unfortunate and persecuted co-religionists. This aid has been organized publicly and internationally (and given diplomatic recognition by Italy) in the name of that Zionism intended to ensure a refuge in exile to those Jews who have been deprived of home and country.

Finally, the recent Geneva meeting (where the statement made by the Italian delegation won universal acclaim for Italy—in Geneva!—as a higher political civilization and a genuinely Roman nation, which would never repudiate its sons) was called and was carried out for the express purpose of studying the means to overcome the recurrent scourge of anti-Semitism; it would not seem that, by participating in the meeting with explicit authorization from the Italian Government, which received an official report of the position we had taken, our Union had in any way failed in its duties of complete loyalty and devotion to Italy.

With your permission, Mr. Farinacci, in conclusion may I say that it is particularly painful for us—and this more than anything else explains my dwelling upon the subject—that it is possible to ask us repeatedly for a new statement and renewed proof of our loyalty and allegiance to Italy and to the Regime; we have the right to consider these requests outrageous, wounding our deepest and most proudest feelings as Italians.

In thanking you, Hon. Editor, I remain yours most sincerely,

Felice Di L. Ravenna

14.

Memorandum [from General Guido Liuzzi
to Victor Emmanuel III]

In the spring of 1934 certain operations carried out by Public Security, particularly in Piedmont, which became public knowledge through the daily newspapers with excessive sensationalism, greatly disturbed the Italian Jewish Communities and particularly that of Turin, where numerous youths were arrested, and accused of conspiracy against the Fascist state. During the criminal investigation, almost all of the arrested were released, and in the end only one young Jew was convicted, receiving a light sentence. It all went up in smoke, blown with too much zeal intended to maintain reasonable security.

The Community became very uneasy, leading to the dismissal of the board of directors, to the appointment of a commissioner and protests by the Community of Turin against the Italian Jewish Community's Union, which had not proved to be a diligent guardian of those it administered in Fascist and Italian spirit.

Under those conditions the elections for the new Community Council took place in June, in Turin, from which this writer emerged as president.

The extraordinary circumstances obligated me to accept the post temporarily, to create a peaceful atmosphere of trust and security, in the area. With the support of the newspaper *La nostra bandiera*, I had proposed to exercise a spiritual Fascist action, purifying the Community of Turin of every trace of Zionism and hastening the sister branches to follow that example.

The Union of the Communities promptly began negotiations with me for the purpose of setting its actions in accordance with my intentions. The results of the said negotiations took place during the first days of 1935, with my entrance and that of two of my associates into the Union's Council. I personally took up a position in the Council and proceeded with a program for a new direction of the Union and the Communities, approved in principle.

But speeding things up during the following May, when I demanded the specific application of my program, and I realized instead that any previous approval given was of no value since it was opposed by the majority of the Council, I handed in my resignation as Councilor of the Union, prompting the resignations of three other councilors.

I believed it my duty to inform the Ministry of Internal Affairs via the Prefect of Turin of those resignations. At the same time I did not miss the opportunity to ask a few but frank and practical questions: my report, however, remained unanswered.

In March of 1936, seeing that my action, if it had been useful in placing a few other communities under Turin's leadership, was useless with respect to the Union, which continued to display apathy and incomprehension. I told the Prefect of Turin of my decision to step down from a position that I did not want to consider as ordinary business. But the prefect at the time begged me to not continue along those lines and advised me to renew the fight against the Union, whose officials he knew, were not well regarded by Rome.

Therefore, I followed this advice, and in May published, in all of the Communities, a pamphlet, *Per il compimento del dovere ebraico nell'Italia Fascista* [For the fulfillment of Jewish duties in Fascist Italy] in which I presented the summary of a complex program that to be enacted required new men educated and motivated by Fascist ideals.

A short while later the first anti-Semitic campaign began in the Italian press, generating much surprise among all Italians and considerable bitterness amongst Italians of the Jewish faith.

The following October, convinced that making the communities completely Fascist could have, quickly and logically, gained favor with the government, and having brought the anti-Semitic campaign in the press to a halt by an appropriate change of leadership of the Union, I arranged to personally send to the Duce an impassioned request for his interest along with an explicit proposal of my modest activity. But I did not receive a reply.

I then went to work so that the other Communities would also be informed regarding my program. And in January '37 a Committee of Italians of Jewish religion was created in Rome, concentrating the fight against the Union.

During that period the anti-Semitic campaign worsened.

The Committee, taking advantage of what had been written in various articles in *Il popolo d'Italia*, sent to that paper, and also to *Il corriere della sera*, a straightforward declaration by Committee officials, expressing the feelings of Italian patriotic spirit of all its associates: the declaration was published with favorable comments and received broad approval.

Finally, adopting more energetic measures, at the beginning of April, the Committee secured the collective resignation of the Union Council. At the same time it presented a request to the Ministry of Internal Affairs for a special Congress for new elections of the Union.

Indeed the Ministry immediately nominated a special commissioner, but then after approximately one and a half months following the resignations, asked the resigning Council to retract them, and reinstated its trust by doing so.

The Committee had to acknowledge in this manner that only at the next ordinary Congress in the spring of '38 would its Fascist action lead it to achieve the goal of giving superior authority to the Communities, which was necessary and desired by Italians of the Jewish religion.

It therefore persisted in propaganda activity. By now I became convinced that I could not count on the government's support and attempted to come to an agreement with the Union's president. But if at first there existed a basis for understanding, drawn up and signed, shortly after that the president did not and could not respect it. Since I was faced with a situation which was unyielding from every angle, I decided to withdraw from any activity whatsoever.

Regarding this decision I discussed the relevant events with Chief Rabbi D. Prato of the Community of Rome.

The Union of the Communities, despite many opinions to the contrary—mine first and foremost—had requested the nomination of the Chief Rabbi. Those opposed based their opinions upon the antecedents of D. Prato, his publications and his political ideas, which were certainly not in harmony with Fascism.

Actually, immediately after his nomination he was strongly attacked by the newspaper *Il Tevere*. And he shortly gave reason for complaint to the Community's Council because of some of his ways and some of his statements during religious and educational ceremonies.

During the meeting of December 5, 1937, which I chaired in Turin, the Committee of Italians of Jewish Religion examined the Prato matter and unanimously voted an agenda inviting the Council of the Community of Rome to proceed as soon as possible with the dismissal of its Chief Rabbi.

That Council, in agreement with the local Fascist Authorities, was setting up the recorded agenda, when the President of the Council was verbally requested by the General Director of Religious Affairs to keep Rabbi Prato in his position. The request, that was seen as an order, was executed by the President, who then felt obliged to resign from his position.

The new and recent attacks by the press against Rabbi Prato lead us to believe that the suggestion given verbally originated in a negative judgment different than that expressed by the Committee and the Community's Council.

In the same meeting of December 5, the Committee of Italians of Jewish Religion even voted to send a message to the Duce, referring to the increasingly cruel insults directed at the Jews, coming indiscriminately from the press during that period, without ever taking into consideration the feelings or the actions that have always been taken by Italians of Jewish Religion, in perfect harmony with all other Italians. It closed its message placing at the orders of the Duce a list of three people, chosen amongst the most worthy of its associates.

But even this message was left unanswered as well.

On March 21, 1938, the ordinary Congress of the Communities I.I., took place, which I was unable to attend, since I had to be in Udine, at the bedside of my son, an officer, seriously wounded in the course of service.

A list was agreed upon by those present at the Congress with the majority of Councilors (9) chosen in the Committee and the minority (6) old councilors, along with the President.

I had taken my name off every list.

Shortly after, regulations also took me off the Council of the Community of Turin. And, if later I had not been urged from all sides to attempt some sort of containment of the overflowing river of hateful threats, launched incessantly against all Jewish Italians by the Italian press; and if the resulting spiritual anguish of all our families had not been comforted by the general and unbroken support by our fellow citizens, I would have remained deaf to my duty of solidarity, since I was disgusted by the numerous precedents. I have summarized only the main events, proving the preconceived intention of not wanting to fascistize the small Italian Jewish sector, wishing to keep it as a possible useful target of future political requirements.

Despite many previous declarations to the contrary made during interviews by the Head of the Government, through the official press and in many other contradictory diplomatic statements, etc., today Italian Jews are outlawed and are called without impunity, by the most zealous of journalists, "twice foreigners in Italy."

What is their fault?

The only real fault today is supposedly being excluded from a purported Italian Aryan race. But it is a fault from which all other Italian citizens who belong to other races (Arabs, Slavs, Greeks, Albanians, Armenians, etc.) are exempt; and so the racial principle proclaimed in Italy acquires the aspect of a mask, used to give to anti-Judaism a logical and reasonable appearance.

The papers continue to speak of a Jewish anti-Fascist International; but I do not believe in the existence of a similar International, and besides, I absolutely reject to the participation of Italian Jews to anything like that. Because they are Italian, they are anti-Bolshevik.

Regarding this repeated accusation, and to avoid misunderstandings, I have to add that I do not consider the Zionist Federation as a Jewish International, approved by the governments with a fundamentally Jewish purpose, but instead as a charitable organization open to all men of any race or religion. If we speak of Zionism as a Jewish International, I must say that since 1935, through the Prefecture, I pointed out to the the Ministry of Internal Affairs the grave disadvantages to Italian Jews coming from the fact that the government, in many circumstances, made use of the most influential Zionists to handle international economic and commercial interests.

History, which should be a lesson for all mankind, unfortunately is conveniently systematically distorted to prove whatever needs to be proved. And history in this sense will presently be used at the inauguration of the academic year, placing the Judaic influence in our beautiful Italy, in a perfidious light!

Meanwhile, those outlawed cannot even use the newspapers, not even to announce their own death! They can no longer send their children to school with other children; they can no longer publicize their research; they can no longer efficiently carry out their professions; in short, they must resign themselves to having their families in continuous spiritual and material anguish, without any possibility of defense.

And, instead, all of this evil, that I do not hesitate to call downright persecution, is said to come from the absolute necessity to defend the Italian race!

15.

**[Bocchini's visit to Germany and the
agreements with Himmler]**

Report on the meetings with Himmler.
Rome April 4, 1936-XIV

The meeting of the Representatives of the Italian and German Police
Forces began March 30 at Gestapo headquarters, a large militarily fortified and
guarded building in downtown Berlin. Himmler, head of the Gestapo, welcomed the Italian Police Force in the name of the German police and with violent language spoke about the action of Communism, Freemasonry, and Judaism, openly attacking the USSR which is really responsible for what was occur-
ring in the world, and whose government directs the rank and file of the Communist Party.

The Italian Delegation cordially replied to that welcome, and even though
declaring the usefulness of a mutual understanding against the common danger,
limited its speech to communism as a political party, without mentioning any
governments.

The entire discussion as far as the Italian delegates were concerned, was
based on such criteria, while the Germans were focused on the Soviet Republic
and the Czechoslovak government, which supports it.

During the first day, the communist problem, the propaganda and methods
of Bolshevism, were discussed at length. The German delegates in particular
spoke about the theoretical part, the Italians about the practical aspects, for which
the Germans did not seem to be prepared.

On the other hand, they do not even know of the recent efforts that the
Communist Party has made for the establishment of a single front, nor the new
standards for legal work, nor what the border service does.

In the evening I had a long meeting with Himmler, to whom I pointed out,
as best I could, how to effect, on the subject of the anti-Communist struggle, a
collaboration between the two police forces.

The following day, March 31, the relevant discussion on Communism had
ended, we went on to Freemasonry and similar organizations.

The German delegation presented a very elaborate report on Freemasonry,
going back to its origins, and maintaining how Internationalism and Masonic
principals had serious consequences as much as Communism.

The Germans essentially attribute their military defeat of '18 to Freemasonry. They indeed maintain that German Freemasonry came from the Grand
Orient of France, hence the obligation of obedience to French policies. Freemasonry had even abundantly infiltrated the German Army, so much so that even at

670

camp, during the war, there were Masonic sessions, as demonstrated by some photographs kept in the Masonic Museum.

Besides, the former enemies of Germany constituted a Masonic coalition. Indeed, the King of England himself was one of the heads of Freemasonry.

Naturally they accuse the Jews, as the founders of Freemasonry, to want to control the world, the entire insidious plot against Germany, and the impetus to destroy German identity.

Himmler told me that he would show me very important documents and very serious proof in support of their argument. Indeed, he took us to see the Masonic Museum that the Gestapo is now arranging in another grandiose building of the German Police. It is a very complete collection of what has been found in the German Masonic Lodges, which have been outlawed two years ago. Other than all the furniture, there are the outfits, bits and pieces, numerous documents, going back to remote times, relevant to nominations and positions. But nothing that confirms the conspiracies to which Himmler alluded. The museum could undoubtedly be useful in the historic reconstruction of the Masonic Organization, but cannot explain recent events to which Germany attributes, as I said, the defeat of 1918, the same applies to the confiscated material could be usable to the police, with regard to the membership lists, but naturally only in Germany.

On the subject of Freemasonry, the Italian Delegation pointed out how Italy's position was very different from Germany's. Indeed, the two Grand Lodges of Italy have been closed for a good eleven years and the Masonic Lodges had been completely destroyed for the same length of time; thus Fascist penetration had succeeded in eliminating all Masonic presence.

Only a few dejected members remain.

The Italian delegation also revealed that there should be absolutely no concern regarding the one representative of Italian Freemasonry who attended the Masonic Congress in Brussels in June 1935 and that he had left Milan where he had returned after speaking at the congress, because the Italian Police knew all about the trip. There is a Grand Lodge of Italy in Paris of which the Grand Master is the noted Jew, Dr. Tedeschi, but that Grand Lodge has a purely symbolic value, inasmuch as it represents, within international Freemasonry a mass of brothers who in reality are nonexistent. The Italian Police actually very carefully controls what Tedeschi tries to stitch together in Italy and has already identified the persons within the Kingdom Tedeschi wants to be in contact with. On the subject of collaboration in this field, the Italian Police could provide Germany with a Masonic report, with particular reference to the matters that are of interest to the Reich.

After the general discussion on Freemasonry, the speakers talked about the organizations that supported it. The attention of the Italian delegates turned particularly to the "Rotary," an association that also exists within the Kingdom and that many eminent leaders of the Regime are part of. The German delegation believes that the "Rotary" is undoubtedly an association of a pro-Masonic nature and is used by Freemasonry for the penetration of delicate circles; in their opinion, it should therefore be placed under surveillance. It was replied that the Italian Police continues to handle single elements associated with the "Rotary," which, due to its political past or for other reasons, has not fully supported the Regime.

The discussion turned also to other affiliations of Freemasonry, J.M.C.A., Knights of Columbus, Sclaraffia (the latter has been dissolved for some time in the Kingdom), and the Italian delegation did not fail to call the attention to the dubious propaganda that the various Protestant Churches carry out.

During the course of the discussions, German delegates found ways at all times to insert lively suggestions against the Jews.

In their opinion the Jewish problem, besides being closely connected with the worldwide phenomenon of Communism, whose heads are, as a matter of fact, all Jews, and with Freemasonry, is threatening in certain aspects. Jewish Internationalism finds excellent allies amongst Communism and Freemasonry, which both deny the fatherland and, therefore, are violently opposed to nationalism.

The Italian delegation pointed out that the Jewish question in Italy has other characteristics, both because of the size of the group, which is irrelevant with respect to the population of the Kingdom, and also because infiltration of the institutions of the Regime and of the State is very small. In this area, as in that of Freemasonry, the Italian Police can supply Germany with a report of a general nature but, naturally, will keep it informed of all matters that may interest the Reich in particular.

The theoretical discussions included detailed visits of the technical plants. The files obviously make up the basis of all police work and the German Political Police have in their possession many files of the most modern kind. But since many of the things shown to the Italian delegation were of a statistical and theoretical nature, it was necessary to point out that the files, even though perfect, do not have those practical characteristics required for the measures employed by the police. For example, whereas with our filing system it is possible to immediately identify the political tendencies of the subversives and the State in which they have taken refuge (or the province for those resident in the Kingdom) therefore in case of emergency immediate action is possible–this is not possible using the German system. The use of graphs and synoptic tables is very widespread and may constitute an important element of judgment for the choice and implementation of police methods, although only when it represents the synthesis of police work, the conclusion of the process; when instead police action is required its practical efficiency is somewhat doubtful.

For example, numerous graphs relevant to the worldwide communist organization and to the illegal communist organization in the Reich were shown to the Italian delegation, the former were of a purely literary nature, the latter were extremely variable and therefore practically ineffective. Anyway, the Italian delegation was able to establish that for Communism and Freemasonry, and finally concerning Judaism, Italy is completely immune.

The Kingdom's privileged status was another reason for the Germans to congratulate us.

The Italian delegation was also able to establish, as further reconfirmation of the judgment that was beginning to form, that the *concrete* fruits of police work in the field of the fight against communism were very modest, actually they consist of a very few examples of underground presses and some modest examples of technical means for conspiracy. At the conclusion of the conversations that took place during the three days of the meetings and the visits that were made to the technical plants, some proposals were drawn up, which, pending final approval, could immediately be put into effect.

Considering what has been discussed regarding Freemasonry and Judaism, where our collaboration can only be generic, in the field of communism instead it could be effective and may generate some results. The two police forces must exchange information on Bolshevik elements of particular danger and mobility in the cities and residing outside the respective state's borders, which could work against both states against their corporative systems, which, having a single type of organization, and differ only in some details of execution. This field could in fact be productive inasmuch as the knowledge of fighting methods is the necessary prerequisite for all police action. The Italian delegation insisted upon the necessity to closely investigate the means for fighting the illegal activity of the Communist Party because only with a good working method is one always able to control and contain the communist movement, not only, but one is capable of preparing the trap for the capture of those very revolutionary elements, of an elusive nationality, carriers of revolutionary seeds and who would not be able to carry out their work if they did not find suitable elements within the State destined to come under Bolshevik influence, and in a suitable political climate.

A matter which seems particularly close to the officials of the German Political Police Force and which is obviously of exceptional importance concerns the capture and delivery of persons belonging to the two states that are considered to be particularly dangerous. The matter was submitted to the Italian delegation for consideration under two aspects: a) the arrest of German elements in Italy, and, respectively of Italian elements in Germany and their delivery, disregarding all diplomatic-judicial procedures to the state requesting them; b) the arrest of the above elements and their internment in concentration camps.

Agreements of that kind have already been reached between the Reich and Poland.

The matter is complex and of an obviously delicate nature and has been formally enunciated in an annex document that safeguards the sovereignty of both parties.

The Gestapo, other than the countless secret agents, strewn both within the Reich and abroad, commands a corps of 4,000 officers, 200,000 men militarily organized over the territory of the Reich and an army of 12,000 men grouped in 3 special regiments that are called "Hitler's Guard." The Italian delegation was invited to visit one of these regiments, which are commanded by the famous [Sepp] Dietrich and which is quite a model of order and power. Quartered in the old cadet school, the regiment is well equipped and mechanized and has complete autonomy inasmuch as it commands all, without distinction, the necessary services for the function of such a complex organization.

The men are chosen both for their physique as well as their political convictions and one gets the impression, visiting the immense barracks, that the Regiment is indeed a powerful instrument of an extremely mobile force which is very compliant to the orders of the leadership.

Commander Dietrich entertained the members of the Italian delegation in the lounges of the Officers' Club where he offered a very cordial hospitality. Many officers of the Reichswehr were also invited and it was said, confidentially, that the fact constituted the beginning of a policy to make relations between the two armed forces of the State more cordial.

The Gestapo is seconded for political action by the ordinary police which must immediately notify the political organs of any evidence that could be relevant to matters concerning the security of the State and the defense of the Nazi regime. The Berlin police, other than the imposing mass of agents assigned to traffic service, includes 16,000 men in uniform. From a political point of view, the most important episode of the Italian delegation's activity, was, without a doubt, the visit made by the delegation to the President of the General Council [of police], General [Hermann] Göring.

General Göring, on two occasions, and in very strong terms, after having summarized the arguments that support a close technical collaboration between the two police forces in the fight against communism, was keen on bringing up the need for a single line of defense, made possible by very close cooperation in the face of the attack that Bolshevism launched with ever renewed energy against the countries having strong governments that undoubtedly constitute the most difficult, if not the only, obstacle encountered by worldwide Bolshevism.

In substance, General Göring was keen on pointing out the need for the agreements between the two States to be not only technical but also political, since it is obvious that resistance to subversive politics can only be efficient through the union of the only two powerful police forces that for the moment can be found in Europe. General Göring, in speaking of the European situation, affected by communist propaganda, mentioned the signing of the French-Soviet pact and made clear reference to the need to be united in the fight against the USSR.

The head of the Italian delegation, replying to the speech by General Göring briefly mentioned the political matters discussed previously, and reaffirmed the necessity of a close collaboration of a technical nature between the two police forces, collaboration which would be regulated by agreements stipulated in the spirit of mutual trust and the foundations of which had already been laid.

The Italian delegation has been informed since the meeting that General Göring in private conversations said he was very satisfied with the visit by the delegation and that he had repeated his ideas insisting on the need to widen the relations that were being established having them proceed beyond the technical field.

On April 2, the two delegations, after a plenary meeting, were in agreement over the main points covered. A protocol was drawn up, both in Italian and German, containing the main points of the practical implementation of the collaboration between the two police forces.

As already mentioned, given the sensitivity of the subject, the matter relevant to the consignment of dangerous elements was dealt with in a separate protocol. The Italian delegation withheld signing the general protocol, giving, however, its full support after superior approval. With regard to the appended protocol it promised to closely examine it without making any commitment, even in general terms.

Text of the agreements.
Berlin, April 1, 1936

Between the Chief of Italian Police, His Excellency Arturo Bocchini, and the "Politischer Polizeikommandeur der deutschen Lander, Reichsführer SS," Heinrich Himmler, the following was agreed upon during the conference, which took place in Berlin from 30.3 to 1.4.1936:

1) The Italian Police and the German Police will keep each other informed of their general experiences and their special observations on the matters of communism and Freemasonry, where these experiences and observations are of interest to the police of the other country.

2) The Italian Police and the German Political Police will each answer questions regarding their general experiences and their special observations about communism and Freemasonry where either State's interests are not hindered.

3) The Italian Police and the German Political Police agree to share material and proof concerning Communism and Freemasonry and those organizations and activities requiring control or suppression in the interests of the two sides, where it is not detrimental to each State's interests.

4) The Italian Police and the German Political Police will cooperate in investigating the activities and intentions against Italy and Germany by Communist and Freemason centers existing outside of Italy and Germany and they will communicate the results of such investigations to each other.

5) The Italian Police and the German Police will receive from one another suggestions regarding the implementation of executive police measures against Communists, Freemasons, and emigrants and will operate in accordance with such suggestions, as far as the legislation of the respective countries allows and where there is no hindering of either State's interests.

6) The Italian Police and the German Political Police will also collaborate in all other matters in this field, even though not mentioned in the above points, or in the present agreement, only if the laws and the interests of the State do not prevent it.

7) The communications, replies and suggestions mentioned under points number 1-6, will be transmitted as follows:

a) written communications, not dealing with urgent affairs, will be conveyed by means of the postal services of the Italian Embassy in Berlin and of the German Embassy in Rome. The internal envelope will carry the name of the chief of Italian Police, His Excellency Bocchini, or that of the "Politischer Polizeikommandeur der deutschen Lander, Reichsführer SS," Himmler, or their substitutes.

b) Particularly urgent affairs will be conveyed by special courier, sent monthly by the Italian Police and by the German Political Police and in extremely urgent cases, immediately. These couriers will travel exclusively by air.

c) To ensure secure telephone communication between the chief of Italian Police and the "Politischen Polizeikommandeur der Lander" each one of the gentlemen will communicate with the other by sending, with each courier, a code name with which he will respond to the telephone calls.

d) To make communications possible in cases when the communications aforementioned in a) and b) fail, the Italian Police will communicate to the German Political Police and the German Political Police to the Italian Police, private code names, to which communications by means of normal post will be conveyed in such cases.

PROPOSAL

From the "Politischer Polizeikommandeur der deutschen Lander, Reichsführer SS" Himmler in addition to the points of April 1, 1936:

A radio telegraphic service will be set up between the Italian Police and the German Political Police. The details will be discussed and arranged through an exchange of letters.

PROPOSAL

From the "Politischer Polizeikommandeur der deutschen Lander, Reichsführer SS" Himmler in addition to the points of April 1, 1936:

The Italian Police and the German Political Police will extradite, with an appropriate reason, political criminals from one to the other, bypassing diplomatic negotiations, where there is no hinderance of one's own State interest.

676

Visit to Camp Dachau.
Milan, April 3, 1936-XIV
To His Excellency, Chief of Police
Rome
Subject: Visit to the German Concentration Camp at Dachau

I have the honor to report to You Excellency regarding the visit made to the German Concentration Camp of Dachau on the 2nd of this month.

The camp is located 18 kilometers outside Münich, in a flat rural zone, completely enclosed by a high wall.

It holds around 1,800 prisoners, of which more than two-thirds are political prisoners and the rest common criminals.

In the camp there are various sheds, at an reasonable distance from each other, assigned as the prisoner's quarters, who are divided according to their status: the political from the criminals, homosexuals from the others, and also Jews who have raped Christian girls.

Such a division though cannot be entirely guaranteed, nor contacts avoided, because the prisoners must work several hours per day, and while working they are divided according to their professional capacities: carpenters, shoemakers, mechanics, bricklayers, gardeners. The intellectuals are assigned, if possible, to office work.

Among all of the existing shops of the camp, there is a very large and well-equipped carpentry, where the inmates themselves have built almost all of the doors, fixtures, and other accessories of the large and very modern barracks recently built inside the camp itself, destined to lodge SS troops, whose task it is to guard the prisoners.

It is possible to reach the barracks from a separate entrance other than that of the Camp.

The prisoners are assigned to the Camp for an indefinite period of time; they are liberated after a certain appropriate time, according to their conduct, the judgment of the commander (a superior officer of the SS) and the opinion of the Münich Chief of Police.

They do not receive any remuneration or check from the State, which provides only for their maintenance, which is reasonable enough, judging by the quality of the soup that was distributed during out visit (an abundant bowl of soup with potatoes, bread, and chopped meat), by the physical aspect of the prisoners, well nourished, and by the small number of patients in the infirmary, less than ten or so out of the 1,800 present in the camp.

The surveillance and discipline in the camp, as already mentioned, is maintained by the units of SS troops, armed with rifles and machineguns. In some turrets, raised a few meters above the level of the camp, machineguns are placed ready to be operated by the guards whenever the need arises. The weapons are aimed to hit every point of the camp in a crossfire and repress any attempt at revolt.

A barbed wire fence contributes to avert any foolish ideas of escape from the Camp at night, which runs parallel to the boundary wall on the inside and through which runs an electric current.

The discipline that the prisoners display is remarkable and even in this particular condition of life they still show the characteristics and temperament of their race. To see them march, when from the separate sheds they go to work, or simply in the kitchens to receive their rations, one would say that they are from military units.

A kind of hierarchy amongst the prisoners is apparent.

Indeed it is a prisoner who is in charge of the more immediate order of the shed and it is he who communicates events to the non-commissioned officer or the officer of the SS who makes an inspection.

The prisoners cannot leave the camp for any reason; neither can they receive any visitors.

The painted red stripes that every prisoner wears on the rear of the jacket and on the outside edge of the pants at the level of the thigh are characteristic; they are evidently signs to distinguish them from a distance so as not to confuse them with the military in charge of surveillance.

In the camp there is even the sale of supplies, where the prisoners who have the means can buy foodstuffs, within well-defined limits which fix the amounts.

There is even a library where books can be requested for reading and some newspapers are allowed.

Finally, there is a swimming pool where the prisoners swim during the summer.

On the occasion of the German elections, which took place on the 29th of last month, the political prisoners of Dachau camp were allowed to express their vote: it was forbidden to the criminal prisoners. Out of approximately 1,300 voters, 1,269 voted Yes; four forms were left blank, the others voted No.

The executives of the camp highlighted the negative votes, even if very marginal in percentage, affirming that those voters were part of the Jewish element: freedom to vote within a prison situation.

Yours respectfully
Commissioner Chief of P. S.
Tommaso Petrillo

16.
[Manifesto of the Racist "Scientists"]

1. *Human races exist.* The existence of human races is not a creation of our mind, but corresponds to a phenomenal material reality, perceptible to our senses. This reality is represented by masses, usually imposing, of millions of men, similar in physical and psychological traits, which are inherited and will continue to be inherited. To say that human races exist does not mean to say *a priori* that superior and inferior human races exist, but only that different human races exist.

2. *Large races and small races exist.* One must not only admit that major groups exist, which are commonly called races and which differ only by a few characteristics, but one must also admit that minor such groups exist (for example, Nordic, Mediterranean, Dinaric, etc.) characterized by a great number of common traits. These groups constitute, from a biological point of view, the real races, whose existence is an obvious fact.

3. *The concept of race is a purely biological concept.* Race is therefore based on other considerations and not the concepts of people and nation, essentially founded on historical, linguistic, and religious considerations. However, at the root of the differences between the people and the nation, there are differences of race. If the Italians are different from the French, the Germans, the Turks, the Greeks, etc., it is not only because they speak a different language and have a different history, but because the racial composition of these peoples is different. It has been the different proportions of different races from ancient times that make up the many peoples, whether one race has absolute dominion over others, whether they all appear to be harmoniously mixed, whether, in the end, they still remain unassimilated one to the other as different races.

4. *The actual population of Italy is of Aryan origin and its culture is Aryan.* This population of Aryan culture has lived in our peninsula for several millennia; very little pre-Aryan culture has remained. The origins of the actual Italians essentially derives from elements of those same races that constitute, and will continue to constitute, the network that has always lived in Europe.

5. *The contribution of great masses of men in historical times is a legend.* After the invasion of the Longobards there have not been other noteworthy population movements in Italy capable of influencing the racial physiognomy of the Nation. The result is that, while for other European Nations racial composition has notably varied even in modern times, for Italy, broadly speaking, the racial composition of today is the same as it was a thousand years ago: the 44,000,000 Italians of today, therefore, date back in absolute majority to families that have lived in Italy for a millennia.

6. *A pure "Italian race" exists at this point.* This statement is not based on the mingling of the biological concept of race with the historical linguistic concept of people and nation, but on the purest blood relationship that unites the Italians of today to the generations that have populated Italy for one thousand years. This ancient purity of blood is the grandest title of nobility of the Italian Nation.

7. *The time has come for Italians to openly proclaim themselves racists.* All the work the Regime has carried out in Italy until now is, after all, racism. Reference to the concept of race has been very frequent in the speeches made by the Leader. The question of racism in Italy must be considered from a purely biological point of view, without philosophic or religious preconceptions. The concept of racism in Italy must be essentially Italian and of Aryan-nordic orientation. This does not mean, though, to simply introduce into Italy the German theories of racism, or affirm that Italians and Scandinavians are the same. But only to point out to the Italians a physical and above all psychological model of human race that because of its purely European characteristics is completely removed from all non-European races, this means elevating the Italians to a higher ideal of self-consciousness and to greater responsibility.

8. *A clear distinction must be made between the Mediterranean people of Europe (Occidentals) on one side, the Orientals and Africans on the other.* The theories that support the claim of the African origins of some Europeans are therefore to be considered dangerous and that include Semitic and Hamitic populations in a common Mediterranean race establishing relationships and ideological sympathies which are absolutely unacceptable.

9. *Jews do not belong to the Italian race.* Nothing remains of the Semites who landed on our sacred soil during the course of centuries. Even the Arab occupation of Sicily left nothing other than the memory of a few names; and besides, the assimilation process in Italy has always been very rapid. The Jews represent the only population, which has never assimilated in Italy because it is made up of racial elements which are not European, differing absolutely from the elements that make up the Italians.

10. *The purely European physical and psychological characteristics of the Italians must not be altered in any way.* Marriage is admissible only between people of European races, in which case there can be no talk of actual hybridism, given that these races belong to a common body and differ only in a few characteristics, whilst they are the same in very many others. The purely European character of the Italians becomes altered by crossbreeding with any non-European race and bearer of a civilization, which is different from the millennial civilization of the Aryans.

17.

[PNF bulletin regarding the "Manifesto of the Racist Scientists"]

Rome, July 25, 1938

The Minister Secretary of the Party received a group of Fascist scholars, professors in Italian Universities who, under the aegis of the Ministry of Popular Culture, have drawn up or have supported the propositions that set the basis of Fascist racism. Present were the Fascists, Dr. Lino Businco, assistant in general pathology at the University of Rome; Prof. Lidio Cipriani, non-tenured lecturer of anthropology at the University of Florence, director of the National Museum of Anthropology and Ethnology of Florence; Prof. Arturo Donaggio, director of the neuropsychiatry clinic at the University of Bologna, president of the Italian Society of Psychiatry; Dr. Leone Franzí, assistant in the Pediatric clinic of the University of Milan; Prof. Guido Landra, assistant of anthropology at the University of Rome; Sen. Nicola Pende, director of the Institute of Special Medical Pathology at the University of Rome; Dr. Marcello Ricci, assistant in zoology at the University of Rome; Prof. Franco Savorgnan, professor of demography at the University of Rome, president of the Central Institute of Statistics; Hon. Sabato Visco, director of the Institute of General Physiology at the University of Rome and director of the National Institute of Biology at the National Council for Research; Prof. Edoardo Zavattari, director of the Institute of Zoology at the University of Rome.

The Minister of Popular Culture participated in the meeting.

The Secretary of the Party, whilst he praised the precision and the conciseness of the theories, reiterated that Fascism, for practically sixteen years, has had a racist policy which consists–through the institutions of the Regime–in bringing about a continuous quantitative and qualitative improvement of the race. The Secretary of the Party added that the Duce, many times–in his articles and speeches–referred to the Italian race as belonging to the so-called Indo-Europeans.

In this field as well the Regime has held to its fundamental policy: first action, then the formulation of a doctrine which must not be considered academic, meaning as an end to itself, but as the starting point of a further political explanation. With the creation of the Empire the Italian race has come into contact with other races; it must therefore be wary of all hybridization and contamination. "Racist" laws in this sense have already been elaborated and applied with fascistic energy in the territories of the Empire.

As far as the Jews are concerned, they have thought of themselves for thousands of years, the world over, as well as in Italy, as a different race superior to others, and it is notorious that, notwithstanding the tolerant politics of the Regime, the Jews have made up, in every nation, with their men and with their means, the general staff of anti-Fascism.

The Secretary of the Party finally announced that the main activity of the institutes of Fascist culture, during the following year, XVII, would be the elaboration and dissemination of Fascist principles on the issue of race, principles which have already raised much interest in Italy and the world.

18.
Informazione Diplomatica n. 18

Responsible circles in Rome note that many of the foreign opinions and impressions concerning Italian racism are dictated by a superficial knowledge of the facts and, in some cases by obvious bad faith. In reality, as it is documented, Italian racism dates back to 1919. Mussolini, in his speech to the Party congress, held in Rome in November 1921–we repeat 1921–explicitly declared:

"I mean to say that Fascism is handling the race problem: Fascists must take charge of the health of the race with which history is made."

If the problem has remained dormant for many years, this happened because of other more urgent problems that had to be solved. But the conquest of the Empire placed racial problems at the top of the agenda, because to ignore them had dramatic and bloody consequences, the details of which we shall not go into today. Other nations send few, well trained officials to the lands of their empires; we send millions of men to Libya, and to the AOI, in the course of time and because it is absolutely necessary. Now, to avoid the catastrophic calamity of half breeding, that is, the creation of a bastard race that is neither European nor African, which will foment disintegration and revolt, the severe laws which Fascism passed and has enacted are not enough. A strong feeling, a strong sense of pride, a clear and ever-present consciousness of race are required.

To discriminate does not mean to persecute. This must be said to the too many Jews in Italy and in other countries who cry useless lamentations to the heavens, passing with typical swiftness from intrusiveness and pride to demoralization and senseless panic. As was clearly stated in note n. 14 of the Informazione Diplomatica and as is repeated today, the Fascist Government has no special plan to persecute the Jews themselves. It deals with another matter. There are 44,000 Jews in the metropolitan territory of Italy, according to Jewish statistical data, which must, though, be confirmed by a special census in the near future; the proportion therefore is supposedly one Jew for every thousand inhabitants.

It is clear that, from now on, the participation of the Jews in the overall life of the State should be, and will be, adapted to such a ratio.

No one will wish to deny this right to the Fascist State, and least of all the Jews, who, as it is solemnly stated in the recent manifesto of the rabbis of Italy, have always been the most integral, intransigent, ferocious apostles, and, from a certain point of view, admirers of Fascism. They have always considered themselves to belong to another bloodline, another race, they self proclaim to be "the chosen people" and have always given proof of their racial solidarity over and above all national borders.

We do not wish to speak here of the historically accurate equation, of these last twenty years of European life, between Judaism, Bolshevism, and Freemasonry.

Thus, there is no doubt that the climate is ready for Italian racism.

There is no doubt that it will become—through the coordinated and determined action of all of the organs of the Regime—part of the spiritual heritage of our nation, a fundamental base of our State, an element of security for our Empire.

19.

[Letter from Roberto Farinacci to Benito Mussolini]

Rome, evening of August 3, 1938-XVI
Chamber of Deputies

Dear President,

As I attempt to cleverly oppose the attitude of the Vatican, I am nevertheless in contact with some of the Cardinals, led by Della Puma (General Secretary of the Congregations) who do not make a mystery of their aversion to the speeches that this now ancient Pope is allowed to make.

From one of these I learned the following:

a) The Pontiff's speech was inspired by Monsignor Pizzardi and by Count della Torre, who has said though, that given his past he does not intend to initiate an anti-racist campaign in the "Osservatore Romano";

b) The speech was made more biting with additions and references to previous declarations of the Pontiff by the Secretariat of State;

c) The Pope was told that the Fascist racist campaign would lead to divorce, the annulment of marriages between Catholics and Jews, the sterilization of the Jews;

d) The Catholics are clearly divided on the racist problem;

e) This morning the Pope asked the Secretary of State to take copies of pages 72-73-74-75 of Ludwig's book on Mussolini, to Castel Gandolfo. I do not have this book at hand but I believe we should expect a coming attack;

f) The well-attuned element of the Vatican feels certain that a few measures on behalf of the Government (seizure of Diocesan and Parish journals and Catholic papers) would get them to backtrack. Monsignor Pizzardi is terrified of an incompatibility between Party members and the Catholic Action.

Dear President, is it true that the Pope's mother is a Jew? If it were true, it would be such a scream.

I am leaving this evening for Cremona where a simple signal would be sufficient for me.

Devoted and affectionate regards.

Yours, Farinacci

20.
[Galeazzo Ciano's report
on Vatican reactions regarding the racial measures]

Confidential
Ministry of Foreign Affairs

Cable n. 00536/c
Addressed to:
Hon. Prime Minister (Cab.)
Royal Ministry of Internal Affairs (Dir. Gen. Religions)
Royal Ministry of Internal Affairs (Dir. Gen. of Demography and Race)
Royal Ministry of Justice (Cab.)
A.E.M. Office of the Holy See

Position SS 4.   Rome, October 10, 1938-XVI

Subject: Resolutions of the Grand Council for the defense of the race with reference to mixed marriages

For all intents and purposes we are honored to transmit the following report, dated the 7th of this month, from the Royal Embassy to the Holy See to this ministry regarding the subject mentioned above:

"Vatican circles have adopted a cautious attitude towards the deliberations of the Grand Council regarding the defense of the race. Some positive points are noted regarding the deliberations themselves, while there is some preoccupation with respect to the regulations on marriage.

"The paragraph that is particularly appreciated in the declaration where 'those born from mixed marriages are not considered of the Jewish race, if they are of a religion different from the Jewish religion as of the date of October 1, XVI'.

Within the lists of motives for discrimination of Jews of Italian citizenship, a great spirit of moderation was observed, as well as for the limitations imposed upon the Jews' occupations.

"The decree which is potentially in direct opposition to ecclesiastic legislation is the prohibition of marriages between Italians and those belonging to Hamite races, Semites and other non-Aryan races. But also on this point it can be said that in church circles the very same canon law opposes the marriage of Jews with Catholics and on this point it is extremely difficult to obtain an exemption for the differences of religion. In fact, instructions given to the bishops to tighten the principles prohibiting mixed marriages and asking the bishops to use every means possible to avoid them are recent. Therefore, one might believe that in exceptional cases a procedure can be found. This is essential since in Italy, following the Concordat between the Vatican State and the Italian State in 1929, civil marriages only exist for non-Catholics and for those who wish to deliberately disregard Catholic principles and discipline. For the rest only religious marriages exist, with civil effects, thanks to the simple notice given to the civil authorities of the celebrated marriage. On the other hand, in approving or denying marriage permits, the church *always takes into consideration the reasons contemplated by the civil legislation of each state.*

"The case of marriages becomes far more difficult regarding converted Jews, who, in the eyes of the church, are Catholics just like everyone else, while the proposed legislation continues to consider them as Jews. In this case the prohibition of marriage imposed by this legislation would come into direct conflict with the doctrine and the discipline of the church. This is the only point of the Grand Council's proclamation the church would object to.

"It is noted, however, that this proclamation alone is not the law still to be issued, but only serves to constitute the basis on which projected laws must be presented, examined and approved. Therefore, before issuing a final judgment it is necessary to wait until such projected laws are known and in the hope meanwhile that the matter can be resolved by keeping in mind all of the factors which influence the objective of considering civil as much as religious needs."

With the following report of the same date (the 7th of this month) the same Royal Representation also communicated the following:

"I have the honor of copying here what the *L'osservatore romano* published this evening regarding the Grand Council's deliberations on the defense of the race:

"'The news following Stefani's announcement can certainly not erase our worries, especially with regard to the principles and the matrimonial discipline of the church.

"'Nevertheless, we await clarification of such a serious matter that can only be given by the related text of the laws, hoping that they shall remove any cause for doubt.'"

CIANO

****

Cable n. 00541/c

Ministry of Foreign Affairs

Addressed to:

Hon. Prime Minister (Cab.)
Royal Ministry of Internal Affairs (Dir. Gen. Religions)
Royal Ministry of Internal Affairs (Dir. Gen. of Demography and Race)
Royal Ministry of Justice (Cab.)
Dir. Gen. Office of the Holy See at the A.E.M. [Ministry of Foreign Affairs]
Rome, October 13, 1938-XVI

Position SS. 32 1 2

Subject: Grand Council's decisions for the defense of the race–mixed marriages

Reference to the cable from the Ministry n. 00536/c of the 10th of this month.

Following the cable cited above, I have the honor of transmitting the following which was communicated on the 10th of this month by the Royal Embassy to the Holy See on the subject at hand:

"As I have already had the honor to inform you, the recent decisions of the Grand Council on the subject of the defense of the race have not, in general, been received unfavorably by the Vatican, referring to the caution expressed also in the brief comment by the *L'osservatore romano* on the 7th of this month, as to the consequences the new regulations could have regarding marriage as it is enforced by the church.

From Monsignor Montini, substitute for Ordinary Affairs at the Secretariat of State, I received confirmation of such impressions and more particularly that the major, if not sole, preoccupation of the Holy See concerns the case of marriage with converted Jews. As H. E. the Ambassador indicated by cable delivered by courier on July 20:

"In anticipation of a possible readjustment of our legislation as far as mixed marriages are concerned, I believe it my duty to draw once again your attention, for your information, to the provision of art. 34 of the Concordat, the first part of which states: 'The Italian State, wishing to restore dignity to the institution of marriage, which is the foundation of the family, in keeping with the Catholic traditions of its people, recognizes the civil effects of the sacrament of marriage disciplined by Canon law.'

"My comment is suggested by the fact that *Canon law recognizes marriages between those baptized as valid (Canon 1012) beyond any other consideration.*"

CIANO

21.

[Exchange of letters Pius XI - Victor Emmanuel III – Mussolini - Tacchi-Venturi]

I. [*Pius XI to Mussolini*]

Dear Son, good health and Apostolic blessings.

A great concern moves Us to address you directly, not doubting the paramount part You played, which We have not forgotten, in the difficult formulation and expected conclusion of the Concordat between the Holy See and Italy; You will understand Our legitimate and dutiful solicitude and thus work efficiently to relieve Our soul, burdened by distressing cares.

Art. 7 of the bill, which next Monday must be presented for approval by the Council of Ministers, does obvious damage to that solemn pact. Such damage can easily be avoided, should there be, instead of the text of the mentioned article ready for approval, the acceptance of what We desired to inform Your closest staff, but that unfortunately We have not had the comfort to see accepted. We therefore send it to You, herewith attached, in the hope that we shall find it within Your wisdom to accept, since You already were able to understand once before how important and beneficial it would be for Italy to regulate the institution of marriage according to the laws of Religion, which is also the official religion of the State.

With these feelings of fatherly faith, We bestow from our heart a token of the divine grace and apostolic blessings.

Made in Rome at Saint Peter's, on November 4, 1938, the seventeenth year of our Pontificate.

PIUS PP. XI

II. [*Pius XI to Victor Emmanuel III*]

Dearest Son, good health and Apostolic blessings.

Yesterday the duty of Our apostolic ministry moved Us to address ourselves to Your Prime Minster to show him the necessity of modifying article 7 of the bill "for the defense of the Italian race" which is in complete contradiction with the solemn Concordat concluded between Us and Your Majesty. To reach this purpose, We send a handwritten fatherly letter, accompanied with the text, which We enclose together here, to substitute the one mentioned before. To Our utmost pain, it has just now been communicated that Our solicitude did not find that complete understanding, which We thought could not be denied, because even accepting the new text up until the words concerning the legitimizing of children, the following were not admitted *also in the case where both contracting parties, even though of a "different race," are of the Catholic religion.*

Considering now that this paragraph constituted the main part of Our text for which We feel We must insist to a greater extent, We do not hesitate for a moment to address to You, Our Royal and Imperial King, who entered into the historical pact with Us, from which much glory has been attached to Your name and to Your August Family, beseeching You to intervene with Your supreme authority to achieve what We, with Our paternal offices, were unable to achieve with Your Prime Minister.

With such faith We bestow Our heartfelt apostolic blessings to Your Majesty and to the Queen Empress, and to all of the Royal and Imperial Family.

Made in Rome at Saint Peter's, November 5, 1938, the seventeenth year of Our Pontificate, to Our Dearest Son Vittorio Emmanuele III King of Italy and Emperor of Ethiopia.

PIUS PP. XI

III. [*Mussolini to Victor Emmanuel III*]

Your Majesty may reply to the Pope telling him that the copy of his letter has been delivered to me and will be held in the highest account in order to reach a conciliatory solution from both points of view, which, I add, are most antithetical.

We have already accepted two of the Pontiff's requests; accepting the third would have violated the law. Nevertheless, we will do our best to find a middle-ground solution which is satisfying to all. It is my impression that the Vatican is pulling at the chain very strongly when it comes to Italy and totally gives in on other issues. I wish to add my devoted regards to Your Majesty.

Mussolini
(November 7, 1938)

IV. [*Victor Emmanuel III to Pius XI*]

Blessed Father,

I thank His Holiness for the letter that he very kindly wished to send me. I hastened to send a copy of His Holiness's letter to His Excellency the Head of the Government. His Holiness's letter will be held in the highest account in order to reach a compromise solution from both points of view.

I devotedly thank His Holiness for the blessing graciously bestowed upon the Queen Empress, my family, and myself.

Would His Holiness accept my sentiments of devoted respect.

Devoted Son of His Holiness.

Victor Emmanuel
San Rossore, November 7, 1938-XVII.

V. [*Father Tacchi-Venturi to Mussolini*]

Rome, November 9, 1938-XVII
Excellency,

It is well into the night as I write this letter to you. The thought that tomorrow, Thursday, the bill of the first item of the law for the defense of our race will inflict a serious breach in the Concordat, a breach that without an extraordinary intervention from Providence will bring very sad consequences to the relations between the Church and the State, prevents me from sleeping. And to think that this trouble could be avoided, when you, not yielding from that spirit of condescension of which you amply displayed during the long elaboration of the Concordat, would be so kind as to modify article 7 in the form that is described in the attached sheet. Give it some thought in the name of grace.

The change that I propose contains *a few things less* than what was in the Holy Father's text sent to Your Excellency and to His Majesty the King Emperor; it saves the principle desired by the legislator, which is that mixed marriages are removed, *notwithstanding that exceptions are made to this agreed-to principle*.

But how many of these exceptions, if ever, will there be? If you bear in mind the small number of Italian citizens of the Semitic race and the aversion that many Jews have towards contracting marriage with Christians and the many Christians with Jews, aversion which the new law will undoubtedly strengthen, I do not fear to declare that not even one hundred marriages in the space of a year will take place between an Aryan spouse and one of the Jewish race professing the Catholic religion. A drop in the ocean! And for so little must there be the violation of a solemn pact which forms one of your most beautiful glories, with immense bitterness to the Father of all Christianity?

Would you, Excellency, reflect further for a moment on the immeasurable gravity of a breach with the Church in this anxious historic moment; I ask you and beseech you and take pleasure in repeating that I, who have never betrayed you in the past, who is incapable of betraying you in the future, who feels shivers in his spine picturing in his mind how much damage, such tremendous ruin, has always been created by going against the desires of the prayers of the Pope! Excuse me, but do not allow my desperate pleas be cast in vain.

With deep religious devotion.
Devoted to Your Excellency
Pietro Tacchi-Venturi

22.

Declaration on Race

I.

[Handwritten text by B. Mussolini]

The Grand Council adopts the ten propositions elaborated by the Fascist university professors, under the aegis of the Ministry of Popular Culture and subsequently approved by the Party Secretary.

The Grand Council declares the urgent relevance of racial problems and the need of a racial consciousness, following the conquest of the Empire and reiterates that Fascism for 16 years has and continues to carry out a positive activity, directed at the quantitative and qualitative improvement of the Italian race that runs the risk of being thwarted, with incalculable political consequences, because of crossbreeding and bastardization.

The Jewish problem is nothing other than the metropolitan aspect of a general problem.

The Grand Council of Fascism establishes:

a) marriages between Italians and those belonging to Hamite, Semite, and other non-Aryan races are forbidden;

b) State employees—civil and military personnel—are forbidden to marry foreign women of any race;

c) the marriage of Italians with foreigners of the Aryan race must have the approval of the Ministry of Internal Affairs;

d) penalties against those who attack the prestige of the race in the territories of the Empire must be increased.

Jews and Judaism.

The Grand Council recalls that worldwide Judaism–especially after the abolition of Freemasonry–has been the instigator of anti-Fascism in all fields and Italian Judaism inside Italy and among those in exile outside Italy has been–in some key moments as in 1924-25 and during the Ethiopian war–unanimously hostile towards Fascism.

The immigration of foreign elements—greatly increased since 1933—has worsened the feelings of Italian Jews towards the Regime, that Italian Judaism cannot sincerely accept since it is antithetical to the psychology, the politics, the internationalism of Israel.

All anti-Fascist efforts can be traced back to a Jew; worldwide Judaism is, in Spain, on the opposite side.

Forbidden entrance and expulsion of foreign Jews.

The Grand Council believes that the law barring the entry of foreign Jews into the Kingdom could no longer be delayed and that the expulsion of the undesirables–to use the expression popular with the great democracies–is indispensable.

The Grand Council decides that, other than individual controversial cases which will be decided by the special commission at the Ministry of Internal Affairs, expulsion shall not apply regarding foreign Jews, when:
a) they are over 60 years of age;
b) they are in poor health;
c) they have three or more minors in their care.

Jews with Italian citizenship.

The Grand Council, establishes the following regarding who is or is not of the Jewish race:
a) those born of parents who are both Jews are of the Jewish race;
b) those born of a Jewish father and a mother of foreign nationality are of the Jewish race;
c) those who, even though they are born of a mixed marriage but profess the Jewish religion, are of the Jewish race;
d) those born of a mixed marriage who practice another religion which is not the Jewish religion, are not of the Jewish race.

Discrimination amongst Jews having Italian citizenship.

No discrimination of an administrative, economic, or moral nature will be applied to Jews having Italian citizenship, as far as they have not, for other reasons, forfeited their citizenship, who belong to:

a) families of those who died in the four wars sustained by Italy during the last century: Libyan, World, Ethiopian, Spanish;

b) families of those maimed, disabled, wounded in the Libyan, World, Ethiopian, Spanish wars;

c) families of those decorated with military medals or with the Military Order of Savoy in the Libyan, World, Ethiopian, Spanish wars;

d) families of those who were volunteers in the Libyan, World, Ethiopian, Spanish wars;

e) families of those who died for the Fascist cause;

f) families of those maimed, disabled, or wounded for the Fascist cause;

g) families of the members of the Fascist action squads during the years '19, '20, '21, '22;

h) families holding undisputed titles of civilian merit.

For the Jews belonging to the categories above an album will be compiled and the reasons why they are not subjected to any discrimination will be made public knowledge. A change of name or other recognition will also be permitted.

Jews of the second category.

Italian citizens of the Jewish race not belonging to the above mentioned categories, pending a new law concerning the acquisition of Italian citizenship, may not:

a) be members of the PNF;

b) own or direct a business of any nature which employs 100 or more people;

c) own more than 50 hectares of land;

d) have domestic servants of the Italian race.

Other conditions.

The Grand Council also decides:

1) that the right to a normal and full pension is recognized for those Jews dismissed from public positions;

2) that every kind of pressure on the Jews to obtain abjurations is strictly forbidden;

3) that nothing is changed with regard to the free practice of religion and the activity of the Jewish Communities according to the laws in force.

The laws that the single ministries are to quickly prepare must be in the spirit of these directives of the Grand Council.

Immigration of Jews to Ethiopia.

The Grand Council does not exclude the possibility of allowing the free and controlled immigration of European Jews into some areas (to be established) of Ethiopia, subject to agreements with leaders of worldwide Jewry. This possibility and the other conditions placed upon the Jews may be cancelled or increased, according to the attitude that Judaism adopts with regard to Italy.

Chairs of Racism.

The Grand Council invites the Ministry of National Education to institute teaching posts on "the study of racism" in the principal universities of the Kingdom, beginning with the oldest: Bologna.

To the Black Shirts.

The Grand Council, while it notes with satisfaction that the complex issue of racial problems has aroused magnificent interest amongst the Italian nation, announces to the Fascists that the Party's directives in substance are to be considered fundamental and binding for all.

Categories of Jews in group A.

1) families of the dead in the Libyan, World, Ethiopian, Spanish wars;
2) families of the maimed, disabled, wounded in the Libyan, World, Ethiopian, Spanish Wars;
3) families of those decorated with military medals in the Libyan, World, Ethiopian, Spanish Wars;
4) families of those who were voluntaries in the Libyan, World, Ethiopian, Spanish Wars;
5) families of of the dead for the Fascist cause;
6) families of those maimed, disabled, or wounded for the fascist cause;
7) families of the Fascist action squad members prior to the March on Rome;
8) families holding indisputable civil titles of merit.

The Jews belonging to the categories mentioned above will not be subjected to any discrimination and will participate in the life of the State in proportion to their numbers: the Jews not belonging to the said categories will not be able to have any participation in aspects of the life of the State.

II.

[Text issued to the members of the Grand Council]

The Grand Council approves and adopts the ten propositions elaborated by the Fascist University Professors, under the aegis of the Ministry of Popular Culture and later approved by the Party Secretary.

The Grand Council declares the urgent relevance of racial problems and the need for racial consciousness, following the conquest of the Empire and reiterates that Fascism has for 16 years, and continues to carry out a positive activity, directed at the quantitative and qualitative improvement of the Italian race, improvement which could be gravely compromised, with incalculable political consequences, through crossbreeding and bastardization.

The Jewish problem is nothing but the metropolitan aspect of a problem of a general character.

The Grand Council of Fascism establishes:

a) marriage between Italians and those belonging to Hamite, Semite, and other non-Aryan races is forbidden;

b) employees of the State–civil and military personnel–may not marry foreign women of any race;

c) Italians marrying foreigners of the Aryan race must be approved by the Ministry of Internal Affairs;

d) the penalties against those who defile the prestige of the race in the territories of the Empire must be increased.

Jews and Judaism.

The Grand Council reiterates that worldwide Judaism–especially following the abolition of Freemasonry–has instigated anti-Fascism in all areas and that foreign and external Italian Judaism has been–at some crucial moments as in 1924-25 and during the Ethiopian war–unanimously hostile to Fascism.

The immigration of foreign elements which has heavily increased since 1933, has worsened the feelings of Italian Jews towards the Regime, which they do not sincerely accept since it is antithetical to the psychology, the politics and the internationalism of Israel.

All anti-Fascist efforts can be traced back to a Jew; worldwide Judaism in Spain is on the opposing side.

Forbidden entry and expulsion of foreign Jews.

The Grand Council believes that the law forbidding the entrance into the Kingdom of foreign Jews could no longer be delayed and that the expulsion of the undesirables–using the expression popular in the great democracies–is indispensable.

The Grand Council decides that, other than singularly controversial cases which will be decided by the special commission of the Ministry of Internal Affairs, expulsion is not applied to foreign Jews, when:

a) they are over 60 years of age;

b) they are in poor health;

c) they have three or more minors in their care;

d) they have entered into a mixed marriage with an Italian before October 1st.

Jews having Italian citizenship.

The Grand Council, concerning who is or is not, of the Jewish race establishes the following:

a) those born of parents who are both Jews are of the Jewish race;

b) those born of a Jewish father and a mother of foreign nationality are of the Jewish race;

c) those who, even though born of a mixed marriage belong to the Jewish religion, are of the Jewish race;

d) those born from a mixed marriage who belong to another religion which is not the Jewish religion, are not of the Jewish race.

Discrimination amongst Jews having Italian citizenship.

No discrimination of an administrative, economic, or moral nature will be applied to Jews who are Italian citizens, as long as they have not, for other reasons, given up citizenship, who belong to:

1) families of those who died in the four wars sustained by Italy during the last century: Libyan, World, Ethiopian, Spanish;

2) families of those maimed, disabled, wounded in the Libyan, World, Ethiopian, Spanish Wars;

3) families of those decorated with military medals or by the Military Order of Savoy in the Libyan, World, Ethiopian, Spanish Wars;

4) families of those who were volunteers in the Libyan, World, Ethiopian, Spanish Wars;

5) families of those who died for the Fascist cause;

6) families of those maimed, disabled, or wounded for the Fascist cause;

7) families of the members of the Fascist action squads during the years '19, 20, 21, 22, and 24;

8) families holding indisputable civil titles of merit.

For the Jews belonging to the categories above a list will be compiled and the reasons why they are not entitled to any discrimination will be made public knowledge. A change of name or other recognition will also be permitted.

According to incomplete survey statistics the war volunteers are 587
Legionnaires at Fiume 79
Maimed and disabled at war 159
Injured in combat 149
Families of those who died at war 141
Families of those died for the Fascist cause 3
Maimed and disabled for the Fascist cause 6
Injured for the Fascist cause 9
Certificate of the March on Rome 210

Jews of the second category.

Italian citizens of the Jewish race not belonging to the categories mentioned above, pending a new law concerning the acquisition of Italian citizenship, may not:

a) be members of the PNF;
b) own or manage a business of any nature which employs 100 or more people;
c) own more than 50 hectares of land;
d) employ domestic servants of the Italian race;
e) be exempt from military service in times of peace and war;
f) the practice of the professions will be the object of further regulations.

Other conditions.

The Grand Council also decides:

1) that the right to the normal and full pension is recognized to those Jews dismissed from public positions;
2) that every kind of pressure on the Jews to obtain abjurations is strictly forbidden;
3) that there is no change with regard to the free practice of religion and the activity of the Jewish Communities according to the law.

The regulations that the single ministries must quickly prepare will be in the spirit of these directives of the Grand Council.

Jewish Immigration to Ethiopia.

The Grand Council does not exclude the possibility of conceding, in order to steer away Jewish immigration from Palestine, a free and controlled immigration of European Jews in some areas (to be established) of Ethiopia, subject to agreements with leaders of worldwide Jewry. This possibility and the other conditions placed upon the Jews may be cancelled or increased, according to the attitude that Judaism adopts vis-à-vis Italy.

Teaching positions of racism.

The Grand Council invites the Ministry of National Education to institute teaching posts for "the study of racism" in the main universities in the Kingdom, beginning with the oldest: Bologna.

To the Black Shirts.

The Grand Council, while it notes with satisfaction that the issue of the racial problem has aroused magnificent interest amongst the Italian nation, announces to the Fascists that the Party's directives in substance are to be considered fundamental and binding for all.

III.
[Text published in the "Order Sheet" of the PNF].

The Grand Council of Fascism, following the conquest of the Empire, declares the urgent relevance of racial problems and the necessity of a racial consciousness and reminds that Fascism for 16 years has, and continues to carry out a positive activity, aimed at the quantitative and qualitative improvement of the Italian race, improvement which could be seriously compromised, with incalculable political consequences, through crossbreeding and bastardization.

The Jewish problem is simply the metropolitan aspect of a more general problem.

The Grand Council of Fascism establishes:

a) marriages between Italians and those belonging to Hamite, Semite, and other non-Aryan races are forbidden;

b) State employees and employees of public institutions—civil and military personnel—are forbidden to marry foreign women of any race;

c) the marriage of Italians to foreigners of the Aryan race must have the prior approval of the Ministry of Internal Affairs;

d) the sanctions must be reinforced against those who attack the prestige of the race in the territories of the Empire.

Jews and Judaism.

The Grand Council of Fascism reiterates that worldwide Judaism–especially after the abolition of Freemasonry–has been the instigator of anti-Fascism in all fields and that foreign and external Italian Judaism—at some crucial moments as in 1924-25 and during the Ethiopian war—were unanimously hostile towards Fascism.

The immigration of foreign elements—strongly increased since 1933—has worsened the frame of mind of Italian Jews, with respect to the Regime, which is not sincerely accepted, since it is antithetical to the psychology, the politics, the internationalism of Israel.

All anti-Fascist efforts can be traced back to a Jew; worldwide Judaism is, in Spain, on the side of the Bolsheviks of Barcelona.

Forbidding the entry and expulsion of foreign Jews.

The Grand Council of Fascism believes that the law concerning the forbidden entry into the Kingdom by foreign Jews could not be further delayed and that the expulsion of the undesirables–using the expression in vogue applied by the great democracies–is absolutely necessary.

The Grand Council of Fascism has decided that, other than particularly controversial cases that will be decided by the special commission of the Ministry of Internal Affairs, expulsion does not apply to the foreign Jews, when:

a) they are over 65 years of age;

b) they have contracted an Italian mixed marriage before October 1, XVI [1938].

Jews of Italian citizenship.

The Grand Council of Fascism establishes the following, regarding who belongs, or not, to the Jewish race,:

a) those born of parents who are both Jews are of the Jewish race;

b) those born of a Jewish father and a mother of foreign nationality are of the Jewish race;

c) those who even though born of a mixed marriage practice the Jewish religion are of the Jewish race;

d) those born of a mixed marriage and practice another religion which is not the Jewish religion, at the date of October 1, XVI, are not of the Jewish race.

Discrimination amongst Jews with Italian citizenship.

No discrimination will be applied–excluding in every instance the teaching profession in all schools and at every grade–to Jews of Italian citizenship, as long as they have not, for other reasons, demerited who belong to:

1) families of the dead in the four wars sustained by Italy during this century: Libyan, World, Ethiopian, Spanish;
2) families of volunteers in the war in Libyan, World, Ethiopian, Spanish Wars;
3) families of those who fought in the Libyan, World, Ethiopian, Spanish Wars decorated with the cross of war merit;
4) families of the dead for the Fascist cause;
5) families of those maimed, disabled, or wounded for the Fascist cause;
6) families of Fascist members of the Party during the years '19, '20, '21, '22, and in the second semester of '24 and the families of Legionnaires in Fiume;
7) families holding exceptional titles of merit which will be ascertained by a special commission.

The other Jews.

Italian citizens of the Jewish race not belonging to the above mentioned categories, pending a new law concerning the acquisition of Italian citizenship, may not:

a) be members of the PNF;
b) own or manage a business of any kind that employs 100 people or more;
c) own more than 50 hectares of land;
d) serve in the military in times of peace and war.

The practice of the professions will be subject to further provisions.

The Grand Council of Fascism also decides:

1) that the normal right to pensions will be recognized for the Jews dismissed from public positions.
2) every form of pressure upon the Jews to obtain abjurations will be rigorously punished;
3) that nothing is changed with regard to the free practice of religion and the activity of the Jewish Communities according to current laws;
4) that, together with elementary schools, the creation of high schools is for the Jews is allowed.

Immigration of Jews in Ethiopia.

The Grand Council of Fascism does not exclude the possibility of allowing, in order to discourage Jewish immigration to Palestine, a controlled immigration of European Jews into some areas of Ethiopia.

This possibility and other conditions placed upon the Jews may be cancelled or increased, according to the attitude that Jewry adopts toward Fascist Italy.

Teaching positions of racism .

The Grand Council of Fascism acknowledges with satisfaction that the Ministry of National Education has created teaching positions for the study of racism in the main universities in the Kingdom.

To the Black Shirts.

The Grand Council of Fascism, while it notes with satisfaction that the racial problems have aroused magnificent interest amongst the Italian nation, announces to the Fascists that the Party's directives in substance are to be considered fundamental and binding for all and that the regulations that will be promptly prepared by the single ministries must be inspired by the directives of the Grand Council.

23.
Measures for the defense of the Italian race

Royal Legal Decree of November 17, 1938-XVII, n. 1728
(GU. N. 264 of 19-11-1938)

Chapter one. Measures relating to marriage.

Art. 1. The marriage of an Italian citizen of the Aryan race with a person belonging to another race is prohibited. A marriage celebrated despite such prohibition is invalid.

Art. 2. Whereas the prohibition in *Art. 1* remains in effect, the marriage of an Italian citizen with a person of foreign nationality is subordinate to the consent of the Minister for Internal Affairs. Offenders will be sentenced to up to three months in prison and a fine of up to 10,000 lire.

Art. 3. Whereas the prohibition in *Art. 1* still remains in effect, the employees of civil and military state administration, of the organizations of the National Fascist Party or those under its control, of the provincial administration, of the municipalities, of state-controlled bodies and of trade associations and collateral agencies cannot enter into marriage with persons of a foreign nationality. Except for the application, when necessary, of the sanctions provided for in *Art. 2*, the violation of the aforementioned article entails the loss of position and rank.

Art. 4. For the purpose of *Articles 2* and *3*, Italians born abroad are not considered as foreigners.

Art. 5. The Registrar of births, deaths and marriages, when requested to publish marriage announcements, must establish, independently of the declarations of the parties, the race and the state of citizenship of both applicants. In the case described in *Art.1*, they will proceed neither with publication nor the celebration of the marriage. The Registrar of births, deaths and marriages who disobeys the provisions of the present article will be punished with a fine of 500 to 5,000 lire.

Art. 6. Marriages celebrated in violation of *Art.1*, shall not be civilly valid and must not, therefore, be entered into the records of the registrar according to art. 5 of the law, May 27, 1929-VII, n. 847. The religious representative, in front of whom the marriage is celebrated, is prohibited from executing what is provided in the first paragraph of *Art. 8* of the above mentioned law. Violators will be punished with a fine of 500 to 5,000 lire.

Art. 7. The Registrar of births, deaths and marriages who has proceeded to publish the acts of marriages celebrated without observing the provisions in *Art. 2* must make an immediate report to the proper authorities.

Chapter two. On those belonging to the Jewish race.
Art. 8. For legal purposes:

a) those born of parents who are both of the Jewish race, even if belonging to religions different from the Jewish religion, are considered of the Jewish race;

b) those born of parents of which one is of the Jewish race and the other of foreign nationality, are considered of the Jewish race;

c) those born of a mother of the Jewish race, if the father is unknown, are considered of the Jewish race;

d) those even though born of parents of Italian nationality, of which only one is of the Jewish race, or belonging to the Jewish religion, or registered in a Jewish community, or have given, in any other way, indications of Judaism, are considered of the Jewish race.

Those born of parents of Italian nationality, of which only one is of the Jewish race, who at the date of October 1, 1938-XVI, belonged to a religion other than the Jewish religion, are not considered of the Jewish race.

Art. 9. Belonging to the Jewish race must be declared and entered in the records of the Registrar of births, deaths and marriages and the bureau of vital statistics.

All of the information in the aforementioned registrars and the related certificates, which confirm belonging to the Jewish race must make clear mention of such records. Equal mention must be made in the acts relating to concessions or authorizations by public authorities. Offenders to the provisions of the present article will be punished with a fine of up to two thousand lire.

Art. 10. Italian citizens of the Jewish race may not:

a) serve in the military in times of peace or war;

b) exercise the function of guardian of minors or the disabled who do not belong to the Jewish race;

c) be owners or managers, with whatever title, of businesses declared as being of interest to the defense of the Nation, according to art. 1 of the Royal Decree-Law November 18, 1929-VIII, n. 2488, nor of a business of any nature which employs one hundred or more persons, nor have, or take the position of administrator or auditor of the said businesses;

d) be owners of land which, in total, has an estimated value of more than five thousand lire;

e) be owners of urban buildings which, in total, have an assessable tax of more than twenty thousand lire. For the buildings where an assessable tax does not exist, it will be established on the base of the ascertainments made as far as the application of a special tax on property as in the Royal Legal Decree October 5, 1936-XIV, n. 1743.

With the Royal Decree, on the proposal of the Minister of Finance, in agreement with the Minister of Internal Affairs, the Minister of Justice, the Minister of Corporations and the Minister of Currency and Exchange, will be issued rules for the implementation of the regulations of the letters c), d), e).

Art.11. A parent of the Jewish race may be deprived of parental authority over children who belong to a religion different from the Jewish religion, if it is demonstrated that they give them an education which does not correspond to their religious principles or to the national purpose.

Art.12. Those belonging to the Jewish race may not have in their employment any domestics who are Italian citizens of the Aryan race. Violators will be punished with the fine of 1,000 to 5,000 lire.

Art. 13. The following may not have persons belonging to the Jewish race in their employment:

a) Civil and Military State Administrations;

b) The PNF and the organizations depending upon it or under its control;

c) The administrations of the Provinces, of the Municipalities, of Public Institutions of Charity and of Boards, Institutes and Businesses, including those of transport under direct management, administered or maintained with assistance from the Provinces, the Municipalities, Public Institutions of Assistance and Charity or their Consortiums;

d) The Administrations of Municipal establishments;

e) The Administrations of State controlled institutes, however constituted and named, of National Works, of Union Associations and Collateral institutions and, in general, of all the Corporations and Institutions of Public Law, even of an autonomous character, subjected to State supervision or safeguard, or which the State participates in the maintenance thereof through contributions of a regular nature;

f) The Administrations of annex establishments or directly dependent upon the Institutions of the preceding letter e) or those which derive from them, in a prevailing manner, the necessary means for achieving their own purposes, as well as companies, whose capital is constituted, at least for half of the amount, with the participation of the State;

g) The Administrations of banks of national interest;

h) The Administrations of private insurance firms.

Art.14. The Minister for Internal Affairs, on the documented application of the interested parties, may, case by case, declare the dispositions of *Articles 10* and *11*, non-applicable, also letter h) of *Article 13*:

a) to the members of families of those who died in the Libyan, World, Ethiopian, and Spanish Wars and of those who died for the Fascist cause;

b) to those who find themselves in the following conditions:

1) maimed, disabled, wounded, war volunteers, or holder of a decoration from the Libyan, World, Ethiopian, and Spanish Wars;

2) servicemen in the Libyan, World, Ethiopian and Spanish Wars, who have at least obtained a war cross;

3) maimed, disabled, or wounded for the Fascist cause;

4) registered in the PNF in the years 1919, 20, 21, 22, and in the second half of 1924;

5) Legionnaires in Fiume;

6) who have acquired exceptional merit, to be evaluated in the terms of art. 16.

In the cases provided for in letter b), benefits may be extended to the members of the families of the persons listed therein, even if these are already deceased. The interested parties may request the entry of the actions of the Minister for Internal Affairs in the Registrar of births, deaths and marriages and the bureau of vital statistics. The action of the Minister for Internal Affairs is not subjected to any encumbrance, either in an administrative sense or in a jurisdictional sense.

Art. 15. For the purposes of the application of *Art. 14*, members of the family are considered, apart from the spouse, ascendants and descendants up to the second degree.

Art. 16. For the evaluation of the special merits in *Article 14* letter b), n. 6, a Commission is established, at the Ministry of Internal Affairs, made up of the

Undersecretary of State of Internal Affairs, who presides, of a vice-secretary of the PNF and the Chief of Staff of the MVSN.

Art. 17. It is prohibited for foreign Jews to take up residence in the Kingdom, in Libya and in the Aegean possessions.

Chapter three. Tempraryand final regulations.

Art. 18. For the period of three months from the effective date of the present decree, authority is given to the Minister for Internal Affairs, the interested Administration having been heard, to override, in special cases, the prohibition in *Art. 3*, these employees who intend to contract marriage with a foreigner of the Aryan race.

Art. 19. For the purposes of the application of *Art. 9*, all those who find themselves in the conditions of *Art. 8*, must make a declaration to the registrar of their municipality of residence, within 90 days of the effectiveness of the present decree. Those who do not fulfill such obligations within the prescribed term or supply incorrect or incomplete information will be arrested for up until one month and given a fine of up to three thousand lire.

Art. 20. The employees of the institutes mentioned in *Art. 13*, who belong to the Jewish race, will be released from service within three months from the effective date of the present decree.

Art. 21. The permanent employees of the State, released from service in application of *Art. 20*, are allowed to receive the pension due to them according to the terms of the law. Making an exception from existing regulations, for those who have not reached the prescribed period of time, the minimum pension is granted if they have completed at least ten years of service; in other cases an indemnity is granted equal to one-twelfth of the last pay for all of the years of service completed.

Art. 22. The dispositions of *Art. 21* are extended, as far as applicable, to the Institutions indicated by the letters b), c), d), e), f), g), h), of art. 13. The Institutions, towards which the dispositions of *Art. 21* are not applicable, will liquidate, to the employees released from service, the checks or indemnities foreseen by their organization or by the rules which regulate the relationship of their employment in the cases of release or dismissal for reasons extraneous to the will of the employees.

Art. 23. Italian citizenship already granted to foreign Jews after January 1, 1919 is revoked in all cases.

Art. 24. Foreign Jews and those to whom *Art. 23* applies, those who began their residence in the Kingdom, in Libya, and in the Aegean possessions after January 1, 1919, must leave the territory of the Kingdom, Libya and the Aegean possessions before March 12, 1939-XVII. Those who do not comply with this obligation within the said term will be arrested for up until three months or fined up to 5,000 lire and will be expelled according to the rule of *Art. 150* of the only text of public security laws, approved by Royal Decree June 18, 1931-IX, n. 773.

Art. 25. The enforcement of *Art. 24* is not applied to Jews of foreign nationality who, prior to October 1, 1938-XVI:

    a) have reached the sixty-fifth year of age;

    b) have contracted marriage with persons of Italian citizenship.

For the purposes of the application of the present article, the interested parties must send a documented application to the Ministry of Internal Affairs within thirty days from the date of effectiveness of the present decree.

Art. 26. Questions relative to the application of the present decree will be resolved case by case by the Minister for Internal Affairs, having heard the interested ministers if necessary, and subject to the opinion of a Commission nominated by him. The action of the Minister for Internal Affairs is not subjected to any encumbrance, either administrative or legal.

Art. 27. Nothing is changed regarding the public practice of religion and the activity of the Jewish communities, according to the laws in effect, except the modifications in case of the need to coordinate such laws with the dispositions of the present decree.

Art. 28. Every contrary regulation is cancelled or, in any case, incompatible with those of the present decree.

Art. 29. The King's Government is authorized to issue regulations necessary for the implementation of the present decree. The present decree will be presented in Parliament for its conversion into law. The DUCE, Minister of Internal Affairs, as proponent, is authorized to present the attached bill. We order that the present decree, sealed with the State Seal, be inserted in the official body of laws and decrees of the Kingdom of Italy, imposing on everyone to observe them and to see that they are observed.

Rome, November 17, 1938-XVII.

Victor Emmanuel
Mussolini-Farinacci–Solmi-Di Revel-Lantini
Endorsed, Minister of Justice: *Solmi.*

Registered at the State Auditor's Department, November 18, 1938-XVII *Acts of Government*, register 403, page 76- *Mancini.*

24.
[Composition of the most
important offices in charge of racial policy]

The superior council of Demography and Race.

The Duce has called to form the Superior Council of Demography and Race, instituted by Royal Decree of September 5, 1938 A.XVI, which by his delegation will be presided by the Undersecretary of State for Internal Affairs, the Fascists:

Prof. Giacomo Acerbo, President of the School of Economics and Commerce, Royal University of Rome; Filippo Bottazzi, Professor of Human Physiology, Royal University of Naples; Alessandro Ghigi, Professor of Zoology, Royal University of Bologna; Raffaele Corso, Professor of Ethnography, Royal University of Florence; Vito De Blasi, Professor of Obstetrics and Gynecology, Royal University of Genoa; Cornelio di Marzio, expert in public law; Cesare Frugoni, Professor of General Clinical Medicine, Royal University of Rome; Livio Livi, Professor of Statistics, Royal University of Florence; Biagio Pace, professor of Topography of Ancient Italy, Royal University of Rome; Prof. Antonio Pagliaro, Professor of Linguistics, Royal University of Rome; Prof. Umberto Pieramonti, non-tenured lecturer of Racial Genetics and Biology, Royal University of Naples; Ugo Rellini, Professor of Paleontology, Royal University of Rome; Giunio Salvi, Professor of Human Anatomy, Royal University of Naples; Sergio Sergi, Professor of Anthropology, Royal University of Rome; Francesco Valagussa, Professor of Clinical Pediatrics, Royal University of Rome.

Also included, as members of law, the Fascists:

Prof. Franco Savorgnan, President of the Central Institute of Statistics; Dr. Antonio Le Pera, Director General of Demography and Race; Prof. Giovanni Petragnani, Director General of Public Health; Advocate Carlo Bergamaschi, Royal Commissioner of OMNI; Eng. Gian Giacomo Borghese, President of the Fascist Union for large families; Dr. Athos Poli, Consul Nino Palmieri, appointed by the PNF; Dr. Renzo Meregazzi; Dr. Ottone Gabelli, appointed by the Ministry of Italian Africa; Dr. Giuseppe Lanzara, appointed by the Ministry of Foreign Affairs; Dr. Giuseppe Lampis, appointed by the Ministry of Justice; Dr. Raffaele Formosa, appointed by the Ministry of Finance; Dr. Collalto Collaltino, appointed by the Ministry of National Education; Dr. Emmanuele Filiberto Carnevale, appointed by the Ministry of Corporations; Prof. Sabato Visco, appointed by the Ministry of Popular Culture.

The functions of the Secretary of Council are practiced by the Director General of Demography and Race.

The Race Court.

H. E. Adv. Gaetano Azzariti, presiding judge of the Court of Appeals, President H. E. Dr. Antonio Le Pera, Prefect, Director General of Demography and Race; Adv. Antonio Manca, Councilor of the Supreme Court; Adv. Giovanni Petraccone, Councilor of the Supreme Court; Dr. Giovanni Ortolani, Vice Prefect. The functions of secretary are filled by Dr. Rodolfo Biancorosso, Councilor of administration of Internal Affairs.

The Commission for Discriminations.

Sen. Stefano De Ruggiero; Prefects: Lorenzo La Via (Dir. Gen. Religious Funds); Antonio Le Pera (Dir. Gen. Demography and Race); Mario Montecchi (Dir. Gen. of Religious Cults), Giuseppe Giovenco (Dir. Gen. of Civil Administration); Michele Magani (Head of Personnel); Vice Prefect Adolfo De Dominicis (in charge of the legal office of the cabinet of the Ministry for Internal Affairs).

Board of Directors of the EGELI.

Sen. Asinari di Bernezzo, president; Ugo Sirovich, President of the Section of the State Auditors' Department; Sen. Giuseppe Mormino, Councilor of the Councilor of State; Dr. Michele Pascolato, National Councilor; Dr. Michele Delle Donne, presiding judge of the Court of Appeals of Rome; Dr. Raffaele Festa Campanile, Superior Inspector of the Ministry of Agriculture; Dr. Erasmo Caravale, Director General of Commerce; Dr. Alessandro Baccaglini, Director General of the Inspectorate for the Defense of Savings and for the Exercise of Credit; Dr. Ettore Usai, National Councilor, president of the Fascist Federation of Owners and Tenant Farmers; Adv. Luigi Biamonti, Consultant of Legal Affairs of the Fascist Confederation of Industrialists.

25.

Race ascertainment

Art. 8 of the Royal Legal Decree 17-11-1938-XVII n. 1728
converted to law 1-5-1939-XVII, n. 274.

1) The attendance of catechism does not constitute evidence of belonging to a different religion than the Jewish religion; the demonstration of timely baptism is required.

2) The automatic registration to a Jewish Community does not constitute by itself, a manifestation of Judaism when the interested party can demonstrate having ignorance of such registration and to have never paid any kind of contribution.

3) Children of mixed marriages who have more than 50% Jewish blood are to be considered in every case of the Jewish race.

4) Children of an Aryan Italian parent and another Jewish foreigner are to be considered, for the purposes of racial ascertainment, in the same way as children of parents who are both of Italian nationality, one Jewish and the other Aryan.

5) Also children of parents who are both of foreign nationality must be judged for the purposes of racial ascertainment according to the Italian racial laws.

6) Those born from mixed marriages after October 1, 1938-XVI, and before October 1, 1939-XVII, are to be considered as not belonging to the Jewish race even if baptized after the said term, except in the case that the Jewish family does not seek a different determination.

7) Those born from mixed marriages after October 1, 1939-XVII, are to be considered as not belonging to the Jewish race if baptized within 10 days of birth, with exception for certain special cases to be evaluated each time.

8) Those born of Italian or mixed foreign marriages, with 50% Jewish blood and baptized before the date of October 1, 1938, but with manifestations of Judaism having married a person of the Jewish race—to be examined:

    a) if the marriage occurred before baptism and there are no children nor unfavorable elements–not belonging to the Jewish race;

    b) if the marriage occurred after baptism and there are no children—in general to be declared Jews;

    c) if the marriage occurred before or after the reception of baptism and there are children—who therefore have 75% Jewish blood, and therefore cannot declare themselves of the Aryan race due to the prevalence of Jewish blood, the parent, in general, is declared as belonging to the Jewish race.

7) Germans can prove their not belonging to the Jewish race through a declaration by the German Government which shows such facts based on national law, and a certificate which shows that they have been baptized prior to October 1, 1938.

26.

["Demography and Race" report to the Duce (August 1940)]

Ministry of Internal Affairs
General Management of Demography and Race

To the Duce

I briefly refer to you the situation of the Jews since more than a year of the application of the various racial laws, in order to receive precise directions from you, DUCE.

STATISTICAL SITUATION

Italian Jews

From an approximate calculation based on the data from the 1938 census, corrected and updated with information from the reports of the Royal Decree of November 17, 1938-XVII n. 1728, around 39,000 Italian Jews present in the Kingdom are residing in the various provinces as in attached n. 1.

The said Jews are assembled in around 11,500 family units.

Of these it appears that around 10,000 Jews are under 15 years of age and around 6,000 Jews are over 65 of age.

Regarding their sex it can be stated that there are 50% males and 50% females.

There are over all 6,820 mixed marriages, of which 2,220 are childless, and the remaining 4,600 marriages with around 13,000 children:

1,200 couples have children who are declared Jewish in the census (around 3,500); 3,400 couples have children who are declared Catholic in the census or other non-Jewish religion (around 9,500).

As professional activities we have noted:

Artisans: approx. 4,350

Professionals: approx. 5,200

Industrialists: approx. 1,000

Clerks: approx. 4,200

Merchants: approx. 1,450

Workers and farm laborers: approx. 700

Farmers: approx. 220

It must be kept in mind that there are more than 150 Jews who are former officers of the Armed Forces and around 250 former State functionaries, of whom many had reached a high rank in the administration.

Roughly, it can be stated that there are:

a) 1,924 *highly distinguished Jews* according to the law who with family extensions form a total of 4,815 persons;

b) 194 *highly distinguished Jews* for exceptional merit or a total of 417 persons.

The moral and political positions of these people have been rigorously assessed by the special Committees and the reasons for the special distinctions are specified in detail in the attached 2;

c) Jews *with an Aryan wife* around 4,000

Many of these have children–not considered as Jews by law—subjected to compulsory military service or civilian draft;

d) Jewish wives of *Aryan heads of family*, around 2,800, many with children practically all non-Jewish, therefore subject to compulsory military service or civil mobilization.

It turns out that many Jews have left the Kingdom permanently, settling abroad, especially in North America. Precise assessments regarding this are in progress.

Foreign Jews or Stateless persons.
  a) Authorized to remain in the Kingdom according to articles 24 and 25—are around 2,950. They are Jews either over the age of 65, or residing in the Kingdom prior to January 1, 1919, or married to Italian citizens;
  b) To be expelled—but still tolerated by the regulations now standing—around 5,200.

Situation of the racial files (Jews).
The revision of the census in each Province and the consequent updating of the general file of the Jews present in the Kingdom are in progress.

Up until October 12 of this year, 3,865 applications for race ascertainment of have been presented, of which 677 have been accepted, 583 rejected, and 2,605 are currently under preliminary investigation.

8,839 cases for special examination have been presented, of which ·4,210 according to the law and 4,625 for exceptional merit.

Of the applications for special distinction examination according to the law:
  2,069 were decided in favor
  837 were rejected
  1,344 are currently under preliminary investigation.
Of the applications for exceptional merit:
  187 were decided in favor
  100 were rejected
  4,342 are currently under preliminary investigation.
  6,369 applications of foreign Jews have been examined.

Political Situation
The application of the racial laws with regard to the Jews has given way to the need to resolve many different matters in the educational, professional, welfare, and social fields etc. which were presented urgently and which have been virtually resolved, pending legislative decisions, always using the principle of expelling Jewish elements from all activities, especially if this is also connected indirectly to national defense.

It was indeed decided that in many sectors Jewish elements were not to carry out any activity, while in other sectors (private insurance, commerce, trade) it was not possible to put the same regulations into effect.

In the field of private insurance—an almost exclusive Jewish monopoly—a radical change in regulations was not believed to be indicated, to avoid serious damage to society and indirectly to national trade.

710

In the field of trade, the application of the Royal legal decree of February 9, 1939-XVII n. 126 gave no practical results: indeed, joint stock companies and businesses which have less then 100 employees were excluded by the limitations, this way the regulations affected very few businesses (around 10 in all of Italy).

Regarding this issue, as you are already aware, a certain discontent was spread within public opinion that many Jews, both by transforming their businesses into joint stock companies and by having Aryan fellow citizens appear as administrators, managed to continue, personally and undisturbed, their commercial or industrial activities without any limitations, but rather continuing to be state contracts for supplies, including supplying the Military Ministries.

Other discontent has spread among Aryans by the fact that in an actual state of emergency the Jews exonerated from military service remained free to speculate and some Jewish elements made themselves far too conspicuous by staying at holiday resorts.

Also, the law which should have limited real estate property was a disappointment in practical terms, both because of the very broad and benevolent interpretation, and because of the donations and other devices accepted as lawful by the Ministry of Finance, almost all the Jews were able to avoid the regulations, as I have already referred to you, with the relevant report.

All of this has generated the opinion that, as you know, it emerges daily, the anti-Jewish law has not yet been applied with severity and that the Jews are left tranquilly to go about their activities.

In contrast to what occurred regarding the Jews in the well off categories (merchants, industrialists, etc.) the Jews belonging to the categories of employees, modest professionals, workers, artisans, and street vendors, etc., who live only from their daily earnings, have been put into conditions where they are unable to meet the daily requirements of their families.

Public opinion displays a certain pity towards them due to the fact that the strong contrast between the two categories of Jews is evident, one has hardly felt anything materially from the regulations while the other has been seriously damaged.

To a major degree the cases of mixed families are worthy of special attention, in which non-Jewish youth suffer the consequences of restrictive dispositions adopted in regard to the Jewish parent.

Indeed you are aware, from reports from several sources, of the serious situation many families are struggling with, which, for marriages celebrated prior to the passage of the racial laws, are made up of one Aryan and one Jewish spouse. Especially when the Jew is the head of the family and the wife the Aryan and there are children who, having been baptized at birth, are considered Aryan, the situation is tragic, inasmuch as the head of the family, placed in the absolute impossibility of being able to work, throws many Aryans into poverty.

Recently the Holy See pointed out the painful situation of many families in which, even though the Jewish spouse had converted to Christianity for many years with the rest of the family being all Christian, the loss of work or position by the head of the family has resulted in the most absolute destitution. Such cases present a serious problem of assistance for many families and many children.

You know, DUCE, that from around 39,000 Italian Jews, grouped in 11,500 family units, there are a good 6,820 mixed families, and 1,200 families have given offspring the Jewish religion *but a good 3,400 couples have given their children a Christian and Catholic education.*

These figures show the seriousness of the situation, which makes it more difficult, if not impossible, to have a more energetic racial policy directed at a clear separation between Jews and Aryans.

To obviate these situations, which almost cancel the effectiveness of racial regulations and often hinder the productive activity of many sectors of the nation, attention has been drawn to the possibility of a radical solution, which would allow the permanent resolution, in a brief period, of the Jewish question in Italy.

Except for the special amendments, which because of public and social order can be imposed, the points on which the measures should be based are three:

1) Legal equality of the Jews achieved through marriage with an Aryan, the Christian education of offspring, religious conversion, and political activity in keeping with the directives of the Regime, etc., offer sufficient guarantees to carry out, without danger, their activities in the organizations and in the institutions of the Regime;

2) Absolute elimination from the nation of all the other Jews—Italian and foreign—who do not qualify for n. 1. To achieve this goal, which does not seem easy, a period of time could be established, promoting the concessions (estates, currencies, etc.) for those who leave Italy faster and aggravating measures (fiscal, estates, limitations of commercial, industrial or professional activities, etc.) proportionate to the time frame for departure from the Kingdom;

3) Absolute prohibition for Jews or foreigners who have already departed to re-enter the Kingdom.

Applying such principles, naturally adapted to all political, social, internal order requirements as well as of special interest to the nation, given the number and the composition of the Jews in Italy, it can be deduced that around 9,000 converted Jews would remain in Italy, who, abandoning their surnames and being appropriately watched in the political field, can easily be absorbed into the 45,000,000 Aryan Italians—and calculating a period of five years for the departure of the other Jews—by 1945 the permanent resolution of the Jewish question could be achieved, without serious repercussions and using a method, if not new historically, at least original in its actual application, also because it can be done only in Italy due to the special numeric situation of the families of the Jews.

Remaining in the kingdom, you will remember that a similar method, perhaps more prompt in its execution, was used in other times to solve the Jewish problem in Sicily and Calabria, where there once prospered numerous Jewish communities; today there remains only the rare Jew brought in from other regions, but many local family surnames indicate a remote Jewish origin.

I am convinced that such a procedure would ensure that we would not even hear about Jews or Judaism in six or seven years time, other than for historical recollection, and allow us to permanently solve the most difficult problem of our policy on the defense of race.

If you do not think such a radical solution is warranted, it would then be, in my opinion, urgent to approve the following directives:

1) A confidential review of Jewish joint stock companies recently transformed or made Aryan only formally in their management;

2) Severe penalties against those Jews who, since they are sheltered abroad, have an anti-Italian attitude, to determine the confiscation of their property in Italy;

3) Imposition of compulsory work, or a special tax, towards the Jews exonerated from military service;

4) Revision into a single legal text of the racial regulations for the Jews, in order to avoid inconvenient complaints.

I submit to you, DUCE, these considerations, and I await your orders before proceeding with a detailed study of the matter.

THE UNDERSECRETARY OF STATE

****

27.

[Draft of the Legal Decree for the resolution of the racial question (October 1940)]

Art. 1. Residence within the Kingdom is forbidden to persons of any nationality or citizenship who, according to the definitions contained in *Art. 8* of the Royal Decree Law of November 17, 1938, no. 1728, are considered members of the Jewish race. The temporary sojourn of Jews within the Kingdom is regulated by the rules described in Art. ...

Art. 2. In compliance with the decree issued by the Minister of Internal Affairs, permission to remain within the Kingdom and to have the same legal rights as Italian citizens of the Aryan race may be granted to those Jews who are members of mixed families as in the situations described in *Art. 3.*

Art. 3. For the purposes of *Art. 2,* a mixed family is considered such wherein one spouse belongs to the Aryan race and the other to the Jewish, as long as at least one possesses Italian citizenship or nationality.

For the same purposes the following are considered to be members of mixed families:

a) a Jew married to a member of the Aryan race;
b) his ascendants;
c) his descendants and their respective spouses;
d) his collateral relatives to and including the 3rd degree of kinship, on condition that they neither live with nor are married to, nor can be assumed as being such, but are instead linked to the specified family by normal family bonds.

The benefits described in *Art. 2* cannot be applied to Jews who have come of age and are members of the Jewish religion as of July 1, 1941, or to Jews who have openly declared their belonging to Judaism or have otherwise behaved in contrast to national instructions.

Art. 4. Jews residing in, or in any case present within, the Kingdom at the date this law becomes effective and who do not benefit from the provisions of *Art. 2* must leave the national territory within five years (starting from ...). For those Jews specifically discriminated by *Art. 14* of the Royal Decree-Law 17-11-1938, n.1728, letters a), b), 1, 3, 4 and 6, this term is extended by another five years.

Art. 5. The penalties defined in the racial laws in effect and currently applicable, remain in effect and during the five-year period to leave the Kingdom granted to non-discriminated Jews, said Jews cannot engage in professional activities nor participate, even indirectly, in the administration of industrial or commercial enterprises, and they cannot leave their usual place of residence without prior permission form the Police Authorities.

Art. 6. These non-discriminated Jews who must leave the Kingdom are authorized to export, under the currency regulations defined by articles ...., their legal estate or the proceeds from the sale of real property, in the following proportions:

a) if they leave the Kingdom during the first year
of the law's application 8/10
b) within the second year 7/10
c) within the third year 6/10
d) within the fourth year 5/10
e) within the fifth year 3/10

714

Those Jews who instead have been specifically discriminated by the law can export their entire estate if they leave the Kingdom within the second year of the law's passage; eight-tenths within the fourth year; seven-tenths within the sixth year; five-tenths within the eighth year and three-tenths within the tenth year.

Art. 7. The Jews not within the category of those specifically distinguished and while waiting to leave the Kingdom will be subject to an increase in all taxes, over-taxes and local rates in the following proportions:

a) first year 10%
b) second year 25%
c) third year 50%
d) fourth year 75%
e) fifth year 100%

Those Jews, not specifically discriminated by the law and who are without property may be, as of the second year of the law's effectiveness, sent to work camps for the construction of public utility projects and under special regulations to be established in a separate provision. For the specifically discriminated Jews the above tax increases will be applied only during the second five-year period.

Art. 8. Those Jews as defined in Art. 4 who have not left the Kingdom by the end of the established term, will be subject to the following sanctions:

a) expulsion from the Kingdom
b) confiscation of property owned
c) assignment to work camps in the Kingdom or the colonies for those who cannot be expelled from the Kingdom.

28.
[Report by Demography and Race (September 1941)]

The Jewish situation in Italy did not present the same exceptional seriousness as in other Nations, both because of the relatively small number of Jews living in the Kingdom, as well as because of the high number of marriages between Jews and Aryans, a phenomenon that was not present in any other Nation. This fact had created a particular situation, since the Jews who had infiltrated the Aryan ranks with bonds of affection as well as economic gain, blunted and greatly reduced the feelings of antagonism in their regard. This contrast was reduced even more by the fact that many Jews, given the important positions they had reached in the Civil Service, the Armed Forces and industry, had been able to create an environment for themselves that was favorable rather than hostile. A genuine feeling of distrust towards the Jews, except for the meager number of anti-Jewish scholars, was widely expressed in Italy only towards the Jews of the lowest social class, who practiced those trades typical of the ghetto.

Indeed, 45,000 Jews (born in Italy) lived in the country: due to emigration, these are now about 39,000.

This number represents about 10,000 families, and a good 6,820 are mixed families, that is, having Aryan relatives: more specifically, there are about 4,000 Jews married to Aryan women and about 2,800 female Jews married to Aryan men. There is therefore a clear tendency among Jews, contrary to their racial spirit, to infiltrate by marrying Aryan women and a smaller number of Aryan men, generally from fairly high social classes, who have chosen a Jew as their life's companion.

The result of these mixed marriages are not demographically important. About 2,200 of mixed couples are without offspring and the other 4,600 have procreated 13,000 children, of whom about one-fourth have been brought into the Jewish religion and three-fourths have been given non-Jewish spiritual instruction.

This situation has no equivalent in any other Nation and explains the large number of individuals of mixed race who have intermarried (various situations have been studied of several generations of individuals of mixed race marrying others like themselves) and who have converted, either spontaneously or because of the effect of the racial laws, to non-Jewish religions and have been the object of a great number of racial verifications effected. There have been up to now more than 10,000; of these, 6,700 have been requested by the persons involved themselves and about 3,500 have been carried out for official reasons, because of the application of racial regulations requiring verification among employees, officers, etc., and the verifications required by the Town Councils to publish wedding announcements.

The same situation, the great percentage of mixed marriages, can explain the decidedly non-hostile environment found in several Italian social classes, which, because of family relations, ways of life and economic interests, have forged strong ties with Jewish or formerly Jewish environments.

The occurrence is limited to northern and central Italy and is rare and exceptional in the southern regions and the islands.

On the other hand, there is no denying that in the Armed Forces (the Army and the Navy), in the Civil Service, in high finance as well as trade, many Jews have reached extremely important positions, that many have been and are Senators of the Kingdom, that many Jews are related to the best known Italian families and, finally, that many Jews have participated both in Italian wars as well as in the Fascist Revolution, and this can explain the high number of requests for discriminations provided by law and that, in fact, wind up being only economic and professional advantages for the wealthy and for professionals whereas they have no practical effect for the less well-to-do and the salaried workers who make up the majority of Italian Jews.

Discriminations have been granted, in fact, to 199 family members of victims of the war and the Fascist Revolution; to more than 1000 Jewish volunteers, amputees, disabled, wounded and decorated because of the war; to about 500 Jews, who were Fascists before the March; and to about 500 Jews included in more than one of the categories above.

Only 213 Jews were awarded discriminations for exceptional merit, an extremely small number considering the requests received and the situation of the Italian Jews as described above.

The most severe and stringent principles were used for racial verification, so much so that some considered them open to too stringent interpretation, but the severity of the principles did create negative feelings both among the subjects of the verification as well as in some Aryan circles, certainly not hostile to the Jews and particularly in some areas, well known to You, who did not hesitate to state their ideas in this regard and to move actively in favor of the Jews who, they thought, deserved kindness and leniency.

After this brief analysis of the real racial situation in Italy regarding the Jews, it is good to consider what practical effects have been created by the anti-Jewish regulations.

The first three articles of the law regarding marriage have been applied in full for marriages between Aryans and persons of other races: none was permitted; in some cases where the marriage was performed against racial regulations, annulment was obtained. Marriages between Italians and foreigners were carefully considered in relation to the particular international situation and after those marriages had already been performed at the date of publication of the law, no new permissions will be granted to state employees or employees of state-controlled bodies.

I have already reported on the application of Art. 8 and 14 regarding racial verification and distinctions. As for Arts. 10 and 13, the law regarding military service, dismissal of employees from state or state-controlled agencies, from the PNF, local civilian administrations, etc., has been rigidly enforced.

The application of those norms regarding limitation of real estate property ownership and industrial and commercial activity on the part of Jews has been ineffective, as this office had in fact expected.

The identical motivations already described regarding mixed families with donations made from Jews to non-Jewish descendents, the recognition of nearly all commercial activities as joint-stock companies, the benevolent interpretation on the part of the competent Ministry in all doubtful cases, have practically cancelled the results the law was intended to produce, leaving nearly unchanged the economic situation of the Jews, both in the private sphere as well as in industry and commerce. The political norms ostracizing Jewish participation did not succeed in changing the strong economic presence of the Jews in commerce and industry since, as You know, the administration and management of the biggest Jewish companies and activities were changed in name only and Aryan names were substituted on paper while management remains, as everyone knows, in Jewish hands.

Regulations regarding national education have been applied inflexibly.

As for professional activities, even though the pertinent legislation has been applied normally, it is not easy, for reasons already mentioned, to obtain a clear separation within the profession itself since, particularly for the legal and medical professions, the environment does not lend itself to strict enforcement of the rules and the application of their repressive provisions.

Many regulations of various kinds have been issued, with administrative orders in each instance, to limit the social activity of the Jews; limiting licenses issued by the Police, forbidding certain trades or activities (building supervisors, hotel owners, landlords, brokers, street vendors, public drivers, second-hand dealers, etc.), forbidding their use of radios, the inclusion of Jews in public telephone directories, refusal of permits to own firearms even for hunting, and expressing the opinion to all those Agencies or various other organizations in the different issues each one raised, that was always intended to limit, in every case, any activity at all by the Jews, even though the opinions issued in some cases by this Office were seen to be legally in excess of the regulations issued by the State Council.

This being a kind of summary of the *current* situation, it is fair to consider which provisions might lead to a fast and thorough solution of the problem, consistent with the principle behind the law voted by the Great Council, and with the real situation and political needs at the present time.

Bearing in mind that every new decision will meet with difficulties as it is applied to Jewish members of mixed families, through legal means it would be possible to set a final date for the presentation by the Jews themselves of requests for race ascertianment and discriminations, in order to complete all the requests already presented as quickly as possible and to accept, after the set date, only official requests for race ascertianment in order to apply the regulations in force and effect.

The solution of the many requests from the provinces, where the majority of Jews live, creates greater difficulties, since many different questions are asked: from simple administrative concessions to Police permits for various authorizations, from requests for housing assistance, permits for importation, etc., and for which regarding the Jewish and even Aryan members of mixed families, there are not always solutions compatible with racial laws or political timeliness, or even with humanitarian impulses when, as often happens, racial intransigence turns into serious damage, often detrimental to the lives of Aryans or people of mixed race and considered non-Jews by the law. In many cases, severity in applying the law can create serious repercussions among the parents or brothers of mixed-non-Jews, as such who might be performing military service, or be at the front, or even prisoners, missing or wounded. These situations, as well as many other very delicate ones (spouses and relatives of well-known persons, of senators, ex-ministers, generals, admirals, national councilmen, famous scientists, etc., the parents of soldiers killed in battle and decorated during the current conflict, parents and relatives of men killed for the Fascist Revolution, etc.) do not allow the issuing and implementation of uniform, rigid racial legislative provisions, which in the vast disparity of the situations themselves could lead to regrettable instances of injustice. Thus, for example, the case of Aryan wives of Jews who have been denied the menas of supporting their family (building supervisors, landlords, street vendors, hotel owners, etc.) which is in blatant contrast to the situation of the Jewish wives of Aryan persons who, belonging to a privileged class, suffer neither moral nor material damage from their racial situation.

On the other hand, a more rapid examination of the existing requests could yield modest results considering the number of requests to be examined and the need for a preliminary investigation that is difficult as well as almost always linked to lengthy research, the present situation would remain practically unchanged for some years and would inevitably worsen the complaints currently being made.

It is the opinion of this Office that a single radical solution could resolve the Jewish question in Italy, in a way most compatible with the political intent of the Great Council, as was already presented in a previous paper, that is: "To confront the problem of mixed families, tolerating within the Kingdom only those Jews who belong to such a family nucleus or who can be considered the same because of special merits, to expel from the Kingdom all other Jews, in a given period of time and with provisions to be applied *automatically* to avoid any suspicion of partiality or favoritism."

Thus, Your Excellency, I refer to the report of which You are aware and that has received the Duce's approval, that would give the Italian Jewish problem, in its very special situation regarding numbers and environment, a radical and permanent solution no other Nation could adopt.

Besides, there are about 7,000 foreign or stateless Jews in the Kingdom: some of these (about 800) are authorized to remain because they are married to Italian citizens.

The planned law regarding persons of mixed background could be applied to foreigners or stateless persons with appropriate modifications in order to arrive at the almost total expulsion from the Kingdom of foreign Jews who have no further reason to continue either their stay or their private or professional activity in Italy.

These provisions, supplemented by proper regulations regarding real estate and personal property belonging to Jews to be expelled, and made simpler by the already approved norms regarding shares of joint stock companies, could resolve the Jewish problem and overcome it in all its aspects, so that in just a few decades it would only be a historical memory.

29.
[Professor Landra's visit to Germany]

Cable n. 9188

Royal Embassy of Italy
Berlin

Royal Ministry of Popular Culture
and for the knowledge of
Royal Ministry of Foreign Affairs
Rome

Berlin, December 23, 1938-XVII

Prof. Landra's visit to Germany.

I am honored to report on the visit to Germany by Prof. Guido Landra, Director of Racial Studies at the Royal Ministry of Popular Culture, and Dr. Lino Buscino, Vice Director of the same.

In accordance with the instructions received by cable from the head of ministerial staff of this ministry, the press agent, Marquess Antinori, on the evening of the 13th went to welcome the two officials along with the Cultural Attaché, Dr. Ridomi. Of the Germans those present at the station were the head of the Racial Office of the National-Socialist Party, Dr. Gross with some of his collaborators in Nazi uniform.

Dr. Gross had prepared a detailed program of visits and meetings for Prof. Landra. Amongst the visits, those to be noted above all are the ones to the Racial Office, the Anthropological Institute directed by Prof. Fischer, the Party's Racial Education School, and the Concentration Camp at Sachsenhausen. Among the meetings, those noteworthy are the meetings with Alfred Rosenberg and with the Chief of the German Police, H. Himmler. All of this has been reported to this ministry by written teletype message on December 14, 15, 18, and 20.

720

Dr. Gross took Prof. Landra and Buscino to Reichenberg, in the Sudeten region, having them attend a meeting on racial propaganda. Upon their return, once the Berlin program was completed, Prof. Landra attended a luncheon offered in his honor by Dr. Gross with the Head of the Doctors of Germany, Prof. Wagner and some other functionaries of the Ministry of Foreign Affairs, the Ministry of Internal Affairs and the Ministry of Education were also present. For the Royal Embassy Prince d'Aquino and Dr. Ridomi were present. Dr. Gross gave a speech on this occasion in which, reminding how Prof. Landra had requested that his visit not be considered official, adding that he was unable to avoid, however, gathering some representatives of German Racial Policy around the Italian comrade, to show the goodwill aroused in Germany by the Italian initiative for the defense of the race.

Gross said that the only worrisome point regarding the Nazi and Fascist programs was the absence, until recently, in the latter, of a racial policy. Now that this point has been eliminated, the Nazi Party is very pleased, not only because of Italian racial policy, but also due to the fact that it uses its own original procedures, that is to say, procedures which its initiators consider to be more in tune with the conditions of the country and the people. The speaker concluded by expressing his admiration for the Duce of Fascist Italy and inviting all those present to raise their glasses to his health.

Prof. Landra replied by declaring himself delighted to have been able to visit the German racial institutes and thankful for the reception he was given; he said that he was only an executor of the Duce's initiatives which were enacted by the competent bodies, in the field of the defense of the race; but he added that it would be incorrect to believe that the racial policy began in Italy since the well-known manifesto. Right from the beginning of Fascism the Duce had a clear vision of national developments also from the racial point of view, and a racial awareness has always existed in Fascism: the speaker concluded with a salute to the Führer.

On the 19th Prof. Landra left for Münich where he was received by the Secretary of the Nazi Party, Minister R. Hess, according to a brief, unofficial communication from the German agency.

The German press followed Prof. Landra's stay in Germany through bulletins of the DNB compiled by the office of Dr. Gross. The *Niedersächsische Tageszeitung* and the *Westdeutscher Beobachter* also published, after conversations between their editor and Prof. Landra, articles of explaining the Italian racial policy.

The Royal Chargé d'Affaires
(Signed) Magistrati

****

30.

[Memos on the draft of the Jews for labor service]

Rome, August 5, 1942-XX

Ministry of Internal Affairs
General Directorate for Demography and Race
To the prefects of the Kingdom
Prot: n.534/30 R

Subject: Draft of Jews for Labor Service

Please follow the regulations below for the mobilization of the Jews for labor service:

1) Generally, except for specifically stated discriminations, the mobilized Jews must be assigned to manual labor, with prior ascertainment, in cases of doubt, of their physical fitness.

2) Those Jews who reached the age of military service in the years from 1910 to 1922, who would have performed military service were it not for the racial laws must be mobilized ahead of all others.

3) Then those Jews who do not have a permanent occupation must be mobilized, and then still further those who have manual occupations.

4) Then those Jews who work in commerce, regular jobs, professions, and students must be mobilized.

5) Finally, in case of need, those Jews who carry out activities in auxiliary establishments and in other establishments of national interest must be mobilized.

6) Pending new regulations, the mobilization of foreigners and doctors remains suspended.

7) Jewish elements who are part of families considered as mixed are exempt from mobilization (for such purposes a mixed family is understood as having one of the spouses Jewish and the other and the children are Aryan).

8) Women who, having children who are minors, directly attend to family duties, only if they do not have dependent domestic staff or there is no other member of the family who can replace them, are exempt from mobilization.

9) For those Jews who are interned or confined, the regulations given by the General Directorate of the PS on July 5, Div. A. G. R. n. 442/18947 are valid.

10) Putting Jews to work must be done gradually when the need is demonstrated. Orders will be given in the case where it will be necessary to transfer Jewish laborers from one province to another.

11) It is also confirmed that especially distinguished Jews are to be mobilized.

12) Those Jews who are confirmed by the Registrar must be mobilized even if a request for recognition as not belonging to the Jewish race is in process.

13) All questions regarding the labor, compensation for labor, the housing of the mobilized laborers, etc., are handled by the Ministry of Corporations.

14) The prohibition of having non-Jews and Jews working together remains in force.

15) There is no need for the consent of this Ministry for the work of the mobilized Jews to begin, although it must be informed per the cable memo of June 23, n. 43738. In cases foreseen by the memo of May 15, n. 26992 M. C. 20 of the Ministry of Corporations (General Directorate of Works) the prior authorization of the said Ministry must be requested.

For the Minister
Buffarini

****

Ministry of Internal Affairs
General Direcorate for Demography and Race

Rome, July 15, 1943-XXI

N. 1366 Cat. 2/19

To the prefects of the Kingdom

Copy for information to:
the Ministry of Corporations
Work Service

To the General Directorate Public Security
Subject: Draft of the Jews for Labor Service.

To explain the recent measures for the total draft for labor service of the Jews of both sexes born between the years 1907 and 1925 included, and in relation to various questions proposed by the prefects, it is to be pointed out that the following are to be excluded from the draft itself:

1) Those confined;

2) Those interned;

3) Those Jews suitable for specialized work, if they are not capable of agricultural work even if not heavy;

4) Generally, those Jews who have already begun compulsory labor due to a formal draft;

5) Of those Jews permanently occupied prior to the order of mobilization those who had serious, stable occupations related to the war or in the public interest with regard to production, are to be distinguished from those whose

occupations had none of the requisites mentioned above; this is left to the cautious discretion of the prefect. Those belonging to the first category of occupations may be excluded, *subject to thorough examination*, from the draft; instead the others will be included.

6) Eligible female Jews, born in the years from 1907 to 1925 included, will be drafted, as a rule, except those who are at an advanced stage of pregnancy or who have minors in their care, considered as such, to the effects of the present draft, when they are not older than 14 years of age.

7) Those Jews evacuated because of the war who possess the desired requirements, will be drafted by the authorities of the province of actual residence, in agreement, where it is necessary, with the authority of the province of the place of origin.

8) For those Jews who are part of mixed-race families, of which the cable of last June 7, n. 41561, must be understood to be Jews, even if they have an Aryan spouse and mixed-race children, even if these were declared as not belonging to the Jewish race.

9) Those of mixed-race will be considered as Jews and therefore included in the draft until there is a formal ministerial declaration on the possible nonbelonging to the Jewish race. The prefects will be able to notify the Ministry of the opportunity of a quick measure in relation to the necessity of ascertaining the racial profile of those drafted, forwarding, where necessary, a formal documented proposal and rapidly completing the judicial inquiry of the cases in progress.

10) Foreign Jews, as already provided, will be normally included in the program of the draft, with the possibility of more precise instructions regarding prospective special discriminations to come from the ministry.

11) In the entire draft of rabbis and doctors born in the years indicated above, it is necessary to keep in mind, within the strict limits necessary, the religious needs and assistance of the remaining Jewish communities in the country.

For the Minister
[illegible]

31.

[Outline for a new declaration of the Italian race]

1) The entire population of Italy has a racial identity with common and unmistakable characteristics.

2) The actual physiognomy of this complex, which traces its origins back to he most remote prehistoric age of the peninsula, distinctly appears since the Roman era. The Italian population presents itself, therefore, in the Roman pe-

riod—after having passed through a few millennia of biological and spiritual permeation, favored by the environment—as one whole unit; and Rome became, right from the beginning, the ethnic center of this formative process.

3) This unity, even its variety of types, stands out because of the evidence of common physical and psychological characteristics. The noble spiritual characteristics of the race correspond to the esthetic harmony of the somatic features.

4) The continuity of the types from the Roman era until today is demonstrated by the persistence of the geographical distribution of the types themselves and by the proof supplied the skeleton documentation of the various periods and by the artistic reproductions from all periods.

5) The racial composition of Italy has been maintained through the historical millennia substantially pure from foreign influence, inasmuch, after the Roman era, Italy was never a land of permanent settlement by alien masses. The demographic effect of immigrations and foreign domination, even of those most remembered for their importance, was extremely weak. From the Roman age onwards the development of the population of Italy was never accentuated in a perceptible way by alien elements, but was instead essentially due to the natural increase of the population itself.

6) This unity and ethnic continuity are confirmed and demonstrated in an even more evident manner by the psychological manifestations of our racial identity.

7) A warlike nature and spirit of enterprise, which took the Romans to the borders of the ancient world, produced the greatest of explorers and scattered our people in every corner of the world, were, and are, the characteristic features still alive in the Italian population at every layer of its social strata. Added to these dynamic inclinations, congenital to the Italian spirit, are, in every era, versatile genius, the capacity of abstract speculation and at the same time concrete application. The inborn, very distinct artistic sense of the race, favored by the superb nature of the country, rises from the anonymous artisans of Roman art and the cathedrals of the medieval period or folk poetry to the powerful artistic personalities which are the pure glory of the Italian spirit. The ethics of the race are revealed in the millenial elaboration of the family institution, characteristic of our people. All of these high qualities harmonize in a spiritual equilibrium, which clearly distinguishes us from other races. The continuity of this spirit is documented by the line of complex and universal geniuses, to be found in every social class, often from the people, and which are the most perfect example of the psychological characteristics of the Italian race. In the Roman era the race is sublime in the fearlessness of the soldiers and in the high political conceptions of Scipio, Caesar, and Augustus, in the poetic vision of Virgil, and, during the most remote and dark medieval times, in the philosophical theories of Sts. Benedict, Gregory the Great, Thomas Aquinas, and of those who conserved

and passed on to us the traditions and the documents of the Roman world. In Saint Francis there is the sublime Italian religious philosophy; in Giotto the first expression in the world of the new pictorial art. The Italy of today lives in the sublime art and the universal conceptions of Dante, in the prophetic power of Machiavelli; the Renaissance culminates in the maximum characters of Leonardo, Michelangelo, and Raphael. The genius of the race is also revealed in its women, such as Vittoria Colonna, Elisabetta Gonzaga, Caterina Sforza. In political decline our race conserves its traditional genius in the works of Galileo, of Vico. In this way the Risorgimento finds, after the political and military glow of [Napoleon] Bonaparte, the vitality of the race alive and integral, that emerges in Cavour, Mazzini, in Garibaldi. Straddling two eras, Marconi, D'Annunzio, and Mussolini pick up the thread, never broken, to resume the inexhaustible value of the race, to inspire in our people the most correct and natural racial pride and to point out to the young and future generations the light and the way which is that of Rome.

8) This ethnic reality finds another confirmation in the consciousness, always ingrained in every social class, and in the aspiration to political unity, which has never been lost, even in the most obscure periods of foreign rule, and which in every moment has radiated a burning love for the homeland, understood in its integral geographical expression, only today almost entirely achieved.

9) In this way the Italian racial element demonstrates its uninterrupted vitality, always prevalent, both on the biological and spiritual side.

The ancient Roman legionnaries live again in the Fascist legionnaries. The local genius of the race continues, its mission of all human greatness unchanged throughout the millennia.

10) The atmosphere created by Fascism today demonstrates the characteristics of this multi-millennial Italic race in the Fascist youth organization, which, carried back the Roman eagles to the land of Africa, revived the Empire, and spreads the new civilization of Mussolini throughout the world.

32.
[Secret report from Dino Alfieri to Galeazzo Ciano]

Secret
Berlin, February 3, 1943-XXI

Mr. Minister,

At this time, as the Jewish problem in Germany seems to be almost "resolved," it is useful to summarize recent history since the end of 1938 to January 30, 1943, the tenth anniversary of the rise to power of National-Socialism.

It was at the beginning of November 1938, after the assassination in Paris of the councilor of the German legation, Von Rath, at the hands of a Jew, that the anti-Jewish measures built up until they became real persecution. Until then the Jews, even if subjected to the severe Nuremberg racial laws and consequently excluded from public positions, journalism, the theatre, and managerial positions in commerce and finance, could with some limitation engage in trade, exercise some professions and benefit from relative tranquility. Therefore it seemed that, after five years of government, National Socialism intended to follow the directives repeated by the Führer in several speeches and limit themselves to treating the Jews as foreigners excluded from positions of command in every sector of the country. The episodes of "pogrom" already taking place in Austria and in Vienna in particular in March of 1938, during the days of the "Anschluss," could still be considered as exceptions that were not destined to be repeated. Gauleiter Burckel himself, a noted anti-Semite, announced after the annexation a relatively moderate program, contemplating accelerated emigration of the Jews from the Ostmark and permission for the elderly to remain in their place of residence continuing their usual occupations. And Seyss-Inquart, inaugurating as well in Vienna in August 1938 the propaganda exhibition of the so-called errant Jew, said that he did not at all intend to push Jewish individuals and families into economic ruin.

After the assassination of Von Rath, the most extreme elements of the party in the entire Reich were able to carry out at least part of the threats repeated for some time in the columns of some of their newspapers, such as Streicher's *Der Stürmer* or Himmler's *Das Schwarze Korps*. The night of November 10, at the same time and with perfect organization, in every large and small center of the Reich, small squads of young members of the party plundered in an orderly way "non-Aryan" shops and systematically set fire to the synagogues. A spontaneous manifestation by the people—this was the definition given at the time by Goebbels; but the people looked on in apathy and many shook their heads—government measures followed, with the transfer of around fifty thousand Jews to concentration camps (the police at the time admitted to having only carried out twenty thousand arrests), the imposition of a fine on the Jews of one billion marks, to be collected by means of a special tax equivalent to 20% of the estate (the contribution was increased to 25% when the initial quote was thought to be insufficient), the "Aryanization" of all businesses, conducted in such a way as to only minimally reimburse the owners, and the ban on using hotels, public premises, cinemas, theatres and even some city neighborhoods.

Nevertheless, it seemed that it would not go further than that and in December of the same year, only a month later, there was talk of a "Schacht plan" to facilitate the exodus of the Jews from Germany and the ex-director of the Reichsbank went to London to negotiate the issue; while in January of 1939

Rublee, the American delegate at the Evian Committee for the Solution of the Jewish Question, came to Berlin, was received by Göring and in a meeting with Ambassador Attolico stated his satisfaction at having reached a provisional agreement.

It went on like this, in the absence of any activity, until the beginning of the war, which marked new discriminatory measures against the Jews. They had to hand in radio sets and, if they received the same ration stamps as Aryans, they did not have the right to clothing stamps nor the stamps in use here for the allotment of poultry, game, fish, and other special distributions. Furthermore, they could enter shops only at a late hour, generally in the afternoon, when non-ticketed items were practically sold out, like fruits and vegetables.

The Führer had announced that the coming of the war would mean the extirpation and total destruction of the Jewish race: and in November of 1939 the first deportations of several thousand people towards former Polish territories, in particular the region near Lublin, were decided. They were not heard from again. After this first experiment, some months of reprieve followed, evidently used by Himmler and his offices—the Reichsführer SS was in the meantime nominated commissioner for the consolidation of the German people and he took charge of the transplantation of millions of Germans and Slavs—to prepare the systematic plans for the transfer. Finally, on October 17, 1940, a plan was systematically put into effect which originally anticipated the evacuation of 150,000 Jews from the Protectorate of Bohemia and Moravia, 65,000 from the Ostmark, 30,000 from the newly annexed provinces of Posen and from East Prussia, and 240,000 from the old territory of the Reich. In total, therefore, around half a million individuals, sent to Nisko on San, a locality southwest of Lublin, to Lublin itself and to Warsaw, where officers of the Death's Head regiments of the SS (SS Totenkopf-Standarten), taken from the noted concentration camps of Buchenwald, Dachau, and Sachsenhausen, took care of the organization of the ghettos, providing also for concentration and the settlement of the Polish Jews, calculated to be around one and a half million.

Regarding the conditions it must be said that those evacuated were allowed to take with them articles of clothing contained in one suitcase and a backpack, as well as the sum of three hundred marks (of which two hundred were immediately taken for the trip, and those who did not have the amount were placed in the cattle carriages), that *mothers were separated from their children and wives from their husbands*, that furniture and decorations and other property were confiscated "for social purposes"—but it was immediately rumored that they were stolen by the men of the party—that there were many suicides innumerable deaths due to exhaustion, pneumonia and typhoid caused by long days passed without nourishment, nights at ten or more degrees below zero spent out in the open, lack of hygiene, doctors and medicine. At this time and later on, those evacuated were not heard from again.

Again there was a reprieve during the first months of 1941—and it is not clear why—then on September 15 of that year, the date when all the Jews had to wear the yellow star, the deportations were intensified and continued methodically without further interruptions, in part also towards Theresienstadt—the fort located between the border of the Reich and the Protectorate—and, recently towards the coal mines of Upper Silesia. Furthermore from October of 1942 the Jews have no right to meat, salami, eggs, wheat, flour products, milk, vegetables, and fruit, being allowed half a kilo of turnips per week. And if at the end of 1942, according to information provided by a reliable source, it was calculated that there were still 35,000 Jews in Germany, of which 25,000 in Berlin, (as well as around 30,000 others, married to Aryans, women in majority) at this point "yellow stars" were almost not to be seen, not in Berlin, Vienna, or Frankfurt, the three German cities with the largest number of Jewish communities (in April of 1940, according to official statistics, the Jews amounted to 91,000 in Vienna, 83,000 in Berlin, 14,000 in Frankfurt).

It is not easy to calculate the number of Jews evacuated from German territory in this manner, mainly because German statistics, even those from the May 1939 census, are based on religious affiliation and not on the basis of race.

According to the information published in 1938 by the National-Socialist Party's office of racial policy, the one hundred percent Jews—that is, according to the laws of Nuremberg, with at least three pure Jewish grandfathers—were 475,000 in the old Reich, in 1933. Given that the emigrants since then until 1939, the year in which the possibility of crossing the border practically ended, were about 150,000, it is possible to calculate that at the end of '39 there remained little more than 300,000, to which must be added the 150,000 remaining in the former Austria and the 50,000 from the other annexed provinces. Therefore those "evacuated" from the actual territory of the Reich were around 500,000.

There can be no doubt as to the fate awaiting them, just like that faced by the Polish, Russian, Dutch, and also French Jews. While the authorities have not made a mystery as to the end result (and in this way Rosenberg, in a speech held at the end of last year at the Works Congress of the German Front, confirmed the desire to fully exterminate the Jewish race, describing the total extermination as a humanitarian act, being the restoration of the European people) admitted that the ghettos of Lublin and Warsaw would be quickly emptied, due to epidemics and hunger, as well as executions. The source to which I have already made reference said just a few days ago that of the 600,000 Jews in the single ghetto of Warsaw, a district where less than 100,000 people lived before, only 53,000 were left.

The SS themselves tell of the mass executions, and even a "Wochenschau" [weekly newsreel], around a year ago, showed films of Russian Jews thrown alive into the flames. Not long ago a similar documentary was said to have been shown to the superior Army command. And a person who was present remembered with horror some scenes of machine-gun executions of naked women and children lined up along the edge of a communal grave. Of the stories that circulate on the scope of the executions I limit myself to relate one which was told to a member of my staff by an SS official, who admitted to having thrown six-month-old babies against a wall, smashing them, as an example to his men, who were tired and shaken from a particularly horrific execution because of the number of people killed.

Given the fanatical attitude with which this is being carried out, it is unlikely that the current drastic labor shortage in Germany can change the fate of the German Jews who are still alive or of the other survivors, those citizens of the countries occupied by the Reich.

Finally, it is well known how German authorities, both at the center and at the fringes, have tried to include the Jewish citizens of non-occupied countries with the Germans. The many steps carried out by foreign diplomats so that the necessary distinctions were observed are also well known.

With the decision of the Royal Government in response to the alternative to deportation or repatriation proposed by the German government, which was communicated by cable n. 150 today, this last problem—as far as Jews of Italian citizenship are concerned—is now heading to its natural conclusion.

Alfieri

33.

Note [from the German
Ministry of Foreign Affairs to Himmler]

On the occasion of the visit by the Reichsführer of the SS to the Duce, the following points can be made:

1) Until now in the zone occupied by Italian troops, Jews and citizens of enemy states have been able to move about freely. There are also many Jews who have emigrated from Germany or who are known for their negative attitude towards the Rome-Berlin Axis; when faced with the advancing German troops they took refuge in the Italian occupied zones. Following a protest, ordered by the RAM, from Ambassador Von Mackensen to the Duce, it was hoped for the immediate enactment of the most rigorous security measures, and precisely through police inspector Lo Spinoso, who was supposed to direct the operation with the Carabinieri, who are not part of the Italian Armed Forces. Initially, in spite of this directive by the Duce, nothing has happened, the embassy in Rome was ordered to handle the matter in May. Bastianini declared, after a telephone conversation with the new Minister of Police, that Lo Spinoso had obtained the

transfer of a larger police force, which was about to leave. The operation was to be executed in a decisive manner. In spite of this renewed promise, until now nothing has happened.

2) The Italians are creating endless difficulties concerning the handing over of the Croatian Jews who were to be transferred to the East, located in the Croatian coastal zones occupied by Italian troops. The negotiations between the German and the Italian legations regarding the matter have not up to now reached a resolution of the issue. We hope that the Italian delegation receives more stringent orders to settle this problem.

3) The Italians have promised to undertake definite measures regarding the Jews (deportation of the stateless Jews and Greek Jews on the Ionian Islands and the extension to persons of Italian nationality of Italian measures regarding the Jews) in the Italian occupied zone of Greece. Similar orders have also been issued to the Italian occupation troops. Nevertheless, no measures have been effective because, according to them, Italian troops are still busy drawing up the lists of the Jews who were in the zone. Assuming the work is concluded, we can expect that the execution of the operation will still be postponed with the excuse that there is not enough space available on the ships for the transport of the Jews. The Rome embassy has been asked to recommend to the Italians to gather the Jews without delay in concentration camps and use them for labor in construction work that must be carried out in Greece.

4) The Italians go to great trouble and search for many reasons to find special merit or other qualifications of "Italian spirit," for some 80 Jews from Salonika who are not of Italian nationality. For particular political reasons in these doubtful cases the offices of the Reichsführer-SS have been requested to allow that the Jews be treated as Italian citizens.

Since, however, a number of these Jews have already been evacuated towards the Eastern territories, it would perhaps be better to draw attention to this difficulty and to the considerations of a defensive nature which prevent the transfer of these Jews to Italy.

5) Regarding this last case the Italians are obstinate in saying that nationality is of no importance, and in fact they ask with insistence for the liberation of a certain Mrs. Cozzi, an Eastern Jew from the Baltic provinces, who after marrying an Italian official, since then deceased, acquired Italian nationality, even though she resided permanently in Riga and hardly spoke any Italian. There are some very serious points against the liberation of Mrs. Cozzi because she has been placed in the ghetto for quite some time.

6) According to a communication from the German Embassy in Rome, the Swedish Honorary Consul in Trieste, Lekner, is a pure Jew and is married to a pure Jew; a certain Portuguese Honorary Consul, Frankel, is a Jew; the Spanish Honorary Vice Consul, Garsolini-Durando is married to a pure Jew; the Bulgarian Honorary Consul, Eliznakoff, is married to a half Jew; the Japanese Honor-

ary Consul, Schnabel, is one quarter Jewish; the Portuguese Honorary Consul in Fiume, Denes, is Jewish. Furthermore there is the suspicion that the Portuguese Honorary Consul in Trieste, Coser, and the Spanish Honorary Consul, Garsolini-Durando are of non-Aryan descent. Although, given the Italian attitude towards the Jewish question, it is not to be expected that the Italians will adopt measures for the expulsion of the Jews from the Consular Corps, it would however be appreciated if the Duce's attention is called to these matters.

Berlin, June 8, 1943.

34.
[The DELASEM for interned children]

DELASEM
Union of the Italian Jewish Communities
Non-Profit Organization R. D., October 30, 1930, n. 1731

Emigrant Assistance Delegation
Genoa
Piazza Vittoria 14 int. 4
Telegram: Delasem-Genova

A PAGE FOR THE CHILDREN
Purim 5701 = 1941

My dear little friends!

Today is Purim; a holiday for all, but above all for you, because you resemble the flowers that exactly today begin to bloom in the fields; because you are capable of being cheerfully gay, as Purim requires.

We will crown our heads with little flowers; we will dress our little Queen Esther, the King Assuerus, the good Mordecai, we will hold hands in a big circle. Do you want to? Then we will sing:

> *Giro giro tondo—giriamo tutto il mondo*
> *Aivola siam di fiori—di vari e bei colori*
> *Bluette cilestrina—e rosa carnicina*
> *Lampone e girasole—garofano e viole*
> *Papavero nostrale—granturco augurale*
> *Giro giro tondo—giriamo tutto il mondo*
> *Noi siamo tutti fiori—di vari e bei colori*

Giriamo in gran corteo–col bravo Mardocheo
E con gl'israeliti–di sacco ancor vestiti
Ed Ester la regina–di bellezza divina
Assuero e il turpe Amanno–che complottò a suo danno.

Then we will all sit down around our teacher who will tell us a long story about Purim. And this story must end like this:

"Mordecai wrote a letter to all the Jews who were in all the provinces of King Assuerus, near and far, to order them to celebrate the fourteenth and fifteenth days of the month of Adar every year, since those were the days the Jews had obtained a truce from the attacks of their enemy, and as the month during which their pain had been changed into happiness, their grief into festivity, and they should turn these days into days of banquets and happiness, in which they would give gifts to each other, and make donations to the needy."

And let's play again because our joy pleases our Lord who protects us, if we have faith in Him.

Your most affectionate friend NAOMI wishes you a happy Purim.

My dear friends,

Your spontaneous letters have moved me very much; your words as thoughtful Jewish children even in joy.

I thank you, because you make me happy; the faith and affection that children have in "grown ups" are gifts that the grown ups do not always know how to appreciate.

I would really like us to continue writing to one another and I hope that you do too. You can ask me all you want, you must speak of yourselves, yes, above all of yourselves, so that I may get to know you, and imagine you, and I will reply using this bulletin, and by writing your names.

I would also love to see the work of the smallest amongst you, with pictures and puppets.

I could print the best of them.

I have a beautiful painting in my mind entitled PESACH 5701, which represents a long table around which many children sit leaning over the illustrated Aggadoth (are they only those of Ferramonti?). We are reading *Had gadjà* and I enjoy passing each child, touching their cheeks to feel the warmth, to look each one in their smiling eyes to read:

ZEMANTOV WILL RETURN

What are worries and suffering compared to such an immense joy?

Naomi

35.
[Report by the Ministry
of Finance on the confiscation of Jewish property]

Note for the DUCE.

Subject: Confiscation of Jewish property—Situation as of December 31, 1944-XXIII.

At the end of the first year of the application of the legal decree of January 4, 1944-XXII, n.4, which ordered the confiscation of property belonging to citizens of the Jewish race, I consider it appropriate to present to you, DUCE, the statistical data relevant to the work carried out until now.

In all, on December 31, 1944-XXIII, 5,768 decrees of confiscation arrived at the EGELI, allocated as follows:

Real estate and fixed property .... 2,590 decrees
Bank deposits .... 2,996 decrees
Companies .... 182 decrees

The transmission of the confiscation decrees is not yet completed in many provinces, among them those with the greatest number of Jews and the property owned by them, because of the complexity of the related assessments, which we are addressing with the greatest possible care and urgency.

Work has not yet begun in the provinces and operational zones of the foothills of the Alps and on the Adriatic Coast (and particularly important in this regard is the Province of Trieste), since the application of L. D. January 4, 1944-XXII, n.2 was suspended by the German authorities; the Ministry of Foreign Affairs has, however, brought the matter to the attention of the German Embassy, to find a solution.

Finally, within the information reported above the decrees issued in some provinces are not included, since they have fallen into enemy hands following the enactment of the D. L. January 4, 1944-XXII, n.2.

As far as the value of the confiscated property is concerned, this can only be precise for certain categories; while for others, even adding up considerable sums (furniture, valuables, linen, various merchandise) accurate data can only be obtained at the time of their sale. For businesses, finally, the value can be given when the EGELI is able to take possession.

As far as the confiscations included in the data reported, bank deposits in cash amount to a total sum of L. 75,089,047.90; State bonds of L. 36,396,831 (nominal value); industrial and other bonds, valued according to the list at the end of December, at L. 731,442,219. Many other bonds exist whose valuation has not been tabulated.

All of the bonds, deposits and cash, are being transferred to pre-established venues, which offer maximum security.

The real estate property has been valued on the basis of the standards established for property tax purposes. The official values calculated in this manner come to: land total of L. 855,348,608, and for houses L. 198,300,003. Naturally, if one wanted to consider today's actual real estate value, these amounts would have to be considerably increased.

As far as what is stated above, I can assure you, DUCE, that the progress of this delicate and important work is to be considered satisfactory in every way and that the offices in charge of it, including those in the provinces (Prefectures, Revenue office, EGELI, etc.) work with dedication and commitment endeavoring to overcome in the best possible way the difficulties associated with the existing situation.

Civilian Mail, 316,1, 12/3/1945-XXIII.

36.
[Memorandum from Giovanni Preziosi to Benito Mussolini]

Munich, January 31, 1944-XXII

Duce!

Hear me out! I have been your faithful follower at every moment and I was famous for the phrase I repeated even in the darkest hours and that I repeated once again at 7 in the evening of July 25th in that letter that was to fall into Badoglio's hands. That letter said, "Duce, now more than ever before: *With You and for You forever.*"

You know that my only ambition and expectation is to serve my Country through scholarship and observation. Among all those "influential" Fascists, I am the only one who, having spent all my days, hour after hour, serving Italy, can say: "I no longer have what I had before the March." Herein lies my wealth; this is the source of the strength that I find which compels me to address this memorandum to you in utmost trust.

You know my work in the press and even with you, as well as with members of the Government, from the very first day after the March on Rome so that this idea would spread: *Fascism has only one real, powerful enemy: the Jew, and along with him his greatest tool, the Mason. Jewish-Masonry dominates the entire national life and is the true Government of Italy.*

You know the weapons Jews and Masons have used to force you to not listen to me. Everything was set up against me from that day (February 22, 1923) when, in agreement with Michele Bianchi (who never would betray!), I promoted a meeting in the Offices of the Chamber of Deputies so that you would receive the proposal–well aware of your ideas and your precedents on the subject–of the statement of incompatibility between the Masonry and Fascism. A man whom we believed not to be a Mason (the Undersecretary of Public Works, Alessandro Sardi) had been invited to attend; and that very evening, even before you were informed, he warned both Masonries and their archives were immediately secreted away. At that point the Masons could guess that the main purposes of the Report on the Reform of Public Administration, that I had been named to present by the High Council, were to have been the elimination of Masons from the bureaucracy and from the army. The Masons knew that since October 15, 1922, *La vita italiana* was publishing in installments the secret yearbook of the Lodges, of the "Triangles" and their trustees. The famous court case called the "Paludi Pontine" thus came about, and Cesare Rossi went to the President of the Court, Caizzi, who was a Mason, in your name telling him that the Court's handing down a conviction was a "political necessity." I have the "Cassis Report," the conclusions of which were never made public, in spite of the solemn promise to do so in an official "Stefani" communiqué, because a shadow was meant to be cast over my life. The report said that I had rendered a great service to the Nation. I know how hard Federzoni, Tittoni, and Baron Fassini worked on you against me at various points in time. I also have the exchange of cables between Cesare Rossi and Scarfoglio, when he became editor of the newspaper, *Il mezzogiorno*, etc., etc. But none of this—if this were all there is!—has succeeded in shaking my faith in you or my feeling about you. You were for me the embodiment of Italy and its grand, new mission in the world. No one has ever heard me say even one word that didn't identify you with the destiny of Italy.

Then came the Matteotti assassination, and you could see then those who were loyal and those who were traitors. It is simple truth for me to say that among the journalists I was indeed in the vanguard of those who remained loyal. And you gave me your trust once again.

Publication of the Masonic documents which I had begun in the *Mezzogiorno*, however, thus revealing that the Masonry of Piazza del Gesù occupied a place within the Party administration, meant the suppression of the newspaper. The Grand Master of this Masonic group had, in the meantime, been placed alongside the most powerful Minister of the moment—Costanzo Ciano—who had taken him on and kept him constantly at the Ministry for Communications. The documents I delivered to the Party obviously disappeared; they mentioned, among others, the names of Marinelli and Melchiori, the Administrative Secretary, the other Deputy Secretary of the Party. And so, for a good five years I was again removed from your presence.

Because of steps taken by my wife, unknown to me, you were given the means to reflect on the "method" used by the Party Masonry, by the Ministry of

Internal Affairs and by your own Press Office, to my detriment (the irresponsible method of that "period" of those daily deceptive information "bulletins" you received). The ice was broken once more and I could again meet and correspond with you.

You know that at every opportunity, I have said and written the truth to you. I have said and written that Judaism and Freemasonry were in power in Italy even under the Fascist Regime. Suppressing the Lodges and the racial laws had the single effect of strengthening Judeo-Freemasonry, which did not want the alliance with Germany and did not want this war. Once the alliance was formed and the war started, Masonry used all its power for the precise purpose of losing the war and overthrowing Fascism.

You have known since November 1939, when, based on a conversation I had with a Cardinal, I wrote to you of the existence of a very specific plan that was known also to the Vatican, to attempt to maintain Italy's neutrality and lead it to disengagement from the Axis and from there to an entente with England and France, and the possibility of a war against Germany. The plan was attributed to the Foreign Minister and was to have been made into an agreement at Lyon. Ciano's speech to the Chamber in which he announced, without Germany's consent, the existence of a secret commitment regarding the date Italy would declare its readiness for war, seemed to be the beginning of Italy's disengagement from the Axis. Also, because during those months the word 'Axis' had disappeared from vocabulary of the newspapers.

And then came the war in Greece. You were aware of the records that General Visconti Prasca presented to the King, with your authorization and following my suggestion. The documents contained therein, but not just those, reveal that Badoglio had prepared the war against Greece for the precise purpose of having Italy lose it (this was part of the anti-Fascist plan prepared in Paris, I had published the relative document at the time and later reproduced it in one of the articles for the *Volkischer Beobachter*). He was, as were the Masons, certain that Fascism would collapse under a defeat at the hands of little Greece; and consequently that Italy would disengage from Germany and would sooner or later enter the coalition forming around England.

You know that the day following Badoglio's resignation as Chief of Staff, I wanted to take a position against him under my own responsibility (as I had already done successfully against Albertini), since "a group was forming around him to create a coalition for the specific purpose of overthrowing Fascism." I had a copy sent to you of the very serious letter General Cadorna had written to me against Badoglio. Badoglio was the center of Masonry within the Army. When everything was ready, the Minister for Popular Culture enjoined me in your name not to attack Badoglio.

Since I sent you a copy myself, I know you are aware of the long letter I had sent to the Prefect Le Pera, Chief of the Racial Affairs Office of the Ministry of the Interior. He had asked me for an interview in the name of the Under Secretary Buffarini-Guidi; therefore you know that I was able to identify and prove that the policy regarding Freemasonry was an act of treason.

You cannot have forgotten, as I saw this treason taking shape, my insistence that you create an "Office" that apparently was to be the "Historical Office of the Revolution" but in fact *was to be used to give you a way to know the truth about the situation and about the men surrounding you from the points of view of race, politics and loyalty.* I said that this office ought to be managed by you directly. At that point you told me to draw up a plan, which I did (one extensive plan and a narrower one) and saw that you received it at Cremona, because I knew that once it became common knowledge, the idea would be sabotaged, as in fact it was. I brought the subject up once again in February, 1942, but you entrusted the Historical Office to the Party (during the Vidussoni period), and Farnesi made the whole idea of the Office seem ridiculous, not dissimilar to how he made the "Exhibition of Judaism and Freemasonry" seem ridiculous: two completely empty galleries. Had that Office, with the specific purposes I had suggested, actually been set up, you would have known the traitors before the betrayal. And instead, in spite of your "orders," it was not even possible to publish the *Financial Biography* that was to have separated the sacred from the profane. The final, insurmountable obstacle was the work of Minister De Marsico, a liberal Mason, whom I had opposed since 1924 (when the Masonic Lodge in Avellino was created under his protection), but, using the tried-and-true system of the information bulletins, you were led to believe that my position was part of some provincial quarrel. And De Marsico, enjoying one triumph after another, finally becoming Minister of Justice and the author of the Grandi agenda.

You know that when they had you declare that "the Jewish question in Italy could be considered solved," and that "the Aryanized (Jews) could be counted on the fingers of one hand," I made my own position known in an article in *La vita italiana* of September 15, 1942 and said that this was "hiding the sores," and I added, "One day or another these sores will become gangrene, and the acts of those who have helped hide them will seem *acts of betrayal.* I do not want to contribute to hiding them." Then, after this introduction, I showed that not only had the Jewish question not been solved, but also that it had become even more serious since it was "a real Trojan Horse in a besieged city." And I described how to resolve the problem. The only effect this statement had was to irritate the Under Secretary Buffarini-Guidi who was the authority for Judeo-Masonic questions, and to provoke a communiqué from the Minister of Popular Culture Pavolini who threatened serious steps against me, naturally.

You know that on November 11, 1942, I wrote an extremely serious letter to General Galbiati as Chief of Staff of the V.S.N. Militia [M.V.S.N.]. As I requested, Galbiati told you about the letter which began with the sentence: "The house is on fire." It was my statement on the acts of treason being perpetrated with impunity and in every sector by ministers and men in the most important offices of the Regime who had more or less fallen prey to mammon ("mammonism is the weapon that Judaism—I wrote—has always used in its conquest of men and nations"). I described the acts committed by the top bureaucracy to sabotage the war and its supplies, to set the people against you and to sow ferocious hatred against Germany. During the days of your imprisonment, you must surely have thought back on that letter. And you must remember also the irritation you felt towards me when you read back to me, on December 12, 1942, the most important passages of that letter, and you said, at the end, "evidently the bombardment of Naples has affected you, as well." You told me that I was worried for no reason and you praised the bureaucracy that was serving the State so well, the State of which you considered yourself the first servant. And you said that I had no right to doubt your collaborators. And when I was about to give you a specific answer, you turned to Undersecretary Russo and told him to prepare the decree naming me Minister of State, but you did not even give me the chance to thank you.

You will remember that, immediately after, during the same month of December, 1942, I succeeded in transmitting to you a 40-page report entitled: "Enemy Propaganda–Judaism–Internal Front," dated November 16, 1942 (prepared in agreement with the Office for the Studies on the Jewish Problem in Trieste) and it had 5 annexes: 1. On espionage; 2. On the position and the responsibility of the betrayal in act through the Jewish "central headquarters" in Trieste; 3. On the Aryanized Jew, the Engineer Cesare Sacerdoti; 4. On the previous records of the plutocratic political group in Trieste which, following the naïve Vidussoni, was to take over inside the Party; 5. A letter which described how the foreign connection was made by the Judeo-plutocratic-espionage group. The only consequence of this Report, which you handed to Undersecretary Buffarini-Guidi to look into and take care of, was the categorical demand by the Party to dismiss the Dean of the Office of Studies of the Jewish Problem in Trieste. And the dismissal would have taken place had I not called you personally. But the Report was left aside, as were many others, which the Centers, through official channels, had sent to Minister of Propaganda Pavolini. If you have the Report brought to you today, you will see that everything was planned, including what was happening around Badoglio.

Already by the end of July 1942, I had sent to you from Cortina a copy of Annex 5 as mentioned above, together with two other very serious letters I had received from Trieste, which also described the sinister work that, through the Jews of the well-known Assicurazioni Generali, presided over (in order to Aryanize it) by … Volpi, was being carried on abroad. You sent that letter to Tamburini, then Prefect of Trieste, and, instead of taking the proper steps, he, not in my own words, "assailed Gastone Bonifacio, an interpreter with the military censorship of Trieste, whom he held guilty of having sent the three letters to Preziosi, and had his house searched; as a result, Bonifacio, a pure Fascist and an honorable man though very sensitive and with a weak heart, died a few days later of heartbreak." Together with Bonifacio, the subject of the three letters was also buried.

You know that following the long conversation between Grandi and de Marsico which took place at the ministry of Justice on June 14, I guessed that serious things were about to take place and I warned Party Secretary Scorza; I know that Scorza spoke to you about the non-fascist De Marsico and that he said I was "the first to be gotten rid of."

You know, because I told you at the Führer's Headquarters, the steps I took to obstruct the meeting of the Grand Council. Up to the last minute I pleaded: "For God's sake don't let the armored division of the Militia leave Rome!" when I found out that the Minister of War had requested that the rifles issued to the GIL be returned, I observed that the plan to disarm the Party was clear.

You know that from Naples, where I had arrived the day before to visit my 85-year-old mother still at Avellino at the mercy of the Anglo-Americans, I wrote you a letter on July 18, that is, as soon as I learned of the meeting of the Grand Council, and in it I said: *"This session of the Grand Council will lead to the suicide of Fascism."*

Here I have only mentioned some of the efforts I made so that you would know what you would never have known through official channels, which were in any case in one of two categories: a) traitors; b) those whose only worry was to make you believe that in their sector everything was going along beautifully. The first category, particularly in the final period, included almost all those who were nearest to you and whom you trusted completely.

But you don't know that when I understood it had become impossible to allow you to see the danger as it was, I summoned an authoritative German scholar who, because of his rank, was a resident of Rome and had always had an excellent relationship with me. After having explained to him that I was aware of the seriousness of the step I was taking, I charged him to inform the German Ambassador—not being listened to in Italy—so that he in turn would inform his Government that a conspiracy was taking place in Italy for the precise purpose of liberating Italy from Germany. The head of the conspiracy was Badoglio and, each for his own purpose, the other members were Federzoni, Grandi, Bottai. Ciano was a declared enemy of Germany. I added that Badoglio had the specific intention of overthrowing Fascism. A year later, I made this declaration twice, and I realize now that the German Ambassador thought well not to lend credence to my words. He was also satisfied with the information he received through official channels; and ... Bottai and Grandi were warmly welcomed in Germany. The only form of protest I had available was to refuse the invitation to visit Germany with men like Baldini whom I considered traitors.

I was able to see all this because I had studied Judaism in its very essence and I followed the way the plan of conquest and subversion was methodically enacted. It was easy to tell what would happen, because similar causes produce similar effects. The difficult part was not to be distracted by secondary facts or by personal interest and in maintaining the rigor of logical reasoning in every circumstance.

My efforts were useless, however. Judeo-Masonic control was so thorough that it is extraordinary that I could continue to write. In the most hopeful view, your Ministers and most of the Party Secretaries as they followed one after the other, were telling you that Preziosi was a fanatic idealist, and someone led you to believe that I was on Hitler's payroll. This is the preferred calumny of that "most moral" Chief of Police, Bocchini, who held in his hands the moral destinies of the Italians, all of them.

And now that the facts have proven me correct?...

Now I know that, among other things, there is a new effort being made to turn you against me. This does not surprise me since the reason behind it is the same for which *if the real causes which brought about July 25th aren't settled, we can only expect similar effects.* And the real causes are: a) the lack of a solution of the Jewish problem; b) the lack of a solution of the problem of Freemasonry in the life of the State and the Party.

Duce, it is my duty to repeat to you what I wrote on last November 9th while leaving Headquarters to return to Germany: "*If we do not decide firmly to thoroughly expel Freemasonry and to achieve a complete solution to the Jewish problem, we shall face new disappointments. God forbid that my voice be again treated like Cassandra's.*"

Aside from all this, I ask, how can we expect collaboration, alongside Germany, in this Jewish war, from all those who have even a drop—I'm saying just one drop—of Jewish blood? Hasn't perhaps history shown that "wherever just a drop of Jewish blood exists, there is loyalty to the Race"? Does it seem a minor question to you that still today in Italy the "Aryanized" people, or those so-called "non-members of the Jewish race" (and just what race do they belong to?) are still not considered Jews and therefore are good Italians? Who doesn't know that these juridical and racial abnormalities hide precisely the most dangerous Jews, who have been Aryanized using huge sums of money. Even General Pugliese—Aryanized as was Engineer Sacerdoti because "indispensable"—continues to move through Italy and goes to visit ... the Pope.

A warning comes to my mind, whose profound truth Italy has met in a terrible experience, and that is written in Hitler's *Mein Kampf.*

"The first duty is not to create a national constitution for the State, but rather to eliminate the Jews. As has often been the case throughout history, the main difficulty is not in forming a new state of things, but rather to make room for it."

The first duty, is not the so-called "national agreement," that others are bleating about along with Gentile, but the total elimination of the Jews, starting with those, and they are numerous, identified as Jews by the census of August 1938 that was never made public. Then, unearth the others, more or less baptized or Aryanized. Then, to exclude from every nerve-center of national life, from the army, from the judiciary, from teaching, from the central and outlying hierarchy of the Party, the half-breeds, the husbands of Jews and all others with drops of Jewish blood. The same goes for those who have belonged to the Masonry. How can we forget that, on the eve of war, in July 19, 1939, the King of England, invested the Duke of Kent to the "lofty position of Grand Master of the Masons," was assured by the Vice Grand Master, Lord Harenwood, that in *case of war* "*he could count on the Brotherhood in that country where Masonry had been abolished*"? The *Times* of August 20, 1939 published this account; in the September 15 issue of *La vita italiana* in that same year, I wrote, in fact: "It will be very useful, in the case of war, that the Chiefs of Staff have a precise list of ex-Masons, to avoid putting delicate duties in their hands" … "Under the patronage of the King of England, the Masons of countries like Italy, where Freemasonry has been abolished for reasons of national security, have been called together. The call invites them, obviously, not to serve their Country, but rather to take the side, in the case of a world war, of universal Masonry. It is, in other words, an invitation to betray their Country." And, in spite of my unequivocal recommendation, that is what happened. When choosing to swear loyalty to their Country or to Freemasonry, always and everywhere, the choice fell to Freemasonry. And it will be that way tomorrow.

Reconstruction cannot begin until Ministers, public officers and Party directors, Army officers, the Republican National Guard, as well as all those holding any and every office within the State Administration, are made to declare that they have never belonged to Masonry and that they demonstrate that they are Aryans in the only serious way that exists, which is through genealogical tables as is done in Germany.

Then there is the *moral question* which was so wonderfully but uselessly raised by Guido Pallotta (Pallotta's problem was indeed "Fascist mysticism"). Someone should tell Gentile, and the other followers of Mammon like himself, that the hackneyed phrase has outlasted its time, comforting as it may be for them: "to once feel the nausea of scandals". For twenty-two years now Italians have heard this Hebrew phrase in every tone, and it has been useful only to hide the ill-deeds of exploiters and embezzlers. "We don't want a scandal," was the guideline every time mud was flung on the Fascist Party. And so, the exploiters and embezzlers increased in number, their very multiplication made the people appear dishonest and the Regime seem like an exploiter. Today, fresh new preachers create the hope of a general absolution, and dare to say that this is the will of the people. The will of the people is something else, and its main characteristic is a *thirst for justice.* The Italian people want the Fascist Leader to be an example to them in every aspect of life. Every time the Italian people have given considerable weight to moral values and have always expressed poor opinions of those who become rich as politicians.

Now, for example, would you like to know the consequences of giving little importance to moral values? And what about that attitude of not considering Fascism as a way of comprehending life and using it? Just ask the Italian Consular representatives, or the Ambassador, or even the German authorities, what kind of a show is being put on right here in Munich by various union organizers, who present themselves as, and take the places of the Republican Fascist leaders in Germany. They have *abandoned* the duties imposed by their initial offices while waiting to take over consular and diplomatic positions as well. Let someone describe, for example, their waste of fuel in a country where even very high-ranking dignitaries cannot use automobiles, and those few who can, are given petrol in minimum quantities. How many automobiles have the Republican Fascists requested? The trip back and forth from Italy to Stuttgart is made by automobile. Some days ago one of these men ran over and killed a German and didn't stop. It took all the good offices of the Consul and the immense indulgence the Germans have for Italians, to avoid his arrest.

Ask what impression they created and what salaries they earned, and that most still earn, that band of Italians working for their country at radio Munich. The director received 6,000 marks per month, the others got from 2,800 to a minimum of 1,400 monthly. And this besides their expenses in one of the biggest hotels of the city. Ask the Consul, or even the hotel manager, about this group, with the exception of two or three: eight or ten men and six or seven young women, for a product which, counting news and a couple of pages of commentary, amounted to somewhere between eight, at the most twenty pages. Salaries like these are unheard of in Germany for any category of work, not just journalists, but even for highly placed dignitaries. Instead they have been paid to Italians so they could create propaganda for Italy and whatever is Italian in what must be the very saddest moment of Italy's entire history. When you told me to look into Radio Munich, I found the above situation and limited my activity to meeting occasionally those two or three young people who stood out for their skill, their integrity, their sense of responsibility.

All this in a Country that is a symbol of discipline and sacrifice, spending all of itself in the enormous war effort. Here, without talking, people see and judge.

I wanted to tell you all of this because I suspect that no one has mentioned a word about it. And I wish to tell you again that there is only one road to regain honor: absolute loyalty to the betrayed Ally. Put an end, therefore, to all the irresponsible, anti-German illusions, in every form; and remember constantly that what is in the making must exist within Aryan European unity, and to achieve this there is no better way than that of the German racial laws. What is needed to enact these laws are men who can be trusted, not those compromised by their unforgotten, unforgettable past.

And I have finished. Think of this letter as my passage from one kind of activity which I performed up to July 25, to another made of the study of those archives, now in German hands (first among them those of the Universal Jewish Alliance and the Rothschild archives), which will be needed to make the real history of Europe known and thus Italy's. History is not what is on the stage. But unfortunately, up to now, this is all we know.

Your devoted
Giovanni Preziosi

37.
[Draft of Legal Decree of the R. S. I. on Race]

THE DUCE OF THE ITALIAN SOCIAL REPUBLIC

In view of the Legal Decree April 18, 1944-XXII, n. 171, regarding the establishment of the General Inspectorate for Race;

GIVEN THE PROPOSAL of the General Inspectorate for Race;

DECREE:

Art. 1. Italian blood. Of Italian blood are those Italian citizens whose ancestors have been residing in Italy at least since January 1, 1800, are of the Aryan race and immune from crossbreeding with Jews or other heterogeneous races. Considered of Italian blood are Italian citizens whose ancestors up until second relatives are of the Aryan race and are immune from crossbreeding with Jews or other heterogeneous races.
Art. 2. Italian kindred blood. Of Italian kindred blood are those who whatever their nationality, are of the Aryan race and immune from crossbreeding with Jews or other heterogeneous races.
Art. 3. Foreign blood. Of foreign blood are Jews and, generally, those who do not belong to the Aryan race.
Art. 4. Half-breeds. Those who have a parent of foreign blood are considered as half-breeds of the first degree. Those who have an ancestor of second-degree foreign blood are considered half-breeds of the second degree.
Art. 5. Half-breeds assimilated to persons of foreign blood. Are considered as being of foreign blood those who have:

744

a) three ancestors of the second degree with foreign blood;

b) two ancestors of the second degree with foreign blood and two ancestors of the same half-breed degree;

c) two ancestors of the second degree with foreign blood and one ancestor of the same half-breed degree.

Art. 6. Half-breeds assimilated to persons of Italian blood. Those who have only one ancestor of the third degree foreign blood are considered of Italian blood. However, the half-breeds of Jews who profess the Jewish religion or are members of an Jewish community or have in any case shown evidence of Judaism, to whichever degree they belong, are considered of foreign blood.

Art. 7. Children of unknown parents. Children of unknown parents are presumed to belong, unless otherwise proven, to the same category of the known parent. Children of parents who are both unknown are presumed, unless proven otherwise, as being of Italian blood if born within the national territory.

Art. 8. Marriage. The marriage of a citizen of Italian blood with a person of foreign blood or a first-degree half-breed is prohibited. A marriage celebrated in spite of this prohibition is considered void.

Art. 9. Crime against the race. A crime against the race is constituted by the procreation of one or more children born out of wedlock between persons of Italian blood and persons of foreign blood or first-degree half-breeds. A subsequent decree will establish the penalties against those guilty.

Art. 10. Change of surname. Citizens of Italian blood who have names which are notoriously common amongst Jews can obtain a change of surname. The change of surname given to Jews and Jewish half-breeds according to the law of July 13, 1939 n. 1055, is revoked. Consequently the Jews and Jewish half-breeds who have modified their surnames in order to not reveal their Jewish origins, must reassume their original surnames. The norms for such changes will be established by a subsequent decree.

Art. 11. Genealogical file. Belonging to a racial category is proven by the "genealogical file" which, at the request of the interested party and upon necessary ascertainments, is issued by the municipal registry office. The characteristics of the genealogical file, the method of its compilation and the procedures and terms for the rejection of the certifications executed by the registry offices will be regulated by a subsequent decree.

Art. 12. On the declarations of not-belonging to the Jewish race. The rule of art. 1 of the law of July 13, 1939 n. 1024 concerning the right to declare the not-belonging to the Jewish race against the evidence shown with the registry office is abolished.

Art. 13. Temporary rules. The declarations of not-belonging to the Jewish race, issued before the enactment of the present decree, will be re-examined piecemeal by the Commission on Race and, following their opinion, these may be revoked by the Inspector General for Race.

Art. 14. Every contradictory rule is cancelled, or in any event is made incompatible with those of the present decree.

Art. 15. The present decree will become effective the day after its publication in the Gazzetta Ufficiale d'Italia and, sealed with the State Seal, will be inserted in the Official Book of Laws and Decrees.

From General Headquarters, on this day…

38.
[Draft of Legal Decree of the R. S. I. regarding the Jews]

THE DUCE OF THE ITALIAN SOCIAL REPUBLIC

IN VIEW OF the decree dated today on the racial definition and differentiation; GIVEN THE PROPOSAL of the Inspector General for Race,

DECREES:

Art. 1. Italian citizens of foreign blood or half-breeds may not perform military service in times of peace or war.

Art. 2. Italian citizens of foreign blood or half-breeds are excluded from all political activity whatsoever.

Art. 3. The following may not have persons of foreign blood or half-breeds in their employment:

a) Civil and Military State Administrations;

b) Administrations of Provinces, Municipalities, public institutions of assistance and charity and non-profit organizations, institutes and businesses administered and maintained by the Provinces, the Municipalities, by public institutions of assistance and charity and non-profit organizations or their unions;

c) The administrations of municipalized businesses;

d) The administrations of State controlled bodies, National Works, Trade associations and collateral bodies and, generally, bodies and institutes of public law even though autonomous;

e) The administrations of annexed businesses or directly dependent upon the bodies to which the preceding section refers or if they obtain from them, to a prevailing extent, the necessary means to achieve their own purposes, also the companies whose capital is constituted, at least fifty percent, by State holdings;

f) The administrations of banks and insurance companies whatever their nature.

Art. 4. Italian citizens of foreign blood or half-breed may not:

a) Practice the duties of tutor or look after minors or handicapped persons of Italian blood;

b) Own land or urban buildings;

c) Own, in full or in part, or administrate in any way, businesses of any nature or consistency, nor manage such businesses, nor assume the duties of director or auditor;

d) Inherit or receive an inheritance from persons of Italian blood.

With a subsequent decree the limits within which citizens of foreign blood or half-breeds may be owners of personal property will be established. With the same decree the conditions and obligations to which the assertion of the rights of ownership of personal property must be subjected, according to its nature, will be established.

Art. 5. The practice of the following professions is prohibited to citizens of foreign blood or half-breeds: notary, journalist, teacher in public schools or in those private schools which are attended by students of Italian blood, surgeon, dentist, pharmacist, veterinarian, obstetrician, lawyer, attorney, counsel, commercial trader, or economist, accountant, engineer, architect, chemist, building surveyor, agronomist, land surveyor and engineer.

Art. 6. Jews and Jewish half-breeds are excluded from the cultural life of the Nation and every activity which is connected to the press, the cinema, the theater, and radio, is prohibited to them.

Art. 7. Jews and Jewish half-breeds may not have in their employment citizens of Italian blood.

Art. 8. Real estate property and industrial and commercial firms existing in the territory of State belonging to Italian citizens of foreign blood or half-breeds, are confiscated by law in favor of the State and given in administration to the Association of Administration and Liquidation. [ndt. EGELI] To such ends a special Section of the said Association will be constituted the manager of which will be nominated in agreement with the Inspector General for race. The revenue from the confiscated property and the profit from the sale of possessions of difficult or costly conservation will be entirely consigned to the Fund for War Pensions.

Art. 9. The Inspector General for Race, upon written request by the interested parties and having consulted the Commission for Race can, case by case, declare non-applicable those parts of *Articles 4, 5,* and *8* of the present decree to persons who find themselves in the following conditions:

a) members of families of those fallen in war or for the Fascist cause;

b) maimed, invalid or injured by war or for the Fascist cause;

c) war volunteers or those holding a war decoration;

d) legionnaires from Fiume;

d) those who have acquired exceptional merit of a national character.

In the cases provided for by the letters b), c) and e) the benefits may be extended to the components of the family, even if the person is deceased.

The decisions issued discrimination proceedings according to legal decree 17-11-1938-XVII n. 1728, converted into the Law of 5-1-1939 n. 274 will be reexamined one by one by the Commission on Race and will be revoked if not in keeping with the regulations contained in the present article.

Art. 10. It is prohibited to foreign Jews and half-breeds to hold permanent residence in the territory of the State.

Art. 11. Every rule contrary or, incompatible with those of the present decree is canceled.

Art. 12. The Inspector General for Race is in charge of issuing regulations for the enactment of the present decree, in accordance with the Ministers for Internal Affairs, of Justice and of Finance.

Art. 13. The present decree will become effective the day after its publication in the Gazzetta Ufficiale d'Italia, and, signed with the State Seal, will be inserted in the official books of laws and decrees.

From General Headquarters, on this day...

39.

Some observations on the racial law

More than the need, we must reflect on the political expediency of issuing new rules regarding racial matters. It remains doubtful that such provisions must be contained in a new "Racial Charter" or if it is not more convenient to issue suitable regulations and overrule some provisions of the existing law and integrate them with others, reaching practically the same result, and perhaps a more concrete and permanent conclusion.

Examination of the individual articles.

Art. 1. It would seem expedient to deal with the problem of the Jewish race in the law in an open manner without hesitation; indeed while scientifically they seem to adopt clear and distinct principles to determine the individuals belonging to the Jewish race, it remains extremely difficult to define precisely the principles of discrimination between the so-called "Aryan race" and the so-called "Heterogeneous race" as well as the "Non-European groups." The law, which from this fundamental point of view of scientific seriousness, appears totally deficient and gives its contents a tone of obvious amateurishness which will be noted in Italy and abroad. As far as our modest racial culture may guide us and allow us the brief period of time available it seems appropriate to propose certain doubts amongst the most obvious which immediately come to mind. The law draws from mixed and, in our opinion, contradictory principles, because it is partly based on "blood" (concept of heterogeneous race, Jewish race and perhaps Aryan race) and partly on territory (concept of non-European groups). For example, according to the principles of the law, crossbreeding would be permitted with the Magyar, with the Finnish, and a part of the Turks, but not with the Turks of the other side of the Bosporus because they belong to a non-European group regardless of the identity of the common Finno-Ugric racial stock to which they all belong. With respect to the text of the article it is impossible to understand the difference between the first paragraph and the second based upon a purely formal and empirical concept.

Art. 2. The contents of this article, rather than clarifying, first of all increase confusion and raise doubts. The concept of affinity of Italian blood is uncertain and anything but scientific. It is not clear if the term "wherever they reside" refers to the residence of the race or the residence of the individual.

Art. 4. The broad extension of the concept of half-breed based on principles completely dissimilar to those of preceding laws creates legal and moral conditions which are very unfair for those subjects legally considered as Aryan and who today suddenly find themselves declared as foreigners (one sole Jewish grandparent today transforms the Aryan grandchild into a Jew—and yes—but just one grandparent of foreign blood declares the grandchild, who had until today all the rights and fulfilled all the obligations of an Italian citizen, as foreign).

Art. 5. The rules of paragraph b) are useless since they are handled by the rules of paragraph c).

Art. 6. It is not clear why in this article the ancestor of the third degree is mentioned when the law does not take into account, in effect, other than the ancestors of the second degree. In any case it would then be necessary to create rules for those cases where there is more than one ancestor of third degree of foreign blood.

Art. 8. The contents of this article are to be considered with and without the modifications added here. That is: first the term "married to" and then the term "who marries." If we consider the original term "married to." In this case the contents of the article are to be considered aberrant, indeed, as it has been considered by the current legislators as absurd to transform, by a simple legal act, a Jew into an Aryan, even more so it seems that one cannot, by the simple act of a mixed marriage, turn an Aryan into a Jew!! The contents of the article are also aberrant for its retroactive application, inasmuch, as along with the proposed law, it would automatically transform into Jews all the pure Aryans who, up until the enactment of the racial laws of 1938, married an individual not belonging to the Aryan race. With the term modified to "who marries" the aberration of the transformation of the Aryan into an individual of foreign blood is eliminated, but it is then allowed in the future for the marriage between Aryan persons and persons of foreign blood or half-breeds of the first degree. In any case the contents of the subsection of article 8 must conform to the provisions of the first paragraph so that that if the term of this first subsection conforms to the amendment of the first paragraph, the marriage between an individual of Italian blood and a half-breed of the second degree, who is still considered by the law, a Jew, will be allowed. With the difference in this case, that contrary to the first, the individual of Italian blood would remain of Italian blood. The above observations on the contents of this article have a fundamental importance regarding the provisions of the racial law which would be completely violated by creating a contradiction, within the law, subject to severe and justified criticism.

Art. 9. Extramarital relations between persons of Italian blood and persons of foreign blood is considered a crime. Conversely, approval of marriage and punishment of an extramarital relationship between persons of Italian blood and persons of foreign blood or half-breeds of the first degree is covered within the same law.

Art. 11. The contents of this article constitute the base of the law because they seek to conduct to the practical application of the principles contained in it. It is entirely useless to state that the "genealogical file" is released at the request of the interested party implying that it deals with the limited application of a few cases. In reality almost all Italians who carry out any kind of activity have the absolute necessity of requesting and obtaining the said certificate. Let us list a partial case record:

Those obliged to request and obtain the certificate are:

1) all Italians who wish or must perform military service;

2) all Italians who wish to carry out a political activity;

3) all Italians belonging to civil or military administrations of the state, administrations of provinces and municipalities, public institutions of assistance and charity, all public and state controlled bodies, municipal companies, insurance companies, trade union associations, banks, etc.;

4) all Italians who are owners or administrators of real estate or firms;

5) all Italians who are professionals;

6) all Italians who carry out a cultural activity of any nature (professors, primary school teachers, etc.);

and finally:

7) all Italians who have or intend to hire domestic servants.

Finally, we must say that until individual genealogical files are produced, each person belonging to these numerous categories is held under the presumption of not being Aryan and is morally damaged in his personality and hindered in the execution of his work.

Regarding this matter we must add that, presently, to obtain the file will be very laborious and difficult for many people and actually impossible for others, creating resentment, discontent, irritation, and protests.

It should not be said that the law is made to not be applied because this would really end up taking away from the Republican Regime, both nationally and abroad, whatever prestige it still has.

Also the proclamation of racial principles, that shall remain, for the most part at least, inoperative, does not foster additional trust in the eyes of the allies.

Quite the opposite.

[Guido Buffarini-Guidi]

40.

[List of religious
establishments in Rome that sheltered the Jews]

Jewish refugees in convents

1. Suore di Nostra Signora di Sion, via Garibaldi, 28 187
2. Suore Adoratrici del Preziosissimo Sangue, via Pannonia, 10 136
3. Suore del Buono e Perpetuo Soccorso, via Merulana, 170 133
4. Maestre Pie Filippini, largo Santa Lucia Filippini, 20; via Caboto, 16;
   via Fornaci 114
5. Oblate Agostiniane di Santa Maria dei 7 Dolori, via Garibaldi, 27 103
6. Suore della Presentazione, via Milazzo, 11a; via Sant'Agata
   dei Goti, 10 102
7. Suore Orsoline dell'Unione Romana, via Nomentana, 234 103
8. Suore Adoratrici Canadesi del Prezioso Sangue, via F. D. Guerrazzi 80
9. Istituto Clarisse Missionarie Francescane del Santissimo Sacramento,
   via Vicenza, 33 76
10. Figlie del Sacro Cuore di Gesù (Verzeri), via Cavour 69
11. Istituto Suore Compassioniste Suore di Maria, via Alessandro
    Torlonia, 14 63
12. Istituto delle Suore di San Giuseppe, via del Casaletto 57
13. Istituto San Giovanni Battista (Suore Medee), via Bartolomeo
    Eustacchio 51
14. Suore di Carità dell'Immacolata Concezione d'Ivrea,
    via Leone IV, 2 50
15. Oblate a Tor de'Specchi, via del Mare, 12 48
16. Istituto "Ravasco," via San Sebastianello, 10 46
17. Istituto delle Suore dell'Assunzione, corso d'Italia 46
18. Suore Alcantarine, via Vasellari, 61 44
19. Suore Francescane Missionarie d'Egitto, via Cicerone, 57; piazza
    Santa Cecilia, 23 43

Jewish refugees in religious residences for men

34. Collegio San Gabriele, viale Parioli, 26 4
35. Collegio di Santa Maria, viale Manzoni, 5 6
36. Ospizi Don Orione 21
37. Parrocchia Santa Croce 80
38. Parrocchia della Divina Provvidenza 65
39. Parrocchia di San Filippo 24
40. Parrocchia del Buon Pastore 5
41. Parrocchia di Santa Maria in Trastevere 2
42. Parrocchia di Santa Maria delle Fornaci 1
43. Parrocchia di Ognissanti 1
44. Parrocchia della Trasfigurazione 100
45. Parrocchia di Santa Maria in Campitelli 38
46. Parrocchia di Santa Maria della Pace 40
47. Parrocchia di San Gioacchino ai Prati 13
48. Reverendi Padri Francescani San Bartolomeo all'Isola 400
49. Reverendi Padri Stimmatini Parrocchia Santa Croce 100
50. Convento di San Bonaventura al Palatino 10
51. Reverendi Padri Domenicani Irlandesi (San Clemente) 2
52. Istituto dell'Immacolata dei Frati Bigi 10
53. Fratelli delle Scuole Cristiane di Irlanda 3
54. Reverendi Padri Gesuiti in case diverse 43
55. Istituto maschile Don Luigi Guanella, via Aurelia Antica 8

Some initiatives to help the Jews in Rome during the most tragic days:

I. Assistance initiatives

1) Opera San Raffaele
   Reverend Father Anthony Weber, General Secretary, with several Pallottini
   Fathers help and rescue between 20,000 to 25,000 persons 25,000
   Help for emigration to North and South America 2,000
   Jewish emigrants 1,500
   Costs incurred are Lire 4,995,000, of which Lire 2,007,000 were covered by
   the Vatican and the Pallottini Fathers
2) DELASEM initiatives by Reverend Father Benedict of Bourg d'Iré
   Capuchin.
   Obtained help for Lire 25,000,000
   Jews of Rome 2,500
   Jewish refugees in Rome 1,500
   Main centers for assembly and distribution of assistance:
       La Casa Generalizia dei Reverendi Padri Cappuccini in via Sicilia.
       La Casa delle Clarisse Missionarie Francescane in Via Vicenza, 33.

The Parish of S. Cuore in Via Marsala.
Parish Priest D. Fio. Brossa assisted by Mrs. Ved. Terzi.
The Parish of S. Maria degli Angeli ed altre.

3) Assistance initiatives of Ruppen-Ambord
Lt. Colonel Ulrico Ruppen and Father Beato Ambord of the General Curia of the Reverend Jesuit Fathers in Borgo S. Spirito as trustees of a Swiss contributor give to Jewish families and individuals the sum of Lire 1,000,000.

II. Charitable initiatives

1) Charity in months
120 homes and 100 religious congregations for women give shelter for many months .... 2,775 persons
60 homes and institutions for men .... 992 persons
2) Shelter for a few days in the buildings owned by churches .... 680 persons

Total .... 4,447 persons

The names and numbers of persons who were given shelter were obtained from the superiors of the religious homes which furnished the lists we have reproduced in this document. Some names are repeated in various lists because the same persons went from one location to another when they thought they would find greater security.

41.

**[Report on the activity
of the DELASEM by Father Benedetto]**

From 1940 to 1943 I worked with my Jewish friends from Marseilles, Cannes and Nice in France, to protect persecuted Jews, in agreement with Italian occupation authorities in the French zone. I was recalled to Rome by my superiors in June 1943, and until September 8 of the same year I helped Mr. Angelo Donati to transfer Jews from France (Italian occupied zone) to Italy and then to North Africa, in agreement on one hand with the Italian government and on the other with the governments of England and the United States. Due to a lack of time this project could not be completed, but after September 8, hundreds of destitute foreign Jews deprived of any means of existence, arrived in Rome from France in large numbers. I was advised of their presence by my friend Lionello Alatri (who unfortunately was deported on October 16, 1943). I went to see them at the Jewish orphanage, where they were temporarily housed and I recognized a good number of those I had previously assisted in Marseilles and Nice. It was impossible for me not to resume the duties of my assistance work; I then made the acquaintance of the Delasem, with whom I worked for nine months, taking part in all of its activities.

I have the greatest esteem for Mr. Sorani and Mr. Levi, because I was able to personally observe, practically on a daily basis, their intelligent, methodic, tireless, disinterested and just work, in spite of the thousands of difficulties and the enormous danger that they continuously faced. Very quickly the offices of the Delasem, Lungo Tevere Sanzio 2, had to be closed and gradually the convent at Via Sicilia 159, with its indoor and outdoor conference rooms and those using the entrance of Via Boncompagni 71, became the central headquarters of the commission. When I say "central headquarters," it was rather a clearing station, because out of necessity other centers were created where those we assisted were divided into categories, and housed. The categories were made up as follows: foreign Jews coming from France, foreign Jews residing in Italy for many years, Yugoslav Jews, Italian Jews from Rome and those not from Rome. Except for the interruption of fifteen or so days when he was arrested, Mr. Sorani always headed the committee, helped by a number of representatives of the group of foreigners, who maintained contact with the masses and handled the multiple assistance tasks. Other than distributing welfare, food, clothing and medicine, the main functions were to provide identity documents which, let us say, were actually false, but in the intentions of those who issued them and those who used them, they were the only means of protection available and legitimate defense against the unjust aggressor. Then there was the need to secure ration cards corresponding to new identity documents because otherwise everyone could not obtain them regularly. The work was immense, and it was a great testimonial to courage because the risk, not to mention the imprudence, was enormous and constant. There was no lack of threatening letters, denunciations, nor spying against our centers and us.

The difficulty in finding the necessary funds for assistance was always acute. To give an idea of our needs it is sufficient to read what the Delasem wrote in a request directed to the Jews in Rome: "On September 8 a little more than 100 foreign Jews were subsidized by us; on June 4 there were 4,000 present, of which 1,500 were foreign and 2,500 Italians. During these nine months there has been around 25,000,000 lire spent even though the welfare distributed was insufficient." The Delasem central headquarters in Genoa had promised to help us, but Mr. Raffaele Cantoni fled to Switzerland after escaping from prison and interrupted his contacts with us. The Delasem in Rome had to turn to the Ambassadors of England and the United States to the Vatican to obtain from the Joint American Committee, through their governments, funds in dollars in England or America that could be sold in Rome. Therefore there were many long negotiations, before receiving a reply from the governments, to find someone willing to buy the dollars under such conditions. Mr. Sorani was always very tactful, persevering and skillful during these negotiations. To confirm this I can mention the testimony of our very dear friend, Monsignor Hérissé of the Vatican, who more than once spoke to me of his admiration for Mr. Sorani's efforts. Furthermore the Delasem wrote more than once to Jewish authorities in Switzerland and kept a prudent but continuous contact with all of the authorities and associations that could be of help to us: the Police and Italian Government Ministries, Food Rationing Offices, the Secretary of State and the Department of Assistance to the war victims of the Vatican, the Vicariate, the International Red Cross, the embassies of Poland, Yugoslavia, Belgium, Spain, and Portugal to the Vatican, the Swiss Legation and the Consulates of Switzerland, Hungary, and France, the political parties of the Liberation who were sympathetic toward us, etc. Everything was attempted to help the Jews and at least with respect to the foreigners, had there not been that very painful episode of the two French spies during the last months, most them would have been saved.

I am aware of the complaints leveled against the Delasem by the very many persons in need that it was assisting. Complaints that on one hand are justified objectively, in the sense that in spite of all the good intentions of the committee the aid distributed was not sufficient, the material help given to the individuals never corresponded to the ever increasing needs of those needing assistance. But knowing the situation, I cannot justify those cmplaints if they mean that those responsible for the committee did not measure up to their most difficult and demanding tasks. I must add that in the end Mr. Sorani never neglected the religious side, taking advantage of every opportunity to remind the Jews of their religious obligations and urging them in this manner to be deserving of God's help. This was always for me a great inspiration, both as a Catholic Priest, as well as a friend, or, as they said, "Father of the Jews," because I cannot imagine a Jew who is not a religious, faithful follower of the God of Abraham, Isaac, and Jacob.

I have outlined above, and without entering into great detail, which could probably be enough to generate a book, my thoughts on the work of the Delasem of Rome, during these nine months, a work that I feel constitutes a beautiful page of its history.

P. Maria Benedetto, Capuchin
159, Via Sicilia 125
July 20, 1944

Index

RENZO DE FELICE, one of the most eminent 20th century Italian historians, is best known not only for *The Jews in Fascist Italy: A History*, but also for his monumental 8-volume biography of Mussolini, also published in Italian by Einaudi. De Felice was born in 1929 in Rieti, near Rome. He studied with the two distinguished modern Italian historians, Federico Chabod and Delio Cantimori, and then taught history at the universities of Salerno and Rome. He died in Rome 1996. This English edition of *The Jews in Fascist Italy: A History* is being published by Enigma Books with the support of the Italian Ministry of Foreign Affairs.

ROBERT L. MILLER, the translator of *The Jews in Fascist Italy: A History*, is the founder and publisher of Enigma Books. Mr. Miller, is a former professor of French and Italian at Saint Peter's College and Herbert Lehman College of CUNY. He was also vice president of Berlitz Publishing and of Macmillan Publishing Company, and is currently the president of Language Publications, Inc. a software publisher. He holds a Licence-ès-Lettres with a Certificate in Contemporary History from the University of Paris at Nanterre, an MA from Middlebury College, and did graduate work at New York University.

Dr. MICHAEL A. LEDEEN holds the Freedom Chair at the American Enterprise Institute in Washington, DC. A student of George L. Mosse, Dr. Ledeen holds a doctorate in modern European history and philosophy from the University of Wisconsin, and taught for many years at the University of Rome. He was variously Rome correspondent for the *New Republic*, founding editor of *The Washington Quarterly* at the Center for Strategic and International Studies, Special Adviser to the Secretary of State, and consultant to the National Security Council during the Reagan Administration. His most recent works include *Machiavelli on Modern leadership* and *Tocqueville on American Character*.

STANISLAO G. PUGLIESE, co-editor of this translation, is Associate Professor of History at Hofstra University and a Visiting Fellow at the Italian Academy for Advanced Studies at Columbia University. Dr. Pugliese holds a Ph.D from the City University of New York and is a specialist in twentieth century Italian history, the Italian anti-fascist resistance and the Italian Jews. He is the author of *Carlo Rosselli: Socialist Heretic and Antifascist Exile*, Harvard University Press 1999, and *Italian Fascism & Antifascism: A Critical Anthology*, Manchester University Press 2001.